THE FILMS OF
20th CENTURY-FOX

THE FILMS OF

A PICTORIAL HISTORY

REVISED AND ENLARGED EDITION

20th CENTURY-FOX

by Tony Thomas and Aubrey Solomon

THE CITADEL PRESS   SECAUCUS, N.J.

ACKNOWLEDGMENTS

As may well be assumed, we received a great deal of help in putting this book together. Initially we are grateful to Jack Haley, Jr., and Martin Groothuis for their encouragement. In the sheer labor of gathering material we thank Jack Yaeger, the head of the studio's records and story files, and for keeping us on the right track we are grateful to Marc W. Pevers, Vice President of 20th Century-Fox Licensing Corporation. Two ladies did fine service in assisting us with research: Lorraine Foreman Thomas and Lori Solomon. That we are grateful to Frank Rodriguez, the head of the studio's still department, is, we hope, obvious. And in those cases where we could not find photos in the studio vaults, we turned to Eddie Brandt and his *Saturday Matinee* photo files in North Hollywood. And for the updated version, we thank Jerry Greenberg, Danny Simon, Emily Cole, Steve Newman, and Gina F. Solomon.

Tony Thomas and Aubrey Solomon

Library of Congress Cataloging in Publication Data

Thomas, Tony, 1927-
    The films of 20th Century-Fox

    Includes index.
    1. Twentieth Century-Fox Film Corporation.
    2. Moving-pictures—Plots, themes, etc.
    I. Solomon, Aubrey, joint author. II. Title.
PN1999.T8T5   384'.8'06579494   79-18210
    ISBN 0-8065-0958-9

CONTENTS

THE LOT THAT WAS

This 1964 photo shows the Fox lot after the sale of the back-lot, the northern half of the property, which is now the popular shopping and business complex called Century City.

The Chicago Lake, built in 1938, for *In Old Chicago* and later used for more than twenty films, including *Little Old New York, Son of Fury, Lydia Bailey, The Farmer Takes a Wife* (1953 version), *Prince Valiant*, and *The Pirates of Tortuga* in 1961.

One of the most used Fox props, the Plantation House built in 1934 for *The Little Colonel* and visible in countless pictures dealing with the South, such as *The Foxes of Harrow, The President's Lady, Jesse James* (1956 version), *The Long Hot Summer*, and finally *Sanctuary* in 1961.

Adano Square, first used in *Son of Fury* in 1942, and later for *A Bell for Adano, Les Miserables* (1952 version), *Soldier of Fortune, Can-Can*, and many others.

Tombstone Street, built for the 1939 *The Cisco Kid* and featured in most Fox Westerns, like *Belle Starr, The Ox-Bow Incident, Yellow Sky, Broken Lance*, and ending with *North to Alaska* in 1960.

The Algerian Street, constructed for *Under Two Flags* in 1936 and used in numerous films dealing with the Middle East or the Far East, such as *Ali Baba Goes to Town, Keys of the Kingdom, The Black Rose, David and Bathsheba, The Robe, The Barbarian and the Geisha,* and *The Story of Ruth.*

Aerial view of the 20th Century-Fox lot in Beverly Hills in the 1950's. The thoroughfare toward the bottom of the photo is Pico Boulevard. The one above the center of the photo is Santa Monica Boulevard. The lot existed between these two lines. The area in the upper right is the elite residential part of Beverly Hills.

Sersen Lake, built for *The Rains Came* in 1939 and appearing in many Fox sea sagas, such as *The Black Swan, Titanic, The Enemy Below,* and lastly *Voyage to the Bottom of the Sea.*

Sligon Castle, built in 1954 for *Prince Valiant* and afterwards used in *The Virgin Queen, The Left Hand of God, The Wizard of Baghdad,* and *Snow White and the Three Stooges.*

Old New York Street, set up for *A Tree Grows in Brooklyn* and used in countless pictures with New York settings, and sometimes doubling for other cities.

Omaha Street, built for *Brigham Young* in 1940 and seen in *Belle Starr, Chicken Every Sunday,* and *The Texas Kid.*

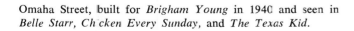

Bernadette Street, laid out for *The Song of Bernadette* in 1944, served European stories like *Forever Amber*, *Les Miserables*, and *Desiree*.

The Old French Street, built for *Forever Amber* in 1947 and seeing its final duty in *Snow White and the Three Stooges* in 1961.

The Waterways, laid out for *Swamp Water* in 1941 and constantly used thereafter. Among the films: *Lydia Bailey*, *The King and I*, the *Adventures in Paradise* television series, and *Voyage to the Bottom of the Sea*.

The New York Street built for *Hello, Dolly* in 1967 at a cost of two million dollars. The street is actually the main entrance of the studio, coming in from Pico Boulevard, and the buildings on the far side of the street are elaborate facades covering office buildings.

8

The Keys of the Kingdom Church, built in 1945 and also seen in *Forever Amber* and *What Price Glory?* This set, like all those in the preceding photos, was leveled when the studio sold its backlot. On these spots today stand the business skyscrapers, hotel, theatres, and shopping plazas of Century City.

The Suburban Street, first used in 1939 for the Jones family pictures and on film repeatedly thereafter, seeing its last service in 1959 in *Rally 'Round the Flag, Boys!*

An aerial shot, showing the filming of the street parade in *Hello, Dolly* and revealing most of the studio's current working area.

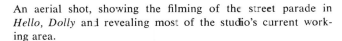

The Parade in New York—in Beverly Hills.

9

THE STUDIO AND THE MEN WHO MADE IT

It doubtlessly was not apparent to William Fox when he went to work as a coat liner for S. Cohen and Son of New York in 1900 that he would one day head a film empire worth hundreds of millions of dollars. It seemed even less apparent to his employer, who considered young Fox overpaid at $25 a week. But this young man, as his name coincidentally implied, had an instinct for survival, plus an irrepressible desire for success.

William Fox, a Jewish Hungarian immigrant, was twenty-one in 1900 and already developing the talents that would result in success on a major scale. Well aware that advancement in the business comes only with capital, he saved hard and deprived himself and his wife of everything but the bare necessities. With a partner he started a business. The Knickerbocker Cloth Examining and Shrinking Company did exactly what its impressive name described, and in its second year it showed a profit of $10,000. By 1904 profits had reached $50,000 and Fox decided to sell the company, and in doing so acquired even more capital. He was on the way.

It is no mere coincidence that men who had flourished in the garment industry would gravitate toward the movie business. Samuel Goldfish had been a glove salesman before he became Samuel Goldwyn, movie mogul. Both Adolph Zukor and Marcus Loew had been furriers. The same tenacity, hard-sell techniques, and inventiveness were the prerequisites of both trades. With similar narrow-margin problems and cutthroat competition, men like Fox, Zukor, and Goldwyn were able to carve out empires where none had been before.

With the profits from the sale of his cloth company, Fox bought a common show—a store remodeled for the exhibition of motion pictures. The term "common show" was a legal phrase for places with fewer than 299 seats and not subject to the fire regulations of larger theatres. With an admission price of five cents, these common shows quickly became known as nickelodeons. Even though initial business was slow, Fox sensed that there would be a great future for this form of entertainment. To bolster attendance he hired a magician to perform in front of the theatre. The magic worked—and once again William Fox was at the helm of a profitable venture. He plowed the profits from the first common show into a second and a third, until he had twenty-five such establishments.

Prior to these common shows, films had been exhibited in so-called "peep shows." Each person would view the film individually. Films were chosen from a catalogue and were bought outright for ten to twenty-five dollars. However, when projection facilities became available, groups of people were able to view films at one time, which led to a saturation of certain films. Rather than the film being discarded, it was given to another exhibitor, which quickly led to the idea of the film exchange. In 1902, Harry Miles, a San Francisco exhibitor, set up the first exchange by purchasing films from producers and then leasing them to other exhibitors for one-week runs. The idea spread and within five years there were almost 150 such exchanges, which paid producers ten cents a foot for films and rented them to exhibitors.

The production of motion pictures was not quite the same as distributing them. In 1909 a group of production companies set up the Motion Picture Patents Company and they alone owned the equipment for production. They organized the General Film Company in 1910 as a distribution subsidiary and through it they regulated the length of films and the rentals exhibitors would pay. Other distributors were bought out or forced out by the withdrawal of the supply of films. With the exception of one remaining distributor, the General Film Company had nationwide exclusivity.

11

William Fox (1879–1952), the man who started it all.

Tom Mix (1880–1940), former cowboy, soldier, lawman, and rodeo rider. Fox signed him in 1918 and held him under contract for ten years, during which time Mix, with his horse Tony, became one of the most popular and highest paid stars in the history of Hollywood.

Theda Bara (b. 1890), the first Fox star; in fact, it was Fox who made a star of her. She had been an extra until 1915, when he devised some garish publicity about her supposed exotic background (she was actually an American) and cast her as a vamp, a word which came into being because of her vampirish seduction of men. Fox starred her in *A Fool There Was,* with instantaneous success. It was this film which gave birth to the line "Kiss me, my fool!"

Fifty-two exchange branches were set up and territories were divided.

William Fox was the one owner of an exchange who remained independent, and even though the monopoly cut off his supply of films, he was determined to fight them. He quickly opened up a studio and began production on his own. Although Fox had been offered $75,000 for his exchange by General, he antagonized them by demanding ten times their offer. Finally, Fox brought a suit against the combine for six million dollars in damages for violation of the Sherman Anti-Trust Act. Victory came in 1912 when the courts ruled against the monopoly and put an end to the stranglehold placed on the industry by Pathé, Biograph, Kalem, Essenay, Selig, Edison, and Vitagraph. No longer were producers, distributors, and exhibitors under the wing of a cartel. The film business was now free and open. And movies became much more interesting, both in terms of business and artistry.

While William Fox was making pictures in New York and New Jersey in 1913, the Los Angeles Chamber of Commerce was promoting its city as a center for film production. Fox, along with Adolph Zukor and Carl Laemmle, decided that the temperate climate might more easily facilitate year-round production. Subsequently, he developed his concerns in Los Angeles and in 1916 opened a studio on Western Avenue, at the junction of Sunset Boulevard. This became the headquarters of his picture-making operation.

Along with the increasing popularity of motion pictures came the ascendancy of the star system. Those actors and actresses who were adored by the public commanded, and received, ever-increasing salaries. Producers soon realized that it was a worthwhile investment. William Fox discovered many of the stars who became so popular in his films: William Farnum, Theda Bara, Tom Mix, and others. These names became veritable gold mines for Fox, since their popularity meant not only profits but prestige as well. Theda Bara's success resulted in one film each month from

1915 to 1919 and a weekly salary of $4,000. Tom Mix began with Fox as a horse trainer, but by the time he ended his Fox contract in 1928 he was making $17,000 weekly.

Fox realized that Europe was a vast potential market, but he had to wait until 1919 before he could set up offices in the major European cities. This he did, and aside from gaining a healthy stream of rentals he also used his various headquarters for the filming of newsreels. The Fox Corporation kept growing—as did the whole motion picture industry—and no one was more compulsively intent on dominating the industry than William Fox. By 1920 he had sold all his common shows and gone on to building up a chain of theatres in the boroughs of New York City. Within ten years this chain claimed 175 houses, in addition to a national network which, by 1927, numbered over one thousand theatres.

At the Fox organization, William Fox was aided by Saul E. Rogers, his attorney, and Winfield Sheehan, an assistant and general manager. Together these men coped with the problems of a constantly expanding and changing business, a business as rife with setbacks as advances. In 1925 Fox bought controlling interest in what was to be the Roxy Theatre for five million dollars. This acquisition gave Fox the distinction of controlling, and later owning, the largest theatre in the world, with a seating capacity of 6,200. Winfield Sheehan, who had been with Fox since 1912, was in charge of reorganizing the studio and he is generally credited with building the distribution arm of the company.

As long as he had been in the film business, William Fox had known that, like any business catering to public taste, it was subject to changes. But there were changes in the late Twenties that surprised even Fox. Theda Bara lost her adoring public to other exotic women, including Greta Garbo and Pola Negri. William Farnum returned to the stage, although in ill health, and Tom Mix left the studio in 1928. By now, other studios had given the public star-studded movies and the Fox policy of building a film around a single star no longer had much impact. Also, more to the point, Fox found himself very short of stars. Winfield Sheehan set out to correct these ills. Rather than depending on stars, he turned toward better material, and in the process of turning out better pictures he also developed talent. Alma Rubens and Edmund Lowe starred in *East Lynne* (1925), which grossed $1,100,-000. In the following year he teamed Lowe with Victor McLaglen in *What Price Glory?*, which not only cleared two million but also began a series of films which continued over the next nine years. The film boosted the career of director Raoul Walsh and under Sheehan's command many other directors were given the opportunities that enabled them to make their names, men like John Ford, Howard Hawks, Irving Cummings, Lewis Seiler, Henry King, Leo McCarey,

and Frank Borzage. Borzage had started his Fox career with *Lazybones* in 1925, but it was not until *Seventh Heaven* two years later that he hit his stride. *Seventh Heaven* was a major hit for the studio and launched the successful teaming of Janet Gaynor and Charles Farrell, both of whom would be well employed by Fox for the next decade.

Sound was on its way to an inevitable marriage with film by 1926, but the major studios rejected the idea of intruding on the audience's enjoyment of movies with "talking." All except William Fox, who in 1925 had already encouraged his engineer Theodore Case to experiment with the possibilities of sound-on-film. The near-bankrupt Warner Brothers had raised $800,000 to invest in sound, and the future of their shaky company rested on that innovation. They soon joined forces with the Bell Telephone Company, which had managed to synchronize pictures with discs. This became the Vitaphone process, which was widely adopted by theatres.

The Fox sound system, devised by Case, operated on somewhat different principles than Vitaphone, and Fox patented it as Movietone, which he hoped to establish as the only sound process in films and thereby control the industry through his patents. Both Vitaphone and Movietone appeared to the public in the late spring and summer of 1926, but only in comedy short subjects and newsreels. At the time, there was no great importance attached to the new processes.

Theatre attendance by 1926 was estimated at one hundred million customers a week, certainly a large number of people capable of making a decision about what they wanted to see. It soon became apparent that they also wanted to hear. Fox's first use of Movietone in a feature came with *What Price Glory?* on January 21, 1927. Whatever doubts remained about sound were cleared away in the following October. *The Jazz Singer* opened to record-breaking business and because many theatres had equipped themselves for Vitaphone short subjects, Warners had an advantage. Their dramatic gamble soon made up the studio losses of the previous two years, and by 1929 their profits stood at seventeen million dollars. A year later, through the acquisition of theatres, Warners' assets reached $230 million.

Sound threw Hollywood into one of its periods of vast reorganization and revitalization. Production was slowed until the overall effect of sound could be evaluated. Millions of dollars were tied up in completed silent films, and it was deemed necessary to salvage them in some way. As a result, many were given sound prologues or epilogues, and sound effects and musical scores were added to other pictures.

At Fox, all this was done through Movietone, and the studio found to its relief that major silent productions such as *Street Angel* and *Four Sons* were not harmed by the addition of sound elements. The films did well and helped build Winfield Sheehan's reputation as he successfully sought to increase the quality of Fox product. The tremendous popularity and widespread acceptance of the talkies made 1929 a year of record profits. Fox's *Sunny Side Up,* a musical starring Janet Gaynor and Charles Farrell, led their program with a gross of more than three million dollars, a record for the company. A sequel to *What Price Glory?,* again pairing Edmund Lowe and Victor McLaglen, called *The Cock-Eyed World* did almost as well.

Amid the coming of sound, William Fox was not one to be satisfied with mere "talkies." In 1929 he released *Happy Days* in 70 mm—twice the normal film gauge, and projected on a much larger screen. The following year he produced *The Big Trail,* John Wayne's first starring vehicle, also in 70 mm. But it was not a successful experiment. Critics felt that the public was too busy adjusting to sound to accept another novelty. Fox had been fortunate in having other studios, such as Paramount, Universal, MGM, and Columbia, adopt his Movietone sound system, but none of them were willing to pick up on his large image scheme. Fox, however, was not a man to be deterred; if one idea failed, there was always another.

Fox had always dreamed of dominating the film industry. His theatre chain was now a thousand strong and it was supplied by his production and distribution arms. His Movietone process of sound reproduction was his own patent and beyond the control of the American Telephone Company. But this strength produced enemies. Any further expansion of his power was considered a threat within the industry, and there were many film businessmen and bankers who believed that something should be done to curtail Fox. Unwittingly, he played into their hands.

William Fox overstepped his bounds on one of his campaigns of expansion. With a fifteen million dollar loan from the Telephone Company and a smiliar loan from Halsey, Stuart and Company of New York, Fox planned a three-way development of his company. The element which caused the most animosity was his acquiring a controlling block of Loew's stock. In early 1929, Fox let it be known that he was interested in acquiring the more powerful Metro-Goldwyn-Mayer and its parent company, Loew's Corporation. President Louis B. Mayer never imagined that Fox would get control of his vast company. Nevertheless, Fox offered to buy all the holdings of the Shubert and Loew families, as well as those of Vice President Nicholas Schenck and Treasurer David Bernstein. Schenck admitted wanting to make a grand profit on the deal, but he thought Fox was bluffing when he offered over-market prices. Fox was not bluffing, and in a surprise transaction he acquired 53 percent of Loew's stock for fifty million dollars. Louis B. Mayer returned from a trip to find himself a Fox employee, and when his contract expired he asked Fox for a raise in salary. Fox's refusal did nothing to aid their relationship.

Fox also paid twenty million dollars for the Poli theatre circuit in New England and bought up half the voting stock of the holding company which controlled Gaumont-British. At this point Fox claimed to have a fortune of a hundred million dollars and a company worth three times that. He intended keeping the company going by issuing stock to refinance his loans and keep up with interest payments.

When William Fox's loans became due in late 1929 and early 1930, he began to feel the full animosity of the people with whom he had been dealing. Halsey, Stuart, the Telephone Company, and Harley Clarke, the president of General Theatres Equipment Corporation, were among those who wanted Fox removed. Halsey, Stuart was representing the Chase Manhattan Bank and various individuals who felt that they could make an easy profit with the Fox empire. Clarke had always wanted to take control and had promised several times to lend money to Fox if ever he was in need. American Telephone wanted to install their sound systems in Fox theatres. It was thought there was something in it for everybody, and when the stock market collapsed Fox found himself without financing. It was late 1929 and he had to secure his loans. His creditors had managed to turn any possible sources of money away from him. So-called friends abandoned him and he spent an unfruitful half-year struggling for survival.

Finally, with no alternatives, Fox was forced to sell off his important holdings to raise some capital and then sell shares in the company he had built up from such a modest beginning. Everyone got what they wanted, including Harley Clarke, who bought his way into the presidency for eighteen million dollars worth of Fox's shares. Fox's situation had been further complicated by an anti-trust suit brought against him for the proposed merger with Loew's. The Loew's shares were then sold back to the corporation. Everything which William Fox had done was about to be undone.

Thus began the looting of the Fox company. Several men and companies made millions from the transactions which followed. The American Telephone Company was now free to control all the sound recording and reproduction patents, and Harley Clarke had all Fox theatres ordered from his own company. Clarke was more concerned with imposing minimum orders on theatres for new seats or marquees than with running a company to produce films. The Fox Film Corporation managed to show a profit of nine and a half million dollars in 1930, the final year of William Fox's presidency, but with Clarke's wasteful administration the following year there was a loss of over five million. It was Harley Clarke's first and final year as president.

When William Fox was ousted in 1930 by the coup perpetrated by Harley Clarke, Halsey Stuart, and the Telephone Company, he was forced to relinquish his shares in the Fox Film Corporation at the prevailing depressed levels. An agreement was also signed not to re-enter feature production. Within two years, Fox dictated his tale of fortunes lost in *Upton Sinclair*

Presents William Fox, a voluminous and biased account centered on the evils of profiteers and speculators. However, even in the depths of defeat, William Fox did not fail to include his monopolistic intentions. To Sinclair, a willing and receptive listener, Fox explained that he would produce educational films and that it would not be long before each of the one million learning institutions across the country would be paying him $5 weekly for the use of his Tri-Ergon sound-on-film process. Unfortunately for Fox, the courts struck down his personal patent claim on the process. Further hardship followed when, in 1932, Fox was called before a Senate Investigations Committee to testify in a Fox stock manipulations charge. By 1936, with $9,935,261 in liabilities and $100 in assets, William Fox declared personal bankruptcy. In the legal proceedings which followed, Fox paid a judge $27,500 and was later charged with bribery. He was sentenced, in 1941, to one year in prison. After his release from the Federal Penitentiary in Lewisburg, he set up a small office in New York City and in 1944, at the age of sixty-five, announced that he planned to build a 1500-acre studio in Los Angeles. He would also organize a complete distribution company to release his productions. To fulfill these grandiose plans again, Fox would need support and financial backing from the industry he once intended to dominate. As in 1930 during his financial crises, support was not forthcoming. Living in the glory that once was, William Fox never realized any further association with the motion picture industry and after a year-long illness, died on May 8, 1952. Ironically there was no one from the film industry to deliver his eulogy.

Despite the industry sages who believed films were exempt from the impact of the Depression, business declined by mid-1930. The novelty of sound had worn off, audiences were more selective as their incomes shrank, and radio had become a viable, and free, form of entertainment. Into the ailing Fox Corporation at this time came Sidney R. Kent. He had previously been at Paramount-Publix, where he had worked his way up from salesman to general manager, and he was therefore far better suited to command a studio than Harley Clarke Kent managed the company's finances and theatres well, but he was never able to secure a more-than-adequate working relationship with Winfield Sheehan, who was still in charge of production in Hollywood. Sheehan, too, had lost some of the "know-how" of previous times. He produced five films in 1931 which grossed over a million dollars but none in that category the following year. The studio was also losing some of its talent, with stars and directors accepting better offers elsewhere. Fox's only new success was Will Rogers, who starred in as many as four films yearly. Sheehan continued to make Janet Gaynor films, Charles Farrell films, and Warner Baxter films, but his policies were not greatly successful. His

Winfield R. Sheehan, the head of production for Fox until Darryl F. Zanuck came on the scene. This photo shows Sheehan on his honeymoon in August of 1935 as he and his bride, opera star Maria Jeritza, take off for Europe on the *Normandie.*

Darryl F. Zanuck at Warners in 1930 while making *Mammy* with Al Jolson. The film's director was Michael Curtiz (at right).

In 1933 George Arliss signs with Zanuck as a star of 20th Century Pictures.

attempt to revive the career of Clara Bow was a decided flop.

If 1932 was a bad year for the film companies, 1933 looked as if it could be worse. When the banks closed in the spring and a new monetary policy was introduced, business dropped twenty percent. However, there were signs of recovery by the summer, although there were circumstances which curtailed any rapid expansion. Fox West Coast theatres was forced into receivership on a note which had been signed by William Fox several years earlier. Charles Skouras, a successful theatre man himself, was appointed receiver of Wesco and became responsible for its finances. Along with Skouras came his two younger brothers, George and Spyros, the latter a future president of 20th Century-Fox.

Aside from the occasional hit, the 1933–34 season under Sheehan was not spectacular. *Cavalcade,* a prestigious filming of the Noel Coward play, brought in three and a half million dollars, a record gross for Fox and the second highest-grossing film since the introduction of sound. Fox in 1933 also had *State Fair* with Will Rogers, the first Fox picture to open at Radio City Music Hall in New York.

Since sound had come in, each of the major studios was refining its product and building up either star power or story power in its vehicles. Fox was clearly lagging behind in these areas. In the period between 1930 and 1935 Warner Brothers boasted such fine product as *Little Caesar, Public Enemy, I Am a Fugitive from a Chain Gang, Gold Diggers of 1933, 42nd Street,* and *Captain Blood,* and elevated such names as James Cagney, Edward G. Robinson, Ruby Keeler, Dick Powell, Ginger Rogers, and Errol Flynn to stardom.

Paramount had introduced audiences to Mae West, the Marx Brothers, Marlene Dietrich, Gary Cooper, and Maurice Chevalier in films like *The Love Parade, Monkey Business, Morocco, I'm No Angel,* and *Love Me Tonight.* In addition, Paramount had made great strides with directors like Ernst Lubitsch, Josef von Sternberg, and Rouben Mamoulian. Even R. K. O. had such popular films as *Cimarron, King Kong, Little Women, Of Human Bondage, Flying Down to Rio,* and the first three-strip Technicolor feature *Becky Sharp.*

Metro-Goldwyn-Mayer was gathering all the stars in the heavens—and everywhere else. Greta Garbo graced *Anna Christie, Susan Lenox, The Painted Veil, Grand Hotel,* and *Queen Christina* with her presence and box-office appeal. *Dinner at Eight, The Champ, Red Dust, The Thin Man, A Tale of Two Cities,* and *Mutiny on the Bounty* displayed the talents of Clark Gable, Jean Harlow, Marie Dressler, Wallace Beery, John Barrymore, Lionel Barrymore, Ronald Colman, Charles Laughton, Myrna Loy, William Powell, and Jackie Cooper.

In addition to the majors was a young company headed by the President of United Artists and the ex-production head at Warner Brothers. Joseph M. Schenck and Darryl F. Zanuck had agreed to form a production company which would release its films through United Artists.

Darryl Zanuck had always been adventurous at heart. At the age of fifteen, he managed to enlist to fight in World War I. By lying about his age, he was able to see the battlefields of Europe. Zanuck was also an avid writer and would grind out his fantasies on paper. After the war, he managed to find a sponsor to publish a collection of his short stories. When *Habit* hit the stands, it contained three original stories and a testimonial to Yuccatone hair restorer—within an adventure story, of course. Once he was published, the next step was to take the material to the film studios. With a need for material, the movies bought all four stories from Zanuck.

By 1922, Zanuck had been hired by the Warner brothers and was creating stories for Rin Tin Tin. With this success behind him, he graduated to "serious" feature films. Zanuck turned out so many screenplays that he decided to use synonyms. Jack Warner agreed to that; he didn't want other studios to think he couldn't afford other writers. In one record year, Zanuck was credited with nineteen screenplays, under all his names.

There are many reasons why Darryl Zanuck later became such a successful producer. Since he had been a writer, he understood the concept of scriptwriting, and as Nunnally Johnson points out, "He would read a script and sometimes a geiger counter would go off when he got to some dull stuff. He'd leaf back to the point where this started." Zanuck possessed an innate sense of pacing and could anticipate an audience's reaction to a story. These abilities became very valuable to him, because within five years at Warner Brothers, Darryl Zanuck was, at age twenty-five, Vice-President in Charge of Production. In this capacity, he supervised the productions of such classics as *Little Caesar, Public Enemy,* and *I Am a Fugitive from a Chain Gang.*

Since Zanuck was the studio's production chief, he was nominated by the Warners to tell producers, directors, and salaried executives of austerity cuts in their weekly paychecks. Zanuck agreed, but when the brothers Warner decided to extend the cut two weeks longer than had been announced, a dispute arose and Zanuck ended his association with the company. On April 15, 1933, Darryl Zanuck left a job which paid $5,000 weekly.

Joseph and Nicholas Schenck, like all the other Hollywood moguls, had come into film from various other enterprises. They, too, were immigrants (from Russia) and became eminently successful in motion pictures. Nicholas took over the presidency of the Loew's Corporation after the death of Marcus Loew in 1927. Joseph had gone into independent production, but eventually wound up as president of United Artists, which was merely a releasing firm for Douglas Fairbanks, Mary

Pickford, Charles Chaplin, and Sam Goldwyn.

Three days after he left Warners, Zanuck met with Joe Schenck, who proposed the formation of a company. He had with him a $100,000 check signed by Louis B. Mayer. The vice president of MGM had given him that check so that Mayer's son-in-law, William Goetz, would be made Zanuck's executive assistant. Both men agreed and soon they were forming their new production unit. Samuel G. Engel, Zanuck's assistant at the time, recalled, "They hadn't yet a name for the company and they were eager to sign George Arliss, whose contract was then expiring with Warners. Zanuck knew that. And so it was that week, I believe, when we had just gotten going over at the Goldwyn lot, and he said he wanted a name for the company. I said I would give him a name that would be good for 67 years. He wanted to know what it was and I replied, 'Twentieth Century Pictures.' And that's how the name came about."

Since Twentieth Century Pictures did not own a studio, they rented space at the United Artists lot. Their offices were set up there and all the equipment they used was rented. Staff was pretty much at a minimum, as Sam Engel remembers: "At Twentieth I served as a story editor and as an assistant to Zanuck. As we only made a limited number of pictures there, I could do everything and anything because it was a very, very small group of people. As a matter of fact I worked as an assistant director, a second assistant —I shot second unit stuff—I did everything."

The first production at the newly founded company was a raucous comedy-drama entitled *The Bowery* and it was released in late 1933. Zanuck had been able to borrow Wallace Beery from Metro through his connections with Mayer, and he signed Raoul Walsh to direct. Walsh had established his easy-going, adventurous style of picture with the McLaglen-Lowe epics at Fox and he proved an ideal choice. *The Bowery* was a great success and Zanuck was on his way.

Under his contract, Zanuck had to personally supervise production on twelve pictures annually. To accomplish this he hired Gregory La Cava, Roy Del Ruth, Rowland V. Lee as directors; Nunnally Johnson, Bess Meredyth, and Garret Ford as writers; and Loretta Young, Ronald Colman, Wallace Beery, George Arliss, Contance Bennett, and Frederick March for needed *star power*. The fact that the producers signed for only six months at a time was a boon to Zanuck. He was thus able to get top talent without having to sign long contracts, which could produce high overhead costs.

In the next two years, Zanuck turned out such hits as *The House of Rothschild, The Mighty Barnum, Clive of India, Folies Bergère, Les Miserables,* and *Call of the Wild.* Of the eighteen films produced at 20th Century, only one lost money.

However, at the Fox Film Corporation, the situation was far less encouraging. They had their Sunset-

Darryl F. Zanuck at the desk and in the office that was his nest for twenty years following his appointment as head of production for 20th Century-Fox in 1935.

In 1941 New York film critic Bosley Crowther represents his colleagues as the president of their association and awards Darryl F. Zanuck their citation for *The Grapes of Wrath* as the best film of 1940.

Will Rogers in *Steamboat Round the Bend* in 1935, released a month after his death in an air crash in August. Rogers had signed with Fox in 1929 and his twenty-one films for the company provided a steady stream of profits.

Western studio in Hollywood and the Westwood Studio in Beverly Hills, which had been built during William Fox's expansive period in 1928. Distribution was still covered by one of the most comprehensive set-ups in the business. Yet this corporation, valued at $36 million, had an annual earning power of $1.8 million, not much more than the earning power of Zanuck's company, which was valued at $4 million despite the fact that it had no studio or distribution arm. Sidney Kent realized that Fox needed a dynamic studio head and that Zanuck needed sound stages and a good distribution organization to expand his output of films. It was a situation that naturally led to thoughts of merger.

At first, Kent thought that Twentieth Century could be bought out just to supply his studio with better product, but Zanuck and Schenck would not agree. A merger was eventually agreed upon and was announced on May 29, 1935. Joseph Schenck became chairman of the board and resigned his presidency at United Artists but stayed on with their theatre circuit. Schenck would be paid an annual $130,000 by Fox. Sidney Kent continued as president at $180,000 and a guarantee of an additional $25,000 as president of National Theatres Corporation, a Fox affiliate.

Darryl Zanuck had been the main reason for the merger and his salary made that obvious. He was made vice-president at an annual salary of $260,000. He had received that salary at Twentieth Century, but now he was also given ten percent of the gross of his films. At the time of the merger he received enough stock in the company to ensure another half million dollars a year.

At both Fox lots, all work stopped on screenplays and on films which were to go into production—all those except the ones which were being personally produced by Winfield Sheehan. He was determined not to be swayed by the dramatic presence of Darryl Zanuck. Other Fox employees were wondering about the future of their projects and their jobs. They did not have to wonder for long, because when Zanuck arrived on the lot it was obvious he had but one objective—to get Twentieth Century-Fox to the top of the business.

Zanuck faced two problems with his new job: the reorganization of studio production, and the weak product it had been turning out. One of the problems was veteran Fox producer Winfield Sheehan, who had also long been accustomed to being vice president in charge of production. Both he and Zanuck knew there could not be two production heads and that one would eventually force the other out. Sheehan realized that Zanuck had the great advantage of being younger, more aggressive, and with a recent track record of success. On July 23, 1935, Sheehan left the company with a settlement of $420,000. This left Zanuck in full command.

Darryl F. Zanuck's track record as a film maker— fully evident in the pages of this book—is legend. The requirements for being a successful film maker over a long period of time are many. It begins with talent and a passion to create, but perhaps even more importantly it takes stamina and a high energy level. Zanuck had all these requirements. From 1935 to 1956 he *was* 20th Century-Fox. Most of his waking hours were spent at the studio and he rode herd on every aspect of picture making. Of particular value to him was his ability as a writer, not a writer in the literary sense but a writer in terms of images and plot lines and personalities. As soon as he took over the studio he brought in people with whom he had worked and for whom he had high regard. They became a Zanuck team. Among them: casting director Lew Schreiber, publicity director Harry Brand, story editor Julian Johnson, and composer-conductor Alfred Newman, whom he would make head of the music department in 1940. Under Newman's leadership, that department became a masterful group of composers, conductors, arrangers, and performers—and Zanuck gave Newman total control.

The first year of 20th Century-Fox was respectable but not overwhelming. But Zanuck found himself with two ace cards: seven-year-old Shirley Temple, whose pictures would be a bonanza for the studio over the next four years, and Will Rogers, whom he had inherited from the previous regime. The five films with Rogers in 1935 were all winners but tragically the winning streak came to an abrupt end with the actor's death in an airplane accident. Ironically, Rogers' *In Old Kentucky* and *Steamboat Round the Bend* turned out to be the studio's two top films of the year. The next three most successful movies were all Temple vehicles.

The slump years were now behind the industry and theatre attendance grew remarkably. With very few star personalities under contract, Zanuck strove to build up a small stable of performers. The public response to young Tyrone Power's small role in *Girl's Dormitory* caused Zanuck to take a gamble on Power as the star of his expensive *Lloyd's of London* in 1936. The gamble paid off handsomely and Power would be a top favorite for years. Zanuck also took a chance on a Norwegian skating star, Sonja Henie, who not only became popular but eventually became one of the richest women in the country.

As time went by Zanuck turned his attention to making films of greater quality and more spectacle. He realized that his stable of talent could not compete with the likes of MGM or Warners and so he made his screenplays his stars. Budgets were raised to make such impressive films as *Suez, In Old Chicago, Jesse James,* and *Stanley and Livingstone.* Zanuck indulged his love of Americana in these and other pictures. Occasionally he won critical acclaim, as he did with *The Grapes of Wrath.* His intense interest in biographies resulted in films like *Brigham Young* and *Wilson,* neither of which would bring in the returns for which he had hoped, but both at least adding to his prestige as a film maker with a sense of idealism.

None of the major studios operated in a vacuum.

Each was directly affected by the fortunes of the others and the industry as a whole. There was an absolute interdependence among the majors for a steady stream of films and playdates. Even the three companies which did not own theatres were dependent on the major chains for key first-run theatres. So vital was this interdependence that when a slump hit, all the companies suffered, and when boom times came, each profited. Such a boom occurred during the second World War and resulted in record-breaking earnings for the industry.

The war boom happened in spite of the loss of talent to the armed forces, including Zanuck. But the studio was so well set up and functional that even his absence did not interrupt efficiency. It was now that Spyros P. Skouras, who had been in charge of the Fox West Coast Theatre chain, came to the studio and assumed command of the company. Skouras and Zanuck were never friends and there was an undercurrent of friction as Skouras tried to one-up Zanuck in production decisions. But those decisions were invariably made by Zanuck.

Zanuck was aware of the gradually changing tastes of the public in the postwar years. Aside from films of obvious entertainment value, like *Leave Her to Heaven* and *Forever Amber,* he began to invest in more trenchant subjects. He tackled corruption in *Boomerang,* anti-semitism in *Gentleman's Agreement,* racial prejudice in *Pinky* and the horrors of mental institutions in *The Snake Pit.* The films not only found a responsive public but added to the prestige of 20th Century-Fox. It was a proud time for the studio, but one that was, sadly, fleeting.

The immediate postwar euphoria which had gripped the film industry was quick to evaporate. Ominous signs loomed over the horizon. The postwar economy was one of inflation and uncertainty. Costs were rising sharply, not only in Hollywood but for the average consumer. Rising costs meant curbing such luxuries as going to the movies. Naturally, the box office felt the pinch and the immediate reaction was to raise prices to make up for the lost audience. At Fox, Zanuck effected economies. The cost of an average Fox picture in 1947 was about $2,400,000; in 1952 Zanuck was making films for half that figure.

What happened, though, in production was a basic change in policy. In 1948 the government outlawed the practice of block booking—the automatic distribution of a film through a chain. From now on every film would have to stand on its own merit to secure a booking, a risk that became greatly accented when the major Hollywood studios were forced by the anti-trust laws to give up their theatre chains, as Fox did in 1952. Studio policy became one of planning films very carefully and keeping a watchful eye on the public.

Among other things, Zanuck turned his thoughts to creating more stars. Tyrone Power had been a valuable asset for many years, but his popularity was waning a little. Betty Grable remained a constant winner at the box office, but time, as it is with all stars, was not on her side. Zanuck found great success with Gregory Peck and Susan Hayward and used them as a pair in *David and Bathsheba* and *The Snows of Kilimanjaro.* Next he began to groom Marilyn Monroe, carefully guiding her from small parts to major vehicles.

With the dawning of the Fifties, the film moguls knew that there was no ignoring the impact of television. The plan now was to offer the public entertainment in the theatres that they could not get in the home—more color, more spectacle, more spice. New devices lured the customers: 3-D, Cinerama, and VistaVision. Fortunately for 20th Century-Fox, Spyros Skouras was able to secure the rights to a patented process which would be called CinemaScope, and the new process would be introduced with much publicity in *The Robe.* The studio wisely decided that the process should not appear as a gimmick but as a legitimate advancement in motion picture photography and used for dramatic effect. *The Robe* was a major success and Zanuck and Skouras made the bold decision to make all their major films in CinemaScope. The studio rode the crest of the wave on the development of the process, which had ostensibly rescued the industry from impending gloom and doom.

The Fifties began as troubled years and soon the initial novelty of CinemaScope wore off and the trouble renewed. Production costs had risen sharply and with fewer films in production, each one was vital to the success or failure of the company. Talent became a cause for alarm as stars asserted their independence, with the approval of writers and directors. The heyday of the major studios as autonomous bodies was drawing to a close. At 20th Century-Fox there were stars who were making life more difficult for Zanuck, such as Marilyn Monroe, with her demands for more money and her tardy work habits. Almost every film after *Gentlemen Prefer Blondes,* which established her popularity, became an ordeal for the studio. Marlon Brando caused Zanuck grief when he refused to turn up for work as the star of the expensive *The Egyptian.* In desperation Zanuck cast the unknown Edmund Purdom in the lead—with disastrous results.

Zanuck's shoulders daily felt the weight of more and more problems. In mid-1956 Skouras tried to quell rumors that Zanuck was about to leave. But leave he did—to go into independent production, although, of course, with 20th Century-Fox as his means of distribution. Under his administration, the studio had become renowned as "the best fanfare in town." But subsequent mismanagement would reduce that studio to a wave of convolutions.

The problems began to shape up with Buddy Adler, the man Zanuck had personally chosen as his successor. Adler, who had won esteem with his production of *From Here to Eternity* at Columbia, signed with 20th Century-Fox in May of 1954 as a producer and pleased

Spyros P. Skouras, the Chairman of the Board and President of 20th Century-Fox from 1943 to 1962, here dines with his star Carmen Miranda and his production head, Darryl F. Zanuck.

On the set of *Cleopatra* in Rome, Joseph L. Mankiewicz gives directions to Hume Cronyn. Rex Harrison, as Caesar, rests on his throne.

the studio with his work on *Anastasia* and *Bus Stop.* But Adler was not a Zanuck and he floundered when left to his own devices as a selector of material. Neither was he a man who followed through on every detail of production. He tended to let the studio go its own way and he was remiss in delegating duties. In short, the job was too big for the man—and it cost him his health. Buddy Adler died of cancer in July of 1960. With his death, Spyros Skouras had Bob Goldstein, the head of Fox's European operation, take over as studio boss. The position was short-lived and Skouras made another choice with Peter Levathes, the head of the studio's television division. He, too, proved insufficient in the complex, demanding job of running a studio. Skouras did everything he could to keep the studio going. Facilities were leased to other companies and the payroll was reduced by almost a thousand workers. Sadly, few films were making profits for the studio and to gain additional funds, the studio made a deal with Webb and Knapp, a land development company, to sell 260 acres of property for the price of $43 million, land that would be used for the development of the business complex now known as Century City.

The studio's luck did not improve. Even such apparently good investments as *Can-Can,* starring Frank Sinatra, and *Let's Make Love,* starring Marilyn Monroe, proved far less profitable than it was thought. And it was at this low ebb that 20th Century-Fox embarked on what would become its most traumatic and most expensive experience—*Cleopatra.* The problems of *Cleopatra* have been well documented elsewhere. Suffice to say that the four years of starts and delays and protracted production ran up to an incredible budget of forty million dollars. Even at the height of the studio's affluence this would have been an alarming investment. For a studio hanging onto life by its fingernails it was an astounding experience. The costs were so great that Skouras kept them from the stockholders. The production was out of control and yet with so much invested, Skouras could not close down production. The films produced at the studio during the *Cleopatra* years were only modestly successful and Skouras was constantly faced with the possibility of bankruptcy. What he needed now, and badly, was a new administration. But who could be brought in to command this Titanic of a situation?

Darryl F. Zanuck had been in Paris for several years, making films that did only moderate business. But his fortunes picked up with his remarkable production of *The Longest Day* in 1962. With that film completed, he found time to think about the situation at the studio. As the largest shareholders in the company, he and his family had the most to lose if Fox went into bankruptcy. The stockholders now voted to make Darryl Zanuck President of 20th Century-Fox, with Spyros Skouras becoming a nominal Chairman of the Board. In the six years he had been away, the studio had gone steadily downhill. Now it was up to him to do something about it.

The industry had changed greatly in Zanuck's absence. None of the once great studios were what they had been. Movies for the theatre were no longer the viable main product of public entertainment. However, it was still an important and profitable industry and Hollywood looked to Zanuck to revitalize 20th Century-Fox. In assuming command he halted production on *Cleopatra* until he could look at all the footage and make his decisions about editing—a talent that had been vital to the studio all through the years of his command. He spent another two million supervising additional footage to complete the long-drawn-out epic and assigned his editors to the task of putting it in shape. What resulted was an impressive film, although one which would have to succeed on a gargantuan scale to earn back its costs. Time has vindicated *Cleopatra*.

Richard Zanuck, who had grown up in the milieu of his father and early showed a passion for production, was given an executive position. He read scripts, put together packages of stars, directors, and writers, and prepared deals. His father was then consulted and would give final approval. The studio's fortunes began to pick up. With the release of *The Sound of Music* in 1965, things reached a state of near euphoria. But it was deceptive. The enormous public response to *The Sound of Music* caused the studio to overinvest in films like *Doctor Doolittle, Star!,* and *The Sand Pebbles*. They were good films, but they cost too much, and the films made in the following years also found smaller audiences. The years 1968 to 1970 were dumbfounding ones for Hollywood. Audiences became fragmented and with the proliferation of sex and violence on the screen the family trade was lost. Neither Darryl nor Richard Zanuck had counted on these changes in public taste, and their decision to go ahead with three blockbuster films—*Hello, Dolly, Tora! Tora! Tora!,* and *Patton*—with a combined budget of sixty million dollars, raised many eyebrows in Hollywood. There was also dismay at the studio caused by the runaway nature of the business in the late Sixties. It became difficult for any film to keep within its budget, largely because management did not have firm control over talent. Things had indeed changed since Zanuck's former regime. The success of certain films with modest budgets, including *M*A*S*H,* proved that selectivity was the key factor in film production and not mammoth projects.

Darryl Zanuck now had to face the ire of the stockholders for the huge losses declared by the studio. But it was not a situation limited to 20th Century-Fox; every major studio in Hollywood was in similar straits. The industry was in a state of upheaval and Darryl Zanuck came to the conclusion that he was no longer capable of controlling the chaos. He withdrew from the job, although because of his long and distinguished association with the studio he was given the title of Chairman Emeritus of the corporation. Richard Zanuck's contract was terminated—and with a touch of irony. He had not been in favor of making the costly *Tora! Tora! Tora!* and had his advice been heeded he would have saved the studio a great deal of money. Also, had he stayed, the success of his production of *The French Connection* would have made him a hero to the stockholders. Richard Zanuck has since gone on to become one of Hollywood's top producers.

With the departure of the Zanucks, Dennis Stanfill became Chairman of the Board and in September of 1971 Gordon Stulberg was put in charge of production. By this time Hollywood had become just what many producers had predicted—a crap shoot. If a studio could hold out long enough, it would have its share of hits. However, the Stanfill management did bring fiscal sanity to Fox. With few films being made on the lot, facilities were made available to independent producers. Films for television were made, using existing sets, and although it was not a high-profit business it provided income and employment. The studio also entered into a coproduction deal which would never have occurred had the studio founding fathers still been in power. Fox and Warners found themselves in coproduction on *The Towering Inferno,* an expensive property that did not seem financially viable for one company alone. Hence it became the first Hollywood film made by two studios. Ironically. *The Towering Inferno* and *The Poseidon Adventure,* both films dealing with terrible disasters, helped restore 20th Century-Fox to security and prestige in the industry. However, Gordon Stulberg resigned as President of 20th Century-Fox in December of 1974 and Dennis Stanfill took over the position, while continuing as Chairman of the Board, resulting in a greater centralization within the Fox structure. Stanfill also assigned Alan Ladd, Jr. to the position of Vice President in Charge of Production; in 1976 Ladd was named President of 20th Century-Fox Pictures. Ladd had been responsible for bringing Mel Brooks, Paul Mazursky, and their successful films to the studio, and in his new position he would be assisted by two former production men with whom he had been associated in London: Jay Kanter and Gareth Wigan.

At the beginning of this regime it was the usual balance of hits and misses. *Lucky Lady* fared poorly at the box office, but *The Adventures of Sherlock Holmes' Smarter Brother* and *The Three Musketeers* made up the slack. Then the luck of the studio began to change. After years of being buffeted by unkind fates, 20th Century-Fox started to take off. Mel Brooks' *Silent Movie* and the stylish horror film *The Omen* were released in June of 1976 and immediately started to bring in impressive returns. Each was made for three million dollars, but the combined incomes would amount to two hundred million in global receipts. *The Silver Streak* proved as good as its title. The studio was at last on a silver streak. That greatly popular picture was but a prelude to another vast success—*Star Wars.* It opened in May of 1977 and within weeks it would seem that Hollywood was back on top. Certainly 20th Century-Fox was back on top with the most profitable movie ever made.

The face of the company and the industry changed with *Star Wars.* Merchandising products related to a motion picture suddenly became an important source of revenue. The impact was felt on Wall Street. Stock in 20th Century-Fox, which had been selling for $6.00 per share in June of 1976 rocketed to $25 one year later, making it one of the most traded stocks on the New York exchange. Fortunately, the studio followed through with a succession of films which were profitable and critically well received, such as *Julia, The Turning Point,* and *An Unmarried Woman.*

In late June, 1979, after a succession of hit movies, Ladd, Kanter, and Wigan announced their resignations in favor of independent production. Following some executive suite maneuverings, Stanfill brought in Alan J. Hirschfield, a former executive of Columbia Pictures, to run the studio. With Hirschfield came Sherry Lansing as president of the feature division and Harris Katleman to take care of the ailing television wing.

Some of the hits during this administration include Lucasfilm's *The Empire Strikes Back, Porky's,* and *Nine to Five.* But it was in television that the company really took off with two extremely successful series, *The Fall Guy* and *Trapper John, M.D.,* and the continuing high-rated *MASH.* Fox also took a leadership position in the burgeoning home video market by setting up a telecommunications division and purchasing Magnetic Video to distribute its product.

Then, in 1981, Marvin Davis, a Denver oil tycoon, surprised the motion picture industry by buying the studio and all its assets. Shortly after, Dennis Stanfill departed the studio and Davis became the first individual in decades to entirely own a major studio.

An important Hollywood executive shuffle which took place in late 1984, involving several studios, brought Fox under the corporate leadership of Barry Diller. With one of the most enviable records of success in the business, Diller came from Paramount, where he had established a program of smash hits year after year. Lawrence Gordon, an independent producer, responsible for the Paramount hit *48 Hrs.,* was named President of the newly-formed Entertainment Group. In addition, in March, 1985, Rupert Murdoch, the Australian publishing tycoon, became a partner of Marvin Davis in the company. Together, these men would be responsible for theatrical and television product as the studio entered its next fifty years as a producer of motion pictures and television shows for the world's audiences.

Lionel Newman, who succeeded brother Alfred as head of the music department. Similarly gifted as a composer, conductor, and executive, Lionel has been with the studio since 1942. He has scored or conducted over 200 films and received eleven Oscar nominations in addition to winning the award for his musical direction of *Hello, Dolly.*

Alfred Newman, a master composer and conductor, and the head of the music department at 20th Century-Fox from 1940 to 1961. A superb administrator as well as a master talent, Newman won nine Oscars and forty-five Academy nominations—by far the greatest winner among film musicians.

Marvin Davis, owner of 20th Century-Fox.

Alan Hirschfield, Chairman of the Board and Chief Executive Officer.

THE FILMS OF
20th CENTURY-FOX

John Boles and Shirley Temple in *The Littlest Rebel*.

1935

BAD BOY

Produced by Edward Butcher
Directed by John Blystone
Screenplay by Alan Rivkin, from a story by Viña Delmar
Photographed by Bert Glennon
Music and lyrics by Lew Pollack and Paul Webber
56 minutes

Cast: James Dunn, Dorothy Wilson, Louise Fazenda, Victor Killian, John Wray, Luis Alberni, Beulah Bondi, Allen Vincent

James Dunn is the "bad boy," a nice, humorous lad who is an expert in the poolrooms but lacking in ability to get a job. He marries his girl friend (Dorothy Wilson), but lets her go back to her family when he cannot get work. He gets a change of luck when he helps round up a couple of gangsters. All is then well.

BLACK SHEEP

Produced by Sol M. Wurtzel
Directed by Alan Dwan
Screenplay by Allen Rivkin, from a story by Allan Dwan
Photography by Arthur Miller
Music by Oscar Levant
Lyrics by Sidney Clare
Musical direction by Samuel Kaylin
73 minutes

Cast: Edmund Lowe, Claire Trevor, Tom Brown, Eugene Pallette, Adrienne Ames, Herbert Mundin, Ford Stirling, Jed Prouty, Billy Bevan, David Torrence

A professional gambler plies his charm and his skill on board a trans-Atlantic liner and dupes wealthy businessmen, society types, and actresses. On one trip he witnesses a young man (Tom Brown) being made the victim of a jewel thief and comes to his aid. The young man is his son by a hapless romance. The film, stylishly directed by the veteran Alan Dwan, who also supplied the story, benefits from an ingratiating performance by Edmund Lowe as the quixotic gambler.

CHARLIE CHAN'S SECRET

Produced by John Stone
Directed by Gordon Wiles
Screenplay by Robert Ellis, Helen Logan, and Joseph
    Hoffman
Photographed by Rudolph Mate
Music by Samuel Kaylin
71 minutes

Cast: Warner Oland, Charles Quigley, Henrietta Crosman, Rosita Lawrence, Edward Trevor, Astrid Allwyn, Herbert Mundin, Arthur Edmund Carewe, Egon Brecher, Gloria Roy, Francis Ford, Ivan Miller, Jonathan Hale, Jerry Miley

Chan is called upon to solve the mysterious disappearance of the heir to a vast fortune. Presumably drowned, the heir returns and is later murdered. Chan grills all the relatives and associates until his usual line, "You are the murderer."

CHARLIE CHAN IN SHANGHAI

Produced by John Stone
Directed by James Tinling
Screenplay by Edward T. Lowe and Gerard Fairlie
Photographed by Barney McGill
Music by Samuel Kaylin
70 minutes

Cast: Warner Oland, Irene Hervey, Charles Locher, Russell Hicks, Keye Luke, Halliwell Hobbes, Frederick Vogeding, Neil Fitzgerald, Max Wagner

Chan is called in on the investigation of a murder in Shanghai that leads to the breaking up of an international opium ring. Chan survives an attempt on his life and his kidnapping by the ring leaders before he brings them to justice.

THE COWBOY MILLIONAIRE

Produced by Sol Lesser
Directed by Edward F. Cline
Screenplay by George Waggner and Dan Jarrett
Photographed by Frank B. Good
Music by Abe Meyer
65 minutes

Cast: George O'Brien, Evalyn Bostock, Edgar Kennedy, Maude Allen, Alden Chase, Dan Jarrett, Lloyd Ingraham, Dean Benton, Thomas Curran

A deviation from the standard Western form, *The Cowboy Millionaire* sports a young Englishwoman

(Evalyn Bostock) who arrives at a dude ranch and falls for its chief cowboy (George O'Brien). She mistakenly gets the impression that he woos her only to win a bet and she returns to England. He follows and persuades her otherwise.

KING OF BURLESQUE

Produced by Darryl F. Zanuck
Directed by Sidney Lanfield
Screenplay by Gene Markey and Harry Tugend, adapted by James Seymour, from a story by Viña Delmar
Photographed by Peverell Marley
Songs by Jimmy McHugh, Ted Koehler, Jack Yellen, and Lew Pollack
Musical direction by Victor Baravalle
88 minutes

Cast: Warner Baxter, Alice Faye, Jack Oakie, Arline Judge, Mona Barrie, Gregory Ratoff, Dixie Dunbar, Fats Waller, Nick Long, Jr., Kenny Baker, Charles Quigley, Keye Luke

Among the best of the backstage musicals, the title refers to a Broadway impresario (Warner Baxter) who graduates from burlesque to the legitimate theatre and does well until he marries a society lady (Mona Barrie), whose influence causes him to produce the wrong vehicles. His top singer, who also loves him (Alice Faye), leaves for London when he marries but returns when he divorces and is in need of help. She and her friends pull him together and get his career going again. Good production numbers and brisk direction helped makes this Alice Faye's best musical to date and paved the way to better films for her.

THE LITTLEST REBEL

Produced by B. G. DeSylva
Directed by David Butler
Screenplay by Edwin Burke, from a story by Edward Peple
Photographed by John Seitz
Musical direction by Cyril Mockridge
70 minutes

Cast: Shirley Temple, John Boles, Jack Holt, Karen Morley, Bill Robinson, Guinn Williams, Willie Best, Frank McGlynn, Sr., Bessie Lyle, Hannah Washington

Shirley Temple in the Civil War, with John Boles as her father, an officer in the Confederate Army. Their plantation home runs down while he is away and her mother becomes gravely ill as the Union forces occupy the area. Father sneaks back through the lines to see his dying wife and is arrested as a spy. A Northern officer (Jack Holt) takes sympathy and arranges for father and daughter to escape, but all are captured and both officers are sentenced to execution. Shirley and Uncle Billy (Bill Robinson) go to see President Lincoln,

who rescinds the orders. A pleasant adventure yarn, *The Littlest Rebel* is prime Temple and highlighted by her dancing with the famed Bill "Bojangles" Robinson.

Warner Oland and Keye Luke in *Charlie Chan in Shanghai.*

Edgar Kennedy, Evelyn Bostock, George O'Brien in *The Cowboy Millionaire.*

25

Rita Cansino (later Hayworth) and Jane Withers in *Paddy O'Day*.

Joan Bennett, Colin Clive, and Ronald Colman in *The Man Who Broke the Bank at Monte Carlo*.

Lawrence Tibbett and Virginia Bruce in *Metropolitan*.

MAN WHO BROKE THE BANK AT MONTE CARLO

Produced by Darryl F. Zanuck
Directed by Stephen Roberts
Screenplay by Howard Smith and Nunnally Johnson, from a play by Illa Surgutchoff and Frederick Albert Swan
Photographed by Ernest Palmer
Songs by Bert Kalmar and Harry Ruby
Musical direction by Oscar Bradley
71 minutes

Cast: Ronald Colman, Joan Bennett, Colin Clive, Nigel Bruce, Montagu Love, Frank Reichef, Lionel Pape, Ferdinand Gottschalk, Charles Fallon, Leonid Snegoff, Sam Ash, Charles Coleman, Lynn Bari

Set in the years after the first World War, the story is that of a refugee Russian prince (Ronald Colman) who goes to Monte Carlo with money earned over a long period by his countrymen in Paris in order to win a fortune for them. He wins ten million francs but refuses the usual etiquette of returning to the tables. The operators scheme to get him back and he does return—with the inevitable result: he loses it all. The film offers some good shots of Monte Carlo and its famed casino, showing the operation of baccarat, and above all it gives the charming Ronald Colman much opportunity to engage in light comedy and romance.

METROPOLITAN

Produced by Darryl F. Zanuck
Directed by Richard Boleslawski
Screenplay by Bess Meredyth and George Marion, Jr., from a story by Bess Meredyth
Photographed by Rudolph Mate
Musical direction by Alfred Newman
76 minutes

Cast: Lawrence Tibbett, Virginia Bruce, Alice Brady, Cesar Romero, Thurston Hall, Luis Alberni, George Marion, Sr., Adrian Rosley, Christian Rub, Ruth Donnelly, Franklyn Ardell, Etienne Giradot, Jessie Ralph

The first 20th Century-Fox film. A vehicle for operatic baritone Lawrence Tibbett, it drew good critical notices but small response from the public. Despite his fine voice, Tibbett was not an engaging film personality and the heavy dosage of arias proved too much for moviegoers in 1935. The story concerns a prima donna (Alice Brady) who walks out on the Metropolitan Opera House and forms her own company, peopling it with promising talent of her acquaintance and Tibbett as her leading man. But the capricious, temperamental lady walks out on this company, too, leaving Tibbett and his friends to pull it all together—which they do to great success. As a reminder of the extraordinary singing of Tibbett, *Metropolitan* deserves to be remembered.

MY MARRIAGE

Produced by Sol M. Wurtzel
Directed by George Archainbaud
Screenplay by Frances Hyland
Photographed by Barney McGill
Musical direction by Samuel Kaylin
73 minutes

Cast: Claire Trevor, Kent Taylor, Pauline Frederick, Paul Kelly, Helen Wood, Thomas Beck, Beryl Mercer, Henry Kolker, Colin Tapley, Noel Madison, Ralf Harolde, Charles Richman, Frank Dawson

A thin soap opera, it deals with an interfering mother-in-law (Pauline Frederick). She tries to stop the marriage of her son (Kent Taylor) to a girl (Claire Trevor) whose father's murder has revealed his connections with racketeers. It turns out that another of her sons (Thomas Beck) is involved in the murder, although unwittingly. The couple are happily married and mother backs down.

MUSIC IS MAGIC

Produced by John Stone
Directed by George Marshall
Screenplay by Edward Eliscu and Lou Breslow, based on a play by Gladys Unger and Jesse Lasky, Jr.
Photographed by L. W. O'Connell
Songs by Oscar Levant, Sidney Clare, Arthur Johnson, and Raul Roulien
Musical direction by Samuel Kaylin
66 minutes

Cast: Alice Faye, Ray Walker, Bebe Daniels, Frank Mitchell, Jack Durant, Rosina Lawrence, Thomas Beck, Andrew Tombes, Luis Alberni, Hattie McDaniel

A Hollywood story, concerning a star (Bebe Daniels) who refuses to recognize the fact that she is getting older and that her popularity is waning. She finally recognizes the facts, but not until she has been replaced in her new film by a movie chorus girl (Alice Faye), who becomes an instant success. Made at the time when Fox was merging with Twentieth Century Pictures, the film shows obvious signs of economy and the shortest running time of any of the Faye musicals. It does, however, contain some amusing comments on Hollywood.

NAVY WIFE

Produced by Sol M. Wurtzel
Directed by Allan Dwan
Screenplay by Sonya Levien, from a story by Kathleen Norris
Photographed by John Seitz
Musical direction by D. Buttolph
69 minutes

Cast: Claire Trevor, Ralph Bellamy, Jane Darwell, Warren Hymer, Ben Lyon, Kathleen Burke, George Irving, Anne Howard

Employing a lot of Hawaiian footage as background, *Navy Wife* centers around a Naval hospital, with Claire Trevor as a nurse. Reluctant to fall in love because of what she has seen of divorce, her views change when she meets an officer (Ralph Bellamy). She is under the impression that he is still in love with his deceased wife, but because he has a crippled daughter, she marries him—and finds that he does indeed love her.

PADDY O'DAY

Produced by Sol M. Wurtzel
Directed by Lewis Seiler
Screenplay by Lou Breslow and Edward Eliscu, from an original story by Sonya Levien
Photographed by Arthur Miller
Music by Harry Akst, Troy Sanders
Lyrics by Sidney Clare, Edward Eliscu
Special song by Pinky Tomlin
Dances by Franchon
Musical direction by Samuel Kaylin
73 minutes

Cast: Jane Withers, Pinky Tomlin, Rita Cansino, Jane Darwell, George Givot, Francis Ford, Vera Lewis, Louise Carter, Russell Simpson, Michael Visaroff, Nina Visaroff

A vehicle to show off the talents of Jane Withers, it displays her as an immigrant who arrives in America to find her mother has died. She escapes Ellis Island and with the aid of friends she has met on the boat she becomes an entertainer. Her success makes it hard for the Immigration officials to do anything except give their approval.

PROFESSIONAL SOLDIER

Produced by Darryl F. Zanuck
Directed by Tay Garnett
Screenplay by Gene Fowler and Howard Ellis Smith, from a story by Damon Runyan
Photographed by Rudolph Mate
Music by Louis Silvers
75 minutes

Cast: Victor McLaglen, Freddie Bartholomew, Gloria Stuart, Constance Collier, Michael Whalen, C. Henry Gordon, Pedro de Cordoba, Lumsden Hare, Walter Kingsford, Lester Matthews, Dixie Dunbar, Rollo Lloyd, Maurice Cass, General Savitsky

In a mythical European country, a rugged soldier-of-fortune (Victor McLaglen) is hired to kidnap a prince (Freddie Bartholomew) so that a new political party can take control. The prince is in favor of the scheme because it will allow him to get away and have fun. His whereabouts are discovered and the kidnapper and his accomplice (Michael Whalen) are thrown into jail. They break out when they realize the prince's life is in danger and that the political party wishing to gain control is an evil one. With that knowledge they do battle and restore the young man to his throne. A good adventure yarn, well played and directed.

SHOW THEM NO MERCY

Produced by Darryl F. Zanuck
Directed by George Marshall
Screenplay by Kubec Glasmon and Henry Lehrman, from a story by Kubec Glasmon
Photographed by Bert Glennon
Musical direction by David Buttolph
76 minutes

Cast: Rochelle Hudson, Cesar Romero, Bruce Cabot, Edward Norris, Edward Brophy, Warren Hymer, Herbert Rawlinson, Robert Gleckler, Charles C. Wilson, Frank Conroy, Edythe Elliott, William Benedict, Orrin Burke, Booth Howard, Paul McVey

The sentiment in the title refers to kidnapping. A young couple (Rochelle Hudson and Edward Norris) take cover from a rainstorm in an abandoned country house used by kidnappers. The toughest of them (Bruce Cabot) wants to kill the intruders, but a more civilized one (Cesar Romero) stops him. Finally, G-Men arrive and save the couple. A well-made crime story, it helped show audiences the government's plans to crack down on the prevalent kidnapping racket.

THANKS A MILLION

Produced by Darryl F. Zanuck
Directed by Roy Del Ruth
Screenplay by Nunnally Johnson
Songs by Arthur Johnston and Gus Kahn
Photographed by Peverell Marley
Musical direction by Arthur Lange
87 minutes

Cast: Dick Powell, Ann Dvorak, Fred Allen, Patsy Kelly, Raymond Walburn, Benny Baker, Alan Dinehart, Andrew Tombes, Paul Harvey, Edwin Maxwell, Margaret Irving, Charles Richman, Paul Whiteman and his band, Ramona Rubinoff, and The Yacht Club Boys

Zanuck borrowed Dick Powell, then greatly popular as a singing leading man, from Warners to head the cast of this fine satire on politics written by Nunnally Johnson. A traveling group of entertainers stop over in a small town and to escape from a downpour, they wander in on a political rally, where the candidate (Raymond Walburn) is making a fool of himself. The entertainer's slick manager (Fred Allen) suggests that his troupe enliven the program. Later the candidate lapses into a drunken stupor and the lead entertainer (Dick Powell) makes a speech in his stead. The political party realizes the young man's power over audiences and talk him into becoming their candidate. Later he exposes his backers as crooks, but he wins office as governor anyway. The Johnson script hits the mark as satire and Fred Allen is perfect with his quips. Powell performs likeably and sings a few good songs, and the Paul Whiteman Orchestra puts in an entertaining appearance.

THIS IS THE LIFE

Produced by Joseph Engel
Directed by Marshall Neilan
Screenplay by Lamar Trotti and Arthur Horman, from a story by Gene Towner, Graham Baker, Lou Breslow, and Sid Brod
Photographed by Daniel Clark
Music and lyrics by Sammy Stepp and Sidney Clare
63 minutes

Cast: Jane Withers, John J. McGuire, Sally Blane, Sidney Toler, Gloria Roy, Gordon Westcott, Francis Ford, Ralf Harolde, Emma Dunn, Del Henderson, Robert Graves, Selmer Jackson, Nick Lucas, Fritzi Brunette, Jayne Hovig, Harry C. Bradley

Jane Withers as a singing-dancing orphan, released from an orphange in the care of a couple who take advantage of her talents. Tired of their treatment, she runs away and after ups-and-downs with the authorities becomes a pro-entertainer.

THUNDER MOUNTAIN

Produced by Sol Lesser
Directed by David Howard
Screenplay by Dan Jarrett and Don Swift, from a story by Zane Grey
Photographed by Frank B. Good
68 minutes

Cast: George O'Brien, Barbara Fritchie, Frances Grant, Morgan Wallace, George F. Hayes, Edward LeSaint, Dean Benton, William Norton Bailey, Sid Jordan

A mining story set in the tall-timber country. George O'Brien is a prospector who stakes a claim to a gold mine with a partner but gets double-crossed by a scheming saloonkeeper. The film, a cut above average in Westerns, concerns his fight to set matters right.

WHISPERING SMITH SPEAKS

Produced by Sol Lesser
Directed by David Howard
Screenplay by Gilbert Wright and Rex Taylor, from a story by Frank H. Spearman
Photographed by Frank Good

Cast: George O'Brien, Irene Ware, Kenneth Thomson,

Maude Allen, Spencer Charters, Vic Potel, Frank Sheridan, William V. Mong, Edward Keane, Maurice Cass

A Western concerning the railroad, with George O'Brien as the son of a railroad president who chooses to go to work as a track walker in order to learn the business. He encounters a girl (Irene Ware) who is about to sell some land, unaware that it contains valuable ore deposits—until George sets her straight.

YOUR UNCLE DUDLEY

Produced by Edward T. Lowe
Directed by James Tinling and Eugene Forde
Screenplay by Dore Schary and Joseph Hoffman, from a
　story by Howard Lindsay and Bertrand Robinson
Photographed by Harry Jackson
Musical direction by Samuel Kaylin
70 minutes

Cast: Edward Everett Horton, Lois Wilson, John McGuire, Rosina Lawrence, Alan Dinehart, Marjorie Gateson, William Benedict, Florence Roberts, Jane Barnes

A good vehicle for the comedic talents of Edward Everett Horton, here playing a timorous citizen who always sacrifices his own interests for the good of the town and ends up with many citations but a lot of debts. He finally asserts himself and gets his business in order.

In 1935 20th Century-Fox also produced the following Spanish-language films:

ANGELITA (Little Angel)

Produced by John Stone
Directed by Louis King

Starring: Rosita Diaz and José Crespo

ASEGURA A SU MUJER (Insure Your Wife)

Produced by John Stone
Directed by Lewis Seiler

Starring: Conchita Montenegro and Raul Roulien

JULIETA COMPRA UN HIJO (Juliet Buys a Baby)

Produced by John Stone
Directed by Louis King

Starring: Catalina Barcena and Gilbert Roland

ROSA DE FRANCIA (Rose of France)

Produced by John Stone
Directed by Gordon Wiles

Starring: Rosita Diaz and Antonio Moreno

SEÑORA CASADA NECEISITA MARIDO (A Married Woman Needs a Husband)

Produced by John Stone
Directed by James Tinling

Starring: Catalina Barcena and Antonio Moreno

TE QUIERO CON LOCURA (I'm Crazy About You)

Produced by John Stone
Directed by John J. Boland

Starring: Rosita Moreno and Raul Roulien

Victor McLaglen and Freddie Bartholomew in *Professional Soldier.*

Andrew Tombes, Alan Dinehart, Paul Harvey, Dick Powell, Fred Allen, and Edwin Maxwell in *Thanks a Million.*

1936

BACK TO NATURE

Produced by Max Golden
Directed by James Tinling
Screenplay by Robert Ellis and Helen Logan
Photographed by Daniel B. Clark
Musical direction by Samuel Kaylin
57 minutes

Cast: Jed Prouty, Shirley Deane, Dixie Dunbar, Tony Martin, Spring Byington, Kenneth Howell, George Ernest, June Carlson, Florence Roberts, Billy Mahan, Ivan Miller

In the third episode of the adventures of the Jones family, they travel to a convention in a trailer. The oldest daughter gets mixed up with an escaped convict, the oldest son has a summer flirtation which turns out badly, and the younger son manages to make some money with photography. The Yosemite backgrounds help the picture, but the family returns home feeling that trailer travel isn't all it's cracked up to be.

BANJO ON MY KNEE

Produced by Nunnally Johnson
Directed by John Cromwell
Screenplay by Nunnally Johnson, from a story by Harry Hamilton
Photographed by Ernest Palmer
Music and lyrics by Jimmy McHugh and Harold Adamson
Musical direction by Arthur Lange
80 minutes

Cast: Barbara Stanwyck, Joel McCrea, Walter Brennan, Buddy Ebsen, Helen Westley, Walter Catlett, Anthony Martin, Katherine DeMille, Victor Killian, Minna Gombell, Spencer Charters, George Humbert, Hilda Vaughn, Cecil Weston, Louis Mason, and the Hall Johnson Choir

A genial account of life on the Mississippi in the late nineteenth century, the story centers on the marriage of a young couple (Joel McCrea and Barbara Stanwyck), with the bridegroom running away on his wedding night because he thinks he has killed one of the guests. His father (Walter Brennan) and his wife eventually find him in New Orleans and persuade him to return, since no crime has been committed. With a few songs by Jimmy McHugh and Harold Adamson and interesting photography of the river and its boats, *Banjo on My Knee* rates as pleasing entertainment.

THE BORDER PATROLMAN

Produced by Sol Lesser
Directed by David Howard
Screenplay by Dan Jarrett and Ben Cohen, from a story by Dan Jarrett and Ben Cohen
Photographed by Frank B. Good
60 minutes

Cast: George O'Brien, Polly Ann Young, William P. Carlton, Roy Mason, Mary Doran, Al Hill, Smiley Burnett, Tom London, George MacQuarrie, Cyril Ring, John St. Polis

Like most of the George O'Brien Westerns, this one is amusing in addition to offering scenery and action. As a border patrolman he arrests a spoiled daughter (Polly Ann Young) of wealthy parents for smoking in a restricted area and is retained by them to keep her in line. For spite she goes across the border into Mexico and gets mixed up with jewel thieves, but after he saves her, she realizes it's George she loves.

CAN THIS BE DIXIE?

Produced by Sol M. Wurtzel
Directed by George Marshall
Screenplay by Lamar Trotti, from a story by Lamar Trotti and George Marshall
Photographed by Bert Glennon and Ernest Palmer
Music and lyrics by Sidney Clare and Harry Akst
70 minutes

Cast: Jane Withers, Slim Summerville, Helen Wood, Thomas Beck, Sara Haden, Claude Gillingwater, Donald Cook, James Burke, Jed Prouty, Hattie McDaniel, Troy Brown, Robert Warwick, Ferdinand Blecher, William Worthington, Otis Harlan

Jane Withers saves a Southern mansion from its creditors. She and her itinerant patent-medicine-peddling father (Slim Summerville) turn up at an ancestral home and organize its cotton pickers into entertainers in order to raise money, and then when more money is needed she turns the place into a nightclub. Light but bright material and a good vehicle for Withers.

CAPTAIN JANUARY

Produced by Darryl F. Zanuck
Directed by David Butler

Screenplay by Sam Heilman, Gladys Lehman, and Harry
    Tugend, from a story by Laura E. Richard
Photographed by John Seitz
Music and lyrics by Lew Pollack, Sidney D. Mitchell, and
    Jack Yellen
Dance direction by Jack Donohue
Musical direction by Louis Silvers
75 minutes

Cast: Shirley Temple, Guy Kibbee, Slim Summerville,
Buddy Ebsen, Sara Haden, Jane Darwell, June Lang,
Jerry Tucker, Nella Walker, George Irving, James Farley,
Si Jenks, John Carradine, Mary McLaren

Among the best of the Temple films, *Captain January*
has her living with a lighthouse keeper (Guy Kibbee),
who rescued her when her parents drowned. All goes
well until a truant officer (Sara Haden) decides the
little girl is not being properly brought up and should
be sent to a boarding school. Shirley is hauled away
but rescued by kind relatives, who give the lighthouse
keeper and his friends jobs as the crew of their boat.
Young Buddy Ebsen plays one of the friends and his
song-and-dance with Shirley, "At the Codfish Ball,"
is impressively staged on a dock set.

Spring Byington and Jed Prouty in *Back to Nature.*

CAREER WOMAN

Produced by Sol M. Wurtzel
Directed by Lewis Seiler
Screenplay by Lamar Trotti, from a story by Gene Fowler
Photographed by James Van Trees and Robert Planck
Musical direction by Samuel Kaylin
70 minutes

Cast: Claire Trevor, Michael Whalen, Isabel Jewell, Eric
Linden, Virginia Field, Gene Lockhart, Edward S. Brophy,
El Brendel, Guinn Williams, Stirling Holloway, Charles
Middleton, Charles Waldron, Sr., Paul Stantin, Kathleen
Lockhart, Frank McGlynn, Sr., June Storey, Lynne Berke-
ley, Ray Brown, George Meeker, Howard Hickman,
Spencer Charters, Erville Alderson, Ely Malyon, Otto
Hoffman

Lamar Trotti's script allows for criticism of theatrical-
ism in conducting murder trials. A fledgling lawyer
(Claire Trevor) and a flamboyant one (Michael
Whalen) defend a girl (Isabel Jewell) accused of killing her father. The flamboyant approach offends the
jury, but the simple, honest one of the new lawyer
saves the girl.

Barbara Stanwyck, Joel McCrea, and Katherine De Mille in
Banjo on My Knee.

CHAMPAGNE CHARLIE

Produced by Edward T. Lowe
Directed by James Tinling
Screenplay by Allen Rivkin
Photographed by Daniel Clark
Musical direction by Samuel Kaylin
60 minutes

Warner Oland in *Charlie Chan at the Circus.*

Jean Hersholt as *The Country Doctor.*

Cast: Paul Cavanagh, Helen Wood, Thomas Beck, Minna Gombell, Herbert Mundin, Noel Madison, Montagu Love

The title role in this film told in flashback is that of a suave gambler (Paul Cavanagh) who is murdered when he double-crosses his backers, who expected him to marry a girl in order to acquire a huge dowry. The murderer plans to blackmail the girl and is himself killed, apparently by his valet (Herbert Mundin), to protect the girl.

CHARLIE CHAN AT THE CIRCUS

Produced by John Stone
Directed by Harry Lachman
Screenplay by Robert Ellis and Helen Logan, based on the character created by Earl Derr Biggers
Photographed by Daniel C. Clarke
Music by Samuel Kaylin
72 minutes

Cast: Warner Oland, Keye Luke, George and Olive Brasno, Francis Ford, Maxine Reiner, John McGuire, Shirley Deane, Paul Stanton, J. Carrol Naish, Boothe Howard, Drue Leyton, Wade Boteler, Shia Jung

Using a real circus in which to set the mystery—and bringing in all of Charlie Chan's twelve children as spectators—the master sleuth deduces that the murderer is the snake charmer (J. Carrol Naish), who commits his crimes while dressed in an ape suit.

CHARLIE CHAN AT THE OPERA

Produced by John Stone
Directed by H. Bruce Humberstone
Screenplay by Scott Darling and Charles S. Belden, based on a story by Bess Meredyth and the character created by Earl Derr Biggers
Photographed by Lucien Andriot
Music direction by Samuel Kaylin
66 minutes

Cast: Warner Oland, Boris Karloff, Keye Luke, Charlotte Henry, Thomas Beck, Margaret Irving, Gregory Gaye, Nedda Harrigan, Frank Conroy, Guy Usher, William Demarest, Maurice Cass, Tom McGuire

Possibly the best of the Charlie Chan pictures, this one benefits from having Boris Karloff in the role of an opera star suffering from amnesia and being suspected of murdering fellow performers. Boris turns out to be innocent. A good use of the theatrical setting and some operatic sequences make this a prime item in the series.

CHARLIE CHAN AT THE RACE TRACK

Produced by John Stone
Directed by H. Bruce Humberstone
Screenplay by Robert Ellis, Helen Logan, and Edward T. Lowe, based on a story by Lou Breslow and Edward T.

Lowe and the character created by Earl Derr Biggers
Photographed by Jarry Jackson
Music by Samuel Kaylin
70 minutes

Cast: Warner Oland, Keye Luke, Helen Wood, Thomas Beck, Alan Dinehart, Gavin Muir, Gloria Day, Jonathan Hale, G. P. Huntley, Jr., George Irving, Frankie Darro

On board a steamship from Honolulu to Los Angeles, Charlie Chan investigates the death of a wealthy race horse owner about to enter his prize stallion in the Santa Anita Handicap. The owner appears to have been kicked to death by his horse. Chan deduces otherwise and also thwarts a possible race track swindle.

THE COUNTRY BEYOND

Produced by Sol M. Wurtzel
Directed by Eugene Forde
Screenplay by Lamar Trotti and Adele Commandini, based on a story by James Cliver Curwood
Photographed by Barney McGill
73 minutes

Cast: Rochelle Hudson, Paul Kelly, Robert Kent, Alan Hale, Alan Dinehart, Andrew Tombes, Claudia Coleman, Matt McHugh, Paul McVey, Holmes Herbert

Based on one of James Oliver Curwood's many stories about the Canadian Northwest and the Mounted Police, this one concerns a young Mountie (Robert Kent) who falls in love with the daughter (Rochelle Hudson) of a man (Alan Hale) he believes to be a fur thief and murderer—until the real culprit (Alan Dinehart) is revealed.

THE COUNTRY DOCTOR

Produced by Darryl F. Zanuck
Directed by Henry King
Screenplay by Sonya Levien, from a story by Charles E. Blake
Photographed by John Seitz and Daniel B. Clark
Musical direction by Louis Silver
110 minutes

Cast: Jean Hersholt, June Lang, Slim Summerville, Michael Whalen, Dorothy Petterson, Robert Barrat, John Qualen, Montagu Love, Jane Darwell, Frank Reicher, David Torrence, George Chandler, Helen Jerome Eddy, Aileen Carlyle, George Meeker, J. Anthony Hughes, William Benedict, the Dionne Quintuplets

A greatly popular film in 1936, because of its enactment of the birth of the Dionne Quintuplets in Canada, with Jean Hersholt playing Dr. Dafoe, who made medical history with his delivery and care of the infants. He was awarded the Order of the British Empire for his services but prior to that he had had a tough

time administering medicine in the small, remote lumber settlement of Moosetown. The film outlines his fight with local businessmen to put up money for a hospital and their electing of another doctor as chief once it is built. Called by a poor local worker (John Qualen) to assist his wife in labor, the doctor brings forth the Quints. The film tells the story well and gives plenty of footage to the actual infants, who seem to be aware of their importance and behave charmingly.

CRACK-UP

Produced by Samuel G. Engel
Directed by Malcolm St. Clair
Screenplay by Charles Kenyon and Sam Mintz, from a story by John Goodrich
Photographed by Barney McGill
Music and lyrics by Sidney Clare and Harry Akst
Musical direction by Samuel Kaylin
65 minutes

Cast: Peter Lorre, Brian Donlevy, Helen Wood, Ralph Morgan, Thomas Beck, Kay Linaker, Lester Matthews, Earl Foxe, J. Carrol Naish, Gloria Roy, Oscar Apfel, Paul Stanton, Howard Hickman

A complicated spy yarn, with Peter Lorre as the head of a foreign espionage group out to get documents about new aircraft. A test pilot (Brian Donlevy) agrees to turn over the plans during a trans-Atlantic trial run, but the plane develops mechanical trouble and crashes, taking the main conspirators to a watery grave.

THE CRIME OF DR. FORBES

Produced by Sol M. Wurtzel
Directed by George Marshall
Screenplay by Frances Hyland and Saul Elkins, from a story by Frances Hyland and Saul Elkins
Music and lyrics by Gene Rose and Sidney Claire
Musical direction by Samuel Kaylin
75 minutes

Cast: Gloria Stuart, Robert Kent, Henry Armetta, J. Edward Bromberg, Sara Haden, Alan Dinehart, Charles Lane, DeWitt Jennings, Taylor Holmes, Paul Stanton, Russell Simpson, Paul McVey, Charles Crocker-King

A medical crime tale, built around the matter of mercy killing, it concerns a scientist (J. Edward Bromberg) who is gravely injured in an accident. He asks his protégé (Robert Kent) to give him an overdose of opiate to put him out of his misery. When the scientist dies, the doctor is accused of murder, but it turns out that the scientist overdosed himself.

DIMPLES

Produced by Darryl F. Zanuck
Directed by William A. Seither
Screenplay by Arthur Sheekman and Nat Perrin

Photographed by Bert Glennon
Songs by Jimmy McHugh and Ted Koehler
Musical direction by Louis Silvers
79 minutes

Cast: Shirley Temple, Frank Morgan, Helen Westley, Robert Kent, Stepin Fetchit, Astrid Allwyn, Delmer Byron, The Hall Johnson Choir, Berton Churchill, Paul Stanton, Julius Tannen, John Carradine, Billy McClain, Jack Clifford, Betty Jean Hainey, Arthur Aylesworth, Leonard Cibrick Warner, Walter and George Weidler, Jesse Scott, Thurman Black

Set in mid-nineteenth century New York City, *Dimples* smacks a little of *Oliver Twist*. Shirley Temple lives with her charming but petty-thieving grandfather (Frank Morgan) and earns pennies as a street entertainer. She upbraids him for picking pockets while she amuses the crowds. They entertain in the home of a society lady (Helen Westley) and Shirley takes the blame for the items grandfather steals. The lady understands the predicament and adopts Shirley, and makes it possible for her to appear on the legitimate stage. The film ends with a performance of "Uncle Tom's Cabin" and success for Shirley. In this Temple attraction, the little star has a hard time keeping Frank Morgan from stealing the scenes.

EDUCATING FATHER

Produced by Max Golden
Directed by James Tinling
Screenplay by Katharine Kavanaugh, Edward T. Lowe, and John Patrick
Photographed by Daniel B. Clark
Musical direction by Samuel Kaylin
59 minutes

Cast: Jed Prouty, Shirley Deane, Dixie Dunbar, Spring Byington, Kenneth Howell, June Carlson, George Ernest, Florence Roberts, William Mahan, Francis Ford, Charles Tannen, J. Anthony Hughes, David Newell, Charles H. Wilson, Jonathan Hale, Erville Alderson

Shirley Temple in *Dimples*.

The Jones family, with well-meaning but bumbling father (Jed Prouty) trying to stop his oldest son (Kenneth Howell) from becoming a pilot, instead of a druggist like himself. But when the son flies Dad back from a fishing trip in order to save the lease on his store, he changes his mind.

EVERY SATURDAY NIGHT

Produced by Max Golden
Directed by James Tinling
Screenplay by Edward Eliscu, from a story by Katharine Kavanaugh
Photographed by Joseph August
Musical direction by Samuel Kaylin
58 minutes

Cast: June Lang, Thomas Beck, Jed Prouty, Spring Byington, Florence Roberts, Kenneth Howell, George Ernest, June Carlson, Paul Stanton, the Paxton Sisters, William Mahan, Kay Hughes, Phyllis Fraser

The first of the Jones family series, with Jed Prouty as the father and Spring Byington as the mother. The five children all disregard father, except when they want help and mother consoles them when they get in trouble. This first film is virtually plotless and gets its impact from a string of familiar family problems, such as the eldest son who wants the family car, and wrecks it, the youngest son who lends money to the others for interest, and the eldest daughter who wants to grow up to be a movie star.

EVERYBODY'S OLD MAN

Produced by Bogart Rogers
Directed by James Flood
Screenplay by Patterson McNutt and A. E. Thomas, from a story by Edgar Franklin
Photographed by Barney McGill
82 minutes

Cast: Irvin S. Cobb, Rochelle Hudson, Johnny Downs, Norman Foster, Alan Dinehart, Sara Haden, Donald Meek, Warren Hymer, Maurice Cass, Charles Coleman, Ramsey Hill, John Miltern, Walter Walker, Frederick Burton, Hal K. Dawson, Delma Byron, Hilda Vaughn

Character actor Irvin S. Cobb in the star role as an elderly businessman who takes a year off when the death of a peer causes him to reflect on the passing years. With the time, he helps straighten out the muddled affairs of the peer's wild children and teaches them about responsibility in life and in business.

FIFTEEN MAIDEN LANE

Produced by Sol M. Wurtzel
Directed by Allan Dwan
Screenplay by Lou Breslow, David Silverstein, and John Patrick, based on a story by Paul Burger

Photographed by John Seitz
65 minutes

Cast: Claire Trevor, Cesar Romero, Douglas Fowley, Lloyd Nolan, Lester Matthews, Robert McWade, Ralf Harolde, Russell Hicks, Holmes Herbert

Cesar Romero as a jewel thief and killer, and Claire Trevor as an insurance investigator who pretends to be a thief in order to gain access to the gang. She inveigles her way to the leader and with the aid of a detective (Lloyd Nolan) arranges for the police to round them all up. A typical Grade B programmer of its time.

THE FIRST BABY

Produced by John Stone
Directed by Lewis Seiler
Screenplay by Lamar Trotti
Photographed by Barney McGill
Music by John W. Green and Edward Heyman
Musical direction by Samuel Kaylin
75 minutes

Cast: Johnny Downs, Shirley Deane, Jane Darwell, Dixie Dunbar, Marjorie Gateson, Gene Lockhart, Taylor Holmes, Willard Robertson, Hattie McDaniel

A domestic comedy-drama, with an overbearing mother-in-law (Marjorie Gateson) interfering in the lives of her daughter (Shirley Deane) and son-in-law (Johnny Downs). By the time the daughter has her second baby, she knows enough to halt the interference.

GENTLE JULIA

Produced by Sol M. Wurtzel
Directed by John Blystone
Screenplay by Lamar Trotti, from a story by Booth Tarkington
Photographed by Ernest Palmer
Musical direction by Samuel Kaylin
62 minutes

Cast: Jane Withers, Tom Brown, Marsha Hunt, Jackie Searl, Francis Ford, George Meeker, Maurice Murphy, Harry Holman, Myra Marsh, Hattie McDaniel, Jackie Hughes, Eddie Buzard

Small-town life, with Jane Withers helping to straighten out the love lives of her friends. A bashful newspaperman (Tom Brown) almost loses his girl (Marsha Hunt) when a charming scoundrel (George Meeker) comes to town, but Jane sees to it that the right parties finally march down the aisle.

GIRLS' DORMITORY

Produced by Raymond Griffith
Directed by Irving Cummings

Screenplay by Gene Markey, from a story by Ladislaus Fodor
Photographed by Merritt Gerstad
Music by Arthur Lange and Charles Maxwell
66 minutes

Cast: Herbert Marshall, Ruth Chatterton, Simone Simon, Constance Collier, J. Edward Bromberg, Dixie Dunbar, John Qualen, Shirley Deane, Tyrone Power, Jr., Frank Reicher, George Hassell, Lynne Berkeley, June Storey, Christian Rub, Rita Gould, Lillian West, Symona Boniface

The head of a girl's private school in Europe (Herbert Marshall) falls in love with a pupil (Simone Simon) and she with him. They prepare to announce their engagement when the girl learns that one of the other teachers (Ruth Chatterton) is also in love with him, and she steps aside for the older woman. *Girls' Dormitory* was the film which introduced the young French star Simone Simon to the American public, but it is memorable as Tyrone Power's debut. The twenty-two-year-old Power was given a small part in a nightclub sequence and provoked so much favorable comment that Zanuck decided to elevate him immediately to stardom.

HALF ANGEL

Produced by Darryl F. Zanuck
Directed by Sidney Lanfield
Screenplay by Bess Meredyth, Gene Fowler, and Allen Rivkin, from a story by F. Tennyson Jesse
Photographed by Bert Glennon
Musical direction by Louis Silvers
65 minutes

Cast: Frances Dee, Brian Donlevy, Charles Butterworth, Helen Westley, Henry Stephenson, Sara Haden, Etienne Giradot, Paul Stanton, Gavin Muir, Julius Tannen, Nigel de Brulier, Hilda Vaughn, Philip Sleeman, William Ingerson, Paul McVey, Bruce Mitchell

A murder comedy, with Frances Dee as a woman acquitted on charges of poisoning her father and then charged again when her benefactor dies from poisoning. A crack reporter (Brian Donlevy) believes in her innocence and digs away until he comes up with evidence revealing the actual culprits.

HERE COMES TROUBLE

Produced by John Stone
Directed by Lewis Seiler
Screenplay by Robert Ellis, Helen Logan, and Barry Trivers, from a story by John Bright and Robert Tasker
Photographed by Harry Jackson
62 minutes

Cast: Paul Kelly, Arline Judge, Mona Barrie, Gregory Ratoff, Halliwell Hobbes, Sammy Cohen, Andrew Tombes, Ed Brophy, Wade Boteler, Stanley Blystone, Ernie Alexander, George Chandler, Frank Hagney, Charles Stevens, Robert Homans, Granville Bates

A routine comedy crime picture, with Paul Kelly getting innocently involved with jewel thieves when one of them (Mona Barrie) gives him a cigarette lighter that contains gems. The crooks try to get it but end up getting caught by the police.

HIGH TENSION

Produced by Sol M. Wurtzel
Directed by Allan Dwan
Screenplay by Lou Breslow, Edward Eliscu, and John Patrick, from a story by J. Robert Bren and Norman Houston
Photographed by Barney McGill
63 minutes

Cast: Brian Donlevy, Glenda Farrell, Norman Foster, Helen Wood, Robert McWade, Theodore von Eltz, Romaine Collander, Jasper Sawyer, Hattie McDaniel, Murray Alper

A knockout comedy concerning the love affair between a flippant, brawling cable layer (Brian Donlevy) and a glib magazine writer (Glenda Farrell). He doesn't want to get married but objects to her seeing any other men. After doing a dangerous job in Hawaii and rescuing a friend (Norman Foster), he decides marriage is best.

HUMAN CARGO

Produced by Sol M. Wurtzel
Directed by Allan Dwan
Screenplay by Jefferson Parker and Doris Malloy, from a story by Kathleen Shepard
Photographed by Daniel B. Clark
Musical direction by Samuel Kaylin
66 minutes

Cast: Claire Trevor, Brian Donlevy, Alan Dinehart, Ralph Morgan, Helen Troy, Rita Cansino, Morgan Wallace, Herman Bing, John McGuire, Ralf Harolde, Wade Boteler, Harry Wood

A pair of rival newspaper reporters (Brian Donlevy and Claire Trevor) go after a smuggling ring who bring illegal aliens into the country. They board a ship in Vancouver, survive being discovered by the crooks, and finally expose the leaders. Appearing as an alien who gets killed is eighteen-year-old Rita Cansino, who had now spent a year at Fox playing bits and was about to leave the studio. Not much more than a year later she would change her surname to Hayworth.

IT HAD TO HAPPEN

Produced by Darryl F. Zanuck
Directed by Roy Del Ruth

Jane Withers and Jackie Searl in *Gentle Julia.*

Simone Simon and Tyrone Power in *Girls' Dormitory.*

Screenplay by Howard Ellis Smith and Kathryn Sola,
from a story by Rupert Hughes
Photographed by Peverell Marley
Musical direction by Arthur Lange
79 minutes

Cast: George Raft, Rosalind Russell, Leo Carrillo, Arline
Judge, Alan Dinehart, Andrew Tombes, Arthur Hohl,
Paul Stanton, Pierre Watkins, Stanley Fields, George
Irving, Thomas Jackson

The story of a poor lad (George Raft) who rises
to power as a political leader, spurred on by his secret
love for the wife (Rosalind Russell) of a wealthy
banker (Alan Dinehart). When the banker tampers
with funds and leaves the country, the politician
replaces the funds. In doing so he makes himself culp-
able and faces a grand jury investigation, which clears
him and brings him the woman he loves.

KING OF THE ROYAL MOUNTED

Produced by Sol Lesser
Directed by Howard Bretherton
Screenplay by Earl Snell, from a story by Zane Grey
Photographed by Herman Neumann
61 minutes

Cast: Robert Kent, Rosalind Keith, Alan Dinehart, Frank
McGlynn, Arthur Loft, Grady Sutton, Jack Luden, Artie
Ortego

Based upon the popular newspaper comic strip, which
in turn was based upon a Zane Grey story, this is another of Hollywood's many versions of life in Canada
with its famed Mounted Police. Here Sergeant King

Loretta Young and Janet Gaynor in *Ladies in Love.*

Tyrone Power, Madeleine Carroll, and Sir Guy Standing in *Lloyds of London.*

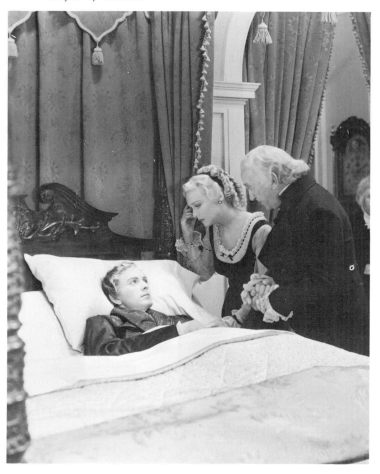

(Robert Kent) protects a girl (Rosalind Keith) who comes to claim a mine owned by her deceased father and runs afoul of a crooked lawyer out to claim the mine for himself.

LADIES IN LOVE

Produced by B. G. DeSylva
Directed by Edward H. Griffith
Screenplay by Malville Baker, from a story by Ladislaus Bus-Fekete
Photographed by Hal Mohr
Musical direction by Louis Silvers
97 minutes

Cast: Janet Gaynor, Loretta Young, Constance Bennett, Simone Simon, Don Ameche, Paul Lukas, Tyrone Power, Jr., Alan Mowbray, Wilfrid Lawson, J. Edward Bromberg, Virginia Field, Frank Dawson, Egon Brecher, Jayne Regan, Vesey O'Davern, John Bleifer, Eleanor Wesselhoeft, William Brisbane

Three Budapest working girls (Loretta Young, Janet Gaynor, and Constance Bennett) pool their resources in order to rent an expensive apartment and hopefully impress the men they date. Loretta falls for a young and wealthy nobleman (Tyrone Power) and when she learns he will marry someone of his own class, she considers taking poison. But the poison is accidentally taken by Janet, whose illness brings her a doctor (Don Ameche), with whom she has long been in love. Constance marries a businessman (Wilfred Lawson) who has been courting her and Loretta consoles herself with the acquisition of a hat shop. *Ladies in Love* is fairly amusing stuff and served to further the public interest in young Tyrone Power, who seemed to like his pairing with Loretta Young, a fact immediately capitalized upon by Darryl Zanuck.

LITTLE MISS NOBODY

Produced by Sol M. Wurtzel
Directed by John Blystone
Screenplay by Lou Breslow, Paul Burger, and Edward Eliscu, from a story by Frederick Hazlitt Brennan
Photographed by Bert Glennon
Music and lyrics by Jack Stern, Henry H. Tobias, Harry Tobias, and Sidney Claire
Musical direction by Samuel Kaylin
65 minutes

Cast: Jane Withers, Jane Darwell, Ralph Morgan, Sara Haden, Harry Carey, Betty Jean Hainey, Thomas Jackson, Jackie Morrow, Jed Prouty, Claudia Coleman, Donald Haines, Clarence H. Wilson, Lillian Harmer

A spirited young girl (Jane Withers), an inmate in an orphanage, gets into lots of jams and is sent to a reform school. On the way she escapes and when she is found, she is given a trial, at which the prosecuting attorney turns out to be her real father.

LLOYD'S OF LONDON

Produced by Darryl F. Zanuck
Directed by Henry King
Screenplay by Ernest Pascal and Walter Ferris, from a
 story by Curtis Kenyon
Photographed by Bert Glennon
Musical direction by Louis Silvers
115 minutes

Cast: Freddie Bartholomew, Madeleine Carroll, Sir Guy
Standing, Tyrone Power, C. Aubrey Smith, Virginia Field,
Forrester Harvey, George Sanders, Montagu Love, J. M.
Kerrigan, Gavin Muir, Will Stanton, Douglas Scott, John
Burton, Lumsden Hare, Una O'Connor, Miles Mander,
Murray Kinell, Ralph Cooper, Fay Chaldecott, Yorke
Sherwood, May Beatty, Robert Grieg, Hugh Huntley,
Billy Bevan, E. E. Clive, Elsa Buchanan, Georges Rena-
vent, Lester Mathews, Arthur Hohl, Reginald Barlow,
Charles Crocker King, Holmes Herbert

Zanuck took a chance on Tyrone Power as the lead in
this grandly scaled quasi-historical romance and
launched the career of one of his most popular stars.
Power here plays Jonathan Blake, who became a
leading light of the great British insurance company,
Lloyds. The film invents a close friendship with Lord
Nelson and assumes that his victory over Napoleon at
Trafalgar in 1815 had a great bearing upon the fortunes
of the company. Blake is presented as an enterprising
young rogue who gradually becomes more responsible.
He falls in love with an English aristocrat (Madeleine
Carroll), whose wastrel husband (George Sanders)
gravely wounds him. As a history lesson *Lloyds of
London* can only be regarded as a whetting of interest,
but it proved a highly popular entertainment and ad-
vanced Zanuck's plans to put 20th Century-Fox in the
Hollywood big league.

A MESSAGE TO GARCIA

Produced by Darryl F. Zanuck
Directed by George Marshall
Screenplay by W. L. Lipscomb and Gene Fowler, from
 a story by Elbert Hubbard and Lieut. Andrew S. Rowan
Photographed by Rudolph Mate
Musical direction by Louis Silvers
77 minutes

Cast: Wallace Beery, Barbara Stanwyck, John Boles, Alan
Hale, Herbert Mundin, Mona Barrie, Enrique Acosta,
Juan Torena, Martin Garralaga, Blanca Vicher, Jose Luis
Tortosa, Lucio Villegas, Frederick Vogeding, Pat Mori-
arity, Octavio Giraud

Set in Cuba during the Spanish-American War, the
film is based on a true incident, that of Lt. Andrew
Rowan (John Boles) carrying a message from President McKinley to General Garcia (Enrique Acosta),
the leader of the Cuban insurgents against the Spanish, telling him of U.S. support. The film invents
fiction around that fact, with Rowan being aided by a

renegade marine (Wallace Beery) and meeting the
daughter (Barbara Stanwyck) of a martyred Cuban
patriot while trekking through the jungle. They share
danger and conflict with vicious spies before the mission is completed.

O'MALLEY OF THE MOUNTED

Produced by Sol Lesser
Directed by David Howard
Screenplay by Dan Jarrett and Frank Howard Clark, from
 a story by William S. Hart
Photographed by Frank B. Good
59 minutes

Cast: George O'Brien, Irene Ware, Stanley Fields, James
Bush, Victor Potel, Reginald Barlow, Dick Cramer, Tom
London, Charles King, Olin Francis, Crawford Kent

George O'Brien in the title role as a Canadian Mountie
assigned to track down a gang of outlaws who are
terrorizing American border towns. He pretends to be
an outlaw and manages to join the gang, and leads them
in a bank hold-up that results in their capture.

ONE IN A MILLION

Produced by Darryl F. Zanuck
Directed by Sidney Lanfield
Screenplay by Leo Praskins and Mark Kelly
Photographed by Edward Cronjager
Songs by Lew Pollack and Sidney D. Mitchell
Musical direction by Louis Silvers
95 minutes

Cast: Sonja Henie, Adolphe Menjou, Don Ameche, Ned
Sparks, Jean Hersholt, Ritz Brothers, Arline Judge, Bor-
rah Minnevitch, Dixie Dunbar, Leah Ray, Shirley Deane,
Montagu Love, Albert Conti, Julius Tannen

Darryl Zanuck introduced Norwegian skating champ
Sonja Henie to movie stardom with this film and
launched a mutually profitable career. Henie would
never become an actress, but her pretty smile and her
grace on skates captured the public. The plot of *One
in a Million* has Henie being discovered in Switzerland
while preparing for the Olympics by an American
theatrical manager (Adolphe Menjou). Complications
occur, but the manager finally gets to bring her to
Madison Square Garden, where she triumphs. With
Don Ameche as the love interest and the Ritz Brothers
for comedy, plus plenty of music, *One in a Million*
was a great success for the studio, bringing in profits
and prestige for Zanuck.

PEPPER

Produced by John Stone
Directed by James Tinling
Screenplay by Lamar Trotti, from a story by Lamar Trotti

Sonja Henie in *One in a Million*.

John Boles, Barbara Stanwyck, and Wallace Beery in *A Message to Garcia*.

Tony Martin, Judy Garland, and Jack Haley in *Pigskin Parade*.

Photographed by Daniel Clark
65 minutes

Cast: Jane Withers, Irvin S. Cobb, Slim Summerville, Dean Jagger, Muriel Roberts, Ivan Lebedeff, George Humbert, Maurice Cass, Romaine Callender, Tommy Bupp, Carey Harrison, Reginald Simpson

Jane Withers butts into the life of an ailing, grouchy millionaire (Irvin S. Cobb) and turns him into a happy man—once she has persuaded him to take her and her gang to Coney Island. She also benefits his health by preventing the marriage of his daughter to a phony nobleman.

PIGSKIN PARADE

Produced by Bogart Rogers
Directed by David Butler
Screenplay by Harry Tugend, Jack Yellen, and William Conselman, from a story by Arthur Sheekman, Jack Yellen, and Mark Kelly
Photographed by Arthur Miller
Music and lyrics by Lew Pollack and Sidney D. Mitchell, and the Yacht Club Boys
Musical direction by David Buttolph
95 minutes

Cast: Stuart Erwin, Patsy Kelly, Jack Haley, the Yacht Club Boys, Johnny Downs, Betty Grable, Arline Judge, Dixie Dunbar, Judy Garland, Anthony Martin, Fred Kohler, Jr., Grady Sutton, Elisha Cook, Jr., Eddie Nugent, Julius Tannen

A mixture of college campus fun and the antics of football games, *Pigskin Parade* is notable as the first feature film appearance of Judy Garland, then fifteen and singing with a lilting voice. Betty Grable, long before her stardom at Fox, also appears in a minor part. The story concerns a married pair of coaches (Jack Haley and Patsy Kelly) who come across a hillbilly (Stuart Erwin) who has a great talent for throwing footballs. Because of him they are invited to play at the Yale Bowl—and win. Light on plot but amusing, the film contains almost a dozen musical numbers, with Garland shining in several.

POOR LITTLE RICH GIRL

Produced by Darryl F. Zanuck
Directed by Irving Cummings
Screenplay by Sam Hellman, Gladys Lehman, and Harry Tugend, based on stories by Eleanor Gates and Ralph Spence
Photographed by John Seitz
Songs by Mack Gordon and Harry Revel
Musical direction by Louis Silvers
72 minutes

Cast: Shirley Temple, Alice Faye, Gloria Stuart, Jack Haley, Michael Whalen, Sara Haden, Jane Darwell,

Claude Gillingwater, Paul Stanton, Henry Armetta, Charles Coleman, Arthur Hoyt, John Wray, Tyler Brooke, Mathilde Comont, Tony Martin

The motherless daughter (Shirley Temple) of a wealthy soap manufacturer (Michael Whalen) gets lost when her nursemaid is involved in a traffic accident. She comes to the attention of a pair of entertainers (Alice Faye and Jack Haley) because of her dancing ability and they decide to make her a part of their act. When the act plays on the radio, the father hears it and is able to locate his daughter. *Poor Little Rich Girl* is contrived but charming and full of good musical material for Temple, Faye, and Haley.

THE PRISONER OF SHARK ISLAND

Produced by Darryl F. Zanuck
Directed by John Ford
Screenplay by Nunnally Johnson
Photographed by Bert Glennon
Musical direction by Louis Silvers
94 minutes

Cast: Warner Baxter, Gloria Stuart, Claude Gillingwater, Arthur Byron, O. P. Heggie, Harry Carey, John McGuire, Francis McDonald, John Carradine, Paul Fix, Joyce Kay, Frank McGlynn, Sr., Ernest Whitman, J. M. Kerrigan, Douglas Wood

The story of Dr. Samuel Mudd (Warner Baxter), who was badly treated by the United States government in 1865 following his treatment of Lincoln's assassin, John Wilkes Booth. Nunnally Johnson's fine script and John Ford's firm direction do justice to the story of a man condemned for following the ethics of his trade. Mudd pleads innocent of conspiracy, being unaware of the identity of the wounded man, but he is sentenced to jail at Shark Island. While there he performs heroic work as a doctor, containing the Yellow Fever which plagues the island and takes many lives. Eventually, through the pleas of friends, he is exonerated and returned to his wife (Gloria Stuart) and child.

PRIVATE NUMBER

Produced by Raymond Griffith
Directed by Roy Del Ruth
Screenplay by Gene Markey, from a story by Cleves Kinkead
Photographed by Peverell Marley
Musical direction by Louis Silvers
80 minutes

Cast: Robert Taylor, Loretta Young, Patsy Kelly, Basil Rathbone, Marjorie Gateson, Paul Harvey, Joe Lewis, Jane Darwell, Paul Stanton, John Miljan, Billy Bevan, Monroe Owsley, George Irving, Frank Dawson, May Beatty

Warner Baxter in *The Prisoner of Shark Island.*

Alice Faye, Jack Haley, and Shirley Temple in *Poor Little Rich Girl.*

41

A contrived and dated romantic melodrama about a serving girl (Loretta Young) who marries the son (Robert Taylor) of the wealthy household against their wishes. The arrogant butler (Basil Rathbone) does his best to break them up, because he wants the girl for himself and because he knows the parents are against the match. But love wins out in the end.

RAMONA

Produced by Sol M. Wurtzel
Directed by Henry King
Screenplay by Lamar Trotti, from a story by Helen Hunt Jackson
Photographed in Technicolor by William Skall and Chester Lyons
Musical direction by Alfred Newman
90 minutes

Cast: Loretta Young, Don Ameche, Kent Taylor, Pauline Frederick, Jane Darwell, Katherine DeMille, John Carradine, Pedro De Cordoba, J. Carrol Naish, Victor Killian, Charles Waldron, Claire Du Brey, Russell Simpson, William Benedict, Robert Spindola, Chief Thunder Cloud

The first 20th Century-Fox film in full Technicolor. Set in early California it tells of a beautiful half-Indian girl (Loretta Young) who is brought up in a wealthy home. When the son of the house (Kent Taylor) falls in love with her, his parents reveal that she is the offspring of a tragic love between an Indian and a member of the household. Learning that she herself is part Indian, the girl feels free to love the handsome Indian (Don Ameche) employed by the home, a decision which brings tragedy as well as happiness. *Ramona* is romantic nonsense by contemporary standards but still a remarkable picture because of the richness of the original three-strip Technicolor.

REUNION

Produced by Bogart Rogers
Directed by Norman Taurog
Screenplay by Sam Hellman, Gladys Lehman, and Sonya Levien, from a story by Bruce Gould
Photographed by Daniel B. Clark
Musical direction by Emil Newman
80 minutes

Cast: Dionne Quintuplets, Jean Hersholt, Rochelle Hudson, Helen Vinson, Slim Summerville, Robert Kent, John Qualen, Dorothy Peterson, Alan Dinehart, J. Edward Bromberg, Sara Haden, Montagu Love, Tom Moore, George Ernest, Esther Ralston, Katherine Alexander, Julius Tannen, Edward McWade, Maude Eburne, George Chandler, Claudia Coleman, Hank Mann, Hattie McDaniel

A follow-up to *The Country Doctor* that takes advantage of the universal fascination with the Dionne Quints. The plot evolves around a Chamber of Commerce plan to honor the Quints' doctor (Jean Hersholt) by staging a reunion of the many people he has brought into the world. This gives him opportunity to dispense advice and help solve some of their problems, in addition to the fun of the reunion.

THE ROAD TO GLORY

Produced by Darryl F. Zanuck
Directed by Howard Hawks
Screenplay by Joel Sayre and William Faulkner
Photographed by Gregg Toland
Music by Louis Silvers
103 minutes

Cast: Fredric March, Warner Baxter, Lionel Barrymore, June Lang, Gregory Ratoff, Victor Killian, Paul Stanton, John Qualen, Julius Tannen, Theodore Von Eltz, Paul Fix, Leonid Kinsky, Jacques Venoire, Edythe Raynore

A somewhat romanticized but largely realistic account of life in the trenches of the first World War, *The Road to Glory* deals with a regiment of the French Army whose men are constantly being killed and replaced. As each new group comes in, the war-weary captain (Warner Baxter) tells them to be proud of the regiment's fine history. His lieutenant (Fredric March) begins his war adventures as a dapper fellow but is soon sobered by the harsh and dirty life in the trenches. Both men fall in love with a pretty nurse (June Lang), but it is the lieutenant who wins her when the captain sacrifices his life in combat. With a good script, fine acting, and the controlled direction of Howard Hawks, *The Road to Glory* remains among the best films about The Great War.

SING, BABY SING

Produced by Darryl F. Zanuck
Directed by Sidney Lanfield
Screenplay by Milton Sperling, Jack Yellen, and Harry Tugend
Photographed by Peverell Marley
Songs by Jack Yellen, Lew Pollack, Sidney Mitchell, Louis Alter, Walter Bullock, and Richard Whiting
Musical direction by Louis Silvers
90 minutes

Cast: Alice Faye, Adolphe Menjou, Gregory Ratoff, Ted Healy, Patsy Kelly, Michael Whalen, The Ritz Brothers, Montagu Love, Dixie Dunbar, Douglas Fowley, Paul Stanton, Tony Martin

A step forward in Zanuck's campaign to make a major star of Alice Faye, *Sing, Baby, Sing* presents her as a nightclub singer whose crazy agent (Gregory Ratoff) gets her involved in schemes to advance her career. One scheme with a wild-living movie star (Adolphe Menjou) finally results in a radio contract. Thin material but whipped along amusingly by director Lan-

Loretta Young and Don Ameche in *Ramona*.

Warner Baxter and Fredric March in *The Road to Glory*.

field and some expert comedy character actors, like Ratoff, Patsy Kelly, and Ted Healy.

SINS OF MAN

Produced by Kenneth Macgowan
Directed by Gregory Ratoff and Otto Brower
Screenplay by Samuel G. Engel, from a story by Joseph Roth
Photographed by Sidney Wagner
Musical director Louis Silver
86 minutes

Cast: Don Ameche, Allen Jenkins, J. Edward Bromberg, Ann Shoemaker, DeWitt Jennings, Fritz Leiber, Francis Ford, Christian Rub, Adrian Roseley, Gene Reynolds, Mickey Rentschler, John Miltern, Paul Stanton, Edward Van Sloan, Egon Brecher, Fred Kohler, Jr., Maxine Reiner, Ruth Robinson

Don Ameche's screen debut, in a dual role as the sons of an Austrian church bell ringer (Jean Hersholt). The father loves music and yearns for his sons to love it too, but is bitterly disappointed when the first leaves for America to become an aeronautical engineer and the second is born deaf and mute. The second son gains his faculties during a first World War bombardment, becomes a musician, and finds success in America as a conductor. The old man, after years of wandering, eventually finds the son and becomes a bell ringer in his orchestra.

THE SONG AND DANCE MAN

Produced by Sol M. Wurtzel
Directed by Allan Dwan
Screenplay by Maude Fulton, from a story by George M. Cohan
Music and lyrics by Sidney Clare and Lew Pollack
Dances by Fanchon
72 minutes

Cast: Claire Trevor, Paul Kelly, Michael Whalen, Ruth Donnelly, James Burke, Helen Troy, Lester Matthews, Ralf Harolde, Gloria Roy, Margaret Dumont, Billy Bevan, Irene Franklin

Taking its title from a George M. Cohan Broadway show, but lacking his dynamic presence, this deals with life in the theatre, chiefly with a dance team (Claire Trevor and Paul Kelly). He drinks and gambles, but the girl goes on to success with a rich, handsome producer (Michael Whalen), until a director substitutes his own girl friend in the show. The reformed gambler-dancer then turns up and set matters right, which saves the show and leads to romance for the girl and the producer.

STAR FOR A NIGHT

Produced by Sol M. Wurtzel
Directed by Lewis Seiler
Screenplay by Frances Hyland and Saul Elkins, from a story by Michaelis Stangeland
Photographed by Ernest Palmer
Music and lyrics by Harry Akst and Sidney Clare
Dance direction by Sammy Lee
Musical direction by Samuel Kaylin
76 minutes

Cast: Claire Trevor, Jane Darwell, Evelyn Venable, Arline Judge, J. Edward Bromberg, Frank Reicher, Joyce Compton, Astrid Allwyn, Dean Jagger, Adrienne Marden, Susan Fleming, Dickie Walters, Chick Chandler, Hattie McDaniel

A blind woman (Jane Darwell) comes to America to visit her three children, all of whom she believes to be greatly successful. But the one she thinks is a great

stage star (Claire Trevor) is a chorus girl, the concert pianist (Evelyn Venable) is a music clerk, and the automobile manufacturer (Dean Jagger) is a taxi driver. The woman regains her sight through an operation and understands the efforts of her children to make her happy.

STOWAWAY

Produced by Buddy DeSylva
Directed by William A. Seiter
Screenplay by William Conselman, Arthur Sheekman, and Nat Perrin, based on a story by Samuel G. Engel
Photographed by Arthur Miller
Songs by Mack Gordon, Harry Revel, Irving Caesar, and Gerald Marks
Musical direction by Louis Silvers
87 minutes

Cast: Shirley Temple, Robert Young, Alice Faye, Eugene Pallette, Helen Westley, Arthur Treacher, J. Edward Bromberg, Astrid Allwyn, Allan Lane, Robert Greig, Willie Fung, Philip Ahn

The ward (Shirley Temple) of missionaries becomes lost in Shanghai and comes across an American playboy (Robert Young) who befriends her. She falls asleep in his car and wakes up to find it in the hold of a ship bound for America. Also on board is a pretty young lady (Alice Faye) who marries the playboy in order to give the child a home. Their differences lead to the divorce court, but with the aid of a sympathetic judge (J. Edward Bromberg), the child brings her new parents together. A well-crafted Temple feature, *Stowaway* gives her plenty of opportunity to sing and dance, notably at an amateur show where she impersonates Al Jolson, Eddie Cantor, and Fred Astaire.

THANK YOU, JEEVES

Produced by Sol M. Wurtzel
Directed by Arthur Greville Collins
Screenplay by Joseph Hoffman and Stephen Gross, from a story by P. G. Wodehouse
Photographed by Barney McGill
Musical direction by Samuel Kaylin
57 minutes

Cast: Arthur Treacher, Virginia Field, David Niven, Lester Matthews, Colin Tapley, John Graham Spacey, Ernie Stanton, Gene Reynolds, Douglas Walton, Willie Best

Arthur Treacher as P. G. Wodehouse's classic butler Jeeves is the main attraction of this thin comedy about crooks on the trail of aeronautical secrets and Jeeves' mistaking them for government agents. Once he knows the true facts, he helps his master (David Niven) bring the crooks to justice.

36 HOURS TO KILL

Produced by Sol M. Wurtzel
Directed by Eugene Forde
Screenplay by Lou Breslow and John Patrick, from a
    story by W. R. Burnett
Photographed by Arthur Miller
Musical direction by Samuel Kaylin
65 minutes

Cast: Brian Donlevy, Gloria Stuart, Douglas Fowley, Isabel Jewell, Stepin Fetchit, Julius Tannen, Warren Hymer, Romaine Callender, James Burke, Jonathan Hale, Gloria Mitzi, Charles Lane

On a train, a top-ranking gangster (Douglas Fowley), on his way to pick up prize money, runs into a G-man (Brian Donlevy) and a newspaperwoman (Claire Trevor), who fall in love once they have brought the gangster to justice.

TO MARY WITH LOVE

Produced by Darryl F. Zanuck
Directed by John Cromwell
Screenplay by Richard Sherman and Howard Ellis Smith,
    from a story by Richard Sherman
Photographed by Sidney Wagner
Musical direction by Louis Silvers
87 minutes

Cast: Warner Baxter, Myrna Loy, Ian Hunter, Claire Trevor, Jean Dixon, Pat Somerset, Helen Brown, Wedgewood Nowell, Harold Forshay, Paul Hurst, Franklin Pangborn, Tyler Brooke, Arthur Aylesworth, Florence Lake, Edward Cooper, Margaret Fielding, Ruth Clifford

A marital yarn, concerning the first ten years in the married life of a businessman (Warner Baxter), starting in 1925, with ups and downs, including his crash in 1929 and his comeback in 1935. His wife (Myrna Loy) stands by him until his character changes with success. She considers divorce, but their best friend (Ian Hunter), who has loved her all along, gets them together again.

UNDER TWO FLAGS

Produced by Darryl F. Zanuck
Directed by Frank Lloyd
Screenplay by W. P. Lipscomb and Walter Ferris, from a
    story by Ouida
Photographed by Ernest Palmer and Sidney Wagner
Musical direction by Louis Silvers
105 minutes

Cast: Ronald Colman, Claudette Colbert, Victor McLaglen, Rosalind Russell, Gregory Ratoff, Nigel Bruce, C. Henry Gordon, Herbert Mundin, John Carradine, Lumsden Hare, J. Edward Bromberg, Onslow Stevens, Fritz Leiber, Thomas Beck, William Ricciardi, Frank Reicher,

Claudette Colbert and Ronald Colman in *Under Two Flags.*

Shirley Temple, Alice Faye, Robert Young, and Allan Lane in *Stowaway.*

Francis McDonald, Harry Semels, Nicholas Soussanin, Douglas Gerrard

One of the more romantic concepts of life in the French Foreign Legion, with Ronald Colman as an elegant, mysterious Englishman who joins the legion after having taken the blame for a crime committed by his brother. A local girl, a Legion mascot called Cigarette (Claudette Colbert) falls in love with him, to the annoyance of the commandant (Victor McLaglen), who loves her. The commandant sends him on dangerous missions, hoping he will not return. On one such mission Cigarette leads relief troops to his rescue, but at the cost of her own life. But Colman has fallen in love with a society visitor (Rosalind Russell) to the garrison, and once cleared of his fake guilt they are free to start a life together. Viewed as pleasing fiction, *Under Two Flags* is an excellent example of Colman at his peak, being charming and gallant and noble.

UNDER YOUR SPELL

Produced by John Stone
Directed by Otto Preminger
Screenplay by Frances Hyland and Saul Elkins, from a story by Bernice Mason and Sy Bartlett
Photographed by Sidney Wagner
Music and lyrics by Arthur Schwartz and Howard Dietz
Musical direction by Arthur Lange
62 minutes

Cast: Lawrence Tibbett, Wendy Barrie, Gregory Ratoff, Arthur Treacher, Gregory Gaye, Berton Churchill, Jed Prouty, Charles Richman

Lawrence Tibbett's flop with *Metropolitan* caused Zanuck to put him in this minor picture, simple because he had him under contract and had to pay him. The story, paper thin, is about a famous singer who tires of publicity and fans and takes off to a ranch in Mexico. His anxious manager (Gregory Ratoff) sends a young lady (Wendy Barrie) to get him back and they end up getting married. This was Otto Preminger's first American assignment as a director.

WHITE FANG

Produced by Darryl F. Zanuck
Directed by David Butler
Screenplay by Hal Long and S. G. Duncan, from a story by Jack London
Photographed by Arthur Miller
Musical direction by Arthur Lange
70 minutes

Cast: Michael Whalen, Jean Muir, Slim Summerville, Charles Winninger, Jane Darwell, John Carradine, Thomas Beck, Joseph Herrick, George Ducount, Marie Chorre

Set in the Klondike in the gold rush days of the 1890's, the Jack London yarn tells of a woman (Jean Muir) and her weakling brother (Thomas Beck) who inherit a mine. The brother finds the going rough and commits suicide, and the guide (Michael Whalen) is accused by those trying to gain the mine of murder. He is almost lynched, but the brother's discovered diary proves him innocent. The guide and the woman then continue with their planned marriage.

WHITE HUNTER

Produced by Darryl F. Zanuck
Directed by Irving Cummings
Screenplay by Sam Duncan and Kenneth Earl, from a story by Gene Markey
Photographed by Chester Lyons
Musical direction by Arthur Lange
65 minutes

Cast: Warner Baxter, June Lang, Gail Patrick, Alison Skipworth, Wilfrid Lawson, George Hassell, Ernest Whitman, Forrester Harvey, Willie Fung, Olaf Hytton, Ralph Cooper, Will Stanton

An African adventure, shot on the back lot and spiked with location footage, with Warner Baxter as a safari guide living in virtual exile because of past grief. He is hired by a man (Wilfrid Lawson) who was responsible for his father's death, but the past is forgotten when the hunter falls in love with the man's daughter (June Lang). A far-fetched but interesting yarn, greatly aided by the skillful editing.

WILD BRIAN KENT

Produced by Sol Lesser
Directed by Howard Bretherton
Screenplay by James Gruen and Earle Snell, from a story by Harold Bell Wright
Photographed by Harry Neumann
60 minutes

Cast: Ralph Bellamy, Mae Clarke, Helen Lowell, Stanley Andrews, Lew Kelly, Richard Alexander, Jack Duffy, Eddie Chandler, Howard Hickman

The title role is that of a polo-playing cad, who learns about responsibility when he stops off in a Kansas town and meets a girl (Mae Clarke) and her aunt (Helen Lowell) who need money to keep their ranch. He becomes a partner with a real estate dealer (Stanley Andrews), but turns on him when he realizes he is a vicious crook out to ruin the women. He saves the situation and wins respect.

ALI BABA GOES TO TOWN

Produced by Darryl F. Zanuck
Directed by David Butler
Screenplay by Harry Tugend and Jack Yellen, from a
     story by Gene Towne, Graham Baker, and Gene Fowler
Photographed by Ernest Palmer
Music and lyrics by Mack Gordon and Harry Revel, and
     Raymond Scott
Dance direction by Sammy Lee
Musical direction by Louis Silver
80 minutes

Cast: Eddie Cantor, Tony Martin, Roland Young, June
Lang, Louise Hovick, John Carradine, Virginia Field,
Alan Dinehart, Douglas Dumbrille, Maurice Cass, Warren
Hayes, Douglas Wood, Sidney Fields, Ferdinand Gott-
schalk, Charles Lane, Raymond Scott Quintet, Peters
Sisters, Jeni Le Gon, Pearl Twins

Eddie Cantor, as a hobo, wanders into the camp of a
movie company on location in the desert and finds
work as an extra. They are making a film about the
Arabian Nights and after drinking a sleeping potion,
he imagines he is back in old Baghdad. He becomes an
advisor to the Sultan and establishes work projects,
taxes the rich, and abolishes the army. The sultan's
enemies try to get rid of him, but with the aid of a
magic carpet he routs them. And then wakes up. A
good spoof on the days of Roosevelt's New Deal—
Cantor performs at his best—with good production
values, songs and dances, and a little satire on Hollywood itself.

ANGEL'S HOLIDAY

Produced by John Stone
Directed by James Tinling
Screenplay by Frank Fenton and Lynn Root, from a story
     by Frank Fenton and Lynn Root
Photographed by Daniel B. Clark
Song by Harold Howard and Bill Telaak
Musical direction by Samuel Kaylin
76 minutes

Cast: Jane Withers, Robert Kent, Joan Davis, Sally Blane,
Harold Huber, Frank Jenks, Ray Walker, John Qualen,
Lon Chaney, Jr., Al Lydell, Russell Hopton, Paul Hurst,
John Kelly, George Taylor, Cy Kendall, Charles Arnt

Jane Withers comes to the rescue of a movie star (Sally
Blane) as she visits her hometown and falls prey to a
group of racketeers, who hold her for ransom. With
the aid of a young newspaper reporter (Robert Kent),
who is an ex-boy friend of the star, plus the police and
the fire department, Jane rounds up the crooks.

BIG BUSINESS

Produced by Max Golden
Directed by Frank R. Strayer
Screenplay by Robert Ellis and Helen Logan, from a story
     by Ron Ferguson and Eleanor De Lamater, based on
     the character created by Katherine Kavanaugh
Photographed by Edward Snyder
Musical direction by Samuel Kaylin
60 minutes

Cast: Jed Prouty, Shirley Deane, Spring Byington, Russell
Gleason, Kenneth Howell, Allan Lane, George Ernest,
June Carlson, Florence Roberts, Billy Mahan, Marjorie
Weaver, Frank Conroy, Wallis Clark

The Jones family gets mixed up in an oil scheme racket,
as a football star (Allan Lane) returns to his hometown
and inveigles Jones (Jed Prouty) and his friends to
invest. The wells contain only mud and water, but an
invention of the older Jones boy (Kenneth Howell)
brings in money to compensate the sorry investors.

BIG TOWN GIRL

Produced by Milton Feld
Directed by Frank R. Strayer
Screenplay by Lou Breslow, John Patrick, Robert Ellis,
     and Helen Logan, from stories by Darrell Ware and
     Frances Whiting Reid
Photographed by Lucien Andriot
Music and lyrics by Sidney Clare and Harry Akst
Musical direction by Samuel Kaylin
66 minutes

Cast: Claire Trevor, Donald Woods, Alan Dinehart, Alan
Baxter, Murray Alper, Spencer Charters, Maurice Cass,
Irving Bacon, George Chandler, Lillian Yarbo, Jonathan
Hale

A department store song plugger (Claire Trevor) is

Louise Hovick and Eddie Cantor in *Ali Baba Goes to Town*.

Tyrone Power and Loretta Young in *Cafe Metropole*.

turned into a radio star by a slick promoter (Alan Dinehart) and becomes the mysterious "Masked Countess." She keeps her identity secret because her estranged husband (Alan Baxter) is a criminal, but a reporter (Donald Woods) discovers her secret and falls in love with her.

BORN RECKLESS

Produced by Sol M. Wurtzel
Directed by Mal St. Clair
Screenplay by John Patrick, Robert Ellis, and Helen Logan, from a story by Jack Andrews
Photographed by Daniel B. Clark
Musical direction by Samuel Kaylin
60 minutes

Cast: Rochelle Hudson, Brian Donlevy, Barton MacLane, Robert Kent, Harry Carey, Pauline Moore, Chick Chandler, William Pawley, Francis McDonald, George Wolcott, Joseph Crehan

An auto racing champ (Brian Donlevy) arrives in town in need of a job and joins a taxi company. It is being harrassed by a racketeer (Barton MacLane), who wants to control all the taxi companies and smashes up those who won't comply. The sister (Rochelle Hudson) of a man framed by the racketeer falls in loves with the champ and together they get the evidence to end the racket.

BORNEO

Produced by Mr. and Mrs. Martin Johnson
Announcer: Lowell Thomas
Supervised by Truman Talley
Continuity by Lew Lehr and Russell Shields
75 minutes

A documentary record of Mr. and Mrs. Martin Johnson's expeditions into Borneo, skillfully edited to convey the lifestyle of the wild and rugged region, showing its animals and terrain, and concentrating on the search for and capture of a huge orangutan.

BORROWING TROUBLE

Produced by Max Golden
Directed by Frank R. Strayer
Screenplay by Robert Chapin and Karen DeWolf, from a story by Robert Chapin and Karen DeWolf, based on the characters created by Katharine Kavanaugh
Photographed by Edward Snyder
Musical direction by Samuel Kaylin
59 minutes

Cast: Jed Prouty, Shirley Deane, Spring Byington, Russell Gleason, Kenneth Howell, George Ernest, June Carlson, Florence Roberts, Billy Mahan, Marvin Stephens, Andrew

Tombes, Howard Hickman, Cy Kendall, Joseph Downing, George Walcott, Dick Wessel, Wade Boteler

The drugstore of the Jones family is robbed and the evidence points to a wayward youngster the family has befriended (Marvin Stephens). It turns out that the boy is protecting his brother, who finally confesses and helps bring in the robbers.

CAFE METROPOLE

Produced by Nunnally Johnson
Directed by Edward H. Griffith
Screenplay by Jaques Deval, from a story by Gregory Ratoff
Photographed by Lucien Andriot
Musical direction by Louis Silver
83 minutes

Cast: Loretta Young, Tyrone Power, Adolphe Menjou, Gregory Ratoff, Charles Winninger, Helen Westley, Ferdinand Gottschalk, Christian Rub, George Renavent, Frederick Vogeding, Leonid Kinsky, Hal K. Dawson, Albert Conti, Leonid Snegoff, Armand Kaliz, Paul Porcasi, Andre Cheron, Marcelle Corday, Louise Clark, Louis Mercier

A further teaming of Tyrone Power and Loretta Young, dubbed by 1937 critics as Hollywood's prettiest twosome. Set in Paris, the slim story is that of a young American (Power) badly in debt to a nightclub owner (Adolphe Menjou), who orders him to pose as a Russian prince and court a wealthy heiress (Young), with the object of marrying her and getting hold of her money. The scheme goes awry when the two fall in love, but from true love comes the solutions to their problems. Cafe Metropole is an amusing frou-frou of a film and a well-designed Zanuck move in increasing the popularity of Power and Young.

THE CALIFORNIANS

Produced by Sol Lesser
Directed by Gus Meins
Screenplay by Gordon Newell and Gilbert Wright, from a story by Harold Bell Wright
Photographed by Harry Neumann
59 minutes

Cast: Ricardo Cortez, Marjorie Weaver, Katherine De-Mille, Maurice Black, Morgan Wallace, Nigel de Brulier, George Regas, Pierre Watkin, James Farley, Edward Keane, Gene Reynolds, Ann Gilles, Helen Holmes, Richard Bottler, Tom Forman, Bud Osborne, Monty Montague, Francisco Del Campo, William Fletcher

Set in California in 1855 and somewhat similar to The Mark of Zorro. A native son (Ricardo Cortez) returns from schooling in Spain and finds crooked politicians trying to deprive old-line Californian, Spanish-speaking families of their properties. He becomes a Robin Hood-like figure in order to set matters right.

CHARLIE CHAN AT MONTE CARLO

Produced by John Stone
Directed by Eugene Forde
Screenplay by Charles Belden and Jerry Cady, based on a story by Robert Ellis and Helen Logan, and the character created by Earl Derr Biggers
Photographed by Daniel C. Clarke
Music by Samuel Kaylin
65 minutes

Cast: Warner Oland, Keye Luke, Virginia Field, Sidney Blackmer, Harold Huber, Kay Linaker, Robert Kent, Edward Raquello, George Lynn, Louis Mercier, George Davis, John Bleifer, George Renavent

On vacation in Monte Carlo, Chan is called upon to help solve the murders of two men. One is a casino messenger bound for Paris with a million dollars' worth of bonds and the other is a small-time crook from Chicago who has been working as a bartender in a local hotel. With almost a third of the dialogue in French and a cast-full of elegant suspects, Chan arrives at his conclusions and points the finger at the murderer. Sadly, this would prove to be Warner Oland's last appearance as Chan. After starting work on the next picture, Charlie Chan at the Ringside, Oland's failing health made it impossible for him to continue. He died on August 6, 1938, at the age of fifty-seven.

CHARLIE CHAN AT THE OLYMPICS

Produced by John Stone
Directed by H. Bruce Humberstone
Screenplay by Robert Ellis and Helen Logan, based on a story by Paul Burger, and the character created by Earl Derr Biggers
Photographed by Daniel C. Clarke
Music by Samuel Kaylin
71 minutes

Cast: Warner Oland, Katherine DeMille, Pauline Moore, Allan Lane, Keye Luke, C Henry Gordon, John Eldredge, Layne Tom, Jr., Jonathan Hale, Morgan Walker, Frederick Vogeding, Andrew Tombes, Howard Hickman

Using footage of the Olympic Games in Berlin in 1936, this edition finds Chan chasing spies in order to regain an invention which will allow for remote-control flying of aircraft. Tracing them to Berlin, Chan cooperates with the German police to nab the culprits. No. One son (Keye Luke) is a member of the U.S. Swimming Team and survives a kidnapping.

CHARLIE CHAN ON BROADWAY

Produced by John Stone
Directed by Eugene Forde
Screenplay by Charles Belden and Jerry Cady, based on a

story by Art Arthur, Robert Ellis, and Helen Logan, and the character created by Earl Derr Biggers
Photographed by Harry Jackson
Music by Samuel Kaylin
67 minutes

Cast: Warner Oland, Keye Luke, Joan March, J. Edward Bromberg, Douglas Fowley, Harold Huber, Donald Woods, Louise Henry, Joan Woodbury, Leon Ames, Marc Lawrence, Tashia Mori, Charles Williams, Eugene Borden

A busy background of New York nightlife is the setting for Chan's unraveling of a nightclub singer's plans to reveal criminals in the city, all of whom are listed in her diary. The singer is murdered and the diary disappears, and Chan probes until he finds the villain to be an ambitious newspaper reporter.

CHECKERS

Produced by John Stone
Directed by H. Bruce Humberstone
Screenplay by Lynn Root, Frank Fenton, Robert Chapin, Karen DeWolf, from a story by Lynn Root and Frank Fenton
Photographed by Daniel B. Clark
Musical direction by Samuel Kaylin
79 minutes

Cast: Jane Withers, Stuart Erwin, Una Merkel, Marvin Stephens, Andrew Tombes, June Carlson, Minor Watson, John Harrington, Spencer Charters, Francis Ford

A horse race yarn, with Jane Withers joining forces with a trainer (Stuart Erwin) to save a horse with a broken leg from being shot. They take it to the ranch of a sympathetic lady (Una Merkel) and nurse it back to health. Its winning of an important race solves the problems of all involved.

CITY GIRL

Produced by Sol M. Wurtzel
Directed by Alfred Werker
Screenplay by Frances Hyland, Robin Harris, and Lester Ziffren, from a story by Frances Hyland, Robin Harris, and Lester Ziffren
Photographed by Harry Jackson
Musical direction by Samuel Kaylin
63 minutes

Cast: Phyllis Brooks, Ricardo Cortez, Robert Wilcox, Douglas Fowley, Chick Chandler, Esther Muir, Adrienne Ames, George Lynn, Charles Lane, Paul Stanton

A crime melodrama about a waitress (Phyllis Brooks) who advances her lifestyle by becoming the girl friend of a racketeer (Ricardo Cortez). He uses her to get information out of a district attorney (Robert Wilcox), whom she comes to love and for whom she eventually sacrifices her life.

DANGER—LOVE AT WORK

Produced by Harold Wilson
Directed by Otto Preminger
Screenplay by James Edward Grant and Ben Markson, from a story by James Edward Grant
Photographed by Virgil Miller
Musical direction by David Buttolph
84 minutes

Cast: Ann Sothern, Jack Haley, Mary Boland, Edward Everett Horton, John Carradine, Walter Catlett, Bennie Bartlett, Maurice Cass, Alan Dinehart, Etienne Giradot, E. E. Clive, Margaret McWade, Margaret Seddon, Elisha Cook, Jr., Hilda Vaughn, Charles Coleman, George Chandler, Spencer Charters, Hal K. Dawson, Stanley Fields, Paul Hurst, Claude Allister, Jonathan Hale, Charles Lane, Paul Stanton

The Pemberton family are rich and crazy. The daughter (Ann Sothern) is playful but a little more sane than the others, and a young lawyer (Jack Haley) is given a rough time in trying to get the signature of the parents on a contract to conclude a land sale— until the daughter falls in love with him and pursues him into marriage. A "screwball" comedy held together by the firm hand of director Otto Preminger.

DANGEROUSLY YOURS

Produced by Sol M. Wurtzel
Directed by Malcolm St. Clair
Screenplay by Lou Breslow and John Patrick
Photographed by Harry Davis
Musical direction by Samuel Kaylin
62 minutes

Cast: Cesar Romero, Phyllis Brooks, Jane Darwell, Alan Dinehart, Natalie Garson, John Harrington, Douglas Wood, Earle Foxe, Leon Ames, Albert Conti, Leonid Snegoff

A crime caper, with Cesar Romero as a detective posing as a jewel thief. He sails from Europe to New York in the company of an assortment of crooks after a famous gem and brings them to justice. But he falls in love with one of them (Phyllis Brooks), who promises to reform and goes on probation, with orders to report to her detective lover.

DINNER AT THE RITZ

Produced by Robert T. Kane
Directed by Harold D. Schuster
Screenplay by Roland Pertwee and Romney Brent
Photographed by Philip Tannura
60 minutes

Cast: Annabella, Paul Lukas, David Niven, Romney Brent, Francis L. Sullivan, Stewart Rome, Norah Swinburn, Tyrell Davis, Frederick Leister, William Dewhurst, Vivienne Chatterton, Ronald Shiner

A confused crime melodrama, starring Annabella as the daughter of a murdered European financier and working as a jewel saleswoman, all the while trying to hunt down the former colleagues of her father who conspired against him. With the aid of David Niven she manages to expose the gang, but none too plausibly.

FAIR WARNING

Produced by Sol M. Wurtzel
Directed by Norman Foster
Screenplay by Norman Foster, from a story by Philip Wylie
Photographed by Sidney Wagner
70 minutes

Cast: J. Edward Bromberg, Betty Furness, John Howard Payne, Victor Killian, Billy Burrud, Gavin Muir, Gloria Roy, Andrew Tombes, Ivan Lebedeff, John Eldredge, Julius Tannen, Paul McVey, Lelah Taylor, Lydia Knott

In the Death Valley area of California, a sheriff (J. Edward Bromberg) is called upon to solve the murder of a mine owner, who has been staying at a posh winter resort. With the aid of a youngster (Billy Burrud), who is a whiz with chemical experiments, they trace the culprit to an abandoned gold mine. An above-average mystery yarn, with Norman Foster directing from his own screenplay.

FIFTY ROADS TO TOWN

Produced by Raymond Griffith
Directed by Norman Taurog
Screenplay by George Marion, Jr. and William Conselman, from a story by Frederick Nebel
Photographed by Joseph H. August
Music and lyrics by Max Gordon and Harry Revel
Musical direction by David Buttolph
80 minutes

Cast: Don Ameche, Ann Sothern, Slim Summerville, Jane Darwell, John Qualen, Douglas Fowley, Allan Lane, Alan Dinehart, Stepin Fetchit, Paul Hurst, Spencer Charters, DeWitt Jennings, Bradley Page, Oscar Apfel, John Hamilton, Russell Hicks, Arthur Aylesworth, Jim Toney

A romantic comedy, with Don Ameche as a man who hides out in the country, so that he will not have to testify in a divorce case involving friends. He is visited by a girl (Ann Sothern), who he thinks is a process server, while she mistakes him for a gangster. They become snowbound in a cabin and surrounded by a sheriff (John Qualen) and his men, who also think Ameche is the gangster. All is forgiven with the clarification of identities.

45 FATHERS

Produced by John Stone
Directed by James Tinling
Screenplay by Frances Hyland and Albert Ray, from a story by Mary Bickel
Photographed by Harry Jackson
Musical direction by Samuel Kaylin
70 minutes

Cast: Jane Withers, Thomas Beck, Louise Henry, The Hartmans, Richard Carle, Nella Walker, Andrew Tombes, Leon Ames, Sammy Cohen, George Givot, Ruth Warren, Hattie McDaniel, Romaine Callendar

A knockabout comedy of an orphan (Jane Withers), adopted by a group of elderly men and placed in the home of one of them. She becomes a little Miss Fixit, amuses everybody with her singing and dancing, and tangles up the love life of a nephew of the house (Thomas Beck). Her intentions are always good and things turn out for the best. *45 Fathers* is simply a showcase for the talents of the likeable Withers.

THE GREAT HOSPITAL MYSTERY

Produced by John Stone
Directed by James Tinling
Screenplay by Bess Meredyth, William Conselman and Jerry Cady, based on a story by Mignon Eberhardt
Photographed by Harry Jackson
Musical direction by Samuel Kaylin
60 minutes

Cast: Jane Darwell, Sig Rumann, Sally Blane, Thomas Beck, Joan Davis, William Demarest, George Walcott, Wade Boteler, Howard Phillips

Jane Darwell as the night superintendent of a hospital and Sally Blane as a nurse whose brother is being hounded by gangsters. They make it look as if he has died as a patient in order to save him, and another patient turns out to be a wanted killer. Jumbled and confused story-telling makes it a great hospital mystery indeed.

HEIDI

Produced by Darryl F. Zanuck
Directed by Allan Dwan
Screenplay by Walter Ferris and Julien Josephson
Photographed by Arthur Miller
Musical direction by Louis Silvers
85 minutes

Cast: Shirley Temple, Jean Hersholt, Arthur Treacher, Helen Westley, Pauline Moore, Thomas Beck, Mary Nash, Sidney Blackmer, Mady Christians, Sig Rumann, Marcia Mae Jones, Delmar Watson, Egon Brecher, Christian Rub, George Humbert

The classic European tale, done up as a vehicle for Shirley Temple. Heidi is an orphan who melts the heart of her bitter grandfather (Jean Hersholt), who has not spoken since his son ran way with a girl. He gets to be fond of Heidi and goes after her when she is abducted by a cruel aunt, who sells her as a servant. She comes to the home of a wealthy man (Sidney Blackmer) and brings happiness to his invalid daughter (Marcia Mae Jones), although menaced by their miserable governess (Mary Nash). Eventually grandfather finds her. The film is the material of fables and an excellent vehicle for Temple, allowing for a couple of musical routines done as dream sequences.

THE HOLY TERROR

Produced by John Stone
Directed by James Tinling
Screenplay by Lou Breslow and John Patrick
Photographed by Daniel B. Clark
Music and lyrics by Sidney Clare and Harry Akst
Musical direction by Samuel Kaylin
68 minutes

Cast: Jane Withers, Anthony Martin, Leah Ray, El Brendel, Joe Lewis, John Eldredge, Gloria Roy, Andrew Tombes, Joan Davis, Gavin Muir, Fred Kohler, Jr., Victor Adams, Raymond Brown

Jane Withers as the daughter of a Naval Air Service officer and the darling of the base. She stages musical shows in which the men participate and at one of them a group of spies cause a brawl because they know it will close the cafe in which it is being held. They want the cafe because it is near a strategic point. When she learns who they are, Jane causes a group of naval aviators to capture the spies. Withers in fine form.

HOT WATER

Produced by Max Golden
Directed by Frank R. Strayer
Screenplay by Robert Chapin and Karen De Wolf, from a story by Ron Ferguson and Eleanor De Lamater
Photographed by Edward Snyder
Musical direction by Samuel Kaylin
55 minutes

Cast: Jed Prouty, Shirley Deane, Spring Byington, Russell Gleason, Kenneth Howell, George Ernest, June Carlson, Florence Roberts, Billy Mahan, Joan Marsh, Marjorie Weaver, Willard Robertson, Robert Gleckler, Arthur Hohl, Selmer Jackson, Joseph King

A Jones family comedy, with father (Jed Prouty) running for mayor and one of his sons secretly printing a newspaper and quoting father's comments on his crooked opponent, which causes consternation. The opposition tries to involve the family in scandal, but the secret paper prints the truth of the frame-ups and father wins the office.

IT HAPPENED OUT WEST

Produced by Sol Lesser
Directed by Howard Bretherton
Screenplay by Earle Snell and Harry Chandler, from a story by Harold Bell Wright
Photographed by Harry Neumann
56 minutes

Cast: Paul Kelly, Judith Allen, Johnny Arthur, Leroy Mason, Steve Clemento, Nina Compana, Frank La Rue, Reginald Barlow

A bank employee (Paul Kelly) is sent to Arizona to advise a rancher (Judith Allen) to sell her failing property. He is suspicious when her foreman (Leroy Mason) feels the same way, and eventually discovers that the foreman and the banker are in league to acquire the silver-laden land. He both downs the scheme and wins the girl.

THE LADY ESCAPES

Produced by Leslie Landau
Directed by Eugene Forde
Screenplay by Don Ettlinger, from a play by Eugene Helta
Photographed by Lucien Andriot
Musical direction by Samuel Kaylin
63 minutes

Cast: Gloria Stuart, Michael Whalen, George Sanders, Cora Witherspoon, Gerald Oliver-Smith, June Brewster, Howard Hickman, Joseph Tozer, Don Alvarado, Maurice Cass, Franklin Pangborn, Tom Ricketts

A marital farce about a couple (Michael Whalen and Gloria Stuart) who are always quarreling. She leaves to go to France and gets involved with a suave playboy (George Sanders), but the husband finds out the playboy is being sued for breach of promise and gets hold of the girl (June Brewster) in order for her to marry the cad. The couple realize their quarreling is silly and agree to give their marriage a new chapter.

LANCER SPY

Produced by Samuel G. Engel
Directed by Gregory Ratoff
Screenplay by Philip Dunne, from a story by Marthe McKenna
Photographed by Barney McGill
Musical direction by Arthur Lange
78 minutes

Cast: Dolores Del Rio, George Sanders, Peter Lorre, Joseph Schildkraut, Virginia Field, Sig Rumann, Maurice Moscovich, Lionel Atwill, Luther Adler, Fritz Feld, Holmes Herbert, Lester Matthews, Carlos De Valdez, Gregory Gaye, Joan Carol, Claude King, Kenneth Hunter, Frank Reicher, Leonard Mudie

Espionage during the first World War, dealing with an Englishman (George Sanders) who is the exact double of a German officer. The Englishman proceeds to Germany in the guise of the escaped German and becomes a national hero but secretly works as a British spy. A German spy (Dolores Del Rio) is assigned by her skeptical boss to cover the bogus hero, but she falls in love with him. *Lancer Spy* rates as one of the more interesting items in wartime spy yarns.

LAUGHING AT TROUBLE

Produced by Max Golden
Directed by Frank R. Strayer
Screenplay by Robert Ellis and Helen Logan, from a story by Adelyn Bushnell
Photographed by Barney McGill
Musical direction by Samuel Kaylin
67 minutes

Cast: Jane Darwell, Sara Haden, Lois Wilson, Margaret Hamilton, Delma Byron, Allan Lane, Pert Kelton, John Carradine, James Burke, Russell Hicks, Edward Acuff, Frank Reicher, William Benedict, Edward McWade

A smalltown newspaper publisher (Jane Darwell) befriends a young man (Allan Lane) who has been convicted of a murder. He escapes from jail and hides in her home. The publisher knows the identity of the real killer and traps him into a confession.

LIFE BEGINS IN COLLEGE

Produced by Harold Wilson
Directed by William A. Seiter
Screenplay by Karl Tunberg and Don Ettlinger, from a series of stories by Darrell Ware
Photographed by Robert Planck
Music and lyrics by Lew Pollack and Sidney D. Mitchell
Musical direction by Louis Silvers
80 minutes

Cast: Ritz Brothers, Joan Davis, Tony Martin, Gloria Stuart, Fred Stone, Nat Pendleton, Dick Baldwin, Joan Marsh, Jed Prouty, Maurice Cass, Marjorie Weaver, Robert Lowery, Ed Thorgersen, Lon Chaney, Jr., J. C. Nugent, Fred Kohler, Jr., Elisha Cook, Charles Wilson, Frank Sully, Norman Willis

A typical college football item of the Thirties, with the Ritz Brothers as campus tailors eager to be involved in football. When the team coach (Fred Stone) is fired, a wealthy Indian student (Nat Pendleton) endows the university with a large sum to keep the coach. The daughter of the coach (Gloria Stuart) thinks her boyfriend (Dick Baldwin) is trying to keep the Indian out of the game by revealing that he has played professionally, but it turns out someone else did the squealing. When the boyfriend is injured in the last two minutes of the game, the Ritz Brothers take to the field and, by comic default, save the game.

Jean Hersholt and Shirley Temple in *Heidi*.

Dolores Del Rio and George Sanders in *Lancer Spy*.

LOVE AND HISSES

Produced by Darryl F. Zanuck
Directed by Sidney Lanfield
Screenplay by Curtis Kenyon and Art Arthur, from a
    story by Art Arthur
Photographed by Robert Planck
Music and lyrics by Mack Gordon and Harry Revel
Musical direction by Louis Silvers
82 minutes

Cast: Walter Winchell, Ben Bernie, Simone Simon, Bert
Lahr, Joan Davis, Dick Baldwin, Peters Sisters, Ruth
Terry, Douglas Fowley, Chick Chandler, Charles Wil-
liams, George Renavent, Chilton and Thomas, Brewster
Twins, Rush Hughs, Gary Breckner, Hal K. Dawson,
Charles Judels, Harry Stubbs, Robert Battier

Columnist Walter Winchell and bandleader Ben Bernie
plays themselves in their well-contrived feud. Here
they are in conflict over a pretty singer (Simone
Simon), who, unknown to Winchell, is under contract
to Bernie for his nightclub. Bernie pretends the girl is
a flop and Winchell builds her up in his column. When
Winchell discovers he has been tricked, he makes
Bernie the victim of a fake kidnapping, which ends up
in his own club, with fun for all.

LOVE IS NEWS

Produced by Harold Wilson and Earl Carroll
Directed by Tay Garnett
Screenplay by Harry Tugend and Jack Yellen, from a
    story by William R. Lopman and Frederick Stephani
Photographed by Ernest Palmer
Musical direction by David Buttolph
72 minutes

Cast: Tyrone Power, Loretta Young, Don Ameche, Slim
Summerville, Dudley Digges, Walter Catlett, George Sanders, Jane Darwell, Stepin Fetchit, Pauline Moore, Elisha
Cook, Jr., Frank Conroy, Edwin Maxwell, Charles Williams, Julius Tannen

Tyrone Power as a breezy newspaper reporter and
Loretta Young as the daughter of a powerful financier.
He writes flashy items about her for his paper and in
retaliation she announces her engagement to him, which
causes embarrassment for him with his employers. They
skirmish but eventually realize they love each other.
Love Is News is a good sample of Hollywood's "screwball" comedies of the Thirties.

LOVE UNDER FIRE

Produced by Nunnally Johnson
Directed by George Marshall
Screenplay by Gene Fowler, Allen Rivkin, and Ernest
    Pascal, from a story by Walter Hackett
Photographed by Ernest Palmer
Musical direction by Arthur Lange
70 minutes

Cast: Loretta Young, Don Ameche, Borah Minnevitch and
his gang, Frances Drake, Walter Catlett, John Carradine,
Sig Rumann, Harold Huber, Katherine DeMille, E. E.
Clive, Don Alvarado, Georges Revanent, Clyde Cook,
George Regas, Claude King

A lightweight crime caper set against the Spanish
Civil War. A Scotland Yard detecuve (Don Ameche)
aims to bring back an alleged jewel thief (Loretta
Young) but discovers that she has been the victim of
an unscrupulous employer. After escaping Spain they
make their way to England—in love.

MIDNIGHT TAXI

Produced by Milton Feld
Directed by Eugene Forde
Screenplay by Lou Breslow and John Patrick, from a
    story by Borden Chase
Photographed by Barney McGill
Musical direction by Samuel Kaylin
73 minutes

Cast: Brian Donlevy, Frances Drake, Alan Dinehart, Sig
Rumann, Gilbert Roland, Harold Huber, Paul Stanton,
Lon Chaney, Jr., Russell Hicks, Regis Toomey

A Federal agent (Brian Donlevy) joins a taxi company
in order to uncover a counterfeit organization. One of
the drivers is a member of the gang and by befriending
him the agent gets to the leader. After various adventures and double-crossing, the agent breaks the
counterfeiters. Brian Donlevy had few chances to play
the hero in his movie career and here he does well as
the tough agent.

NANCY STEELE IS MISSING

Produced by Nunnally Johnson
Directed by George Marshall
Screenplay by Gene Fowler and Hal Long
Photographed by Barney McGill
Musical direction by David Buttolph
84 minutes

Cast: Victor McLaglen, Walter Connolly, Peter Lorre,
June Lang, Robert Kent, Shirley Deane, John Carradine,
Jane Darwell, Frank Conroy, Granville Bates, George
Taylor, Kane Richmond, Margaret Fielding, DeWitt Jen-
nings, George Chandler, George Hubert, Robert Murphy

A minor criminal (Victor McLaglen) returns to society
after seventeen years in jail and is greeted by the girl
(June Lang) who thinks he is her father. She is
actually someone he kidnapped when she was a baby.
He returns her to her wealthy father, who offers him a
reward and a job. A former jailmate (Peter Lorre) tries
to confuse the issue and steal the reward. A well-written
and tightly directed minor melodrama.

OFF TO THE RACES

Produced by Max Golden
Directed by Frank R. Strayer
Screenplay by Robert Ellis and Helen Logan, based on
    the characters created by Katharine Kavanaugh
Photographed by Barney McGill
Musical direction by Samuel Kaylin
58 minutes

Cast: Slim Summerville, Jed Prouty, Shirley Deane, Spring
Byington, Russell Gleason, Kenneth Howell, George
Ernest, June Carlson, Florence Roberts, Bill Mahan, Ann
Gillis, Fred Toones, Chick Chandler, Ruth Gillette

The Jones family get involved with Uncle George
(Slim Summerville) and his trotting horse. George
enters his trotter in the race at the fair grounds and
needs the help of the family to care for the horse and
raise money for the entrance fees. George's ex-wife
turns up in pursuit of alimony and father Jones (Jed
Prouty) takes the reins and leads the horse to victory.

ON THE AVENUE

Produced by Darryl F. Zanuck
Directed by Roy Del Ruth
Screenplay by Gene Markey and William Conselman
Photographed by Lucien Andriot
Songs by Irving Berlin
Musical direction by Arthur Lange
90 minutes

Cast: Dick Powell, Madeleine Carroll, Alice Faye, The
Ritz Brothers, George Barbier, Alan Mowbray, Cora Witherspoon, Walter Catlett, Douglas Fowley, Stephin Fetchit,
Joan Davis, Sig Rumann, Billy Gilbert, Paul Gerrits, Douglas Wood

One of the best of the Fox musicals of the Thirties, due
largely to a fine set of songs from Irving Berlin. Zanuck again borrowed Dick Powell from Warners—
Powell was among the top ten at the box office in
1937—and starred him as a Broadway producer who
stages a satire on a prominent New York society family.
The family sues, but the daughter (Madeleine Carroll)
and the producer fall in love. Complications are made
by a jealous member of the cast (Alice Faye), but she
finally decides to dabble with the daughter's wealthy
father. A good script and fine playing make *On the
Avenue* a top item in its class.

ONE MILE FROM HEAVEN

Produced by Sol M. Wurtzel
Directed by Allan Dwan
Screenplay by Lou Breslow and John Patrick, from the
    stories of Judge Ben B. Lindsey, adapted by Robin
    Harris and Alfred Golden
Photographed by Sidney Wagner
Musical direction by Samuel Kaylin
67 minutes

Tyrone Power, Slim Summerville, and Loretta Young in *Love
Is News.*

Cast: Claire Trevor, Sally Blane, Douglas Fowley, Fredi
Washington, Joan Carol, Ralf Harolde, John Eldredge,
Paul McVey, Ray Walker, Russell Hopton, Chick Chan-
dler, Eddie Anderson, Howard Hickman, Bill Robinson

A brash and likeable newspaper reporter (Claire
Trevor) likes to scoop her colleagues and seizes what
she thinks is an arresting item—a young black woman,
claiming to be the mother of a white child. It turns
out that the child is actually that of a woman (Sally
Blane) now remarried into wealth. Crooks try to take
advantage of the situation. The child is reunited with
her mother, the black woman is hired as her nurse, and
a judge persuades the reporter that the story is best
left unprinted.

ROLL ALONG COWBOY

Produced by Sol Lesser
Directed by Gus Meins
Screenplay by Dan Jarrett, based on a story by Zane Grey
Photographed by Harry Neumann
57 minutes

Cast: Smith Ballew, Cecelia Parker, Stanley Fields, Wally
Albright, Jr., Ruth Robinson, Gordon Elliott, Frank
Milan, Monte Montague, Bud Osbourne, Harry Bernard,
Budd Buster, Buster Fite and His Six Saddle Tramps.

Singing cowboy Smith Ballew turns up for work on a
ranch owned by a woman (Ruth Robinson) and finds
her to be in trouble with crooks. He straightens out
her problems and also falls in love with her daughter
(Cecelia Parker). A very minor Western.

Alice Faye, Dick Powell, and Madeleine Carroll in *On the Avenue*.

SECOND HONEYMOON

Produced by Raymond Griffith
Directed by Walter Lang
Screenplay by Kathryn Scola and Darrel Ware, from a story by Philip Wylie
Photographed by Ernest Palmer
Musical direction by David Buttolph
84 minutes

Cast: Tyrone Power, Loretta Young, Stuart Erwin, Claire Trevor, Marjorie Weaver, Lyle Talbot, J. Edward Bromberg, Paul Hurst, Jayne Regan, Hal K. Dawson, Mary Treen

A giddy comedy, typical of the Thirties and the tendency to ridicule the rich. A recently remarried young woman (Loretta Young) is bored with her stuffy, businessman husband (Lyle Talbot) and begins to yearn for the crazy times she had with her first husband (Tyrone Power), a wealthy playboy. When she meets him again during a vacation in Florida, love again rears its head and the dull second husband gets short shrift.

SECRET VALLEY

Produced by Sol Lesser
Directed by Howard Bretherton
Screenplay by Dan Jarrett and Earl Snell, from a story by Harold Bell Wright
Photographed by Charles Schoenbaum
60 minutes

Cast: Richard Arlen, Virginia Grey, Jack Mulhall, Norman Willis, Sid Saylor, Russell Hicks, Willie Fung, Maude Allen

A contemporary Western, with Richard Arlen as a rancher entertaining a girl (Virginia Grey) who has arrived in Nevada to get a divorce from her gangster husband (Jack Mulhall). The gangster follows her and runs afoul of both Arlen and the law.

SEVENTH HEAVEN

Produced by Darryl F. Zanuck
Directed by Henry King
Screenplay by Melville Baker, based on the play by Austin Strong
Photographed by Merritt Gerstad
Musical direction by Louis Silvers
102 minutes

Cast: Simone Simon, James Stewart, Jean Hersholt, Gregory Ratoff, Gale Sondergaard, J. Edward Bromberg, John Qualen, Victor Killian, Thomas Beck, Sig Rumann, Mady Christians, Rollo Lloyd, Rafaela Ottiano, Georges Renavent, Edward Keane, Irving Bacon, John Hamilton

A remake of the 1927 film, which had been a great hit for Charles Farrell and Janet Gaynor. Here the Parisian sewer worker is James Stewart, a man who yearns to have a beautiful wife and rise in the social order, and the waif he rescues from the police and takes as his wife is Simone Simon. Their home is a bleak flat on the seventh floor, but to them it is heaven. He marches off to war, but she never doubts his return. The remake failed to make anywhere near the impact of the original. Such a love fantasy as this seemed better suited to the unreality of the silent era.

SHE HAD TO EAT

Produced by Samuel G. Engel
Directed by Malcolm St. Clair
Screenplay by Samuel G. Engel, from a story by M. M. Musselman and James Edward Grant
Photographed by Barney McGill
Songs and lyrics by Sidney Clare and Harry Ault
Musical direction by Samuel Kaylin
74 minutes

Cast: Jack Haley, Rochelle Hudson, Arthur Treacher, Eugene Pallette, Douglas Fowley, John Qualen, Maurice Cass, Wallis Clark, Lelah Tyler, Tom Kennedy, Tom Dugan, Franklin Pangborn

The owner of a filling station in Arizona (Jack Haley) undergoes a string of comic adventures when he is mistaken for an escaped killer and rival gangsters kidnap him for ransom. A pleasant vehicle for Haley, with Rochelle Hudson as his fun-loving girl friend, Eugene Pallette as an eccentric millionaire, and Arthur Treacher as the millionaire's butler.

Loretta Young and Tyrone Power in *Second Honeymoon.*

Simone Simon and James Stewart in *Seventh Heaven*.

Warner Baxter and Wallace Beery in *Slave Ship*.

SING AND BE HAPPY

Produced by Milton Feld
Directed by James Tinling
Screenplay by Ben Markson, Lou Breslow, and John
 Patrick
Photographed by Daniel B. Clark
Songs and lyrics by Sidney Clare and Harry Akst
Musical direction by Samuel Kaylin
64 minutes

Cast: Tony Martin, Leah Ray, Joan Davis, Helen Westley,
Allan Lane, Dixie Dunbar, Chick Chandler, Berton Churchill, Andrew Tombes, Luis Alberni, Frank McGlynn, Sr.

A lightweight comedy built around radio, *Sing and
Be Happy* deals with rival advertising agencies com-
peting over a pickle-manufacturing account. Mostly a
vehicle to boost singer Tony Martin, here playing the
son of an ad man in love with the daughter (Leah Ray)
of a rival ad man.

SLAVE SHIP

Produced by Darryl F. Zanuck
Directed by Tay Garnett
Screenplay by Sam Hellman, Lamar Trotti, and Gladys
 Lehman, from a story by William Faulkner based on a
 novel by George S. King
Photographed by Ernest Palmer
Musical score by Alfred Newman
100 minutes

Cast: Warner Baxter, Wallace Beery, Elizabeth Allan,
Mickey Rooney, George Sanders, Jane Darwell, Joseph
Schildkraut, Arthur Hohl, Minna Gombell, Billy Bevan,
Francis Ford, J. Farrell MacDonald, Paul Hurst, Holmes
Herbert, Edwin Maxwell

A captain of the slave trade (Warner Baxter) decides
to end his career transporting Africans to America and
instructs his first mate (Wallace Beery) to discharge
the crew and engage another, in order to become a
respectable merchant mariner. When he brings his
bride (Elizabeth Allan) on board, he finds the mate
and the old crew in command and still shipping slaves.
With the aid of a few trustworthy crew members he
defeats the mutineers and clears his name. *Slave Ship*
is a solid adventure yarn and an interesting view of the
last years of the slave trade.

STEP LIVELY, JEEVES!

Produced by John Stone
Directed by Eugene Forde
Screenplay by Frank Fenton and Lynn Root, from a story
 by Frances Hyland
Photographed by Daniel B. Clark
Musical direction by Samuel Kaylin
69 minutes

Cast: Arthur Treacher, Patricia Ellis, Robert Kent, Alan Dinehart, George Givot, Helen Flint, John Harrington, George Cooper, Arthur Housman, Max Wagner, Franklin Pangborn

Arthur Treacher, Hollywood's personification of the English butler, was a logical choice for this filming of the adventures of Jeeves, the character invented by P. G. Wodehouse. Frances Hyland's concoction has the disdainful butler whisked off to America, tricked by con men into thinking he is the heir to the fortunes of Sir Francis Drake but actually is being used as a dupe. The mixture of Jeeves and mobsters provides a goodly amount of amusement.

THANK YOU, MR. MOTO

Produced by Sol M. Wurtzel
Directed by Norman Foster
Screenplay by Willis Cooper and Norman Foster, from a
    story by John P. Marquand
Photographed by Virgil Miller
Musical direction by Samuel Kaylin
66 minutes

Cast: Peter Lorre, Thomas Beck, Pauline Frederick, Jayne Regan, Sidney Blackmer, Sig Rumann, John Carradine, William Von Brincken, Nedda Harrigan, Philip Ahn, John Bleifer

An intrigue develops around a series of Chinese scrolls. Six of them are in the possession of a respected family and the seventh is eagerly sought by various parties, because when the seven scrolls are pieced together they form a map indicating the whereabouts of the treasures of Genghis Khan. When Mr. Moto (Peter Lorre) finally gets all the scrolls together, he burns them so no one will ever disturb the treasures.

THAT I MAY LIVE

Produced by Sol M. Wurtzel
Directed by Allan Dwan
Screenplay by Ben Mardson and William Conselman
Photographed by Robert Planck
Musical direction by Samuel Kaylin
70 minutes

Cast: Rochelle Hudson, Robert Kane, J. Edward Bromberg, Jack La Rue, Frank Conroy, Frank Kelsey, George Cooper, DeWitt Jennings, Russell Simpson, William Benedict

A young man (Robert Kent) is sent to jail after crooks use his ability as a safe expert. When he comes out after three years, they pick him up and involve him in more crime. He falls in love with a waitress and they takes jobs as helpers to a kindly traveling merchant (J. Edward Bromberg). The law catches up with the young man, but the resourceful merchant provides evidence to show that he was framed.

THIN ICE

Produced by Darryl F. Zanuck
Directed by Sidney Lanfield
Screenplay by Boris Ingster and Milton Sperling from the
    play *Der Komet* by Attila Obok
Photographed by Robert Planck and Edward Cronjager
Songs and lyrics by Lew Pollock, Sidney D. Mitchell,
    Mack Gordon, and Harry Revel
Musical direction by Louis Silvers
78 minutes

Cast: Sonja Henie, Tyrone Power, Arthur Treacher, Raymond Walburn, Joan Davis, Sig Rumann, Alan Hale, Leah Ray, Melville Cooper, Maurice Cass, George Givot, Greta Meyer, Egon Brecher, Torben Meyer, George Davis, Lon Chaney, Jr.

Sonja Henie's second film was among the biggest money makers for Fox in 1937. The theme was a popular one in those times—a commoner in love with a member of royalty. Here Sonja is a Swiss hotel ski instructor, who falls in love with a young man (Tyrone Power) who likes to go skiing every morning. Their affair attracts attention, but the girl is among the last to know that her young man is a prince and that she is about to become a princess. The film gives Henie plenty of opportunity to skate amid pretty scenery and reveal the skill that had made her a champion.

THINK FAST, MR. MOTO

Produced by Sol M. Wurtzel
Directed by Norman Foster
Screenplay by Howard Ellis Smith and Norman Foster,
    from a story by J. P. Marquand
Photographed by Harry Jackson
Song by Sidney Clare and Harry Akst
Musical direction by Samuel Kaylin
70 minutes

Cast: Peter Lorre, Virginia Field, Thomas Beck, Sig Rumann, Murray Kinnell, John Rogers, Lotus Long, George Cooper, J. Carrol Naish, Frederick Vogeding

The first of the Mr. Moto series, based on John Marquand's novels and starring Peter Lorre as the nimble-minded Japanese detective. Here much of the action takes place on a freighter going from San Francisco to Shanghai, with Moto solving the mysteries caused by a gang of international smugglers.

THIS IS MY AFFAIR

Produced by Kenneth Macgowan
Directed by William A. Seiter
Screenplay by Allen Rivkin and Lamar Trotti, from a
    story by Allen Rivkin and Lamar Trotti
Photographed by Robert Planck
Songs and lyrics by Mack Gordon and Harry Revel
Musical direction by Arthur Lange
100 minutes

Shirley Temple and Victor McLaglen in *Wee Willie Winkie.*

gone, the doctor's work suffers and he also starts to neglect his wife. The matter is solved when the nurse returns to resume her job and the wife realizes her husband needs the nurse, too. Walter Lang's nimble direction keeps this thin material alive.

WILD AND WOOLLY

Produced by John Stone
Directed by Albert Werker
Screenplay by Lynn Root and Frank Fenton
Photographed by Harry Jackson
Songs by Sidney Clare and Harry Akst
Musical direction by Samuel Kaylin
65 minutes

Cast: Jane Withers, Walter Brennan, Pauline Moore, Carl "Alfalfa" Switzer, Jack Searl, Berton Churchill, Douglas

Fowley, Robert Wilcox, Douglas Scott, Lon Chaney, Jr., Frank Melton, Syd Saylor

A comedy Western, with Jane Withers as a lively lass who delights in the celebrations of her home town's fiftieth anniversary. Her ex-badman grandfather (Walter Brennan) continues his feud with a local politician (Berton Churchill) and challenges him to a duel, but for reasons beyond him, he doesn't turn up. He gets a chance to save face when Jane and her friend (Carl "Alfalfa" Switzer) overhear a pair of crooks planning to stage a bank robbery during the celebrations. Armed with this foreknowledge, grandfather saves the day. *Wild and Woolly* is among the best of the Jane Withers features.

WINGS OF THE MORNING

Produced by Robert T. Kane
Directed by Harold Schuster
Screenplay by Tom Geraghty, based on stories by Donn Byrne
Photographed in Technicolor by Henry Imus and Jack Cardiff
Musical direction by Arthur Benjamin
87 minutes

Cast: Annabella, Henry Fonda, John McCormack, Leslie Banks, D. J. Williams, Philip Sydney Frost, Stewart Rome, Irene Vanbrugh, Harry Tate, Helen Haye, Teddy Underdown, Mark Daley, Sam Livesy, E. V. H. Emmett, R. C. Lyle, Steve Donahue

The first film shot in the British Isles in Technicolor, *Wings of the Morning* retains its charm because of the beautiful quality of the softly toned colors in the variety of scenes done in England and Ireland. The story involves French actress Annabella in a dual role, that of a gypsy princess in 1889 who loses her aristocratic husband when he is killed in an accident, and that of her granddaughter in 1937. The young girls falls in love with a Canadian horse trainer (Henry Fonda) working to prepare entries for the Epsom Downs Derby, and he gradually comes to love her. Complete with gypsy lore, some songs by the great Irish tenor John McCormack, scenes of horse racing, lovely scenery and a good screenplay based on the stories of Donn Byrne, *Wings of the Morning* holds much interest for film students.

WOMAN WISE

Produced by Sol M. Wurtzel
Directed by Allan Dwan
Screenplay by Ben Markson
Photographed by Robert Planck
Song by Sidney Clare and Harry Akst
Musical direction by Samuel Kaylin
62 minutes

Ben Bernie, Jack Haley, Walter Winchell, and Alice Faye in
Wake Up and Live.

Henry Fonda and Annabella in *Wings of the Morning*.

Musical direction by Samuel Kaylin
69 minutes

Cast: Jane Withers, Leo Carrillo, Pauline Moore, William Henry, Henry Wilcoxon, Douglas Fowler, Etienne Giradot, Harry Woods, Rosita Harlan

A comic Western, with Jane Withers upsetting the plans of gold robbers in the Arizona of 1870. She discovers that the local sheriff is a crook and she comes to the aid of her ex-bandit foster-father (Leo Carrillo) when he is falsely accused of being the man behind the robberies. The villains stand no chance against mischievous, spirited Jane.

THE BARONESS AND THE BUTLER

Produced by Darryl F. Zanuck
Directed by Walter Lang
Screenplay by Sam Hellman, Lamar Trotti, and Kathryn Scola, based on a story by Ladislaus Bus-Fekete
Photographed by Arthur Miller
Musical direction by Louis Silvers
75 minutes

Cast: William Powell, Annabella, Helen Westley, Henry Stephenson, Joseph Schildkraut, J. Edward Bromberg, Nigel Bruce, Lynn Bari, Maurice Cass, Ivan Simpson, Alphonse Ethier, Claire DuBrey, Frank Baker, Wilfred Lucas, Sidney Bracy, George Davis, Margaret Irving

The gentleman of the title (William Powell) is the holder of a position that has been handed down for generations. The lady is the daughter of the man for whom he works. He rules the household of the prime minister of Hungary, until the day he is elected to parliament and finds himself the leader of the opposition. The daughter (Annabella) resents the stand the butler takes against her father, but comes to realize that the passion the butler evokes in her is caused by love and not hatred. An amusing if not accurate entry among the many Hollywood versions of life amid European high society.

BATTLE OF BROADWAY

Produced by Sol M. Wurtzel
Directed by George Marshall
Screenplay by Lou Breslow and John Patrick, from a story by Norman Houston
Photographed by Barney McGill
Musical direction by Louis Silvers
84 minutes

Cast: Victor McLaglen, Brian Donlevy, Louise Hovick, Raymond Walburn, Lynn Bari, Jane Darwell, Robert Kellard, Sammy Cohen, Esther Muir, Eddie Holden, Hattie McDaniel, Paul Irving, Frank Moran, Andrew Tombes

A pair of bickering buddies (Victor McLaglen and Brian Donlevy), both American Legionnaires on a con-

Jack Haley (drums), Alice Faye, Don Ameche, and Tyrone Power in *Alexander's Ragtime Band.*

vention in New York, look up the son (Robert Kellard) of their steel-mill boss (Raymond Walburn), with instructions to break up his affair with a showgirl. They get involved in capers with the theatrical crowd and both fall for a stunning entertainer (Louis Hovick, as Gypsy Rose Lee was billed by Hollywood), until the boss turns up and she goes for him.

CHANGE OF HEART

Produced by Sol M. Wurtzel
Directed by James Tinling
Screenplay by Frances Hyland and Albert Ray
Photographed by Daniel B. Clark
Musical direction by Samuel Kaylin
59 minutes

Cast: Gloria Stuart, Michael Whalen, Lyle Talbot, Delmar Watson, Jane Darwell

A champion golfer (Gloria Stuart) finds it impossible to interest her busy businessman husband (Michael Whalen) in the game—until she teams up with another pro (Lyle Talbot) and starts winning tournaments with him, which also involves his affections. Then the husband takes up golf, becomes good at it, and wins back his wife.

CHARLIE CHAN IN HONOLULU

Produced by John Stone
Directed by H. Bruce Humberstone
Screenplay by Charles Belden, based on the character created by Earl Derr Biggers
Photographed by Charles Clarke
Music by Samuel Kaylin
65 minutes

Cast: Sidney Toler, Phyllis Brooks, Sen Yung, Eddie Collins, John King, Claire Dodd, George Zucco, Robert Barrat, Marc Lawrence, Richard Kane, Layne Tom, Jr., Philip Ahn, Paul Harvey

Sidney Toler's first appearance as Charlie Chan, the role made famous by Warner Oland. Here Chan is a passenger on a freighter en route to Honolulu and when murder is committed he finds out who and why it was done. Toler, who did not imitate Oland, was accepted by the public, and the studio, with a giant sigh of relief, continued to churn out Chan pictures for the numberless fans around the world.

DOWN ON THE FARM

Produced by John Stone
Directed by Malcolm St. Clair
Screenplay by Robert Ellis and Helen Logan, from stories by Homer Croy, Frank Fenton, and Lynn Root
Photographed by Edward Snyder
Musical direction by Samuel Kaylin
61 minutes

Cast: Jed Prouty, Spring Byington, Louise Fazenda, Russell Gleason, Ken Howell, George Ernest, June Carlson, Florence Roberts, Billy Mahan, Eddie Collins, Dorris Bowdon, Roberta Smith, Marvin Stephens, William Haade, John T. Murray, William Irving

The further adventures of the Jones family, in which a country aunt (Louise Fazenda) invites them to spend a vacation with her. The youngsters get involved in local romances and father Jones (Jed Prouty) enters, and wins, a cornhusking contest, which leads to his involvement in politics. Skullduggery among politicians and the ways of country folks provide the humor.

FIVE OF A KIND

Produced by Sol M. Wurtzel
Directed by Herbert I. Leeds
Screenplay by Lou Breslow and John Patrick
Photographed by Daniel B. Clark, Bernard Herzbrun, and Chester Gore
Musical direction by Samuel Kaylin
83 minutes

Cast: Dionne Quintuplets, Jean Hersholt, Claire Trevor, Cesar Romero, Slim Summerville, Henry Wilcoxon, Inez Courtney, John Qualen, Jane Darwell, Pauline Moore, John Russell, Andrew Tombes, David Torrence, Marion Byron, Hamilton MacFadden, Spencer Charters, Charles D. Brown

Making their third screen appearance, the Dionne Quints are four-and-a-half years of age and charming as they dance, sing, play with puppies, and ride hobby horses. They roughhouse Dr. Dafoe (Jean Hersholt) and generally bring pleasure into the lives of all around them. Which is why this film was made.

FOUR MEN AND A PRAYER

Produced by Darryl F. Zanuck
Directed by John Ford
Screenplay by Richard Sherman, Sonya Levien, and Walter Ferris, from a book by David Garth
Photographed by Ernest Palmer
Musical direction by Louis Silver
85 minutes

Cast: Loretta Young, Richard Greene, George Sanders, David Niven, C. Aubrey Smith, J. Edward Bromberg, William Henry, John Carradine, Alan Hale, Reginald Denny, Berton Churchill, Barry Fitzgerald, Claude King, Cecil Cunningham, Frank Dawson, John Sutton

The four men of the title are the sons of an unjustly cashiered British Army officer (C. Aubrey Smith), who has served with distinction in India and who has been murdered by crooked businessmen. The sons—Richard Greene, David Niven, George Sanders, and William Henry—are implacable as they follow clues halfway around the world. Love interest is supplied by Loretta Young as the breezy American who loves and supports Greene. Good production values and John Ford's brisk direction make *Four Men and a Prayer* a zesty adventure mystery.

GATEWAY

Produced by Darryl F. Zanuck
Directed by Alfred Werker
Screenplay by Lamar Trotti, from a story by Walter Reisch
Photographed by Edward Cronjager
Musical direction by Arthur Lange
73 minutes

Cast: Don Ameche, Arleen Whalen, Gregory Ratoff, Binnie Barnes, Gilbert Roland, Raymond Walburn, John Carradine, Maurice Moscovich, Harry Carey, Majorie Gateson, Lyle Talbot, Fritz Leiber, Warren Hymer, Eddy Conrad, E. E. Clive, Russell Hicks, Charles Coleman

An immigration melodrama, with much of the action taking place on an ocean liner bound for New York. On board is a returning war corespondent (Don Ameche), who makes friends with an Irish girl (Arleen Whelan), sailing to meet her fiancé in America. A lecherous older man (Raymond Walburn) molests her and is slightly injured when she pushes him away. The resultant charges brought against her cause her to be detained at Ellis Island by the Immigration Service, but the correspondent makes a good case for her. The film is an interesting reminder of 1938 immigration procedures.

HAPPY LANDING

Produced by Darryl F. Zanuck
Directed by Roy Del Ruth
Original screenplay by Milton Sperling and Boris Ingster
Photographed by John Mescal
Songs by Jack Yellen, Sam Pokrass, Walter Bullock, Harold Spina, and Raymond Scott
Musical direction by Louis Silvers
102 minutes

Cast: Sonja Henie, Don Ameche, Cesar Romero, Ethel Merman, Jean Hersholt, Billy Gilbert, Wally Vernon, El Brendel, Marcelle Corday, Joseph Crehan, Eddie Conrad, Ben Welden, Leah Ray

A glib and amusing plotline serve as the basis for skating routines by Sonja Henie and a variety of songs. Cesar Romero is an amorous bandleader and Don Ameche is his manager. They turn up in Norway, where Romero woos Henie, who takes him seriously and follows him when he returns to America. There she becomes a sensational skating star. Ameche tricks Romero into marrying his singer (Ethel Merman) and then concentrates on winning Henie, whom he has loved all along. The smile and the skates of Henie helped make this another box-office winner for Zanuck.

HAWAIIAN BUCKAROO

Produced by Sol Lesser
Directed by Ray Taylor
Screenplay by Dan Jarrett, from a story by Dan Jarrett
Photographed by Allen Thompson
Songs by Albert von Tilzer, Eddie Grant, and Harry MacPherson
Musical direction by Abe Meyer
58 minutes

Cast: Smith Ballew, Evalyn Knapp, Benny Burt, Harry Woods, Pat O'Brien, George Regas, Laura Treadwell. Carl Stockdale, Snowflake

A Western set in Hawaii, with cowboys and herds of cattle mixed with tropical scenery and songs. Singing cowboy Smith Ballew and his sidekick Benny Burt go to work for a beautiful but snooty ranches (Evalyn Knapp) and save her from her crooked foreman and his colleagues.

HOLD THAT CO-ED

Produced by Darryl F. Zanuck
Directed by George Marshall
Screenplay by Karl Tunberg, Don Ettlinger, and Jack Yellen, from a story by Karl Tunberg and Don Ettlinger
Photographed by Robert Planck
Music and lyrics by Mack Gordon and Harry Revel; Lew Pollack and Lew Brown: Jule Styne and Nicholas Castle, and Geneva Sawyer
Musical direction by Arthur Lange
80 minutes

Cast: John Barrymore, George Murphy, Majorie Weaver, Joan Davis, Jack Haley, George Barbier, Ruth Terry, Donald Meek, Johnny Downs, Paul Hurst, Guinn Williams, Brewster Twins, Bill Benedict, Frank Sully, Charles Wilson, Glenn Morris

The best of John Barrymore's last films, with the great but tired actor appearing as a glib and conniving politician appearing at a college at the height of the football season and drumming up votes. He seeks re-election as a state governor and aids a needy university, which includes scheming to see that their football team wins. Barrymore's caricatured politico was thought to be Huey Long and his Louisiana state machine. *Hold That Co-Ed* is a satirical gem of a film.

I'LL GIVE A MILLION

Produced by Darryl F. Zanuck
Directed by Walter Lang
Screenplay by Boris Ingster and Milton Sperling, from a story by Cesare Zazarrini and Giaci Mondaini
Photographed by Lucien Andriot
Musical direction by Louis Silvers
70 minutes

Cast: Warner Baxter, Majorie Weaver, Peter Lorre, Jean

Jean Hersholt and the Dionne Quints in *Five of a Kind*.

George Sanders, Loretta Young, William Henry, Richard Greene, and David Niven in *Four Men and a Prayer*.

Sen Yung, Eddie Collins, and Sidney Toler in *Charlie Chan in Honolulu*.

Sonja Henie in *Happy Landing*.

Louise Hovick, Brian Donlevy, and Victor McLaglen in *Battle of Broadway*.

Jane Withers and Leo Carrillo in *The Arizona Wildcat*.

Alice Brady, Tyrone Power, and Alice Faye in *In Old Chicago*.

Hersholt, John Carradine, J. Edward Bromberg, Lynn Bari, Fritz Feld, Sig Rumann, Christian Rub, Paul Harvey, Charles Halton, Frank Reicher, Frank Dawson, Harry Hayden, Stanley Andrews, Lillian Porter

A millionaire (Warner Baxter) has long grown weary of human leeches and disillusioned with people who befriend him only because of his money. After saving a tramp (Peter Lorre) from suicide, he takes his tattered clothing and disappears, but lets it be known that he will give a million dollars for any genuine act of kindness he meets. Tramps are then royally entertained all over town. The millionaire meets a circus performer (Marjorie Weaver) and finds the kindness he has sought, which leads to marriage.

IN OLD CHICAGO

Produced by Darryl F. Zanuck
Directed by Henry King
Screenplay by Lamar Trotti and Sonya Levien, based on a story by Niven Busch
Photographed by Peverell Marley
Special effects photographer: Daniel B. Clarke
Title song by Mack Gordon and Harry Revel, other songs by Sidney Clare and Lew Pollack

Musical direction by Louis Silvers
115 minutes

Cast: Tyrone Power, Alice Faye, Don Ameche, Alice Brady, Andy Devine, Brian Donlevy, Phyllis Brooks, Tom Brown, Madame Sultewan, Berton Churchill, Sidney Blackmer, June Storey, Paul Hurst, J. Anthony Hughes, Gene Reynolds, Bobs Watson, Spencer Charters, Russell Hicks, Rondo Hatton

A pet project of Darryl Zanuck and one of the most expensive Hollywood films of its day ($1,800,000), *In Old Chicago* gives a splendidly staged account of the great fire of 1871, mounted on the backlot and edited to twenty minutes of screen time. It takes its cue from the incident of Mrs. O'Leary (Alice Brady) and her cow kicking over a lantern in a stable and triggering the immense holocaust, but precedes it with a fictional tale of her two sons—one a charming rogue (Tyrone Power) who wants to become a wealthy impresario, and the other, a solid lawyer (Don Ameche) who becomes the mayor. The mayor dies in his heroic direction of the campaign to control the terrible fire, and the other son, presumably, learns to be a better citizen. Despite the fiction, the film is entertaining throughout and its re-creation of the fire remains a magnificent piece of filmmaking.

INSIDE STORY

Produced by Howard J. Green
Directed by Ricardo Cortez
Screenplay by Jerry Cady, from a story by Ben Ames
  Williams
Photographed by Virgil Miller
Musical direction by Samuel Kaylin
60 minutes

Cast: Michael Whalen, Jean Rogers, Chick Chandler,
Douglas Fowley, John King, Jane Darwell, June Gale,
Spencer Charters, Theodore Von Eltz, Cliff Clark, Charles
D. Brown, Charles Lane, Jan Duggan, Louise Carter,
Bert Roach

A newspaper yarn, with Michael Whalen as a crack
reporter, looking for the loneliest girl in New York to
treat her to an old-fashioned Christmas on a farm. A
club hostess (Jean Rogers) poses as a stenographer to
get the story, but the contact with the spirit of Yule-
tide softens her attitudes and she helps the reporter file
his evidence against a murderer.

INTERNATIONAL SETTLEMENT

Produced by Darryl F. Zanuck
Directed by Eugene Forde
Screenplay by Lou Breslow and John Patrick, from a
  story by Lynn Root and Frank Fenton
Photographed by Lucien Andriot
Musical direction by Samuel Kaylin
75 minutes

Cast: Dolores Del Rio, George Sanders, June Lang, Dick
Baldwin, Ruth Terry, John Carradine, Keye Luke, Harold
Huber, Leon Ames, Pedro de Cordoba

Set in Shanghai during the Sino-Japanese warfare. An
adventurer (George Sanders) takes on the job of collecting money from suppliers of guns and ammunition
and gets enmeshed in double-crossing and espionage.
He falls in love with a French singer (Dolores Del
Rio), who helps him survive the complicated situation
and leaves with him on a refugee ship. A good spy
story, enlivened by newsreel clips of the bombing and
fighting in Shanghai.

ISLAND IN THE SKY

Produced by Sol M. Wurtzel
Directed by Herbert I. Leeds
Screenplay by Frances Hyland and Albert Ray, from a
  story by Jerry Cady
Photographed by Edward Cronjager
Musical direction by Samuel Kaylin
61 minutes

Cast: Gloria Stuart, Michael Whalen, Paul Kelly, Robert
Kellard, June Storey, Paul Hurst, Leon Ames, Willard
Robertson, George Humbert, Aggie Herring, Charles D.
Brown

An investigator (Michael Whalen) for the district attorney is about to begin his honeymoon when a man
is indicted for murder on what looks like an open-and-
shut case. But his bride (Gloria Stuart) believes otherwise and with the aid of a friend (Paul Kelly) who
used to be a racketeer, she digs up the evidence that
reveals the real killer.

JOSETTE

Produced by Gene Markey
Directed by Allan Dwan
Screenplay by James Edward Grant, from a play by
  Paul Frank and Georg Fraser, from a story by Ladislaus
  Vadnai
Photographed by John Mescall
Songs by Mack Gordon and Harry Revel
Musical direction by David Buttolph
70 minutes

Cast: Don Ameche, Simone Simon, Robert Young, Joan
Davis, Bert Lahr, Paul Hurst, William Collier, Sr., Tala
Birell, Lynn Bari, William Demarest, Ruth Gillette,
Armand Kaliz, Ferdinand Gottschalk, Maurice Cass

An elderly gentleman (William Collier, Sr.) marries
a gold digger (Tala Birell). His two sons (Don
Ameche and Robert Young) try to get him out of her
clutches, but they have never met her and through a
mistake they assume her to be a young singer (Simone
Simon) in a nightclub. They both fall in love with
her and once her identity is established, she responds
to Ameche.

JUST AROUND THE CORNER

Produced by Darryl F. Zanuck
Directed by Irving Cummings
Screenplay by Ethel Hill, J. P. McEvoy, and Darrell Wise,
  from a story by Paul Gerrard Smith
Photographed by Arthur Miller
Songs by Walter Bullock and Harold Spina
70 minutes

Cast: Shirley Temple, Joan Davis, Charles Farrell,
Amanda Duff, Bill Robinson, Bert Lahr, Franklin Pangborn, Cora Witherspoon, Bennie Bartlett, Claude Gillingwater, Hal K. Dawson, Charles Williams, Eddy Conrad,
Tony Hughes, Orville Caldwell

Shirley Temple as the daughter of a once wealthy architect and widower (Charles Farrell), now flattened by
the Depression and working as a maintenance man of
an apartment building, in which his girl friend
(Amanda Duff) lives in the penthouse. Shirley refuses
to accept their drop in the world and carries on happily. She makes friends with an eccentric old man
(Claude Gillingwater), who turns out to be a millionaire and backs her father's engineering plans. Story-
book material, made enjoyable by Shirley's personality

and particularly by her tap dance routines with Bill Robinson.

KEEP SMILING

Produced by John Stone
Directed by Herbert I. Leeds
Screenplay by Frances Hyland and Albert Ray, from a story by Frank Fenton and Lynn Root
Photographed by Edward Cronjager
Musical direction by Samuel Kaylin
75 minutes

Cast: Jane Withers, Gloria Stuart, Henry Wilcoxon, Helen Westley, Jed Prouty, Douglas Fowley, Robert Allen, Pedro De Cordoba, Claudia Coleman, Paula Rae Wright, Etta McDaniel, Carmencita Johnson, Mary McCarthy, Hal K. Dawson, the Three Nelsons

A good spoof on Hollywood, with Jane Withers as a talented youngster trying to break into the business. Her uncle is a veteran film director (Henry Wilcoxon) now down on his luck but still loved by his faithful secretary (Gloria Stuart). Through Jane's energetic conniving, she not only gets into films but revives her uncle's career and gets him married.

KENTUCKY

Produced by Darryl F. Zanuck
Directed by David Butler
Screenplay by Lamar Trotti and John Taintor Foote, from a story by John Taintor Foote
Photographed in Technicolor by Ernest Palmer and Ray Rennahan
Musical direction by Louis Silvers
95 minutes

Cast: Loretta Young, Richard Greene, Walter Brennan, Douglas Dumbrille, Karen Morley, Moroni Olsen, Russell Hicks, Willard Robertson, Charles Waldron, George Reed, Bobs Watson, Delmar Charles Middleton, Harry Hayden, Robert Clark, Meredith Howard

A Romeo and Juliet story filmed in Kentucky in color and revealing much about the state's association with race horse breeding, with the Kentucky Derby serving as the climax. Loretta Young and Richard Greene are lovers but also the product of families who have been feuding since the Civil War. The girl's uncle (Walter Brennan) is the keeper of the feud, which began when Union soldiers under the command of the other family took over his stables. But when he dies, it is a member of that family who reads the eulogy. The girl's horse, trained by her lover, wins the Derby and all traces of the feud vanish. *Kentucky* is especially interesting for lovers of horses and their training as racers. Walter Brennan won an Oscar as best supporting actor for his performance as the testy old feud-keeper.

KENTUCKY MOONSHINE

Produced by Darryl F. Zanuck
Directed by David Butler
Screenplay by Art Arthur and M. M. Musselman, from a story by M. M. Musselman and Jack Lait, Jr.
Photographed by Robert Planck
Songs by Lew Pollack and Sidney Mitchell
Musical direction by Louis Silvers
87 minutes

Cast: The Ritz Brothers, Tony Martin, Marjorie Weaver, Slim Summerville, John Carradine, Wally Vernon, Berton Churchill, Eddie Collins, Cecil Cunningham, Paul Stanton, Mary Treen, Francis Ford, Brian Sisters, Charles Hummel Wilson, Claude Allister

The Ritz Brothers and Tony Martin as radio personalities seeking higher ratings. To try a different angle, Martin goes to Kentucky to do hillbilly music and discovers the brothers, who are actually from New York and just pretending to be hillbillies in order to get on Martin's show. Their wild antics impress him and he takes them back to New York, where they confess the ruse, but by that time it doesn't matter. Among Ritz Brothers admirers, *Kentucky Moonshine* is considered to be just about their best work.

KIDNAPPED

Produced by Darryl F. Zanuck
Directed by Alfred Werker
Screenplay by Sonya Levien, Eleanor Harris, Ernest Pascal, and Edwin Blum, from a novel by Robert Louis Stevenson
Photographed by Gregg Toland
Musical direction by Arthur Lange
85 minutes

Cast: Warner Baxter, Freddie Bartholomew, Arleen Whelan, C. Aubrey Smith, Reginald Owen, John Carradine, Nigel Bruce, Miles Mander, E. E. Clive, Halliwell Hobbes, H. B. Warner, Arthur Hohl, Montague Love, Donald Hainer, Moroni Olsen, Leonard Mudie, Mary Gordon, Forrester Harvey

Warner Baxter as the Scottish rebel Alan Breck and Freddie Bartholomew as David Balfour, in a screenplay loosely derived from two of Robert Louis Stevenson's novels about the warfare between Scotland and England in the late eighteenth century. Young Balfour is the heir to an estate and his evil uncle arranges for him to be kidnapped in order to gain the property. The boy is sent to sea but meets the exiled adventurer Breck and together they make their way back to Scotland. A good advenure yarn, although not very faithful to Stevenson.

John Barrymore and Jack Haley in *Hold That Co-Ed*.

Shirley Temple and Bill Robinson in *Just Around the Corner*.

LITTLE MISS BROADWAY

Produced by Darryl F. Zanuck
Directed by Irving Cummings
Screenplay by Harry Tugend and Jack Yellen
Photographed by Arthur Miller
Songs by Walter Bullock and Harold Spina
Musical direction by Louis Silvers
70 minutes

Cast: Shirley Temple, George Murphy, Jimmy Durante, Phyllis Brooks, Edna May Oliver, George Barbier, Edward Ellis, Jane Darwell, El Brendel, Donald Meek, Patricia Wilder, Claude Gillingwater

Shirley Temple is once again an orphan, this time placed in provisional adoption with the manager (Edward Ellis) of a hotel catering to entertainers. The owner of the hotel (Edna May Oliver) objects to the noise the show biz people make and moves to have Shirley sent back to the orphanage. Her nephew (George Murphy) looks into the matter and takes the side of the entertainers, and the crusty old owner finally changes her mind. The film is highlighted by Temple's dancing with Murphy and her clowning with Jimmy Durante, playing one of the hotel guests.

LOVE ON A BUDGET

Produced by Sol M. Wurtzel
Directed by Herbert I. Leeds
Screenplay by Robert Ellis and Helen Logan, from the characters created by Katherine Kavanaugh

Walter Brennan and Loretta Young in *Kentucky*.

H. B. Warner, Arleen Whelan, Freddie Bartholomew, and Warner Baxter in *Kidnapped*.

Photographed by Edward Snyder
Musical direction by Samuel Kaylin
60 minutes

Cast: Jed Prouty, Shirley Deane, Spring Byington, Russell Gleason, Kenneth Howell, George Ernest, June Carlson, Florence Roberts, Billy Mahan, Alan Dinehart, Dixie Dunbar, Marvin Stephens, Paul Harvey, Joyce Compton

The Jones family involved in the get-rich-quick schemes of Uncle Charlie (Alan Dinehart). When daughter Bonnie (Shirley Deane) gets married, she and her husband (Russell Gleason) try living on a meager budget, until Uncle Charlie plans to increase their wealth. He almost spoils their marriage until an investment miraculously pays off.

MEET THE GIRLS

Produced by Sol M. Wurtzel
Directed by Eugene Forde
Screenplay by Marguerite Roberts
Photographed by Edward Snyder
Musical direction by Samuel Kaylin
60 minutes

Cast: June Lang, Lynn Bari, Robert Allen, Ruth Donnelly, Gene Lockhart, Wally Vernon, Eric Rhodes, Constantine Romanoff, Jack Norton, Emmet Vogan

A pair of entertainers (Lynn Bari and June Lang) lose their jobs in Honolulu and also lose their passage money back to San Francisco. They become stowaways and get involved with jewel thieves on board before proving their innocence and solving their predicament.

MR. MOTO'S GAMBLE

Produced by John Stone
Directed by James Tinling
Screenplay by Charles Belden and Jerry Cady, based on the character "Mr. Moto," created by John P. Marquand
Photographed by Lucien Andriot
Musical direction by Samuel Kaylin
60 minutes

Cast: Peter Lorre, Keye Luke, Dick Baldwin, Lynn Bari, Douglas Fowley, Jane Regan, Harold Huber, Maxie Rosenbloom, John Hamilton, George Stone, Bernard Nedell, Charles Williams, Ward Bond, Cliff Clark, Edward Marr, Lon Chaney, Jr., Russ Clark

With a background of gambling and prize fighting, Mr. Moto (Peter Lorre) accepts the challenge of finding out who poisoned a fighter in the ring. This film started out as *Charlie Chan at the Ringside,* but with Warner Oland's death during production, the course was changed to a Moto. So much footage was shot of Keye Luke for the Chan film that the producers decided to use the footage and make him a leading character in this one.

MR. MOTO TAKES A CHANCE

Produced by Sol M. Wurtzel
Directed by Norman Foster
Screenplay by Lou Breslow and John Patrick, from a story by Willia Cooper and Norman Foster
Photographed by Virgil Miller
Musical direction by Samuel Kaylin
63 minutes

Cast: Peter Lorre, Rochelle Hudson, Robert Kent, J. Edward Bromberg, Chick Chandler, George Regas, Frederick Vogeding

Set in Sumatra, with Moto (Peter Lorre) helping an American agent (Rochelle Hudson) get to a potentate (J. Edward Bromberg) in need of aid in quelling a possible rebel insurrection led by a priest (George Regas). One of the more wildly improbable of the Moto adventures.

MY LUCKY STAR

Produced by Darryl F. Zanuck
Directed by Roy Del Ruth
Screenplay by Harry Tugend and Jack Yellen, from a story by Karl Tunberg and Don Ettlinger
Photographed by John Mescall
Music and lyrics by Mack Gordon and Harry Revel
Musical direction by Louis Silvers
90 minutes

Cast: Sonja Henie, Richard Greene, Joan Davis, Cesar Romero, Buddy Ebsen, Arthur Treacher, George Barbier, Louise Hovick, Billy Gilbert, Patricia Wilder, Paul Hurst, Elisha Cook, Jr., Robert Kellard, Brewster Twins, Kay Griffith

A department store sports clerk (Sonja Henie) is seen skating by the son (Cesar Romero) of the owner. He decides to enroll her as a student at a university, so that she will be a walking advertisement for the store's fashion department. Her extensive sports wardrobe causes jealousy among the students and she falls in love with a teacher (Richard Greene). For these and other reasons she is expelled, but the publicity pays off and she stars in a lavish ice fashion show staged at the store. The skating of Henie is the real star of the film, especially in the costumed ice ballet of "Alice in Wonderland."

MYSTERIOUS MR. MOTO

Produced by Sol M. Wurtzel
Directed by Norman Foster
Screenplay by Philip MacDonald and Norman Foster, based on the character created by J. P. Marquand
Photographed by Virgil Miller
Musical direction by Samuel Kaylin
62 minutes

Cast: Peter Lorre, Mary Maguire, Henry Wilcoxon, Erick Rhodes, Harold Huber, Leon Ames, Forrester Harvey, Frederick Vogeding, Lester Matthews, John Rogers, Karen Sorrell, Mitchell Lewis

Moto (Peter Lorre) picks up clues in his pursuit of a group of international killers and has himself imprisoned on Devil's Island as a cellmate of one of them (Leon Ames). He aids the man in his escape and goes with him, which leads to Moto's apprehending the rest of the gang.

ONE WILD NIGHT

Produced by John Stone
Directed by Eugene Forde
Screenplay by Charles Belden and Jerry Cady, based on an original idea by Edwin Dial Torgenson
Photographed by Harry Davis
Musical direction by Samuel Kaylin
72 minutes

Cast: June Lang, Dick Baldwin, Lyle Talbot, J. Edward Bromberg, Sidney Toler, Andrew Tombes, William Demarest, Romaine Callender, Jan Duggan, Spencer Charters, Harlan Briggs

A comedy whodunit concerning the disappearance of four wealthy big-city men after each has withdrawn a large sum from a bank. A crime student (Dick Baldwin) and an eager reporter (June Lang) find that it's all a plot between the men, who want to escape their wives, and a bank manager (J. Edward Bromberg) short on funds.

PANAMINT'S BAD MAN

Produced by Sol Lesser
Directed by Ray Taylor
Screenplay by Luci Ward and Charles Arthur Powell, from a story by Edmund Kelso and Lindsley Parsons
Photographed by Allen Thompson
60 minutes

Cast: Smith Ballew, Evelyn Daw, Noah Beery, Sr., Stanley Fields, Harry Wood, Pat O'Brien, Armand Wright

A routine Western, with Smith Ballew posing as a bad man in order to discover the outlaws and pausing every now and then to sing a song to the heroine (Evelyn Daw). Noah Beery, Sr. scowls as the villain.

RASCALS

Produced by John Stone
Directed by H. Bruce Humberstone
Screenplay by Robert Ellis and Helen Logan
Photographed by Edward Cronjager
Songs and lyrics by Sidney Clare and Harry Akst
Musical direction by Samuel Kaylin
77 minutes

Jimmy Durante and Shirley Temple in *Little Miss Broadway*.

Dick Baldwin, Peter Lorre, and Keye Luke in *Mr. Moto's Gamble*.

Richard Greene, Sonja Henie, and Cesar Romero in *My Lucky Star*.

Cast: Jane Withers, Rochelle Hudson, Robert Wilcox, Borrah Minnevitch and Gang, Steffi Duna, Katharine Alexander, Chester Clute, José Crespo, Paul Stanton, Frank Reicher, Edward Cooper, Kathleen Burke, Myra March, Frank Puglia

Jane Withers as the main fixer and inspiration of a band of Gypsy rovers who lightheartedly purloin everything they come across but always in a commendable cause. They pick up a society girl (Rochelle Hudson) suffering from amnesia and make her their ace fortune teller, which raises enough money for the girl to have an operation and regain her memory.

RAWHIDE

Produced by Sol Lesser
Directed by Ray Taylor
Screenplay by Dan Jarrett and Jack Natteford, from a
    story by Dan Jarrett
Photographed by Allen Thompson
58 minutes

Cast: Lou Gehrig, Smith Ballew, Evalyn Knapp, Arthur Loft, Carl Stockdale, Si Jenks, Cy Kendall, Lafe McKee, Dick Curtis, Cecil Kellogg, Slim Whitaker, Tom Foreman, Cliff Parkinson, Harry Tenbrook

A Western starring the great baseball player Lou Gehrig as a rancher being coerced, along with others, to give up their properties to a gang of bandits. His sister (Evalyn Knapp) loves a young lawyer (Smith Ballew) and together they organize the ranchers to defeat the outlaws.

REBECCA OF SUNNYBROOK FARM

Produced by Darryl F. Zanuck
Directed by Allan Dwan
Screenplay by Karl Tunberg and Don Ettlinger, from a
    story by Kate Douglas Wiggin
Photographed by Arthur Miller
Songs and lyrics by Mack Gordon and Harry Revel,
    Lou Pollack and Sidney D. Mitchell, Sam Pokras and
    Jack Yellen, and Raymond Scott
Musical direction by Arthur Lange
80 minutes

Cast: Shirley Temple, Randolph Scott, Jack Haley, Gloria Stuart, Phyllis Brooks, Helen Westley, Slim Summerville, Bill Robinson, J. Edward Bromberg, Alan Dinehart, Raymond Scott Quintet, Dixie Dunbar, Paul Hurst

Little but the title remains in this Shirley Temple vehicle loosely based on Kate Douglas Wiggin's famous children's tale. Here Shirley is a singing child, in the care of an uncle (William Demarest) who tires of trying to get her a contract and dumps her on the farm of an aunt (Helen Westley). Her aunt forbids her to have anything to do with show business people, but a neighbor (Randolph Scott) happens to be a talent scout and secretly arranges for her to broadcast. Success, as in all Temple pictures, brings complete understanding from all concerned. Ten-year-old Shirley was such a veteran by this time that the film actually featured a song medley from her previous movies—songs with which she was already uniquely identified.

ROAD DEMON

Produced by Jerry Hoffman
Directed by Otto Brower
Screenplay by Robert Ellis and Helen Logan
Photographed by Edward Snyder
Musical direction by Samuel Kaylin
65 minutes

Cast: Henry Arthur, Joan Valerie, Henry Armetta, Tom Beck, Bill Robinson, Jonathan Hale, Murray Alper, Edward Marr, Lon Chaney, Jr., Eleanor Virzie, Betty Greco

Set against a background of the Indianapolis Speedway and using much stock footage, this minor auto-race thriller deals with racketeers trying to dominate the business. They attempt to get rid of a young driver (Henry Arthur) whose father they have previously killed in a race, but he gets the better of them. The film is interesting in that Bill (Bojangles) Robinson appears as a junk yard owner and does a little tap dancing.

SAFETY IN NUMBERS

Produced by John Stone
Directed by Malcolm St. Clair
Screenplay by Joseph Hoffman, Karen De Wolf, and
    Robert Chapin, from a story by Dorothy Manney and
    Zena George, based on characters created by Katherine
    Kavanaugh
Photographed by Charles Clarke
Musical direction by Samuel Kaylin
55 minutes

Cast: Jed Prouty, Shirley Deane, Spring Byington, Russell Gleason, Ken Howell, George Ernest, June Carlson, Florence Roberts, Billy Mahan, Marvin Stephens, Iva Stewart, Helen Freeman, Henry Kolker, Paul McVey

The Jones family comes up against swindlers who have persuaded father (Jed Prouty), who is also the mayor, that the town swamp is actually the site of valuable mineral deposits. When some of the youngsters accidentally fall into the swamp, they find it has been doctored, which causes an uproar and a lot of effort to set things right.

SALLY, IRENE AND MARY

Produced by Darryl F. Zanuck
Directed by William S. Seiter
Screenplay by Harry Tugend and Jack Yellen, from a story by Karl Tunberg and Don Ettinger, based on the play by Edward Dowling and Cyril Wood
Photographed by Peverell Marley
Songs by Mack Gordon and Harry Revel, Raymond Scott, Walter Bullock, and Harold Spina
Musical direction by Arthur Lange
86 minutes

Cast: Alice Faye, Tony Martin, Fred Allen, Jimmy Durante, Joan Davis, Gregory Ratoff, Marjorie Weaver, Louis Hovick, Barnett Parker, Mary Treen, J. Edward Bromberg

Sally (Alice Faye), Irene (Joan Davis), and Mary (Marjorie Weaver) are manicurists hoping to become Broadway entertainers. Their agent (Fred Allen) gets them jobs in a Greenwhich Village nightclub and Sally falls in love with the star (Tony Martin). Their careers go nowhere until Mary inherits a broken-down old ferry boat, which with the aid of friends they turn into a successful supper club. The film is typical of its kind, and made the more interesting by the antics of Fred Allen and Jimmy Durante. Publicity value was derived from the fact that Faye and Tony Martin were man and wife at the time of filming.

SHARPSHOOTERS

Produced by Sol M. Wurtzel
Directed by James Tinling
Screenplay by Robert Ellis and Helen Logan, from a story by Maurice Rapf and Lester Ziffren
Photographed by Barney McGill
Musical direction by Samuel Kaylin
63 minutes

Cast: Brian Donlevy, Lynn Bari, Wally Vernon, John King, Douglas Dumbrille, C. Henry Gordon, Sidney Blackmer, Martin Joseph Spellman, Jr., Frank Puglia, Hamilton MacFadden, Romaine Callendar

The adventures of newsreel cameramen, with Brian Donlevy as a crack lensman of an American outfit operating in Europe. When the king of a mythical nation is assassinated, Donlevy is the only one enterprising enough to get his negatives out of the country. Later he finds the young crown prince is also slated for death and schemes to save his life.

SPEED TO BURN

Produced by Jerry Hoffman
Directed by Otto Brower
Screenplay by Robert Ellis and Helen Logan, from a story by Edwin Dial Torgerson
Photographed by Edward Snyder

Evalyn Knapp and Smith Ballew in *Rawhide.*

Musical direction by Samuel Kaylin
60 minutes

Cast: Michael Whalen, Lynn Bari, Marvin Stephens, Henry Armetta, Chick Chandler, Sidney Blackmer, Johnnic Pirrone, Charles D. Brown, Inez Palange

A horse racing yarn, about a youngster (Marvin Stephens) who raises a horse for a trainer and sees it sold to the police. With the aid of a policeman (Michael Whalen) he finds the horse was detoured by race crooks to eliminate possible competition. Eventually they reclaim the horse and bring it in a winner.

STRAIGHT, PLACE AND SHOW

Produced by Darryl F. Zanuck
Directed by David Butler
Screenplay by M. M. Musselman and Allen Rivkin, from a play by Damon Runyan and Irvin Ceasar
Photographed by Ernest Palmer
Music and lyrics by Lew Brown and Lew Pollack; Sid Kuller, Ray Golden, and Jule Styne
Musical direction by Louis Silvers
66 minutes

Cast: The Ritz Brothers, Richard Arlen, Ethel Merman, Phyllis Brooks, George Barbier, Sidney Blackmer, Will Stanton, Ivan Iebedeff, Gregory Gaye, Rafael Storm, Stanley Fields, Tiny Roebuck, Ben Welden, Ed Gargan, Pat McKee

The Ritz Brothers at the races. The trio are the proprietors of a pony ride outfit who team up with a young man (Richard Arlen) to train the horse of his fiancée (Phyllis Brooks). To raise training and entry money they engage in a wrestling match and when they hear that a team of Russian jockeys plan to foul the race, they imprison the Russians and take their place. A madcap comedy, tailor made for the Ritz Brothers, and leavened here and there with songs sung by Ethel Merman.

Loretta Young and Tyrone Power in *Suez*.

Adolphe Menjou, Tony Martin, Jack Oakie, and Binnie Barnes in *Thanks for Everything*.

Loretta Young, Pauline Moore, David Niven, and Marjorie Weaver in *Three Blind Mice*.

SUBMARINE PATROL

Produced by Darryl F. Zanuck
Directed by John Ford
Screenplay by Rian James, Darrell Ware, and Jack Yellen, from a story by Ray Milholland
Photographed by Arthur Miller
Musical direction by Arthur Lange
95 minutes

Cast: Richard Greene, Nancy Kelly, Preston Foster, George Bancroft, Slim Summerville, John Carradine, Joan Valerie, Henry Armetta, Warren Hymes, Douglas Fowley, J. Farrell MacDonald, Maxie Rosenbloom, Dick Hogan, E. E. Clive, Ward Bond, Charles Tannen, Robert Lowery

A World War One naval adventure about an officer (Preston Foster) who is demoted for negligent duty and put in charge of a run-down old submarine chaser and finds himself with a motley crew. With the aid of an old sea dog (J. Farrell MacDonald) he whips his men into a crack outfit and they perform heroically in the Adriatic, sinking several subs. One of his officers is a playboy (Richard Greene) who learns about responsibility during this assignment and wins the love of a tough ship owners' daughter (Nancy Kelly). The film gets it spark from director John Ford—just prior to his making of *Stagecoach*.

SUEZ

Produced by Darryl F. Zanuck
Directed by Allan Dwan
Screenplay by Philip Dunne and Julien Josephson, from a story by Sam Duncan
Photographed by Peverell Marley
Musical direction by Louis Silvers
100 minutes

Cast: Tyrone Power, Loretta Young, Annabella, J. Edward Bromberg, Joseph Schildkraut, Henry Stephenson, Sidney Blackmer, Maurice Moscovich, Sig Rumann, Nigel Bruce, Miles Mander, George Zucco, Leon Ames, Rafaela Ottiano, Victor Varconi

A well-mounted historical romance but a meager history lesson, with Tyrone Power at the age of 24 playing the great French engineer Ferdinand De Lesseps, who was 64 when he completed building the Suez Canal. Here De Lesseps is a young aristocrat who falls in love with a girl (Loretta Young) who later marries Louis Napoleon and becomes the Empress Eugénie. In Egypt, where his father is a diplomat of France, he conceives the idea of a canal linking the Mediterranean and the Red Sea and raises funds to start a company, largely with the help of a local prince (J. Edward Bromberg) and the love of a tomboyish secretary (Annabella), who loses her life when she saves his in a sandstorm. Napoleon lets De Lesseps down, but Disraeli and his new British parliament come to his aid in finishing the canal. *Suez* is among Hollywood's most spurious historical forays but nonetheless entertaining in its production values.

TARZAN'S REVENGE

Produced by Sol Lesser
Directed by D. Ross Lederman
Screenplay by Robert Lee Johnston and Jay Vann, from a novel by Edgar Rice Burroughs
Photographed by George Meehan
Musical score by Abe Meyer
Musical direction by Hugo Riesenfeld
70 minutes

Cast: Glenn Morris, Eleanor Holm, George Barbier, C. Henry Gordon, Hedda Hopper, George Meeker, Corbett Morris, Joseph Sawyer, John Lester Johnson

Glenn Morris is Tarzan in this minor entry in the series and swimming star Eleanor Holm is the heroine. The story concerns her abduction by a villainous jungle sultan and her rescue by the omnipresent Tarzan.

THANKS FOR EVERYTHING

Produced by Darryl F. Zanuck
Directed by William A. Seiter
Screenplay by Harry Tugend, based on a story by Gilbert Wright
Photographed by Lucien Andriot
Songs and lyrics by Mack Gordon and Harry Revel
Musical direction by Louis Silvers
70 minutes

Cast: Adolphe Menjou, Jack Oakie, Jack Haley, Arleen Whelan, Tony Martin, Binnie Barnes, George Barbier, Warren Hymer, Gregory Gaye, Andrew Tombes, Renie Riano, Jan Duggan, Charles Lane, Charles Trowbridge, Frank Sully

An advetising agency produces a radio contest and offers a $25,000 prize to the winner, who must be the paragon of the average, normal American. He turns out to be Jack Haley, and the promoters (Adolphe Menjou and Jack Oakie) make money by merchandising him as a man with unerring taste in food, apparel, and notions. All goes well until he falls in love with a girl (Arleen Whelan) who is wise to the tricksters and helps him upset their elaborate schemes to control the business world. A brisk and amusing comedy.

THREE BLIND MICE

Produced by Darryl F. Zanuck
Directed by William A. Seiter
Screenplay by Brown Holmes and Lynn Starling, from a play by Stephen Powys
Photographed by Ernest Palmer
Songs and lyrics by Lew Pollack and Sidney D. Mitchell
Musical direction by Arthur Lange
75 minutes

Cast: Loretta Young, Joel McCrea, David Niven, Stuart Erwin, Marjorie Weaver, Pauline Moore, Binnie Barnes, Jane Darwell, Leonid Kinsky, Spencer Charters, Franklin Pangborn, Herb Heywood

Three sisters set out from Kansas to California with a small inheritance and the object of landing rich husbands. One (Loretta Young) poses as a wealthy socialite and the others (Marjorie Weaver and Pauline Moore) pretend to be her staff. The man they think is rich (Joel McCrea) is not, but after misunderstandings, he's the one the older sister loves. The second is paired with a rancher (David Niven) and the third loves a bartender (Stuart Erwin), who is indeed a millionaire. A well scripted and directed love comedy, *Three Blind Mice* would serve as a blueprint for other movies to come.

TIME OUT FOR MURDER

Produced by Howard J. Green
Directed by H. Bruce Humberstone
Screenplay by Jerry Cady, from a story by Irving Reis
Photographed by Virgil Miller
Musical direction by Samuel Kaylin
58 minutes

Cast: Gloria Stuart, Michael Whalen, Douglas Fowley, Robert Kellard, Chick Chandler, Jane Darwell, Jean Rogers, June Gale, Ruth Hussey, Cliff Clark, Peter Lynn, Edward Marr, Lester Mathews

A murder mystery, in which a bank runner (Robert Kellard) is accused of killing a lady (Ruth Hussey) for whom he is depositing a large sum of money. A crack reporter (Michael Whalen) and a bank collector (Gloria Stuart) combine forces to discover who committed the murder.

A TRIP TO PARIS

Produced by Max Gordon
Directed by Malcolm St. Clair
Screenplay by Robert Ellis and Helen Logan, based on the characters created by Katherine Kavanaugh
Photograph by Edward Snyder
Musical direction by Samuel Kaylin
64 minutes

Cast: Jed Prouty, Shirley Deane, Spring Byington, Russell Gleason, Ken Howell, George Ernest, June Carlson, Florence Roberts, Billy Mahan, Marvin Stephens, Joan Valerie, Harold Huber, Nedda Harrigan, Leonid Kinskey

Father (Jed Prouty) and Mother (Spring Byington) celebrate their 25th wedding anniversay by taking the Jones family to Paris. Their adventurers include being taken advantage of by small-time crooks, amorous advances, and an accidental involvement in a spy plot, with the family pleased to get back to simple values at home.

Victor McLaglen and Gracie Fields in *We're Going to Be Rich*.

Billy Mahan, Spring Byington, and Jed Prouty in *A Trip to Paris*.

UP THE RIVER

Produced by Sol M. Wurtzel
Directed by Alfred Werker
Screenplay by Lou Breslow and John Patrick, from an
    original story by Maurine Watkins
Photographed by Peverell Marley
Songs and lyrics by Sidney Clare and Harry Akst
Musical direction by Samuel Kaylin
75 minutes

Cast: Preston Foster, Tony Martin, Phyllis Brooks, Slim
Summerville, Arthur Treacher, Alan Dinehart, Eddie Collins, Jane Darwell, Sidney Toler, Bill Robinson, Edward
Gargan, Robert Allen, Dorothy Dearing

A pair of confidence tricksters (Preston Foster and
Arthur Treacher) are sent to jail, where they become
stars of the football team. A fellow prisoner (Tony
Martin) learns that his mother (Jane Darwell) is being
fleeced by crooks. The confidence pair break out of
prison, settle the crooks, and return to jail and their
success with its football victories over other prisons.
Up the River is a good lampoon on prison movies.

WALKING DOWN BROADWAY

Produced by Sol M. Wurtzel
Directed by Norman Foster
Screenplay by Robert Chapin and Karen DeWolf
Photographed by Virgil Miller
Songs and lyrics by Sidney Clare and Harry Akst
Musical direction by Samuel Kaylin
75 minutes

Cast: Claire Trevor, Phyllis Brooks, Leah Ray, Dixie
Dunbar, Lynn Bari, Jayne Regan, Michael Whalen,
Woolf King, Jed Prouty, Robert Kellard, Joan Carol,
Leon Ames, William Benedict

With a misleading title, the film is about six girls, all
of them Broadway dancers, who make a pact at the
closing of their revue to have a reunion one year later.
In that time, two die in accidents, one is jailed for
murder, one marries wealth, another marries her sweetheart when his innocence in a robbery is proven, and
the other (Claire Trevor) achieves success in business.

WE'RE GOING TO BE RICH

Produced by Samuel G. Engel
Directed by Monty Banks
Screenplay by Sam Hellman and Rohama Siegel, from
    a story by James Edward Grant
Photographed by Mutz Greenbaum
Music and lyrics by Lew Pollack and Sidney D. Mitchell,
    Harry Parr-Davies, Will Haynes, Jim Harper, Noel
    Forrester, Greatrex Newman, Howard Flynn, and Ralph
    Butler
78 minutes

Cast: Gracie Fields, Victor McLaglen, Brian Donlevy, Coral Brown, Ted Smith, Gus McNaughton, Charles Carson, Syd Crossley, Hal Gordon, Robert Nainby, Charles Harrison, Tom Payne, Don McCorkindale, Joe Mott, Alex Davies

Set in the gold mine country of South Africa but made in England, the film is a vehicle for the comedic and musical talents of Gracie Fields. It concerns a charming drifter (Victor McLaglen) who leaves Australia and goes to South Africa in the 1880's with his wife (Fields), hoping to gain wealth but continuing his improvident ways. She finally realizes that he cannot be changed and that home is wherever her shiftless but good-hearted husband happens to be. Fields has plenty of scope to sing in her role as a tavern entertainer.

WHILE NEW YORK SLEEPS

Produced by Sol M. Wurtzel
Directed by H. Bruce Humberstone
Screenplay by Frances Hyland and Albert Ray, from a story by Frank Fenton and Lynn Root

Photographed by Lucien Andriot
Songs by Sidney Clare and Arthur Johnston
Musical direction by Samuel Kaylin
63 minutes

Cast: Michael Whalen, Jean Rogers, Chick Chandler, Robert Kellard, Joan Woodbury, Harold Huber, Marc Lawrence, Sidney Blackmer, William Demarest, June Gale, Cliff Clark, Edward Gargan, Minor Watson, Robert Middlemass

A glib newspaper yarn, about a flippant reporter (Michael Whalen) who unravels the mystery of the deaths of a number of bond-carriers while carrying on a romance with a show girl (Jean Rogers).

20TH CENTURY-FOX ACADEMY AWARDS FOR 1938

WALTER BRENNAN: Best supporting actor in *Kentucky*.
ALFRED NEWMAN: Best scoring of a musical picture for *Alexander's Ragtime Band*.

1939

THE ADVENTURES OF SHERLOCK HOLMES

Produced by Darryl F. Zanuck
Directed by Alfred Werker
Screenplay by Edwin Blum and William Drake, based on a play by William Gillette
Photographed by Leon Shamroy
Musical direction by Cyril J. Mockridge
85 minutes

Cast: Basil Rathbone, Nigel Bruce, Ida Lupino, Alan Marshall, Terry Kilburn, George Zucco, Henry Stephenson, E. E. Clive, Arthur Hohl, May Beatty, Peter Willes, Mary Gordon, Holmes Herbert, George Regas

Basil Rathbone as Sherlock Holmes, in contest with his venerable adversary, the brilliant but evil Professor Moriarty (George Zucco). Moriarty devises a scheme to steal the crown jewels from the Tower of London, but first performs two murders to engage Holmes in other directions. One of the murders involves a young girl (Ida Lupino) who is menaced by a clubfooted gaucho. Moriarty spins a confusing trail of clues to challenge Holmes, but the master sleuth proves more than equal. The film is possibly Rathbone's finest appearance as Holmes and allows for him to appear in disguise, including a scene in which he does a Cockney song and dance.

BARRICADE

Produced by Darryl F. Zanuck
Directed by Gregory Ratoff
Screenplay by Granville Walker
Photographed by Karl Freund
Music by David Buttolph
71 minutes

Cast: Alice Faye, Warner Baxter, Charles Winninger, Arthur Treacher, Keye Luke, Willie Fong, Doris Lloyd, Eily Malyon, Joan Carroll, Leonid Snegoff, Philip Ahn, Jonathan Hale, Moroni Olsen, Harry Hayden

Set in China in the Thirties. Two Americans, a singer (Alice Faye) and a journalist (Warner Baxter), meet on a train when that is attacked by bandits. They fall in love and undergo various adventures in the war-torn country before being able to make their escape.

Limp and confusing, the film lingered on the shelf for a year before the studio decided to take a chance and release it.

BOY FRIEND

Produced by John Stone
Directed by James Tinling
Screenplay by Joseph Hoffman and Barry Trivers, from a story by Lester Ziffren and Louis Moore
Photographed by Lucien Andriot
Song by Sidney Clare and Harry Akst
Musical direction by Samuel Kaylin
70 minutes

Cast: Jane Withers, Arleen Whelan, Richard Bond, Douglas Fowley, Warren Hymer, Robert Shaw, Robert Kellard, George Ernest, Minor Watson, Ted Pearson, William H. Conselman, Jr.

Jane Withers' big brother (Richard Bond) is a cop pretending to be a crook in order to ferret out the gang. The villains run a night club as a front, which gives Jane a chance to get up and do a song, as she helps her brother do his job. The gentleman of the title is a military school cadet and this picture marks Jane's first cinematic love affair.

CHARLIE CHAN AT TREASURE ISLAND

Produced by Sol M. Wurtzel
Directed by Norman Foster
Screenplay by John Larkin, based on the character created by Earl Derr Biggers
Photographed by Virgil Miller
Musical direction by Samuel Kaylin
71 minutes

Cast: Sidney Toler, Cesar Romero, Pauline Moore, Sen Yung, Douglas Fowley, June Gale, Douglas Dumbrille, Sally Blane, Billie Seward, Wally Vernon, Donald McBride, Charles Halton, Trevor Bardette, Louis Jean Heydt

At a San Francisco exposition, Chan cuts through the displays of magic shows and psychic claims to discover why a novelist friend of his has committed suicide. Blackmail is the reason and a phony psychic is the villain.

CHARLIE CHAN IN CITY IN DARKNESS

Produced by John Stone
Directed by Herbert I. Leeds
Screenplay by Robert Ellis and Helen Logan, from a
    play by Gina Kaus and Ladislaus Fodor, based on the
    character created by Earl Derr Biggers
Photographed by Virgil Miller
Musical direction by Samuel Kaylin
72 minutes

Cast: Sidney Toler, Lynn Bari, Richard Clarke, Harold
Huber, Pedro de Cordoba, Dorothy Tree, C. Henry
Gordon, Douglas Dumbrille, Noel Madison, Leo Carroll,
Lon Chaney, Jr., Louis Mercier, George David, Barbara
Leonard

Chan attends a reunion with war buddies in Paris and
gets involved with spies. The film cashes in on the
Munich crisis of the previous year and concerns the
murder of a munitions manufacturer (Douglas Dumbrille) who supplies arms to the enemy. The film
ends with a warning from Chan to beware of peace
table conferences.

CHARLIE CHAN IN RENO

Produced by John Stone
Directed by Norman Foster
Screenplay by Frances Hyland, Albert Ray, and Robert
    E. Kent, based on a story by Philip Wylie and the
    character created by Earl Derr Biggers
Photographed by Virgil Miller
Music by Samuel Kaylin
65 minutes

Cast: Sidney Toler, Richardo Cortez, Phyllis Brooks,
Slim Summerville, Kane Richmond, Sen Yung, Pauline
Moore, Eddie Collins, Kay Linaker, Louise Henry, Robert Lowery, Charles D. Brown, Iris Wong, Morgan Conway, Hamilton MacFadden

When a young Hawaiian lady (Pauline Moore) is arrested in Reno as a murder suspect, Chan leaves his
Honolulu home and travels to Nevada to defend her.
The victim is a fellow guest at a hotel catering to di-
vorcees and there are a lot of people who wanted her
out of the way. Chan, of course, finds out which one
actually did the job.

CHASING DANGER

Produced by Sol M. Wurtzel
Directed by Ricardo Cortez
Screenplay by Robert Ellis and Helen Logan, from a
    story by Leonardo Bercovici
Photographed by Virgil Miller
Musical direction by Samuel Kaylin
60 minutes

Cast: Preston Foster, Lynn Bari, Wally Vernon, Henry
Wilcoxon, Joan Woodbury, Harold Huber, Jody Gilbert,
Pedro de Cordoba, Stanley Fields, Roy D'Arcy

Basil Rathbone, Richard Greene, and Lionel Atwill in *The
Hound of the Baskervilles.*

More adventures of newsreel cameramen, with Preston
Foster as a crack lensman stationed in Paris and sent
to cover an Arab rebellion. He discovers that a supposedly deceased financier is actually alive and promoting the desert warfare.

CHICKEN WAGON FAMILY

Produced by Sol M. Wurtzel
Directed by Herbert I. Leeds
Screenplay by Viola Brothers Shore, based on a novel by
    Barry Benefield
Photographed by Edward Cronjager
Musical direction by Samuel Kaylin
63 minutes

Cast: Jane Withers, Leo Carrillo, Marjorie Weaver,
Spring Byington, Kane Richmond, Hobart Cavanaugh,
Hamilton MacFadden, Inez Palange

A story of an itinerant merchant (Leo Carrillo) and his
family, who tire of rural life and head for New York.
Father has a weakness for poker, as he looks for work,
but his youngest daughter (Jane Withers) energetically
solves all the family problems. Originally purchased as
a Will Rogers vehicle but shelved with his death,
Chicken Wagon Family was redesigned as a Withers
film—with limp results.

CLIMBING HIGH

Directed by Carol Reed
Screenplay by Lesser Samuels and Marion Dix
Photographed by Mutz Greenbaum
67 minutes

Linda Darnell and Tyrone Power in *Daytime Wife*.

Claudette Colbert and Henry Fonda in *Drums Along the Mohawk*.

Cast: Jessie Matthews, Michael Redgrave, Noel Madison, Margaret Vyner, Alistair Sim, Tucker McGuire, Torin Thatcher, Francis L. Sullivan, Mary Clare, Enid Taylor, Leo Pokorny, Basil Radford

A British production, with Jessie Matthews as a model who meets a young man (Michael Redgrave) of high society who pretends to be poor in order to be near her. He is almost engaged to an aggressive aristocrat (Margaret Vyner), but in the end it's the model who gets him.

DAYTIME WIFE

Produced by Darryl F. Zanuck
Directed by Gregory Ratoff
Screenplay by Art Arthur and Robert Harari, from a story by Rex Taylor
Photographed by Peverell Marley
Musical direction by Cyril J. Mockridge
71 minutes

Cast: Tyrone Power, Linda Darnell, Warren William, Binnie Barnes, Wendy Barrie, Joan Davis, Joan Valerie, Leonid Kinskey, Mildred Grover, Renie Riano

A marital farce, about an executive (Tyrone Power) whose wife (Linda Darnell) feels he doesn't pay enough attention to her. He seems to be having an affair with his secretary (Wendy Barrie), but it's only friendship. Her friend (Binnie Barnes) suggests she take action, so she gets a job as a secretary to a wealthy playboy and architect (Warren William), which causes the inevitable jealousy—and solution. The film helped widen Power's popularity by giving him a lightly comedic role, supplementing the drama and heroism of his other features.

DRUMS ALONG THE MOHAWK

Produced by Raymond Griffith
Directed by John Ford

Screenplay by Lamar Trotti and Sonya Levien, based on the novel by Walter D. Edmonds
Photographed in Technicolor by Bert Glennon and Ray Rennahan
Music by Alfred Newman
103 minutes

Cast: Claudette Colbert, Henry Fonda, Edna May Oliver, Eddie Collins, John Carradine, Dorris Bowden, Jessie Ralph, Arthur Shields, Robert Lowery, Roger Imof, Francis Ford, Ward Bond, Kay Linaker, Russell Simpson, Chief Big Tree, Spencer Charters, Arthur Aylesworth, Si Jenks

John Ford's lusty and enlightening account of the life of farmers in the Mohawk Valley in the years prior to the Revolutionary War. A young farmer (Henry Fonda) brings a bride (Claudette Colbert) from the East and they settle down in a new home, until they are burned out by Indians. Neighbors take them in and the young farmer joins the militia and marches away to fight the Indians. When he returns, there is even more fighting, but the Indians eventually retreat and life in the valley goes on. Ford's film is spendidly photographed in handsome scenery in Technicolor and gives a fine account of the hardships and the courage of frontier life. As an exciting evocation of this period and location of American history it has few peers.

THE ESCAPE

Produced by Sol M. Wurtzel
Directed by Ricardo Cortez
Screenplay by Robert Ellis and Helen Logan
Photographed by Edward Cronjager
Musical direction by Samuel Kaylin
58 minutes

Cast: Kane Richmond, Amanda Duff, Henry Armetta, Edward Norris, June Gale, Frank Reicher, Leona Roberts, Scotty Beckett

A time-worn yarn of youths growing up in the dingy

Sonja Henie and Ray Milland in *Everything Happens at Night.*

Randolph Scott and Cesar Romero in *Frontier Marshal.*

city tenements, with one growing up to be a policeman (Kane Richmond) and one becoming a criminal (Edward Norris). The sister of the criminal (Amanda Duff) is in love with the cop, whose father has been murdered. The criminal opposes the marriage, but when mortally wounded changes his mind and also reveals the name of the killer.

EVERYBODY'S BABY

Produced by John Stone
Directed by Malcolm St. Clair
Screenplay by Karen De Wolf, Robert Chapin, Frances Hyland, and Albert Ray, based on a story by Hilda Stone and Betty Reinhardt and the characters created by Katherine Kavanaugh
Photographed by Edward Snyder
Musical direction by Samuel Kaylin
61 minutes

Cast: Jed Prouty, Shirley Deane, Spring Byington, Russell Gleason, June Carlson, Florence Roberts, Billy Mahan, Reginald Denny, Robert Allen, Claire Du Brey, Marvin Stephens, Hattie MacDaniel, Arthur Loft, Howard Hickman

The Jones family get mixed up with modern theories on childbirth, as an author (Reginald Denny) arrives in town and lectures on how to raise babies. His schemes cause friction in local families and when some of the local fathers find that he is a fraud, they devise a means of ending his influence.

EVERYTHING HAPPENS AT NIGHT

Produced by Darryl F. Zanuck
Directed by Irving Cummings
Screenplay by Art Arthur and Robert Harari
Photographed by Edward Cronjager
Musical direction by Cyril J. Mockridge
77 minutes

Cast: Sonja Henie, Ray Milland, Robert Cummings, Maurice Moscovich, Leonid Kinsky, Alan Dinehart, Fritz Feld, Jody Gilbert, Victor Varconi, William Edmunds, George Davis, Paul Porcasi, Michael Visaroff, Eleanor Wesselhoeft, Lester Matthews

A British newspaperman (Ray Milland) and an American newspaperman (Robert Cummings) both discover a supposedly slain political commentator (Maurice Moscovich) living in Switzerland and vie to tell his story. The situation is complicated by both of them falling in love with his daughter (Sonja Henie), but with the American settling for romance and the Briton opting for an exclusive story. The film offers a few solo skating scenes for Henie but no production numbers, and was intended to broaden her dramatic and romantic image. Like all Henie films in these years, it made money for the studio.

FRONTIER MARSHAL

Produced by Sol M. Wurtzel
Directed by Allan Dwan
Screenplay by Sam Hellman, based on a book by Stuart N. Lake
Photographed by Charles Clarke
Musical direction by Samuel Kaylin
70 minutes

Cast: Randolph Scott, Nancy Kelly, Cesar Romero, Binnie Barnes, John Carradine, Edward Norris, Eddie Foy, Jr., Ward Bond, Lon Chaney, Jr., Chris-Pin Martin, Joe Sawyer, Don Henderson, Harry Hayden

Randolph Scott as Wyatt Earp, the marshal of Tombstone, Arizona, in a very romanticized account, based on Stuart Lake's popular book. Earp accepts the offer to become marshal and quiet the rowdy, raucous town —except for Curly Bell (Joe Sawyer) and his gang. When Earp's friend Doc Holliday (Cesar Romero) is killed because of Curly, it remains for the marshal to settle the score with the gang at the O. K. Corral.

THE GORILLA

Produced by Darryl F. Zanuck
Directed by Allan Dwan
Screenplay by Rian James and Sid Silvers, based on a play by Ralph Spence
Photographed by Edward Cronjager
Musical direction by David Buttolph
67 minutes

Cast: Ritz Brothers, Anita Louise, Patsy Kelly, Lionel Atwill, Bela Lugosi, Joseph Calleia, Edward Norris, Wally Vernon, Paul Harvey, Art Miles

A knockabout mystery, with the Ritz Brothers as three incompetent detectives hired by a wealthy man (Lionel Atwill) when his life is threatened by a killer known as The Gorilla, who does his killing dressed as one. They go to the mansion, which is a maze of secret passageways, and await the killer. A real gorilla escapes from a zoo and turns up at the mansion at the same time. Slapstick à la Ritz.

HEAVEN WITH A BARBED WIRE FENCE

Produced by Sol M. Wurtzel
Directed by Ricardo Cortez
Screenplay by Dalton Trumbo, Leonard Hoffman, and Ben Grauman Kohn, from a story by Dalton Trumbo
Photographed by Edward Cronjager
Musical direction by Samuel Kaylin
61 minutes.

Cast: Jean Rogers, Raymond Walburn, Marjorie Rambeau, Glenn Ford, Nicholas Conte, Eddie Collins, Ward Bond, Irving Bacon, Kay Linaker

A New York department store clerk (Glenn Ford) saves his money and buys a piece of land in Arizona and then hitchhikes his way out west. En route he teams up with a hobo (Richard Conte) and a Spanish girl (Jean Rogers) who is an illegal alien. They undergo a variety of adventures before reaching Arizona, where the former clerk saves the girl from deportation by marrying her.

HERE I AM A STRANGER

Produced by Darryl F. Zanuck
Directed by Roy Del Ruth
Screenplay by Milton Sperling and Sam Hellman, from a story by Gordon Malherbe Hillman
Photographed by Arthur Miller
Song by Mack Gordon and Harry Revel
Musical direction by Louis Silvers
82 minutes

Cast: Richard Greene, Richard Dix, Brenda Joyce, Roland Young, Gladys George, Katharine Aldridge, Russell Gleason, George Zucco, Edward Norris, Henry Kolker, Richard Bond

A young man (Richard Greene) brought up in England by his mother (Gladys George) and her second husband gets to meet his real father (Richard Dix) in America. The father is a former alcoholic who gains strength from getting to know his son, and the boy benefits from the knowledge and experience of the father.

HOLLYWOOD CAVALCADE

Produced by Darryl F. Zanuck
Directed by Irving Cummings
Screenplay by Irving Pascal, based on a story by Hilary Lynn and Brown Holmes
Photographed in Technicolor by Ernest Palmer and Allen M. Davey
Music by Louis Silvers
96 minutes

Cast: Alice Faye, Don Ameche, J. Edward Bromberg, Alan Curtis, Stuart Erwin, Jed Prouty, Donald Meek, George Givot, Chick Chandler, Russell Hicks, Robert Lowery, Ben Weldon. *Guest stars:* Buster Keaton, Ben Turpin, Chester Conklin, Al Jolson, Mack Sennett, the Keystone Kops

Starting in New York in 1913, the cavalcade gets underway when movie director Michael Linnett Connors (Don Ameche) spots refreshing young singer Molly Adair (Alice Faye) and talks her into a movie contract. Together their fortunes build as they go from comedy shorts to features, until Molly becomes a major star. She loves Mike, but he is always too busy to notice and she marries an actor (Alan Curtis), which causes the angry director to fire them both. Their careers grow bigger as his declines. To save him, she asks for him as the director of her next film. It is the time of the coming of sound to the movies, and the success of their film augurs a new era for them. *Hollywood Cavalcade* is strung together with a thin thread, but offers movie buffs prime footage in dealing with the early years of making silent movies and actually involving the likes of Buster Keaton, Ben Turpin, Mack Sennett, and the Keystone Kops.

THE HONEYMOON'S OVER

Produced by Sol M. Wurtzel
Directed by Eugene Forde
Screenplay by Hamilton MacFadden, Clay Williams, and Leonard Hoffman, from a play *Six Cylinder Love* by William Anthony McGuire
Photographed by Virgil Miller
Musical direction by Samuel Kaylin
69 minutes

Cast: Stuart Erwin, Marjorie Weaver, Patric Knowles, Russell Hicks, Jack Carson, Hobart Cavanaugh, June Gale, E. E. Clive, Renie Riana, Harrison Green, Lelah Tyler, Harry Hayden

A young newly married couple (Stuart Erwin and Mar-

MR. MOTO IN D[...]

Produced by John Stone
Directed by Herbert I. L[...]
Screenplay by Peter Milr[...]
    Reinhard and George
    W. Vandercook, based
    Marquand
Photographed by Lucien
Musical direction by Sar
64 minutes

Cast: Peter Lorre, Jean [...]
Hymer, Richard Lane, [...]
Charles D. Brown, Paul
Marr, Harry Woods

The island is Puerto Ric[...]
by the U.S. government [...]
after a previous investig
plots against himself
which frees certain offici
fallen. Fist fights, gunpl
help the visual impact o
which was released thr
cessor, *Mr. Moto Takes*

MR. MOTO'S LAS[...]

Produced by Sol M. Wur
Directed by Norman Fos
Screenplay by Philip Ma
    created by J. P. Marq
Photographed by Virgil
Musical direction by Sar
74 minutes

Cast: Peter Lorre, Ricar
Carradine, George Sande
Margaret Irving, Robert

The story begins in Por[...]
to cause friction betwe
Moto (Peter Lorre) fi[...]
sink several ships of th
the British. Moto prever

MR. MOTO TAKE[...]

Produced by Sol M. Wu
Directed by Norman Fos
Screenplay by Phillip N
    based on a character
Photographed by Charles
Musical direction by Sa[...]
65 minutes

Cast: Peter Lorre, Jose
Virginia Field, John Kin
ley, Victor Varconi, Joh[...]
Wallace, Anthony Warde

Mr. Moto (Peter Lorre)
Schildkraut) who has [...]

jorie Weaver) become the victims of confidence tricksters and have their lives almost wrecked as they are pushed into debt. They struggle their way back to solvency after learning that young couples should live within their means.

HOTEL FOR WOMEN

Produced by Darryl F. Zanuck
Directed by Gregory Ratoff
Screenplay by Kathryn Scola and Darrell Ware, from a
    story by Elsa Maxwell and Kathryn Scola
Photographed by Peverell Marley
Song by Elsa Maxwell
Musical direction by David Buttolph
83 minutes

Cast: Ann Sothern, Linda Darnell, James Ellison, Jean Rogers, Lynn Bari, June Gale, Joyce Compton, Elsa Maxwell, John Halliday, Katharine Aldridge, Alan Dinehart, Sidney Blackmer, Amanda Duff, Ruth Terry, Chick Chandler

The movie debut of sixteen-year-old Linda Darnell, playing a girl from Syracuse who goes to New York to see her boyfriend (James Ellison) and finds him a great success as an architect but no longer interested in her. With the encouragement of fellow guests in a women's hotel she becomes a top model, which brings the boyfriend back, by which time he has a lot of competition. The screenplay is based on a story by famed party-giver Elsa Maxwell, who also appears in the picture, dispensing advice to young ladies.

THE HOUND OF THE BASKERVILLES

Produced by Gene Markey
Directed by Sidney Lanfield
Screenplay by Ernest Pascal, from a story by Arthur
    Conan Doyle
Photographed by Peverell Marley
Musical direction by Cyril J. Mockridge
80 minutes

Cast: Richard Greene, Basil Rathbone, Wendy Barrie, Nigel Bruce, Lionel Atwill, John Carradine, Barlowe Borland, Beryl Mercer, Morton Lowry, Ralph Forbes, E. Mary Gordon, Peter Willes, Ivan Simpson, Ian MacLaren, John Burton, Dennis Greene

The first casting of Basil Rathbone as Sherlock Holmes and Nigel Bruce as Dr. Watson, but with Richard Greene getting top billing as Sir Henry Baskerville, the lord of an ancestral hall on the bleak moors of Devonshire. Sir Henry returns from abroad and opens up the closed mansion after the death of an uncle. Holmes is hired and predicts that there is a plot to kill Sir Henry, in order for the culprit to gain his wealth. The means of death is a huge, trained hound, which Holmes manages to kill just in time. The film remains one of the best depictions of Conan Doyle's classic mystery tale,

with fine settings, and a performance from Rathbone that made sequels inevitable.

IT COULD HAPPEN TO YOU

Produced by David Hempstead
Directed by Alfred Werker
Screenplay by Allen Rivkin and Lou Breslow, from a
    story by Charles Hoffman
Photographed by Ernest Palmer
Musical direction by Samuel Kaylin
70 minutes

Cast: Stuart Erwin, Gloria Stuart, Raymond Walburn, Douglas Fowley, June Gale, Clarence Korb, Paul Hurst, Richard Lane, Robert Greig

A comedy mystery concerning an ad man (Stuart Erwin) who is jailed on suspicion of murdering a beautiful girl and whose wife (Gloria Stuart) goes about solving the crime and clearing her husband.

Alice Faye and Buster Keaton in *Hollywood Cavalcade.*

Nigel Bruce, Ida Lupino, and Basil Rathbone in *The Adventures of Sherlock Holmes.*

87

JESSE

Produced
Directed b
Screenplay
 Rosalind
Photograpl
 George
Music by I
105 minute

Cast: Tyr(
dolph Sco
Bromberg,
John Russ(
Breakston,
Tannen, (
Goodwin,

Handsome
in Missou
Jesse Jam
post-Civil '
James (H(
a represei
farmers fc
take to a l
Robin Ho
giving up
colleague
the way o|
ful, actioi
continues

THE JC

Produced l
Directed b;
Screenplay
 Hoffman
 created l
Photograpl
Musical di
60 minutes

Henry Fond

A flat attempt to widen Alice Faye's image, *Tail Spin* presents her as a spirited flying enthusiast who enters a cross-country aerial derby and loses when her plane cracks up, but manages to persuade people to help carry on. She becomes a rival with a rich society flyer (Constance Bennett) and gets involved in competitions, parachute jumps, business dealings, and love affairs. A dated item, the film is of some interest to aviation buffs because it involves footage shot at the Cleveland Air Meet of 1938, displaying the latest planes.

THE THREE MUSKETEERS

Produced by Raymond Griffith
Directed by Allan Dwan
Screenplay by M. M. Musselman, William A. Drake, and
 Sam Hellman
Photographed by Peverell Marley
Music and lyrics by Samuel Pokrass and Walter Bullock
Musical direction by David Buttolph
72 minutes

Cast: Don Ameche, the Ritz Brothers, Binnie Barnes, Lionel Atwill, Gloria Stuart, Pauline Moore, Joseph Schildkraut, John Carradine, Miles Mander, Douglas Dumbrille, John King, Russell Hicks, Gregory Gaye, Lester Matthews, Egon Brecher

Don Ameche is a singing D'Artagnan in this knock-about version of the Dumas classic and the Ritz Brothers are comic cowards posing as musketeers. Miles Mander is Cardinal Richelieu, Binnie Barnes is Lady de Winter, Joseph Schildkraut is the King, and Lionel Atwill is De Rochefort. Long on slapstick and music and woefully short on genuine swashbuckling.

TOO BUSY TO WORK

Produced by Sol M. Wurtzel
Directed by Otto Brower
Screenplay by Robert Ellis, Helen Logan, and Stanley
 Rauh, based on *The Torchbearers* by George Kelley
 and *Your Uncle Dudley* by Howard Lindsay and Bert-
 rand Robinson
Photographed by Edward Cronjager
Musical direction by Samuel Kaylin
64 minutes

Cast: Jed Prouty, Spring Byington, Ken Howell, George Ernest, June Carlson, Florence Roberts, Billy Mahan, Joan Davis, Chick Chandler, Marjorie Gateson, Andrew Toombes, Marvin Stephens, Irving Bacon, Helen Ericson, Harold Goodwin

A Jones family comedy, in which the females decide that it is time to teach father (Jed Prouty) a lesson, when they feel he is neglecting his drugstore business in favor of politics and his running for mayor. They show him what happens when wives and daughters neglect their domestic chores.

20,000 MEN A YEAR

Produced by Sol M. Wurtzel
Directed by Alfred E. Green
Screenplay by Lou Breslow and Owen Francis, from a
 story by Frank Wead
Photographed by Ernest Palmer
Musical direction by Samuel Kaylin
82 minutes

Cast: Randolph Scott, Preston Foster, Margaret Lindsay, Robert Shaw, Mary Healy, George Ernest, Kane Richmond, Maxie Rosenbloom, Douglas Wood, Sen Yung, Paul Stanton, Tom Seidel, Edward Gargan, Harry Tyler, Sidney Miller

A crack transport pilot (Randolph Scott) disobeys orders he considers unsafe and loses his job. He buys a rundown private airport and starts a flying school, but almost goes under until the government announces a new program to promote aerial education. A government inspector (Preston Foster) with whom Scott has had difficulties sends his reluctant brother (Robert Shaw) to be trained, which almost costs Scott his life. The film tied in with the government's actual attempts to promote aviation, in the hope that twenty thousand young men each year would become pilots.

WIFE, HUSBAND AND FRIEND

Produced by Darryl F. Zanuck
Directed by Gregory Ratoff
Screenplay by Nunnally Johnson, from a novel by James
 M. Cain
Photographed by Ernest Palmer
Music and lyrics by Samuel Pokrass, Walter Bullock,
 and Armando Hauser
Musical direction by David Buttolph
75 minutes

Cast: Loretta Young, Warner Baxter, Binnie Barnes, Cesar Romero, George Barbier, J. Edward Bromberg, Eugene Pallette, Helen Westley, Ruth Terry, Alice Armand, Iva Stewart, Dorothy Dearing, Helen Ericson, Kay Griffith

A genial comedy about a businessman (Warner Baxter) whose wife (Loretta Young) has delusions about being a great singer, with the encouragement of her calculating teacher (Cesar Romero). She flops when she appears in a theatre. Then the husband is encouraged to sing by a philandering professional singer (Binnie Barnes) and has a little success, which leads him to opera, where he makes a fool of himself. Husband and wife come to their senses and decide to remain amateurs. The Nunnally Johnson script scores a few points about musical pretentiousness.

WINNER TAKE ALL

Produced by Jerry Hoffman
Directed by Otto Brower

Screenplay by Frances Hyland and Albert Ray, from a story by Jerry Cady
Photographed by Edward Cronjager
Musical direction by Samuel Kaylin
61 minutes

Cast: Tony Martin, Gloria Stuart, Henry Armetta, Slim Summerville, Kane Richmond, Robert Allen, Inez Palange, Johnnie Pirrone, Jr., Pedro de Cordoba

A waiter (Tony Martin) scores a lucky knockout in a benefit prizefight and is picked up by gamblers, who rig some fights for him to win. A reporter (Gloria Stuart) who likes him arranges for a fighter friend (Kane Richmond) to teach him a lesson and deflate his swelled head. She then encourages him to become a pro and go into training, which he does with success.

YOUNG MR. LINCOLN

Produced by Darryl F. Zanuck
Directed by John Ford
Screenplay by Lamar Trotti
Photographed by Bert Glenon
Music by Alfred Newman
100 minutes

Cast: Henry Fonda, Alice Brady, Majorie Weaver, Arleen Whelan, Eddie Collins, Pauline Moore, Richard Cromwell, Donald Meek, Dorris Bowden, Eddie Quillan, Spencer Charters, Ward Bond, Milburn Stone, Cliff Clark, Robert Lower, Charles Tannen, Francis Ford, Kred Kohler, Jr.

Ten years in the early life of Abraham Lincoln, with Henry Fonda giving a masterly performance of a simple, good-natured man moving toward maturity in his experiences as a lawyer and politician. The awkward Kentucky cabin youth proceeds to Springfield, Illinois, sets up a law practice, and soon gains clients with his honesty and his humor. He comes to wide attention when he defends two young men accused of murder in a political brawl and he suffers his first tragedy with the death of his sweetheart Ann Rutledge (Pauline Moore). Later he courts Mary Todd (Marjorie Weaver), an ambitious girl who would become his wife, and he agrees to go into politics to represent the common people. The film, firmly directed by John Ford, presents a clear portrait of Lincoln prior to his years of great exposure.

20TH CENTURY-FOX ACADEMY AWARDS FOR 1939

FRED SERSEN and E. H. HANSEN: Special award for technical developments.

Pauline Moore and Henry Fonda in *Young Mr. Lincoln.*

THE BLUE BIRD

Produced by Darryl F. Zanuck
Directed by Walter Lang
Screenplay by Ernest Pascal, from a play by Maurice
 Maeterlinck
Photographed in technicolor by Arthur Miller and Ray
 Rennahan
Music by Alfred Newman
84 minutes

Cast: Shirley Temple, Spring Byington, Nigel Bruce,
Gale Sondergaard, Eddie Collins, Sybil Jason, Jessie
Ralph, Helen Ericson, Johnny Russell, Laura Hope
Crews, Russell Hicks, Cecilia Loftus, Al Shean, Gene
Reynolds

Visually beautiful and full of imaginative sets, splendidly photographed in rich Technicolor, *The Blue
Bird* was the first Shirley Temple film to flop at the
box office. It did not allow for the Temple image,
being confined by its strict fantasy-fable framework,
and confused youngsters with its allegory of the search
for the bluebird of happiness. The plot visits the future
and the past and deals with the wide range of human
nature. The Germanic, gingerbread story, somewhat
like *Hansel and Gretel*, did nothing to help Temple's
gradually sagging public appeal.

BRIGHAM YOUNG

Produced by Darryl F. Zanuck
Directed by Henry Hathaway
Screenplay by Lamar Trotti, from a story by Louis
 Bromfield
Photographed by Arthur Miller
Music by Alfred Newman
110 minutes

Cast: Tyrone Power, Linda Darnell, Dean Jagger, Brian
Donlevy, Jane Darwell, John Carradine, Mary Astor,
Vincent Price, Jean Rogers, Ann Todd, Willard Robert-
son, Moroni Olsen, Marc Lawrence, Stanley Andrews,
Frank Thomas

An admirable attempt to interest a wide audience in
the story of the pioneering Mormons and their founding of Salt Lake City, but less successful than Zanuck
had hoped. It tells the story of the death of the Mormon leader Joseph Smith (Vincent Price) and the
decision to trek westward in the early nineteenth century to escape religious persecution under the leadership of Brigham Young (Dean Jagger). The film
graphically outlines the toil and hazards of the long
wagon trip and the choosing of Utah as the promised
land for the Mormons. The scene of the locusts raiding
the farmlands is a major cinematic achievement. Tyrone Power was given top billing for obvious box
office reasons, but his role as a young Mormon pioneer
is secondary.

CHAD HANNA

Produced by Nunnally Johnson
Directed by Henry King
Screenplay by Nunnally Johnson, based on the story *Red
 Wheels Rolling* by Walter D. Edmonds
Photographed in Technicolor by Ernest Palmer
Music by David Buttolph
86 minutes

Cast: Henry Fonda, Dorothy Lamour, Linda Darnell,
Guy Kibbee, Jane Darwell, John Carradine, Ted North,
Roscoe Ates, Ben Carter, Frank Thomas, Olin Howard,
Frank Conlan, Edward Conrad, Edward McWade, Ed-
ward Mundy, George Davis

The title role is that of a genial country boy (Henry
Fonda) who joins a circus in the upstate New York
of the 1840's and falls in love with a bare-back rider
(Dorothy Lamour). He follows the circus life and
performs all manner of chores and finally falls in love
with a fellow runaway (Linda Darnell), a drab girl
who blossoms into a beauty with the circus life. The
story is slight, but director Henry King sparks it
with good circus atmosphere and depictions of its
attractions.

CHARLIE CHAN AT THE WAX MUSEUM

Produced by Walter Morosco and Ralph Dietrich
Directed by Lynn Shores
Screenplay by John Larkin, based on the character
 created by Earl Derr Biggers
Photographed by Virgil Miller
Musical direction by Emil Newman
63 minutes

Cast: Sidney Toler, Sen Yung, C. Henry Gordon, Marc Lawrence, Joan Valerie, Marguerite Chapman, Ted Osburn, Michael Visaroff, Hilda Vaughn, Charles Wagenheim, Archie Twitchell, Edward Marr, Joe King, Harold Goodwin

A wax museum run by a demented doctor is the locale of this Chan mystery, with the master sleuth trying to establish the identity of an arch criminal who has taken refuge in the wax chamber of horrors. The doctor also performs facial surgery on criminals, making it difficult to tell humans from dummies. But nothing can stop Chan arriving at his conclusions.

CHARLIE CHAN IN PANAMA

Produced by Sol M. Wurtzel
Directed by Norman Foster
Screenplay by John Larkin and Lester Ziffren, based on the character created by Earl Derr Biggers
Photographed by Virgil Miller
Music by Samuel Kaylin
66 minutes

Cast: Sidney Toler, Jean Rogers, Lionel Atwill, Mary Nash, Sen Yung, Kane Richmond, Chris-Pin Martin, Lionel Royce, Helen Ericson, Jack La Rue, Edwin Stanley, Don Douglas, Frank Puglia, Addison Richards, Edward Keane

Chan takes on big responsibilities in this adventure, working for the American government and solving spy plots that would interfere with the Navy, as it moves the fleet through the canal back to the Pacific after a training campaign in the Atlantic.

CHARLIE CHAN'S MURDER CRUISE

Produced by Sol M. Wurtzel
Directed by Eugene Forde
Screenplay by Robertson White and Lester Ziffren, based on a story by Earl Derr Biggers
Photographed by Virgil Miller
Music by Sidney Kaylin
77 minutes

Cast: Sidney Toler, Marjorie Weaver, Lionel Atwill, Sen Yung, Robert Lowery, Don Beddoe, Leo Carroll, Cora Witherspoon, Kay Linaker, Harlan Briggs, Charles Middleton, Claire Du Brey, Leonard Mudie, James Burke, Richard Keene, Layne Tom, Jr., Montague Shaw

Chan joins a world cruise at Honolulu and proceeds to San Francisco in order to unravel the murder of a Scotland Yard friend who has been tracking a strangler. Four more murders occur before Chan reveals the culprit to be a maniac who bears a grudge against a former wife and her husband.

CHARTER PILOT

Produced by Sol M. Wurtzel

Directed by Eugene Forde
Screenplay by Stanley Rauh and Lester Ziffren, from a story by J. Robert Bren and Norman Houston
Photographed by Lucien Andriot
Music direction by Emil Newman
70 minutes

Cast: Lloyd Nolan, Lynn Bari, Arleen Whelan, George Montgomery, Hobart Cavanaugh, Henry Victor, Etta McDaniel, Andrew Tombes, Charles Wilson, Chick Chandler

An ace pilot (Lloyd Nolan) for a freighting service between the U.S. and Central America marries a radio broadcaster (Lynn Bari) and promises to take a desk job. But the urge to adventure is much too strong and he resumes flying. She compromises by using him as the hero of a radio series. Togther they smash a sabotage plot.

THE CISCO KID AND THE LADY

Produced by Sol M. Wurtzel
Directed by Herbert I. Leeds
Screenplay by Frances Hyland, from a story by Stanley Rauh, suggested by the character created by O. Henry
Photographed by Barney McGill
Music direction by Samuel Kaylin
74 minutes

Cast: Cesar Romero, Marjorie Weaver, Chris-Pin Martin, George Montgomery, Robert Barrat, Virginia Field, Harry Green, Gloria Ann White, John Beach, Ward Bond, J. Anthony Hughes, James Burke, Harry Hayden

Johnny Russell and Shirley Temple in *The Blue Bird.*

Tyrone Power and Linda Darnell in *Brigham Young.*

Cisco (Cesar Romero), the benevolent bandit, tackles a gang of bandits out to acquire a gold mine owned by an orphan whose father has been shot by the leader (Robert Barrat). The mine is saved and the child is deposited with a local schoolteacher (Marjorie Weaver), who turns out to be the actual mother of the child.

CITY OF CHANCE

Produced by Sol M. Wurtzel
Directed by Ricardo Cortez
Screenplay by John Larkin and Barry Trivers
Photographed by Lucien Andriot
Music direction by Samuel Kaylin
56 minutes

Cast: Lynn Bari, C. Aubrey Smith, Donald Woods, Amanda Duff, June Gale, Richard Lane, Robert Lowery, Alexander D'Arcy, George Douglas, Harry Shannon, Edward Marr, Robert Allen, Charlotte Wynters

A Texas girl (Lynn Bari) goes to New York and gets a job as a newspaper reporter, with the object of trying to get her gambling addict boyfriend (Donald Woods) to return home. She gathers enough evidence on the illicit gambling house where he works to arrange a police raid and talks him into giving up his involvement in petty crime.

DOWN ARGENTINE WAY

Produced by Darryl F. Zanuck
Directed by Irving Cummings
Screenplay by Darrell Ware and Karl Tunberg, from a story by Rian James and Ralph Spence
Photographed in technicolor by Leon Shamroy and Ray Rennahan
Songs and lyrics by Harry Warren and Mack Gordon
Musical direction by Emil Newman
94 minutes

Cast: Don Ameche, Betty Grable, Carmen Miranda, Charlotte Greenwood, J. Carrol Naish, Henry Stephenson, Katharine Aldridge, Leonid Kinskey, Chris-Pin Martin, Robert Conway, Gregory Gaye, Bobby Stone, Charles Judels, Nicholas Brothers

With much of the European market cut off by the war, Hollywood concentrated on Latin America, particularly with musicals, of which *Down Argentine Way* was a leading item. It introduced Brazilian bombshell Carmen Miranda to the movies and triggered Betty Grable's success as a star of color musicals. The film, like almost all the other Latin musicals, pictured South America in only the most glowing touristic splendor, constantly bubbling over with songs and dances . . . a fiction which pleased audiences everywhere. Here Grable is an American girl on vacation in Argentina who falls in love with a wealthy race horse owner (Don Ameche) and after sundry misunderstandings agrees to marry him. In the meantime moviegoers have seen beautiful shots of Argentina, its fiestas and its racetracks, with pauses here and there for sparkling musical numbers. *Down Argentine Way* is lightweight entertainment but an important opening-up of the market for the studio.

EARTHBOUND

Produced by Sol M. Wurtzel
Directed by Irving Pichel
Screenplay by John Howard Lawson and Samuel Engel, from a story by Basil King
Photographed by Lucien Andriot
Music by Alfred Newman
67 minutes

Cast: Warner Baxter, Andrea Leeds, Lynn Bari, Charles Grapewin, Henry Wilcoxon, Elizabeth Patterson, Russell Hicks, Christian Rub, Ian Wolfe, Lester Scharff, Reginald Sheffield, Pedro de Cordoba

A ghostly whodunit, about a murdered man (Warner Baxter) who helps his widow (Andrea Leeds) bring to justice the woman (Lynn Bari) who shot him as a final act of an outlived secret passion. The widow is able to save her husband's good name and the husband (Henry Wilcoxon) of the murderess steps up to speak of trying to save him. A not very plausible film but well staged and acted.

FOUR SONS

Produced by Darryl F. Zanuck
Directed by Archie Mayo
Screenplay by John Howard Lawson, from a story by I. A. R. Wylie
Photographed by Leon Shamroy
Musical direction by David Buttolph
89 minutes

Cast: Don Ameche, Eugenie Leontovich, Mary Beth Hughes, Alan Curtis, George Ernest, Robert Lowery, Lionel Rovce, Sig Rumann, Ludwig Stossel, Christian Rub, Torben Meyer, Egon Brecher, Eleanor Wesselhoeft, Michael Visaroff

Set in Czechoslovakia at the time of the German invasion. The four sons of a Czech-German family go their separate ways according to their beliefs. One (Don Ameche) is a Czech patriot, another (Alan Curtis) sides with the Nazis, another (Robert Lowery) goes to America and becomes an artist, and the youngest (George Ernest) dies a German soldier and wins the Iron Cross. *Four Sons* clearly outlines not only the horrors of war but its confused issues, and helped American audiences feel the impact of the war in Europe.

FREE, BLONDE AND 21

Produced by Sol M. Wurtzel

Directed by Ricardo Cortez
Screenplay by Frances Hyland
Photographed by George Barnes
Musical direction Samuel Kaylin
75 minutes

Cast: Lynn Bari, Mary Beth Hughes, Joan Davis, Henry Wilcoxon, Robert Lowery, Alan Baxter, Katharine Aldridge, Helen Ericson, Chick Chandler, Joan Valerie, Elsie Knox, Dorothy Dearing, Herbert Rawlinson, Kay Linaker, Thomas Jackson

A woman's magazine-type yarn, about a hotel catering exclusively to women and presenting several of their stories. Chief among them is an attractive, glib blonde (Mary Beth Hughes) who cheats men and ends up in jail, and a hard-working artist (Lynn Bari) who is honest and ends up with a millionaire.

THE GAY CABALLERO

Produced by Walter Morosco and Ralph Dietrich
Directed by Otto Brower
Screenplay by Albert Duffy and John Larkin, from a story by Walter Bullock and Albert Duffy, based on the character created by O. Henry
Photographed by Edward Cronjager
Musical direction by Emil Newman
59 minutes

Cast: Cesar Romero, Sheila Ryan, Robert Sterling, Chris-Pin Martin, Janet Beecher, Edmund MacDonald, Jacqueline Daly, Montague Shaw, Hooper Atchley

O. Henry's dashing bandit, the Cisco Kid, appears in the guise of Cesar Romero. Here he arrives in a small town with his side-kick (Chris-Pin Martin) and finds himself posted as deceased and with a stigma attached to his name. He discovers that crimes have been committed in his name by a female crook (Janet Beecher), and he puts an end to her operation.

GIRL FROM AVENUE A

Produced by Sol M. Wurtzel
Directed by Otto Brower
Screenplay by Frances Hyland, based on the play *The Brat* by Maude Fulton
Photographed by George Barnes and Lucien Andriot
Musical direction by Emil Newman
71 minutes

Cast: Jane Withers, Kent Taylor, Katharine Aldridge, Elyse Knox, Laura Hope Crews, Jessie Ralph, Harry Shannon, Vaughan Glaser, Rand Brooks, Ann Shoemaker, George Humbert

A turn-of-the-century comedy-drama about a street urchin (Jane Withers) with a theatrical background, who is taken into a wealthy but eccentric family in order to inspire a playwright son (Kent Taylor). She does that, and also indulges in comic capers. A kind of poor man's *Pygmalion*.

GIRL IN 313

Produced by Sol M. Wurtzel
Directed by Ricardo Cortez
Screenplay by Barry Trivers and Clay Adams, from a story by Hilda Stone
Photographed by Edward Cronjager
56 minutes

Cast: Florence Rice, Kent Taylor, Lionel Atwill, Katharine Aldridge, Mary Treen, Jack Carson, Elyse Knox, Joan Valerie, Dorothy Dearing, Dorothy Moore, Jacqueline Wells, Charles C. Wilson, William Davidson

A police agent (Florence Rice) eases her way into a gang of jewel thieves in order to discover the ringleader. She finds a crooked insurance company at the roots and falls in love with a suave thief (Kent Taylor), who loses his life in a police trap.

THE GRAPES OF WRATH

Produced by Darryl F. Zanuck
Directed by John Ford
Screenplay by Nunnally Johnson, based on a novel by John Steinbeck
Photographed by Gregg Toland
Music by Alfred Newman
128 minutes

Cast: Henry Fonda, Jane Darwell, John Carradine, Charles Grapewin, Dorris Bowdon, Russell Simpson, P. Z. Whitehead, John Qualen, Eddie Quillan, Zeffie Tilbury

John Ford's classic film about the Oklahoma farmers who left their drought-ridden lands in the Thirties and migrated to California. They left not only because the land turned to dust but because they were dispossessed, and having arrived in California—after long and grueling treks across the southwest—they became virtual slave labor. The story centers on the Joad family and particularly their son Tom (Henry Fonda), a common man who refuses to be beaten down by adversity. *The Grapes of Wrath* is an American tragedy fashioned into cinematic art, with magnificent photography by Gregg Toland and a script that finely distills the Steinbeck novel. The performance of Fonda is a testament to courage and stamina and is among the most indelible impressions ever made on the screen.

THE GREAT PROFILE

Produced by Darryl F. Zanuck
Directed by Walter Lang
Screenplay by Milton Sperling and Hilary Lynn
Photographed by Ernest Palmer
Musical direction by Cyril J. Mockridge
82 minutes

Cast: John Barrymore, Mary Beth Hughes, Gregory Ratoff, John Payne, Anne Baxter, Lionel Atwill, Edward

Brophy, Willie Fung, Joan Valerie, Charles Lane, Marc Lawrence, Cecil Cunningham

John Barrymore in the last years of his career, lampooning himself and his legend as a great actor. Here he plays a famous stage actor, given to excessive drinking, whose wild antics almost wreck the show in which he is appearing. His leading lady (Mary Beth Hughes) walks out but eventually comes back and pulls the show together. In the meantime a young girl (Anne Baxter) tries to reform the amorous, eccentric actor. *The Great Profile* is interesting because of Barrymore, but it is a sad reminder of what he did to himself in those last years.

HE MARRIED HIS WIFE

Produced by Darryl F. Zanuck
Directed by Roy Del Ruth
Screenplay by Sam Hellman, Darrell Ware, Lynn Starling, and John O'Hara, from a story by Erna Lazarus and Scott Darling
Photographed by Ernest Palmer
Musical direction by David Buttolph
83 minutes

Cast: Joel McCrea, Nancy Kelly, Roland Young, Mary Boland, Cesar Romero, Mary Healy, Lyle Talbot, Elisha Cook, Jr., Barnett Parker

A romantic farce, with Joel McCrea as a dedicated race horse owner whose love for his work brings about a divorce, even though he still loves his wife (Nancy Kelly). His alimony payments are so heavy he contrives with his lawyer (Roland Young) to get her married to someone, but when she picks on a sly lothario (Cesar Romero), he decides to remarry his wife.

HIGH SCHOOL

Produced by Sol M. Wurtzel
Directed by George Nicholls, Jr.
Screenplay by Jack Jungmeyer, Jr., Edith Skouras, and Harold Tarshis, based on an idea by Robert Ellis and Helen Logan
Photographed by Lucien Andriot
Musical direction by Samuel Kaylin
74 minutes

Cast: Jane Withers, Joe Brown, Jr., Paul Harvey, Lloyd Corrigan, Cliff Edwards, Claire Du Brey, Lillian Porter, Lynn Roberts, John Kellogg, Margaret Brayton, Marvin Stephens, Johnnie Pironne, Mary McCarty, Emma Dunn

A boisterous teenager (Jane Withers) is sent from a Texas ranch to a San Antonio school, where her commanding ways bring her many snubs from fellow students. Gradually she learns humility and regard for others, and then becomes a model student.

HUDSON'S BAY

Produced by Kenneth Macgowan
Directed by Irving Pichel
Screenplay by Lamar Trotti
Photographed by Peverell Marley and George Barnes
Music by Alfred Newman
95 minutes

Cast: Paul Muni, Gene Tierney, Laird Cregar, John Sutton, Virginia Field, Vincent Price, Nigel Bruce, Morton Lowry, Robert Greig, Chief Thundercloud, Frederick Worlock, Florence Bates, Montague Love, Ian Wolfe, Chief John Big Tree, Jody Gilbert

The early history of Canada, heavily romanticized and laced with a great deal of fiction. Paul Muni plays the famed trapper and explorer Pierre Radison and makes him out to be a charming rogue, as he envisions a great empire in the lands around Hudson's Bay. Radison's adventures take him through the wild regions of the north, where he makes friends with the Indians and clashes with the French, and then to England, where he interests King Charles II (Vincent Price) in sponsoring an expedition to claim the lands for the British crown. He and his band run into problems, which result in their being sentenced to the gallows when they return to England. They are saved by a last-minute revelation of their triumphs in setting up the Hudson's Bay Company, which helped bring Canada into British hands. The film is fairly good entertainment but a cockeyed history lesson.

I WAS AN ADVENTURESS

Produced by Darryl F. Zanuck
Directed by Gregory Ratoff
Screenplay by Karl Tunberg, Don Ettlinger, and John O'Hare, from an original production by Gregor Rabinovitch written by Jacques Companeez, Herbert Juttke, Hans Jacoby, and Michel Duran
Photographed by Leon Shamroy and Edward Cronjager
Musical direction by David Buttolph
81 minutes

Paul Muni in *Hudson's Bay.*

Cesar Romero and Marjorie Weaver in *The Cisco Kid and the Lady.*

Betty Grable and Don Ameche in *Down Argentine Way.*

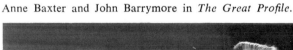

Henry Fonda, Jane Darwell, and Russell Simpson in *The Grapes of Wrath.*

Anne Baxter and John Barrymore in *The Great Profile.*

Cast: Zorina, Richard Greene, Erich von Stroheim, Peter Lorre, Sig Rumann, Fritz Feld, Cora Witherspoon, Anthony Kemble Cooper, Paul Porcasi, Inez Palange, Egon Brecher, Roger Imhoff, Rolfe Sedan, Eddie Conrad

A light comedy drama, starring ballerina Vera Zorina as a bogus countess in league with a pair of slick crooks (Erich von Stroheim and Peter Lorre) and working as their decoy. She falls in love with one of their victims (Richard Greene) and marries him, with the pair afterwards blackmailing her. She finally confesses all, which leads to a solution. The plot is thin but the lines are good and Zorina shines at the end of the film in a ballet sequence directed by George Balanchine.

101

Tyrone Power and Dorothy Lamour in *Johnny Apollo*.

JOHNNY APOLLO

Produced by Darryl F. Zanuck
Directed by Henry Hathaway
Screenplay by Philip Dunne and Rowland Brown, from a story by Samuel G. Engel and Hal Long
Photographed by Arthur Miller
Songs by Lionel Newman, Frank Loesser, and Mack Gordon
Musical direction by Cyril J. Mockridge
94 minutes

Cast: Tyrone Power, Dorothy Lamour, Edward Arnold, Lloyd Nolan, Charley Grapewin, Lionel Atwill, Marc Lawrence, Jonathan Hale, Harry Rosenthal, Russell Hicks, Fuzzy Knight, Charles Lane, Selmar Jackson

A powerful Wall Street broker (Edward Arnold) is convicted and jailed for embezzling, which earns him the disgust of his college graduate son (Tyrone Power). However, when the son goes out in the world to make a living he finds it hard, and he resorts to crime in order to raise money to help his father out of jail. He becomes the assistant to a mobster (Lloyd Nolan) and falls in love with his girl (Dorothy Lamour). The proud father, a model prisoner, deplores the course his son has taken, but they are united when the son is put in the same prison. The son goes into jail with plans to break out, which he does. *Johnny Apollo* is a solid crime melodrama, and helped to further Power's range as a popular actor.

LILLIAN RUSSELL

Produced by Darryl F. Zanuck
Directed by Irving Cummings
Screenplay by William Anthony McGuire
Photographed by Leon Shamroy
Music by Alfred Newman
127 minutes

Cast: Alice Faye, Don Ameche, Henry Fonda, Edward Arnold, Warren William, Leo Carrillo, Helen Westley, Dorothy Peterson, Ernest Truex, Lynn Bari, Nigel Bruce, Claude Allister, Joe Weber, Lew Fields, Una O'Connor, Eddie Foy, Jr., Joseph Cawthorn, William D. Davidson

The story of the famous musical star of the turn of the century, *Lillian Russell* is a lengthy account of her career from the time bandleader Tony Pastor (Leo Carrillo) discovered her in 1880 to her retirement in 1912 when she married newspaperman Alexander Moore (Henry Fonda). It details her rise on Broadway, her great successes in London, her marriage with composer Edward Solomon (Don Ameche) and his death, and her associations with many celebrated personalities of the theatre. It is also an elaborate showcase for Alice Faye. The costly film proved popular but critics noted that the great American beauty was a more interesting woman than here presented.

LITTLE OLD NEW YORK

Produced by Darryl F. Zanuck
Directed by Henry King
Screenplay by Harry Tugend, based on a story by John Balderston
Photographed by Leon Shamroy
Music by Alfred Newman
100 minutes

Cast: Alice Faye, Fred MacMurray, Richard Greene, Brenda Joyce, Andy Devine, Henry Stephenson, Ben Carter, Ward Bond, Fritz Feld, Clarence Hummel Wilson, Robert Middlemass, Roger Imhof, Theodore Von Eltz, Virginia Brissac

Inventor Robert Fulton (Richard Greene) arrives in New York in 1807 with his plans to build a steamboat and finds little encouragement. A tavern keeper (Alice Faye) giveshim accommodations and believes in him, to the chagrin of her sailor boyfriend (Fred MacMurray). Fulton raises funds to build his boat, but a

group of sailors, fearful that it will put them out of work, burn it. The tavern keeper then raises money herself and persuades her friends to help Fulton rebuild. The day arrives when he launches his steamboat and a new era in maritime history begins. As a history lesson *Little Old New York* is minimal, but it is amusing and exciting, and makes a good point of departure for a study of Fulton.

LUCKY CISCO KID

Produced by Sol M. Wurtzel
Directed by H. Bruce Humberstone
Screenplay by Robert Ellis and Helen Logan, from a story by Julian Johnson, based on the character created by O. Henry
Photographed by Lucien Andriot
Musical direction by Cyril J. Mockridge
67 minutes

Cast: Cesar Romero, Mary Beth Hughes, Dana Andrews, Evelyn Venable, Chris-Pin Martin, Willard Robertson, Joseph Sawyer, John Sheffield, William Royle, Francis Ford

The Cisco Kid (Cesar Romero) resents being blamed for other people's crimes, so he finds time to round up a gang of crooks led by a dishonest judge (Willard Robertson) who are driving settlers off their land and blaming the Kid for it. Then he goes back to romancing an attractive widow (Evelyn Venable).

THE MAN I MARRIED

Produced by Darryl F. Zanuck
Directed by Irving Pichel
Screenplay by Oliver H. P. Garrett, based on a story by Oscar Schisgall
Photographed by Peverell Marley
Musical direction by David Buttolph
77 minutes

Alice Faye as *Lillian Russell.*

Fred MacMurray, Alice Faye, and Richard Greene in *Little Old New York.*

Cast: Joan Bennett, Francis Lederer, Lloyd Nolan, Anna Sten, Otto Kruger, Maria Ouspenskaya, Ludwig Stossel, Johnny Russell, Lionel Royce, Frederick Vogeding, Ernst Deutsch, Egon Brecher

A melodrama about an American girl (Joan Bennett) who marries a German (Francis Lederer) in 1938 and her shock when he gradually turns into a Nazi. She strives to leave Germany and take her young son back to America, and finds an ally in her father-in-law (Otto Kruger), who tells his son that his mother was Jewish. With this knowledge the son agrees to release his wife. A topical anti-Nazi tract, backed up with newsreel footage of the times.

MANHATTAN HEARTBEAT

Produced by Sol M. Wurtzel
Directed by David Burton
Screenplay by Harold Buchman, Clark Andrews, Jack Jungmeyer, Jr., and Edith Skouras, from a play by Viña Delmar and Brian Marlow, from a novel by Viña Delmar
Photographed by Virgil Miller
Musical direction by Cyril J. Mockridge
72 minutes

Cast: Robert Sterling, Virginia Gilmore, Joan Davis, Edmund MacDonald, Don Beddoe, Paul Harvey, Irving Bacon, Mary Carr

A remake of *Bad Girl* (1931). A young couple (Robert Sterling and Virginia Gilmore) get married and have troubles keeping up with expenses, with the wife expecting too much and the husband getting surly. He is an airplane mechanic and makes some needed money testing aircraft. Once they have their baby they seem to settle down to domestic life, with all its daily problems.

THE MAN WHO WOULDN'T TALK

Produced by Sol M. Wurtzel
Directed by David Burton
Screenplay by Robert Ellis, Helen Logan, Selter Ziffren,
    and Edward Ettinger, from a play by Holworthy Hall
    and Robert M. Middlemass
Photographed by Virgil Miller
Musical direction by Samuel Kaylin
74 minutes

Cast: Lloyd Nolan, Jean Rogers, Richard Clarke, Onslow
Stevens, Eric Blore, Joan Valerie, Mae Marsh, Paul
Stanton, Douglas Wood, Irving Bacon, Lester Scharff,
Harlan Briggs

A somber melodrama with Lloyd Nolan in the leading
role as a martyr who chooses to die rather than expose
others. Involved in a crime, he inadvertently kills his
key witness and bitterly resigns himself to death,
changing his name in order not to harm his family.
But the law is not content with his explanation and
events leading up to the murder are disclosed, resulting
in his life being spared.

THE MARK OF ZORRO

Produced by Raymond Griffith
Directed by Rouben Mamoulian
Screenplay by John Taintor Foote, adapted by Garrett
    Fort and Bess Meredyth from the novel *The Curse of
    Capistrano* by Johnston McCulley
Photographed by Arthur Miller
Music by Alfred Newman
93 minutes

Tyrone Power and Basil Rathbone in *The Mark of Zorro*.

John Payne and Brenda Joyce in *Maryland*.

Cast: Tyrone Power, Linda Darnell, Basil Rathbone, Gale
Sondergaard, Eugene Pallette, J. Edward Bromberg,
Montague Love, Janet Beecher, Robert Lowery, Chris-
Pin Martin, George Regas, Belle Mitchell, John Bleifer,
Frank Puglia, Eugene Borden, Pedro de Cordoba

Douglas Fairbanks, Sr. set the style for movie swashbuckling with his version of *The Mark of Zorro* in
1920. With no one like Fairbanks to perform heroic
acrobatics, Rouben Mamoulian concentrated on style
and atmosphere to turn this remake into one of the
best of the genre. Tyrone Power performs engagingly
as the son of a California nobleman, circa 1820, who
returns home from Madrid to find the state under the
control of a dictatorship. He dons the guise of a
masked avenger and deposes the villains. The film
benefits greatly by having Basil Rathbone as the principal villain. His final duel with Power (largely
doubled by Albert Cavens) is a masterpiece of screen
swordplay.

MARYLAND

Produced by Gene Markey
Directed by Henry King
Screenplay by Ethel Hill and Jack Andrews
Photographed in Technicolor by George Barnes
Musical direction by Alfred Newman
92 minutes

Cast: Walter Brennan, Fay Bainter, Brenda Joyce, John
Payne, Charles Ruggles, Hattie McDaniel, Marjorie
Weaver, Sidney Blackmer, Ben Carter, Ernest Whitman,
Paul Harvey, Robert Lowery, Spencer Charters

A saga of the horsey set in Maryland, with Fay Bainter
as a woman haunted by the death of her husband in a
hunt and forbidding her son (John Payne) to have
anything to do with horses. But he falls in love with
the daughter (Brenda Joyce) of his father's old trainer
(Walter Brennan) and decides to ride their horses in
the Maryland Hunt. He wins the race and cures his

mother's phobia about horses. The film offers insights into Maryland's history and its famous steeplechase, with much footage for horse lovers.

MICHAEL SHAYNE, PRIVATE DETECTIVE

Produced by Sol M. Wurtzel
Directed by Eugene Forde
Screenplay by Stanley Rauh and Manning O'Connor, from a novel by Brett Halliday
Photographed by George Schneiderman
Musical direction by Emil Newman
77 minutes

Cast: Lloyd Nolan, Marjorie Weaver, Joan Valerie, Donald MacBride, Queenie Vassar, Walter Abel, Charles Coleman, Clarence Kolb, George Meeker

The first of the Michael Shayne series, with Lloyd Nolan as the slick Irish-American sleuth. Here he is hired by a wealthy race track executive (Clarence Kolb) as a bodyguard for his daughter (Marjorie Weaver), who has a weakness for gambling. In the maze of crooked gambling manipulations, the daughter's gambler boyfriend is murdered, and in trying to protect her Shayne finds himself a suspect. But once he solves the case he also wins the love of the girl. The film retains its impact as a top-notch private eye yarn thanks to Nolan's performance and a superior script.

MURDER OVER NEW YORK

Produced by Sol M. Wurtzel
Directed by Harry Lachman
Screenplay by Lester Ziffren, based on a character created by Earl Derr Biggers
Photographed by Virgil Miller
Musical direction by Emil Newman
65 minutes

Cast: Sidney Toler, Marjorie Weaver, Robert Lowery, Ricardo Cortez, Donald MacBride, Melville Cooper, Joan Valerie, Kane Richmond, Sen Yung, John Sutton, Leyland Hodgson, Clarence Muse, Frederick Worlock

Charlie Chan (Sidney Toler) attends a police convention in New York and while there learns about sabotage in airplane plants. He offers his services to discover who is killing who and why, and pinpoints the enemy agents responsible for hampering production.

NIGHT TRAIN

Produced by Maurice Ostrer
Directed by Carol Reed
Screenplay by Sydney Gilliat and Frank Launder, from a story by Gordon Wellesley
Photographed by Otto Kanturek
Musical direction by Louis Levy
90 minutes

Cast: Margaret Lockwood, Rex Harrison, Paul von Hernreid, Basil Radford, Naunton Wayne, James Harcourt, Felix Aylmer, Wyndham Goldie, Roland Culver, Eliot Makeham, Raymond Huntley, Austen Trevor

A British-produced adventure yarn set in the early days of the second World War, dealing with the daughter (Margaret Lockwood) of a Czech industrialist who is used by a Gestapo agent (Paul von Hernreid—before he changed his name to Paul Henreid) as a means of locating her wanted father. A British agent (Rex Harrison) poses as a Nazi officer and helps the father and the daughter escape Germany.

ON THEIR OWN

Produced by Sol M. Wurtzel
Directed by Otto Brower
Screenplay by Harold Buchman and Val Burton, from a story by Val Burton, Jack Jungmeyer, Jr., and Edith Skouras, based on Katharine Kavanaugh characters
Photographed by Arthur Miller
Musical direction by Samuel Kaylin
65 minutes

Cast: Spring Byington, Ken Howell, George Ernest, June Carlson, Florence Roberts, Billy Mahan, Marguerite Chapman, John Qualen, Charles Judels, Chick Chandler, Forrester Harvey

The Jones family, minus father on this outing, face financial losses and decide to head for California, where they open a bungalow court. Business is bad until they advertise for families with children and pets, which causes a neighboring landlord to sue them for noise. But the court rules in favor of the motley collection of tenants and owners.

Lloyd Nolan and Marjorie Weaver in *Michael Shayne, Private Detective.*

Paul Henreid and Rex Harrison in *Night Train.*

PIER 13

Produced by Sol M. Wurtzel
Directed by Eugene Forde
Screenplay by Stanley Rauh and Clark Andrews, from a
   story by Harry Connors and Philip Klein
Photographed by Virgil Miller
Musical direction by Cyril J. Mockridge
64 minutes

Cast: Lynn Bari, Lloyd Nolan, Joan Valerie, Douglas
Fowley, Chick Chandler, Oscar O'Shea, Michael Morris,
Louis Jean Heydt, Frank Orth

A police officer (Lloyd Nolan) flirts with a waitress
(Lynn Bari) in a waterfront restaurant and learns that
her sister (Joan Valerie) is implicated in a robbery
pulled off by a crook (Douglas Fowley) he is trailing.
The policeman ferrets out the crook and clears the
sister, which brings him a promise of marriage from
the waitress.

PUBLIC DEB NO. 1

Produced by Darryl F. Zanuck
Directed by Gregory Ratoff
Screenplay by Karl Tunberg and Darrell Ware, from a
   story by Karl Tunberg and Don Ettinger
Photographed by Ernest Palmer
Musical direction by Alfred Newman
79 minutes

Cast: George Murphy, Brenda Joyce, Ralph Bellamy,
Elsa Maxwell, Mischa Auer, Charlie Ruggles, Maxie
Rosenbloom, Berton Churchill, Franklin Pangborn, Ho-
bart Cavanaugh, Lloyd Corrigan, Ivan Lebedeff, Charles
Judels, Elisha Cook

A super rich society girl (Brenda Joyce) causes consternation when she supports a Communist rally and
a waiter (George Murphy) gives her a public spanking,
which makes headlines and brings the waiter an offer
from a soup tycoon (Charlie Ruggles), the girl's uncle,
to be a vice-president of the company. He helps the
company forge ahead and he tames the spoiled girl of
her red leanings.

THE RETURN OF FRANK JAMES

Produced by Darryl F. Zanuck
Directed by Fritz Lang
Screenplay by Sam Hellman
Photographed in Technicolor by George Barnes and
   William V. Skall
Music by David Buttolph
92 minutes

Cast: Henry Fonda, Gene Tierney, Jackie Cooper, Henry
Hull, John Carradine, J. Edward Bromberg, Donald
Meek, Eddie Collins, George Barbier, Ernest Whitman,
Charles Tannen, Lloyd Corrigan, Russell Hicks, Victor
Killian, Edward McWade, George Chandler, Irving
Bacon, Frank Shannon, Barbara Pepper

Henry Hull, Gene Tierney, and Henry Fonda in *The Return
of Frank James.*

The inevitable sequel to *Jesse James* and an excellent
film, due very largely to the skill of director Fritz
Lang, who gave it more mood and character than is
usually found in Westerns. Henry Fonda continued the
fine characterization he had set in the previous picture,
that of a quiet, tobacco-chewing farmer, here dedicated
to tracking down the killers of his brother. At first he
leaves the law to find them. But when the killers are
pardoned, Frank takes the law into his own hands and
gets the job done. The film is notable as Gene Tierney's
debut in the movies—as a reporter who wants to tell
the story of Frank James and who comes to love him.

SAILOR'S LADY

Produced by Sol M. Wurtzel
Directed by Allan Dwan
Screenplay by Frederick Hazlett Brennan, from a story
   by Frank Wead
Photographed by Ernest Palmer
Musical direction by Samuel Kaylin
67 minutes

Cast: Nancy Kelly, Jon Hall, Joan Davis, Dana Andrews,
Mary Nash, Larry Crabbe, Katharine Aldridge, Harry
Shannon, Wally Vernon, Bruce Hampton, Charles D.
Brown, Selmar Jackson, Edgar Dearing

A sailor (Jon Hall) plans to marry his girl (Nancy
Kelly) when he returns from sea, but things become
complicated when the bride-to-be becomes foster
mother to a one-year-old boy when his parents are
killed in an accident. The baby is left on board a
battleship during a visit and is later discovered during
a battle maneuver, which causes a naval uproar before
the facts can be explained.

SHIPYARD SALLY

Produced by Robert Kane
Directed by Monty Banks

Screenplay by Karl Tunberg and Don Ettlinger
Photographed by Otto Kanturek
Musical direction by Louis Levy
77 minutes

Cast: Gracie Fields, Sydney Howard, Morton Selton, Norma Varden, Oliver Wakefield, Tucker McGuire, McDonald Parke, Richard Cooper

Gracie Fields as a music hall performer who takes over the management of the saloon bought by her well-meaning but bumbling father (Sydney Howard). Among her customers are a group of shipyard workers who have lost their jobs, but with Gracie's aid they get them back. The plot is slight, but it provides Fields with plenty of opportunity to sing and amuse.

SHOOTING HIGH

Produced by John Stone
Directed by Alfred E. Green
Screenplay by Lou Breslow and Owen Francis
Photographed by Ernest Palmer
Songs by Felix Bernard, Paul Francis Webster, Gene Autry, Johnie Marvin, Harry Tobias, Charles Newman, and Fred Glickman
Musical direction by Samuel Kaylin
65 minutes

Cast: Jane Withers, Gene Autry, Marjorie Weaver, Robert Lowery, Katharine Aldridge, Hobart Cavanaugh, Frank M. Thomas, Jack Carson, Hamilton MacFadden, Charles Middleton, Ed Brady

A movie company arrives in a little town to make a film about its legendary sheriff of former years and hires his grandson (Gene Autry) to be a stand-in for the actor (Robert Lowery) playing the role of the sheriff. His friend (Jane Withers) scares the leading man out of town in order that Autry can get the starring part himself and win the love of Jane's sister (Marjorie Weaver). He also proves himself a real hero by foiling a bank robbery. Hollywood does a little self-spoofing in this one.

SO THIS IS LONDON

Produced by Robert T. Kane
Directed by Thornton Freeland
Screenplay by William Conselman, from a play by George M. Cohan
Photographed by Otto Kanturek
70 minutes

Cast: Robertson Hare, Alfred Drayton, George Sanders, Berton Churchill, Fay Compton, Carla Lehman, Stewart Granger, Lily Cahill, Mavis Clair, Ethel Revnell, Gracie West

Filmed in London and a remake of the 1930 Will Rogers picture, based on the George M. Cohan play, this is a comic yarn about an American businessman

Gene Autry and Jane Withers in *Shooting High.*

(Berton Churchill) who goes to London to negotiate a deal with an English Lord (Alfred Drayton). Both are cantankerous men and the American doesn't enjoy England, until his daughter (Carla Lehmann) falls in love with the Englishman's son (Stewart Granger).

STAR DUST

Produced by Darryl F. Zanuck
Directed by Walter Lang
Screenplay by Robert Ellis and Helen Logan, from a story by Jesse Malo, Kenneth Earl, and Ivan Kahn
Photographed by Peverell Marley
Songs by Mack Gordon
Musical direction by David Buttolph
90 minutes

Cast: Linda Darnell, John Payne, Roland Young, Charlotte Greenwood, William Gargan, Mary Beth Hughes, Mary Healy, Donald Meek, Harry Green, Jessie Ralph, Walter Kingsford, George Montgomery, Robert Lowery

A young girl (Linda Darnell) is given a crack at a Hollywood contract by a roving talent scout (Roland Young) and is then rejected because she is too young. She falls in love with another contractee (John Payne), who helps her in her plans to become a star. With the aid of the talent scout she gets her chance and proves a hit. *Star Dust* is an interesting insight into Hollywood and partly based on Linda Darnell's own early experiences. It also has William Gargan, as a studio boss, doing a take-off on Darryl Zanuck.

STREET OF MEMORIES

Produced by Lucien Hubbard
Directed by Shepard Traube
Screenplay by Robert Lees and Frederic I. Rinaldo
Photographed by Charles Clarke
Musical direction by Emil Newman
71 minutes

Cast: Lynne Roberts, Guy Kibbee, John McGuire, Ed Gargan, Hobart Cavanaugh, Jerome Cowan, Charles Waldron, Sterling Holloway, Scotty Beckett, Adele Horner, Pierre Watkins

A farm worker suffering from amnesia (John McGuire), frequently unemployed and in trouble with the police, is befriended by a girl (Lynne Roberts) in a small town and they marry. In a fight he is hit on the head, which causes his memory to return. He recalls that he is the son of a wealthy Chicago businessman, but he can remember nothing about his recent activity. Eventually his mind clears and he realizes his love for his wife.

THEY CAME BY NIGHT

Produced by Maurice Ostrer
Direction by Harry Lachman
Screenplay by Sidney Gilliat and Michael Pertwee, from a play by Barre Lyndon
Photographed by Jack Cox
73 minutes

Cast: Will Fyffe, Phyllis Calvert, Anthony Hulme, George Merett, Kathleen Harrison, John Glyn Jones, Athole Setwart, Cees Leseur, Hal Walters, Kuda Bux, Leo Britt, Sylvia St. Clair

A British crime caper, starring the famed Scottish actor Will Fyffe as a jeweler who aids Scotland Yard in recovering the theft of an expensive ruby. He inveigles his way into the gang responsible and sets them up with a bank robbery so that the police can nab them.

TIN PAN ALLEY

Produced by Darryl F. Zanuck
Directed by Walter Lang
Screenplay by Robert Ellis and Helen Logan
Photographed by Leon Shamroy
Musical direction by Alfred Newman
92 minutes

Cast: Alice Faye, Betty Grable, Jack Oakie, John Payne, Allen Jenkins, Esther Ralston, John Loder, Elisha Cook, Jr., Fred Keating, Billy Gilbert, Lionel Pape, Ben Carter, Lillian Porter, the Nicholas Brothers

Song writers Harrigan and Calhoun (John Payne and Jack Oakie) struggle to make their way in the bustling music district of New York called Tin Pan Alley. They get the Blane Sisters, Katie (Alice Faye) and Lily (Betty Grable), to introduce a new song of theirs. Katie decides to join the company, while Lily goes off to London to success on the stage. The company does well until the boys give a song Katie wants to introduce at a benefit to Nora Bayes (Esther Ralston) instead. She leaves in a pique and joins Lily. Later, with the boys in England with the army in 1918 they are reunited happily. With one new song by Harry Warren

and Mack Gordon ("You Say the Sweetest Things, Baby") and a raft of oldies, Tin Pan Alley is indeed tuneful, as well as brashly entertaining.

VIVA CISCO KID

Produced by Sol M. Wurtzel
Directed by Norman Foster
Screenplay by Samuel G. Engel and Hal Long, from a character created by O. Henry
Photographed by Charles Clark
Musical direction by Samuel Kaylin
65 minutes

Cast: Cesar Romero, Jean Rogers, Chris-Pin Martin, Minor Watson, Stanley Fields, Nigel De Brulier, Harold Goodwin, Francis Ford, Charles Judels

The Cisco Kid (Cesar Romero) and his sidekick (Chris-Pin Martin) rescue a stagecoach from robbery and the Kid falls for one of the passengers (Jean Rogers). It turns out that the girl's father (Minor Watson) is involved in crime with a vicious partner (Stanley Fields), who plans to kill him. Cisco sees that it doesn't happen and that the villain's career comes to a swift end.

YESTERDAY'S HEROES

Produced by Sol M. Wurtzel
Directed by Herbert I. Leeds
Screenplay by Irving Cummings, Jr. and William Counselman, Jr., from a serial by William Brent
Photographed by Charles Clarke
Musical direction by Emil Newman
66 minutes

Cast: Jean Rogers, Robert Sterling, Ted North, Katharine Aldridge, Russell Gleason, Richard Lane, Edmund MacDonald, George Irving, Emma Dunn, Harry Hayden, Isabel Randolph, Pierre Watkin

Yesterday's hero is a doctor (Robert Sterling) looking at his scrapbook and recalling his college days as a medical student, when because of his prowess as a footballer he was coerced into becoming a member of the team. His success interferes with his studies and his flirting with a college widow (Katharine Aldridge) almost kills his romance with his true love (Jean Rogers). A college roommate (Russell Gleason) helps to straighten him out.

YOUNG AS YOU FEEL

Produced by Sol M. Wurtzel
Directed by Malcolm St. Clair
Screenplay by Joseph Hoffman and Stanley Rauh, from a play Merry Andrew by Lewis Beach, based on characters created by Katharine Kavanaugh
Photographed by Charles Clarke
Musical direction by Samuel Kaylin
60 minutes

Cast: Jed Prouty, Spring Byington, Joan Valerie, Russell Gleason, Ken Howell, George Ernest, June Carlson, Florence Roberts, Billy Mahan, Helen Ericson, George Givot, Marvin Stephens, Harlan Briggs, Harry Shannon, Jack Carson, Guy Repp, Gladys Blake, Esther Brodelet

The Jones family go to New York after father (Jed Prouty) sells his drugstore, with the object of enjoying life among the sophisticates. They are taken advantage of by all manner of con men and bilked of their funds before coming to their senses and going home. The last of the Jones family films.

YOUNG PEOPLE

Produced by Harry Joe Brown
Directed by Allan Dwan
Screenplay by Edwin Blum and Don Ettlinger
Photographed by Edward Cronjager
Music and lyrics by Mack Gordon and Harry Warren
Musical direction by Alfred Newman
78 minutes

Cast: Shirley Temple, Jack Oakie, Charlotte Greenwood, Arleen Whelan, George Montgomery, Kathleen Howard, Minor Watson, Frank Swann, Frank Sully, Mae Marsh, Sarah Edwards, Irving Bacon, Charles Halton, Arthur Aylesworth, Olin Howard, Billy Wayne, Harry Tyler

Shirley Temple's concluding film on her 20th Century-Fox contract. Now twelve years old and at the awkward age, the film presents her as the daughter of a show business couple (Jack Oakie and Charlotte Greenwood) who decide that it is time to retire, in order to give her a normal upbringing in a small town. The leaders of the townspeople don't care much for the newcomers, but during a great storm the show biz types prove their courage and the town takes them to heart. Not a major film, but an interesting one for Temple fans, using footage from her previous pictures to show the background of the child within the story.

YOUTH WILL BE SERVED

Produced by Lucien Hubbard
Directed by Otto Brower
Screenplay by Wanda Tuchock, from a story by Ruth Fasken and Hilda Vincent
Photographed by Edward Cronjager
Music and lyrics by Frank Loesser and Louis Alter
Musical direction by Emil Newman
68 minutes

Cast: Jane Withers, Jane Darwell, Joe Brown, Jr., Robert Conway, Elyse Knox, John Qualen, Charles Holland, Lillian Porter, Clara Blandick, Tully Marshall, Edwin Stanley, Mildred Gover, Richard Lane, Cy Kendall, James Flavin, Eddie Marr

Jane Withers at camp. Here she is a Southern girl whose father has been sent to jail for moonshining,

while she goes to a National Youth Association camp, which seems doomed when a local tycoon wants to buy up the land. Jane leads the campers in staging a show, which softens his heart. Her father escapes from prison and captures two bandits who have stolen the tycoon's payroll. The camp is saved!

20TH CENTURY-FOX ACADEMY AWARDS FOR 1940

JANE DARWELL: Best supporting actress in *The Grapes of Wrath.*
JOHN FORD: Best direction for *The Grapes of Wrath.*
ALFRED NEWMAN: Best scoring of a musical picture for *Tin Pan Alley*
20TH CENTURY-FOX CAMERA DEPT.: Special award for technical developments.

Alice Faye and Betty Grable in *Tin Pan Alley.*

Jack Oakie, Shirley Temple, and Charlotte Greenwood in *Young People.*

109

1941

ACCENT ON LOVE

Produced by Walter Morosco and Ralph Dietrich
Directed by Ray McCarey
Screenplay by John Larkin, from a story by Dalton
    Trumbo
Photographed by Charles Clarke
Musical direction by Emil Newman
61 minutes

Cast: George Montgomery, Osa Massen, J. Carrol Naish,
Cobina Wright, Jr., Stanley Clements, Minerva Urecal,
Thurston Hall, Irving Bacon, Leonard Carey, Oscar
O'Shea, John T. Murray

A young man (George Montgomery) tires of his idle
life as an employee of his rich father-in-law (Thurston
Hall) and takes a job as a ditch digger with the WPA.
He meets and falls in love with an immigrant girl (Osa
Massen) and convinces his father-in-law that some-
thing should be done about the tenements in which
poor workers live. He also divorces his wife (Cobina
Wright, Jr.) and finds new purpose in life.

BELLE STAR

Produced by Kenneth Macgowan
Directed by Irving Cummings
Screenplay by Lamar Trotti, from a story by Niven
    Busch and Cameron Rogers
Photographed in Technicolor by Ernest Palmer and Ray
    Rennahan
Music by Alfred Newman
87 minutes

Cast: Randolph Scott, Gene Tierney, Dana Andrews,
John Shepperd, Elizabeth Patterson, Chill Wills, Louise
Beavers, Olin Howland, Paul Burns, Joseph Sawyer,
Joseph Doning, Howard Hickman

A greatly romanticized account of Missouri's famous
lady bandit in the years of the Civil War and after,
with Gene Tierney as Belle, a member of the landed
gentry who resents the loss of her lands to the Yankees
and who marries Confederate guerrilla leader Sam
Starr (Randolph Scott). Together they continue the
fight against the exploiters of the defeated South, until
the day Belle is shot as she rides to warn her husband
of a trap. The film makes no great claim to history, but
presents a legend, splendidly color photographed and
full of Western action—and the radiantly beautiful
Gene Tierney.

BLOOD AND SAND

Produced by Darryl F. Zanuck
Directed by Rouben Mamoulian
Screenplay by Jo Swerling, based on a novel by Vicente
    Blasco Ibañez
Photographed in Technicolor by Ernest Palmer and Ray
    Rennahan
Musical direction by Alfred Newman
124 minutes

Cast: Tyrone Power, Linda Darnell, Rita Hayworth,
Nazimova, Anthony Quinn, J. Carrol Naish, John Carra-
dine, Laird Cregar, Lynn Bari, Vicente Gomez, William
Montague (Monty Banks), George Reeves, Pedro de
Cordoba, Fortunio Bonanova, Victor Killian, Michael
Morris, Charles Stevens

Rudolph Valentino had scored one of his biggest successes with *Blood and Sand* in 1922 and the same
story served as a Tyrone Power vehicle a generation
later. The Power version is a romantic classic, telling
the story of a talented but naive young bullfighter
who is led astray by adulation and particularly by the
attentions of a beauteous society lady (Rita Hayworth),
causing him to slight the girl (Linda Darnell) who
has always loved him. She stands by him to the inevitable end, when he is gored in the ring. The film,
thanks to the direction of Rouben Mamoulian, is a
masterly depiction of the elegance and the brutality of
bullfighting. It is also one of the greatest examples of
Technicolor filmmaking, with Mamoulian and his
photographers using color to accent dramatic effect
and to approximate the moods of certain Spanish
paintings.

BLUE, WHITE AND PERFECT

Produced by Sol M. Wurtzel
Directed by Herbert I. Leeds
Screenplay by Samuel G. Engel, from a story by Borden
    Chase and a character by Brett Halliday

Photographed by Glen MacWilliams
73 minutes

Cast: Lloyd Nolan, Mary Beth Hughes, Helene Reynolds, George Reeves, Steve Geray, Henry Victor, Curt Bois, Marie Blake, Emmett Vogan, Mae Marsh, Frank Orth, Ivan Lebedeff, Wade Boteler, Charles Trowbridge, Edward Earle, Cliff Clark

Detective Michael Shayne (Lloyd Nolan) gets involved in the war effort and helps end the antics of a group of smugglers, who steal industrial diamonds, disguise them as buttons, and ship them off to the enemy, via Hawaii. Some of the action takes place on a luxury liner bound for Honolulu.

THE BRIDE WORE CRUTCHES

Produced by Lucien Hubbard
Directed by Shepard Traube
Screenplay by Ed Verdier, from a story by Alan Drady and Ed Verdier
Photographed by Charles Clarke
Musical direction by Emil Newman
55 minutes

Cast: Lynne Roberts, Ted North, Edgar Kennedy, Robert Armstrong, Lionel Stander, Richard Lane, Grant Mitchell, Harry Tyler, Edmund MacDonald, Horace MacMahon, Anthony Caruso, Billy Mitchell

A struggling young reporter (Ted North) becomes an eye witness to a bank robbery, which eventuates his tracking down the robbers, joining them, and then bringing about their arrest. This impresses his employers and his girl friend (Lynne Roberts).

CADET GIRL

Produced by Sol M. Wurtzel
Directed by Ray McCarey
Screenplay by Stanley Rauh and H. W. Hanemann, from a story by Jack Andrews and Richard English
Photographed by Charles Clarke
Songs by Leo Robin and Ralph Rainger
Musical direction by Emil Newman
69 minutes

Cast: Carole Landis, George Montgomery, John Shepperd, William Tracy, Janis Carter, Robert Lowery, Basil Walker, Charles Tannen, Chick Chandler, Otto Han, Irving Bacon, Jane Hazzard, Edna Mae Jones, Charles Trowbridge

A wartime morale booster about a West Point cadet (George Montgomery) who falls in love with a lovely girl (Carole Landis) who sings with his brother's band. They decide to marry even though it means the cadet's giving up his appointment at the Academy. But his brother (John Shepperd) writes a patriotic ballad, which makes the cadet realize he must postpone his marriage and serve his country.

Jack Benny and Kay Francis in *Charley's Aunt.*

CHARLEY'S AUNT

Produced by William Perlberg
Directed by Archie Mayo
Screenplay by George Seaton, from a play by Brandon Thomas
Photographed by Peverell Marley
Music by Alfred Newman
83 minutes

Cast: Jack Benny, Kay Francis, James Ellison, Anne Baxter, Edmund Gwenn, Reginald Owen, Laird Cregar, Arleen Whelan, Richard Haydn, Ernest Cossart, Morton Lowry, Lionel Pape, Will Stanton, Montague Shaw, Claude Allister, William Austin

The classic piece of theatre comedy is here filmed almost literally, with little leeway given for Jack Benny starring in the title role—but with fine results. It is one of the best of Benny's films, despite his obvious miscasting as an English undergraduate at Oxford. James Ellison and Richard Haydn are the two students

Gene Tierney and Randolph Scott in *Belle Starr.*

Rita Hayworth and Tyrone Power in *Blood and Sand.*

who coerce Benny into masquerading as Ellison's aunt in order to be a fake chaperone to make things easy for them with their girl friends (Anne Baxter and Arleen Whelan). Much of the comedy comes from Benny's being courted by the girls' ardent guardian (Edmund Gwenn) until the real aunt (Kay Francis) shows up.

CHARLIE CHAN IN RIO

Produced by Sol M. Wurtzel
Directed by Harry Lachman
Screenplay by Samuel G. Engel and Lester Ziffren, based on the character created by Earl Derr Biggers
Photographed by Joseph P. MacDonald
Musical direction by Emil Newman
61 minutes

Cast: Sidney Toler, Mary Beth Hughes, Cobina Wright, Jr., Ted North, Victor Jory, Harold Huber, Sen Yung, Richard Derr, Jacqueline Dalya, Kay Linaker, Truman Bradley, Hamilton McFadden, Leslie Denison, Iris Wong, Eugene Borden, Ann Codee

In Rio de Janiero, Chan works with the local police—intelligently depicted—to solve a pair of murders. With one of the murderers being killed by the widow of the first victim, Chan's deductive powers are exercised. The Rio background allows more music and romance than usual in the Chan pictures.

CONFIRM OR DENY

Produced by Len Hammond
Directed by Archie Mayo
Screenplay by Jo Swerling, from a story by Henry Wales and Samuel Fuller
Photographed by Leon Shamroy
74 minutes

Cast: Don Ameche, Joan Bennett, Roddy McDowall, John Loder, Raymond Walburn, Arthur Shields, Eric Blore, Helene Reynolds, Claude Allister, Roseanne Murray, Stuart Robertson, Queenie Leonard, Jean Prescott, Alan Napier, Billy Bevan

Wartime London, with Don Ameche as the head of an American news bureau and Joan Bennett as a British government teletype operator assigned to see that he does not send any news items out of the country without first checking for permission. Together they spend a lot of time dodging bombs in the blitz and gradually falling in love, with the hot-shot newsman finally becoming more responsible about flashing the news.

THE COWBOY AND THE BLONDE

Produced by Ralph Dietrich and Walter Morosco
Directed by Ray McCarey

Screenplay by Walter Bullock, from a story by Walter Bullock and William Brent
Photographed by Charles Clarke
Musical direction by Cyril J. Mockridge
68 minutes

Cast: Mary Beth Hughes, George Montgomery, Alan Mowbray, Robert Conway, John Miljan, Richard Lane, Robert Emmet Keane, Minerva Urecal, Fuzzy Knight, George O'Hara, Monica Bannister

A rodeo cowboy (George Montgomery) takes a crack at the movies and does well in Wesetrns, until he comes up against a temperamental actress (Mary Beth Hughes) who gives everybody a rough time with her tantrums. But the cowboy won't take any nonsense from her, which causes her to fall in love with him and surrender. A "taming of the shrew" comedy and one containing some good digs at Hollywood.

DANCE HALL

Produced by Sol M. Wurtzel
Directed by Irving Pichel
Screenplay by Stanley Rauh and Ethel Hill, from a novel by W. R. Burnett
Photographed by Lucien Andriot
Songs by Mack Gordon, Harry Revel, Jimmy McHugh, and Harold Adamson
Musical direction by Emil Newman
72 minutes

Cast: Carole Landis, Cesar Romero, William Henry, June Storey, J. Edward Bromberg, Charles Halton, Shimen Ruskin, William Haade, Trudi Marsdon, Russ Clark, Frank Fanning

A dance hall singer (Carole Landis) is at first interested by the advances of the dashing manager (Cesar Romero), but cools when she realizes he is a lothario. He becomes serious but she no longer cares, and with that he decides to put in a good word for his protégé-composer (William Henry). A slim comedy romance, but with some nice singing by Landis, especially of "There's a Lull in My Life" by Mack Gordon and Harry Revel.

DEAD MEN TELL

Produced by Walter Morosco and Ralph Dietrich
Directed by Harry Lachman
Screenplay by John Larkin, based on the character created by Earl Derr Biggers
Photographed by Charles Clarke
Musical direction by Emil Newman
61 minutes

Cast: Sidney Toler, Sheila Ryan, Robert Weldon, Sen Yung, Don Douglas, Katharine Aldridge, Paul McGrath, George Reeves, Truman Bradley, Ethel Griffies, Lenita Lane, Milton Parsons

Charlie Chan (Sidney Toler) is called in when an eccentric old lady (Ethel Griffies) is killed just as she is about to embark on a treasure hunt for a family fortune. She is frightened to death by someone disguised as the ghost of a pirate ancestor. Chan goes on the trip and discovers which of the other hunters is a killer.

DRESSED TO KILL

Produced by Sol M. Wurtzel
Directed by Eugene Forde
Screenplay by Stanley Rauh and Manning O'Connor, from a novel by Richard Burke and characters created by Brett Halliday
Photographed by Glenn MacWilliams
Musical direction by Emil Newman
75 minutes

Cast: Lloyd Nolan, Mary Beth Hughes, Sheila Ryan, William Demarest, Ben Carter, Virginia Brissac, Erwin Kalser, Henry Daniel, Dick Rich, Milton Parsons, Charles Arnt, Charles Trowbridge, Hamilton MacFadden

Detective Michael Shayne (Lloyd Nolan) leaves a marriage licensing bureau with his long-suffering girl friend (Mary Beth Hughes) and hears shots fired in a nearby theatre. He investigates and find a strange string of murders, all linked to a theatrical production of the past, with victims dying in the costumes they wore in the play. Shayne digs away until he spots the murderer—a porter (Erwin Kalser) who was once jilted. Then Shayne is jilted by his girl friend.

FOR BEAUTY'S SAKE

Produced by Lucien Hubbard
Directed by Shepard Traube
Screenplay by Wanda Tuchock, Ethel Hill, and Walter Bullock, from a story by Clarence Budington Kelland
Photographed by Charles Clarke
Musical direction by Emil Newman
62 minutes

Cast: Ned Sparks, Marjorie Weaver, Ted North, Joan Davis, Pierre Watkin, Lenita Lane, Richard Lane, Lotus Long, Glenn Hunter, Lois Wilson, John Hylten, Isabel Jewell, Nigel De Brulier, Janet Beecher

A young astronomy professor (Ted North) must run his aunt's beauty shop for two years if he wants to inherit her wealth. His girl friend (Marjorie Weaver) brings in a veteran press agent (Ned Sparks) to hype the business. Murder and blackmail are just some of the adventures the professor experiences before his tenure is up.

GOLDEN HOOFS

Produced by Walter Morosco and Ralph Dietrich
Directed by Lynn Shores

Screenplay by Ben Grauman Kohn, from a story by Roy Chanslor and Thomas Langan
Photographed by Lucien Andriot
Musical direction by Cyril J. Mockridge
68 minutes

Cast: Jane Withers, Charles Rogers, Katharine Aldridge, George Irving, Buddy Pepper, Cliff Clark, Philip Hurlick, Sheila Ryan, Howard Hickman

Jane Withers saves a trotting horse farm. Her grandfather (George Irving) has to sell his old farm, on which trotting horses have been trained for many years, and a commercially minded young man (Charles "Buddy" Rogers) buys it. Jane develops a crush on the handsome newcomer and manages to persuade him not to get rid of the farm and its horses but to enjoy the world of trotting.

THE GREAT AMERICAN BROADCAST

Produced by Darryl F. Zanuck
Directed by Archie Mayo
Screenplay by Don Ettlinger, Edwin Blum, Robert Ellis, and Helen Logan
Photographed by Leon Shamroy and Peverell Marley
Songs by Mack Gordon and Harry Warren
Musical direction by Alfred Newman
90 minutes

Cast: Alice Faye, Jack Oakie, John Payne, Cesar Romero, The Ink Spots, James Newill, Mary Beth Hughes, Eula Morgan, William Pawley, Lucien Littlefield, Edward Conrad, Eddie Acuff, Mildred Gover, the Wiere Brothers, and the Nicholas Brothers

Following the first World War, a pair of enterprising fellows (Jack Oakie and John Payne) try several businesses without success before going into the new field of radio broadcasting. They are initially successful, but soon become left behind by the major stations. The two men part company and Payne's singer wife (Alice Faye) goes to an old boyfriend (Cesar Romero) for money to build up their radio station. The husband resents this and walks out, and the wife goes on to become a big star. The former partner hears about the split and devises a scheme to get them all together again—a coast-to-coast broadcast, the first of its kind. Payne reappears, claiming that it was his idea anyway, which it was. *The Great American Broadcast* has a better than average plot and some interesting insights into the early days of radio.

GREAT GUNS

Produced by Sol M. Wurtzel
Directed by Monty Banks
Screenplay by Lou Breslow
Photographed by Glen MacWilliams
Musical direction by Emil Newman
74 minutes

113

Cast: Stan Laurel, Oliver Hardy, Sheila Ryan, Dick Nelson, Edmund MacDonald, Charles Trowbridge, Ludwig Stossel, Kane Richmond, Mae Marsh, Ethel Griffies, Paul Harvey, Charles Arnt

Laurel and Hardy join the army when their young and spoiled employer (Dick Nelson) is drafted. They feel he needs them around, even though they themselves are hopeless soldiers. Their sergeant (Edmund MacDonald) is frustrated in his efforts to train them, and more so when he sees a pretty post worker (Sheila Ryan) being courted by their boy. The film ends with a maneuvers campaign in which Stan and Ollie, miraculously, aid their side to victory.

HOW GREEN WAS MY VALLEY

Produced by Darryl F. Zanuck
Directed by John Ford
Screenplay by Philip Dunne, based on the novel by Richard Llewellyn
Photographed by Arthur Miller
Music by Alfred Newman
118 minutes

Cast: Walter Pidgeon, Maureen O'Hara, Donald Crisp, Anna Lee, Roddy McDowall, John Loder, Sara Allgood, Barry Fitzgerald, Patric Knowles, Morton Lowry, Arthur Shields, Ann Todd, Fredric Worlock, Richard Fraser, Evan S. Evans, James Monk, Rhys Williams, Clifford Severn, Lionel Pape, Ethel Griffies, Eve Marsh, Marten Lamont, Irving Pichel (narrator)

How Green Was My Valley won an Oscar as the best film of 1941, as well as Oscars for director John Ford, photographer Arthur Miller, and actor Donald Crisp. Set in Wales around the turn of the century, it tells of a family headed by a stern father (Crisp) and a gentle mother (Sara Allgood), whose five eldest sons are all coal miners and whose youngest (Roddy McDowall) is a sensitive lad they hope will find his way into a better life. Fox built a Welsh village on location and created a warm sense of atmosphere to convey the sentiments of the central character (the boy played by McDowall but grown to manhood) looking back on a past way of life and the many people he remembered, including a minister (Walter Pidgeon) and his thwarted love for sister Angharad (Maureen O'Hara). Welsh critics found the film overly sentimental in its treatment of a sad period in their history—the squalor of coal mining prior to trade unionism—but generally the film remains a firm favorite and a testament to the story-telling ability of John Ford.

I WAKE UP SCREAMING

Produced by Milton Sperling
Directed by H. Bruce Humberstone
Screenplay by Dwight Taylor, from a novel by Steve Fisher

Photographed by Edward Cronjager
Musical direction by Cyril J. Mockridge
82 minutes

Cast: Betty Grable, Victor Mature, Carole Landis, Laird Cregar, William Gargan, Alan Mowbray, Allyn Joslyn, Elisha Cook, Jr., Chick Chandler, Cyril Ring, Morris Ankrum, Charles Lane, Frank Orth

A beautiful young girl (Carole Landis) is murdered and the chief suspect is the man (Victor Mature) who has been promoting her for possible stardom as an entertainer. Her sister (Betty Grable) demands action from the police and a detective is assigned to the case. The detective (Laird Cregar) is a huge, seemingly amiable, but menacing man who hounds the promoter and promises to "get him." But the murderer is the detective himself, who had idolized the girl from afar and resented the possibility of sharing her with the world. *I Wake Up Screaming* is a classy suspense picture with a haunting performance by Cregar as the pathetic and sinister detective.

THE LAST OF THE DUANES

Produced by Sol M. Wurtzel
Directed by James Tinling
Screenplay by Irving Cummings, Jr. and William Conselman, Jr., based on the novel by Zane Grey
Photographed by Charles Clarke
Musical direction by Cyril Mockridge
57 minutes

Cast: George Montgomery, Lynne Roberts, Eve Arden, Francis Ford, George E. Stone, William Farnum, Joseph Sawyer, Truman Bradley, Russell Simpson, Don Costello, Harry Woods, Andrew Tombes

Last made in 1931 and starring George O'Brien, the familiar story has the hero (George Montgomery) in the Texas of 1870 coming home to find his father murdered. He trails an outlaw to a border town and discovers him to be a member of an organized gang, and then brings in the Texas Rangers to break up the gang. A conventional Western sparked by the appearance of Eve Arden as a dance hall entertainer.

MAN AT LARGE

Produced by Ralph Dietrich
Directed by Eugene Forde
Screenplay by John Larkin
Photographed by Virgil Miller
Musical direction by Emil Newman
69 minutes

Cast: Marjorie Weaver, George Reeves, Richard Derr, Steve Geray, Milton Parsons, Spencer Charters, Lucien Littlefield, Elisha Cook, Jr., Minerva Urecal, Bodil Ann Rosing, Richard Lane

A German aviator escapes from a Canadian camp and

enters the United States and a British agent (Richard Derr) captures him and takes his place. Then, in league with an FBI man (George Reeves) they set out to discover a German espionage ring, with some help and a lot of hindrance from an avid newspaperwoman (Marjorie Weaver).

MAN HUNT

Produced by Kenneth Macgowan
Directed by Fritz Lang
Screenplay by Dudley Nichols, based on a novel by
   Geoffrey Household
Photographed by Arthur Miller
Music by Alfred Newman
95 minutes

Stan Laurel, Sheila Ryan, and Oliver Hardy in *Great Guns.*

Alice Faye, John Payne, and Jack Oakie in *The Great American Bandstand.*

Roddy McDowall and Walter Pidgeon in *How Green Was My Valley.*

Carole Landis, Victor Mature, and Betty Grable in *I Wake Up Screaming.*

Walter Pidgeon in *Man Hunt.*

Cast: Walter Pidgeon, Joan Bennett, George Sanders, John Carradine, Roddy McDowall, Ludwig Stossel, Heather Thatcher, Frederick Worlock, Roger Imhof, Egon Brecher, Lester Matthews

A British sportsman-hunter (Walter Pidgeon) on vacation in Bavaria comes close to the home of Adolf Hitler and gets him in his gun sights. He is apprehended in the act, accused of being an assassin, beaten, and left for dead by the Gestapo. He recovers and returns to London, where he finds himself hunted by German agents, led by an apparently very British gentleman (George Sanders). He is also befriended by a loving girl (Joan Bennett) who is a prostitute and who helps him dodge the agents. The hunter is finally trapped, but survives when he kills the head agent. *Man Hunt* is a classic suspense and chase thriller, thanks to the direction of the masterly Fritz Lang and the darkly dramatic photography of Arthur Miller.

MARRY THE BOSS'S DAUGHTER

Produced by Lou Ostrow
Directed by Thornton Freeland
Screenplay by Jack Andrews, from a story by Sandor Farago and Alexander G. Kenedi
Photographed by Charles Clarke
60 minutes

Cast: Brenda Joyce, Bruce Edwards, George Barbier, Hardie Albright, Ludwig Stossel, Bodil Ann Rosing, Brandon Tynan, Charles Arnt, George Meeker, Frank McGlynn, Eula Guy

A brash young Kansan (Bruce Edwards), with a passion for business methods, comes to Manhattan and gets a job with a tycoon (George Barbier) he idolizes. He discovers errors in the files and when his immediate superiors won't listen to him, he barges in on the boss and tells him how to run his business. This results in promotion and the final step in courting his daughter (Brenda Joyce).

MOON OVER HER SHOULDER

Produced by Walter Morosco
Directed by Alfred Werker
Screenplay by Walter Bullock, from a story by Helen Vreeland Smith and Eve Golden
Photographed by Lucien Andriot
Musical direction by Emil Newman
68 minutes

Cast: Lynn Bari, John Sutton, Dan Dailey, Jr., Alan Mowbray, Leonard Carey, Irving Bacon, Joyce Compton, Lillian Yarbo, Eula Guy, Shirley Hill, Sylvia Arslan

A spoof on marital counseling, with a doctor (John Sutton), a famed authority on marriage, advising his bored wife (Lynn Bari) to take up painting. This

brings her into contact with a young yachtsman (Dan Dailey) and a lot of fun on his boat, which causes the doctor to put up a fight for his wife.

MURDER AMONG FRIENDS

Produced by Ralph Dietrich and Walter Morosco
Directed by Ray McCarey
Screenplay by John Larkin
Photographed by Charles Clarke
Musical direction by Emil Newman
67 minutes

Cast: Marjorie Weaver, John Hubbard, Cobina Wright, Jr., Mona Barrie, Douglas Dumbrille, Sidney Blackmer, Truman Bradley, Lucien Littlefield, Bill Halligan, Don Douglas

An insurance clerk (Marjorie Weaver) becomes suspicious when a number of elderly men die, all of whom are beneficiaries to a large policy devised by them when they were in college. She persuades her doctor boyfriend (John Hubbard) that it is a plot and they rush from holder to holder warning them, although most die before the killer is revealed.

MOON OVER MIAMI

Produced by Harry Joe Brown
Directed by Walter Lang
Screenplay by Vincent Lawrence and Brown Holmes, based on a story by Stephen Powys, adapted by George Seaton
Photographed in Technicolor by Peverell Marley and Leon Shamroy
Songs by Leo Robin and Ralph Rainger
Musical direction by Alfred Newman
91 minutes

Cast: Betty Grable, Don Ameche, Robert Cummings, Charlotte Greenwood, Jack Haley, Carole Landis, Cobina Wright, Jr., George Lessey, Robert Conway, The Condos Brothers, Robert Grieg, Minor Watson, Fortunio Bonanova, George Humbert, Stephen Charters, Lynn Roberts, Larry McGrath

This musical remake of *Three Blind Mice* did much to establish Betty Grable with the public and set off a whole stream of Grable color musicals throughout the decade. With a few establishing shots of a 1941 Miami, the story has Grable and her sister (Carole Landis) arriving from Texas in pursuit of rich husbands. After a mishmash of romantic adventures, she ends up with a handsome but penniless Don Ameche, and Landis lands millionaire Robert Cummings. *Moon Over Miami* is a genial film of its kind, with some notable dancing by the Condos Brothers and a pleasant set of songs by Robin and Rainger, of which "You Started Something" is the most memorable.

THE PERFECT SNOB

Produced by Walter Morosco
Directed by Ray McCarey
Screenplay by Lee Loeb and Harold Buchman
Photographed by Charles Clarke
Musical direction by Emil Newman
63 minutes

Cast: Charlie Ruggles, Charlotte Greenwood, Lynn Bari, Cornel Wilde, Anthony Quinn, Alan Mowbray, Chester Clute, LeRoy Mason, Jack Chefe, Biddle Dorsey

A family comedy, about a girl (Lynn Bari) taught by her mother (Charlotte Greenwood) to look for wealth in a marriage and advised by her kindly father (Charlie Ruggles) to seek love. In Hawaii she happily gets the best of both views, with a young man (Cornel Wilde) who appears to be poor but actually owns a sugar plantation.

PRIVATE NURSE

Produced by Sol M. Wurtzel
Directed by David Burton
Screenplay by Samuel G. Engel
Photographed by Virgil Miller
61 minutes

Cast: Jane Darwell, Brenda Joyce, Sheldon Leonard, Robert Lowery, Ann Todd, Kay Linaker, Frank Sully, Ferike Boros, Claire Dubrey, Leonard Carey, Clara Blandick, Myra Marsh, George Chandler

A young girl (Ann Todd) is brought up by her ex-racketeer father (Sheldon Leonard) to believe that her mother is dead, but at a birthday party given for her nurse (Jane Darwell) she learns the mother is alive. The facts are then relayed to her, about how the father gave up his old ways in order to provide her with a proper environment.

REMEMBER THE DAY

Produced by William Perlberg
Directed by Henry King
Screenplay by Tess Slesinger, Frank Davis, and Allan Scott, from a novel by Philo Higley and Philip Dunning
Photographed by George Barnes
Music by Alfred Newman
86 minutes

Cast: Claudette Colbert, John Payne, John Shepperd, Ann Todd, Douglas Croft, Jane Seymour, Anne Revere, Frieda Inescort, Harry Hayden, Francis Pierlot, Marie Blake, William Henderson, Chick Chandler, John Hiestand

The recollections of a schoolteacher (Claudette Colbert) told in sentimental flashbacks. As an elderly woman awaiting a meeting with a nominee (John Shepperd) for the Presidency, her mind drifts back to 1916, when he was a student of hers and of his asso-

ciation with the man (John Payne) she loved and married and lost in early death. A charming film and a fine showcase for Colbert.

RIDE, KELLY, RIDE

Produced by Sol M. Wurtzel
Directed by Norman Foster
Screenplay by William Conselman, Jr. and Irving Cummings, Jr., based on a story by Peter H. Kyne
Photographed by Virgil Miller
Musical direction by Emil Newman
59 minutes

Cast: Eugene Pallette, Marvin Stephens, Rita Quigley, Mary Healy, Richard Lane, Charles D. Brown, Chick Chandler, Dorothy Peterson, Lee Murray, Frankie Burke, Cy Kendall, Hamilton Burke, Walter "Speck" O'Donnell, Ernie Adams, Edwin Stanley

A race track drama, about an ambitious young jockey (Marvin Stephens) and his triumph over crooks who want him to throw a race. He is encouraged by a veteran stable trainer (Eugene Pallette) and the daughter (Rita Quigley) of a horse owner.

Charlotte Greenwood, Betty Grable, and Carole Landis in *Moon Over Miami.*

John Payne and Claudette Colbert in *Remember the Day.*

RIDE ON, VAQUERO

Produced by Sol M. Wurtzel
Directed by Herbert I. Leeds
Screenplay by Samuel G. Engel, from characters created
    by O. Henry
Photographed by Lucien Andriot
Musical direction by Emil Newman
64 minutes

Cast: Cesar Romero, Mary Beth Hughes, Lynne Roberts,
Chris-Pin Martin, Robert Lowery, Ben Carter, William
Demarest, Robert Shaw, Edwin Maxwell, Paul Sutton,
Don Costello, Arthur Hohl, Irving Bacon, Dick Rich

The Cisco Kid (Cesar Romero) offers his services to
the law when he learns a gang of kidnappers are at
work. An honest robber himself, he despises kidnapping. The gang is firmly entrenched in the community,
but Cisco ferrets them out, with enough time on the
side to flirt with a lusty dance hall girl (Mary Beth
Hughes).

THE RIDERS OF THE PURPLE SAGE

Produced by Sol M. Wurtzel
Directed by James Tinling
Screenplay by William Bruckner and Robert Metzier,
    based on the novel by Zane Grey
Photographed by Lucien Andriot
58 minutes

Cast: George Montgomery, Mary Howard, Robert Barrat,
Lynne Roberts, Kane Richmond, Patsy Patterson, Richard
Lane, Oscar O'Shea, James Gillette, Frank McGrath, Le-
roy Mason

The classic Zane Grey Western in its fourth filming,
with George Montgomery as Jim Lassiter, who finds
that the judge (Robert Barrat) who cheated his niece
out of her inheritance is also the leader of a gang who
pose as vigilantes but who are actually outlaws who
rob and murder to control the territory. Lassiter puts
an end to their operation and settles down to a peaceful
life in the beautiful valley with the girl he has found.

RISE AND SHINE

Produced by Mark Hellinger
Directed by Allan Dwan
Screenplay by Herman Mankiewicz, based on *My Life
    and Hard Times* by James Thurber
Photographed by Edward Cronjager
Songs by Leo Robin and Ralph Rainger
Musical direction by Emil Newman
92 minutes

Cast: Jack Oakie, George Murphy, Linda Darnell, Walter
Brennan, Milton Berle, Sheldon Leonard, Donald Meek,
Ruth Donnelly, Raymond Walburn, Donald MacBride,
Emma Dunn, Charles Waldron, Mildred Gover, William
Haade, Dick Rich, John Hiestand

A knockabout football musical, with Jack Oakie as a
dumb ox of a player who is kidnapped by racketeers
in order to prevent him from playing, and George
Murphy as an ex-football star turned song-and-dance
man. Linda Darnell is the daughter of a professor
(Donald Meek) who is mad about magic and Milton
Berle is a gangster who brays like a horse when he
gets excited. The script by Herman Mankiewicz, inspired by Thurber, is peopled with lunatic types and
makes *Rise and Shine* the most amusing of all college
musicals.

ROMANCE OF THE RIO GRANDE

Produced by Sol M. Wurtzel
Directed by Herbert I. Leeds
Screenplay by Harold Buchman and Samuel G. Engel,
    based on a novel by Katherine Fullerton Gerould, sug-
    gested by the character created by O. Henry
Photographed by Charles Clarke
Musical direction by Emil Newman
72 minutes

Cast: Cesar Romero, Patricia Morison, Lynne Roberts,
Ricardo Cortez, Chris-Pin Martin, Aldrich Bowker,
Joseph McDonald, Pedro de Cordoba, Inez Palange,
Raphael Bennett, Trevor Bardette, Tom London

An aging cattle baron (Pedro de Cordoba) finds that
running his empire is getting too much for him and
sends for a grandson to take over. The grandson is
wounded by an assassin en route and the Cisco Kid
(Cesar Romero) takes his place in order to discover
who is planning to inherit the ranch and its fortunes.
He finds another relative (Ricardo Cortez) to be the
culprit.

SCOTLAND YARD

Produced by Sol M. Wurtzel
Directed by Norman Foster
Screenplay by Samuel G. Engel and John Balderston,
    from a play by Denison Clift
Photographed by Virgil Miller
Musical direction by Emil Newman
68 minutes

Cast: Nancy Kelly, Edmund Gwenn, John Loder, Henry
Wilcoxon, Melville Cooper, Gilbert Emery, Norma Varden, Leyland Hodgson, Lionel Pape, Lilian Bond, Leo
Carroll, Frank Dawson, Eugene Borden, Edward Fielding, Robert De Bruce, Denis Green

Intrigue in wartime England, with Inspector Cork
(Edmund Gwenn) of Scotland Yard relentlessly pursuing a bank robber (John Loder) over a period of
time. The robber serves in the army and receives
severe facial injuries. With plastic surgery he assumes
the features and the identity of a bank president and
as such he plans a huge robbery. But Inspector Cork
stops it all from happening, as does the robber's sense

of patriotism. When he runs into a German spy plot, he exposes it.

SLEEPERS WEST

Produced by Sol M. Wurtzel
Directed by Eugene Forde
Screenplay by Lou Breslow and Stanley Rauh, based on a novel by Frederick Nebel and the character created by Brett Halliday
Photographed by Peverell Marley
74 minutes

Cast: Lloyd Nolan, Lynn Bari, Mary Beth Hughes, Louis Jean Heydt, Edward Brophy, Don Costello, Ben Carter, Don Douglas, Oscar O'Shea, Harry Hayden, Hamilton MacFadden, Ferike Boros

Lloyd Nolan as detective Michael Shayne bound for San Francisco to deliver a surprise witness (Mary Beth Hughes) at a murder trial. Much of the action takes place on a train and Shayne is kept busy protecting the girl from all the parties who would like to keep her from testifying.

SMALL TOWN DEB

Directed by Harold Schuster
Screenplay by Ethel Hill, from a story by Jerrie Walters
Photographed by Virgil Miller
Musical direction by Emil Newman
73 minutes

Cast: Jane Withers, Jane Darwell, Bruce Edwards, Cobina Wright, Jr., Cecil Kellaway, Katharine Alexander, Jack Searl, Buddy Pepper, Robert Cornell, Margaret Early, Douglas Wood, John T. Murray, Ruth Gillette

A family comedy, with Jane Withers as the younger daughter favored by her father (Cecil Kellaway) and Cobina Wright, Jr., as the attractive but snooty older daughter, championed by her snobbish mother (Katharine Alexander). Their bickering provides a little amusement, but *Small Town Deb* was designed as a transition for Withers, going from young hoyden to a slightly more subdued teenager interested in clothes and boys.

SUN VALLEY SERENADE

Produced by Milton Sperling
Directed by H. Bruce Humberstone
Screenplay by Robert Ellis and Helen Logan, from a story by Art Arthur and Robert Harari
Photographed by Edward Cronjager
Songs by Mack Gordon and Harry Warren
Musical direction by Emil Newman
86 minutes

Cast: Sonja Henie, John Payne, Glenn Miller, Milton Berle, Lynn Bari, Joan Davis, Nicholas Brothers, William Davidson, Dorothy Dandridge, Almira Sessions, Mel Ruick, Forbes Murray

A lively musical set in the famed Idaho ski resort, with Sonja Henie skiing all over the landscape and the Glenn Miller Orchestra providing memorable support. The plot has the Miller band arriving at Sun Valley to keep an engagement and the pianist (John Payne) finding himself stuck with a Norwegian refugee (Henie) he has sponsored. But she turns out to be a champ skater and when the Miller soloist (Lynn Bari) quits in a fit of jealousy, Sonja stages an ice show as a substitute, which is a big hit. *Sun Valley Serenade* is Henie at her best, aided by choreographer Hermes Pan and the songs of Harry Warren and Mack Gordon. Outstanding is "Chattanooga Choo Choo," sung and danced by The Nicholas Brothers and Dorothy Dandridge.

George Montgomery and Mary Howard in *Riders of the Purple Sage.*

Linda Darnell, George Murphy, and Milton Berle in *Rise and Shine.*

Glenn Miller, Sonja Henie, and John Payne in *Sun Valley Serenade.*

SWAMP WATER

Produced by Irving Pichel
Directed by Jean Renoir
Screenplay by Dudley Nichols, from a story by Vereen Bell
Photographed by Peverell Marley
Music by David Buttolph
88 minutes

Cast: Walter Brennan, Walter Huston, Anne Baxter, Dana Andrews, Virginia Gilmore, Eugene Pallette, John Carradine, Mary Howard, Ward Bond, Guinn Williams, Russell Simpson, Joseph Sawyer

The first American film of the eminent French director Jean Renoir, set in the Okeefenokee swamps of Georgia. Walter Brennan is a fugitive living in the depths of the marshlands with his young daughter (Anne Baxter). A wandering hunter (Dana Andrews) happens upon them, falls in love with the daughter, and persuades the fugitive to return to town. The film gets its value from Renoir's imaginative moods and the photography of the mysterious swamplands with its tangled vegetation and trackless waterways.

TALL, DARK AND HANDSOME

Produced by Fred Kohlmar
Directed by H. Bruce Humberstone
Screenplay by Karl Tunberg and Darrell Ware
Photographed by Ernest Palmer
Musical direction by Emil Newman
78 minutes

Cast: Cesar Romero, Virginia Gilmore, Charlotte Greenwood, Milton Berle, Sheldon Leonard, Stanley Clements, Frank Jenks, Barnett Parker, Marc Lawrence, Paul Hurst, Frank Bruno, Anthony Caruso, Marion Martin

The story of a suave gangster (Cesar Romero) in the Chicago of 1929, who dresses stylishly and behaves like a gentleman. A girl (Virginia Gilmore) falls in love with him despite her resolve to resist and he behaves almost like a father to a New York hoodlum (Stanley Clements). In fact, he turns out to be more of a Robin Hood than a crook and he wipes out a really nasty gangster (Sheldon Leonard). More of a comedy than a crime drama, with a fine performance from Romero.

THAT NIGHT IN RIO

Produced by Darryl F. Zanuck
Directed by Irving Cummings
Screenplay by George Seaton, Bess Meredyth, and Hal Long, based on a play by Rudolph Lothar and Hans Adler
Photographed in Technicolor by Leon Shamroy and Ray Rennahan
Songs by Mack Gordon and Harry Warren
Musical direction by Alfred Newman
90 minutes

Cast: Alice Faye, Don Ameche, Carmen Miranda, S. Z. Sakall, J. Carrol Naish, Curt Bois, Leonid Kinsky, Frank Puglia, Lillian Porter, Maria Montez, George Renavent, Edward Conrad, Fortunio Bonanova, the Flores Brothers

A remake of *Folies Bergère*, with Don Ameche in the dual role of an entertainer and a wealthy aristocrat, with the former doing an impersonation of the latter in his night club act in Rio de Janiero. Complications ensue when the impersonator accepts an invitation from the wife of the aristocrat to attend a party in the guise of her husband, so that business associates will not know he is out of town and having trouble with finances. The impersonator falls in love with the wife and behaves much more lovingly than her husband, which causes the husband to realize he should be more appreciative of his wife. Colorful sets and costumes support the involved plot and Carmen Miranda is prominent as the impersonator's jealous girl friend and also singing cheerful songs like "Chica, Chica Boom Chic."

TOBACCO ROAD

Produced by Darryl F. Zanuck
Directed by John Ford
Screenplay by Nunnally Johnson, from the play by Jack Kirkland and the novel by Erskine Caldwell
Photographed by Arthur Miller
Musical direction by David Buttolph
84 minutes

Cast: Charley Grapewin, Marjorie Rambeau, Gene Tierney, William Tracy, Elizabeth Patterson, Dana Andrews, Slim Summerville, Ward Bond, Grant Mitchell, Zeffie Tilbury, Russell Simpson, Spencer Charters

Erskine Caldwell's spicy story of life among the poor white folks of the South—turned into a play by Jack Kirkland which ran eight years on Broadway—is somewhat cleaned up in the screen version, stressing comedy rather than the ignorance and crudeness of its rural characters. Charley Grapewin stars as Jeeter Lester, the lazy but lovable old reprobate, with Elizabeth Patterson as his long-suffering wife. Despite the fine acting and the direction of John Ford, the purely physical behavior of the characters, almost entirely shiftless, makes for a heavy-handed depiction of the lifestyle it examines.

A VERY YOUNG LADY

Produced by Robert T. Kane
Directed by Harold Schuster
Screenplay by Ladislas Fodor and Elaine Ryan, from a play by Ladislas Fodor
Photographed by Edward Cronjager
Musical direction by Cyril J. Mockridge
80 minutes

Cast: Jane Withers, Nancy Kelly, John Sutton, Janet Beecher, Richard Clayton, June Carlson, Charles Halton,

A st[...]
grea[...]
bottl[...]
devo[...]
towa[...]
man[...]
whic[...]
her.[...]
to a[...]
excel[...]
as a[...]

GIRL TROUBLE

Produced by Robert Bassler
Directed by Harold Schuster
Screenplay by Ladislas Fodor[...]
   from a story by Ladislas F[...]
   Trosper
Photographed by Edward Cro[...]
Music by Alfred Newman
82 minutes

Cast: Don Ameche, Joan B[...]
Craven, Alan Dinehart, Helen[...]
nova, Ted North, Doris Mer[...]
Murray, Janis Carter, Vivia[...]
Robert Greig, Joseph Crehan[...]

A wartime comedy, with [...]
civil defense, about a South[...]
who comes to New York in [...]
for his father's rubber plan[...]
lems when he rents the a[...]
(Joan Bennett) who prefer[...]
mantic and business compli[...]
satisfactions. *Girl Trouble*[...]
example of Hollywood's [...]
known as "the screwball co[...]

ICELAND

Produced by William LeBar[...]
Directed by H. Bruce Humbe[...]
Screenplay by Robert Ellis ar[...]
Photographed by Arthur Mil[...]
Songs by Mack Gordon and [...]
Musical direction by Emil Ne[...]
79 minutes

Cast: Sonja Henie, John Pa[...]
sart, Osa Massen, John Mer[...]
and his orchestra, Sterling [...]
Reynolds, Ludwig Stossel, D[...]

A wartime musical, with [...]
land and running into ro[...]
ladykiller (John Payne) m[...]
(Sonja Henie) and is am[...]
proposal of marriage. Icel[...]
for casual propositions. Hi[...]
to help him out of the pre[...]
the idea of marriage to th[...]
appealing. In *Iceland* the [...]
matters are the skating rou[...]
explanation is given for su[...]
staged in a Reykjavik ni[...]
Harry Warren and Mack G[...]
ballad "There Will Never[...]

John Pa[...]

Cecil Kellaway, Marilyn Kinsely, JoAnn Ransom, Catherine Henderson, Lucita Ham, June Horne

Tomboyish Jane Withers is packed off to a finishing school to acquire some refinement and resists the treatment until she starts entertaining romantic notions about the handsome headmaster (John Sutton). She pours out her heart in love letters which she never intends to send, but they are discovered and cause a scandal. She renounces the letters and gives her approval to the headmaster's love for a teacher (Nancy Kelly)—and gets her first kiss from a juvenile admirer (Richard Clayton).

WE GO FAST

Produced by Lou Ostrow
Directed by William McGann
Screenplay by Thomas Lennon and Adrian Scott, based on a story by Doug Welch
Photographed by Harry Jackson
Musical direction by Emil Newman
64 minutes

Cast: Lynn Bari, Alan Curtis, Sheila Ryan, Don Deforest, Ernest Truex, Gerald Mohr, George Lessey, Paul McGrath, Thomas Dugan, Arthur Hohl, James Flavin, Arthur Loft, Charles Arnt

A waitress in a highway restaurant (Lynn Bari) is the subject of rivalry between two motorcycle cops (Alan Curtis and Don Deforest). She falls for an Oriental executive (Gerald Mohr), but he turns out to be a crook and she goes back to flirting with the cops.

WEEKEND IN HAVANA

Produced by William Le Baron
Directed by Walter Lang
Screenplay by Karl Tunberg and Darrell Ware
Photographed in Technicolor by Ernest Palmer
Songs by Mack Gordon, Harry Warren, and Jimmy Monaco
Musical direction by Alfred Newman
80 minutes

Cast: Alice Faye, Carmen Miranda, John Payne, Cesar Romero, Cobina Wright, Jr., George Barbier, Sheldon Leonard, Leonid Kinskey, Billy Gilbert, Chris-Pin Martin, Hal K. Dawson, William Davidson, Leona Roberts

A New York salesgirl (Alice Faye) takes a cruise to Havana on a ship that runs aground. The company sends a man (John Payne) to see that she gets to Havana and has a good time. He doesn't tell her that he has a fiancée in New York and she is disappointed in his lack of romantic interest. But a suave gambler (Cesar Romero) mistakes her for a wealthy tourist and romances her, to the annoyance of his jealous singer girlfriend (Carmen Miranda). The company man doesn't take long to realize he is engaged to the wrong girl. A pleasant frou-frou of a musical, with beguiling

Charley Grapewin and Gene Tierney in *Tobacco Road*.

---

singing by Faye and some vigorous singing and dancing by Miranda.

WESTERN UNION

Produced by Harry Joe Brown
Directed by Fritz Lang
Screenplay by Robert Carson, from a novel by Zane Grey
Photographed in Technicolor by Edward Cronjager and Allen Davey
Musical direction by David Buttolph
95 minutes

Cast: Randolph Scott, Robert Young, Dean Jagger, Virginia Gilmore, Chill Wills, Slim Summerville, Barton MacLane, John Carradine, Russell Hicks, Victor Killian, Minor Watson, George Chandler, Chief Big Tree

A superior Western, beautifully color photographed in Utah, with a minimal historical basis—about the connecting by telegraph wires of Omaha and Salt Lake City—and a good deal of fiction, about two brothers, one (Randolph Scott) who gives up his outlaw ways and works for the Western Union and the other (Barton MacLane) who leads a band of outlaws in trying to stop the laying of the lines. In the end the good brother shoots the bad one, but loses his own life in doing so. In the meantime there is a lot of conflict with Indians, who resent the pioneers intruding on their land, and outlaws pretending to be Indians. *Western Union* has the distinction of being directed by the eminent Fritz Lang, who gave the film swift pacing and deeper characterization than are usually found in Western epics.

Carmen Miranda, Don Ameche, Alice Faye, and Leonid Kinskey in *That Night in Rio*.

121

pretending to
security leaks. S
Ellison), but fi
on the right sid

CASTLE IN

Produced by Ra
Directed by Har
Screenplay by Jc
  by Earl Derr I
Photographed b
Musical directio
63 minutes

Cast: Sidney To
las Dumbrille, I
Yung, Lenita La
Geray, Lucien I

Chan is called
family and cor
scheme to acq
house, with its
artifacts, provic
and murderous

CHINA GIR

Produced by Be
Directed by Hei
Screenplay by B
  man
Photographed b
Musical directio
93 minutes

Cast: Gene Tie
len, Lynn Bari,
mick, Bobby B
Neal, Paul Fung

A tough Am
Montgomery)
period before
He escapes a J
lay, where he
Chinese girl ((
the spies who
back to the Ja
book containir
Ben Hecht and
China Girl an

DR. RENAI

Produced by Sc
Directed by Ha
Screenplay by \
Photographed I
Music by David
58 minutes

124

ing, including the affection of the promoter's lovely
partner (Lynn Bari), who even agrees to marry him.
With Fonda as the pleasant dope, the film strikes a
blow for lack of ambition.

MAN IN THE TRUNK

Produced by Walter Morosco
Directed by Malcolm St. Clair
Screenplay by John Larkin
Photographed by Glen MacWilliams
Music by Cyril J. Mockridge
70 minutes

Cast: Lynne Roberts, George Holmes, Raymond Walburn,
J. Carrol Naish, Dorothy Peterson, Eily Malyon, Arthur
Loft, Milton Parsons, Matt McHugh, Charles Cape. Theo-
dore von Eltz, Joan Marsh, Syd Saylor

The man in the trunk has been there ten years, the
victim of a murder, and all that remains is a skeleton.
When the trunk is finally opened, the man's ghost (Raymond Walburn) appears and helps a young attorney
(George Holmes) find the man who killed him.

THE MAN WHO WOULDN'T DIE

Produced by Sol M. Wurtzel
Directed by Herbert I. Leeds
Screenplay by Arnaud d'Usseau, based on a novel by
  Clayton Rawson, and the character created by Brett
  Halliday
Photographed by Joseph P. MacDonald
73 minutes

Cast: Lloyd Nolan, Marjorie Weaver, Helene Reynolds,
Henry Wilcoxon, Richard Derr, Paul Harvey, Billy Bevan,
Olin Howard, Robert Emmett Keane, LeRoy Mason, Jeff
Corey

Michael Shayne (Lloyd Nolan) is hired to pose as the
husband of the daughter (Marjorie Weaver) of a
millionaire (Paul Harvey) in order to find out who is
trying to kill them. Shayne discovers that the culprit
is a man considered dead and buried and who is in
league with the millionaire's young second wife
(Helene Reynolds) to acquire his wealth.

MANILA CALLING

Produced by Sol M. Wurtzel
Directed by Herbert I. Leeds
Screenplay by John Larkin
Photographed by Lucien Andriot
Music by Cyril J. Mockridge and Emil Newman
79 minutes

Cast: Lloyd Nolan, Carole Landis, Cornel Wilde, James
Gleason, Martin Kosleck, Ralph Byrd, Charles Tannen,
Ted North, Elisha Cook, Jr., Harold Huber, Lester Mat-
thews, Louis Jean Heydt, Sen Yung

128

Jean Gabin and Ida Lupino in *Moontide*.

A war adventure, with Lloyd Nolan as the leader of a
band of Americans who form a guerrilla unit and fight
on after the Japanese invasion of Mindanao. With
him is an entertainer (Carole Landis) who chooses to
stay rather than leave, and an army officer (Cornel
Wilde) who is a telephone engineer. They build a
short wave radio station and send out information
about Japanese movements until the enemy closes in
and wipes them out.

MOONTIDE

Produced by Mark Hellinger
Directed by Archie Mayo
Screenplay by John O'Hara, from a novel by Willard
  Robertson
Photographed by Charles Clarke
Musical direction by Cyril J. Mockridge and David
  Buttolph
95 minutes

Cast: Jean Gabin, Ida Lupino, Thomas Mitchell, Claude
Rains, Jerome Cowan, Helene Reynolds, Ralph Byrd,
William Halligan, Sen Yung, Chester Gan, Robin Ray-
mond, Arthur Aylesworth, Arthur Hohl, John Kelly

A moody waterfront melodrama, staring Jean Gabin
in his first American film, as a rough, itinerant seaman
with a bad temper, who wakes up with a hangover
and wonders if he was responsible for a murder. A
derelict friend (Thomas Mitchell) strings him along
with the possibility so that he can be taken care of,
but the seaman finds happiness when he rescues a girl
(Ida Lupino) from suicide and is rewarded with love.
The rather gloomy picture is made interesting by the
macho presence of Gabin.

MY GAL SAL

Produced by Robert Bassler
Directed by Irving Cummings

Screenplay by Seton I. Miller, Darrel Ware, and Karl Tunberg, based on *My Brother Paul* by Theodore Dreiser
Photographed in Technicolor by Ernest Palmer
Musical direction by Alfred Newman
103 minutes

Cast: Rita Hayworth, Victor Mature, John Sutton, Carole Landis, James Gleason, Phil Silvers, Walter Catlett, Mona Maris, Frank Orth, Stanley Andrews, Margaret Moffat, Libby Taylor, John Kelly, Curt Bois, Gregory Gaye, Andrew Tombes

The story of songwriter Paul Dresser, *My Gal Sal* is a handsome musical set in the Midwest and in New York of the late nineteenth century. Dresser was a colorful personality and something of a rogue, who died in 1905 at the age of forty-six after a few glittering years on Broadway. Victor Mature was a good choice for the role and Rita Hayworth is glamour personified as Sally Elliott, the musical comedy star who was the love of Dresser's life. The title song was written for her. For its evocation of period and for some fine production numbers, *My Gal Sal* rates as one of the best musicals dealing with the career of a songwriter.

THE NIGHT BEFORE THE DIVORCE

Produced by Ralph Dietrich
Directed by Robert Siodmak
Screenplay by Jerry Sackheim, based on a play by Gina Kaus and Ladislas Fodor
Photographed by Peverell Marley
Musical direction by Emil Newman
67 minutes

Cast: Lynn Bari, Mary Beth Hughes, Joseph Allen, Jr., Truman Bradley, Nils Asther, Kay Linaker, Lyle Latell, Mary Treen, Thurston Hall, Spencer Charters, Leon Belasco, Tom Fadden

A bright, intelligent wife (Lynn Bari) is sued for divorce by her husband (Joseph Allen, Jr.) because he feels she bests him in everything. He goes off with a blonde charmer (Mary Beth Hughes) and she dates a bandleader (Nils Asther), who is murdered. With the aid of a detective friend, the wife pretends she is in trouble with the police, which challenges her husband's male image and brings him back to marriage.

ON THE SUNNY SIDE

Produced by Lou Ostrow
Directed by Harold Shuster
Screenplay by Lillie Hayward and George Templeton, from a story by Mary C. McCall, Jr.
Photographed by Lucien Andriot
Musical direction by Emil Newman
69 minutes

Rita Hayworth in *My Gal Sal.*

Cast: Roddy McDowall, Jane Darwell, Stanley Clements, Katharine Alexander, Don Douglas, Freddie Mercer, Ann Todd, Jill Esmond, Freddie Walburn, Leon Tyler, Billy Benedict, Stuart Robertson, Whiskers

The sunny side is America—in the estimation of a group of British children shipped across the Atlantic to escape the blitz. Among them is a boy (Roddy McDowall) with refined English manners who delights his hosts (Don Douglas and Katharine Alexander) so much that they neglect their own son (Freddie Mercer). The resultant jealousy ends when the two boys team up to fight a common bully at school.

ORCHESTRA WIVES

Produced by William LeBaron
Directed by Archie Mayo
Screenplay by Karl Tunberg and Darrel Ware, from a story by James Prindle
Photographed by Lucien Ballard
Songs by Mack Gordon and Harry Warren
Musical direction by Alfred Newman
97 minutes

Cast: George Montgomery, Ann Rutherford, Cesar Romero, Glenn Miller and his Band, Lynn Bari, Carole Landis, Virginia Gilmore, Mary Beth Hughes, Nicholas Brothers, Tamara Geva, Frank Orth, Grant Mitchell, Henry Morgan

Possibly the best dance band movie ever made, thanks to the involvement of Glenn Miller (unfortunately his last screen appearance) and a number of memorable songs by Harry Warren and Mack Gordon, including "I Got a Gal in Kalamazoo," "At Last," and "Serenade in Blue." The central characters are a trumpeter (George Montgomery) and his bride (Ann Rutherford) whose marriage isn't given much of a chance by the wives of the other musicians, partly because of the sultry band singer (Lynn Bari). But true love does triumph over the affairs and the gossip, and the great Miller performances live on, thanks to the movie and its soundtrack recordings.

OVER MY DEAD BODY

Produced by Walter Morosco
Directed by Malcolm St. Clair
Screenplay by Edward James, from a novel by James O'Hanlon
Photographed by Lucien Andriot
Music by Emil Newman and Cyril J. Mockridge
68 minutes

Cast: Milton Berle, Mary Beth Hughes, Reginald Denny, Frank Orth, William Davidson, Wonderful Smith, J. Patrick O'Malley, George M. Carleton, John Hamilton, Jill Warren, Milton Parsons, Leon Belasco, Charles Trowbridge, Bud McCallister, Cyril Ring

Milton Berle as a mystery writer who gets so confused by his own plots he can't finish them, and who is supported by his wife (Mary Beth Hughes). In her office he overhears three men talking about the suicide of their senior partner, who knew that they were involved in crooked plans. Intrigued with the probable plot ideas, he suggests that he take the blame as a murderer, confident that he can figure out a way of extricating himself. He does, but not until he has almost been tried for murder. An ingenious comedy, with Berle in fine (early) form.

THE PIED PIPER

Produced by Nunnally Johnson
Directed by Irving Pichel
Screenplay by Nunnally Johnson, from a novel by Nevil Shute
Photographed by Edward Cronjager
Music by Alfred Newman
87 minutes

Cast: Monty Woolley, Roddy McDowall, Anne Baxter, Otto Preminger, J. Carrol Naish, Lester Matthews, Jill Esmond, Ferike Boros, Peggy Ann Garner, Merrill Rodin, Maurice Tauzin, Fleurette Zama, William Edmunds, Marcel Dalio

A charming war story about an elderly Englishman (Monty Woolley) who is vacationing in France when the Germans invade. He claims not to like children but agrees to get a couple of them to England, and along the way picks up several more of various nationalities. He is aided by a French girl (Anne Baxter) and hindered by a German officer (Otto Preminger), who finally lets the Englishman go ahead with his evacuation scheme provided he takes his own niece with him. The seemingly irascible Woolley dominates

Ann Rutherford and George Montgomery in *Orchestra Wives.*

the film, but he is well supported by a fine script and production values.

THE POSTMAN DIDN'T RING

Produced by Ralph Dietrich
Directed by Harold Schuster
Screenplay by Mortimer Braus, from a story by Mortimer Braus and Leon Ware
Photographed by Joseph MacDonald
Musical direction by Emil Newman
68 minutes

Cast: Richard Travis, Brenda Joyce, Spencer Charters, Stanley Andrews, William Bakewell, Emma Dunn, Joseph Cawthorn, Oscar O'Shea, Erville Alderson, Jeff Corey, Frank M. Thomas, Will Wright, Betty Jean Hainey, Ethel Griffies

Fifty years after a mail sack is stolen it is found in the attic of an old house. The letters are delivered and make a change in the lives of several people, particularly a young man (Richard Travis) whose father had money coming to him. His farming interests blossom with the cash and affect the whole community. He falls in love with an avid stamp collector (Brenda Joyce) and gets a call from his draft board just as they are about to leave for their honeymoon.

QUIET PLEASE, MURDER

Produced by Ralph Dietrich
Directed by John Larkin
Screenplay by John Larkin from a story by Lawrence G. Bluchman
Photographed by Joseph MacDonald
Music by Emil Newman
70 minutes

Cast: George Sanders, Gail Patrick, Richard Denning, Lynne Roberts, Sidney Blackmer, Kurt Katch, Margaret Brayton, Charles Tannen, Byron Foulger, Arthur Space, George Walcott, Chick Collins

Musical direction by Alfred New[...]
90 minutes

Cast: Betty Grable, John Payne, [...]
Romero, Charlotte Greenwood, [...]
Harry James and his Music Mak[...]
Gleason, Harry Hayden

A show biz musical with Betty [...]
as a pair of entertainers who lo[...]
squabble over jealousies. He hir[...]
(Carmen Miranda) and preten[...]
Grable teams up with a Latin d[...]
and announces her engagement[...]
triumphs, but not until many s[...]
been performed against Techn[...]
including Lake Louise, Alberta[...]
Warren and Mack Gordon pr[...]
Miranda, and Harry James wit[...]
ties, with "I Had the Craziest [...]
standard.

SUNDOWN JIM

Produced by Sol M. Wurtzel
Directed by James Tinling
Screenplay by Robert F. Metzler
    from a novel by Ernest Haycox
Photographed by Glen MacWillia[...]
Musical direction by Emil Newma[...]
53 minutes

Cast: John Kimbrough, Virginia G[...]
Joseph Sawyer, Paul Hurst, Moro[...]
LeRoy Mason, Lane Chandler, Ja[...]
en, Cliff Edwards

A Western set in the mountair[...]
giving a different background, [...]
a U.S. Marshall (John Kimbr[...]
clean up a town and rid it of i[...]

TALES OF MANHATTAN

Produced by Boris Morros and S. [...]
Directed by Julien Duvivier
Screenplay by Ben Hecht, from st[...]
    Donald Ogden Stewart, Samu[...]
    Campbell, Ladislas Fodor, C. V[...]
    Trotti, and Henry Blankfort
Photographed by Joseph Walker
Songs by Leo Robin and Ralph [...]
Music by Sol Kaplan
Musical direction by Edward Pau[...]
118 minutes

Cast: Charles Boyer, Rita Hayw[...]
Henry Fonda, Charles Laughton, [...]
Paul Robeson, Ethel Waters, Roch[...]
Eugene Pallette, Cesar Romero, [...]

An ingenious crime caper, set mostly in a large public library, with George Sanders as a highly intelligent murderer who deals in fake copies of priceless books. He employs fake police to protect him as he steals rare volumes, but his assistant and girl friend (Gail Patrick) becomes terrified of him and brings in a detective (Richard Denning) to end his mad and killing schemes.

THE REMARKABLE MR. KIPPS

Produced by Edward Black
Directed by Carol Reed
Screenplay by Sidney Gilliat, from a novel by H. G.
    Wells
Photographed by Arthur Crabtree
Musical direction by Louis Levy
87 minutes

Cast: Michael Redgrave, Diana Wynyard, Phyllis Calvert, Arthur Riscoe, Philip Frost, Diana Calderwood, Max Adrian, Helen Haye, Michael Wilding, Lloyd Pearson, Edward Rigby, Mackenzie Ward, Hermione Baddeley

A charming English film about a shop clerk (Michael Redgrave) who inherits a lot of money and makes many friends, some of whom are dubious in their intentions. An ambitious girl (Diana Wynyard) almost traps him into marriage, but he finds real happiness after he loses his money, marries a serving girl (Phyllis Calvert), and returns to his former, simple life.

RIGHT TO THE HEART

Produced by Sol M. Wurtzel
Directed by Eugene Forde
Screenplay by Walter Bullock, from a story by Harold
    McGrath
Photographed by Virgil Miller
Musical direction by Emil Newman
72 minutes

Monty Woolley, Roddy McDowall, Anne Baxter, and Otto Preminger in *The Pied Piper*.

Spring Byington, Gene Tierney, and Henry Fonda in *Rings on Her Finger*.

Cast: Brenda Joyce, Joseph Allen, Jr., Cobina Wright, Jr., Stanley Clements, Don DeFore, Hugh Beaumont, Charles D. Brown, Ethel Griffies, Frank Orth, Phil Tead, William Haade, Spencer Charters

A young New Yorker (Joseph Allen, Jr.) is disinherited by his wealthy aunt (Ethel Griffies) because of his irresponsible behavior. He enrolls in a camp for fighters in order to get in shape to beat a boxer who made him look foolish and falls in love with the daughter (Brenda Joyce) of the camp trainer (Charles D. Brown). At the camp he learns the humility he needs to win back the approbation of his aunt.

RINGS ON HER FINGERS

Produced by Milton Sperling
Directed by Rouben Mamoulian
Screenplay by Ken Englund, based on a story by Robert
    Pirosh and Joseph Schrank
Photographed by George Barnes
Music by Cyril Mockridge
86 minutes

Cast: Henry Fonda, Gene Tierney, Spring Byington, Laird Cregar, John Shepperd, Frank Orth, Henry Stephenson, Marjorie Gateson, George Lessey, Iris Adrian, Harry Hayden, Gwendolyn Logan, Eric Wilton, Bill Benedict, Sarah Edwards, Thurston Hall, Clara Blandick

An amiable comedy about a pair of confidence tricksters (Laird Cregar and Spring Byington) who recruit a pretty shop girl (Gene Tierney) in order to find a millionaire off whom they all might live. They pick a young man (Henry Fonda) at a fashionable beach resort whom they assume to be rich because he speaks eloquently and passionately about yachts. He is actually penniless, but he and the girl fall in love and marry, and ruin the plans of the tricksters. The material is lightweight, but the acting gives it style.

ROXIE HART

Produced by Nunnally
Directed by William A
Screenplay by Nunnall
Watkins
Photographed by Leon
Music by Alfred Newr
74 minutes

Cast: Ginger Rogers,
gomery, Lynne Overm
Allgood, William Fra
Helene Reynolds, Geo

First filmed in 1928
as the basis for a sta
Hart is that of a bra:
allows her murder
farce because she th
publicity. In this s
(Adolphe Menjou) or
trial is a farce becaus
Roxie's husband (Ge
wards dumps. She tl
Montgomery) who ha
covering her "ordeal."
on American jurispr
whipping it along fra
a field day as the wily

SECRET AGENT

Produced by Sol M. W
Directed by Irving Picl
Screenplay by John La:
Photographed by Lucie
Musical direction by Er
72 minutes

Cast: Preston Foster, L
Janis Carter, Steve Ger
Ian Wolfe, Hermaine
Puglia, Leyland Hodgs

A night club owner
wanted in America fc
patriotism when he r
priating property an
abusing people of othe
a British agent (Lyr
activities to their res
a typical "B" war e
for the enemy.

SON OF FURY

Produced by William P
Directed by John Cron
Screenplay by Philip
Marshall
Photographed by Arthu

132

1943

BATTLE OF RUSSIA

Produced by Anatole Litvak, with supervision by Frank
Capra
Written and narrated by Anthony Veiller
80 minutes

A documentary of the Russian campaigns to contain
and turn back the German invasion, with stress on the
actual fighting, using much Russian footage and an
amount of captured German material.

BOMBER'S MOON

Produced by Sol M. Wurtzel
Directed by Charles Fuhr
Screenplay by Kenneth Gamet, from a story by Leonard
Lee
Photographed by Lucien Ballard
Music by David Buttolph
Musical direction by Emil Newman

Cast: George Montgomery, Annabella, Kent Taylor,
Walter Kingford, Martin Kosleck, Dennis Hoey, Robert
Barrat, Richard Graham, Kenneth Brown, Lionel Royce,
Victor Killian, Felix Basch

An American pilot (George Montgomery) crash lands
in wartime Germany and is imprisoned with a Czech
(Kent Taylor) who is actually a German agent. They
escape in the company of a Russian (Annabella) and
make for the coast. The agent is killed as he is about
to expose the underground workers, the Russian manages to get on a fishing boat, the American steals a
German plane and is romantically reunited in England
with the Russian girl. A fair war adventure, the film
was directed by Edward Ludwig and Harold Schuster,
who decided to put their work out under the invented
name of Charles Fuhr.

CHETNIKS

Produced by Sol M. Wurtzel
Directed by Louis King
Screenplay by Jack Andrews and Edward E. Paramore,
from a story by Frank Andrews
Photographed by Glen MacWilliams
Music by Hugo W. Friedhofer

138

Musical direction by Emil Newman
73 minutes

Cast: Philip Dorn, Anna Sten, John Shepperd, Virginia
Gilmore, Martin Kosleck, Felix Basch, Frank Lackteen,
Patricia Prest, Merrill Rodin, Leroy Mason

A tribute to the Yugoslavian war effort, highlighting the
guerrilla campaign against the Germans, with Philip
Dorn as General Draja Mihailovitch, the leader of the
Yugoslav resistance brigades known as Chetniks. Based
on the general's own accounts, the film graphically
depicts the ferocity of the fighting between the invaders and the defenders in the villages and the rugged
mountains. An excellent war picture made with Yugoslavian cooperation.

CLAUDIA

Produced by William Perlberg
Directed by Edmund Goulding
Screenplay by Morrie Ryskind, from a play by Rose
Franken
Photographed by Leon Shamroy
Song by Alfred Newman and Charles Henderson
Music by Alfred Newman
90 minutes

Cast: Dorothy McGuire, Robert Young, Ina Claire, Reginald Gardiner, Olga Baclanova, Jean Howard, Frank
Tweddell, Elsa Janssen, John Royce, Frank Fenton, Ferdinand Munier, Winifred Harris

Dorothy McGuire in her screen debut, as Claudia, the
naive young bride for whom almost everything about
marriage, sex, running a home, and childbirth comes
as a vast surprise. McGuire had been a success on
Broadway in the play and was instantly successful in
the screen version, triggering off a distinguished film
career. The role is that of an impulsive, vague, and
erratic but basically charming and loving child-woman,
with Robert Young as the tolerant husband sometimes giving way to anger. A warm domestic comedy,
with touches of anguish, delicately directed by Edmund Goulding.

CONEY ISLAND

Produced by William Perlberg
Directed by Walter Lang

Screenplay by George Seaton
Photographed in Technicolor by Ernest Palmer
Songs by Leo Robin and Ralph Rainger
Musical direction by Alfred Newman
90 minutes

Cast: Betty Grable, George Montgomery, Cesar Romero,
Charles Winninger, Phil Silvers, Matt Briggs, Paul Hurst,
Frank Orth, Phyllis Kennedy, Carmen D'Antonio, Hal K.
Dawson, Andrew Tombes, Harry Seymour, Byron Foulger

A pleasant musical comedy, set around New York's
Coney Island at the turn-of-the-century, dealing with a
pair of rival saloon owners (George Montgomery and
Cesar Romero) who pull elaborate schemes on one
another in order to prosper and come to serious differences when they want the same girl, a flashy entertainer (Betty Grable). Montgomery teaches her some
finesse, which increases her fame and wins her love,
which Romero finally comes to accept. *Coney Island*
is a prime example of Technicolor at its richest, with
excellent decor, and memorable for Grable singing
"Cuddle Up a Little Closer."

CRASH DIVE

Produced by Milton Sperling
Directed by Archie Mayo
Screenplay by Jo Swerling, from a story by W. R. Burnett
Photographed in Technicolor by Leon Shamroy
Music by David Buttolph
Musical direction by Emil Newman
105 minutes

Cast: Tyrone Power, Anne Baxter, Dana Andrews, James
Gleason, Dame May Whitty, Henry Morgan, Ben Carter,
Charles Tannen, Frank Conroy, Florence Luke, John
Archer, George Holmes, Minor Watson, Kathleen Howard

A tribute to the submarine service, made with Naval
Department cooperation and partly filmed at the New
London, Connecticut, submarine base. Tyrone Power
is the young officer transferred from PT boats to be
the executive of a submarine commanded by Dana
Andrews and falling in love with his fiancée (Anne
Baxter). The two men learn to respect each other's
bravery, particularly when they raid a German naval
base, and the commander gives up the girl when he
realizes the love between her and Power is genuine.
An obvious wartime morale booster but done with
style and excitement. After completing the film, Power
left Hollywood for his own war service, with the
Marines.

THE DANCING MASTERS

Produced by Lee Marcus
Directed by Malcolm St. Clair
Screenplay by W. Scott Darling, from a story by George
    Bricker
Photographed by Norbert Brodine

Dorothy McGuire and Robert Young in *Claudia*.

George Montgomery and Betty Grable in *Coney Island*.

Tyrone Power and Dana Andrews in *Crash Dive*.

139

Alice Faye and Carmen Miranda in *The Gang's All Here*.

William Bendix, Anthony Quinn, Lionel Stander (at right) and Lloyd Nolan (cigarette in mouth) in *Guadalcanal Diary*.

Don Ameche and Gene Tierney in *Heaven Can Wait*.

Pangborn, Ethel Griffies, Eric Blore, Montagu Love, Richard Fraser, Edwin Maxwell, Ian Wolfe, Alec Craig

Producer-scenarist Nunnally Johnson tailored *Holy Matrimony* to fit the special image of Monty Woolley, the Yale professor of haughty manner and diction who made a late acting debut and won fame as *The Man Who Came to Dinner*. Here he appeared as a painter who is recalled after twenty years abroad to receive a knighthood from the Crown. Not interested in fame and loath to give up his reclusiveness, he proceeds grudgingly. But he takes the opportunity to evade the issue when his valet dies and he assumes his identity. This opens up problems he never imagined, such as marriage to a lady (Gracie Fields) who has been corresponding, sight unseen, with the valet—and a case of bigamy when the valet's previous family turns up. *Holy Matrimony* is an appealing and civilized comedy, and a fond reminder of Woolley and Fields at their peaks.

IMMORTAL SERGEANT

Produced by Lamar Trotti
Directed by John Stahl
Screenplay by Lamar Trotti, from the novel by John Brophy
Photographed by Arthur Miller
Music by David Buttolph
Musical direction by Alfred Newman
90 minutes

Cast: Henry Fonda, Maureen O'Hara, Thomas Mitchell, Allyn Joslyn, Reginald Gardiner, Melville Cooper, Bramwell Fletcher, Morton Lowry, Bob Mascagno, Italia De Nubla, Jean Prescott

Henry Fonda as a timorous Canadian, serving with the British Eighth Army in North Africa and lost with a squad of comrades in the Libyan desert. During his lonely stands on watch duty he thinks of his girl (Maureen O'Hara) back home and under the guidance of a tough old sergeant (Thomas Mitchell) he gradually changes from shyness to certainty as a leader of men. The sergeant dies and it remains for the Canadian to bring the small group of survivors back to their lines, which results in a medal and a positive reunion with his girl.

JITTERBUGS

Produced by Sol M. Wurtzel
Directed by Malcolm St. Clair
Screenplay by Scott Darling
Photographed by Lucien Andriot
Songs by Charles Newman and Lew Pollock
Musical direction by Emil Newman
74 minutes

Cast: Stan Laurel, Oliver Hardy, Vivian Blaine, Bob

June Havoc, Jack Oakie, Alice Faye, and John Payne in *Hello, Frisco, Hello*.

Una O'Connor, Gracie Fields, and Monty Woolley in *Holy Matrimony*.

Bailey, Douglas Fowley, Noel Madison, Lee Patrick, Robert Emmett Keane, Charles Halton

Laurel and Hardy help a girl (Vivian Blaine) regain money swindled from her mother by a pair of crooks. It involves their going to New Orleans, where Hardy poses as a Southern colonel, with Laurel as his valet, and later Laurel poses as the girl's aunt. The climax takes place on a riverboat which slips its mooring. *Jitterbugs* is perhaps the best of the famed comics' last films and served to introduce Vivian Blaine, whose two songs helped give the picture a lift.

MARGIN FOR ERROR

Produced by Ralph Dietrich
Directed by Otto Preminger
Screenplay by Lillie Hayward, from a play by Clare Boothe
Photographed by Edward Cronjager
Music by Leigh Harline
Musical direction by Emil Newman
74 minutes

Cast: Joan Bennett, Milton Berle, Otto Preminger, Carl Esmond, Howard Freeman, Poldy Dur, Clyde Fillmore, Ferike Boros, Joe Kirk, Hans Von Twardowski, Ted North, Elmer Jack Semple, J. Norton Dunp

A Brooklyn Jewish policeman (Milton Berle) is assigned to the prewar German consulate to guard the threatened life of its chief officer (Otto Preminger), whose personal use of consulate funds is known to his assistant (Carl Esmond) and to the consul's wife (Joan Bennett), who is married to him only because her father is in a concentration camp. The consul is killed by poison, stabbing, and gunshot and the policeman finds it was a suicide, but under odd circumstances. The wild comedy was a hit on Broadway, with Preminger as directed and portraying the consul. When he was assigned to do the film it seemed obvious for him to repeat his role as the arrogant Nazi.

THE MEANEST MAN IN THE WORLD

Produced by William Perlberg
Directed by Sidney Lanfield
Screenplay by George Seaton and Allan House, based on a play by George M. Cohan
Photographed by Peverell Marley
Music by Cyril J. Mockridge
Musical direction by Emil Newman
57 minutes

Cast: Jack Benny, Priscilla Lane, Rochester, Edmund Gwenn, Matt Briggs, Anne Revere, Margaret Seddon, Helene Reynolds, Don Douglas, Harry Hayden, Arthur Loft, Andrew Tombes, Paul Burns

Jack Benny cashing in on his celebrated image as a skinflint. Here he is a small-town lawyer with a strong sense of justice and love for humankind but hardly any business. His valet (Rochester) suggests that he change his style and become tough and mean instead of nice. Business then picks up, but his girl friend (Priscilla Lane) doesn't like the change and leaves him. Her father (Matt Briggs) brings the two of them together. Not the best of Benny, but still amusing.

THE MOON IS DOWN

Produced by Nunnally Johnson
Directed by Irving Pichel
Screenplay by Nunnally Johnson, from a novel by John Steinbeck
Photographed by Arthur Miller
Music by Alfred Newman
90 minutes

Cast: Sir Cedric Hardwicke, Henry Travers, Lee J. Cobb, Dorris Bowdon, Margaret Wycherly, Peter Van Eyck, William Post, Jr., Henry Rowland, E. J. Ballentine, Violette Wilson, Hans Schumm

Henry Fonda in *The Immortal Sergeant.*

The German invasion of Norway, centering upon a small town and the conflict between the citizens and the Germans, particularly the commandant (Sir Cedric Hardwicke) and the mayor (Henry Travers), two civilized men in an uncivilized situation. The Germans try to organize the townspeople to work in iron mines and meet resistance in many forms, resulting in death for both sides. The film is a harsh, somber portrait of life under occupation, revealing the various shades of character and courage, or the lack of it, among the people involved.

MY FRIEND FLICKA

Produced by Ralph Dietrich
Directed by Harold Schuster
Screenplay by Lillie Hayward, from a story by Mary O'Hara
Photographed in Technicolor by Dewey Wrigley
Music by Alfred Newman
89 minutes

Cast: Roddy McDowall, Preston Foster, Rita Johnson, James Bell, Jeff Corey, Diana Hale, Arthur Loft

A classic horse story about a boy (Roddy McDowall) who daydreams about having his own colt and whose rancher father (Preston Foster) finally agrees but doesn't like the choice the boy makes. He chooses the product of a mare who has shown madness, but he trains the colt through various trials and tribulations. The boy's faith is justified and the colt grows into a beautiful animal. The film is a gem among animal pictures, magnificently color photographed in ranching country in the Rockies, with a memorable performance by McDowall as the boy who loves the horse he calls Flicka (the Swedish word for girl).

THE OX-BOX INCIDENT

Produced by Lamar Trotti
Directed by William Wellman
Screenplay by Lamar Trotti, based on the novel by Walter Van Tilberg Clark
Photographed by Arthur Miller
Music by Cyril Mockridge
75 minutes

Cast: Henry Fonda, Dana Andrews, Mary Beth Hughes, Anthony Quinn, William Eythe, Henry Morgan, Jane Darwell, Matt Briggs, Harry Davenport, Frank Conroy, Marc Lawrence, Victor Killian, Paul Hurst, Chris-Pin Martin, Ted North, George Meeker, Almira Sessions, Margaret Hamilton, Dick Rich, Francis Ford

Darryl Zanuck was correct in believing *The Ox-Bow Incident* would not do well at the box office. This darkly hued, downbeat picture met with critical acclaim and has since taken its place as a Western classic, but in 1943 it offered little in the way of conventional en-

tertainment. In effect it is a Greek tragedy in an American setting, telling the story of three men who are summarily tried and hung for cattle rustling and murder, but with no evidence. The film is a searing indictment of mob violence and an honest depiction of the crude values of frontier life, leavened here and there with figures of decency and compassion. *The Ox-Bow Incident* came to be only because Henry Fonda and director William Wellman insisted on making it, and it will forever be a tribute to their integrity.

PARIS AFTER DARK

Produced by Andre Daven
Directed by Leonide Moguy
Screenplay by Harold Buchman, from a story by George Kessel
Photographed by Lucien Andriot
Music by Hugo W. Friedhofer
Musical direction by Emil Newman
86 minutes

Cast: George Sanders, Philip Dorn, Brenda Marshall, Madeleine LeBeau, Marcel Dalio, Robert Lewis, Henry Rowland, Raymond Roe, Gene Gary, Jean Del Val, Curt Bois, Ann Codee, Louis Borell, John Wengref

A story of the French underground activities against the German invasion, with George Sanders as a cultured doctor who goes about his work unrestricted, but who is actually a leader of the resistance. His nurse (Brenda Marshall) supports his cause, but her husband (Philip Dorn), brainwashed by the Nazis, is a hindrance, until he comes to his senses. A good impression of the subject matter, doubtless due to director Leonide Moguy, a Frenchman who escaped his country during the invasion.

THE SONG OF BERNADETTE

Produced by William Perlberg
Directed by Henry King
Screenplay by George Seaton, from a novel by Franz Werfel
Photographed by Arthur Miller
Music by Alfred Newman
156 minutes

Cast: Jennifer Jones, William Eythe, Charles Bickford, Vincent Price, Lee J. Cobb, Gladys Cooper, Anne Revere, Roman Bohnen, Mary Anderson, Patricia Morison, Aubrey Mather, Charles Dingle, Edith Barrett, Sig Ruman, Blanche Yurka

The story of the French peasant girl Bernadette Soubirous, who saw a vision of the Virgin Mary in the town of Lourdes and from which point a spring poured forth. That spring became the healing place of multitudes of sick and needy people. *The Song of Bernadette* tells the story with respect, combining the facts with the legend and benefiting from a superb performance by

Jennifer Jones as the girl who claimed she was not very bright, but who never wavered from her claim of heavenly contact. No evidence can refute her story and the village of Lourdes has been a mecca ever since. Henry King's direction keeps a firm focus on the story and its many characters, ranging from simple villagers to the highest ranks of the church. Alfred Newman's score supplies an almost spiritual added dimension.

STORMY WEATHER

Produced by William Le Baron
Directed by Andrew Stone
Screenplay by Frederick Jackson and Ted Koehler, from a story by Jerry Horwin and Seymour B. Robinson
Photographed by Leon Shamroy
Musical direction by Emil Newman
77 minutes

Cast: Lena Horne, Bill Robinson, Cab Calloway and his Band, Katherine Dunham and her troupe, Fats Waller, Nicholas Brothers, Ada Brown, Dooley Wilson, The Tramp Band, Babe Wallace, Ernest Whitman, Zutty Singleton

Some of the enormous contributions of black Americans to the musical culture of their country receive a good showcase in this highly entertaining picture. The plot is a simple one, about a dancer (Bill Robinson) and his rise to fame, his split with his singer wife (Lena Horne), and their final reconciliation. Spread through the film are fourteen musical numbers, demonstrating the talents of such legendary entertainers as Fats Waller, the Nicholas Brothers, Katherine Dunham and her dance troupe, Cab Calloway, and Dooley Wilson. Plus Lena Horne and the great Bojangles. A remarkable film.

SWEET ROSIE O'GRADY

Produced by William Perlberg
Directed by Irving Cummings
Screenplay by Ken Englund, from stories by William R. Kipman and Frederick Stephani and Edward Van Every
Photographed in Technicolor by Ernest Palmer
Songs by Mack Gordon and Harry Warren
Musical direction by Alfred Newman and Charles Henderson
76 minutes

Cast: Betty Grable, Robert Young, Adolphe Menjou, Reginald Gardiner, Virginia Grey, Phil Regan, Sig Rumann, Alan Dinehart, Hobart Cavanaugh, Frank Orth, Jonathan Hale, Stanley Clements, Byron Foulger

Betty Grable is the girl of the title, a Brooklyn singer and dancer at the turn-of-the-century who desires more than success in the beer halls and goes to London to try to snare a duke (Reginald Gardiner). A *Police Gazette* reporter (Robert Young), who wants her for himself, spoils her chances of becoming a titled wife

Rita Johnson, Preston Foster, and Roddy McDowall in *My Friend Flicka.*

and once she recovers from her anger she comes to return his love. The slight plot is enough to support a great deal of singing and dancing by Grable, with solos like "My Heart Tells Me," and elaborate production numbers like "Going to the Country Fair." The Technicolor does justice to the rich period decor and costuming.

Laurel and Hardy in *Jitterbugs.*

Henry Travers, William Post, Jr., and Henry Rowland in *The Moon Is Down.*

Anthony Quinn, Francis Ford, Dana Andrews, Henry Fonda, Frank Conroy, and Jane Darwell in *The Ox-Bow Incident*.

Jennifer Jones in *The Song of Bernadette*.

Bill Robinson, Lena Horne, and Cab Calloway in *Stormy Weather*.

THEY CAME TO BLOW UP AMERICA

Produced by Lee Marcus
Directed by Edward Ludwig
Screenplay by Aubrey Wisberg, from a story by Michael Jacoby
Photographed by Lucien Andriot
Music by Hugo W. Friedhofer
Musical direction by Emil Newman
73 minutes

Cast: George Sanders, Anna Sten, Ward Bond, Dennis Hoey, Sig Rumann, Ludwig Stossel, Robert Barrat, Poldy Dur, Ralph Byrd, Elsa Janssen, Rex Williams, Charles McGraw, Sven Hugo Borg

A wartime warning to the American home front about the possibilities of German sabotage. An FBI man of German parentage (Gearge Sanders) is ordered to take the place of an American Nazi and go to Germany to join a school of sabotage. He manages to pull off the masquerade and returns with a team, who are then arrested. An interesting account of German sabotage methods, although with wartime sentiments.

TONIGHT WE RAID CALAIS

Produced by Andre Daven
Directed by John Brahm
Screenplay by Waldo Salt, from a story by L. Willinger and Rohama Lee
Photographed by Lucien Ballard
Music by Emil Newman and Cyril J. Mockridge
70 minutes

Cast: Annabella, John Sutton, Lee J. Cobb, Beulah Bondi, Blanche Yurka, Howard Da Silva, Marcel Dalio, Ann Codee, Nigel de Brulier, Robert Lewis, Richard Derr, Leslie Denison, Billy Edmunds

A British intelligence officer (John Sutton) leads a unit into occupied France to locate a German munitions plant and thereby pave the way for a bombing raid. He is aided and somewhat hindered by a French girl (Annabella) who hates the British. He is captured before he can complete the mission, but others bring about the desired result. A well-crafted war adventure tale.

WINTERTIME

Produced by William Le Baron
Directed by John Brahm
Screenplay by E. Edwin Moran and Jack Jevne and Lynn Starling, from a story by Arthur Kober
Photographed by Joe MacDonald
Songs by Leo Robin and Nacio Herb Brown
Musical direction by Alfred Newman
90 minutes

Cast: Sonja Henie, Jack Oakie, Cesar Romero, Carole Landis, S. Z. Sakall, Cornel Wilde, Woody Herman and his orchestra, Helene Reynolds, Don Douglas, Geary Steffen, Georges Renavent

A skating musical set in Canada, with Sonja Henie as a Norwegian champion. She arrives in Quebec with her millionaire uncle (S. Z. Sakall), who is persuaded to invest in an old hotel by its owner (Jack Oakie), who runs the place for entertainers. One of them (Cesar Romero) makes a play for Sonja, who agrees to star in an ice show to raise money for the hotel and ends up in the arms of another man (Cornel Wilde). Again it's the skating of Henie and the music that support the story, in this instance with the aid of Woody Herman and his orchestra.

20TH CENTURY-FOX ACADEMY AWARDS FOR 1943

JENNIFER JONES: Best actress in *The Song of Bernadette.*

JAMES BASEVI and WILLIAM DARLING: Art direction, black and white, for *The Song of Bernadette.*

ARTHUR MILLER: Cinematography, black and white, for *The Song of Bernadette.*

THOMAS LITTLE: Set decoration, black and white, for *The Song of Bernadette.*

ALFRED NEWMAN: Best scoring of a dramatic picture for *The Song of Bernadette.*

HARRY WARREN and MACK GORDON: Best song, "You'll Never Know," from *Hello, Frisco, Hello.*

CHARLES GALLOWAY CLARKE and 20TH CENTURY-FOX CAMERA DEPARTMENT: Honorable mention for technical developments.

FRED SERSEN and ROGER HEMAN: Special effects for *Crash Dive.*

Betty Grable and Robert Young in *Sweet Rosie O'Grady.*

Sonja Henie in *Wintertime.*

1944

BERMUDA MYSTERY

Produced by William Girard
Directed by Benjamin Stoloff
Screenplay by W. Scott Darling, from a story by John Larkin
Photographed by Joseph La Shelle
Music by Arthur Lange
Musical direction by Emil Newman
65 minutes

Cast: Preston Foster, Ann Rutherford, Charles Butterworth, Helene Reynolds, Jean Howard, Richard Lane, Roland Drew, John Eldredge, Theodore von Eltz, Pierre Watkin, Jason Robards, Kane Richmond

A man dies after smoking a cigarette from a gift package and his niece (Ann Rutherford) hires a detective (Preston Foster) to solve the crime. Several men die in the same manner and it is found that they were all friends who invested in an insurance policy just about to pay off. The detective finds the culprit to be the wife of one of the men.

THE BIG NOISE

Produced by Sol M. Wurtzel
Directed by Malcolm St. Clair
Screenplay by Scott Darling
Photographed by Joe MacDonald
Music by Cyril J. Mockridge
Musical direction by Emil Newman
75 minutes

Cast: Stan Laurel, Oliver Hardy, Doris Merrick, Arthur Space, Veda Ann Borg, Bobby Blake, Frank Fenton, James Bush, Phil Van Zandt, Esther Howard, Robert Dudley, Edgar Dearing

Laurel and Hardy as janitors in a detective agency, who are hired to guard a newly invented bomb against a gang of crooks who want it. The boys suffer discomfort in their attempts to evade the crooks, including getting stuck in a radio-directed plane over a desert target range. Amusing, but not the best of Laurel and Hardy.

BUFFALO BILL

Produced by Harry A. Sherman
Directed by William A. Wellman
Screenplay by Aeneas MacKenzie, Clements Ripley, and Cecile Kramer, from a story by Frank Winch
Photographed in Technicolor by Leon Shamroy
Music by David Buttolph
Musical direction by Emil Newman
90 minutes

Cast: Joel McCrea, Maureen O'Hara, Linda Darnell, Thomas Mitchell, Edgar Buchanan, Anthony Quinn, Moroni Olsen, Frank Fenton, Matt Briggs, Gene Lessey, Frank Orth

A colorful but highly romanticized account of the career of William Cody (Joel McCrea), promoted into fame by press agent Ned Buntline (Thomas Mitchell). The film follows his adventures as a hunter-scout for the army, his courtship and marriage of a refined Eastern girl (Maureen O'Hara), his separation from her when he returns to frontier duty and his personal conflict with Chief Yellow Hand (Anthony Quinn), his arguments with politicians over the treatment being meted out to the Indians, and finally his success as a dandified Wild West showman. The accent is definitely on the legend rather than the facts, but the production values are spacious and exciting.

CANDLELIGHT IN ALGERIA

Produced by John Stafford
Directed by George King
Screenplay by Brock Williams and Katherine Strueby, from a story by Dorothy Hope
Photographed by Otto Heller
Music by Roy Douglas
Musical direction by Jack Beaver
85 minutes

Cast: James Mason, Carla Lehmann, Raymond Lovell, Enid Stamp-Taylor, Walter Rilla, Pamela Sterling, Lea Seidl, Hella Kurty, Leslie Bradley, MacDonald Parke, Michel Morel, Albert Whelan

A British war film, concerning the planning and the intrigue involved in the meeting of Allied leaders at a secret place on the Algerian coast to make preparations for the landings in North Africa. A British agent (James Mason) and an American girl (Carla Lehmann) defeat the efforts of German agents to locate a roll of film which would betray the meeting place. A good spy

picture, weaving fiction around some well-illustrated facts.

THE EVE OF ST. MARK

Produced by William Perlberg
Directed by John M. Stahl
Screenplay by George Seaton, based on the play by
  Maxwell Anderson
Photographed by Joseph La Shelle
Music by Cyril J. Mockridge
Musical direction by Emil Newman
96 minutes

Cast: Anne Baxter, William Eythe, Michael O'Shea, Vincent Price, Ruth Nelson, Ray Collins, Stanley Prager, Henry Morgan, Robert Bailey, Joann Dolan, Toni Favor, George Mathews, John Archer

The story of a young country boy (William Eythe) whose courtship of a local girl (Anne Baxter) is interrupted by his call to service and his being sent to the Philippines. Her letters help sustain him as he suffers the discomforts of military life and the terror of warfare. The film ends with the boy and his buddies still overseas, with no indication as to whether they will or will not survive. Seaton's script, from the Maxwell Anderson play, gives a more sensitive than usual account of service life.

THE FIGHTING LADY

Produced by Louis de Rochemont
Narration written by John Stuart Martin and Eugene
  Ling
Narrated by Lt. Robert Taylor, USNR
Music by David Buttolph
Musical direction by Alfred Newman
61 minutes

A documentary about naval warfare in the South Pacific in World War II, with the title referring to an aircraft carrier of the American fleet. All the footage was shot by service cameramen and graphically shows the ferocity of the air and sea combat with the Japanese.

FOUR JILLS IN A JEEP

Produced by Irving Starr
Directed by William A. Seiter
Screenplay by Robert Ellis, Helen Logan, and Snag Werris, from a story by Froma Sand and Fred Niblo, Jr.
Photographed by Peverell Marley
Songs by Jimmy McHugh and Harold Adamson
Musical direction by Emil Newman
89 minutes

Cast: Alice Faye, Betty Grable, Carmen Miranda, George Jessel, Dick Haymes, John Harvey, Phil Silvers, Jimmy Dorsey and his Orchestra, Kay Francis, Carole Landis, Martha Raye, Mitzi Mayfair

The four Jills are Carole Landis, Martha Raye, Kay Francis, and Mitzie Mayfair, playing themselves and recounting their adventures entertaining servicemen in England and North Africa. Dick Haymes made his debut as a singing soldier and Georgie Jessel played master of ceremonies for a benefit show, which allowed for guest appearances by Alice Faye, Betty Grable, and Carmen Miranda, all doing songs associated with them. *Four Jills in a Jeep* is interesting as a war souvenir.

GREENWICH VILLAGE

Produced by William Le Baron
Directed by Walter Lang
Screenplay by Earl Baldwin and Walter Bullock, from a
  story by Frederick Hazlitt Brennan
Photographed in Technicolor by Leon Shamroy and Harry
  Jackson
Songs by Leo Robin and Nacio Herb Brown
Musical direction by Emil Newman and Charles
  Henderson
81 minutes

Cast: Carmen Miranda, Don Ameche, William Bendix, Vivian Blaine, Felix Bressart, Tony and Sally De Marco, The Revuers, B. S. Pully, Four Step Brothers, Emil Rameau, Frank Orth, Torben Meyer

A backstage musical about a composer (Don Ameche) who comes to New York in 1922 to raise interest in his piano concerto and becomes involved with the owner (William Bendix) of a Greenwich Village speakeasy. The owner stages a costume ball to raise money for a stage show he wants to produce and the composer pitches in as pianist, which brings him into loving contact with the speakeasy's singing star (Vivian Blaine), leading to success for everyone, including Carmen Miranda and her antic Latin songs, plus some fine ballroom dancing by Tony and Sally De Marco and jazz dancing by the Four Step Brothers.

HOME IN INDIANA

Produced by Andre Daven
Directed by Henry Hathaway
Screenplay by Winston Miller, from a story by George
  Agney Chamberlain
Photographed in Technicolor by Edward Cronjager
Music by Hugo W. Friedhofer
Musical direction by Emil Newman
106 minutes

Cast: Walter Brennan, Lon McAllister, Jeanne Crain, Charlotte Greenwood, June Haver, Ward Bond, Charles Dingle, Robert Condon, Charles Saggau, Willie Best, George Reed, Noble "Kid" Chissell

Technicolored Americana concerning the training of trotting horses and partly filmed on the trotting tracks of Indiana, Ohio, and Kentucky. A farming couple (Walter Brennan and Charlotte Greenwood) are down

Joel McCrea and Maureen O'Hara in *Buffalo Bill*.

Carole Landis, Mitzi Mayfair, Kay Francis, and Martha Raye in *Four Jills in a Jeep*.

Carmen Miranda in *Greenwich Village*.

to their last horse when their nephew (Lon McAllister) arrives from the city to learn about country life. His education is aided by the attentions of two lovely girls (Jeanne Crain and June Haver) and he decides to become a champion trotting racer. He supplies his uncle with a promising filly and settles down to a good life in his new home state. An apple pie story, attractively produced.

IN THE MEANTIME DARLING

Produced by Otto Preminger
Directed by Otto Preminger
Screenplay by Arthur Kober and Michael Uris
Photographed by Joe MacDonald
Music by David Buttolph
Musical direction by Emil Newman
76 minutes

Cast: Jeanne Crain, Frank Latimore, Eugene Pallette, Mary Nash, Stanley Prager, Gale Robbins, Jane Randolph, Doris Merrick, Cara Williams, Ann Corcoran, Reed Hadley, Heather Angel, Bonnie Bannon, William Colby, Cliff Clark, Elizabeth Risdon, Marjorie Massow

The lives of wartime service wives, and one in particular, the daughter (Jeanne Crain) of a wealthy man (Eugene Pallette). She marries an army lieutenant (Frank Latimore) and quickly learns about the discomforts of traveling from base to base and trying to find accommodations in crowded quarters. She causes a rift with her husband when she has her father try to get him a permanent posting, but they are reconciled when she accepts the reality of wartime conditions.

IRISH EYES ARE SMILING

Produced by Damon Runyon
Directed by Gregory Ratoff
Screenplay by Earl Baldwin and John Tucker Battle, from a story by E. A. Ellington
Photographed in Technicolor by Harry Jackson
Musical direction by Alfred Newman and Charles Henderson
90 minutes

Cast: June Haver, Dick Haymes, Monty Woolley, Anthony Quinn, Beverly Whitney, Maxie Rosenbloom, Veda Ann Borg, Clarence Kolb, Leonard Warren, Blanche Thebom, Chick Chandler, Kenny Williams, Michael Dalmatoff

A pleasing but blarney account of the Irish-American songwriter Ernest R. Ball (Dick Haymes) and his rise to success in the years prior to the first World War. He arrives in New York and achieves success as a singer-pianist in saloons, falls in love with a show girl (June Haver), and steadily turns out a stream of sentimental songs about Ireland. The story is merely an excuse for a parade of songs and dances, all splendidly packaged in Technicolor decor, including some operatic

Lon McAllister and Jeanne Crain in *Home in Indiana*.

sequences involving Leonard Warren and Blanche Thebom, and some verbal wit by Monty Woolley as an impresario.

JANE EYRE

Produced by William Goetz
Directed by Robert Stevenson
Screenplay by Aldous Huxley, Robert Stevenson, and John Houseman, based on the book by Charlotte Brontë
Photographed by George Barnes
Music by Bernard Herrmann
96 minutes

Cast: Orson Welles, Joan Fontaine, Margaret O'Brien, Peggy Ann Garner, John Sutton, Sara Allgood, Henry Daniell, Agnes Moorehead, Aubrey Mather, Edith Barrett, Barbara Everest, Hilary Brooke, Ethel Griffies, Mae Marsh, Yorke Sherwood, John Abbott, Ronald Harris

A natural subject for filming, *Jane Eyre* is a darkly romantic Victorian melodrama about cruelty, madness, and love amid the brooding Yorkshire moors. This version benefited by the performance of Orson Welles as Edward Rochester, the troubled master of a great estate, and Joan Fontaine as the demure young lady who brings him peace and love. It also benefitted from stylish sets, strikingly photographed by George Barnes, and by a masterly score from Bernard Herrmann. The contributions of so many fine artists makes this a classic item of gothic cinema.

THE KEYS OF THE KINGDOM

Produced by Joseph L. Mankiewicz
Directed by John M. Stahl
Screenplay by Joseph L. Mankiewicz and Nunnally Johnson, from a novel by A. J. Cronin
Photographed by Arthur Miller
Music by Alfred Newman
137 minutes

Cast: Gregory Peck, Thomas Mitchell, Vincent Price, Rose Stradner, Roddy McDowall, Edmund Gwenn, Sir Cedric Hardwicke, Peggy Ann Garner, Anne Revere, Ruth Nelson, Benson Fong, Leonard Strong, Philip Ahn, Arthur Shields

Gregory Peck's first major film (following his debut in the war film *Days of Glory*) and a lengthy account of the career of a Scottish priest from his childhood and his many years in China to his return to Scotland as an elderly man. An orphan, he finds purpose in the church, although not a good student, and when assigned to a mission in China he finds the challenge of his life. With his Chinese wards he suffers all kinds of problems and privation, including civil war, but he sees his influence grow throughout the years. He finds it hard to accept retirement, but friendship with children in his Scottish village gives him another sense of purpose.

Fine acting and an intelligent script give *The Keys of the Kingdom* a lasting impact as a film that communicates the basics of Christianity.

LADIES OF WASHINGTON

Produced by William Girard
Directed by Louis King
Screenplay by Wanda Tuchock
Photographed by Charles Clarke
Music by Cyril Mockridge
61 minutes

Cast: Trudy Marshall, Ronald Graham, Anthony Quinn, Sheila Ryan, Robert Bailey, Beverly Whitney, Jackie Paley, Carleton Young, John Philiber, Robin Raymond, Doris Merrick, Barbara Booth

Melodrama in wartime, involving girls employed in government jobs and living together in crowded apartments. One of them (Sheila Ryan) is embittered over an unhappy love affair with a married executive and allows herself to become involved with an enemy agent (Anthony Quinn) who needs information on the man. The affair results in death and the girl ends up in an institution.

LAURA

Produced and directed by Otto Preminger
Screenplay by Jay Dratler, Samuel Hoffenstein, and Betty Reinhardt, based on the novel by Vera Caspary
Photographed by Joseph La Shelle
Music by David Raksin
88 minutes

Cast: Gene Tierney, Dana Andrews, Clifton Webb, Vincent Price, Judith Anderson, Dorothy Adams, James Flavin, Clyde Fillmore, Ralph Dunn, Grant Mitchell, Kathleen Howard

Laura remains one of the most stylish murder mysteries ever filmed. It established Otto Preminger as a director and introduced the grandly mannered Clifton Webb to the screen. In addition, it produced a music score by David Raksin that is a textbook example of the deft usage of music in filmmaking. Webb appears as a bitchy intellectual accused of the murder of the lovely girl of the title (Gene Tierney), whom he loves so much he will not accept losing her to another man. It evolves that Laura is not dead and that the body, with gunshot obliterated face, is that of a model. In the meantime a detective assigned to the case (Dana Andrews) has fallen in love with her, via a portrait, and continues the love when she turns out to be alive. With a fine script and sensitive performances, *Laura* holds her own at the top of this particular class of mystery melodrama.

Dick Haymes and June Haver in *Irish Eyes Are Smiling*.

Joan Fontaine and Orson Welles in *Jane Eyre*.

Thomas Mitchell and Gregory Peck in *The Keys of the Kingdom*.

Clifton Webb, Gene Tierney, and Dana Andrews in *Laura*.

John Hodiak and Tallulah Bankhead in *Lifeboat*.

LIFEBOAT

Produced by Kenneth Macgowan
Directed by Alfred Hitchcock
Screenplay by Jo Swerling, from a story by
  John Steinbeck
Photographed by Glen MacWilliams
Music by Hugo W. Friedhofer
Musical direction by Emil Newman
97 minutes

Cast: Tallulah Bankhead, William Bendix, Walter Slezak, Mary Anderson, John Hodiak, Henry Hull, Heather Angel, Hume Cronyn, Canada Lee

Eight people survive a sinking in the Atlantic, among them an elegant writer (Tallulah Bankhead), a tough seaman (John Hodiak), and a nurse (Mary Anderson). Also sunk is the German U-boat responsible for the sinking, and they pick up its one survivor (Walter Slezak), who turns out to be its captain. With none of them experienced in navigation they give the job to the German, but he is a dedicated Nazi and plans to get rid of some of them before navigating to a German supply ship. They get rid of him and try to make it by themselves. *Lifeboat* is remarkable for the degree of drama Alfred Hitchcock packs into the confined space of his story, which is set entirely in one small boat for the whole film.

THE LODGER

Produced by Robert Bassler
Directed by John Brahm
Screenplay by Barre Lyndon, based on the novel by Marie
  Belloc-Lowndes
Photographed by Lucien Ballard
Music by Hugo Friedhofer
84 minutes

Cast: Merle Oberon, George Sanders, Laird Cregar, Sir Cedric Hardwicke, Sara Allgood, Aubrey Mather, Queenie Leonard, Doris Lloyd, David Clyde, Helena Pickard, Lumsden Hare, Frederic Worlock, Olaf Hytten, Colin Campbell, Harold DeBecker

Marie Belloc-Lowndes' novel *The Lodger* won attention and popularity not only because it dealt with the hideous crimes of Jack the Ripper, but because it explored the psychology of crime. The film version follows the style of the novel, with a splendidly sullen and haunted portrayal of the mysterious gentleman of the title, who finds accommodations in the Whitechapel district of London in the late 1880's and roams the streets at night, killing women he deems unworthy. It is a film drenched with swirling fog and damp night air, and peopled with Hollywood's then extensive British colony. But it is the presence of Laird Cregar, a greatly talented but doomed actor which gives the film its major asset. He would die at the age of twenty-eight, as the result of crash-dieting, the same year *The Lodger* was released.

Laird Cregar in *The Lodger.*

PIN-UP GIRL

Produced by William Le Baron
Directed by Bruce Humberstone
Screenplay by Robert Ellis, Helen Logan, and Earl Baldwin, from a story by Libbie Block
Photographed in Technicolor by Ernest Palmer
Songs by Mack Gordon and James Monaco
Musical direction by Emil Newman and Charles
  Henderson
83 minutes

Cast: Betty Grable, John Harvey, Martha Raye, Joe E. Brown, Eugene Pallette, Skating Vanities, Dorothea Kent, Dave Willock, Condos Brothers, Charles Spivak and his Orchestra, Robert Homans

With Betty Grable the No. 1 Pin-Up Girl of World War II servicemen, it was logical to make a musical with this title. What little story there is concerns Grable as a secretary who visits a USO canteen and falls for a sailor (John Harvey). In order to be near him on other occasions she pretends to be a Broadway star, which causes the USO people to ask her to perform. From that comes real stardom. Half the running time of the film is filled with songs and dances, highlighted by Grable's Apache number with choreographer Hermes Pan, and her leading sixty girls in a military drill routine of "I'll Be Marching to a Love Song."

THE PURPLE HEART

Produced by Darryl F. Zanuck
Directed by Lewis Milestone
Screenplay by Jerry Cady, from a story by Melville Crossman
Photographed by Arthur Miller
Music by Alfred Newman
99 minutes

Cast: Dana Andrews, Richard Conte, Farley Granger, Kevin O'Shea, Donald Barry, Trudy Mrashall, Sam Levene, Charles Russell, John Craven, Tala Birell, Richard Loo, Peter Chong, Gregory Gaye, Torben Meyer

A harrowing wartime story of a group of American airmen tried by the Japanese as war criminals and executed. The men survive being shot down while making a bombing raid over Japan and are then given a military trial, the object of which is to reveal them as barbarians and also to squeeze information from them about their bases. Eight airmen, led by a captain (Dana Andrews), individually undergo torture, but none breaks or cooperates. One of the judges (Richard Loo) commits suicide in court because of his failure to break the Americans, who march to their execution with a degree of pride. Clearly wartime propaganda, but well and convincingly produced.

ROGER TOUHY—GANGSTER

Produced by Lee Marcus
Directed by Robert Florey
Screenplay by Crane Wilbur and Jerry Cady, from a story by Crane Wilbur
Photographed by Glen MacWilliams
Music by Hugo W. Friedhofer
Musical direction by Emil Newman
73 minutes

Cast: Preston Foster, Victor McLaglen, Lois Andrews, Kent Taylor, Anthony Quinn, William Post, Jr., Henry Morgan, Matt Briggs, Moroni Olsen, Reed Hadley, Trudy Marshall, John Archer, Frank Jenks

A gangster story based on facts and made with FBI cooperation, with scenes filmed at the Illinois State Penitentiary. The story is that of Roger Touhy (Preston Foster), one of Al Capone's chief associates, and his years as a thief, extortionist, and kidnapper in Chicago. The film is highlighted by an excitingly staged prison break-out and it ends with Touhy and his men being tracked down by the FBI and sentenced to life terms.

SOMETHING FOR THE BOYS

Produced by Irving Starr
Directed by Lewis Seiler
Screenplay by Robert Ellis, Helen Logan, and Frank Gabrielson, based on a musical comedy by Herbert and Dorothy Fields
Songs by Cole Porter
Photographed in Technicolor by Ernest Palmer
Musical direction by Emil Newman and Charles Henderson
87 minutes

Cast: Carmen Miranda, Michael O'Shea, Vivian Blaine, Phil Silvers, Sheila Ryan, Perry Como, Glenn Langan, Roger Clark, Cara Williams, Thurston Hall, Clarence Kolb, Paul Hurst, Andrew Tombes

Loosely based on the Cole Porter Broadway musical— but with a couple of added new songs by Jimmy McHugh and Harold Adamson—it tells of three cousins (Carmen Miranda, Vivian Blaine, and Michael O'Shea) who turn a bankrupt plantation, which they have inherited, into a home for the wives of servicemen. In order to run the place, they devise a theatrical production on the grounds, which allows for plenty of music from the cast—including young Perry Como in his film debut.

THE SULLIVANS

Produced by Sam Jaffe
Directed by Lloyd Bacon
Screenplay by Mary C. McCall, Jr., from a story by Edward Doherty and Jules Schermer
Photographed by Lucien Andriot
Music by Cyril J. Mockridge
Musical direction by Alfred Newman
112 minutes

Cast: Thomas Mitchell, Anne Baxter, Selena Royle, Edward Ryan, Trudy Marshall, John Campbell, James Cardwell, John Alvin, George Offerman, Jr., Roy Roberts, Ward Bond, Mary McCarty, Bobby Driscoll

The true story of five brothers from the small town of Waterloo, Iowa, who were lost in the sinking of the cruiser *Juneau* off Guadalcanal. The film is largely a flashback and shows the lives of the brothers, with their father (Thomas Mitchell) and mother (Selena Royle). The romance and marriage of the youngest (Edward Ryan) is traced and his widow (Anne Baxter) joins the parents when they are visited by a naval officer with the tragic news. The film is sentimental but honest and it had a bearing on the Navy's decision to never again allow all the members of one family to serve on the same vessel.

SUNDAY DINNER FOR A SOLDIER

Produced by Walter Morosco
Directed by Lloyd Bacon

Screenplay by Wanda Tuchock and Melvin Levy, from a story by Martha Cheavens
Photographed by Joe MacDonald
Music by Alfred Newman
87 minutes

Cast: Anne Baxter, John Hodiak, Charles Winninger, Anne Revere, Connie Marshall, Chill Wills, Robert Bailey, Bobby Driscoll, Jane Darwell, Billy Cummings, Marietta Canty, Barbara Sears

A charming story about a family living on a houseboat along the Florida shore. Grandfather (Charles Winninger) is an old seaman and with him are four children, the eldest of whom (Anne Baxter) leads them in their plan to entertain a serviceman with a dinner and a family evening. They have little success in getting one until a soldier (John Hodiak) ambles along the beach and he accepts their invitation. In two hours his loneliness is dispelled and he and the elder daughter start to fall in love. Thus his life is changed by their act of hospitality. A warm and genial picture of a nice family.

SWEET AND LOW-DOWN

Produced by William Le Baron
Directed by Archie Mayo
Screenplay by Richard English, from a story by Richard English and Edward Haldeman
Photographed by Lucien Ballard
Songs by Mack Gordon and James Monaco
Musical direction by Emil Newman and Charles Henderson
76 minutes

Cast: Benny Goodman and his band, Linda Darnell, Lynn Bari, Jack Oakie, James Cardwell, Allyn Joslyn, John Campbell, Roy Benson, Dickie Moore, Buddy Swan, Beverly Hudson, Dorothy Vaughan

Benny Goodman (playing himself) and his orchestra perform for a settlement house in Chicago and pick up a talented trombone player (James Cardwell). Goodman promotes the young man, which results in a swelled head and the attentions of a society girl (Linda Darnell), who persuades an agent (Allyn Joslyn) to set the boy up with his own band at a ballroom. He flops and returns to his factory job in Chicago, until Goodman comes to town again and gives him another chance. The society girl realizes she was wrong and accepts him as a bandsman. The film's real value is Goodman, and it comes alive whenever he and his musicians play.

TAKE IT OR LEAVE IT

Produced by Bryan Foy
Directed by Benjamin Stoloff
Screenplay by Harold Buchman, Snag Werris, and Mac Benoff

Photographed by Joseph La Shelle
Musical direction by Emil Newman
68 minutes

Cast: Phil Baker, Phil Silvers, Edward Ryan, Marjorie Massow, Stanley Prager, Roy Gordon, Nana Bryant, Carleton Young, Ann Corcoran, Nella Walker, Renie Riano, Frank Jenks

A movie quiz, based upon Phil Baker's long-running radio quiz series, and using clips from many Fox films as items for participants to guess. Baker plays himself and the film offers the story of a sailor (Edward Ryan) entering the quiz in order to raise money for his expectant wife (Majorie Massow). The sailor wins, with clips involving scenes from the films of Shirley Temple, Sonja Henie, Jack Oakie, the Ritz Brothers, Alice Faye, Al Jolson, and others.

TAMPICO

Produced by Robert Bassler
Directed by Lothar Mendes
Screenplay by Kenneth Gamet, Fred Niblo, Jr., and Richard Macaulay, from a story by Ladislas Fodor
Photographed by Charles Clarke
Music by David Raksin
Musical direction by Emil Newman
75 minutes

Cast: Edward G. Robinson, Lynn Bari, Victor McLaglen, Robert Bailey, Marc Lawrence, E. J. Ballantine, Mona Maris, Tonio Selwart, Carl Ekberg, Roy Roberts, George Sorel, Charles Lang, Ralph Byrd, Louis Hart

A nautical melodrama about an oil tanker captain (Edward G. Robinson) who marries a girl (Lynn Bari) he rescues after her ship has been sunk by a U-boat. The captain's ship is sunk and the girl comes under suspicion because she has no identification. The captain sets out to clear her name and finds his first mate (Victor McLaglen) is a German agent. A fairly exciting yarn, with many scenes filmed in the port of Tampico, Mexico.

UNCENSORED

Produced by Edward Black
Directed by Anthony Asquith
Screenplay by Rodney Ackland and Terence Rattigan, from a story by Wolfgang Wilhelm, based on a book by Oscar E. Millard
Photographed by Arthur Crabtree
Musical direction by Louis Levy
85 minutes

Cast: Eric Portman, Phyllis Calvert, Griffith Jones, Raymond Lovell, Peter Glenville, Frederick Culley

A story of the Belgian underground and the publication of an anti-Nazi newspaper in Brussels. A cafe entertainer (Eric Portman) is the publisher, although

Betty Grable in *Pin Up Girl*.

John Hodiak and Anne Baxter in *Sunday Dinner for a Soldier*.

Richard Loo and Dana Andrews in *The Purple Heart*.

he is thought to be a collaborator, and one of the chief writers (Griffith Jones) is actually employed by the Germans. The paper almost goes under, but the publisher manages to defeat the Nazis. A conventional war story given some distinction by the tight direction of Anthony Asquith.

WILSON

Produced by Darryl F. Zanuck
Directed by Henry King
Screenplay by Lamar Trotti
Photographed in Technicolor by Leon Shamroy
Music by Alfred Newman
154 minutes

Cast: Alexander Knox, Charles Coburn, Geraldine Fitzgerald, Thomas Mitchell, Ruth Nelson, Sir Cedric Hardwicke, Vincent Price, William Eythe, Mary Anderson, Ruth Ford, Sidney Blackmer, Madeleine Forbes, Stanley Ridges, Eddie Foy, Jr.

The most ambitious of Darryl Zanuck's biographical pictures and a commendable account of the presidency of Woodrow Wilson, played by Alexander Knox. The film begins with Wilson as the president of Princeton University and the author of books on the democratic process. He accepts a nomination as governor of New Jersey, the success of which leads to his successfully being nominated for the Presidency. His vow to keep America out of the first World War becomes impossible in his second term, and his postwar plan for a League of Nations is doomed to eventual failure by the refusal of Congress to grant American participation. In his later years Wilson meets more disappointment when his warnings of the coming second war are largely ignored. *Wilson* is a superb, albeit idealistic, political film, with top-notch production values and a fine performance from Knox as the American champion of humanity.

WING AND A PRAYER

Produced by William A. Bacher and Walter Morosco
Directed by Henry Hathaway
Screenplay by Jerome Cady, from a story by Jerome Cady
Photographed by Glen MacWilliams
Music by Hugo W. Friedhofer
Musical direction by Emil Newman
98 minutes

Cast: Don Ameche, Dana Andrews, William Eythe, Richard Jaeckel, Charles Bickford, Sir Cedric Hardwicke, Kevin O'Shea, Henry Morgan, Richard Crane, Glenn Langan, Benny McEvoy, Robert Bailey

The story of an aircraft carrier and her involvement in the Pacific campaigns against the Japanese. Director Henry Hathaway spent several weeks aboard a carrier prior to making the film and picked up footage of actual combat and operational activities. The story concerns a new group of pilots and how they experience defeats and losses before victory. Don Ameche is the tough flight officer whose unwavering control of his pilots brings resentment before it brings understanding and respect. An excellent war film.

WINGED VICTORY

Produced by Darryl F. Zanuck
Directed by George Cukor
Screenplay by Moss Hart, from a play by Moss Hart
Photographed by Glen MacWilliams
Music by Sgt. David Rose
130 minutes

Cast: Pvt. Lon McCallister, Jeanne Crain, Sgt. Edmond O'Brien, Jane Ball, Sgt. Mark Daniels, Jo-Carroll Dennison, Cpl. Don Taylor, Judy Holliday, Cpl. Lee Cobb, T/Sgt. Peter Lind Hayes, Cpl. Red Buttons, Cpl. Barry Nelson, Sgt. Rune Hultman

Moss Hart's stage play is here transferred to the screen with his own scenario and expert direction from George Cukor. Many actors in the film were actually in the services at the time and were seconded from duty. The story concerns a number of young men, with Lon McAllister as the central figure, who are called in to the Air Force and who undergo training as pilots, navigators, bombardiers, etc., with incidents about their backgrounds, their families, and girl friends. The film also follows the men to their assignments in the Pacific war, with some comedy and tragedy and action. *Winged Victory* holds its value as a broad yet finely detailed picture of the second World War.

20TH CENTURY-FOX ACADEMY AWARDS FOR 1944

DARRYL F. ZANUCK: Irving G. Thalberg Award for outstanding achievement in motion picture production.

LAMAR TROTTI: Best original screenplay for *Wilson*.

WIARD IHNEN: Art direction, color, for *Wilson*.

JOSEPH LA SHELLE: Cinematography, black and white, for *Laura*.

LEON SHAMROY: Cinematography, color, for *Wilson*.

E. H. HANSEN: Sound recording for *Wilson*.

BARBARA McLEAN: Film editing for *Wilson*.

THOMAS LITTLE: Set decoration, color, for *Wilson*.

The Fighting Lady: Special award for distinctive achievement in documentaries.

GROVER LAUBE and 20TH CENTURY-FOX CAMERA DEPT.: Honorable mention for technical developments.

Thomas Mitchell, Alexander Knox, and Geraldine Fitzgerald in *Wilson*.

Mark Daniels, Edmund O'Brien, and Lon McAllister in *Winged Victory*.

1945

AND THEN THERE WERE NONE

Produced by Harry M. Popkin
Directed by René Clair
Screenplay by Dudley Nichols, from a story by Agatha Christie
Photographed by Lucien Andriot
97 minutes

Cast: Barry Fitzgerald, Walter Huston, Louis Hayward, Roland Young, June Duprez, Sir C. Aubrey Smith, Judith Anderson, Mischa Auer, Richard Haydn, Queenie Leonard, Harry Thurston

Agatha Christie's classic murder mystery is here given added dimensions of artistry through the clever direction of René Clair, full of moods and shaded photography. The story concerns ten people who are invited to a house party on an island off the coast of Cornwall. They are stranded for the weekend after finding that their host is unknown to any of them. One by one they fall victim to a murderer with a maniacal design for justice. Only three survive, when the murderer unmasks himself and commits suicide with the knowledge that he has been outwitted. Barry Fitzgerald heads the cast as a fanatical judge, and Louis Hayward and June Duprez play the lovers—who survive, of course.

A BELL FOR ADANO

Produced by Louis D. Lighton and Lamar Trotti
Directed by Henry King
Screenplay by Lamar Trotti and Norman Reilly Raine, from a novel by John Hersey
Photographed by Joseph La Shelle
Music by Alfred Newman
104 minutes

Cast: John Hodiak, Gene Tierney, William Bendix, Glenn Langan, Richard Conte, Stanley Prager, Henry Morgan, Montague Banks, Reed Hadley, Roy Roberts, Hugo Haas, Marcel Daltro, Fortunio Bonanova, Henry Armetta

Adano is a little Italian town and the time is the end of the second World War, with the U.S. Army conducting its civil administration program in liberated areas. An army major (John Hodiak) is put in charge of the town and all its problems, including hunger and red tape. He falls in love with a beautiful local girl (Gene Tierney) and is taken advantage of by certain citizens, but he eventually brings order back to the town. He also retrieves the town bell, which was taken by the Germans and around which the life of the town revolves. The film is a touching account of difficult times.

THE BULLFIGHTERS

Produced by William Girard
Directed by Malcolm St. Clair
Screenplay by W. Scott Darling
Photographed by Norbert Brodine
Music by David Buttolph
61 minutes

Cast: Stan Laurel, Oliver Hardy, Margo Woode, Richard Lane, Carol Andrews, Diosa Costello, Frank McCown, Ralph Sanford, Irving Gump, Ed Gargan, Lorraine De Wood, Emmett Vogan, Rober Neury, Gus Glassmire, Rafael Storm, Jay Novello, Guy Zanetto

Laurel and Hardy blunder their way around Mexico as private detectives sent from the States in search of a lady criminal. The best part of the film is the sequence in which Hardy is inveigled by a bullfight manager (Richard Lane) into taking the place of a look-alike matador.

CAPTAIN EDDIE

Produced by Winfield R. Sheehan
Directed by Lloyd Bacon
Screenplay by John Tucker Battle
Photographed by Joe MacDonald
Musical score by Cyril J. Mockridge
Musical direction by Emil Newman
107 minutes

Cast: Fred MacMurray, Lynn Bari, Charles Bickford, Thomas Mitchell, Lloyd Nolan, James Gleason, Mary Phillips, Darryl Hickman, Spring Byington, Richard Conte, Charles Russell, Richard Crane, Stanley Ridges, Clem Bevans, Grady Sutton, Chick Chandler

The story of Eddie Rickenbacker (Fred MacMurray), America's leading aviator of the first World War, told in flashback form as he and a group of survivors from an airplane crash at sea drift in a rubber raft and reminisce. Rickenbacker's career is clearly covered from his early days as a pioneer, his involvement in war, his marriage, and his attempts to make aviation a respectable and progressive industry. The film ends with his rescue near exhaustion. It presents an interesting portrait of an extraordinary man.

THE CARIBBEAN MYSTERY

Produced by William Girard
Directed by Robert Webb
Screenplay by Jack Andrews and Leonard Praskins, from the novel by John W. Vandercook
Photographed by Clyde De Vinna
Music by David Buttolph
Musical direction by Emil Newman
65 minutes

Cast: James Dunn, Sheila Ryan, Edward Ryan, Jackie Paley, Reed Hadley, Roy Roberts, Richard Shaw, Daral Hudson, William Forrest, Roy Gordon, Virginia Walker, Lal Chand Mehra, Katherine Connors, Robert Filmer, Lucien Littlefield

A Brooklyn detective (James Dunn) arrives on a Caribbean island in search of a murderer and wades his way through quicksands, swamps, alligators, corpses, and clues before nabbing the villain (Roy Roberts).

CIRCUMSTANTIAL EVIDENCE

Produced by William Girard
Directed by John Larkin
Screenplay by Robert Metzler, based on a story by Nat Ferber and Sam Duncan
Photographed by Harry Jackson
Music by David Buttolph
Musical direction by Emil Newman
68 minutes

Cast: Michael O'Shea, Lloyd Nolan, Trudy Marshall, Billy Cummings, Ruth Ford, Reed Hadley, Roy Roberts, Scotty Beckett, Leon Tyler, Marvin Davis, Harry McKim, Hugh McGuire, Byron Foulger, William Frambes

A murder mystery, with much of the action played in courts and in prisons, and with the accent on the fallibility of witnesses. A violent-tempered man (Michael O'Shea) kills a grocer in a fight when the man attacks his son for chopping up a packing box with an axe. Witnesses swear that the grocer was killed with the axe, but it is proven that such was not the case.

COLONEL EFFINGHAM'S RAID

Produced by Lamar Trotti
Directed by Irving Pichel

Louis Hayward, Walter Huston, and Roland Young in *And Then There Were None.*

Gene Tierney and John Hodiak in *A Bell for Adano.*

Fred MacMurray as *Captain Eddie.*

Betty Grable in *Diamond Horseshoe.*

Screenplay by Kathryn Scola, based on a novel by Berry Fleming
Photographed by Edward Cronjager
Music by Cyril J. Mockridge
Musical direction by Emil Newman
70 minutes

Cast: Charles Coburn, Joan Bennett, William Eythe, Allyn Joslyn, Elizabeth Patterson, Frank Craven, Donald Meek, Thurston Hall, Cora Witherspoon, Emory Parnell, Henry Armetta, Michael Dunne, Roy Roberts, Michael Dunne

A retired army colonel (Charles Coburn) returns to the scene of his young years in Fredericksville, Georgia, and is disturbed by the lack of civic pride. He writes a newspaper column and attacks those who would do away with traditions, particularly those moving to tear down the old city hall and those who would rename Confederate Square after a politician. The film has charm and humor, and rests largely on the talents of the grandly elegant Coburn.

DIAMOND HORSESHOE

Produced by William Perlberg
Directed by George Seaton
Screenplay by George Seaton, suggested by a play by John Kenyon Nicholson
Photographed in Technicolor by Ernest Palmer
Songs by Harry Warren and Mack Gordon
Musical direction by Alfred Newman and Charles Henderson
106 minutes

Cast: Betty Grable, Dick Haymes, Phil Silvers, William Gaxton, Beatrice Kay, Carmen Cavallaro, Willie Solar, Margaret Dumont, Roy Benson, George Melford, Hal K. Dawson, Kenny Williams, Reed Hadley, Eddie Acuff, Edward Gargan

George Seaton's first assignment as a director, and working from his own screenplay. A bright and amusing

musical, supposedly set in Billy Rose's New York night club, with William Gaxton as the owner-MC of the club and Betty Grable as its leading entertainer. The owner's medical student son (Dick Haymes) falls in love with Betty and opts for a life in show business—against the wishes of his father. She gets blamed for the defection, but it's Betty who puts him back on the road to becoming a doctor. The film is the birth-place of the classic song "The More I See You," sung and made famous by Haymes, as well as other Harry Warren–Mack Gordon standards such as "In Aca-pulco," and "I Wish I Knew." For allowing Fox to use the name of his club for a fee of $76,000—the studio also found itself legally committed to releasing the film as *Billy Rose's Diamond Horseshoe.*

DOLL FACE

Produced by Bryan Foy
Directed by Lewis Seiler
Screenplay by Leonard Praskins, from a play by Louise Hovick
Photographed by Joseph La Shelle
Songs by Jimmy McHugh and Harold Adamson
Musical direction by Emil Newman
81 minutes

Cast: Vivian Blaine, Dennis O'Keefe, Perry Como, Carmen Miranda, Martha Stewart, Michael Dunne, Reed Hadley, Stanley Prager, Charles Tannen, George E. Stone, Frank Orth

A backstage musical, based on a play by Louise (Gypsy Rose Lee) Hovick and full of her observations about life in burlesque. A star stripper (Vivian Blaine) under-goes refining when her boyfriend-boss (Dennis O'Keefe) decides she needs educating in order to make the grade in the legitimate theatre. Among other things he hires a writer (Michael Dunne) to ghost a book for her. The slight plot is greatly aided by a half dozen songs written by Jimmy McHugh, and performed by Blaine, Perry Como, and Carmen Miranda.

THE DOLLY SISTERS

Produced by George Jessel
Directed by Irving Cummings
Screenplay by John Larkin and Marian Spitzer
Photographed in Technicolor by Ernest Palmer
Songs by Mack Gordon and James Monaco
Musical direction by Alfred Newman
114 minutes

Cast: Betty Grable, John Payne, June Haver, S. Z. Sakall, Reginald Gardiner, Frank Latimore, Trudy Marshall, Gene Sheldon, Sig Rumann, Colette Lyons, Evan Thomas, Donna Jo Gribble, Robert Middlemass

A lavish account of the careers of the fabled musical comedy stars Jenny and Rosie Dolly, played by Betty

Grable and June Haver. The story starts in New York in 1904 with the young girls performing in the care of their uncle (S. Z. Sakall) and progressing from small theatres to the major stages of Broadway, London, and Paris. Eventually they become the toast of Europe and America. The film contains a large amount of music, both of the period and several new songs by Mack Gordon and James Monaco, with ample opportunity to display the talents of Grable and Haver.

DON JUAN QUILLIGAN

Produced by William Le Baron
Directed by Frank Tuttle
Screenplay by Arthur Kober and Frank Gabrielson, from a story by Herbert Clyde Lewis
Photographed by Norbert Brodine
Music by David Raksin
Musical direction by Emil Newman
75 minutes

Cast: William Bendix, Joan Blondell, Phil Silvers, Mary Treen, Anne Revere, B. S. Pully, John Russell, Veda Ann Borg, Thurston Hall, Cara Williams, Richard Gaines, Hobart Cavanaugh, Rene Carson, George MacReady

A broad comedy about a Hudson River barge captain (William Bendix) with overly romantic notions about women, due to his great love for his mother. This leads him to become engaged to two girls simultaneously, one in Brooklyn (Joan Blondell) and one in Utica (Mary Treen). He marries both of them and his friend (Phil Silvers) invents a murder, so that the naive bigamist can be supposedly sentenced and sent away to prison, and thus escape his married life. Runyon-esque nonsense but a good showcase for Bendix.

FALLEN ANGEL

Produced by Otto Preminger
Directed by Otto Preminger
Screenplay by Harry Kleiner, from a novel by Matty Holland
Photographed by Joseph La Shelle
Song by David Raksin and Kermit Goell
Music by David Raksin
Musical direction by Emil Newman
98 minutes

Cast: Alice Faye, Dana Andrews, Linda Darnell, Charles Bickford, Anne Revere, Bruce Cabot, John Carradine, Percy Kilbride, Olin Howlin, Hal Taliaferro, Mira McKinney, Jimmy Conlin, Gus Glassmire, Leila McIntyre

A cynical press agent (Dana Andrews) marries a wealthy girl (Alice Faye) in order to get her money. He then hopes to divorce her and marry a sultry waitress (Linda Darnell) with whom he has become smitten. When the waitress is murdered, the suspicion falls on the press agent, but it turns out that she was killed by another lover, a retired policeman (Charles Bickford). The agent returns to his loving wife and a better sense of values. *Fallen Angel,* despite some stylish direction by Preminger, fails to convince fully. It offers Alice Faye in a dramatic role and one which turned out to be her last film before her retirement.

HANGOVER SQUARE

Produced by Robert Bassler
Directed by John Brahm
Screenplay by Barre Lyndon, based on a novel by Patrick Hamilton
Photographed by Joseph La Shelle
Music by Bernard Herrmann
78 minutes

Cast: Laird Cregar, Linda Darnell, George Sanders, Glenn Langan, Faye Marlowe, Alan Napier, Fredric Worlock, J. W. Austin, Leyland Hodgson, Clifford Brooke, John Goldsworthy, Michael Dyne

A juicy gothic melodrama about a madman (Laird Cregar) in Victorian London, who is also a composer and pianist. He lapses into manic depressions whenever he hears violently discordant noises and his pent-up hatreds lead to murder. He stabs an antique dealer who treats him unfairly and he strangles a woman who hires him to write music and then rejects him. A psychologist (George Sanders) befriends him and comes to understand his malady, as does the sad genius himself. He dies in a fire as he sits at the piano playing his concerto. *Hangover Square* is memorable for its fine score by Bernard Herrmann, who later adapted the final sequence into a one-movement concerto, and for the impressive performance of Laird Cregar, whose last screen appearance this is. He died shortly after the filming at the age of twenty-eight.

THE HOUSE ON 92nd STREET

Produced by Louis de Rochemont
Directed by Henry Hathaway
Screenplay by Barre Lyndon, Charles G. Booth, and John Monks, Jr., from a story by Charles G. Booth
Photographed by Norbert Brodine
Music by David Buttolph
Musical direction by Emil Newman
89 minutes

Cast: William Eythe, Lloyd Nolan, Signe Hasso, Gene Lockhart, Leo G. Carroll, Lydia St. Clair, William Post, Jr., Harry Bellaver, Bruno Wick, Harro Meller, Charles Wagenheim, Alfred Linder, Edwin Jerome, Elizabeth Neumann, Salo Douday

Louis de Rochemont, the skilled documentarist who had excelled with his *March of Time* series, brought the documentary style to Hollywood with *The House on 92nd Street,* an espionage story based on fact and filmed with the cooperation of the FBI. It deals with the pursuit and capture of a German spy ring in

161

Washington, a ring attempting to gain U.S. atomic program secrets. William Eythe plays a federal undercover man posing as a member of the ring led by Signe Hasso, and Lloyd Nolan is the chief of the FBI unit involved. Director Hathaway skillfully matches his live action with actual FBI footage and gives an exciting account of this particular operation. The film proved to be a pioneer in bringing documentary techniques to films dealing with crime and espionage.

JUNIOR MISS

Produced by William Perlberg
Directed by George Seaton
Screenplay by George Seaton, from the play by Jerome Chodorov and Joseph Fields, based on stories by Sally Benson
Photographed by Charles Clarke
Music by David Buttolph
Musical direction by Emil Newman
94 minutes

Cast: Peggy Ann Garner, Allyn Joslyn, Michael Dunne, Faye Marlowe, Mona Freeman, Sylvia Field, Barbara Whiting, Stanley Prager, John Alexander, Connie Gilchrist, Scotty Beckett, Alan Edwards, Dorothy Christy, William Franbes, Ray Klinge

George Seaton's amusing scripting and directing of the Broadway play, here starring Peggy Ann Garner in the title role of the ebullient teenager whose enthusiastic meddlings in the lives of her family causes consternation as well as humor. Among other things she is instrumental in marrying off her uncle (Michael Dunne) to the daughter (Faye Marlowe) of her father's boss, which almost costs her father (Allyn Joslyn) his job. The film is an appealing and understanding portrait of a young girl going through the "awkward" age and deriving humor along the way.

LEAVE HER TO HEAVEN

Produced by William A. Bacher
Directed by John M. Stahl
Screenplay by Jo Swerling, from a novel by Ben Ames Williams
Photographed in Technicolor by Leon Shamroy
Music by Alfred Newman
111 minutes

Cast: Gene Tierney, Cornel Wilde, Jeanne Crain, Vincent Price, Mary Philips, Ray Collins, Gene Lockhart, Darryl Hickman, Reed Hadley, Chill Wills, Paul Everton, Olive Blakeney, Addison Richards, Harry Depp, Grant Mitchell, Milton Parsons

The portrait of a villainess (Gene Tierney), a beautiful girl who murders in order to keep the man (Cornel Wilde) she loves. She is selfish and jealous and wants to share no other life with her husband. She allows his crippled brother (Darryl Hickman) to drown and deliberately causes her own miscarriage so she will not have to share his love with a child. When she finally realizes she has lost him, she commits suicide and makes it seem that her sister (Jeanne Crain) murdered her. But evidence proves otherwise and the sister marries the husband. Juicy melodrama, but well played and made vivid with colorful locations in Arizona, Georgia, and Maine.

MOLLY AND ME

Produced by Robert Bassler
Directed by Lewis Seiler
Screenplay by Leonard Praskins, from a novel by Frances Marion
Photographed by Charles Clarke
Music by Cyril J. Mockridge
Musical direction by Emil Newman
77 minutes

Cast: Gracie Fields, Monty Woolley, Roddy McDowall, Reginald Gardiner, Natalie Schafer, Edith Barrett, Clifford Brooke, Aminta Dyne, Queenie Leonard, Doris Lloyd, Patrick O'Moore, Lewis L. Russell

A group of out-of-work English entertainers, led by a feisty singer (Gracie Fields), take up domestic positions in the home of a grumpy old gentleman (Monty Woolley) and change his life. They bring music and laughter to the house, they reconcile him with his son (Roddy McDowall), save him from the schemes of his ex-wife (Doris Lloyd), and persuade him to pick up his career in politics. The film is a genial comedy, allowing Woolley to be elegantly caustic and Fields to charm with her songs and folksy personality.

NOB HILL

Produced by Andre Daven
Directed by Henry Hathaway
Screenplay by Wanda Tuchock and Norman Reilly Raine, from a story by Eleanore Griffin
Photographed in Technicolor by Edward Cronjager
Songs by Jimmy McHugh and Harold Adamson
Musical direction by Emil Newman and Charles Henderson
95 minutes

Cast: George Raft, Joan Bennett, Vivian Blaine, Peggy Ann Garner, Alan Reed, B. S. Pully, Emil Coleman, Edgar Barrier, George Anderson, Joe Smith and Charles Dale, Don Costello, Joseph J. Greene, J. Farrell McDonald, Three Swifts, William Haade

A colorful musical, set in the San Francisco of the turn-of-the-century, and dealing with a tough Barbary Coast saloon owner (George Raft) who wins the love of a society girl (Joan Bennett) and tries to live in her upper-crust milieu. But he finds it the wrong setting and returns to his own lively neighborhood and the cabaret singer (Vivian Blaine) who has loved him all along. A slight yarn, but well staged and helped by a large amount of music, both period pieces and new songs by Jimmy HcHugh and Harold Adamson.

Betty Grable and June Haver as *The Dolly Sisters*.

Dana Andrews and Alice Faye in *Fallen Angel*.

Gene Tierney and Cornel Wilde in *Leave Her to Heaven*.

Laird Cregar and Linda Darnell in *Hangover Square*.

George Raft and Joan Bennett in *Nob Hill*.

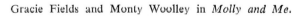

Gracie Fields and Monty Woolley in *Molly and Me*.

A ROYAL SCANDAL

Produced by Ernst Lubitsch
Directed by Otto Preminger
Screenplay by Edwin Justus Mayer, based on a play by
    Lajos Biro and Melchior Lengyel
Photographed by Arthur Miller
Musical score by Alfred Newman
94 minutes

Cast: Tallulah Bankhead, Charles Coburn, Anne Baxter,
William Eythe, Vincent Price, Mischa Auer, Sig Ruman,
Vladmir Sokoloff, Mikhail Rasumny, Grady Sutton, Don
Douglas, Egon Brecher

Russia's Catherine the Great (Tullalah Bankhead),
ever amorous, takes a fancy to a young officer (William
Eythe) whom she pampers and promotes. But he turns
out to be the leader of a revolution against her,
so she orders his execution. However, she lets him off
when she finds he is engaged to her faithful lady-in-
waiting (Anne Baxter). The film is really a showcase
for the florid acting of Bankhead, but also gives opportunities to Charles Coburn as the royal chancellor
and Vincent Price as the French ambassador who is
seduced by Catherine. The film was to have been directed by Lubitsch, but he withdrew because of illness
and assigned Preminger to do it. Good as it is, this
stylish material would have been even better with the
famed Lubitsch touch.

THE SPIDER

Produced by Ben Silvey
Directed by Robert Webb
Screenplay by Jo Elsinger and W. Scott Darling, based
    on a play by Charles Fulton Oursler and Lowell Bren-
    tano
Photographed by Glen MacWilliams
Music by David Buttolph
Musical direction by Emil Newman
62 minutes

Cast: Richard Conte, Faye Marlowe, Kurt Kreuger, John
Harvey, Martin Kosleck, Mantan Moreland, Walter Sande,
Cara Williams, Charles Tannen, Margaret Brayton, Harry
Seymour, Ann Savage, Jean Del Val

A murder mystery set in New Orleans' French Quarter,
with Richard Conte as a tough private detective, hired
by a girl (Faye Marlowe) who does a mind reading act
at a carnival and who fears for her life. Several people
are murdered before the detective nails the killer.

STATE FAIR

Produced by William Perlberg
Directed by Walter Lang
Screenplay by Oscar Hammerstein II, based on the novel
    by Phil Stong
Photographed in Technicolor by Leon Shamroy
Songs by Richard Rodgers and Oscar Hammerstein II

Anne Baxter and Tallulah Bankhead in *A Royal Scandal.*

Musical direction by Alfred Newman and Charles
    Henderson
100 minutes

Cast: Jeanne Crain, Dana Andrews, Dick Haymes, Vivian
Blaine, Charles Winninger, Fay Bainter, Donald Meek,
Frank McHugh, Percy Kilbride, Henry Morgan, Jane
Nigh, William Marshall, Phil Brown, Paul Burns, Tom
Fadden, William Frambes

With their success on Broadway with *Oklahoma* and
Carousel, Richard Rodgers and Oscar Hammerstein II
were a natural choice for this musical version of classic
Americana, first filmed a dozen years previously with
Will Rogers. Hammerstein agreed to write the screen-
play, which with his lyrics and Rodgers' music elevated
State Fair to great popularity. Set in Iowa in the sum-
mertime, the story tells of the Frake family and their
adventures at the state fair, with father (Charles
Winninger) winning a prize for his hog, mother (Fay
Bainter) winning one for her cooking, and their chil-
dren (Jeanne Crain and Dick Haymes) finding ro-
mance, respectively, in the form of a newspaperman
(Dana Andrews) and a dance-band singer (Vivian
Blaine). "It Might As Well Be Spring" won the
Oscar as best original song of the year.

THUNDERHEAD, SON OF FLICKA

Produced by Robert Bassler
Directed by Louis King
Screenplay by Dwight Cummins and Dorothy Yost, based
    on a novel by Mary O'Hara
Photographed in Technicolor by Charles Drake
Music by Cyril J. Mockridge
Musical direction by Emil Newman
77 minutes

Cast: Roddy McDowall, Preston Foster, Rita Johnson,
James Bell, Diana Hale, Carleton Young, Ralph Sanford,
Robert Filmer, Alan Bridge

Jeanne Crain and Dana Andrews in *State Fair*.

A sequel to the greatly successful *My Friend Flicka*, with most of the same cast. The horse of the title is a white colt trained by the son (Roddy McDowall) of a rancher and whose adventures help bring maturity to the boy. The horse helps round up the stray stallions roaming the wild ranges and brings back those that were stolen, which helps the rancher (Preston Foster) at a critical time. In the end Thunderhead indicates his desire to be released and the boy lets him go, realizing that the horse requires his freedom. The film offers a great deal to horse lovers, with obvious care and training of the animals used, and rich color landscapes of Utah.

A TREE GROWS IN BROOKLYN

Produced by Louis D. Lighton
Directed by Elia Kazan
Screenplay by Tess Slesinger and Frank Davis, based on a novel by Betty Smith
Photographed by Leon Shamroy
Musical score by Alfred Newman
128 minutes

Cast: Dorothy McGuire, Joan Blondell, James Dunn, Lloyd Nolan, Peggy Ann Garner, Ted Donaldson, James Gleason, Ruth Nelson, John Alexander, B. S. Pully, Ferike Boros, J. Farrell MacDonald, Adeline De Walt Reynolds

Betty Smith's novel of life in a working-class district of Brooklyn in the early years of the century, beautifully translated to the screen by Elia Kazan. The story details the happiness and the tragedies of a family barely able to keep its head above water, with a kindly but alcoholic father (James Dunn) and a strong mother (Dorothy McGuire), and two children (Peggy Ann Garner and Ted Donaldson). The father makes a spotty living as a singing waiter and constantly talks of better times ahead, but he never lives to see them. A little

joy is brought into their lives by the visits of their aunt (Joan Blondell), the kind of woman who survives no matter what. The film is rich with detail and conviction.

A WALK IN THE SUN

Produced by Lewis Milestone
Directed by Lewis Milestone
Screenplay by Robert Rossen, based on a story by Harry Brown
Photographed by Russell Harlan
Songs by Millard Lampell and Earl Robinson
Musical score by Frederic Efrem Rich
117 minutes

Cast: Dana Andrews, Richard Conte, George Tyne, John Ireland, Lloyd Bridges, Sterling Holloway, Norman Lloyd, Herbert Rudley, Richard Benedict, Huntz Hall, James Cardwell, George Offerman

A realistic, unsentimental account of war, detailing the infantrymen engaged in a landing in Italy and assigned to capture an isolated farmhouse from the Germans. The plot is simple, but the film focuses on each of the men in the platoon and reveals their background and character. They are ordinary men forced into an extraordinary situation and hoping to survive. Milestone's film has an almost documentary style and offers no glorification of warfare.

THE WAY AHEAD

Produced by Norman Walker and John Sutro
Directed by Carol Reed
Screenplay by Eric Ambler and Peter Ustinov, from a story by Eric Ambler
Photographed by Guy Green
Music by William Alwyn
Musical direction by Muir Mathieson
106 minutes

Dorothy McGuire, James Dunn, Peggy Ann Garner, and Ted Donaldson in *A Tree Grows in Brooklyn*.

Eythe, Walter Brennan, Constance Bennett, Dorothy Gish, Barbara Whiting, Larry Stevens, Kathleen Howard, Buddy Swan, Charles Dingle, Avon Long, Gavin Gordon, Eddie Dunn, Lois Austin, Harry Strang, Frances Morris, Reginald Sheffield, William Frambes, Paul Everton

Philadelphia in the summer of 1876 and lots of celebration to mark America's first hundred years. The Rogers family are visited by their Aunt Zenia (Constance Bennett), who brings with her a young Frenchman (Cornel Wilde) in charge of the French pavilion. Both daughters (Jeanne Crain and Linda Darnell) fall for him, while father (Walter Brennan) tries to promote his inventions and hang on to his job with the railroad. With Zenia's help he does both, while Jeanne wins the love of the Frenchman and Linda finally says yes to her devoted doctor-suitor (William Eythe). With fine period decor, *Centennial Summer* is memorable mostly as the last music score written by Jerome Kern, and released after his death.

CLAUDIA AND DAVID

Produced by William Perlberg
Directed by Walter Lang
Screenplay by William Brown Meloney, from the story by Rose Franken
Photographed by Joseph Le Shelle
Music score by Cyril Mockridge
78 minutes

Cast: Dorothy McGuire, Robert Young, Mary Astor, John Sutton, Gail Patrick, Rose Hobart, Harry Davenport, Florence Bates, Jerome Cowan, Else Jansen, Frank Twedell, Anthony Sydes, Pierre Watkin, Henry Mowbray, Clara Blandick, Eric Wilton, Frank Darien

Three years after her film debut as *Claudia*, Dorothy McGuire appeared in this sequel, with Robert Young again the husband. She is still charming and slightly scatterbrained, picking up her husband at the station and driving none too well, and worrying over the health of her son. She is disturbed by the attentions of another man (John Sutton) and jealous over the interest of another woman (Mary Astor) in David, but both know their home means more than anything else. A light but pleasing domestic comedy.

CLUNY BROWN

Produced by Ernst Lubitsch
Directed by Ernst Lubitsch
Screenplay by Samuel Hoffenstein and Elizabeth Reinhardt, based on the novel by Marjorie Sharp
Photographed by Joseph La Shelle
Music by Cyril Mockridge
Musical direction by Emil Newman
100 minutes

Cast: Charles Boyer, Jennifer Jones, Peter Lawford, Helen Walker, Reginald Owen, Reginald Gardiner, Margaret Bannerman, Sir C. Aubrey Smith, Richard Haydn, Sara Allgood, Ernest Cossart, Una O'Connor, Florence Bates, Billy Bevan, Queenie Leonard, Michael Dyne, Christopher Severn

A sophisticated comedy with the Lubitsch touch, set in England just before the war, concerning the love of a Czech author (Charles Boyer), a refugee from the Nazis, and a plumber's niece (Jennifer Jones). She becomes a maid in the country manor where the author is a guest and together they upset the serenity of the upper crust customs, and then get married. Fine performances from Jones as the spirited girl and from Boyer as the suave European, plus many notables of Hollywood's once-flourishing British colony.

DANGEROUS MILLIONS

Produced by Sol M. Wurtzel
Directed by James Tinling
Screenplay by Irving Cummings, Jr. and Robert G. North, from a story by Irving Cummings, Jr. and Robert G. North
Photographed by Benjamin Kline
69 minutes

Cast: Kent Taylor, Donna Drake, Tala Birell, Leonard Strong, Konstantin Shayne, Robert H. Barrat, Rex Evans, Rudolph Anders, Otto Reichow, Franco Cosaro, Henry Rowland, Victor Sen Yung

A millionaire shipping magnate (Robert Barrat), located in China, announces that eight of his far-flung relatives should gather after his death at his remote mountaintop home to share his vast fortunes. Once gathered, there are two murders and several near disasters before the magnate appears to tell them that he made a false announcement of his death in order to test their worthiness, and that he finds them all unworthy.

THE DARK CORNER

Produced by Fred Kohlmar
Directed by Henry Hathaway
Screenplay by Jay Dratler and Bernard Schoenfeld, from a story by Leo Rosten
Photographed by Joe MacDonald
Music by Cyril J. Mockridge
99 minutes

Cast: Lucille Ball, Clifton Webb, William Bendix, Mark Stevens, Kurt Kreuger, Cathy Downs, Reed Hadley, Constance Collier, Eddie Heywood and orchestra, Molly Lamont, Forbes Murray, Regina Wallace, John Goldsworthy

An excellent example of the private detective genre, with Mark Stevens as a tough operator, with an adoring secretary (Lucille Ball), who finds himself involved in a complicated case in which he has been cleverly framed for murder. He solves the case and saves himself in the nick of time. Hathaway's taut direction and Clifton Webb's portait of an art gallery proprietor who is insanely jealous of his young wife (Cathy Downs) make *The Dark Corner* memorable.

DEADLINE FOR MURDER

Produced by Sol M. Wurtzel
Directed by James Tinling
Screenplay by Irving Cummings, Jr.
Photographed by Benjamine Kline
66 minutes

Cast: Paul Kelly, Kent Taylor, Sheila Ryan, Jerome Cowan, Renee Carson, Joan Blair, Marian Martin, Leslie Vincent, Matt McHugh, Jody Gilbert, Edward Marr, Thomas Jackson, Larry Blake, Ray Teal, Andre Charlot, Emory Parnell, Lester Derr

A crime melodrama about a series of killings that are motivated by the possession of important documents wanted by an overseas power. A detective (Paul Kelly) and an affluent gambler (Kent Taylor) combine forces to solve the mystery, but are somewhat hampered by an overly zealous newspaperwoman (Sheila Ryan).

DO YOU LOVE ME?

Produced by George Jessel
Directed by Gregory Ratoff
Screenplay by Robert Ellis and Helen Logan, from a story by Bert Granet
Photographed in Technicolor by Edward Cronjager
Music direction by Emil Newman and Charles Henderson
89 minutes

Cast: Maureen O'Hara, Dick Haymes, Harry James, Reginald Gardiner, Richard Gaines, Stanley Prager, Harry James' Music Makers, B. S. Pully, Chick Chandler, Alma Kruger, Almira Sessions, Douglas Wood, Harlan Briggs, Julia Dean, Harry Hays Morgan

A slim musical about the dean (Maureen O'Hara) of a music school who goes to New York to engage a symphony conductor and on the train runs up against a dance band leader (Harry James), who tells her she is dowdy. She changes her image and becomes glamorous, which causes both the band leader and a crooner (Dick Haymes) to fall in love with her. Her association with dance music causes her to lose her job, but the band and the crooner give a concert at her school and prove the value of swing music. The film gets its value from the playing of Harry James, the singing of Dick Haymes, and a raft of songs written by Jimmy McHugh, Harold Adamson, Lionel Newman, Charles Henderson, Harry Ruby, Herbert Magidson, and Matty Malneck.

Irene Dunne and Rex Harrison in *Anna and the King of Siam.*

Jeanne Crain, Linda Darnell, and Cornel Wilde in *Centennial Summer.*

Charles Boyer and Jennifer Jones in *Cluny Brown.*

Mark Stevens and Lucille Ball in *Dark Corner.*

Gene Tierney, Vincent Price, and Jessica Tandy in *Dragonwyck*.

Dick Haymes and Maureen O'Hara in *Do You Love Me?*

Jeanne Crain and Alan Young in *Margie*.

Victor Mature and Henry Fonda in *My Darling Clementine*.

SENTIMENTAL JOURNEY

Produced by Walter Morosco
Directed by Walter Lang
Screenplay by Samuel Hoffenstein and Elizabeth Reinhardt, from a story by Nelia Gardner White
Photographed by Norbert Brodine
Music by Cyril J. Mockridge
94 minutes

Cast: John Payne, Maureen O'Hara, William Bendix, Sir Cedric Hardwicke, Glen Langan, Mischa Auer, Connie Marshall, Kurt Kreuger, Trudy Marshall, Ruth Nelson, Dorothy Adams, Mary Gordon, Lillian Bronson, Olive Blakeney, James Flavin

A very sentimental journey, about a Broadway couple, a producer and an actress (John Payne and Maureen O'Hara) who yearn to have a child but cannot. She comes across a little orphan (Connie Marshall), a girl with a strange, gentle quality, and they adopt her. The mother dies of a heart attack shortly after and the father finds it hard to relate to the child. He buries himself in work, but the youngster finally succeeds in filling the void.

SHOCK

Produced by Aubrey Schenck
Directed by Alfred Werker
Screenplay by Eugene Ling, from a story by Albert De Mond
Photographed by Glen MacWilliams and Joe MacDonald
Music by David Buttolph
Musical direction by Emil Newman
68 minutes

Cast: Vincent Price, Lynn Bari, Frank Latimore, Anabel Shaw, Michael Dunne, Reed Hadley, Renee Carson, Charles Trowbridge, John Davidson, Selmer Jackson, Pierre Watkin, Mary Young, Cecil Weston

A girl (Anabel Shaw) is shocked into amnesia by witnessing a man (Vincent Price) murdering his wife in a hotel room. The man is motivated by a beautiful but evil woman (Lynn Bari) and together they seek out the girl to silence her. But the girl's husband is a police officer (Frank Latimore) and in a battle of wits and time he sees to it that his wife is saved and the killer apprehended.

SMOKY

Produced by Robert Bassler
Directed by Louis King
Screenplay by Lily Hayward, Dwight Cummins, and Dorothy Yost, from a novel by Will James
Photographed in Technicolor by Charles Clarke
Music by David Raksin
Musical direction by Emil Newman
87 minutes

Herbert Marshall, Tyrone Power, Gene Tierney, Anne Baxter, and John Payne in *The Razor's Edge*.

Cast: Fred MacMurray, Anne Baxter, Burl Ives, Bruce Cabot, Esther Dale, Roy Roberts, J. Farrell MacDonald

Will James' classic horse story, beautifully color photographed in Utah, with Fred MacMurray as the roving cowboy who spots an intelligent, handsome black stallion as it defies round-up. He captures the horse and trains it, and finds it responsive. The horse is stolen during a cattle raid and the cowboy loses contact with it, but never stops looking for it. In the meantime it has been maltreated and finally ends up pulling a junk wagon. One day during a parade the horse steps out jauntily at the sound of music and it is there the cowboy sees him. A delightful modern Western, with a splendid animal in the title role.

SOMEWHERE IN THE NIGHT

Produced by Anderson Lawler
Directed by Joseph L. Mankiewicz
Screenplay by Howard Dimsdale and Joseph L. Mankiewicz, from a story by Marvin Borowsky
Photographed by Norbert Brodine
Music by David Buttolph
Musical direction by Emil Newman
110 minutes

Cast: John Hodiak, Nancy Guild, Lloyd Nolan, Richard Conte, Josephine Hutchinson, Fritz Kortner, Margo Wood, Sheldon Leonard, Lou Nova, John Russell, Houseley Stevenson, Charles Arnt, Al Sparlis, Richard Benedict

A Marine combat casualty (John Hodiak) suffers from amnesia and returns to civilian life with only a name. He learns that his last address before the war was a hotel in Los Angeles and he goes there to begin retracing his steps. His only clue is a baggage check. With it he claims a briefcase, containing information about a bank account, which leads to information that suggests he is a murderer. With the aid of a night club singer (Nancy Guild) and a police detective (Lloyd Nolan) the amnesiac learns that he was involved in a crime but that he was an innocent party. A clever but complicated mystery yarn and well directed by the skillful Mankiewicz.

STRANGE JOURNEY

Produced by Sol M. Wurtzel
Directed by James Tinling
Screenplay by Charles Kenyon and Irving Elman, from a story by Charles Kenyon
Photographed by Benjamin Kline
67 minutes

Cast: Paul Kelly, Osa Massen, Hillary Brooke, Lee Patrick, Bruce Lester, Gene Stutenroth, Fritz Leiber, Kurt Katch

A reformed gangster (Paul Kelly) and his wife (Hillary Brooke) crash land their plane on a Caribbean

Connie Marshall and Maureen O'Hara in *Sentimental Journey.*

island and come across a group stranded from a shipwreck. Some of them are Nazis and when news of a uranium deposit is revealed there is a struggle for survival, with the ex-gangster patriotically gaining the upper hand for America.

STRANGE TRIANGLE

Produced by Aubrey Schenck
Directed by Ray McCarey
Screenplay by Mortimer Braus, from a story by Jack Andrews
Photographed by Harry Jackson
Music by David Buttolph
65 minutes

Cast: Signe Hasso, Preston Foster, Anabel Shaw, John Shepperd, Roy Roberts, Emory Parnell, Nancy Evans, Gladys Blake, Frank Pershin, Robert Malcolm

A traveling bank supervisor (Preston Foster) spends a few days with a seductive woman (Signe Hasso) and is later surprised to find her the wife of a business associate. Her extravangances have driven the husband (John Shepperd) to gambling with bank funds, and the supervisor himself is involved in crime before he realizes she is a worthless woman.

THREE LITTLE GIRLS IN BLUE

Produced by Mack Gordon
Directed by H. Bruce Humberstone
Screenplay by Valentine Davis, from a play by Stephan Powys
Photographed in Technicolor by Ernest Palmer
Songs by Mack Gordon, Josef Myrow, and Harry Warren
Musical direction by Alfred Newman
90 minutes

Cast: June Haver, George Montgomery, Vivian Blaine, Celeste Holm, Vera-Ellen, Frank Latimore, Charles Smith, Charles Halton, Ruby Dandridge, Thurston Hall, Clinton Rosemond, William Forrest, Jr.

Another remake of *Three Blind Mice,* this time set in

left Spain after being dispossessed and tortured by the Inquisition, and bringing with him a peasant girl (Jean Peters) as his wife. Their hopes of finding a new life in the New World are dampened by the appearance of the officer (John Sutton) who instigated the false charges against the nobleman in order to covet his lands. The officer is murdered, with the blame falling on the nobleman, who is cleared when an Indian prince admits to the murder. The film contains a good story, with splendidly photographed locations and a magnificent music score by Alfred Newman.

CARNIVAL IN COSTA RICA

Produced by William A. Bacher
Directed by Gregory Ratoff
Screenplay by John Larkin, Samuel Hoffenstein, and
   Elizabeth Reinhardt
Photographed in Technicolor by Harry Jackson
Songs by Ernesto Lecuona, Harry Ruby, Sunny Skylar,
   and Albert Stillman
Musical direction by Emil Newman
96 minutes

Cast: Dick Haymes, Vera-Ellen, Cesar Romero, Celeste Holm, Anne Revere, J. Carrol Naish, Lecuona Cuban Boys, Pedro de Cordoba, Barbara Whiting, Nestor Paiva, Fritz Feld, Tommy Ivo, Mimi Aguglia, Anna Demetrio, Severo Lopez

A pleasing color musical, benefiting from some footage shot in Costa Rica. The slight story concerns two well-established families who have betrothed their two children (Cesar Romero and Vera-Ellen) without taking their own wishes into consideration. He is in love with an American night club singer (Celeste Holm) and she is smitten with a young American visitor (Dick Haymes). The family leaders (J. Carroll Naish and Pedro de Cordoba) have to accept the fact that their children will choose their own mates. Songs and carnival scenes, with plenty of spirited dancing, make up for the lack of plot.

THE CRIMSON KEY

Produced by Sol M. Wurtzel
Directed by Eugene Forde
Screenplay by Irving Elman, from a story by Irving
   Elman
Photographed by Benjamin Kline
Musical direction by Morton Scott
75 minutes

Cast: Kent Taylor, Doris Dowling, Dennis Hoey, Louise Currie, Ivan Triesault, Arthur Space, Vera Marshe, Edwin Rand, Bernadene Hayes, Victoria Horne, Doug Evans, Ann Doran, Victor Sen Yung, Chester Clute, Ralf Harolde, Milton Parsons, Jimmy Magill, Marietta Canty, Stanley Mann

A mild whodunit, with Kent Taylor as a private detective hired by an attractive woman (Doris Dowling) to tail her husband. He finds a confusing web of intrigues and murder.

DAISY KENYON

Produced and directed by Otto Preminger
Screenplay by David Hertz, based on the novel by
   Elizabeth Janeway
Photographed by Leon Shamroy
Music by David Raksin
99 minutes

Cast: Joan Crawford, Dana Andrews, Henry Fonda, Ruth Warrick, Martha Stewart, Peggy Ann Garner, Connie Marshall, Nicholas Joy, Art Baker, Robert Karnes, John Davidson, Victoria Horne, Charles Meredith, Roy Roberts, Griff Barnett

Daisy Kenyon (Joan Crawford) is a commercial artist living in New York and having a "black street" affair with a married lawyer (Dana Andrews), until she meets and marries a nice man (Henry Fonda) who truly loves her. When the lawyer divorces his nagging wife, he tries to persuade Daisy to leave her husband. She almost does. A Joan Crawford film entirely, allowing her to perform her specialty—the emotionally distraught professional lady.

FOREVER AMBER

Produced by William Perlberg
Directed by Otto Preminger
Screenplay by Philip Dunne and Ring Lardner, Jr., from
   the novel by Kathleen Winsor
Photographed in Technicolor by Leon Shamroy
Music by David Raksin
Musical direction by Alfred Newman
140 minutes

Cast: Linda Darnell, Cornel Wilde, Richard Greene, George Sanders, Glenn Langan, Richard Haydn, Jessica Tandy, Anne Revere, Jane Ball, Robert Coote, Leo G. Carroll, Natalie Draper, Margaret Wycherly, Alma Kruger, Edmund Breon, Alan Napier

A gargantuan historical romance set in the England of King Charles II, but a disappointing transfer of Kathleen Winsor's spicy, erotic novel because of the censorship restrictions of 1947. Linda Darnell is a pretty but lackluster Amber, a girl who rebels against her Puritan upbringing and becomes a courtesan in London. She falls in love with a titled soldier (Cornel Wilde), but falls on hard times when he goes abroad. She bears his child and then goes on to affairs with various men, eventually becoming a favorite of the King, but never regaining the one man she loves, who leaves England and takes their child to America. *Forever Amber* is visually attractive, with splendid depictions of court life, banditry, warfare, the great fire of London—all done in magnificent Technicolor and backed by a classic musical score by David Raksin. But it lacks the earthiness that made the book an enormous success.

THE FOXES OF HARROW

Produced by William A. Bacher
Directed by John M. Stahl
Screenplay by Wanda Tuchock, from the novel by Frank Yerby
Photographed by Joseph La Shelle
Musical score by David Buttolph
Musical direction by Alfred Newman
118 minutes

Cast: Rex Harrison, Maureen O'Hara, Richard Haydn, Victor McLaglen, Vanessa Brown, Patricia Medina, Gene Lockhart, Charles Irwin, Hugo Haas, Dennis Hoey, Roy Roberts, Marcel Journet, Kenneth Washington, Helen Crozier, Libby Tylor, Renee Beard

A historical romance, set in the American South in the years before the Civil War, dealing with the adventures of a charming Irish scoundrel (Rex Harrision) who parlays his skill as a gambler into membership in New Orleans society and land ownership. He wins a plantation in a card game and seeks to establish a dynasty in the South, such as the kind he had known in Ireland, but had been forced to leave because he was illegitimate. He woos a society girl (Maureen O'Hara) into marriage and offends her with his interests in other women. But with the financial collapse of the South, they find new strengths in themselves to survive their misfortunes. *The Foxes of Harrow* is expensive soap opera, made interesting by the acting of Harrison as the elegant cad and the lavish depictions of New Orleans and plantation life.

GENTLEMAN'S AGREEMENT

Produced by Darryl F. Zanuck
Directed by Elia Kazan
Screenplay by Moss Hart, based on the novel by Laura Z. Hobson
Photographed by Arthur Miller
Musical direction by Alfred Newman
118 minutes

Cast: Gregory Peck, Dorothy McGuire, John Garfield, Celeste Holm, Anne Revere, June Havoc, Albert Dekker, Jane Wyatt, Dean Stockwell, Nicholas Joy, Sam Jaffe, Harold Vermilyea, Ransom M. Sherman, Roy Roberts, Kathleen Lockhart, Curt Conway, John Newland

Hollywood's first major attack on anti-Semitism, involving major talents in all departments. The central character is a writer (Gregory Peck) who is given an assignment by a magazine to explore the subject of anti-Semitism. It occurs to him to pose as a Jew and he then comes into contact with more prejudice, direct and subtle, than he ever imagined. He finds his girl

Boomerang, with Lee J. Cobb, Karl Malden, and Dana Andrews.

Dick Haymes and Vera-Ellen in *Carnival in Costa Rica.*

Cornel Wilde and Linda Darnell in *Forever Amber.*

Tyrone Power in *Captain from Castile.*

Dana Andrews and Joan Crawford in *Daisy Kenyon*.

Maureen O'Hara and Rex Harrison in *The Foxes of Harrow*.

friend (Dorothy McGuire), the daughter of his publisher, not fully understanding the power of racial intolerance, even though she thinks herself free of bigotry. The exposure to these revelations changes their attitudes for the better. Shot largely in New York, the film has a realistic approach to its subject and a fine performance by Peck as a man stunned by his experiences in posing as a man of a different faith.

THE GHOST AND MRS. MUIR

Produced by Fred Kohlmar
Directed by Joseph L. Mankiewicz
Screenplay by Philip Dunne, based on the novel by R. A. Dick
Photographed by Charles Lang
Music by Bernard Herrmann
104 minutes

Cast: Gene Tierney, Rex Harrison, George Sanders, Edna Best, Vanessa Brown, Anna Lee, Robert Coote, Natalie Wood, Isobel Elsom, Victoria Horne, Whitfield Kane, Brad Slaven, William Stelling, Helen Freeman, David Thursby

Dorothy McGuire, Gregory Peck, and John Garfield in *Gentleman's Agreement*.

The Ghost and Mrs. Muir is the least frightening ghost story ever filmed. It is more a piece of romantic make-believe about the relationship between a young widow (Gene Tierney) and the spirit of a deceased sea captain (Rex Harrison) in turn-of-the-century England. She buys an old house on the coast, despite warnings that it is haunted. When the spirit shows himself, he and the widow find themselves becoming friends, and when her funds run out, he devises a method of income for her—he dictates his memoirs, which turn into a profitable book. The ghost comes to love her, but realizing that nothing can ever come of such a love, he departs. Under Mankiewicz's fine direction, the actors make this a delightful picture. In this they are aided by an especially touching music score from Bernard Herrmann.

Gene Tierney and Rex Harrison in *The Ghost and Mrs. Muir*.

THE HOMESTRETCH

Produced by Robert Bassler
Directed by H. Bruce Humberstone
Screenplay by Wanda Tuchock
Photographed in Technicolor by Arthur Arling
Music by David Raksin
99 minutes

Cast: Cornel Wilde, Maureen O'Hara, Glenn Langan, Helen Walker, James Gleason, Henry Stephenson, Margaret Bannerman, Ethel Griffies, Tommy Cook

A race track picture, but with the accent more on the people than the horses. A charming young gambler

June Haver in *I Wonder Who's Kissing Her Now*.

(Cornel Wilde) marries a girl (Maureen O'Hara) from a sheltered Boston background. She cheerfully follows him as he makes the rounds of the famous race tracks, until he has to borrow money from a former girl friend (Helen Walker), who behaves as if she owned him. The wife considers divorce but comes to realize her husband's true love—both for her and for racing. The story is thin, but the film offers exciting color photography of many race courses, such as Churchill Downs, Hialeah, Saratoga, Palermo in South America, the Ascot in England and, for its climax, the Kentucky Derby.

I WONDER WHO'S KISSING HER NOW

Produced by George Jessel
Directed by Lloyd Bacon
Screenplay by Lewis R. Foster
Photographed in Technicolor by Ernest Palmer
Songs by Joseph E. Howard, George Jessel, and Charles Henderson
Musical direction by Alfred Neman
104 minutes

Cast: June Haver, Mark Stevens, Martha Stewart, Reginald Gardiner, Lenore Aubert, William Frawley, Gene Nelson, Truman Bradley, George Cleveland, Harry Seymour, Lewis L. Russell, John "Skins" Miller, Lew Hearn, Eve Miller, Florence O'Brien, Emmett Vogan, Milton Parsons

A pleasant turn-of-the-century color musical based on the career of vaudeville songwriter and troubadour Joe Howard (Mark Stevens), tracing his early days as an organ salesman in Weehawken to his success on Broadway. He falls for a European musical star (Lenore Aubert), but it's a pert little American singer-dancer (June Haver) who wins his heart. The film presents some of Howard's best-remembered songs, such as the title number and "Hello, My Baby," together with some special material written by producer George Jessel and composer Charles Henderson.

THE INVISIBLE WALL

Produced by Sol M. Wurtzel
Directed by Eugene Forde
Screenplay by Arnold Belgard, from a story by Howard J. Green and Paul Frank
Photographed by Benjamin Kline
Music score by Dale Butts
Musical direction by Morton Scott
73 minutes

Cast: Don Castle, Virginia Christine, Richard Gaines, Arthur Space, Edward Keane, Jeff Chandler, Harry Cheshire, Mary Gordon, Harry Shannon, Rita Duncan

A mystery tale, about a gambler (Don Castle) accused of murder but cleared when it is learned that the man was a crook actually shot by the police. Told in flashback, the story follows the gambler through adventures in Las Vegas, Los Angeles, Denver, and St. Louis, with confusion all the way.

JEWELS OF BRANDENBURG

Produced by Sol M. Wurtzel
Directed by Eugene Forde
Screenplay by Irving Cummings, Jr., Robert G. North, and Irving Elman, from a story by Irving Cummings, Jr. and Robert G. North
Music score by Darrell Calker
65 minutes

Cast: Richard Travis, Micheline Cheirel, Carol Thurston, Leonard Strong, Fernando Alvarado, Eugene Bordon, Lewis Russell, Louis Mercier, Otto Reichow, Ralf Harolde, Harro Meller, Emmett Vogan, William Gould, Joel Friedkin

Filmed in Europe and dealing with the theft of jewels by a wartime spy (Leonard Strong) who worked for both sides. An American agent (Richard Travis), who had been involved with the spy during the war, is sent by the U.S. government to clear up the case and thereby avoid an international incident.

KISS OF DEATH

Produced by Fred Kohlmar
Directed by Henry Hathaway
Screenplay by Ben Hecht and Charles Lederer, based on a story by Eleazar Lipsky
Photographed by Norbert Brodine
Music by David Buttolph
98 minutes

Cast: Victor Mature, Brian Donlevy, Richard Widmark, Taylor Holmes, Howard Smith, Robert Keith, Karl Malden, Anthony Ross, Mildred Dunnock, Millard Mitchell, Temple Texas, J. Scott Smart, Jay Jostyn

Kiss of Death continued Hollywood's concern with realism, particularly in depicting crime. Henry Hathaway insisted on shooting this film entirely in New York, achieving an authenticity that made backlot depictions of that city a thing of the past. The central character is a small-time crook (Victor Mature) who would prefer to go straight but who is caught in circumstances he cannot control. He is given a twenty-year jail sentence for robbery. A district attorney (Brian Donlevy) who feels the sentence was unjust offers to help him if he will reveal his accomplices. At first the man refuses, but agrees when he learns his wife has committed suicide and his children are being threatened by the accomplices, particularly one of them, a psychopath named Tommy Udo (Richard Widmark). *Kiss of Death* met with excellent critical and public response and served to debut the film career of Widmark.

THE LATE GEORGE APLEY

Produced by Fred Kohlmar
Directed by Joseph L. Mankiewicz
Screenplay by Philip Dunne, from a play by John P.
  Marquand and George S. Kaufman, based on a novel
  by John P. Marquand
Photographed by Joseph La Shelle
Music by Cyril J. Mockridge
Musical direction by Alfred Newman
98 minutes

Cast: Ronald Colman, Peggy Cummins, Vanessa Brown,
Richard Haydn, Charles Russell, Richard Ney, Percy
Waram, Mildred Natwick, Edna Best, Nydia Westman,
Francis Pierlot, Kathleen Howard, Paul Harvey, Helen
Freeman, Theresa Lyon, William Moran

John P. Marquand collaborated with George S. Kaufman to make a play of his Pulitzer prize-winning novel, and Philip Dunne turned the play into this fine picture. It contains a superb performance by Ronald Colman as an exceedingly proper, turn-of-the-century Bostonian, who tenaciously clings to tradition and regards all innovations as radical. His son (Richard Ney) must go only to Harvard and his daughter must marry into the right family. But the march of time forces Mr. Apley to compromise, and those compromises form the basis for this gentle satire. The quality of the comedy even amused Bostonians.

THE MIRACLE ON 34th STREET

Produced by William Perlberg
Directed by George Seaton
Screenplay by George Seaton, based on a story by
  Valentine Davies
Photographed by Charles Clarke and Lloyd Aherne
Music by Cyril Mockridge
96 minutes

Cast: Edmund Gwenn, Maureen O'Hara, John Payne,
Gene Lockhart, Natalie Wood, Porter Hall, William
Frawley, Jerome Cowan, Philip Tonge, James Seay,
Harry Antrim, Thelma Ritter, Mary Field

As a Christmas movie, *The Miracle on 34th Street* has little competition. Much of it was shot in New York City in the winter of 1946 and writer-director George Seaton secured the cooperation of Macy's Department Store to tell this tale of an advertising executive (Maureen O'Hara) who has to quickly find a replacement for a drunk she has hired to play Santa Claus. On hand is a genial gentleman who calls himself Kris Kringle (Edmund Gwenn). He delights children and parents, but concerns his employers with his frank criticism of some of their products and his habit of guiding customers elsewhere. He claims that he really is Santa Claus, which eventually leads to his arrest and trial. The trial proves nothing, except that this gentleman may indeed be who he says he is. The role brought

Edmund Gwenn a well-deserved Oscar—and an image that is perpetually appealing.

MOSS ROSE

Produced by Gene Markey
Directed by Gregory Ratoff
Screenplay by Jules Furthman and Tom Reed, from a
  novel by Joseph Shearing
Photographed by Joe MacDonald
Music by David Buttolph
Musical direction by Alfred Newman
82 minutes

Cast: Peggy Cummins, Victor Mature, Ethel Barrymore,
Vincent Price, Margo Woode, George Zucco, Patricia
Medina, Rhys Williams, Felippa Rock, Carol Savage,
Victor Wood, Patrick O'Moore, Billy Bevan, Michael
Dyne, John Rogers, Charles McNaughton, Alex Frazer

An eerie murder mystery set in the fog-bound London of the turn-of-the-century, concerning the deaths of several chorus girls, with the finger of suspicion pointing toward a wealthy young man (Victor Mature) who has been dating one of the girls. A friend of hers (Peggy Cummins) takes advantage of the knowledge and forces an invitation to his elegant home, presided over by his elegant mother (Ethel Barrymore). Another death occurs at the mansion and the girl herself barely escapes being killed—before the murderer is revealed. Old-fashioned melodrama, but darkly stylish.

MOTHER WORE TIGHTS

Produced by Lamar Trotti
Directed by Walter Lang
Screenplay by Lamar Trotti, based on the book by
  Miriam Young
Photographed in Technicolor by Harry Jackson
Songs by Mack Gordon and Joseph Myrow
Musical direction by Alfred Newman
107 minutes

Cast: Betty Grable, Dan Dailey, Mona Freeman, Connie
Marshall, Vanessa Brown, Robert Arthur, Sara Allgood,
William Frawley, Ruth Nelson, Anabel Shaw, Michael
Dunne, George Cleveland, Veda Ann Borg, Lee Patrick,
Señor Wences, Maude Eburne, Kathleen Lockhart

A nostalgic and glorifying look at the heyday of vaudeville, with Betty Grable and Dan Dailey as song-and-dance artists who meet, marry, and raise a family, while never giving up the theatre. With almost no plot but a series of vignettes of a happy family, interspersed with a great variety of musical numbers, the film has a pleasant glow about it, and is made even more warm by its narrative, spoken by Nan Bryant. The film was among the most successful made by Betty Grable and the one she claimed as her personal favorite. The teaming with Dan Dailey was especially favorable and resulted in three more pictures together.

NIGHTMARE ALLEY

Produced by George Jessel
Directed by Edmund Goulding
Screenplay by Jules Furthman, based on the novel by
　William Lindsay Gresham
Photographed by Lee Garmes
Music by Cyril Mockridge
Musical direction Lionel Newman
111 minutes

Cast: Tyrone Power, Joan Blondell, Colleen Gray, Helen
Walker, Taylor Holmes, Mike Mazurki, Ian Keith, Julia
Dean, James Flavin, Roy Roberts, James Burke

A radical change of style for Tyrone Power, here trying
to expand his romantic-heroic image by playing an
ambitious con man who masters a mind-reading act
and teams up with an unscrupulous psychiatrist (Helen
Walker) to fleece wealthy clients. He forces his wife
(Colleen Gray) to be part of his act, but during one
bout of phony spiritualism she panics and inadvertently
reveals him as a fake. He escapes, takes to the bottle,
becomes a drifting hobo, and ends up working for a
circus as a freak attraction. His wife finds him and
hopes to bring him back to normalcy. *Nightmare Alley*
is a fine gothic horror film, offering an excellent performance from Power. He regarded it as one of his
best pieces of work, but the public in general did not
agree—and Power had to return to his romantic guise.

ROSES ARE RED

Produced by Sol M. Wurtzel
Directed by James Tinling
Screenplay by Irving Elman
Photographed by Benjamin Kline
Musical score by Rudy Schrager
65 minutes

Cast: Don Castle, Peggy Knudsen, Patricia Knight, Joe
Sawyer, Edward Keane, Jeff Chandler, Charles McGraw,
Charles Lane, Paul Guilfoyle, Doug Fowley, James Arness

A newly elected district attorney (Don Castle) is kidnapped by a big city crime boss (Edward Keane) and
an exact look-alike is put in his place, with the boss
thus controlling the city. But the DA manages to
escape, the double is removed and the DA pretends to
be the double—until he can get enough evidence to
wipe out the crime boss and his gang.

SECOND CHANCE

Produced by Sol M. Wurtzel
Directed by James S. Tinling
Screenplay by Arnold Belgard, from a story by Lou
　Breslow and John Patrick
Photographed by Benjamine Kline
68 minutes

Cast: Kent Taylor, Louise Currie, Dennis Hoey, Larry

Blake, Ann Doran, John Eldredge, Paul Guilfoyle, William
Newell, Guy Kingford, Charles Flynn, Eddie Fetherston,
Francis Pierlot, Betty Compson, Edwin Maxwell, Michael
Brandon

The leader of a gang of jewel thieves (Kent Taylor)
falls in love with a girl (Louise Currie) who seems to
be a jewel thief herself. She joins the gang and aids
in planning a million dollar heist, but actually she is
an insurance detective. She tries to persuade him to
give up his crooked ways and when he does not, she
leads the police in rounding up the gang.

THE SHOCKING MISS PILGRIM

Produced by William Perlberg
Directed by George Seaton
Screenplay by George Seaton, from a story by Ernest
　Maas Fredricka
Photographed in Technicolor by Leon Shamroy
Songs by George and Ira Gershwin
Musical direction by Alfred Newman and Charles
　Henderson
87 minutes

Cast: Betty Grable, Dick Haymes, Anne Revere, Allyn
Joslyn, Gene Lockhart, Elizabeth Patterson, Elizabeth
Risdon, Arthur Shields, Charles Kemper, Roy Roberts,
Stanley Prager, Ed Laughton, Hal K. Dawson, Likkian
Bronson, Raymond Largay, Constance Purdy, Mildred
Stone

An interesting attempt to give Betty Grable a different
kind of vehicle and made even more interesting by
digging up hitherto unused songs by George and Ira
Gershwin. The setting is Boston in 1874, with Betty as
a typist in a shipping company and falling in love,
and vice versa, with her boss (Dick Haymes). What is
shocking about this young lady, Miss Pilgrim, is that
she is an advocate of women's rights and joins the
suffragette movement. Her boss is a little stuffy about
it, but comes to see her point of view. Despite its
pleasing decor and its songs, the public did not take
kindly to a Betty Grable film with her famous legs
hidden in long skirts, and it proved to be one of the
least successful of her films.

13 RUE MADELEINE

Produced by Louis de Rochemont
Directed by Henry Hathaway
Screenplay by John Monks and Sy Bartlett
Photographed by Norbert Brodine
Music by Alfred Newman
95 minutes

Cast: James Cagney, Annabella, Richard Conte, Frank
Latimore, Walter Abel, Melville Cooper, Sam Jaffe,
Marcel Rousseau, Richard Gordon, Everett G. Marshall,
Blanche Yurka, Peter Von Zerneck, Alfred Linder, James
Craven, Roland Belanger, Horace MacMahon, Alexander
Kirkland, Donald Randolph

Richard Widmark and Victor Mature in *Kiss of Death*.

Betty Grable and Dan Dailey in *Mother Wore Tights*.

Maureen O'Hara, Edmund Gwenn, Natalie Wood, and John Payne in *The Miracle on 34th Street*.

Filmed in semi-documentary fashion by newsreel expert Louis de Rochemont, *13 Rue Madeleine* derives its title from the address of a Gestapo unit in Paris in World War II. A group of allied agents headed by a tough adventurer (James Cagney) prepare to infiltrate German files in France and discover the whereabouts of a rocket-projectile site, so that it may be bombed before the Allied invasion of Europe. The situation becomes more risky with the knowledge that one among them is a German agent. The film is among the very best to deal with war espionage and gains statue by its use of actual OSS accounts and footage. Cagney is its driving force and he is especially effective in the early part of the film, in which he is shown putting agents through their arduous mental and physical training.

THUNDER IN THE VALLEY

Produced by Robert Bassler
Directed by Louis King
Screenplay by Jerome Cady, from a novel by Alfred Ollivant
Photographed in Technicolor by Charles Clarke
Music by Cyril Mockridge
110 minutes

Cast: Lon McAllister, Peggy Ann Garner, Edmund Gwenn, Reginald Owen, Charles Irwin, Dave Thursby, John Rogers, Leyland Hodgson, Harry Allen, Edgar Norton, Norma Varden

Peggy Cummins and Victor Mature in *Moss Rose*.

A story of the Scottish highlands, color photographed in Utah, about a crochety old sheepherder (Edmund Gwenn), who loves his prize collie dog but little else, not even his son (Lon McAllister). The son, with the love of a neighbor's daughter (Peggy Ann Garner), raises his own prize dog and beats out his father in a contest. The father also has to shoot his dog when it turns killer. Based on the classic animal book *Bob, Son of Battle,* the film is a fine account of the raising of dogs as sheepherders.

20TH CENTURY-FOX ACADEMY AWARDS FOR 1947

GENTLEMAN'S AGREEMENT: Best picture.

CELESTE HOLM: Best supporting actress in *Gentleman's Agreement.*

EDMUND GWENN: Best supporting actor in *The Miracle on 34th Street.*

ELIA KAZAN: Best direction for *Gentleman's Agreement.*

VALENTINE DAVIES: Best original film story for *Miracle on 34th Street.*

GEORGE SEATON: Best written screenplay for *Miracle on 34th Street.*

ALFRED NEWMAN: Best scoring of a musical picture for *Mother Wore Tights.*

Charles Russell, Peggy Cummins, and Ronald Colman in *The Late George Apley.*

Coleen Gray, Joan Blondell, Tyrone Power, and Mike Mazurki in *Nightmare Alley.*

Peggy Ann Garner and Lon McAllister in *Thunder in the Valley.*

Dick Haymes and Betty Grable in *The Shocking Miss Pilgrim.*

1948

ANNA KARENINA

Produced by Sir Alexander Korda
Directed by Julien Duvivier
Screenplay by Jean Anouilh, Guy Morgan, and Julien
  Duvivier, based on a novel by Count Leo Tolstoy
Photographed by Henri Alekan
Music by Constant Lambert
110 minutes

Cast: Vivien Leigh, Ralph Richardson, Kieron Moore,
Hugh Dempster, Mary Kerridge, Marie Lohr, Frank
Tickle, Sally Ann Howes, Niall Macginnis, Michael
Gough, Martita Hunt, Heather Thatcher, Helen Haye,
Mary Martlew, Ruby Miller, Austin Trevor, Guy Verney,
John Longden, Leslie Bradley, Beckett Bould

Tolstoy's classic romantic tragedy in a strong, darkly
hued version directed by Julien Duvivier. Set among
the Russian aristocracy of the late nineteenth century,
the story is that of a beautiful woman (Vivien Leigh)
who is happily married to a distinguished Czarist statesman (Ralph Richardson) until she meets a dashing
young soldier and nobleman (Kieron Moore). Ostra-
cized by society when she runs off with the officer, she
is denied a divorce by her husband, who won't even
let her see her son. The hopelessness of the situation,
compounded by her lover's lack of understanding
about her disgrace, leads her to suicide. The Korda
version has fine production values, but it is the
beauty and the performance of Vivien Leigh which
lingers in the memory.

APARTMENT FOR PEGGY

Produced by William Perlberg
Directed by George Seaton
Screenplay by George Seaton, from a story by Faith
  Baldwin
Photographed in Technicolor by Harry Jackson
Music by David Raksin
Musical direction by Lionel Newman
96 minutes

Cast: Jeanne Crain, William Holden, Edmund Gwenn,
Gene Lockhart, Griff Barnett, Randy Stuart, Marion Mar-
shall, Pati Behrs, Henri Letondal, Houseley Stevenson,
Helen Ford, Almira Sessions, Charles Lane, Ronald Burns,
Gene Nelson, Bob Patten

Postwar problems are the substance of this light
comedy-drama about a returning soldier (William
Holden) who continues his education under the GI Bill
of Rights with the enthusiastic help of his young wife
(Jeanne Crain), but at the embarrassment of not having
enough money to provide her with a good home. He
considers ending his frugal plan and getting a job, but
they move in with a college professor (Edmund
Gwenn), who persuades him to go through with the
education. A warm and genial picture, with Gwenn
stealing the scenes.

ARTHUR TAKES OVER

Produced by Sol M. Wurtzel
Directed by Malcolm St. Clair
Screenplay by Mauri Grashin
Photographed by Benjamin Kline
Music by Darrel Calker
63 minutes

Cast: Lois Collier, Richard Crane, Skip Homeier, Ann E.
Todd, Jerome Cowan, Barbara Brown, William Bakewell,
Howard Freeman, Joan Blair, Almira Sessions

A thin little comedy about a bride (Lois Collier) who
persuades her husband (Richard Crane) to keep their
marriage a secret until she can break the news gently
to her mother (Barbara Brown), who had planned
for her a marriage with a richer man. The bride's
young brother (Skip Homeier) pretends to be engaged
in order to take the pressure off, but only makes things
worse. Mother finally accepts the situation.

BELLE STARR'S DAUGHTER

Produced by Edward L. Alperson
Directed by Lesley Selander
Screenplay by W. R. Burnett
Photographed by William Sickner
Music by Dr. Edward Kilenyi
86 minutes

Cast: George Montgomery, Rod Cameron, Ruth Roman,
Wallace Ford, Charles Kemper, William Phipps, Edith
King, Jack Lambert, Fred Libby, Isabel Jewell, J. Farrell
MacDonald, Cris-Pin Martin, Kenneth MacDonald, Wil-
liam Perrott, William Ruhl, Frank Darien

A Western concoction, with Ruth Roman playing the title role and out to get the marshall (George Montgomery) she believes killed her famous outlaw mother. Actually some of her own men killed her, but they are eager to have the daughter think it was the marshall. One of them (Rod Cameron) persuades the girl to join their band, but the marshall eventually catches up with them and reveals the truth, as well as his love.

BUNGALOW 13

Produced by Sam Baerwitz
Directed by Edward L. Cahn
Screenplay by Richard G. Hubler
Photographed by Jackson C. Rose
Musical direction by Edward J. Kay
65 minutes

Cast: Tom Conway, Margaret Hamilton, Richard Cromwell, James Flavin, Frank Cady, Marjorie Hoshelle, Eddie Acuff, Mildred Coles, Lyle Latell, John Davidson, Jody Gilbert, Robert Malcolm

A private detective (Tom Conway) gives up his chase for a valuable piece of jade when the police kill his last suspect. He goes to a motel for a rest and finds the owner involved in the mystery. The owner (Frank Cady) is arrested when two more murders take place, but the detective sets a trap for the real culprit.

CALL NORTHSIDE 777

Produced by Otto Lang
Directed by Henry Hathaway
Screenplay by Jerome Cady and Jay Dratler, based on articles by James P. McGuire, adapted by Leonard Hoffman and Quentin Reynolds
Photographed by Joe MacDonald
Music by Alfred Newman
111 minutes

Cast: James Stewart, Richard Conte, Lee J. Cobb, Helen Walker, Betty Garde, Kasia Orzazewski, Joanne de Bergh,

Ralph Richardson and Vivien Leigh in *Anna Karenina.*

William Holden and Jeanne Crain in *Apartment for Peggy.*

Howard Smith, Moroni Olsen, John McIntire, Paul Harvey, George Tyne, Richard Bishop, Otto Waldis, Michael Chapin, E. G. Marshall

Henry Hathaway's success with *Kiss of Death* led to this film, which is a similar depiction of street crime, except that it is set in Chicago, where it was filmed. It is a true story, based on a newspaperman's dogged attempts to clear a falsely convicted man (Richard Conte). The journalist (James Stewart) at first considers the case a routine assignment, but then becomes intrigued as he discovers discrepancies in given evidence, including that of the police. With little help from anyone, he finally manages to free the man. In making the film, the producers involved the Polish community of Chicago and achieved an effective sense of reality. The film also helped progress the postwar career of Stewart, who here defined a tougher persona than before.

THE CHALLENGE

Produced by John Temple-Smith
Directed by John Gilling
Screenplay by John Gilling, from a story by John Gilling
Photographed by Gordon Dines
Music by Bill McGuffie
93 minutes

Cast: Jayne Mansfield, Anthony Quayle, Carl Mohner, Peter Reynolds, John Bennett, Barbara Mullen, Peter Pike, Robert Brown, Dermot Welsh, Edward Judd, John Stratton, Patrick Holt, Lorraine Clewes, Percy Herbert, Liane Marelli, Bill McGuffie

An American girl (Jayne Mansfield) in London heads a gang of crooks and persuades an infatuated businessman (Anthony Quayle) to join them in making a large heist. He is caught and sentenced to five years, but not until he has secreted the money in a safe place. When he is released, he wants to keep the money in order to bring up his motherless son, but the gang

Richard Conte and James Stewart in *Call Northside 777*.

wants it and kidnaps the child. With the help of the police the man recovers his child and puts an end to the gang.

THE CHECKERED COAT

Produced by Sam Baerwitz
Directed by Edward L. Cahn
Screenplay by John C. Higgens, from a story by Seleg Lester and Merwin Gerard
Photographed by Jackson Rose
Musical direction by Edward J. Kay
66 minutes

Cast: Tom Conway, Noreen Nash, Hurd Hatfield, James Seay, Garry Owen, Marten Lamont, Rory Mallinson, Leonard Mudie, Eddie Dunn, John R. Hamilton, Fred Brown, Lee Tung Foo, Julian Rivero, Dorothy Porter

A mystery yarn, wih Tom Conway as a psychiatrist whose life is complicated by a psychotic patient (Hurd Hatfield) who occasionally collapses but refuses to go to a hospital. The psychiatrist gives him a letter which explains his condition but which also involves him in the patient's crimes, causing much embarrassment before the solution.

THE COUNTERFEITERS

Produced by Maurice Conn
Directed by Peter Stewart
Screenplay by Fred Myton and Barbara Worth, from a story by Maurice Conn
Photographed by James Brown, Jr.
Musical score by Irving Gertz
74 minutes

Cast: John Sutton, Doris Merrick, Hugh Beaumont, Lon Chaney, Jr., George O'Hanlon, Douglas Blackley, Herbert Rawlinson, Pierre Watkins, Don Harvey, Fred Coby, Joyce Lansing, Gerard Gilbert

A Scotland Yard detective (John Sutton) works with

the U.S. Secret Service to track down a band of international counterfeiters. He finds their leader (Hugh Beaumont) but never with the evidence. The leader's daughter (Doris Merrick) complicates things by falling in love with the detective and also trying to protect her father. But justice prevails.

THE CREEPER

Produced by Bernard Small
Directed by Jean Yarbrough
Screenplay by Maurice Tombragel, from a story by Don Martin
Photographed by George Robinson
Musical score by Milton Rosen
63 minutes

Cast: Eduardo Ciannelli, Onslow Stevens, June Vincent, Ralph Morgan, Janis Wilson, John Baragrey, Richard Lane, Philip Ahn, Lotte Stein, Ralph Peters, David Hoffman

A minor horror item, about the discovery of a serum which changes humans into cats. Two scientists (Onslow Stevens and Ralph Morgan) return from an expedition to the West Indies with the serum. One believes they should continue with their experiments and the other does not, which disagreement costs him his life. Several deaths occur before the first scientist is halted in his mad plans.

CRY OF THE CITY

Produced by Sol C. Siegel
Directed by Robert Siodmak
Screenplay by Ralph Murphy, from a novel by Henry Edward Helseth
Photographed by Lloyd Ahern
Music by Alfred Newman
Musical direction by Lionel Newman
96 minutes

Victor Mature and Richard Conte in *Cry of the City*.

Cast: Victor Mature, Richard Conte, Fred Clark, Shelley Winters, Betty Garde, Berry Kroeger, Tommy Cook, Debra Paget, Hope Emerson, Roland Winters, Walter Baldwin, June Storey, Tito Vuolo, Mima Aguglia, Dolores Castle, Claudette Ross, Tine Francone

Crime in New York City, with Victor Mature as a police lieutenant tracking down a former school chum (Richard Conte) who shoots a policeman and later breaks out of jail to commit more murder before he is himself killed. What gives the film distinction is the vigorous direction of Robert Siodmak, a master of suspense and fluid camera movement, plus the performance of Conte as a chillingly vicious killer.

DANGEROUS YEARS

Produced by Sol M. Wurtzel
Directed by Arthur Peirson
Screenplay by Arnold Belgard, from a story by Arnold Belgard
Photographed by Benjamin Kline
Musical score by Rudy Schrager
65 minutes

Cast: William Halop, Ann E. Todd, Jerome Cowan, Anabel Shaw, Richard Shaw, Richard Gaines, Scotty Beckett, Darryl Hickman, Harry Shannon, Dickie Moore, Donald Curtis, Harry Harvey, Jr., Gill Stratton, Jr., Joseph Vitale, Marilyn Monroe, Nana Bryant

A young hoodlum (William Halop) recruits students into his gang and on one particular warehouse raid he kills a man. At his trial a young girl (Ann E. Todd) speaks up for him as her protector in the days when she lived in an orphanage. She is the adopted daughter of the district attorney (Richard Gaines) and when the hoodlum is sentenced to life imprisonment, the defense attorney (Jerome Cowan) lays the blame at the feet of the parents of delinquents. What the district attorney doesn't know is that the hoodlum is his son.

DEEP WATERS

Produced by Samuel G. Engel
Directed by Henry King
Screenplay by Richard Murphy, based on the novel *Spoonhandle* by Ruth Moore
Photographed by Joseph La Shelle
Music by Cyril Mockridge
Musical direction by Lionel Newman
86 minutes

Cast: Dana Andrews, Jean Peters, Cesar Romero, Dean Stockwell, Anne Revere, Ed Begley, Leona Powers, Mae Marsh, Will Geer, Bruno Wick, Cliff Clark, Harry Tyler, Raymond Greenleaf

Set in Maine and dealing with the lives of lobster fishermen, the story concerns an orphan (Dean Stockwell) who is placed in the home of a woman (Anne Revere) and causes trouble by stealing. A state welfare worker (Jean Peters) makes herself responsible for him, which brings him into contact with her boyfriend, a lobsterman (Dana Andrews), who takes a liking to the boy. The friendship between the two gives the boy substance, and he in turn promotes the romance between the girl and the lobsterman. Light on story but well photographed on location in Maine and revealing facets of life among the seafaring people.

ESCAPE

Produced by William Perlberg
Directed by Joseph L. Mankiewicz
Screenplay by Philip Dunne, based on the novel by John Galsworthy
Photographed by Frederick A. Young
Musical score by William Alwyn
Musical direction by Muir Mathieson
78 minutes

Cast: Rex Harrison, Peggy Cummins, William Hartnell, Norman Wooland, Jill Esmond, Frederick Piper, Marjorie Rhodes, Betty Ann Davies, Cyril Cusack, John Slater, Frank Pettingell, Michael Golden, Maurice Denham

Filmed in England, with Rex Harrison as a returned air force ace who gets mixed up in a scuffle in a London park in which a policeman is killed. He stands trial and is sentenced to three years, which he considers a gross miscarriage of justice. He escapes prison and becomes a hunted man, until he meets a girl (Peggy Cummins), with whom he falls in love and who helps him realize it is better to surrender to the law and tackle the injustice in another way. A mild melodrama, given some impact by the quality of its actors.

FIGHTING BACK

Produced by Sol M. Wurtzel
Directed by Malcolm St. Clair
Screenplay by John Stone
Photographed by Benjamin Kline
Musical score by Darrell Calker
Musical direction by David Chudnow
60 minutes

Cast: Paul Langton, Jean Rogers, Cary Grey, Joe Sawyer, Morris Ankrum, John Kellogg, Dorothy Christy, Tommy Ivo, Lela Tyler, Pierre Watkin, Daisy

A convict (Paul Langdon) wins his freedom by serving in the army and is afterwards given a job by a manufacturer (Morris Ankrum). An old crony turns up, steals an expensive bracelet from the employer, with the suspicion falling on the ex-convict. With the aid of his talented performing dog, the suspect is able to clear himself.

FURY AT FURNACE CREEK

Produced by Fred Kohlmar
Directed by H. Bruce Humberstone
Screenplay by Charles G. Booth, from a story by David Garth
Photographed by Harry Jackson
Musical score by David Raksin
Musical direction by Alfred Newman
88 minutes

Cast: Victor Mature, Colleen Gray, Glenn Langan, Reginald Gardiner, Albert Dekker, Fred Clark, Charles Kempler, Robert Warwick, George Cleveland, Roy Roberts, Willard Robertson, Griff Barnett, Frank Orth, J. Farrell MacDonald, Charles Stevens, Jay Silverheels

A military outpost in the West is wiped out by Indians and the commanding officer (Robert Warrick) is court-martialed on a charge of conspiracy. He dies of a heart attack during the trial and his two sons, an adventurer (Victor Mature) and an officer (Glenn Langan), set about finding the evidence to clear their father's name. They discover that he had been framed in order to pave the way for a crooked mining enterprise. The film is a superior Western, with well-staged action and good characterizations.

THE GAY INTRUDERS

Produced by Frank Seltzer
Directed by Ray McCarey
Screenplay by Francis Swann, from a story by Francis Swann and Ray McCarey
Photographed by Mack Stengler
Music by Ralph Stanley
Musical direction by David Chudnow
68 minutes

Cast: John Emery, Tamara Geva, Leif Erickson, Roy Roberts, Virginia Gregg, Si Wills, Sara Berner, Harry Lauter, Marilyn Williams

A pair of temperamental stage stars decide to resolve their differences by consulting psychiatrists. The stars (John Emery and Tamara Geva) each pretend that their doctors (Leif Erickson and Virginia Gregg) are old school chums. By the end of the film the doctors are the quarreling ones and the two stars are getting along well. An amusing lampoon on psychiatry.

GIVE MY REGARDS TO BROADWAY

Produced by Walter Morosco
Directed by Lloyd Bacon
Screenplay by Samuel Hoffenstein and Elizabeth Reinhardt, from a story by John Klempner
Photographed in Technicolor by Harry Jackson
Musical direction by Lionel Newman
82 minutes

Cast: Dan Dailey, Charles Winninger, Nancy Guild, Charlie Ruggles, Fay Bainter, Barbara Lawrence, Jane Nigh, Charles Russell, Sig Ruman, Howard Freeman, Herbert Anderson, Pat Flaherty, Harry Seymour, Paul Harvey, Lela Bliss, Georgie Caine, Matt McHugh

A sentimental show biz story about an old vaudevillian (Charles Winninger) who takes a job in a factory but never loses hope that he may one day return to the spotlight. To this end he brings his children up to be performers, but they gradually become interested in other lines and the old man finally realizes that the past cannot be re-created. The film is a showcase for the talents of the charming Winninger and contains some interesting peeks into the world of vaudeville.

GREEN GRASS OF WYOMING

Produced by Robert Bassler
Directed by Louis King
Screenplay by Martin Berkeley, based on the novel by Mary O'Hara
Photographed in Technicolor by Charles Clarke
Musical score by Cyril Mockridge
Musical direction by Lionel Newman
92 minutes

Cast: Peggy Cummins, Charles Coburn, Robert Arthur, Lloyd Nolan, Burl Ives, Geraldine Wall, Robert Adler, Will Wright, Herbert Heywood, Richard Garrick, Charles Hart, Charles Tannen

Idealized Americana, beautifully color photographed, about two families who compete in the trotting race business. The niece (Peggy Cummins) of a veteran owner (Charles Coburn) falls in love with the son (Robert Arthur) of another owner (Lloyd Nolan) and complicates the rivalry, but their love brings a solution. The film is light on story but appealing in its fine settings and its insights into the training of trotting horses.

HALF PAST MIDNIGHT

Produced by Sol M. Wurtzel
Directed by William F. Claxton
Screenplay by Arnold Belgard, from a story by Arnold Belgard
Photographed by Benjamin Kline
Musical score by Darrell Calker
Musical direction by David Chudnow
70 minutes

Cast: Kent Taylor, Peggy Knudsen, Joe Sawyer, Walter Sande, Gil Stratton, Jr., Martin Kosleck, Mabel Paige, Jean Wong, Jane Everett, Damien O'Flynn, Richard Loo, Tom Dugan, Jean de Briac, Willie Best, Victor Sen Yung, Beetlepuss Lewis

A mystery yarn, concerning a detective (Kent Taylor) who meets a girl (Peggy Knudsen) and finds she is being blackmailed by a dancer. The dancer is murdered and the girl is the suspect, until the detective finds out the identity of the real murderer.

THE IRON CURTAIN

Produced by Sol C. Siegel
Directed by William A. Wellman
Screenplay by Milton Krims, based on the personal
  history of Igor Gouzenko
Photographed by Charles G. Clarke
Musical direction by Alfred Newman
88 minutes

Cast: Dana Andrews, Gene Tierney, June Havoc, Berry
Kroeger, Edna Best, Stefan Schnabel, Nicholas Joy,
Eduard Franz, Frederic Tozere, Noel Cravat, Christopher
Robin Olsen, Peter Whitney, Leslie Barrie, Mauritz Hugo,
John Shay, Victor Woon, Anne Curson, Helena Dare,
Eula Morgan, Reed Hadley

Based on actual material concerning a major espionage
case in Canada, *The Iron Curtain* is an exciting depiction in semidocumentary style of the plight of a
Russian code clerk in Ottawa (Dana Andrews) who
defects and asks for Canadian asylum. He does so
after tipping off the Western allies about Soviet espionage schemes for infiltration and control of intelligence, which causes the Russians to demand his return.
The demands are denied and the clerk's life is protected
against their plans to kill him. A true story, told with
skillful matter-of-factness, and shot largely on location
in Canada.

JUNGLE PATROL

Produced by Frank N. Seltzer
Directed by Joe Newman
Screenplay by Francis Swann, based on the play by
  William Bowers
Photographed by Mack Stengler
Musical score by Emil Newman and Arthur Lange
72 minutes

Cast: Kristine Miller, Arthur Franz, Ross Ford, Tom
Noonan, Gene Reynolds, Richard Jaeckel, Mickey Knox,
Harry Lauter, Bill Murphy, C. Pat Collins

A war story about a squadron of fliers commanded by
a young veteran (Ross Ford) whose mission it is to
hold an air strip against the Japanese. They do so
until almost all of them are wiped out, but not until
the commander has enjoyed a little romance with a
visiting USO entertainer (Kristine Miller).

LET'S LIVE AGAIN

Produced by Frank Seltzer
Directed by Herbert Leeds
Screenplay by Rodney Carlisle and Robert Smiley, from a
  story by Herman Wohl and John Vlahos
Photographed by Mack Stengler
Music by Ralph Stanley
Musical direction by David Chudnow
68 minutes

Jean Peters and Dana Andrews in *Deep Waters.*

Charles Winninger and Dan Dailey in *Give My Regards to
Broadway.*

Peggy Cummins, Charles Coburn, and Robert Arthur in *Green
Grass of Wyoming.*

Gene Tierney and Dana Andrews in *The Iron Curtain.*

Tyrone Power and Anne Baxter in *The Luck of the Irish*.

Celeste Holm, Ida Lupino, and Cornel Wilde in *Road House*.

Lon McAllister, June Haver, and Geraldine Wall in *Scudda Hoo! Scudda Hay!*

Clifton Webb makes a point with the baby in *Sitting Pretty*.

Cast: John Emery, James Millican, Taylor Holmes, Diana Douglas, Hillary Brooke, Charles D. Brown, Jeff Corey, Percy Helton, John Parrish, Earle Hodgins, Dewey Robinson, Ralph D. Sanford, Rags

A wacky comedy, about an atomic scientist (John Emery) whose personality is overshadowed by that of his colorful explorer-brother (James Millican). When the brother is reported killed, the scientist imagines that a stray dog is the brother reincarnated. This causes complications in his work and his home-life, and he is put in an institution—and cured after a number of comic capers.

THE LUCK OF THE IRISH

Produced by Fred Kohlmar
Directed by Henry Koster
Screenplay by Philip Dunne, from a novel by Guy and Constance Jones
Photographed by Joseph La Shelle
Music by Cyril J. Mockridge
Musical direction by Lionel Newman
99 minutes

Cast: Tyrone Power, Anne Baxter, Cecil Kellaway, Lee J. Cobb, James Todd, Jayne Meadows, J. M. Kerrigan, Phil Brown, Charles Irwin, Louise Lorimer, Tim Ryan, Harry Antrim, Margaret Wells, John Galsworthy, Dorothy Neumann, Ruth Clifford, Douglas Gerrard, Tito Vuolo

A whimsical comedy about an American newspaper-man (Tyrone Power) on holiday in Ireland who comes across a leprechaun (Cecil Kellaway) and is adopted by him. He follows the newsman to New York, guides him toward a lovely colleen (Anne Baxter), and becomes his conscience. Gradually the newsman loses his ambitions for power and success and returns to Ireland with his new wife and a job as an open-minded writer for a liberal publication. A bit of a strain on credulity, but amusing, and a fine platform for the engaging Cecil Kellaway.

MEET ME AT DAWN

Produced by Marcel Hellman
Direction by Thornton Freeland
Screenplay by Lesley Storm and James Seymour
Photographed by Gunther Krampf
Music by Mischa Spoliansky
89 minutes

Cast: William Eythe, Stanley Holloway, Beatrice Campbell, George Thorpe, Irene Browne, Hazel Court, Basil Sydney, Margaret Rutherford, Ada Reeve, Graeme Muir, James Harcourt, Wilfred Hyde White, Charles Victor, John Salew, Percy Walsh, Hy Hazell, Diana Decker, John Ruddock, Katie Johnson

A comedy adventure, made in England, about a professional duellist (William Eythe) in the Paris of

1902, who makes a living hiring himself to those who want opponents put out of circulation. Complications arise when he is hired to duel a politician, but he is saved by the love of a beautiful woman (Hazel Court) who is also involved.

MINE OWN EXECUTIONER

Produced by Anthony Kimmins and Jack Kitchin
Directed by Anthony Kimmins
Screenplay by Nigel Balchin, from a novel by Nigel Balchin
Photographed by Wilkie Cooper
Musical score by Benjamin Frankel
105 minutes

Cast: Burgess Meredith, Dulcie Gray, Michael Shepley, Christine Norden, Kieron Moore, Barbara White, Walter Fitzgerald, Edgar Norfolk, John Laurie, Martin Miller, Clive Morton, Joss Ambler, Jack Raine, Lawrence Hanray

In London an acclaimed psychiatrist (Burgess Meredith) takes on a schizophrenic (Kieron Moore) who is an ex-fighter pilot and prisoner of the Japanese. The patient is more dangerous than the psychiatrist bargained for. He murders his wife and later commits suicide. The film pinpoints some of the problems of psychoanalysis and the dangers of a doctor taking on more than he should.

NIGHT WIND

Produced by Sol M. Wurtzel
Directed by James Tinling
Screenplay by Arnold Belgard and Robert G. North, from a story by Robert G. North
Photographed by Benjamin Kline
Music by Ralph Stanley
65 minutes

Cast: Charles Russell, Virginia Christine, Gary Gray, John Ridgely, James Burke, Konstantin Shayne, William Stelling, Flame

The hero is a dog called Flame, trained in wartime, whose master is killed by the Germans. Years later three men turn up at a hunting lodge where Flame lives. Because one is wearing a trenchcoat worn by his former master's killer, the dog attacks, causing the men to be revealed as agents spying on a nearby atomic project.

ROAD HOUSE

Produced by Edward Chodorov
Directed by Jean Negulesco
Screenplay by Edward Chodorov, based on a story by Margaret Gruen and Oscar Saul
Photographed by Joseph La Shelle
Music by Cyril Mockridge
95 minutes

Cast: Ida Lupino, Cornel Wilde, Celeste Holm, Richard Widmark, O. Z. Whitehead, Robert Karnes, George Beranger, Ian MacDonald, Grandon Rhodes, Jack G. Lee, Marion Marshall, Jack Edwards, Jr., Don Kohler

The owner (Richard Widmark) of a roadhouse becomes jealous when his singer (Ida Lupino) falls in love with his manager (Cornel Wilde). He frames him on a robbery charge and then has him released in his custody. To flaunt his control over them, the owner takes them along on a trip to his hunting lodge, where he is knocked unconscious during his drunken attack on the manager. The lovers try to escape and in pursuing them, the owner is killed by the singer. The murky melodrama is conspicuous for Widmark's playing of the psychotic owner and for Lupino's singing of the song "Again."

SCUDDA-HOO! SCUDDA-HAY!

Produced by Walter Morosco
Directed by F. Hugh Herbert
Screenplay by F. Hugh Herbert, based on a novel by Agnew Chamberlain
Photographed in Technicolor by Ernest Palmer
Musical score by Cyril Mockridge
Musical direction by Lionel Newman
95 minutes

Cast: June Haver, Lon McCallister, Walter Brennan, Anne Revere, Natalie Wood, Robert Karnes, Henry Hull, Tom Tully, Lee MacGregor, Geraldine Wall, Ken Christy, Tom Moore, Matt McHugh, Charles Wagenheim

The title refers to the yells made in training mules, which is what this genial bit of rural Americana is all about. A young man (Lon McCallister) goes to work for a farmer, Tom Tully) who once owned the pair of mules the boy now owns, and which he has trained with the help of a veteran mule man (Walter Brennan). The farmer connives to get the mules back, but his daughter (June Haver) sides with the boy in seeing that he keeps them. The film is amusing and exciting, and probably the only major film to take such a sympathetic interest in the character and welfare of mules. *Note:* A bit role by Marilyn Monroe ended on the cutting room floor.

SITTING PRETTY

Produced by Samuel G. Engel
Directed by Walter Lang
Screenplay by F. Hugh Herbert, based on a novel by Gwen Davenport
Photographed by Norbert Brodine
Musical score by Alfred Newman
84 minutes

Cast: Robert Young, Maureen O'Hara, Clifton Webb, Richard Haydn, Louise Allbritton, Randy Stuart, Ed Begley, Larry Olsen, John Russell, Betty Ann Lynn,

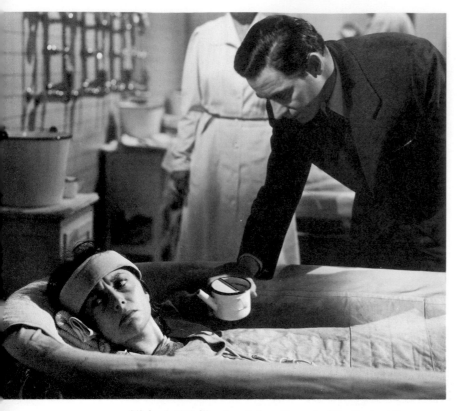

Olivia de Havilland and Leo Genn in *The Snake Pit*.

Betty Grable and Douglas Fairbanks, Jr., in *That Lady in Ermine*.

Willard Robertson, Anthony Sydes, Roddy McCaskill, Grayce Hampton

Lynn Belvedere (Clifton Webb), a self-declared genius, decides to add baby sitting to his list of accomplishments and takes a job with a suburban couple (Robert Young and Maureen O'Hara), who have been unable to hang on to maids because of the obstreperous behavior of their three children. Belvedere, who is actually an author doing research on a book about suburbia, is a master of all skills and under his caustic command the children become models of decorum. *Sitting Pretty* is a classic comedy and a high point in the career of Clifton Webb, a master of timing and haughty personal style.

THE SNAKE PIT

Produced by Darryl F. Zanuck
Directed by Anatole Litvak
Screenplay by Frank Partos and Millen Brand, based on the novel by Mary Jane Ward
Photographed by Leo Tover
Musical direction by Alfred Newman
108 minutes

Cast: Olivia de Havilland, Mark Stevens, Leo Genn, Celeste Holm, Glenn Langan, Helen Craig, Leif Erickson, Beulah Bondi, Lee Patrick, Howard Freeman, Natalie Schafer, Ruth Donnelly, Katherine Locke, Frank Conroy, Minna Gombell, June Storey, Lora Lee Mitchel

A breakthrough in film realism in Hollywood, *The Snake Pit* tackles the subject of insanity and the facts of life in mental institutions with no romantic notions or false hope. The story is that of a woman (Olivia de Havilland) who, soon after marriage, loses her mind and is sent to a state hospital for treatment. Her husband (Mark Stevens) remains loyal, and a kindly psychiatrist (Leo Genn) probes her past to understand the reasons for her aberration. With their support, she is saved from permanent confinement, but in the meantime she is exposed to the tragedies of other inmates and to the brutal conditions of an overcrowded asylum. Olivia de Havilland's performance as an intelligent woman skirting the borders of madness is a masterpiece.

THE STREET WITH NO NAME

Produced by Samuel G. Engel
Directed by William Keighley
Screenplay by Harry Kleiner
Photographed by Joe MacDonald
Musical direction by Lionel Newman
94 minutes

Cast: Mark Stevens, Richard Widmark, Lloyd Nolan, Barbara Lawrence, Ed Begley, Donald Buka, Joseph Pevney, John McIntire, Walter Greaza, Howard Smith,

192

Gene Tierney and Tyrone Power in *That Wonderful Urge*.

Bill Mauch, Sam Edwards, Don Kohler, Roger McGee, Vincent Donahue

A crime melodrama in semidocumentary style, concerning the FBI and its methods of tackling organized gangsterism. A bureau chief (Lloyd Nolan) sends an agent (Mark Stevens) to infiltrate a gang led by a slick criminal (Richard Widmark). The agent poses as a crook, but the leader of the gang frames him on a theft charge in order to get his background and exposes the FBI scheme to capture the gang. Other devices are then employed. The film gives a good indication of FBI methods in fighting crime, as well as the intelligence used by methodical criminals.

THAT LADY IN ERMINE

Produced and directed by Ernst Lubitsch
Screenplay by Samson Raphaelson
Photographed in Technicolor by Leon Shamroy
Songs by Leo Robin and Frederick Hollander
Musical direction by Alfred Newman
88 minutes

Cast: Betty Grable, Douglas Fairbanks, Jr., Cesar Romero, Walter Abel, Reginald Gardiner, Harry Davenport, Virginia Campbell, Whit Bissell, Edmund MacDonald, David Bond, Harry Cording, Belle Mitchell, Mary Bear

The last film of the master cinematic farceur Ernst Lubitsch and a disappointment, mostly because of an old-fashioned musical comedy script. The setting is a Ruritanian country in the nineteenth century, and a castle taken over by an invading army led by a dashing officer (Douglas Fairbanks, Jr.) who falls in love with the owner, a countess (Betty Grable). In a dream, her great-great-grandmother advises her to do as she did —pretend to fall in love with the invader and then kill him. But the countess falls in love with this one, period. Beautiful sets and costumes, and some nice songs, but the fantasy is flat. Lubitsch died during the course of production and the remainder of the film was directed by Otto Preminger.

THE TENDER YEARS

Produced by Edward L. Alperson
Directed by Harold Schuster
Screenplay by Jack Jungmeyer, Jr. and Harold Belgard, from a story by Jack Jungmeyer, Jr.
Photographed by Henry Freulich
Musical score and direction by Dr. Edward Kilenyi
81 minutes

Cast: Joe E. Brown, Richard Lyon, Noreen Nash, Charles Drake, Josephine Hutchinson, James Millican, Griff Barnett, Jeanne Gail, Harry V. Cheshire, Jimmie Dodd

A sentimentalized attack on cruelty to animals, about a kindly minister (Joe E. Brown) in a small town who comes across a barn in which the sport of dog fighting is being conducted. To save a dog to which his son (Richard Lyon) has become attached, the preacher steals it and prepares to stand trial for theft. The trial is called off, but it leads to legislation outlawing the sport.

THAT WONDERFUL URGE

Produced by Fred Kohlmar
Directed by Robert Sinclair
Screenplay by Jay Dratler, based on a story by William R. Lipman and Frederick Stephani
Photographed by Charles G. Clarke
Musical score by Cyril Mockridge
Musical direction by Alfred Newman
81 minutes

Cast: Tyrone Power, Gene Tierney, Reginald Gardiner, Arleen Whelan, Lucille Watson, Gene Lockhart, Lloyd Gough, Porter Hall, Richard Gaines, Taylor Holmes, Chill Wills, Hope Emerson, Frank Ferguson, Charles Arnt, Francis Pierlot, Mickey Simpson, Robert Foulke

A remake of *Love Is News* (1937), with Tyrone Power reprising his old role and Gene Tierney doing Loretta Young's part. He is again the newspaperman writing a story on a prominent society woman (Tierney), who tires of his invasion of her privacy and issues a statement announcing that she has married him. This leads to a variety of comic embarrassments for the writer and an eventual realization on the part of both that they really love each other.

13 LEAD SOLDIERS

Produced by Bernard Small
Directed by Frank McDonald
Screenplay by Irving Elman, from a story by "Sapper"
Photographed by George Robinson
Musical direction by Milton Rosen
66 minutes

Cast: Tom Conway, Maria Palmer, Helen Westcott, John Newland, Terry Kilburn, William Stelling, Gordon Richards, Harry Cording, John Goldworthy, William Edmunds

Tom Conway as master sleuth Bulldog Drummond on the trail of thieves who have taken several lead soldiers made 900 years previously by King Harold of the Normans. The complete set gives the key to the location of a treasure trove, so Drummond announces he has two of the lead soldiers himself, which leads him to nab the culprits.

TROUBLE PREFERRED

Produced by Sol M. Wurtzel
Directed by James Tinling
Screenplay by Arnold Belgard
Photographed by Benjamin Kline
Musical score by Lucien Cailliet

Musical direction by David Chudnow
62 minutes

Cast: Peggy Knudsen, Lynn Roberts, Charles Russell, Mary Bear, Paul Langton, James Cardwell, June Storey, Paul Guilfoyle, Marcia Mae Jones

The training and the duties of policewomen, with a pair of rookies (Peggy Knudsen and Lynne Roberts) bridling at being given desk jobs and bending rules in order to get more exciting assignments. They gain some credit when they save a suicide (Marcia Mae Jones) and effect her reunion with her husband.

UNFAITHFULLY YOURS

Produced by Preston Sturges
Directed by Preston Sturges
Screenplay by Preston Sturges
Photographed by Victor Milner
Musical direction by Alfred Newman
105 minutes

Cast: Rex Harrison, Linda Darnell, Barbara Lawrence, Rudy Vallee, Kurt Kreuger, Lional Stander, Edgar Kennedy, Alan Bridge, Julius Tannen, Torben Meyer, Robert Greig, Evelyn Beresford, Georgia Caine, Harry Seymour, Isabel Jewell, Marion Marshall

A marital farce, delightfully whipped up by the wit and style of Preston Sturges, in which a famous and temperamental British conductor (Rex Harrison) imagines his pretty young wife (Linda Darnell) is having an affair with his secretary (Kurt Kreuger). During a concert, his mind wanders as he conducts various pieces of music and he imagines ways of dramatically dealing with the situation. His suspicions prove groundless, but in the meantime he manages to make a fool of himself. The Sturges dialogue allows for many barbs at marriage and Harrision has plenty of scope to be grandly imperious, while also being amusingly human.

THE WALLS OF JERICHO

Produced by Lamar Trotti
Directed by John M. Stahl
Screenplay by Lamar Trotti, based on the novel by Paul Wellman
Photographed by Arthur Miller
Music by Cyril Mockridge
111 minutes

Cast: Cornel Wilde, Linda Darnell, Anne Baxter, Kirk Douglas, Ann Dvorak, Marjorie Rambeau, Henry Hull, Colleen Townsend, Barton MacLane, Griff Barnett, William Tracy, Art Baker, Frank Ferguson, Ann Morrison, Hope Landis

The Walls of Jericho takes its title from the Bible and such biblical factors as love, hate, greed, envy, and murder, but it is set in a small town called Jericho in the Kansas of 1908. It concerns a married doctor (Cornel Wilde) who spurns the wife (Linda Darnell) of his best friend (Kirk Douglas) and thereupon becomes the victim of her spite. The doctor's alcoholic wife (Ann Dvorak) shoots him when he falls in love with a young lawyer (Anne Baxter), but he survives and true love wins in the end. Such is the stuff of *The Walls of Jericho.*

WHEN MY BABY SMILES AT ME

Produced by George Jessel
Directed by Walter Lang
Screenplay by Lamar Trotti, based on the play *Burlesque* by George Manker Watters and Arthur Hopkins
Photographed in Technicolor by Harry Jackson
Songs by Mack Gordon and Joseph Myrow
Musical direction by Alfred Newman
98 minutes

Cast: Betty Grable, Dan Dailey, Jack Oakie, June Havoc, Richard Arlen, James Gleason, Vanita Wade, Kenny Williams, Jean Wallace, Pati Behrs, Robert Emmet Keane, Jerry Maren, George "Beetlepuss" Lewis, Tom Stevenson

A period musical, about a vaudeville couple, Bonnie (Betty Grable) and Skid (Dan Dailey), who lead a happy life until he graduates to success on Broadway. Success goes to his head and he starts to drink and ends up a confined alcoholic. She divorces him and plans to marry a rancher(Richard Arlen), but Skid's friend (Jack Oakie) pulls him together and gets him to go back on the stage. The attempt fails until Bonnie turns up, resulting in reconciliation and a resumption of their act. Light on plot but charming in its use of the vaudeville setting and its musical numbers.

THE WINNER'S CIRCLE

Produced by Richard Polimer
Directed by Felix Feist
Screenplay by Howard J. Green
Photographed by Elmer Dyer
Musical direction by Lucien Caillet
75 minutes

Cast: Johnny Longden, Morgan Farley, Bob Howard, William Gould, John Benardono, Frank Day, Russ Conway, Jean Willes

A story of a race horse, told from the point of view of the horse, from his birth on a Kentucky farm to his winning of a race at Santa Anita. It tells of his training, his initial failures, his relegation to menial work and eventual triumph, due to the devotion of his owner (Jean Willes). Johnny Longden appears as himself, riding the horse to victory, and the film is hyped by newsreel footage of celebrated race events.

YOU WERE MEANT FOR ME

Produced by Fred Kohlmar
Directed by Lloyd Bacon
Screenplay by Elick Moll and Valentine Davies
Photographed by Victor Milner
Musical direction by Lionel Newman
91 minutes

Cast: Jeanne Crain, Dan Dailey, Oscar Levant, Barbara Lawrence, Selena Royle, Percy Kilbride, Herbert Anderson, Les Clark, Kenny Williams, Harry Barris, Bob McCord, Lee McGregor

A genial and very musical slice of nostalgia, about a bandleader (Dan Dailey), his smalltown bride (Jeanne Crain), and his manager (Oscar Levant), and how they stumble through the Depression. They tour the towns of the Midwest but their chance to play New York disappears with the Wall Street crash. They go to live with her parents, but the bandleader finds it impossible to adjust to small town life and takes off by himself. When he lands a job with a hotel band in New York he sends for his wife, with the manager settling for the quiet life in the small town. The film offers a wide selection of songs of the Twenties and Thirties, with appearances by famous musicians like Harry Barris and Bob McCord, and a little of Levant at the piano playing Gershwin.

20TH CENTURY-FOX ACADEMY AWARDS FOR 1948

Symphony of a City: Best short subject (one reel). Produced by Edmund H. Reek.

SOUND RECORDING: *The Snake Pit.*

NICK KALTEN and LOUIS WITTE: Technical and scientific award (class 2).

Cornel Wilde and Linda Darnell in *The Walls of Jericho.*

Betty Grable and Dan Dailey in *When My Baby Smiles at Me.*

Rex Harrison and Linda Darnell in *Unfaithfully Yours.*

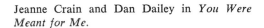

Jeanne Crain and Dan Dailey in *You Were Meant for Me.*

THE BEAUTIFUL BLONDE FROM BASHFUL BEND

Produced by Preston Sturges
Directed by Preston Sturges
Screenplay by Preston Sturges, from a story by Earl Felton
Photographed in Technicolor by Harry Jackson
Music by Cyril Mockridge
76 minutes

Cast: Betty Grable, Cesar Romero, Rudy Vallee, Olga San Juan, Sterling Holloway, Hugh Herbert, El Brendel, Porter Hall, Pati Behrs, Margaret Hamilton, Danny Jackson, Emory Parnell, Alan Bridge, Chris-Pin Martin, J. Farrell MacDonald, Richard Hale, Georgia Caine

A farce Western by Preston Sturges, with Betty Grable as the title heroine, a girl who has grown up in the Wild West and learned marksmanship as a way of protecting herself. Her boyfriend (Cesar Romero) starts to fool around with other girls, so she takes a shot at him, which misses and hits a judge in the rear end. She takes off for a different town and gets a job as a schoolteacher. When two of her students are reported killed, their father comes into town and shoots it up, and kidnaps Betty's new suitor (Rudy Vallee). She rescues him but dumps him when the boys are found to have played hookey and the former boyfriend promises to be true. Not the best of Sturges, but still containing some wacky lines and situations.

CANADIAN PACIFIC

Produced by Nat Holt
Directed by Edwin L. Marin
Screenplay by Jack DeWitt and Kenneth Gamet, from a story by Jack DeWitt
Photographed in Cinecolor by Fred Jackman, Jr.
Music by Dimitri Tiomkin
94 minutes

Cast: Randolph Scott, Jane Wyatt, J. Carrol Naish, Victor Jory, Nancy Olson, Robert Barrat, Walter Sande, Don Haggerty, Mary Kent, John Parrish, John Hamilton, Richard Wessel, Howard Negley

More fiction than fact, but aided by being filmed in the Rockies, *Canadian Pacific* purports to tell the story of the building of that railroad, with Randolph Scott as the tough surveyor and troubleshooter who blazes the trail for the tracks to follow. His main opposition comes from the leader (Victor Jory) of the trappers, who feel that the railroad will end their monopoly on the territory, and who whip the Indians up in revolt against the rail pioneers. An exciting Western, with spectacle and action, but with no approval from Canadian scholars.

CHICKEN EVERY SUNDAY

Produced by William Perlberg
Directed by George Seaton
Screenplay by George Seaton and Valentine Davies, from a play by Julius J. and Philip E. Epstein, based on a book by Rosemary Taylor
Photographed by Harry Jackson
Music by Alfred Newman
91 minutes

Cast: Dan Dailey, Celeste Holm, Colleen Townsend, Alan Young, Natalie Wood, William Frawley, Connie Gilchrist, William Callahan, Veda Ann Borg, Porter Hall, Whitney Bissell, Katherine Emory

A domestic comedy set in Tucson in the early years of the century about a married couple (Dan Dailey and Celeste Holm) who part company after years of problems caused by his vague schemes to get rich and by her practical approach to life. The husband is a charmer, but he never has the money to complete his ideas and his wife takes in boarders to support her family. When he uses the mortgage money to back a mining investment that proves a bust, she decides she has had enough. But friends contrive to bring the loving couple together. The playing of Dailey and Holm and Seaton's script and direction give the picture a warm and amusing quality.

COME TO THE STABLE

Produced by Samuel G. Engel
Directed by Henry Koster
Screenplay by Oscar Millard and Sally Benson, from a story by Clare Boothe Luce
Photographed by Joseph La Shelle
Song by Mack Gordon and Alfred Newman

Music by Cyril Mockridge
Musical direction by Lionel Newman
95 minutes

Cast: Loretta Young, Celeste Holm, Hugh Marlowe, Elsa Lanchester, Thomas Gomez, Dorothy Patrick, Basil Ruysdael, Dooley Wilson, Regis Toomey, Mike Mazurki, Henri Letondal, Walter Baldwin, Tim Huntley

The charming story of two French nuns (Loretta Young and Celeste Holm) who come to America with the object of building a hospital for children and achieve that object despite all the problems involved. They choose a small New England town called Bethlehem and their first friend is a painter (Elsa Lanchester) of religious canvases, who lets them use her studio, a converted stable. From there they set out to raise money, which includes persuading gamblers to invest and playing tennis for profit. With the help of local nuns the project comes to fruition. A delightful story, well set and played.

DANCING IN THE DARK

Produced by George Jessel
Directed by Irving Reis
Screenplay by Mary C. McCall, Jr., based on the musical revue *The Bandwagon* by George S. Kauffman, Howard Dietz, and Arthur Schwartz
Photographed in Technicolor by Harry Jackson
Songs by Howard Dietz and Arthur Schwartz
Musical direction by Alfred Newman
92 minutes

Cast: William Powell, Mark Stevens, Betsy Drake, Adolphe Menjou, Randy Stuart, Lloyd Corrigan, Hope Emerson, Walter Catlett, Don Beddoe, Jean Hersholt, Sid Grauman, Helen Wescott, Frank Ferguson, Charles Tannen

A Hollywood story, which begins with a famous star (William Powell) being feted at Grauman's Chinese

Rudy Vallee, Cesar Romero, Betty Grable, and Olga San Juan in *The Beautiful Blonde from Bashful Bend.*

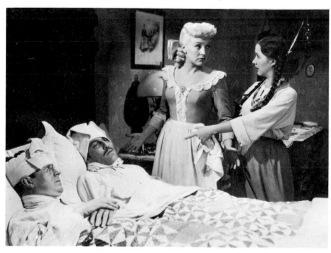

Nancy Olsen, Jane Wyatt, and Randolph Scott in *Canadian Pacific.*

Theatre and then moves to the present, twenty years later, when he is out of work and forgotten. The head of a studio (Adolphe Menjou) offers him the job of a talent scout, in order to sign a Broadway star who has been avoiding Hollywood. But the scout takes a liking to an unknown (Betsy Drake) and coaches her for the part. The studio rejects the idea but changes its mind when she gets publicity. It turns out she is the daughter of the washed-up movie star. An improbable tale, but with good views of Hollywood, a stylish performance by Powell, and an interesting use of the Arthur Scwartz-Howard Dietz songs from *The Bandwagon,* which is the musical being considered for filming within this film.

DOWN TO THE SEA IN SHIPS

Produced by Louis D. Lighton
Directed by Henry Hathaway
Screenplay by John Lee Mahin and Sy Bartlett, from a story by Sy Bartlett
Photographed by Joe MacDonald
Music by Alfred Newman
120 minutes

Cast: Richard Widmark, Lionel Barrymore, Dean Stockwell, Cecil Kellaway, Gene Lockhart, Berry Kroeger, John McIntire, Henry Morgan, Harry Davenport, Paul Harvey, Jay C. Flippen, Fuzzy Knight

A nineteenth-century whaling yarn about a grizzled old captain (Lionel Barrymore), his grandson (Dean Stockwell), who is eager to leave school and go to sea, and his first mate (Richard Widmark), who represents the new breed of seaman with his nautical education. The old man resents the new breed, but comes to respect him, even though he has to relieve him of his duties for rescuing his grandson and leaving the ship to do it. When the ship is damaged by contact with an iceberg, it is the old captain who saves the day and is fatally injured in the process. A fine sea saga, with a memorable performance from Barrymore and a good account of the whaling men out of New Bedford, Massachusetts.

EVERYBODY DOES IT

Produced by Nunnally Johnson
Directed by Edmund Goulding
Screenplay by Nunnally Johnson, from a story by James M. Cain
Photographed by Joseph La Shelle
Music by Mario Castelnuovo-Tedesco
Musical direction by Alfred Newman
98 minutes

Cast: Paul Douglas, Linda Darnell, Celeste Holm, Charles Coburn, Millard Mitchell, Lucile Watson, John Hoyt, George Tobias, Leon Belasco, Tito Vuolo, Geraldine Wall, Ruth Gilette, Gilbert Russell, John Ford

A businessman (Paul Douglas) cares little about music but indulges his wife (Celeste Holm) in her ambition to be an opera star. He hires a hall and she pleases the friendly audience. In the course of having produced the concert, he meets an opera star (Linda Darnell), who discovers that the businessman has a marvelous baritone voice. With her persuasion he takes lessons and proves a hit at recitals, but when he co-stars with her in an opera he makes a fool of himself with his awkwardness. He then decides to give up singing and stick to business, which pleases his wife. The film is a sophisticated comedy, well scripted and directed and with a fine performance from the amusing Douglas.

THE FAN

Produced by Otto Preminger
Directed by Otto Preminger
Screenplay by Walter Reisch, Dorothy Parker, and Ross Evans, from a play by Oscar Wilde
Photographed by Joseph La Shelle
Music by Daniele Amfitheatrof
80 minutes

Celeste Holm, Dan Dailey, and Alan Young in *Chicken Every Sunday*.

Celeste Holm and Loretta Young in *Come to the Stable*.

Cast: Jeanne Crain, Madeleine Carroll, George Sanders, Richard Greene, Martita Hunt, John Sutton, Hugh Dempster, Richard Ney, Virginia McDowall, Hugh Murray, Frank Elliott, John Burton, Trevor Ward

The fan belongs to Lady Windermere in Victorian London. This version of the Oscar Wilde play sacrifices some of the wit in order to build a story of amorous intrigue. An attractive widow (Madeleine Carroll) inveigles her way into London society, mostly by knowing the influential Lord Windermere (Richard Greene). Lady Windermere (Jeanne Crain) is having an affair with Lord Darlington (George Sanders) and leaves her fan in his apartment. When the fan is found and likely to cause a scandal, the widow claims that it is hers and leaves London in dishonor but with some satisfaction. It seems that she is the long-lost mother of Lady Windermere, and because of her the Windermeres go on to a long married life. The Preminger film misses the pungent style of the original material, but is well mounted and benefits from Sanders' playing, to the manner born, of the amorous aristocrat.

FATHER WAS A FULLBACK

Produced by Fred Kohlmar
Directed by John M. Stahl
Screenplay by Aleen Leslie, Casey Robinson, Mary Loos, and Richard Sale, from a play by Clifford Goldsmith
Photographed by Lloyd Ahern
Music by Cyril Mockridge
Musical direction by Lionel Newman
84 minutes

Cast: Fred MacMurray, Maureen O'Hara, Betty Lynn, Rudy Vallee, Thelma Ritter, Natalie Wood, James G. Backus, Richard Tyler, Buddy Martin, Mickey McCardle, John MeKee, Charles J. Flynn

A college football coach (Fred MacMurray) suffers through a losing season, with the sympathy of his wife (Maureen O'Hara), but with no help from his teenage

he slowly poisons her. It seems his family [...]
the house and its lands and he wants to r[...]
The other sister calls in an English doctor[...]
dleton), who diagnoses the malady. Whe[...]
the man of the house with the evidence, th[...]
the man falls to his death over a cliff. A[...]
amid charming settings.

MR. BELVEDERE GOES TO CO[...]

Produced by Samuel G. Engel
Directed by Elliott Nugent
Screenplay by Richard Sale, Mary Loos, an[...]
   Call, Jr., from a character created by Gwe[...]
Photographed by Lloyd Ahern
Music by Alfred Newman
84 minutes

Cast: Clifton Webb, Shirley Temple, Tom [...]
Young, Jessie Royce Landis, Kathleen Hug[...]
Holmes, Alvin Greenman, Paul Harvey, B[...]
Bob Patten, Lee MacGregor, Helen Westcot[...]
dler, Clancy Cooper, Evelynn Eaton, Judy B[...]

Shirley Temple returned to 20th Century-[...]
nine-year absence, but took second billing[...]
Webb, here reprising the delightful char[...]
he had registered in *Sitting Pretty.* Lynn B[...]
cides he needs to complete college in order[...]
for an award given only to men with d[...]
college agrees to enroll him, provided[...]
nothing to cause them undue publicity. Th[...]
is made difficult by a journalism major (T[...]
sees Belvedere's presence as the opportun[...]
an exciting magazine article. He outwits her[...]
when her behavior causes a rift with he[...]
(Tom Drake), he gets the young lovers tog[...]
The film gets its comedic value almost er[...]
Webb's presence.

MISS MINK OF 1949

Produced by Sol M. Wurtzel
Directed by Glenn Tyron
Screenplay by Arnold Belgard
Photographed by Benjamin Kline
Music by Mahlon Merrick
Musical direction by David Chudnow
69 minutes

Cast: Jimmy Lydon, Lois Collier, Richard L[...]
Brown, Paul Guilfoyle, June Storey, Gran[...]
Walter Sande, Don Kohler, Vera Mars[...]
Granger, Iris Adrian

An office clerk (Lois Collier) wins a te[...]
dollar mink coat in a radio contest and [...]
sternation for her husband (Jimmy Lydon)[...]
lifestyle is expected to be more grand. [...]

daughters (Natalie Wood and Betty Lynn), whose own problems with boys cause the father even more travail. When one of them publishes an article about her supposed sex life, father is almost fired, but a football champion (Richard Tyler) comes to his aid with guidance that puts the team on top—and all is well. A knockabout comedy and a good vehicle for the fumbling but genial comic talents of MacMurray.

FIGHTING MAN OF THE PLAINS

Produced by Nat Holt
Directed by Edwin L. Marin
Screenplay by Frank Gruber
Photographed in Cinecolor by Fred Jackman, Jr.
Music by Paul Sawtell
93 minutes

Cast: Randolph Scott, Bill Williams, Victor Jory, Jane Nigh, Douglas Kennedy, Joan Taylor, Berry Kroeger, Rhys Williams, Barry Kelley, James Todd, Paul Fix, James Millican, Burk Symon, Dale Robertson, Herbert Rawlinson, J. Farrell MacDonald, Harry Cheshire, James Griffith

In post-Civil War Kansas, an ex-member of Quantrill's Raiders (Randolph Scott) kills a man he believes murdered his brother. He is wrong and becomes a fugitive. Later, because of his skill as a gunfighter, he becomes the marshal of the Kansas town of Lanyard, where, with assistance of Jesse James (Dale Robertson), he drives out the gang who have been terrorizing the district. A good action tale, with Scott as its solid asset.

FORBIDDEN STREET

Produced by William Perlberg
Directed by Jean Negulesco
Screenplay by Ring Lardner, Jr., from the novel by
   Margery Sharp
Photographed by Georges Perinal
Music by Malcolm Arnold
Musical direction by Muir Mathieson
88 minutes

Cast: Dana Andrews, Maureen O'Hara, Dame Sybil Thorndike, Fay Compton, A. E. Matthews, Diane Hart, Ann Butchart, Wilfred Hyde White, Anthony Tancred, Herbert Walton, Mary Martlew, June Allen

A Victorian melodrama, filmed in London, about a well-bred young lady (Maureen O'Hara) who loves and marries an art teacher (Dana Andrews) and lives in poverty with him until he dies in an accident. A

William Powell and Betsy Drake in *Dancing in the Dark.*

Richard Widmark, Lionel Barrymore, and Dean Stockwell in *Down to the Sea in Ships.*

street harridan (Dame Sybil Thorndike) blackmails her, claiming she is a murderer, until a young barrister (also Dana Andrews) comes along with legal advice. They fall in love and together devise a puppet show that proves a great success, which brings the girl a reunion with her estranged family and another marriage. The melodrama creaks a little, especially with Andrews in a dual role.

HOUSE OF STRANGERS

Produced by Sol C. Siegel
Directed by Joseph L. Mankiewicz
Screenplay by Philip Yordan, from a novel by Jerome
   Weidman
Photographed by Milton Krasner
Music by Daniele Amfitheatrof
101 minutes

Cast: Edward G. Robinson, Susan Hayward, Richard Conte, Luther Adler, Paul Valentine, Efrem Zimbalist, Jr., Debra Paget, Hope Emerson, Esther Minciotti, Diana Douglas, Tito Vuolo, Sid Tomack

A dark drama about a hard, unscrupulous self-made banker (Edward G. Robinson) on New York's Lower East Side who employs his four sons at meager salaries and shows them little regard. When the father is arrested for illegal practices, the sons take over the business and deny the father access to his bank when he returns from prison. One son (Richard Conte) tries to help, but his brothers cause him to be jailed. When he is freed, he turns his back on them and proceeds to California with the girl (Susan Hayward) he loves. A grim account of a grim family, but well directed by Mankiewicz and acted by Robinson.

I CHEATED THE LAW

Produced by Sam Baerwitz
Directed by Edward L. Cahn
Screenplay by Richard G. Hubler, from a story by Sam
   Baerwitz
Photographed by Jackson A. Rose

199

Musical direction by Edward J. [...]
64 minutes

Cast: Tom Conway, Steve Brodie[...]
bara Billingsley, Russell Hicks, [...]
ley, Ton Noonan, William Goul[...]
Owen, Charles Waggenheim

A lawyer (Tom Conway) def[...]
Brodie) on a murder charge a[...]
He then finds the man is guilt[...]
be tried again, the lawyer devise[...]
other charge on him. Once he [...]
tricks the gangster into revealin[...]

I WAS A MALE WAR BRI[...]

Produced by Sol C. Siegel
Directed by Howard Hawks
Screenplay by Charles Lederer, [...]
    Hagar Wilde, from a story by [...]
Photographed by Norbert Brodin[...]
Musical direction by Lionel New[...]
105 minutes

Cast: Cary Grant, Ann Sheridan, [...]
Stuart, William Neff, Eugene Ger[...]
Lester Sharpe, John Whitney, Ker[...]
son, Alfred Linder, David McMa[...]

A French army officer (Cary Gr[...]
WAC officer are assigned to a p[...]
many and after a bickering cour[...]
marriage requires a great deal of [...]
the Frenchman decides to prc[...]
finds he qualifies for entry un[...]
act governing war brides, but [...]
husbands. His wife devises a wa[...]
—by getting him on a troop shi[...]
WAC. The paper work is finall[...]
until the Frenchman has under[...]
but, for the audience, amusing ex[...]
is top notch, thanks mostly to G[...]
in pretending to be a woman.

IT HAPPENS EVERY SF[...]

Produced by William Perlberg
Directed by Lloyd Bacon
Screenplay by Valentine Davies, [...]
    W. Smith and Valentine Davie[...]
Photographed by Joe MacDonald
Music by Leigh Harline
Musical direction by Lionel New[...]
87 minutes

Cast: Ray Milland, Jean Pete[...]
Begley, Ted de Corsia, Ray Colli[...]
Alan Hale, Jr., Bill Murphy, Wil[...]
Keane, Gene Evans, Al Eben, [...]
Jane Van Duser, Ray Teal, Gr[...]
Simpson, Johnny Calkins, Harry [...]
mour, Robert B. Williams, Charle[...]

200

Maureen O'Hara, Natalie Wood, and Fred MacMurray in
Father Was a Fullback.

Cary Grant and Ann Sheridan in *I Was a Male War Bride.*

Edward G. Robinson and Richard Conte in *House of
Strangers.*

Jean Peters and Ray Milland in *It Happens Every Spring.*

Clifton Webb and Shirley Temple in *Mr. Belvedere Goes to
College.*

Linda Darnell, Ann Sothern, and Jeanne Crain in *A Letter to
Three Wives.*

Loretta Young and Van Johnson in *Mother Is a Freshman*.

Mark Stevens and June Haver in *Oh, You Beautiful Doll*.

PINKY

Produced by Darryl F. Zanuck
Directed by Elia Kazan
Screenplay by Philip Dunne and Dudley Nichols, from
  a novel by Cid Ricketts Sumner
Photographed by Joe MacDonald
Music by Alfred Newman
102 minutes

Cast: Jeanne Crain, Ethel Barrymore, Ethel Waters,
William Lundigan, Basil Ruysdael, Kenny Washington,
Nina Mae McKinney, Griff Barnett, Frederick O'Neal,
Evelyn Varden, Raymond Greenleaf, Dan Riss

An indictment of racial bigotry and a major step forward for Hollywood in bringing to the screen the
problems of black Americans. The story is of a light-
complexioned girl (Jeanne Craine), the granddaughter
of a washerwoman (Ethel Waters), who returns to the
South after her northern education because of her love
for a white doctor (William Lundigan). When the
grandmother's employer (Ethel Barrymore), a kindly
but sharp-tongued dowager, becomes ill, the girl becomes her nurse and stays with her to the end. She
receives an inheritance, which is bitterly contested by
the dowager's relatives, but a court upholds the will,
despite the abuse leveled against the girl. She then
decides to dispense with her love for the doctor and to
open a nursery school. *Pinky* does not date, thanks to
Kazan's direction and the fine performances of Crain,
Waters, and Barrymore.

PRINCE OF FOXES

Produced by Sol C. Siegel
Directed by Henry King
Screenplay by Milton Krims, based on the novel by
  Samuel Shellabarger
Photographed by Leon Shamroy
Music by Alfred Newman
111 minutes

Cast: Tyrone Power, Orson Welles, Wanda Hendrix,
Marina Berti, Everett Sloane, Katina Paxinou, Felix
Aylmer, Leslie Bradley, Njntsky, Rena Lennart, Giuseppe
Faeti

A magnificently filmed adventure story about Renais-
sance Italy—unfortunately not in Technicolor—using
actual locations. The central story is of Cesare Borgia
(Orson Welles) and his ambition to control even wider
areas of Italy. He employs a soldier (Tyrone Power) to
act as a roving ambassador to the kingdoms he hopes to
acquire and pave the way for him. After some success
the ambassador goes to a mountain state ruled by an
elderly, peace-loving nobleman (Felix Aylmer) and
there learns of more honorable ways to live. He turns
against the Borgias and after suffering imprisonment
and torture leads a revolt against them. The film is interesting because of its sense of history, but is lacking
in excitement, because of a regrettable decision to shoot
in black-and-white, thereby losing the gorgeous color
potential of its costumes and locations.

SAND

Produced by Robert Bassler
Directed by Louis King
Screenplay by Martin Berkeley and Jerome Cady, from
  a novel by Will James
Photographed in Technicolor by Charles G. Clarke
Music by Daniele Amfitheatrof
88 minutes

Cast: Mark Stevens, Colleen Gray, Rory Calhoun,
Charley Grapewin, Bob Patten, Mike Conrad, Tom
London, Paul Hogan, Jack Gallagher, William (Bill)
Walker, Davison Clark, Ben Erwey, Harry Cheshire

A Will James horse story color-photographed in Colorado. A horseman (Mark Stevens) loses his prize
stallion as the result of a railroad accident and enlists
the aid of another horse lover (Colleen Gray) in

Jeanne Crain and Ethel Waters in *Pinky*.

Wanda Hendrix and Tyrone Power in *Prince of Foxes*.

John Russell, Linda Darnell, Veronica Lake and Richard Widmark in *Slattery's Hurricane*.

tracking the animal. The horse responds wildly to freedom and presents problems in dealing with those who treat it badly. By the time the owner locates the horse there is the fear it may have turned killer. But he wins its confidence and restores it to its former state of training. Definitely a film for horse lovers.

SLATTERY'S HURRICANE

Produced by William Perlberg
Directed by Andre de Toth
Screenplay by Herman Wouk and Richard Murphy, from a story by Herman Wouk
Photographed by Charles G. Clarke
Music by Cyril J. Mockridge
Musical direction by Lionel Newman
83 minutes

Cast: Richard Widmark, Linda Darnell, Veronica Lake, John Russell, Gary Merrill, Walter Kingsford, Raymond Greenleaf, Stanley Waxman, Joseph De Santis, David Wolf, Amelita Ward, William Hawes, Lee MacGregor

Adventures along the coasts of Florida, with weather experts and dope smugglers. A former Navy pilot (Richard Widmark) makes a comfortable and irresponsible living flying for a smuggling ring and making love to a secretary (Veronica Lake) of one of the leaders. He meets an old Navy colleague (John Russell), whose wife (Linda Darnell) was once his girl friend. He tries to get her back, but she brings him to his senses about his wild life and he reforms. He also performs heroic service for the weather bureau during a terrible hurricane. Widmark at his heel-hero best, together with good use of Florida locations and remarkable special effects in the filming of the fearful storm.

THIEVES' HIGHWAY

Produced by Robert Bassler
Directed by Jules Dassin
Screenplay by A. L. Bezzerides, based on his novel
Photographed by Norbert Brodine
Music by Alfred Newman
Musical direction by Lionel Newman
94 minutes

Cast: Richard Conte, Valentina Cortese, Lee J. Cobb, Barbara Lawrence, Jack Oakie, Millard Mitchell, Joseph Pevney, Morris Carnovsky, Tamara Shayne, Kasia Orzazewski, Norbert Schiller, Hope Emerson

A melodrama about the trucking of fruit and produce in California, with Lee J. Cobb as a crook who controls various truckers and merchants. He causes a man who will not cooperate to be badly injured and the man's son (Richard Conte) plans to break the crook. He becomes a trucker and gets involved with the crook's operation, and with the aid of a girl friend (Valentina Cortese) of the crook, who turns against him, he brings

204

in the police. Jules Dassin keeps the story moving at a brisk pace, with good use of highways and the produce district of San Francisco.

THIS WAS A WOMAN

Produced by Marcel Hellman
Directed by Tim Whelan
Screenplay by Val Valentine, from a play by Joan Morgan
Photographed by Gunther Krampf and Hal Britten
Music by Mischa Spoliansky
102 minutes

Cast: Sonia Dresdel, Walter Fitzgerald, Emrys Jones, Barbara White, Julian Dallas, Cyril Raymond, Marjorie Rhodes, Celia Lifton, Lesley Osmond, Kynaston Reeves, Noel Howlett

A British melodrama about a psychotic woman (Sonia Dresdel) who vents her frustrations on her family. She resents the announced marriage of her daughter (Barbara White) and upsets the girl emotionally. When she takes a fancy to another man, she poisons her husband (Walter Fitzgerald). Her son (Emrys Jones) is the only one who realizes how dangerous she is and calls the police. Although convicted of murder, she is certified insane and put in an institution.

TUCSON

Produced by Sol M. Wurtzel
Directed by William Claxton
Screenplay by Arnold Belgard
Photographed by Benjamin Kline
Music by Darrell Calker
60 minutes

Cast: Jimmy Lydon, Penny Edwards, Deanna Wayne, Charles Russell, Joe Sawyer, Walter Sande, Lyn Wilde, Marcia Mae Jones, John Ridgely, Gandon Rhodes, Gil Stratton, Harry Lauter

A student (Jimmy Lydon) at the University of Arizona does badly in class because most of his time is spent training his horse for the intercollegiate rodeo, which his father wants him to win in order to annoy a rival rancher. But he first has to learn responsibility in the classrooms before he can tackle the rodeo.

TWELVE O'CLOCK HIGH

Produced by Darryl F. Zanuck
Directed by Henry King
Screenplay by Cy Bartlett and Beirne Lay, Jr., based on the novel by Cy Bartlett
Photographed by Leon Shamroy
Music by Alfred Newman
132 minutes

Cast: Gregory Peck, Hugh Marlowe, Gary Merrill, Millard Mitchell, Dean Jagger, Robert Arthur, Paul Stewart, John Kellogg, Robert Patten, Lee McGregor, Sam Edwards, Roger Anderson, John Zilly

Based upon the wartime career of Major General Frank A. Armstrong, *Twelve O'Clock High* (air force jargon for "bombers over target") was a major step forward for Hollywood in taking a realistic look at war, with no flag waving or fiendish depictions of the enemy. It is a compassionate account of the stress and trauma of command, in which a general of the 8th Air Corps in England (Gregory Peck) gradually moves from being a martinet to being the victim of breakdown as his concern for his men undermines his health. He is daily involved in sending men to their deaths and he grows ever more protective about them. The film is among the very best made on the subject and Gregory Peck won much respect for the skill of his performance.

YELLOW SKY

Produced by Lamar Trotti
Directed by William Wellman
Screenplay by Lamar Trotti, from a story by W. R. Burnett
Photographed by Joe MacDonald
Music by Alfred Newman
99 minutes

Cast: Gregory Peck, Anne Baxter, Richard Widmark, Robert Arthur, John Russell, Henry Morgan, James Barton, Charles Kemper, Robert Adler, Harry Carter, Victor Killian, Paul Hurst, Hank Worden, Jay Silverheels

A classic Western, due to Lamar Trotti's fine script and William Wellman's firm direction. A group of outlaws arrive at a ghost town near exhaustion and find it occupied by an old man (James Barton) and his granddaughter (Anne Baxter). When they learn there is gold on the premises, the men make a deal with the old man to share it, but a few of them choose to cheat him. Their leader (Gregory Peck), who has a fondness for the girl, faces the dissension in his ranks and battles the main doublecrosser (Richard Widmark) and kills him. Filmed entirely on location in the California desert near Death Valley and with a fine performance from Peck as the lusty outlaw with heart.

YOU'RE MY EVERYTHING

Produced by Lamar Trotti
Directed by Walter Lang
Screenplay by Lamar Trotti and Will H. Hays, Jr., from a story by George Jessel
Photographed in Technicolor by Arthur E. Arling
Musical direction by Alfred Newman
94 minutes

205

Cast: Dan Dailey, Anne Baxter, Anne Revere, Stanley Ridges, Shari Robinson, Henry O'Neill, Selena Royle, Alan Mowbray, Robert Arthur, Buster Keaton, Phyllis Kennedy, Chester Jones, Nyas and Warren Berry, John Hiestand

A charming musical, largely set in Hollywood and dealing with the early days of sound films. A successful stage dancer (Dan Dailey) gets a screen test and his wife (Anne Baxter) steps into the scene to give him someone to play against. But it's the wife who gets the studio contract and goes on to become a major movie star, while the husband settles for his career as a dancer. When their daughter (Shari Robinson) shows talent as an entertainer, the father coaches her and she becomes another Shirley Temple, which displeases the mother, who would prefer the child not be in the business. The parents separate but are brought together by their daughter. With plenty of songs and dances, nice performances from Dailey and

Baxter, *You're My Everything* offers some interesting shots of old Hollywood, including a campy appearance by Alan Mowbray as a silent movie director.

20TH CENTURY-FOX ACADEMY AWARDS FOR 1949

JOSEPH L. MANKIEWICZ: Best direction for *A Letter to Three Wives.*

JOSEPH L. MANKIEWICZ: Best screenplay for *A Letter to Three Wives.*

DEAN JAGGER: Best performance by a supporting actor in *Twelve O'Clock High.*

THOMAS MOULTON, W. D. FLICK, and ROGER HEMAN: Best sound recording for *Twelve O'Clock High.*

A Chance to Live: Most distinctive documentary short (tie), March of Time, Richard de Rochemont, producer.

Anne Baxter and Dan Dailey in *You're My Everything.*

Dean Jagger and Gregory Peck in *Twelve O'Clock High.*

Gregory Peck and Anne Baxter in *Yellow Sky.*

ALL ABOUT EVE

Produced by Darryl F. Zanuck
Directed by Joseph L. Mankiewicz
Screenplay by Joseph L. Mankiewicz, based on the story
 The Wisdom of Eve by Mary Orr
Photographed by Milton Krasner
Music by Alfred Newman
138 minutes

Cast: Bette Davis, Anne Baxter, George Sanders, Celeste Holm, Gary Merrill, Hugh Marlowe, Thelma Ritter, Marilyn Monroe, Gregory Ratoff, Barbara Bates, Walter Hampden, Randy Stuart, Craig Hill, Leland Harris, Claude Stroud, Eugene Borden, Steve Geray, Bess Flowers, Stanley Orr

It is doubtful if there will ever be a more revealing film about the theatre and its people than *All About Eve.* The girl of the title is an aspiring actress (Anne Baxter) who dotes on veteran Broadway star Margo Channing (Bette Davis) and insinuates her way into her employment and eventually into a successful career. Along the way she cajoles, charms, seduces, and sometimes tramples on a variety of writers, directors, producers, and sundry wives. One critic (George Sanders) sees through her and her machinations but loves her nonetheless. He is the one who knows "all about Eve." The film is writer-director Mankiewicz's masterpiece, sparkling with wit and knowledge about the theatrical profession. It is also one of Bette Davis' finest vehicles, as well as being a showcase for the acting skills of Anne Baxter, George Sanders, and almost everyone who appears in it.

AMERICAN GUERRILLA IN THE PHILIPPINES

Produced by Lamar Trotti
Directed by Fritz Lang
Screenplay by Lamar Trotti, based on the novel by Ira
 Wolfert
Photographed in Technicolor by Harry Jackson
Music by Cyril J. Mockridge
Musical direction by Lionel Newman
105 minutes

Cast: Tyrone Power, Micheline Presle, Tom Ewell, Bob Patten, Tommy Cook, Juan Torena, Jack Elam, Robert Barrat, Carleton Young

The guerrilla warfare against the Japanese in the Philippines, partly filmed in the South Pacific, with Tyrone Power as a young naval officer whose ship is sunk off Leyte, and who joins with other stranded Americans to help the Filipinos organize their resistance campaign. They build radio stations to spread news of the war and harass the enemy at every turn. The navy man falls in love with the French wife (Micheline Presle) of a local hero, who is killed by the Japanese. At the end, General MacArthur (Robert Barrat) keeps his promise to return to the islands. A conventional war story, but well mounted and paced by director Lang.

THE BIG LIFT

Produced by William Perlberg
Directed by George Seaton
Screenplay by George Seaton
Photographed by Charles G. Clarke
Music by Alfred Newman
119 minutes

Cast: Montgomery Clift, Paul Douglas, Cornell Borchers, Bruni Loebel, O. E. Hasse, Danny Davenport

An excellent account of adventures during the Berlin air lift, with the American Air Force bringing in supplies in the face of the Russian blockade. Filmed entirely in Berlin and making exciting use of Tempelhof Airport, the story has Montgomery Clift as a pilot and Paul Douglas as a ground operations sergeant doing their jobs successfully despite the pilot's unhappy love affair with a local girl (Cornell Borchers) and the sergeant's hatred for Germans, due to war experiences. Clift and Douglas are the only Hollywood personalities; the rest are German actors and members of the armed forces. Writer-director Seaton makes this an entertaining as well as informative picture.

THE BLACK ROSE

Produced by Louis D. Lighton
Directed by Henry Hathaway
Screenplay by Talbot Jennings, based on the novel by
 Thomas B. Costain
Photographed in Technicolor by Jack Cardiff
Music by Richard Addinsell

207

Anne Baxter, Bette Davis, Marilyn Monroe, and George Sanders in *All About Eve*.

Musical direction by Muir Matheison
120 minutes

Cast: Tyrone Power, Orson Welles, Cecile Aubry, Jack Hawkins, Michael Rennie, Finlay Currie, Herbert Lom, Mary Clare, Bobby Blake, Alfonso Bedoya, Gibb McLaughlin, James Robertson Justice

A large-scaled historical romance, about a thirteenth-century Saxon nobleman (Tyrone Power) who leaves England, disgusted with Norman subjugation and heads for the Far East in search of adventure. He takes with him his warrior friend (Jack Hawkins) and while traversing North Africa they meet a powerful war lord (Orson Welles), who dreams of conquering the world, and with whom they dally for a while. Eventually, the nobleman and his friend reach China, where they are treated like gods, until they want to leave. Then they have to fight their way out. The friend is killed, but the Saxon makes his way back to England, taking with him the discovery of gunpowder, printed books, and tales of the other side of the world. The long story lumbers a little, but the color photography by Jack Cardiff of locations in England and Morocco is superb.

BROKEN ARROW

Produced by Julian Blaustein

Directed by Delmer Daves
Screenplay by Michael Blankfort, from the novel by Elliott Arnold
Photographed by Ernest Palmer
Musical direction by Alfred Newman
93 minutes

Cast: James Stewart, Jeff Chandler, Debra Paget, Basil Ruysdael, Will Geer, Joyce MacKenzie, Arthur Hunnicutt, Raymond Bramley, Jay Silverheels, Argentina Brunetti, Jack Lee

A superb Western, beautifully photographed in Arizona, and accurately dealing with the conflict between the whites and the Apaches in the 1870's. A veteran scout (James Stewart) reasons that intelligence must be used in halting the warfare. He learns the Apache language, confers with their leader Cochise (Jeff Chandler) and prevails upon him to allow the mail riders to pass unmolested. The two men become friends and the scout falls in love with an Indian girl (Debra Paget), whom he marries. When she is killed by renegade whites, the scout cries for revenge, but Cochise advises him to contain his anger. Peace is finally brought about through conferences and agreement. *Broken Arrow* retains its distinction of being one of the first major Westerns to deal with the Indians with respect and knowledge.

THE CARIBOO TRAIL

Produced by Nat Holt
Directed by Edwin L. Marin
Screenplay by Frank Gruber, from a story by John Rhodes Sturdy
Photographed in Cinecolor by Fred Jackman, Jr.
Music by Paul Sawtell
82 minutes

Cast: Randolph Scott, George "Gabby" Hayes, Bill Williams, Karin Booth, Victor Jory, Douglas Kennedy, Jim Davis, Dale Robertson, Mary Stuart, James Griffith, Lee Tung Foo, Tony Hughes

Gold-mining adventures in the Cariboo district of British Columbia in the 1890's, with Randolph Scott as a prospector from Montana. An enterprising crook (Victor Jory) sets himself up as the boss of the territory and makes things hard for everyone, including Scott, who finally realizes the folly of chasing gold and turns to cattle ranching. Action and scenery makes this a solid Western.

CHEAPER BY THE DOZEN

Produced by Lamar Trotti
Directed by Walter Lang
Screenplay by Lamar Trotti, from a novel by Frank B. Gilbreth, Jr., and Ernestine Gilbreth Carey
Photographed in Technicolor by Leon Shamroy
Music by Cyril J. Mockridge
Musical direction by Lionel Newman
85 minutes

Cast: Clifton Webb, Jeanne Crain, Myrna Loy, Betty Lynn, Edgar Buchanan, Barbara Bates, Mildred Natwick, Sara Allgood, Anthony Sydes, Roddy McCaskill, Norman Ollestad, Carole Nugent, Jimmy Hunt, Teddy Driver

A charming comedy about a turn-of-the-century family, with twelve children, ruled over by a stern but loving father (Clifton Webb), with the aid of a gentle wife (Myrna Loy). The film is a series of incidents, such as the father escorting the eldest daughter (Jeanne Crain) to her first high school prom and becoming the hit of the evening himself, and father accompanying his children to the hospital to supervise a mass taking-out of tonsils. His death comes as a shattering blow to a family for whom he has been the captain. Clifton Webb dominates the picture with his commanding but amusing style.

DAKOTA LIL

Produced by Edward L. Alperson
Directed by Lesley Selander
Screenplay by Maurice Geraghty, from a story by Frank Gruber
Photographed in Cinecolor by Jack Greenhalgh
Music by Dimitri Tiomkin
87 minutes

Cast: George Montgomery, Rod Cameron, Marie Windsor, John Emery, Wallace Ford, Jack Lambert, Larry Johns, Marion Martin, Walter Sande, Kenneth MacDonald

A Western about counterfeiters. An agent (George Montgomery) of the Secret Service is sent west to uncover a gang in control of large amounts of fake money. He finds a dance hall girl (Marie Windsor) to be a ring leader and ingratiates himself with her, which leads to his meeting the bandit leader (Rod Cameron). By the time she realizes he is a government man, she is in love with him and helps him bring the gang to justice.

FAREWELL TO YESTERDAY

Produced by Edmund Reek
Writen by Joseph Kenas
Narrated by Sidney Blackmer, John Larkin, Kermit Murdock, and William Post, Jr.
Music by Louis Applebaum and Richard Mohaupt
Musical direction by Jack Shaindlin
60 minutes

A documentary concerning the errors of twentieth-century history, the diplomatic mistakes and blunders which resulted in the second World War. The footage is taken from newsreels, armed services films, and material drawn from foreign countries, all of it expertly edited to form a warning history lesson.

THE FIREBALL

Produced by Bert Friedlob
Directed by Tay Garnett
Screenplay by Tay Garnett and Horace McCoy
Photographed by Lester White
Music by Victor Young
85 minutes

Cast: Mickey Rooney, Pat O'Brien, Beverly Tyler, James Brown, Marilyn Monroe, Ralph Dumke, Bert Begley, Milburn Stone, Sam Flint, John Hedloe, Glen Corbett

The thrills and spills of the roller derby, with Mickey Rooney as an orphan who runs away from a school presided over by a priest (Pat O'Brien) and discovers an interest in roller skating, which he devolps into a great skill. Seeing him become a success, the priest does nothing to stop him. But the boy becomes arrogant with his success and at the height of his popularity he is struck down with polio. With great determination he exercises and reclaims his health, and reenters the sport. By now he has learned some humility and allows the young players to win points. Good action sequences and Rooney's vitality carry the film.

Tyrone Power and Micheline Prelle in *An American Guerilla in the Philippines*.

Paul Douglas and Montgomery Clift in *The Big Lift*.

Tyrone Power, Orson Welles, and Jack Hawkins in *The Black Rose*.

FOR HEAVEN'S SAKE

Produced by William Perlberg
Directed by George Seaton
Screenplay by George Seaton, based on a play by Harry Segall
Photographed by Lloyd Ahern
Music by Alfred Newman
92 minutes

Cast: Clifton Webb, Joan Bennett, Robert Cummings, Edmund Gwenn, Joan Blondell, Gigi Perreau, Jack La Rue, Harry von Zell, Tommy Rettig, Dick Ryan, Charles Lane, Robert Kent, Whit Bissell, Ashmead Scott

A supernatural satire, with Clifton Webb as an angel sent from above to help solve the problems of a theatrical producer (Robert Cummings) and his actress wife (Joan Bennett). The couple bicker, and they have been too busy to have children. The angel takes the form of a wealthy rancher in order to meet the couple, who need backing for their new show. The social life appeals to the angel and he finds he has a gift for gambling and winning, which brings the income tax people on his trail. With the aid of a sober fellow angel (Edmund Gwen) he is rescued from his predicament and returns to heaven. Seaton's script and direction make this a charming comedy, with a bravura performance from Webb.

THE GUNFIGHTER

Produced by Nunnally Johnson
Directed by Henry King
Screenplay by William Bowers and William Sellers, from a story by William Bowers and Andre de Toth
Photographed by Arthur Miller
Music by Alfred Newman
85 minutes

Cast: Gregory Peck, Helen Westcott, Millard Mitchell, Jean Parker, Karl Malden, Skip Homeier, Anthony Ross, Verna Felton, Ellen Corby, Richard Jaeckel, Alan Hale, Jr., David Clarke, John Pickard, B. G. Norman, Angela Clarke, Cliff Clark, Jean Inness

A famed gunfighter (Gregory Peck) rides into a town to see his estranged wife (Helen Westcott) and their small son. The sheriff (Millard Mitchell) is an old friend, but warns him that his presence is upsetting to the town and that he must move on. After seeing his wife, and arranging a possible future reconciliation, he starts to leave town, but is challenged by a young hoodlum (Skip Homeier) and mortally wounded. Before he dies he warns the hoodlum that all he can look forward to is a smiliar fate. *The Gunfighter* is a masterly Western, darkly shaded and tautly directed by Henry King, with an indelible performance by Peck as the outlaw, weary and doomed by his reputation.

Debra Paget, Jeff Chandler, and James Stewart in *Broken Arrow*.

I'LL GET BY

Produced by William Perlberg
Directed by Richard Sale
Screenplay by Mary Loos and Richard Sale, from a story
  by Robert Ellis, Helen Logan, and Pamela Harris
Photographed in Technicolor by Charles G. Clarke
Musical direction by Lionel Newman
86 minutes

Cast: June Haver, William Lundigan, Gloria De Haven,
Dennis Day, Harry James, Thelma Ritter, Steve Allen,
Danny Davenport, Tom Hanlon

A musical comedy about song writers and using the title
song and a number of other standards for its score.
A publisher (William Lundigan) on the verge of poverty is joined by a singer (Dennis Day) who has written "Deep in the Heart of Texas." They meet a couple
of sisters (June Haver and Gloria De Haven) who are
singing with Harry James' band and try to get the song
plugged. With that and "I'll Get By" they start to be
prosperous, but a boycott by the song writers union
(ASCAP) against radio soon dissipates their profits.
Their problems are solved by the war and they join
the Marines in the South Pacific, where they are reunited with their girls, now touring as entertainers.
A pleasant musical, with familiar music and guest appearances by Jeanne Crain, Victor Mature, and Dan
Dailey. The film is actually an updating of *Tin Pan
Alley.*

Cheaper By the Dozen, with (in back row) Barbara Bates,
Clifton Webb, Myrna Loy, and Jeanne Crain.

Gregory Peck as *The Gunfighter.*

THE JACKPOT

Produced by Samuel G. Engel
Directed by Walter Lang
Screenplay by Phoebe and Henry Ephron, based on an
  article in the *New Yorker* by John McNulty
Photographed by Joseph La Shelle
Music by Lionel Newman
87 minutes

Cast: James Stewart, Barbara Hale, James Gleason, Fred
Clark, Alan Mowbray, Patricia Medina, Natalie Wood,
Tommy Rettig, Robert Gist, Lyle Talbot, Charles Tannen,
Bigelow Sayre, Dick Cogan, Jewel Rose, Eddie Firestone

A satire on radio quiz programs, with James Stewart
as a typical, small-town married man who answers a
phone call from a radio show and wins the jackpot
with his replies to their questions. As the prizes pour in
his life changes. His favorite furniture is relegated to
the garage, the house is decorated against his tastes,
he has no place to keep a Shetland pony or the tons
of foodstuffs delivered to him. Worst of all he has the
income tax people on his tail. After losing his job
and spending a night in jail, he is more than content
to go back to his ordinary dull life. Stewart makes
the winner's anguish amusingly painful.

211

LOVE THAT BRUTE

Produced by Fred Kohlmar
Directed by Alexander Hall
Screenplay by Karl Tunberg, Darrell Ware, and John Lee Mahin
Photographed by Lloyd Ahern
Music by Cyril Mockridge
Musical direction by Lionel Newman
86 minutes

Cast: Paul Douglas, Jean Peters, Cesar Romero, Keenan Wynn, Joan Davis, Arthur Treacher, Peter Price, Jay C. Flippen, Barry Kelley, Leon Belasco, Edwin Max, Sid Tomack, Phil Tully, Clara Blandick

A soft-hearted racketeer (Paul Douglas) falls in love with the recreation director (Jean Peters) of a city park and hires her to be the governess of his children, even though he has none. He has his lieutenant (Keenan Wynn) find a child for him, but the governess threatens to walk out when she learns that her boss is an underworld figure, about to merge with another gangster (Cesar Romero). She changes her mind when she realizes that he is not a killer and that he is willing to change his ways.

MR. 880

Produced by Julian Blaustein
Directed by Edmund Goulding
Screenplay by Robert Riskin, based on the *New Yorker* article by St. Clair McKelway
Photographed by Joseph La Shelle
Music by Sol Kaplan
Musical direction by Lionel Newman
90 minutes

Cast: Burt Lancaster, Dorothy McGuire, Edmund Gwenn, Millard Mitchell, Minor Watson, Howard St. John, Hugh Sanders, James Millican, Howland Chamberlain, Larry Keating, Kathleen Hughes, Geraldine Wall

The charming story of an old counterfeiter (Edmund Gwenn) who turns out a few badly made dollar bills, just enough to support himself but enough to confound the Federal agents, to whom he is known by his file number, Mr. 880. The top agent (Burt Lancaster) falls in love with a girl (Dorothy McGuire) who gets stuck with one of the bills, which comes about because she lives in the same apartment building as the counterfeiter. Eventually he is caught, but his charm and his reputation as a kindly man cause the judges to minimize his sentence. The agreeable yarn, based on an actual case, is genial tour-de-force for Edmund Gwenn.

MOTHER DIDN'T TELL ME

Produced by Fred Kohlmar
Directed by Claude Binyon

Screenplay by Claude Binyon, from a book by Mary Bard
Photographed by Joseph La Shelle
Musical direction by Lionel Newman
83 minutes

Cast: Dorothy McGuire, William Lundigan, June Havoc, Joyce MacKenzie, Gary Merrill, Jessie Royce Landis, Leif Erickson, Reiko Sato, Anthony Cobb, Tracy Cobb, Georgia Backus, Everett Glass, Michael Brandon, Mary Bear, Larry Keating, Jean "Babe" London, Wilton Graff

A marital comedy about a young woman (Dorothy McGuire) who visits a doctor (William Lundigan) because of a cold and falls in love with him at first sight. They marry and she finds it hard to be a doctor's wife, dealing with his hours and his many women patients. She makes mistake after mistake and annoys the doctor's haughty mother (Jessie Royce Landis). She has a real battle when his assistant (Joyce MacKenzie) makes a play for the boss. Finally she settles down to the realities of life with the doctor and he, too, makes the necessary adjustments. The film rests on the talents of the charming and amusing McGuire.

THE MUDLARK

Produced by Nunnally Johnson
Directed by Jean Negulesco
Screenplay by Nunnally Johnson, from a novel by Theodore Bonnet
Photographed by George Perinal
Music by William Alwyn
Musical direction by Muir Mathieson
100 minutes

Cast: Irene Dunne, Alec Guinness, Andrew Ray, Beatrice Campbell, Finlay Currie, Anthony Steel, Raymond Lovell, Marjorie Fielding, Constance Smith, Ronan O'Casey, Edward Rigby, Robin Stevens, William Strange, Kynaston Reeves

Irene Dunne as Queen Victoria and Alec Guinness as Benjamin Disraeli. A scruffy street urchin (Andrew Ray) breaks into Windsor Castle and meets the Queen, who cannot be convinced that the boy has anything to do with possible assassination plot. The Queen, depressed after many years of seclusion, is taken by the boy's cheerful nature and through their friendship she agrees to reenter public life. A charming story, with a splendid performance from Dunne and backed up by the skillful use of locations such as Windsor Castle, the Tower of London, and the Parliament buildings.

MY BLUE HEAVEN

Produced by Sol C. Siegel
Directed by Henry Koster
Screenplay by Lamar Trotti and Claude Binyon, from a story by S. K. Lauren

Photographed in Technicolor by Arthur E. Arling
Songs by Harold Arlen and Ralph Blane
Musical direction by Alfred Newman
96 minutes

Cast: Betty Grable, Dan Dailey, David Wayne, Jane Wyatt, Mitzi Gaynor, Una Merkel, Louise Beavers, Laura Pierpont, Don Hicks, Beulah Parkington, Ann Burr, Melinda Plowman, Vicki Lee Blunt, Gary Pagett

Betty Grable and Dan Dailey as a husband and wife team of radio entertainers. They badly want to become parents, but when her doctor tells her she may not conceive, they try to adopt. As theatrical people they find the agencies are not well disposed toward them. They acquire a child through devious means and then have it taken away from them. A kindly head of a home for foundlings lets them have a child, at the same time the first child is returned to them—as well as getting the news that Betty is really pregnant. The slim story is well supported by plenty of top-notch dancing by Grable and Dailey, and the film debut of Mitzi Gaynor.

NIGHT AND THE CITY

Produced by Samuel C. Engel
Directed by Jules Dassin
Screenplay by Jo Eisinger, from the novel by Gerald Kersh
Photographed by Max Greene
Music by Franz Waxman
95 minutes

Cast: Richard Widmark, Gene Tierney, Googie Withers, Hugh Marlowe, Francis L. Sullivan, Herbert Lom, Stanislaus Zbyszko, Mike Mazurki, Charles Farrell

Crime in the murky depths of the London underground, with Richard Widmark as a conniving promoter with more ambition than talent. He is a tout for a night club partly owned by a woman (Googie Withers) who feels some sympathy for him. She lends him money to set up a new club, but he uses it for his own scheme, to break into the wrestling racket, which puts him into conflict with a czar (Herbert Lom) of that racket. The tout's lies and double dealings end with him being killed. A conventional crime plot, but given some style by director Dassin and the use of London locations.

NO WAY OUT

Produced by Darryl F. Zanuck
Directed by Joseph L. Mankiewicz
Screenplay by Joseph L. Mankiewicz and Lesser Samuels
Photographed by Milton Krasner
Music by Alfred Newman
106 minutes

Cast: Richard Widmark, Linda Darnell, Stephen McNally, Sidney Poitier, Mildred Joanne Smith, Harry Bel-laver, Stanley Ridges, Dots Johnson, Amanda Randolph, Bill Walker, Ruby Dee, Ossie Davis, Ken Christy

A vividly dramatic account of racial prejudice, with Sidney Poitier, in his film debut, as a graduate doctor assigned to a municipal hospital with a liberal administrator (Stephen McNally). Two hoodlums, brothers, are brought in and the doctor operates on one because he detects something more than a gunshot wound. The man dies and his brother (Richard Widmark), a psychotic who hates blacks vows he will kill the doctor. He engineers a riot, but the widow (Linda Darnell) of the dead man realizes the stupidity of it all and moves to save the doctor. *No Way Out* retains its validity as an indictment of prejudice, as well as being excellent drama, thanks to the writing and direction of Mankiewicz.

PANIC IN THE STREETS

Produced by Sol C. Siegel
Directed by Elia Kazan
Screenplay by Richard Murphy, from a story by Edna and Edward Anhalt
Photographed by Joe MacDonald
Music by Alfred Newman
96 minutes

Cast: Richard Widmark, Paul Douglas, Barbara Bel Geddes, Walter (Jack) Palance, Zero Mostel, Dan Riss, Alexis Minotis, Guy Tomajan, Tommy Cook, Edward Kennedy, H. T. Tsiang

Filmed in New Orleans and making excellent use of its streets and its dock area, the story is that of a medical officer (Richard Widmark) who finds that an illegal alien has died not only of gunshot wounds but of plague, and that the two men responsible for killing him have no doubt picked up the germs. He alerts the city and keeps the news from reaching the papers, and with the aid of a police captain (Paul Douglas) he leads a manhunt that traces the two men (Jack Palance and Zero Mostel). By the time the fugitives are located, they are indeed suffering from the plague. A fictional story, but mounted with almost documentary technique and made convincing by Kazan's tight direction.

STELLA

Produced by Sol C. Siegel
Directed by Claude Binyon
Screenplay by Claude Binyon, based on a novel by Doris Miles Disney
Photographed by Joe MacDonald
Music by Cyril Mockridge
83 minutes

Cast: Ann Sheridan, Victor Mature, David Wayne, Randy Stuart, Marion Marshall, Frank Fontaine, Leif Erickson, Evelyn Varden, Lea Penman, Joyce MacKenzie, Hobart

Cavanaugh, Charles Halton, Walter Baldwin, Larry Keating, Mary Bear, Paul Harvey

A black comedy about a crazy family whose uncle dies right after an argument with his nephew Carl (David Wayne). Carl is convinced no one will believe it isn't murder and buries the body in a remote graveyard. An insurance investigator (Victor Mature) falls for the one sane member of the family, Stella (Ann Sheridan), and comes to learn of their strange behavior. When is it revealed that the uncle had a 20,000 insurance policy, the family try to identify various bodies as that of the uncle, while Carl has trouble finding where he planted the corpse.

THREE CAME HOME

Produced by Nunnally Johnson
Directed by Jean Negulesco
Screenplay by Nunnally Johnson, from a book by Agnes Newton Keith
Photographed by Milton Krasner
Music by Hugo Friedhofer
Musical direction by Lionel Newman
106 minutes

Cast: Claudette Colbert, Patric Knowles, Florence Desmond, Sessue Hayakawa, Sylvia Andrew, Phyllis Morris, Mark Keuning, Howard Chuman, Drue Mallory, Carol Savage

A harshly realistic study of prison camp conditions under the Japanese during the invasion of Borneo and largely filmed on location. Agnes Newton Keith's book about her experiences is here depicted, with Claudette Colbert as Mrs. Keith. The film clearly shows the manner in which British and Americans were interned, with privations, near starvation, and frequent humiliations. Conditions deteriorate to the point where many prisoners die and the others are near exhaustion by the time of liberation. Aside from the fine Colbert performance, Sessue Hayakawa is impressive as a Japanese colonel torn between the brutality of his orders and his own innate decency.

A TICKET TO TOMAHAWK

Produced by Robert Bassler
Directed by Richard Sale
Screenplay by Mary Loos and Richard Sale
Photographed in Technicolor by Harry Jackson
Music by Cyril J. Mockridge
Musical direction by Lionel Newman
91 minutes

Cast: Dan Dailey, Anne Baxter, Rory Calhoun, Walter Brennan, Charles Kemper, Connie Gilchrist, Arthur Hunnicutt, Will Wright, Chief Yowlachie, Victor Sen Yung, Mauritz Hugo, Raymond Greenleaf, Harry Carter

A spoof Western, centering around the rivalry between a stage coach line and a new railroad trying to establish a franchise in the Colorado territory. The coach line promoter (Rory Calhoun) uses Indians, bandits, and a touring theatrical company to keep the railroad from meeting its deadline. A train expedition led by a sharpshooting young lady (Anne Baxter), the granddaughter of the injured owner, is aided by an enterprising traveling salesman (Dan Dailey) to get the train in on time and win the fight with the coach line. Comedy and Colorado scenery make this a pleasing picture. Marilyn Monroe appears briefly as a chorus girl in the traveling theatrical company.

TWO FLAGS WEST

Produced by Casey Robinson
Directed by Robert Wise
Screenplay by Casey Robinson, from a story by Frank S. Nugent and Curtis Kenyon
Photographed by Leon Shamroy
Music by Hugo Friedhofer
Musical direction by Alfred Newman
92 minutes

Cast: Joseph Cotten, Linda Darnell, Jeff Chandler, Cornel Wilde, Dale Robertson, Jay C. Flippen, Noah Beery, Harry von Zell, John Sands, Arthur Hunnicutt, Jack Lee, Robert Adler, Harry Carter, Ferris Taylor

In the closing days of the Civil War, a contingent of Confederate prisoners led by a colonel (Joseph Cotten) agree to serve the Union Army, provided they are used in the West in the Indian campaigns. They are sent to a post in New Mexico, where the commandant is a rebel hater (Jeff Chandler) because of the loss of his brother in the war. The commandant is also tortured by his love for his sister-in-law (Linda Darnell). He refuses to use the Southerners, but when the fort is ferociously attacked by Indians because of the commandant's ruthless killing of a chief's son, he sacrifices himself to the Indians and relieves the fort from further attack. An interesting Western, with fine characterizations and brisk direction from Robert Wise.

UNDER MY SKIN

Produced by Casey Robinson
Directed by Jean Negulesco
Screenplay by Casey Robinson, from a story by Ernest Hemingway
Photographed by Joseph La Shelle
Music by Daniele Amfitheatrof
86 minutes

Cast: John Garfield, Micheline Presle, Luther Adler, Orley Lindgren, Noel Drayton, A. A. Merola, Ott George, Paul Bryar, Ann Codee, Steve Geray, Joseph Warfield, Eugene Borden

A horse racing story filmed in France, with John Garfield as a has-been jockey who doublecrosses a big gambler (Luther Adler) in order to make some fast money and get away. He desposits his young son (Orley Lindgren) with a girl friend (Micheline Presle), a night club singer in Paris. Between the love of the girl and the jockey's love for his son, he decides to reform and lead a good life. But the gambler catches up with him and demands that he throw a race in order to repay the money he stole. The jockey chooses to win the race, at the cost of his life, and thereby leave a good name and memory for his son.

WABASH AVENUE

Produced by William Perlberg
Directed by Henry Koster
Screenplay by Harry Tugend and Charles Lederer
Photographed in Technicolor by Arthur E. Arling
Songs by Mack Gordon and Josef Myrow
Musical direction by Lionel Newman
92 minutes

Cast: Betty Grable, Victor Mature, Phil Harris, Reginald Gardiner, James Barton, Barry Kelley, Margaret Hamilton, Jacqueline Dalya, Robin Raymond, Hal K. Dawson, Dorothy Neumann, Alexander Pope, Henry Kulky

The plot lines are those of *Coney Island*, with Victor Mature and Phil Harris as business partners who don't trust each other and Betty Grable again the brassy singer-dancer who is turned into a classier entertainer by the love of the producer (Mature), despite the manipulations of the saloon owner (Harris) to keep her for himself. The setting is Chicago and most of the action takes place in a Wabash Avenue casino, until the producer gets his girl into a Hammerstein show in New York, following much tricky business with his partner and many amorous misunderstandings. An excellent Grable musical.

WHEN WILLIE COMES MARCHING HOME

Produced by Fred Kohlmar
Directed by John Ford
Screenplay by Mary Loos and Richard Sale, from a story by Sy Gomberg
Photographed by Leo Tover
Music by Alfred Newman
86 minutes

Cast: Dan Dailey, Corinne Calvet, Coleen Townsend, William Demarest, James Lydon, Lloyd Corrigan, Evalyn Varden, Kenny Williams, Les Clark, Charles Halton, Mae Marsh, Jack Penick, Mickey Simpson

A satire on the war spirit, dealing with an eager young man (Dan Dailey) who is the first in his home town to enlist and the last, because he is assigned locally as an instructor, to leave. No matter how hard he tries, he can't get an overseas shipment until a gunner is taken ill and he replaces him. The eager young man has to bail out over France and there meets a beautiful re-

Victor Mature and Betty Grable in *Wabash Avenue*.

June Haver and William Lundigan in *I'll Get By*.

Burt Lancaster, Dorothy McGuire, and Edmund Gwenn in *Mr. 880*.

Rory Calhoun, Anne Baxter, and Dan Dailey in *A Ticket to Tomahawk*.

Irene Dunne and Andrew Ray in *The Mudlark*.

Jack Palance and Zero Mostel in *Panic in the Streets*.

Richard Widmark and Sidney Poitier in *No Way Out*.

Joseph Cotten, Cornel Wilde, Roy Gordon, and Jeff Chandler in *Two Flags West*.

Sessue Hayakawa and Claudette Colbert in *Three Came Home*.

Dan Dailey and Coleen Townsend in *When Willie Comes Marching Home*.

sistance fighter (Corinne Calvet). With her help he witnesses German rocket emplacements and escapes. Back in America and reporting this vital information to the government, he is sworn to secrecy. As far as his home town is concerned, he has never been away. The young hero has to wait a long time for recognition. John Ford's direction keeps the comedy on edge, with Dailey performing well as the constantly frustrated warrior.

WHERE THE SIDEWALK ENDS

Produced by Otto Preminger
Directed by Otto Preminger
Screenplay by Ben Hecht, from a novel by William A. Stuart
Photographed by Joseph La Shelle
Music by Cyril J. Mockridge
Musical direction by Lionel Newman
95 minutes

Cast: Dana Andrews, Gene Tierney, Gary Merrill, Bert Freed, Tom Tully, Karl Malden, Ruth Donnelly, Craig Stevens, Robert Simon, Harry von Zell, Dick Appell, Neville Brand, Grace Mills

A police detective (Dana Andrews) with a violent temper and a hatred of crooks, partly due to his being the son of one, kills a man during an investigation and disposes of the body to make it look like the work of hoodlums. The body is found and a taxi driver (Tom Tully) is charged with murder. He helps the daughter (Gene Tierney) get a lawyer, but no one will take the case and the detective signs a confession that incriminates him but also brings him the love of the girl. The drama is far-fetched, but the settings and the acting help bring it off.

WHIRLPOOL

Produced by Otto Preminger
Directed by Otto Preminger
Screenplay by Ben Hecht and Andrew Solt, from a novel by Guy Endore
Photographed by Arthur Miller
Music by David Raksin
Musical direction by Alfred Newman
97 minutes

Cast: Gene Tierney, Richard Conte, Jose Ferrer, Charles Bickford, Barbara O'Neil, Eduard Franz, Constance Collier, Fortunio Bonanova, Ruth Lees, Ian MacDonald, Bruce Hamilton, Alex Gerry, Larry Keating, Mauritz Hugo, John Trebach

The wife (Gene Tierney) of a successful psychiatrist (Richard Conte) has a weakness—shoplifting. She is caught in the act in a store, but rescued by a smooth-talking gentleman (Jose Ferrer), a fortune-teller who moves in high society. He offers to help her, but he is actually using her as a shield for his murder of a client. She comes to realize his guilt and with the aid of her husband, she manages to extricate herself from his alibi and bring about his capture. A good suspense mystery, with an excellent performance by Ferrer as the villainous charlatan.

20TH CENTURY-FOX ACADEMY AWARDS FOR 1950

DARRYL F. ZANUCK: Irving G. Thalberg Memorial Award.

ALL ABOUT EVE: Best picture.

GEORGE SANDERS: Best supporting actor in *All About Eve*.

JOSEPH L. MANKIEWICZ: Best direction for *All About Eve*.

JOSEPH L. MANKIEWICZ: Best screenplay for *All About Eve*.

EDNA and EDWARD ANHALT: Best motion picture story for *Panic in the Streets*.

EDITH HEAD, CHARLES LEMAIRE: Best costume design, black and white, for *All About Eve*.

W. D. FLICK, ROGER HEMAN: Best sound recording for *All About Eve*.

WHY KOREA: Best documentary short.

JAMES B. GORDON and the 20TH CENTURY-FOX CAMERA DEPARTMENT: Class II award for the design and development of a Multiple Image Film Viewer.

Richard Conte and Gene Tierney in *Whirlpool*.

1951

ANNE OF THE INDIES

Produced by George Jessel
Directed by Jacques Tourneur
Screenplay by Philip Dunne and Arthur Caesar, from a story by Herbert Ravenel Sass
Photographed in Technicolor by Harry Jackson
Music by Franz Waxman
82 minutes

Cast: Jean Peters, Louis Jourdan, Debra Paget, Herbert Marshall, Thomas Gomez, James Robertson Justice, Francis Pierlot, Sean McClory, Holmes Herbert, Byron Nelson, Douglas Bennett, Mario Siletti, Bob Stephenson, Carleton Young

A colorful, action-packed pirate picture about a girl (Jean Peters) who becomes a feared captain of the Spanish Main and a French officer (Louis Jourdan) who sets out to trap her. He woos the beautiful buccaneer, but she catches on to his duplicity and escapes his plans. In revenge she captures the officer and his wife (Debra Paget) and sets them down on a desert isle to die. But she has a change of heart and comes back for them. She then battles to the death her pirate rival, Blackbeard (Thomas Gomez), and dies bravely. A lusty nautical fable, handsomely mounted and with Jean Peters playing the none-too-credible role with great bravura and displaying admirable style in swordplay.

AS YOUNG AS YOU FEEL

Produced by Lamar Trotti
Directed by Harmon Jones
Screenplay by Lamar Trotti, from a story by Paddy Chayefsky
Photographed by Joe MacDonald
Music by Cyril J. Mockridge
Musical direction by Lionel Newman
77 minutes

Cast: Monty Woolley, Thelma Ritter, David Wayne, Jean Peters, Constance Bennett, Marilyn Monroe, Albert Dekker, Clinton Sundberg, Minor Watson, Ludwig Stossel, Renie Riano, Wally Brown, Rusty Tamblyn

A comedic defense of old age, with Monty Woolley as a gentleman who resents being laid off at the age of 65. He dies his hair black and poses as the president of a holding company and tours the printing plant from which he has been dismissed. He advises the rehiring of similarly dismissed personnel and addresses a Chamber of Commerce meeting in which he brilliantly outlines the country's economic woes. The president (Minor Watson) whom he has been impersonating gets the credit for the nationally reported wisdom and has no choice but to see the old man gets his job back.

BIRD OF PARADISE

Produced by Delmer Daves
Directed by Delmer Daves
Screenplay by Delmer Daves
Photographed in Technicolor by Winston C. Hoch
Music by Daniele Amfitheatrof
101 minutes

Cast: Louis Jourdan, Debra Paget, Jeff Chandler, Everett Sloane, Maurice Schwartz, Jack Elam, Prince Lei Lani, Otto Waldis, Alfred Zeisler, Mary Ann Ventura, David K. Bray, Sam Monsarat

A remake of the 1932 film about an adventurer in the South Seas who falls in love with a Polynesian princess. A French seaman (Louis Jourdan) joins his friend (Jeff Chandler) when he returns to his island home after education in America. There he meets the friend's sister (Debra Paget) and falls in love with her. She responds and they break native traditions by courting without first getting formal approval. They marry and live happily, despite the protests of the witch doctors, who believe the Frenchman's presence will bring disaster. When a volcano erupts and threatens to destroy the island, the bride, who is the chief's daughter, follows tradition and sacrifices herself to the volcano. The story strains belief, but the film offers gorgeous Technicolor settings in Hawaii and an attractive cast.

CALL ME MISTER

Produced by Fred Kohlmar
Directed by Lloyd Bacon
Screenplay by Albert E. Lewin and Burt Styler, from a revue by Harold J. Rome and Arnold Aurbach
Photographed in Technicolor by Arthur E. Arling

Songs by Mack Gordon, Sammy Fain, Jerry Seelen, Earl K. Brent, Harold Rome, and Frances Ash
Musical direction by Alfred Newman
96 minutes

Cast: Betty Grable, Dan Dailey, Danny Thomas, Dale Robertson, Benay Venuta, Richard Boone, Jeffrey Hunter, Frank Fontaine, Harry Von Zell, Dave Willock, Robert Ellis, Jerry Paris, Lou Spencer, Art Stanley

Harold Rome's postwar Broadway musical brought to the screen after a long delay and minus much of his material. Here Betty Grable is an entertainer touring Japan and putting on shows for the servicemen, and running into her ex-husband (Dan Dailey). He is still in the army and still hoping to reconcile with her, despite the attention she is getting from a handsome captain (Dale Robertson). Dan helps her stage a show and does indeed win her back. The film's main assets are the dancing of Grable and Dailey, with choreography of the bigger numbers by Busby Berkeley, and Danny Thomas as the man who can't adapt to military life.

DAVID AND BATHSHEBA

Produced by Darryl F. Zanuck
Directed by Henry King
Screenplay by Philip Dunne
Photographed in Technicolor by Leon Shamroy
Music by Alfred Newman
123 minutes

Cast: Gregory Peck, Susan Hayward, Raymond Massey, Kieron Moore, James Robertson Justice, Jayne Meadows, John Sutton, Dennis Hoey, Walter Talun, Paula Morgan, Francis X. Bushman, Teddy Infuhr, Leo Pessin, Gwyneth Verdon, Gilbert Barnett, John Burton

The love affair of King David, the Lion of Judah, and Bathsheba, the wife of one of his soldiers. The vast biblical canvas is brought into focus by the excellent screenplay of Philip Dunne and the intensity of Gregory Peck's portrait of the mighty monarch almost destroyed by his passion. His infatuation with Bathsheba (Susan Hayward) leads him to neglect his duties, to the point of almost sacrificing his kingdom. The wrath of God falls heavily upon his land, bringing about a realization that leads to his atonement. The film is among the very best of all the biblical epics, with superb photography by the veteran Leon Shamroy and a masterly music score by Alfred Newman.

THE DAY THE EARTH STOOD STILL

Produced by Julian Blaustein
Directed by Robert Wise
Screenplay by Edmund H. North, from a story by Henry Bates
Photographed by Leo Tover

Gregory Peck and Susan Hayward in *David and Bathsheba.*

Jean Peters and Louis Jourdan in *Anne of the Indies.*

Jeff Chandler, Louis Jourdan, and Debra Paget in *Bird of Paradise.*

Dan Dailey and Betty Grable in *Call Me Mister.*

Music by Bernard Herrmann
92 minutes

Cast: Michael Rennie, Patricia Neal, Hugh Marlowe, Sam Jaffe, Billy Gray, Frances Bavier, Lock Martin, Drew Pearson, Frank Conroy, Carleton Young, Fay Roope, Robert Osterloh, Tyler McVey

A masterpiece of science fiction, about a visitor (Michael Rennie) from another planet who lands his space craft in Washington in the hope of seeing the President and discussing peace in the universe. He finds it impossible to get an appointment and takes a room in a boarding house, run by a lady (Patricia Neal) with a young son (Billy Gray). The boys arranges a meeting with a mathematician (Sam Jaffe), who quickly realizes the genius of the visitor and agrees to try and bring about a gathering of scientists. But the visitor is by now a hunted man. He is wounded by the police, but manages to make an escape in his space ship, after warning that the world must solve its problems or face eventual conflict with other planets. The script is literate, the effects plausible, and the acting impressive, as is Bernard Herrmann's eerie music score.

DECISION BEFORE DAWN

Produced by Anatole Litvak
Directed by Anatole Litvak
Screenplay by Peter Viertel, from a novel by George Howe
Photographed by Frank Planer
Music by Franz Waxman
119 minutes

Cast: Richard Basehart, Gary Merrill, Oskar Werner, Hildegarde Neff, Dominique Blanchar, O. E. Hasse, Wilfried Seyfert, Hans Christian Blech, Helene Thimig

In the last year of the second World War, the U.S. Army recruits a number of German prisoners to use as spies against their own people. One of them (Oskar Werner) is a sensitive young idealist who truly believes that by working with the Americans he can bring the war to an end faster and save his country from further degradation. He is trained in espionage and performs his duties, but he sacrifices his life when he saves an American officer (Richard Basehart) as they are making their way back to their lines. The film ranks as one of the finest accounts of the functions of military intelligence, with a fine performance from Werner and dramatic use of actual war-scarred German locations.

THE DESERT FOX

Produced by Nunnally Johnson
Directed by Henry Hathaway
Screenplay by Nunnally Johnson, from a book by Brigadier Desmond Young
Photographed by Norbert Brodine

Music by Daniele Amfitheatrof
91 minutes

Cast: James Mason, Cedric Hardwicke, Jessica Tandy, Luther Adler, Everett Sloane, Leo G. Carroll, George McReady, Richard Boone, Eduard Franz, Desmond Young, William Reynolds, Charles Evans, Walter Kingsford

A sober if slightly romanticized account of the career of Erwin Rommel, with James Mason giving a measured performance as the distinguished German soldier. Most of the film deals with his experiences as a commander in North Africa, where he won the admiration of both sides with his tactical skill, which almost defeated the Allies. As the war wears on he shares the disgust of other German officers with Hitler's mad policies and allows himself to be drawn into a plan of assassination. The failure of the plan reveals his participation and he is coerced into suicide in order to save his family and his good name with the German public. Produced with good taste and accuracy, *The Desert Fox* tells a solid story about a fascinating but tragic soldier.

ELOPEMENT

Produced by Fred Kohlmar
Directed by Henry Koster
Screenplay by Bess Taffel
Photographed by Joseph La Shelle
Music by Cyril J. Mockridge
Musical direction by Lionel Newman
81 minutes

Cast: Clifton Webb, Anne Francis, Charles Bickford, William Lundigan, Reginald Gardiner, Evelyn Varden, Margalo Gilmore, Tommy Rettig, J. Farrell MacDonald, Julia Dean, Howard Price, William Bouchey

A successful functional designer (Cliffton Webb) brings up his daughter (Anne Francis) to follow in his footsteps, but the day she graduates from college she elopes with her psychology teacher (William Lundigan). Father is furious and so are the parents of the groom. Both families set up to chase the fleeing couple and persuade them to annul, but with time the two sets of parents, at first antagonistic, comes to like each other. The young couple start to have doubts about their elopement, but the parents then rally round to bolster the marriage. Nonsense made amusing by the haughty playing of Webb.

FIXED BAYONETS

Produced by Jules Buck
Directed by Samuel Fuller
Screenplay by Samuel Fuller, from a novel by John Brophy
Photographed by Lucien Ballard
Music by Roy Webb

Musical direction by Lionel Newman
92 minutes

Cast: Richard Basehart, Gene Evans, Michael O'Shea, Richard Hylton, Craig Hill, Skip Homeier, Henry Kulky, Richard Monohan, Paul Richards, Tony Trent, Don Orlando, Patrick Fitzgibbon

The Korean war and the story of a small group of infantrymen covering the rear as the American army withdraws through a snowy mountain pass. The central character is a corporal (Richard Basehart), a sensitive scholarly man who has to take command of the handful protecting the rear and who has to overcome his fear of killing, which he does. A good account of tired, rugged foot soldiers doing their grimy jobs.

FOLLOW THE SUN

Produced by Samuel G. Engel
Directed by Sidney Lanfield
Screenplay by Frederick Hazlitt Brennan
Photographed by Leo Tover
Music by Cyril J. Mockridge
Musical direction by Lionel Newman
96 minutes

Cast: Glenn Ford, Anne Baxter, Dennis O'Keefe, June Havoc, Larry Keating, Roland Winters, Nana Bryant, Sam Snead, James Demaret, Dr. Cary Middlecoff, Harold Blake, Ann Burr, Harmon Stevens, Louise Lorimer, Esther Somers

The story of golf champ Ben Hogan, played with quiet charm by Glenn Ford, with Anne Baxter as the loving, supportive wife. The story is relatively simple, as it relates Hogan's early years as a man determined to master golf and make it his life. His success is slow and gradual as he travels the circuits with his wife, and his success is halted by a car accident. He recovers and goes on to beat the great Sammy Snead. Ford conveys the dignity of Hogan and the film gives golf a loving coverage.

FOURTEEN HOURS

Produced by Sol C. Siegel
Directed by Henry Hathaway
Screenplay by John Paxton, from a story by Joel Sayre
Photographed by Joe MacDonald
Music by Alfred Newman
91 minutes

Cast: Paul Douglas, Richard Basehart, Barbara Bel Geddes, Debra Paget, Agnes Moorehead, Robert Keith, Howard da Silva, Jeffrey Hunter, Martin Gabel, Grace Kelly, Frank Faylen, Jeff Corey

Based on a Manhattan suicide in 1938, *Fourteen Hours* describes the actual time a man, played by Richard Basehart, stood on a ledge high above the streets before he jumped. A likeable policeman (Paul Douglas)

wins his confidence and is able to talk to him. All others—reporters, religious counselors, doctors, and relatives—are turned back by his threat to jump. Finally he falls into a net the police have rigged and he is saved, which is not what happened to the man in 1938, who killed himself. The film is a study in the effect the man has on the people around him, from those who genuinely care to those who are simply morbidly curious. It is also a study in cinematic suspense and a credit to director Hathaway.

THE FROGMEN

Produced by Samuel G. Engel
Directed by Lloyd Bacon
Screenplay by John Tucker Battle, from a story by Oscar Millard
Photographed by Norbert Brodine
Music by Cyril J. Mockridge
Musical direction by Lionel Newman
96 minutes

Cast: Richard Widmark, Dana Andrews, Gary Merrill, Jeffrey Hunter, Warren Stevens, Robert Wagner, Harvey Lembeck, Robert Rockwell, Henry Slate, Robert Adler, Bob Patten, Harry Flowers, William Bishop, Fay Roope

The war adventures of the underwater demolition divers known as frogmen. The central character is a tough commander (Richard Widmark) who is put in charge of a squad of frogmen and wins no love with his martinet ways. It is not until he risks his own life to detonate a live torpedo that his men realize his courage and the fact that his kind of discipline is necessary for their hazardous work. The film offers a graphic account of what frogmen do, especially in the long sequence in which they move into a Japanese submarine base, set their underwater explosives, and destroy the base.

THE GIRL ON THE BRIDGE

Produced by Hugo Haas
Directed by Hugo Haas
Screenplay by Hugo Haas and Arnold Phillips
Photographed by Paul Ivano
Music by Harold Byrns
76 minutes

Cast: Hugo Haas, Beverly Michaels, Robert Dane, Tony Jochim, John Close, Darr Smith

A young unwed mother (Beverly Michaels) is saved from suicide by a kindly, elderly man (Hugo Haas), who then employs her in his watch store. He comes to love her and offers her marriage, which she accepts. The cousin (John Close) of the girl's jilted lover (Robert Dane) blackmails the old man, who kills him. The lover is tried for murder, but the old man, stricken with guilt, commits suicide so that the girl and her lover can start a new life together.

GOLDEN GIRL

Produced by George Jessel
Directed by Lloyd Bacon
Screenplay by Walter Bullock, Charles O'Neal, and
   Gladys Lehman, from a story by Albert and Arthur
   Lewis and Edward Thompson
Photographed in Technicolor by Charles G. Clarke
Songs by George Jessel, Sam Lerner, Lionel Newman,
   Eliot Daniel, and Ken Darby
Musical direction by Lionel Newman
108 minutes

Cast: Mitzi Gaynor, Dale Robertson, Dennis Day, James
Barton, Una Merkel, Raymond Walburn, Gene Sheldon,
Carmen D'Antonio, Michael Ross, Harry Carter, Lovyss
Bradley, Emory Parnell, Luther Crockett, Harris Brown,
Kermit Maynard, Robert Nash, Jessie Arnold

The story of Lotta Crabtree, a musical comedy star of
the Civil War era, with a vivacious performance from
Mitzi Gaynor, but with a script much more full of
fiction than fact. Here she is the product of a gambler
father (James Barton) who loses his house and takes to
life in a caravan, with his daughter entertaining in California mining camps. She falls in love with a Confederate spy (Dale Robertson) who steals a gold shipment
with which she has been entrusted. by the government,
but she continues to love him despite the war. She triumphs in San Francisco and on the occasion of her
debut in New York she is reunited with her ex-spy.
The title may refer to Crabtree, but it should refer to
the fabulous Mitzi.

THE GUY WHO CAME BACK

Produced by Julian Blaustein
Directed by Joseph Newman
Screenplay by Allan Scott, from a story by William Fay
Photographed by Joseph La Shelle
Music by Leigh Harline
92 minutes

Cast: Paul Douglas, Joan Bennett, Linda Darnell, Don
DeFore, Billy Gray, Zero Mostel, Edmon Ryan, Ruth
McDevitt, Walter Burke, Henry Kulky, Dick Ryan, Rob-
ert B. Williams, Ted Pearson, Mack Williams

A pro football player (Paul Douglas) refuses a job as a
coach when his days as a player come to an end. He
idly dreams of making a comeback, leaves his wife
(Joan Bennett), takes up with another woman (Linda
Darnell), and picks up a little money as a wrestler.
The other woman comes to realize he will never divorce
his wife, so she joins forces with her to get him back
on his old team. Because of the shortage of manpower
caused by the war, he gets his chance to play again
but soon comes to his senses about his ability and
settles for the job as the coach. Paul Douglas makes
the vain chump understandable and likeable.

222

HALF ANGEL

Produced by Julian Blaustein
Directed by Richard Sale
Screenplay by Robert Riskin, from a story by George
   Carleton Brown
Photographed in Technicolor by Milton Krasner
Songs by Alfred Newman and Ralph Blane
Music by Cyril J. Mockridge
Musical direction by Alfred Newman
77 minutes

Cast: Loretta Young, Joseph Cotten, Cecil Kellaway,
Basil Ruysdael, Jim Backus, Irene Ryan, John Ridgely,
Therese Lyon, Mary George, Mary Tarcal, Steve Pritko,
Gayle Pace, Edwin Max, Art Smith

A comedy of romantic errors, with Loretta Young as a
nurse who meets a former sweetheart, now a big lawyer
(Joseph Cotten), and falls in love with him despite
being engaged to another man (John Ridgely). She is
prim and proper but is also given to sleepwalking,
when the subconscious part of her personality takes
over, causing her to proceed to the lawyer's house and
behave amorously. He has trouble making her believe
that the girl who sleepwalks is the true nature of the
nurse—but he does.

HALLS OF MONTEZUMA

Produced by Robert Bassler
Directed by Lewis Milestone
Screenplay by Michael Blankfort
Photographed in Technicolor by Winton C. Hoch
Music by Sol Kaplan
Musical direction by Lionel Newman
113 minutes

Cast: Richard Widmark, Walter (Jack) Palance, Regi-
nald Gardiner, Robert Wagner, Karl Malden, Richard
Hylton, Richard Boone, Skip Homeier, Don Hicks, Jack
Webb, Bert Freed, Neville Brand

A tribute to the Marine Corps and their campaigns
against the Japanese in the South Pacific. The focus
of the film is the capture of an island on which the
enemy have set up rocket sites. A Marine patrol is
sent out, with orders to take prisoners and bring them
back for interrogation. From that comes enough information to locate the sites and achieve the objective.
Richard Widmark is a former schoolteacher who becomes a fine officer and assembles a disparate group of
men into an effective fighting unit. The production
values convey the sound and fury and bloodshed of
the ferocious warfare and director Lewis Milestone
keeps the long and broad account exciting and convincing.

HOUSE ON TELEGRAPH HILL

Produced by Robert Bassler
Directed by Robert Wise

Screenplay by Elick Moll, from a novel by Dana Lyon
Music by Sol Kaplan
Musical direction by Alfred Newman
93 minutes

Cast: Richard Basehart, Valentina Cortese, William Lundigan, Fay Baker, Gordon Gebert, Kei Thing Chung, Steve Geray, Herbert Butterfield, John Burton, Katherine Meskill, Mario Siletti, Tamara Schee, Natasha Lytess, Ashmead Scott

A Polish woman (Valentina Cortese) in a German concentration camp assumes the identity of a girl who dies in the camp. After the war she makes her way to the girl's wealthy relatives in San Francisco, where she finds the girl has a son who is heir to a fortune. She marries the boy's guardian (Richard Basehart) and after a while starts to fear for her life when it becomes apparent that he means to kill her and the boy. A lawyer (William Lundigan) befriends her and gradually comes to realize her fears are just. The husband becomes the victim of one of his own plans to poison the wife, and she and the lawyer are free to make their future. A quietly effective thriller, well paced by director Wise.

I CAN GET IT FOR YOU WHOLESALE

Produced by Sol C. Siegel
Directed by Michael Gordon
Screenplay by Abraham Polonsky, from a novel by Jerome Weidman
Photographed by Milton Krasner
Music by Sol Kaplan
93 minutes

Cast: Susan Hayward, Dan Dailey, George Sanders, Sam Jaffe, Randy Stuart, Marvin Kaplan, Harry von Zell, Barbara Whiting, Vicki Cummings, Ross Elliott, Richard Lane, Jan Kayne, Marion Marshall, Jayne Hazard

An ambitious New York model (Susan Hayward) works her way through the dress business of Seventh Avenue and becomes a designer. She persuades a top salesman (Dan Dailey) and a cutter (Sam Jaffe) to come into business with her. They prosper until she meets a suave gown tycoon (George Sanders), who hires her for her designing talent. She tries to break her contract with her partners, which results in their declaring bankrupcy, but she realizes her own duplicity and the fact that she loves her salesman-partner. With that they plan their future together. Susan Hayward is excellent as the almost ruthless designer and the film gives good insights into New York's garment trade.

I'D CLIMB THE HIGHEST MOUNTAIN

Produced by Lamar Trotti
Directed by Henry King

Screenplay by Lamar Trotti, from a novel by Corra Harris
Photographed in Technicolor by Edward Cronjager
Music by Sol Kaplan
Musical direction by Lionel Newman
88 minutes

Cast: Susan Hayward, William Lundigan, Rory Calhoun, Barbara Bates, Gene Lockhart, Lynn Bari, Ruth Donnelly, Kathleen Lockhart, Alexander Knox, Jean Inness, Frank Tweddell, Jerry Vandiver

A charming slice of rural Americana, about a circuit-riding preacher (William Lundigan) in the South who marries a city girl (Susan Hayward) and takes her to his assignment in a small Georgia community. They tend to the needs of various people and among other things they persuade a gruff businessman (Gene Lockhart) that he should allow his daughter (Barbara Bates) to marry a local scoundrel because they believe marriage will settle him down. It does. They also suffer through a severe epidemic and help save lives. They leave at the end of three years, with the wife having learned a great deal about life. Henry King, a master of Americana, directed this agreeable tale, beautifully shot on location in Georgia.

I'LL NEVER FORGET YOU

Produced by Sol C. Siegel
Directed by Roy Baker
Screenplay by Ranald MacDougall, from a play by John L. Balderston
Photographed in Technicolor by Georges Perinal
Music by William Alwyn
Musical direction by Muir Mathieson
91 minutes

Cast: Tyrone Power, Ann Blyth, Michael Rennie, Dennis Price, Beatrice Campbell, Kathleen Byron, Raymond Huntley, Irene Browne

A remake of *Berkeley Square* (1933) and made in England. An atomic scientist (Tyrone Power) lives in the home of his ancestors in London and dreams of the past. He finds himself back in time a couple of centuries and appalled at social conditions, but enchanted with a cousin (Ann Blyth). She is the only one who understands he is a visitor from the future and when he sets up a laboratory to manufacture twentieth-century inventions, he is arrested and sentenced to Bedlam. With that he wakes up in the present time and shortly thereafter finds a contemporary version of his beautiful cousin. A romantic fantasy and a strain on credibility, but made pleasant by colorful sets and costumes and a fine cast of British players in support of Power and Blyth.

JOURNEY INTO LIGHT

Produced by Joseph Bernhard and Anson Bond

Directed by Stuart Heisler
Screenplay by Stephanie Nordi and Irving Shulman,
   from a story by Anson Bond
Photographed by Elwood Bredell
Music by Emil Newman and Paul Dunlap
88 minutes

Cast: Sterling Hayden, Viveca Lindfors, Thomas Mitchell, Ludwig Donath, H. B. Warner, Jane Darwell, John Berkes, Peggy Webber, Paul Guilfoyle, Charles Evans, Marian Martin, Everett Glass, Raymond Bond, Billie Bird

After the suicide of his alcoholic wife, a minister (Sterling Hayden) gives up his church and wanders in depression. He ends up in a sleazy part of downtown Los Angeles, where he is arrested after collapsing in front of a bar. After a number of experiences on skid row, he is taken into the home of a preacher (Ludwig Donath), who helps him regenerate himself. With the love of the preacher's blind daughter (Viveca Lindfors) he finds new purpose in life.

LET'S MAKE IT LEGAL

Produced by Robert Bassler
Directed by Richard Sale
Screenplay by F. Hugh Herbert and I. A. L. Diamond,
   from a story by Mortimer Braus
Photographed by Lucien Ballard
Music by Cyril J. Mockridge
Musical direction by Lionel Newman
79 minutes

Cast: Claudette Colbert, Macdonald Carey, Zachary Scott, Barbara Bates, Robert Wagner, Marilyn Monroe, Frank Cady, Jim Hayward, Carol Savage, Paul Gerrits, Betty Jane Bowen, Vici Raaf

An attractive grandmother (Claudette Colbert) divorces her husband (Macdonald Carey) because he is an inveterate gambler. Their daughter (Barbara Bates) does all she can to get them together, but a problem arises when an old beau (Zachary Scott) arrives in town. He is now a millionaire and eager to pick up where he left off years ago. The ex-husband tries to break them up and pulls some wild stunts. When the lady finds out how she came to be married—by her husband gambling with loaded dice against the other boyfriend to see which one would get her—she gives in and remarries him. A charming spoof on marriage, with young Marilyn Monroe doing a bit as a man hunter.

LOVE NEST

Produced by Jules Buck
Directed by Joseph Newman
Screenplay by I. A. L. Diamond, from a novel by Scott
   Corbett
Photographed by Lloyd Ahern
Music by Cyril J. Mockridge

Musical direction by Lionel Newman
84 minutes

Cast: June Haver, William Lundigan, Frank Fay, Marilyn Monroe, Jack Paar, Leatrice Joy, Henry Kulky, Marie Blake, Patricia Miller, Maude Wallace, Joe Ploski, Martha Wentworth, Faire Binney, Caryl Lincoln

A domestic comedy about a serviceman (William Lundigan) who returns to civilian life in the hope of becoming a writer. He and his wife (June Haver) live in the basement of the apartment building they have bought, but they find that running the building and catering to the tenants takes up all their time. Among the nonstop round of problems is a voluptuous young tenant (Marilyn Monroe) and a slick confidence man (Frank Fay) who bilks widows of their cash. He becomes news when he is jailed and the writer earns his first credit writing the life story of the lothario tenant.

LUCKY NICK CAIN

Produced by Joseph Kaufman
Directed by Joseph Newman
Screenplay by George Callahan and William Rose
Photographed by Otto Heller
Music by Walter Goehr
85 minutes

Cast: George Raft, Coleen Gray, Enzo Staiola, Charles Goldner, Walter Rilla, Martin Benson, Peter Illing, Hugh French, Peter Bull, Elwyn Brook-Jones, Greta Gynt, Margot Grahame, Constance Smith

An American gambler (George Raft) goes to Italy and is welcomed at a casino where it is thought his name will help bring in customers. He befriends an American girl (Coleen Gray) who has lost her money at the tables. They are framed on a murder charge, but the gambler breaks away from the police and finds out that the murdered man was a Treasury Department inspector on the trail of counterfeiters in possession of plates stolen from the Nazis. He solves the mystery and goes back to gambling and romancing his new girl friend.

THE MAN WHO CHEATED HIMSELF

Produced by Jack M. Warner
Directed by Felix E. Feist
Screenplay by Seton I. Miller and Philip MacDonald,
   from a story by Seton I. Miller
Photographed by Russell Harlan
Music by Louis Forbes
86 minutes

Cast: Lee J. Cobb, John Dall, Jane Wyatt, Lisa Howard, Alan Wells, Harlan Warde, Tito Vuolo, Mimi Aguglia, Charles Arnt, Marjorie Bennett, Bud Wolfe, Morgan Farley, Howard Negley, William Gould

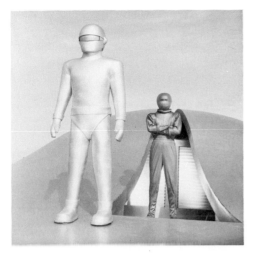

The Day the Earth Stood Still.

Hildegarde Neff and Oskar Werner in *Decision Before Dawn*.

Ann Blyth and Tyrone Power in *I'll Never Forget You*.

James Mason as *The Desert Fox*.

Richard Basehart and Paul Douglas in *Fourteen Hours*.

Gary Merrill and Richard Widmark in *The Frogmen*.

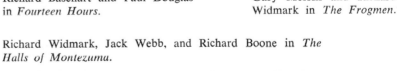

Richard Widmark, Jack Webb, and Richard Boone in *The Halls of Montezuma*.

Mitzi Gaynor in *Golden Girl*.

Dan Dailey and Susan Hayward in *I Can Get It For You Wholesale*.

A police lieutenant in San Francisco (Lee J. Cobb) has an affair with a society woman (Jane Wyatt) who shoots and kills her husband (Harlan Warde). The lieutenant leaves the body in such a manner as to suggest a robbery at his home. He is then assigned by his department to investigate the case, as is his brother (John Dall), a fellow policeman. Despite his efforts to deflect the younger brother, he is found out and sentenced to stand trial for murder along with the lady.

MEET ME AFTER THE SHOW

Produced by George Jessel
Directed by Richard Sale
Screenplay by Mary Loos and Richard Sale, from a story by Erna Lazarus and W. Scott Darling
Photographed in Technicolor by Arthur E. Arling
Songs by Jule Styne and Leo Robin
Musical direction by Lionel Newman
86 minutes

Cast: Betty Grable, Macdonald Carey, Rory Calhoun, Eddie Albert, Fred Clark, Lois Andrews, Irene Ryan, Steve Condos, Jerry Brandow, Arthur Walge, Edwin Max, Robert Nash, Don Kohler, Gwen Verdon

Betty Grable as a star of the musical theatre and furious because she believes her producer husband (Macdonald Carey) is playing around with other women. She leaves his show, feigns amnesia, and returns to Miami, where she started her career in night clubs. She resumes her old name and act, and accepts the attentions of a local playboy (Rory Calhoun). When she has driven her husband mad with jealousy and become convinced of his love, she admits her false amnesia and returns to him. The giddy yarn is backed up with some fine dancing, choreographed by Jack Cole, and highlighted by a street urchin routine by Grable and Gwen Verdon.

A MILLIONAIRE FOR CHRISTY

Produced by Bert E. Friedlob
Directed by George Marshall
Screenplay by Ken Englund, from a story by Robert Harari
Photographed by Harry Stradling
Musical score and direction by Victor Young
91 minutes

Cast: Fred MacMurray, Eleanor Parker, Richard Carlson, Una Merkel, Kay Buckley, Douglass Dumbrille, Raymond Greenleaf, Nestor Paiva, Chris-Pin Martin, Walter Baldwin, Ralph Hodges, Byron Foulger

A wacky comedy about a genial radio entertainer (Fred MacMurray) who inherits a fortune and can't believe it, and a secretary (Eleanor Parker), who decides that she is going to marry him. He is already engaged to another girl (Kay Buckley), who is loved by a doctor

(Richard Carlson). The secretary and the doctor join forces to get the mates they want—and they do. George Marshall, a director with a flair for brisk and airy comedic material, makes this one work.

MR. BELVEDERE RINGS THE BELL

Produced by Andre Hakim
Directed by Henry Koster
Screenplay by Ranald MacDougall, from the play by Robert E. McEnroe and the character "Belvedere" created by Gwen Davenport
Photographed by Joseph LaShelle
Music by Cyril J. Mockridge
Musical direction by Lionel Newman
88 minutes

Cast: Clifton Webb, Joanne Dru, Hugh Marlowe, Zero Mostel, Billy Lynn, Doro Merande, Frances Brandt, Kathleen Comegys, Jane Marbury, Harry Hines, Warren Stevens, William and Ludwig Provaznik, Cora Shannon

Lynn Belvedere (Clifton Webb) interrupts a lecture tour to help the inmates of an old folks' home administered by a poor church. He is appalled by the drab conditions, which make the people seem even older than their years, so he pretends to be a very fit man of 77 and gains admission. Once inside he starts to inject vitality into the place and even makes a pitch for the fiancée (Joanne Dru) of the minister (Hugh Marlowe) in charge, so that he will be jealous and marry the long-patient girl. Eventually he is found out, but by that time he has done so much good nobody minds.

THE MODEL AND THE MARRIAGE BROKER

Produced by Charles Brackett
Directed by George Cukor
Screenplay by Charles Brackett, Walter Reisch, and Richard Breen
Photographed by Milton Krasner
Music by Cyril J. Mockridge
Musical direction by Lionel Newman
103 minutes

Cast: Jeanne Crain, Scott Brady, Thelma Ritter, Zero Mostel, Michael O'Shea, Helen Ford, Frank Fontaine, Dennie Moore, John Alexander, Jay C. Flippen, Nancy Kulp, Bunny Bishop, Kathryn Card

The model is Jeanne Crain and the marriage broker is Thelma Ritter. The broker actually runs a dating service and she has the heart of a Miss Fix-It. She is perturbed to find that the lovely model is carrying on an affair with a married man and she arranges for her to meet an X-ray technician (Scott Brady). The model is at first offended, but when she comes to love the young man, she returns the favor and fixes the broker up with a prospective husband. An appealing comedy, with some compassion for the lonely, a witty script, and with Ritter stealing every scene in which she appears.

NO HIGHWAY IN THE SKY

Produced by Louis D. Lighton
Directed by Henry Koster
Screenplay by R. C. Sherriff, Oscar Millard, and Alec Coppel, based on the novel by Nevil Shute
Photographed by Georges Perinal
98 minutes

Cast: James Stewart, Marlene Dietrich, Glynis Johns, Jack Hawkins, Ronald Squire, Janette Scott, Nial McGinnis, Elizabeth Allan, Kenneth More, David Hutcheson, Ben Williams, Maurice Denham, Wilfred Hyde White, Hector MacGregor, Basil Appleby, Michael Kingsley, Peter Murray, Dora Bryan

Filmed in England, *No Highway in the Sky* deals with commercial aviation and its possible hazards. A scientist (James Stewart) is sent to Labrador to investigate an air crash and finds he is traveling on a plane which has logged 1420 hours in the air, a situation he believes disastrous and likely to result in disintegration from metal fatigue. Few give him credit for his alarming views. One who does is a famous movie star (Marlene Dietrich), who later speaks up for him when he wrecks the plane in Labrador to prevent it from taking off. He begs for time and resources to prove his theories. At first considered out of his mind, he finally gets permission and comes up with evidence that completely vindicates him. With the expert performances of Stewart and Dietrich, director Koster's fine creation of suspense and the dabbling with information relevent to the safety of flying, the film makes for a solid piece of entertainment.

OF MEN AND MUSIC

Produced by Rudolph Polk and Bernard Luber
Directed by Irving Reis
Screenplay by Liam O'Brien, Harry Kurnitz, John Paxton, and David Epstein
Photographed by Floyd Crosby
85 minutes

Cast: Artur Rubinstein, Jan Peerce, Nadine Conner, Jascha Heifetz, Deems Taylor, Dimitri Mitropoulos, Philharmonic Symphony Orchestra of New York, Emanuel Bay, Victor Young and Orchestra, William Johnstone, Alvin Hammer, Frank Ferguson

A documentary for music lovers, with several great musicians being seen in concert and in conversation. Jascha Heifetz and Artur Rubinstein play short and well known classical pieces, Jan Peerce and Nadine Conner perform opera, and Dimitri Mitropoulos is seen rehearsing the New York Philharmonic. Time makes the film an ever more valuable document.

ON THE RIVIERA

Produced by Sol C. Siegel
Directed by Walter Lang
Screenplay by Valentine Davies and Phoebe and Henry Ephron, from a play by Rudolph Lothar and Hans Adler
Photographed in Technicolor by Leon Shamroy
Songs by Sylvia Fine
Musical direction by Alfred Newman
89 minutes

Cast: Danny Kaye, Gene Tierney, Corinne Calvet, Marcel Dalio, Jean Murat, Henri Letondal, Clinton Sunberg, Sig Ruman, Joyce MacKenzie, Monique Chantal, Marina Koshetz, Ann Codee, Mari Blanchard, Ethel Martin

Another remake of *Folies Bergere* (1935)—following the 1941 *That Night in Rio* — with Danny Kaye as the entertainer who does impressions of famous people. He poses as a heroic aviator-industrialist in order to please the man's wife (Gene Tierney), who becomes confused when the impersonator turns out to be more loving than her husband. And he sits in on an important business deal when the husband is indisposed, which results in a major success for the industrialist—and some advice from the impersonator that he treat the wife more kindly. Again the story amuses, plus a generous amount of singing, dancing, and clowning from Kaye.

PEOPLE WILL TALK

Produced by Darryl F. Zanuck
Directed by Joseph L. Mankiewicz
Screenplay by Joseph L. Mankiewicz, from a play by Curt Goetz
Photographed by Milton Krasner
Musical direction by Alfred Newman
110 minutes

Cast: Cary Grant, Jeanne Crain, Finlay Currie, Hume Cronyn, Walter Slezak, Sidney Blackmer, Basil Ruysdael, Katherine Locke, Will Wright, Margaret Hamilton, Esther Somers, Carleton Young, Larry Dobkin

A brilliant comedy-drama about an unconventional doctor (Cary Grant), who shocks fellow medicos but pleases his patients and his students with his claim that a doctor needs to know about the human soul as well as the body. One of his students is a pregnant girl (Jeanne Crain), whom he saves from a suicide attempt and whom he marries. A jealous rival doctor (Hume Cronyn) calls an inquiry into his practices, but it proves only that the unconventional doctor is more compassionate and reasonable than any of them. He continues his career, which includes conducting the medical school's symphony orchestra. Cary Grant is superb as the suave and wordly doctor, and the script and direction of Mankiewicz make *People Will Talk* one of the most sophisticated of film comedies.

RAWHIDE

Produced by Samuel G. Engel
Directed by Henry Hathaway
Screenplay by Dudley Nichols
Photographed by Milton Krasner
Music by Sol Kaplan
Musical direction by Lionel Newman
86 minutes

Cast: Tyrone Power, Susan Hayward, Hugh Marlowe, Dean Jagger, Edgar Buchanan, Jack Elam, George Tobias, Jeff Corey, James Millican, Louis Jean Heydt, William Haade, Milton R. Corey, Sr., Ken Tobey

A Western suspense yarn, with Tyrone Power as the assistant to the manager (Edgar Buchanan) of a stage coach way station. When news of a band of outlaws reaches the station, the manager advises a young mother (Susan Hayward) to stay at the station and not continue her journey. The outlaws turn up, kill the manager, and mistake the woman and the assistant as a married couple. They lock the pair up as they await a coach containing gold. The couple then work toward making their escape and while the outlaws are arguing among themselves, they make their move. A slim story given tension by director Hathaway and his players.

THE SECRET OF CONVICT LAKE

Produced by Frank P. Rosenberg
Directed by Michael Gordon
Screenplay by Oscar Saul, from a story by Anna Hunger and Jack Pollexfen
Photographed by Leo Tover
Music by Sol Kaplan
Musical direction by Lionel Newman
83 minutes

Cast: Glenn Ford, Gene Tierney, Ethel Barrymore, Zachary Scott, Ann Dvorak, Barbara Bates, Cyril Cusack, Richard Hylton, Helen Westcott, Jeanette Nolan, Ruth Donnelly, Harry Carter, Jack Lambert

A group of convicts escape from a Nevada prison and make their way to a village they find occupied only by women, because all the men are away on a silver strike. The leader of the men (Glenn Ford) tries to control them, and the leader of the women (Ethel Barrymore) hides all the guns in the village. When it is known that there is $40,000 in stolen currency in the village, the men find the guns and then find the money. As they prepare to leave, they are engaged in battle by the village's returning menfolk, with the convicts losing. Their leader is declared innocent of the crime for which he was imprisoned and claims the love of one of the village ladies (Gene Tierney).

THE SWORD OF MONTE CRISTO

Produced by Edward L. Alperson
Directed by Maurice Geraghty
Screenplay by Maurice Geraghty
Photographed in Supercinecolor by Jack Greenhalgh
Music by Raoul Kraushaar
80 minutes

Cast: George Montgomery, Paula Corday, Berry Kroeger, William Conrad, Rhys Williams, Steve Brodie, Robert Warwick, David Bond, Lillian Bronson, Acquanetta, Trevor Bardette, Crane Whitley, Leonard Mudie

A swashbuckling story about a sword left by the Count of Monte Cristo which gives clues to a fortune left by him. The scheming chief minister (Berry Kroeger) of France learns about it and strives to get it in order to wrest control of the country from Louis Napoleon (David Bond). He is foiled in his plans by an officer (George Montgomery) of the emperor and a noblewoman (Paula Corday)—which leads to the fortune being turned over to France and love for the two heroic leaders.

TAKE CARE OF MY LITTLE GIRL

Produced by Julian Blaustein
Directed by Jean Negulesco
Screenplay by Julius J. and Philip G. Epstein, from the novel by Peggy Goodin
Photographed in Technicolor by Harry Jackson
Music by Alfred Newman
94 minutes

Cast: Jeanne Crain, Dale Robertson, Mitzi Gaynor, Jean Peters, Jeffrey Hunter, Betty Lynn, Helen Westcott, Lenka Peterson, Carol Brannon, Natalie Schafer, Beverly Dennis, Kathleen Hughes, Peggy O'Connor

A dramatic criticism of college sorority life, with Jeanne Crain as an intelligent girl who, after the first few weeks of frenetic rushing and bidding, begins to find the whole thing silly—and in some instances dangerous. She is appalled by the social significance placed on sorority decisions, with their snobbism, their rejection of certain girls, and their indifference to academic studies. Her boyfriend (Dale Robertson) convinces her that she has no need to belong to a sorority in order to succeed in school.

THE 13th LETTER

Produced and directed by Otto Preminger
Screenplay by Howard Koch, from a story by Louis Chavance
Photographed by Joseph La Shelle
Music by Alex North
Musical direction by Lionel Newman
88 minutes

Cast: Linda Darnell, Charles Boyer, Michael Rennie, Constance Smith, François Rosay, Judith Evelyn, Guy Sorel, June Hedin, Paul Guevremont, George Alexander, J. Leo Gagnon, Ovila Legare

Betty Grable, Eddie Albert, and Macdonald Carey in *Meet Me After the Show*.

Clifton Webb and Joanne Dru in *Mr. Belvedere Rings the Bell*.

Marlene Dietrich and James Stewart in *No Highway in the Sky*.

Danny Kaye in *On the Riviera*.

An intriguing tale of poison pen writing in a small Canadian town. A newly arrived doctor (Michael Rennie) receives abusive letters accusing him of an affair with the young wife (Constance Smith) of a respected middle-aged doctor (Charles Boyer). The culprit is thought to be a nurse (Judith Evelyn), who is imprisoned. But the letters continue and the new doctor himself tracks down the culprit, who turns out to be the middle-aged doctor, a man insanely jealous of his young wife. The film's dramatic impact is aided by its having been filmed on location in Quebec with good use of scenic values.

YOU'RE IN THE NAVY NOW

Produced by Fred Kohlmar
Directed by Henry Hathaway
Screenplay by Richard Murphy, based on an article by
    John W. Hazard
Photographed by Joe MacDonald
Music by Cyril Mockridge
93 minutes

Cary Grant and Jeanne Crain in *People Will Talk*.

Tyrone Power, Susan Hayward, and Hugh Marlowe in *Rawhide*.

Cast: Gary Cooper, Jane Greer, Millard Mitchell, Eddie Albert, John McIntire, Ray Collins, Harry Von Zell, Jack Webb, Richard Erdman, Harvey Lembeck, Henry Slate, Ed Begley, Fay Roope, Charles Tannen, Charles Buchinsky (later Bronson), Lee Marvin

During World War II, a reserve officer (Gary Cooper) with little naval experience is put in command of an experimental patrol vessel fitted with steam engines instead of the usual diesel. He is dismayed to find all of his officers and most of his crew are also wartime draftees. Trouble plagues the ship and the crew flounder through their adventures, but they serve the purposes of the Navy in proving that steam is impractical in warships. The film is a genial comedy, with an appealing performance from Gary Cooper as the mild-mannered captain operating under unfair conditions. This was Cooper's first starring vehicle at 20th Century-Fox and the first time he had worked at the studio since being an extra in a 1925 Tom Mix Western.

Jane Greer and Gary Cooper in
You're in the Navy Now.

Michael Rennie and Charles Boyer
in *The 13th Letter.*

BELLES ON THEIR TOES

Produced by Samuel G. Engel
Directed by Henry Levin
Screenplay by Phoebe and Henry Ephron, from the book
  by Frank B. Gilbreth, Jr., and Ernestine Gilbreth Carey
Photographed in Technicolor by Arthur E. Arling
Music by Cyril J. Mockridge
Musical direction by Lionel Newman
89 minutes

Cast: Jeanne Crain, Myrna Loy, Debra Paget, Jeffrey
Hunter, Edward Arnold, Hoagy Carmichael, Barbara
Bates, Robert Arthur, Verna Felton, Roddy McCaskill,
Carole Nugent, Tina Thompson, Teddy Driver, Tommy
Ivo

A sequel to *Cheaper By the Dozen,* with the twelve
children and their mother (Myrna Loy) carrying on
after the death of the father. She continues her husband's business of industrial engineering and meets bias
against a woman being so involved. An industrialist
friend (Edward Arnold) gives mother an opportunity
to train fledgling engineers and she shines. With the
income the children continue their education and the
eldest daughter (Jeanne Crain) is romanced by a
young doctor (Jeffrey Hunter), resulting in marriage.
Charm, humor, and colorful settings make this almost
as pleasing as its predecessor.

BLOODHOUNDS OF BROADWAY

Produced by George Jessel
Directed by Harmon Jones
Screenplay by Sy Gomberg, from a story by Damon
  Runyon
Photographed in Technicolor by Edward Cronjager
Musical direction by Lionel Newman
93 minutes

Cast: Mitzi Gaynor, Scott Brady, Mitzi Green, Mar-
guerite Chapman, Michael O'Shea, Wally Vernon, Henry
Slate, George E. Stone, Edwin Max, Richard Allan,
Sharon Baird, Ralph Volkie, Charles Buchinski, Timothy
Carey

A wacky musical comedy, definitely Runyonesque,
about a slick New York bookie (Scott Brady) who
ducks out of town to avoid a crime investigating committee. He gets lost in the wilds of Georgia and
meets a lovely hillbilly (Mitzi Gaynor), who sings and
dances and aims for a career in show business. She persuades the bookie to take her to Broadway, where she
quickly scores a hit. With her love, he decides to reform. He goes before the committee, makes a confession, and gets off with a one-year sentence. Knockabout
nonsense, greatly aided by the appealing talents of
Gaynor.

DEADLINE—U. S. A.

Produced by Sol C. Siegel
Directed by Richard Brooks
Screenplay by Richard Brooks
Photographed by Milton Krasner
Music by Cyril J. Mockridge and Sol Kaplan
87 minutes

Cast: Humphrey Bogart, Ethel Barrymore, Kim Hunter,
Ed Begley, Warren Stevens, Paul Stewart, Martin Gabel,
Joe De Santis, Joyce MacKenzie, Audrey Christie, Fay
Baker, Jim Backus, Carlton Young, Selmer Jackson

Deadline U.S.A. is a tough account of journalism
under fire from both crime and business pressures.
An uncompromising editor (Humphrey Bogart) backs
his reporters as they expose crime and political col-
lusion, but is dismayed when his employer (Ethel
Barrymore) tells him that it has become necessary to
close the company. Nothing can be done to save the
newspaper, but the editor decides to pursue his attempts to reveal a major criminal (Martin Gabel)
rather than observe warnings that he should not. The
final edition proves to be a moral victory. The film
did much to advance the career of writer-director
Richard Brooks, and provided another fine characterization for the solid image of Bogart.

DIPLOMATIC COURIER

Produced by Casey Robinson
Directed by Henry Hathaway
Screenplay by Casey Robinson and Liam O'Brien, from
  a novel by Peter Cheyney
Photographed by Lucien Ballard
Music by Sol Kaplan
97 minutes

Cast: Tyrone Power, Patricia Neal, Stephen McNally, Hildegarde Neff, Karl Malden, James Millican, Stefan Schnabel, Herbert Berghof, Arthur Blake, Helene Stanley, Michael Ansara, Sig Arno, Alfred Linder

Tyrone Power as the top agent of the U.S. State Department's communications branch, sent to Trieste to retrieve papers stolen from a murdered fellow agent. In conjunction with a military intelligence officer (Stephen McNally), he finds that the man had found the Soviet's plans for invading Yugoslavia. He meets an American girl (Patricia Neal) and romances her, but she turns out to be a Russian agent. By the time he succeeds in his mission, agent Power has seen a lot of Europe, survived murder attempts, and has been involved in much chasing and being chased.

DON'T BOTHER TO KNOCK

Produced by Julian Blaustein
Directed by Roy Baker
Screenplay by Daniel Taradash, from a novel by Charlotte Armstrong
Photographed by Lucien Ballard
Musical direction by Lionel Newman
76 minutes

Cast: Richard Widmark, Marilyn Monroe, Anne Bancroft, Donna Corcoran, Jeanne Cagney, Lurene Tuttle, Elisha Cook, Jr., Jim Backus, Verna Felton, Willis B. Bouchey, Don Beddoe, Gloria Blondell, Grace Hayle

The story of a beautiful but psychotic young lady (Marilyn Monroe) who babysits a child (Donna Corcoran) in a hotel and flirts with a guest (Richard Widmark). He has just been given a brush-off by his girl friend (Anne Bancroft) and takes a fancy to the babysitter. The child wakes up and disturbs the lovemaking couple and the babysitter reveals homicidal tendencies. It is revealed that she is lately released from an asylum, with a record of suicide attempts. She is prevented from killing the child and restrained from another try at suicide. An interesting suspense film, with Monroe giving her first major dramatic performance.

DREAMBOAT

Produced by Sol C. Siegel
Directed by Claude Binyon
Screenplay by Claude Binyon, from a story by John D. Weaver
Photographed by Milton Krasner
Music by Cyril J. Mockridge
Musical direction by Lionel Newman
83 minutes

Cast: **Clifton Webb, Ginger Rogers, Anne Francis, Jeffrey Hunter, Elsa Lanchester, Fred Clark, Paul Harvey, Ray Collins, Helene Stanley, Richard Garrick, George Barrows, Jay Adler, Marietta Canty, Laura Brooks**

A delightful satire on television, with Clifton Webb as a long-retired silent movie idol, now a respected college professor and resentful of any mention of his Hollywood past. When his old movies start to play on television, his co-star (Ginger Rogers) takes full advantage in order to promote her own career and tries to inveigle him back into the spotlight. His academic life is shattered, but he eventually agrees to go back into the film industry, on what he thinks are his terms but are actually hers. *Dreamboat* succeeds as an attack on commercial television and contains amusing flashbacks to the silent screen, with Webb and Rogers disporting themselves in spoofs on films about first World War aviators, Zorro, legionnaires, and musketeers.

FIVE FINGERS

Produced by Otto Lang
Directed by Joseph L. Mankiewicz
Screenplay by Michael Wilson, from a book by L. C. Moyzisch
Photographed by Norbert Brodine
Music by Bernard Herrmann
108 minutes

Cast: James Mason, Danielle Darrieux, Michael Rennie, Walter Hampden, Oscar Karlweis, Herbert Berghof, John Wengraf, A. Ben Astar, Roger Ployden, Michael Pate, Ivan Triesault, Hannelore Axman, David Wolfe

A masterly account of the wartime espionage experiences of L. C. Moyzisch, on whose book *Operation Cicero* it is based, with James Mason playing the author —perhaps the most daring spy of the second World War. Known as Cicero, he works as a valet at the British Embassy in Ankara and sells their secret files to the Germans at high price. They pay the price, but regard the information as too fantastic to be believed. With the money Cicero sets up a palatial home for a friend (Danielle Darrieux), which he uses to meet German officials. Eventually he is doublecrossed—by the girl and by the Germans, who pay him off in counterfeit British currency. *Five Fingers* is superbly paced by director Mankiewicz, with a sophisticated script, stylish acting, and a fascinating story.

THE I DON'T CARE GIRL

Produced by George Jessel
Directed by Lloyd Bacon
Screenplay by Walter Bullock
Photographed in Technicolor by Arthur E. Arling
Musical direction by Lionel Newman
91 minutes

Cast: Mitzi Gaynor, David Wayne, Oscar Levant, Bob Graham, Craig Hill, Warren Stevens, Hazel Brooks, Marietta Canty, Sam Hearn, Wilton Graff, Dwayne Ratliff, Bill Foster, Gwyneth Verdon, George Jessel

The story of vaudeville star Eva Tanguay, played with

great gusto by Mitzi Gaynor, and with the film's producer, George Jessel, seen in conferences with his writers, trying to figure out how to tell the story. They get the views and anecdotes of a number of people who knew her, allowing for flashbacks to her days of glory. The story lines are slim and barely matter. What matters are the many opportunities given Gaynor to sing and dance, along with David Wayne as a Tanguay partner and Oscar Levant as his acerbic, piano-playing self.

JAPANESE WAR BRIDE

Produced by Joseph Bernhard
Directed by King Vidor
Screenplay by Catherine Turney, from a story by Anson Bond
Photographed by Lionel Lindon
Music by Emil Newman and Arthur Lange
90 minutes

Cast: Shirley Yamaguchi, Don Taylor, Cameron Mitchell, Marie Windsor, James Bell, Louise Lorimer, Philip Ahn, Sybil Merritt, Jane Nakano, Kathleen Mulqueen, Orley Lindgren, George Wallace, May Takasugi

An army officer, wounded in Korea and hospitalized in Japan (Don Taylor), falls in love with the girl (Shirley Yamaguchi) who nurses him back to health. They marry and return to America to face certain adjustments, mostly of the family kind. His parents try to understand, but his sister-in-law (Marie Windsor) tries to break them up by writing an anonymous letter accusing the wife of an affair with a Japanese-American, which causes trouble. When the furor is settled, it brings about a closer marriage and better understanding all round.

KANGAROO

Produced by Robert Bassler
Directed by Lewis Milestone
Screenplay by Harry Kleiner, from a story by Martin Berkeley
Photographed in Technicolor by Charles G. Clarke
Music by Sol Kaplan
Musical direction by Alfred Newman
84 minutes

Cast: Maureen O'Hara, Peter Lawford, Finlay Currie, Richard Boone, Chips Rafferty, Letty Craydon, Charles Tingwell, Ron Whelan, John Fegan, Guy Doleman, Reg Collins, Frank Ransom, Clyde Combo, Henry Murdoch

An Australian Western, with superb Technicolor photography of the awesome landscapes and a turn-of-the-century story about a pair of crooks (Peter Lawford and Richard Boone) who try to swindle an old rancher (Finlay Currie). Their plans fall apart when the younger man falls in love with the rancher's daughter (Maureen O'Hara). When a mounted policeman

(Chips Rafferty) comes after them, they escape, resulting in the death of the older crook and the wounding of the younger. By surrendering himself and confessing, the younger man stands to get a light sentence and a bright future with the daughter. A conventional story made arresting by the sight of cattle drives, forest fires, aborigine dancing, and herds of kangaroos.

LADY IN THE IRON MASK

Produced by Walter Wanger and Eugene Frenke
Directed by Ralph Murphy
Screenplyay by Jack Pollexfen and Aubrey Wisberg
Photographed in Natural Color by Ernest Laszlo
Music by Dimitri Tiomkin
78 minutes

Cast: Louis Hayward, Patricia Medina, John Sutton, Steve Brodie, Alan Hale, Jr., Judd Holdren, Hal Gerard, Lester Matthews

A pleasing swashbuckling yarn, inspired by Dumas, with D'Artagnan (Louis Hayward) and the musketeers rallying to the rescue of the royal throne of France when the Princess Anne (Partricia Medina in a dual role) is kidnapped and her long-lost sister Louise is put in her place. The plotters (John Sutton and company) want a marriage with Philip of Spain, which would ensure their control of France. The musketeers see that the villains are stopped, and once they are stopped Princess Anne marries D'Artagnan and leaves her sister on the throne in her place.

LES MISERABLES

Produced by Fred Kohlmar
Directed by Lewis Milestone
Screenplay by Richard Murphy, from the novel by Victor Hugo
Photographed by Joseph La Shelle
Music by Alex North
Musical direction by Alfred Newman
105 minutes

Cast: Michael Rennie, Debra Paget, Robert Newton, Edmund Gwenn, Sylvia Sidney, Cameron Mitchell, Elsa Lanchester, James Robertson Justice, Joseph Wiseman, Rhys Williams, Florence Bates, Merry Anders, John Rogers

The fourth Hollywood version of the Dumas classic, with Michael Rennie as Jean Valjean and Robert Newton as the fanatically dedicated policeman Javert. Richard Murphy's screenplay follows the main line of the book, tracing Valjean's arrest for stealing bread and his ten years of imprisonment, his making a success in business and becoming the mayor of his town. But by not reporting for parole approval he violates the letter of the law, which is enough for Javert to hound him and turn him into a fugitive again. The question is one of justice versus compassion—with the spirit of the law finally recognized, even by Javert, as the more important factor.

LURE OF THE WILDERNESS

Produced by Robert L. Jacks
Directed by Jean Negulesco
Screenplay by Louis Lantz, from a story by Vereen Bell
Photographed in Technicolor by Edward Cronjager
Music by Franz Waxman
93 minutes

Cast: Jean Peters, Jeffrey Hunter, Constance Smith, Walter Brennan, Tom Tully, Harry Shannon, Will Wright, Jack Elam, Harry Carter, Pat Hogan, Al Thompson, Robert Adler, Sherman Sanders, Robert Karnes

A remake of *Swamp Water* (1941), with almost the same plot lines. Set in the Okefenokee swamps of Georgia in the early years of the century and concerning a man (Walter Brennan) who has been living as a fugitive from justice in the depths of the swamp with his daughter (Jean Peters). A young hunter (Jeffrey Hunter) finds them and by selling their pelts raises enough money to bring in a good lawyer to clear the old man of the false charges laid against him by the actual culprits. They cause him to again retreat into the swamps, but in following him, one is killed and the other captured and made to confess. Color and locations add to the lure of the melodrama.

LYDIA BAILEY

Produced by Jules Schermer
Directed by Jean Negulesco
Screenplay by Michael Blankfort and Philip Dunne, from a novel by Kenneth Roberts
Photographed in Technicolor by Harry Jackson
Music by Hugo Friedhofer
Musical direction by Lionel Newman
89 minutes

Cast: Dale Robertson, Anne Francis, Charles Korvin, William Marshall, Luis Van Rooten, Adeline de Walt Reynolds, Angos Perez, Bob Evans, Gladys Holland, Will Wright, Roy E. Glenn, Ken Renard

A colorful grand adventure, set in Haiti during the island's conflict with Napoleon. An American lawyer (Dale Robertson) arrives to conclude a contract with an aristocratic land owner (Anne Francis) and gets involved with the Haitian revolt against the French. He is befriended by a rebel general (William Marshall), who gets him across the island to the lady's estate, whose life he later saves. The lady, at first sympathetic to the French, comes to share the rebel point of view and falls in love with the American. Together they escape the turmoil. The film is a limited versions of Kenneth Roberts' vast novel but gorgeously scenic.

MONKEY BUSINESS

Produced by Sol C. Siegel
Directed by Howard Hawks
Screenplay by Ben Hecht, Charles Lederer, and I. A. L. Diamond, from a story by Harry Segall
Photographed by Milton Krasner
Music by Leigh Harline
Musical direction by Lionel Newman
97 minutes

Cast: Cary Grant, Ginger Rogers, Charles Coburn, Marilyn Monroe, Hugh Marlowe, Henri Letondal, Robert Cornthwaite, Larry Keating, Douglas Spencer, Esther Dale, George Winslow, Emmett Lynn, Jerry Sheldon

A screwball comedy about a brilliant research chemist (Cary Grant) who invents a formula for delaying the aging process. A champanzee in the laboratory pours all the formula into the water cooler. When the chemist takes a drink, he becomes an adolescent and when his wife takes several drinks, she starts to behave like a child. The chemist recovers and comes to realize that the formula is only temporarily effective, but he has the pleasure of seeing his staid old employer (Charles Coburn) romping around the lab like a wild baby. Marilyn Monroe adds to the pleasure of the picture as a sexy and amusing secretary.

MY COUSIN RACHEL

Produced by Nunnally Johnson
Directed by Henry Koster
Screenplay by Nunnally Johnson, from a novel by Daphne du Maurier
Photographed by Joseph La Shelle
Music by Franz Waxman
98 minutes

Cast: Olivia de Havilland, Richard Burton, Audrey Dalton, Ronald Squire, George Dolenz, John Sutton, Tudor Owen, J. M. Kerrigan, Margaret Brewster, Alma Lawton

A Daphne du Maurier period mystery about a young man (Richard Burton) who goes to Italy when he receives letters from his cousin (John Sutton) claiming that his wife (Olivia de Havilland) is poisoning him. When he gets there, he finds the cousin dead and the widow gone. He swears revenge, but when the beautiful lady turns up in England, he falls in love with her. Though he turns over his estate to her, she refuses to marry him; but she nurses him through his sickness when he falls ill, apparently from a poison. When she seems about to leave with an Italian friend, he angrily faces her and accidentally causes her to fall to her death from a cliff. Later he receives a letter from a friend which suggests that she was innocent of her husband's death. He is left with the riddle: was Rachel a villainess or was she not?

Myrna Loy and Jeanne Crain in *Belles on Their Toes*.

Humphrey Bogart and Kim Hunter in *Deadline—USA*.

Mitzi Gaynor in *The I Don't Care Girl*.

Marilyn Monroe and Richard Widmark in *Don't Bother to Knock*.

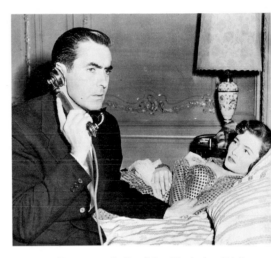

Tyrone Power and Patricia Neal in *Diplomatic Courier*.

James Mason and Danielle Darrieux in *5 Fingers*.

Clifton Webb and Ginger Rogers in *Dream Boat*.

Maureen O'Hara and Peter Lawford in *Kangaroo*.

Michael Rennie and Robert Newton in *Les Miserables*.

235

MY PAL GUS

Produced by Stanley Rubin
Directed by Robert Parrish
Screenplay by Fay and Michael Kanin
Photographed by Leo Tover
Music by Leigh Harline
Musical direction by Lionel Newman
83 minutes

Cast: Richard Widmark, Joanne Dru, Audrey Totter, George Winslow, Joan Banks, Regis Toomey, Ludwig Donath, Ann Morrison, Lisa Golm, Christopher Olsen, Robert Foulk, Mimi Gibson, Sandy Descher

A divorced industrial tycoon (Richard Widmark) is bothered by the pranks of his young son (George Winslow) and places him in a playtime school. His teacher (Joanne Dru) improves the boy's behavior and falls in love with the father, and vice versa. The tycoon's ex-wife (Audrey Totter) appears and claims their divorce is not legal and that if he wants it to be he must pay a large sum or lose custody of the boy to her. She loses the court case but gets the boy. Then the father, with the teacher's love and approval, realizes his son means more than money and pays out the large sum to get him back.

MY WIFE'S BEST FRIEND

Produced by Robert Bassler
Directed by Richard Sale
Screenplay by Isobel Lennart, from a story by John Briard Harding
Photographed by Leo Tover
Music by Leigh Harline
Musical direction by Lionel Newman
87 minutes

Cast: Anne Baxter, Macdonald Carey, Cecil Kellaway, Casey Adams, Catherine McLeod, Leif Erickson, Frances Bavier, Mary Sullivan, Martin Milner, Billie Bird, Wild Red Berry, Henry Kulky, John Hedloe

A marital comedy about a husband (Macdonald Carey) who admits to his wife (Anne Baxter) that he had an affair with her best friend (Catherine McLeod). In her mind she invents revenge and imagines how she would behave if she were Joan of Arc, Cleopatra, and other past figures. In the end it evolves that the affair was a mild flirtation and nothing more, and the tranquility of their marriage is restored.

NIGHT WITHOUT SLEEP

Produced by Robert Bassler
Directed by Roy Baker
Screenplay by Frank Partos and Elick Moll, from a story by Elick Moll
Photographed by Lucien Ballard
Musical direction by Lionel Newman
77 minutes

Cast: Linda Darnell, Gary Merrill, Hildegarde Neff, Joyce MacKenzie, June Vincent, Donald Randolph, Hugh Beaumont, Louise Lorimer, William Forrest, Steven Geray, Mauri Lynn, Bill Walker, Mae Marsh, Ben Carter

A composer (Gary Merrill), who has been warned by a psychiatrist that he has a dangerous tendency, awakens in a stupor after a night of drinking with the feeling that in his drunkenness he has killed a woman. The three women in his life are his rich wife (June Vincent), with whom he frequently quarrels, an ex-mistress (Hildegarde Neff), and a movie actress (Linda Darnell), an old friend. In flashback he recalls his sometimes stormy association with all of them and calls to find if they are alive. He is relieved to find the mistress and the actress still alive, but on entering his bedroom finds his wife dead. He then calls the police.

O. HENRY'S FULL HOUSE

Produced by Andre Hakim
Directed by Henry Koster, Henry Hathaway, Jean Negulesco, Howard Hawks, and Henry King
Screenplays by Richard Breen, Walter Bullock, Ivan Goff, Ben Roberts, and Lamar Trotti, from the stories of O. Henry
Photographed by Lloyd Ahern, Lucien Ballard, Joe MacDonald, and Milton Krasner
Musical direction by Alfred Newman
117 minutes

Cast: Charles Laughton, Marilyn Monroe, David Wayne, Dale Robertson, Richard Widmark, Joyce MacKenzie, Anne Baxter, Jean Peters, Gregory Ratoff, Fred Allen, Oscar Levant, Jeanne Crain, Farley Granger, Fred Kelsey

An interesting grouping of five short stories of O. Henry: *The Cop and the Anthem,* with Charles Laughton as an old hobo who gets himself arrested every winter in order to have the comfort of jail; *The Clarion Call,* with Richard Widmark as a killer who is finally and ironically caught by an old detective friend (Dale Robertson); *The Last Leaf,* with Anne Baxter as an invalid who recovers because of the sacrifice of an old painter (Gregory Ratoff); *The Ransom of Red Chief,* with Fred Allen and Oscar Levant as a pair of kidnappers who gladly give up their fiendish subject (Lee Acker) and pay his father money to take him back; and *The Gift of the Magi,* with Jeanne Crain and Farley Granger as a poor but loving young couple who sell their only prize possessions in order to buy Christmas gifts for one another. Five directors, a host of fine actors and a veritable stable of writers make this a very full and fascinating house.

THE OUTCASTS OF POKER FLAT

Produced by Julian Blaustein
Directed by Joseph M. Newman
Screenplay by Edmund H. North, from a story by Bret Harte

Jean Peters and Jeffrey Hunter in *Lure of the Wilderness.*

Photographed by Joseph La Shelle
Music by Hugo Friedhofer
Musical direction by Lionel Newman
80 minutes

Cast: Anne Baxter, Dale Robertson, Miriam Hopkins, Cameron Mitchell, Craig Hill, Barbara Bates, Billy Lynn, Dick Rich, Tom Greenway, Russ Conway, John Ridgely

A grimly dramatic Western about a group of people marooned in a mountain cabin during a raging snowstorm and terrorized by a murderous bandit (Cameron Mitchell). He holds them at gunpoint and eats all the food. With him is his wife (Anne Baxter), who has learned to fear him, and a gambler (Dale Robertson), who waits for the opportunity to jump the bandit. The bandit kills one of the group (Billy Lynn) and when another (Miriam Hopkins) runs out to get the attention of an approaching man, he kills her too. But it is then that the gambler gets his chance to tackle the bandit and kill him.

PHONE CALL FROM A STRANGER

Produced by Nunnally Johnson
Directed by Jean Negulesco
Screenplay by Nunnally Johnson, based on a story by I. A. R. Wylie
Photographed by Milton Krasner
Music by Franz Waxman
96 minutes

Cast: Shelley Winters, Gary Merrill, Michael Rennie, Keenan Wynn, Evelyn Varden, Warren Stevens, Beatrice Straight, Ted Donaldson, Craig Stevens, Helen Westcott, Bette Davis, Sydney Perkins, Hugh Beaumont, Thomas Jackson, Harry Cheshire, Tom Powers, Freeman Lusk, George Eldridge, Nestor Paiva, Perdita Chandler, Genevieve Bell

Flying to Los Angeles to escape what he thinks is a failed marriage, David Trask (Gary Merrill) passes the time in conversation with a number of passengers, all of whom pour out the stories of their tangled lives to him. The plane crashes and Trask is the survivor among those whose lives he has touched en route. He makes it his mission to visit their families. The last visit takes him to a lady (Bette Davis) who reveals that her seemingly brash and vulgar late husband (Keenan Wynn) was actually a very tender man, who had forgiven her after she had an affair with another man and who had taken her back when she became an invalid. She advices Trask to phone his wife and see what he can do about saving his marriage. Basically a soap opera, *Phone Call from a Stranger* gains greatly from the quality of its actors.

PONY SOLDIER

Produced by Samuel G. Engel
Directed by Joseph M. Newman
Screenplay by John C. Higgins, from a story by Garnett Weston
Photographed in Technicolor by Harry Jackson
Music by Alex North
Musical direction by Alfred Newman
81 minutes

Cast: Tyrone Power, Cameron Mitchell, Thomas Gomez, Penny Edwards, Robert Horton, Anthony Earl Numkena, Adeline de Walt Reynolds, Howard Petrie, Stuart Randall, Richard Shackleton, James Hayward, Muriel Landers, Frank De Kova, Louis Hemminger (Shooting Star), Grady Galloway, Nipo T. Strongheart

Tyrone Power in the Canadian West in the early years of the Royal Canadian Mounted Police (late 1870's) and their actions in containing the Indians. As a con-

Cary Grant and Marilyn Monroe in *Monkey Business.*

237

stable he is assigned to persuade the Crees to return to their reservation and to claim two white captives, one a girl (Penny Edwards) and the other an escaped convict (Robert Horton). The convict complicates matters by killing the brother of a chief (Cameron Mitchell), but despite the Mountie's promise to the Indians to see the man will receive punishment according to the law, the convict brings about his own death. Beautifully color photographed in Coconimo National Forest, but at variance with the supposed Canadian setting of the story.

THE PRIDE OF ST. LOUIS

Produced by Jules Schermer
Directed by Harmon Jones
Screenplay by Herman J. Mankiewicz, from a story by Guy Trosper
Photographed by Leo Tover
Music by Arthur Lange
Musical direction by Lionel Newman
93 minutes

Cast: Dan Dailey, Joanne Dru, Richard Hylton, Richard Crenna, Hugh Sanders, James Brown, Leo T. Cleary, Kenny Williams, John McKee, Stuart Randall, William Frambes, Damian O'Flynn, Cliff Clark

Dan Dailey as baseball great Dizzy Dean, in a warm and amusing account of his career. Dean, a lovable clown of a man, works his way up from poverty and the minor leagues and becomes famous with his pitching for the St. Louis Cardinals. His brother Paul (Richard Crenna) plays on the same team and together they help take the World Series away from Detroit. As a result of an injury his days as a pitcher come to an end, which he finds hard to accept. His wife (Joanne Dru) leaves him in order to shake him into a sense of reality. It works and he discovers another career as a sports commentator. *The Pride of St. Louis* is a major movie about baseball, with a winning performance from Dailey.

RETURN OF THE TEXAN

Produced by Frank P. Rosenberg
Directed by Delmer Daves
Screenplay by Dudley Nichols, from a novel by Fred Gipson
Photographed by Lucien Ballard
Music by Sol Kaplan
88 minutes

Cast: Dale Robertson, Joanne Dru, Walter Brennan, Richard Brennan, Richard Boone, Tom Tully, Robert Horton, Helen Westcott, Lonnie Thomas, Dennis Ross, Robert Adler, Kathryn Sheldon, Aileen Carlyle

A homey yarn, about a young widower (Dale Robertson) who returns to his rundown Texas farm with his two sons and his father (Walter Brennan) determined to start life again. He takes a job with a mean neighbor (Richard Boone), whose sister-in-law (Joanne Dru) falls in love with him. He is obsessed with memories of his wife, but with the love of the new woman in his life and his sons happy in their new home, he finds the life he wants.

ROSE OF CIMARRON

Produced by Edward L. Alperson
Directed by Harry Keller
Screenplay by Maurice Geraghty
Photographed in Natural Color by Karl Struss
Music by Raoul Kraushaar
74 minutes

Cast: Jack Buetel, Mala Powers, Bill Williams, Jim Davis, Dick Curtis, Lane Bradford, William Phipps, Bob Steele, Alex Gerry, Lillian Bronson, Art Smith, Monte Blue, Argentina Brunetti, Irving Bacon

The lady of the title (Mala Powers) is a white brought up by Cherokee Indians after the killing of her parents by Comanches. When outlaws plunder and murder her Indian parents, she vows vengeance. She teams up with a young marshall (Jack Buetel) on the same mission, and together they bring the culprits to justice.

RUBY GENTRY

Produced by Joseph Bernhard and King Vidor
Directed by King Vidor
Screenplay by Silvia Richards, from a story by Arthur Fitz-Richard
Photographed by Russell Harlan
Music by Heinz Roemheld
85 minutes

Cast: Jennifer Jones, Charlton Heston, Karl Malden, Tom Tully, Bernard Phillips, James Anderson, Josephine Hutchinson, Phyllis Avery, Herbert Heyes, Myra Marsh, Charles Cane, Sam Flint

A steamy Southern melodrama about a sultry beauty (Jennifer Jones) born to a lowly family but desirous of rising in the world. Her handsome boyfriend (Charlton Heston) doesn't consider her good enough to marry, so she marries a wealthy businessman (Karl Malden). When he dies in a sailing accident, there is talk of murder and she retaliates by driving local businesses into bankrupcy. When the old boyfriend starts to woo her again, her mad brother (James Anderson) shoots and kills him. Ruby then kills her brother, leaving the audience to decide whether she was of evil heart or mostly a victim of circumstances.

RED SKIES OF MONTANA

Produced by Samuel G. Engel
Directed by Joseph M. Newman
Screenplay by Harry Kleiner, from a story by Art Cohn
Photographed in Technicolor by Charles G. Clarke

Music by Sol Kaplan
Musical direction by Lionel Newman
99 minutes

Cast: Richard Widmark, Constance Smith, Jeffrey Hunter, Richard Boone, Warren Stevens, James Griffith, Joe Sawyer, Gregory Wolcott, Richard Crenna, Robert Adler, Charles Buchinsky, Bob Nichols, Ralph Reed

An exciting, colorful tribute to the Forestry Service and their facilities for fighting fires—with modern communication, helicopters, chemicals, tactics, and courage. The story concerns a veteran firefighter (Richard Widmark) who is accused of cowardice by a rookie (Jeffrey Hunter) when the young man loses his father in a forest fire campaign supervised by the veteran. It seems the veteran blacked out during the fire, and when the young man comes to serve under him, he realizes the veteran is a tough, capable commander. The story is slight, but the color photography of the forests and the fires is magnificent.

THE SNOWS OF KILIMANJARO

Produced by Darryl F. Zanuck
Directed by Henry King
Screenplay by Casey Robinson, from a story by Ernest Hemingway
Photographed in Technicolor by Leon Shamroy
Music by Bernard Herrmann
114 minutes

Cast: Gregory Peck, Susan Hayward, Ava Gardner, Hildegarde Neff, Leo G. Carroll, Torin Thatcher, Ava Norring, Helene Stanley, Marcel Dalio, Vincente Gomez, Richard Allan, Leonard Carey, Paul Thompson, Emmett Smith

A handsome, colorful canvas of adventure as a Hemingway hero (Gregory Peck) lies wounded on the slopes of an African mountain, in the company of his lady love (Susan Hayward), and reflects on his life. He thinks of himself largely as a failure, as a writer who chose trivia instead of worthy literature, and he recalls his times in Paris, on the Riviera and in Spain, where he lost his wife (Ava Gardner) when they both fought for the Loyalists. In reviewing his life he forms a degree of self-respect and a realization that he loves his lady companion. With new resolve he aims to do better with his life and his writing. Peck makes the hero an interesting and believable man. The photography of many fine locations, the music of Bernard Herrmann, and the clear direction of Henry King combine to make this an epic picture.

SOMETHING FOR THE BIRDS

Produced by Samuel G. Engel
Directed by Robert Wise
Screenplay by I. A. L. Diamond and Boris Ingster, from stories by Alvin M. Josephy, Joseph Petracca, and Boris Ingster
Photographed by Joseph La Shelle
Music by Sol Kaplan
Musical direction by Lionel Newman
81 minutes

Cast: Victor Mature, Patricia Neal, Edmund Gwenn, Larry Keating, Gladys Hurbut, Hugh Sanders, Christian Rub, Wilton Graff, Walter Baldwin, Archer MacDonald, Richard Garrick, Ian Wolfe

A comedy about lobbying in Washington, with Patricia Neal as a Californian bent on preserving the condors of her state. She is befriended by an old fraud (Edmund Gwenn), who prints his own invitations to high society parties in the capitol, and through him she meets another lobbyist (Victor Mature). He represents the oil company whose bill threatens the existence of the birds, but after exposure to her, he changes his views and helps defeat the bill. A genial comedy, with Edmund Gwenn walking away with every scene in which he appears.

THE STAR

Produced by Bert E. Friedlob
Directed by Stuart Heisler
Screenplay by Katherine Albert and Dale Eunson
Photographed by Ernest Laszlo
Music by Victor Young
90 minutes

Cast: Bette Davis, Sterling Hayden, Natalie Wood, Warner Anderson, Minor Watson, June Travis, Katherine Warren, Kay Riehl, Barbara Woodel, Fay Baker, Barbara Lawrence, David Alpert, Paul Frees

The Star is one of Hollywood's less flattering movies about itself. The title lady (Bette Davis) is a film luminary who has fallen on rough times, mostly because of bad films and bad investments, and a refusal to realize her age that keeps her from the parts in which she once excelled. Her personal effects are sold off at auction and the relatives whom she had kept on allowances now turn their backs on her. Her salvation comes in the form of an ex-actor (Sterling Hayden) who once appeared with her and now runs his own business. He has harbored a love for her and can now offer her a home. After a number of humiliations in the movie industry, she realizes she had best forget having been a star and start a new life with him. The film offers interesting insights into Hollywood, but it is Davis' intense performance as a woman driven almost to breaking which makes it worthwhile.

STARS AND STRIPES FOREVER

Produced by Lamar Trotti
Directed by Henry Koster
Screenplay by Lamar Trotti, from the book *Marching*

Along by John Philip Sousa
Photographed in Technicolor by Charles G. Clarke
Musical direction by Alfred Newman
89 minutes

Cast: Clifton Webb, Debra Paget, Robert Wagner, Ruth Hussey, Finlay Currie, Roy Roberts, Tom Brown Henry, Lester Matthews, Maude Prickett, Erno Verebes, Richard Garrick, Romo Vincent, Florence Shirley

A colorful and tuneful account of the career of John Philip Sousa, with Clifton Webb as the great bandmaster and composer of memorable marches. The film concentrates on the 1890's, when Sousa left the Marine Corps and formed his own concert band, which continuously toured America and the world. The story is one of total success, with a little fiction about a musician (Robert Wagner) who invents a giant horn which becomes known as a Sousaphone and who marries a singer-dancer (Debra Paget) and gets her a job singing with the band even though Sousa opposes wives touring with the band. The story barely matters; what matters is the evocation of an era, the colorful costumes, and a generous amount of Sousa's music under the direction of Alfred Newman.

THE STEEL TRAP

Produced by Bert E. Friedlob
Directed by Andrew Stone
Screenplay by Andrew Stone
Photographed by Ernest Laszlo
Music by Dimitri Tiomkin
84 minutes

Cast: Joseph Cotten, Teresa Wright, Eddi Marr, Aline Towne, Bill Hudson, Benny Burt, Joey Ray, Sam Flint, Charlie Collins, Kurt Martell, Jonathan Hale, Stephanie King

A Los Angeles assistant bank manager (Joseph Cotten) finally yields to temptation and steals a million dollars. He plans to fly to Brazil with his wife (Teresa Wright) and child, but on arrival in New Orleans they find they have missed the plane to Brazil. It is there that the wife learns her husband has stolen the money and with that she leaves him and returns home. On reflection he realizes his values and what being branded as a thief would mean to his family. The money he stole on Friday he then returns on Monday.

THE THIEF OF VENICE

Produced by Robert Haggiag
Directed by John Brahm
Screenplay by Jesse L. Lasky, Jr., from a story by
    Michael Pertwee
Photographed by Anchise Brizzi
Music by Alessandro Cicognini
91 minutes

Cast: Maria Montez, Paul Christian, Massimo Serato, Faye Marlowe, Aldo Silvani, Louis Saltamerenda, Guido Celano, Humberto Sacripanti, Camillo Pilotto, Ferdinand Tamberlani, Liana Del Balzo

Intrigue and adventures in eighth-century Venice, during its war with Turkey, with Maria Montez as a tavern keeper on whose premises a plot to take over the city is hatched. She combines forces with a naval captain (Paul Christian) to keep the chief plotter (Massimo Serato) from completing his greedy aims. Made in Italy, the film offers plenty of action and masses of extras in battle. It was the last screen appearance of Montez, who died in 1951 at the age of thirty-three.

VIVA ZAPATA!

Produced by Darryl F. Zanuck
Directed by Elia Kazan
Screenplay by John Steinbeck
Photographed by Joe MacDonald
Music by Alex North
112 minutes

Cast: Marlon Brando, Jean Peters, Anthony Quinn, Joseph Wiseman, Arnold Moss, Alan Reed, Margo, Harold Gordon, Lou Gilbert, Mildred Dunnock, Frank Silvera, Nina Varela, Florenz Ames, Bernie Gozier, Frank De Kova, Joseph Granby

It was Elia Kazan who persuaded Darryl F. Zanuck that there was a film in the story of the almost legendary Mexican revolutionary Emiliano Zapata, and once persuaded Zanuck poured out his enthusiasm and resources. He hired John Steinbeck for the screenplay and engaged Marlon Brando to play the lead, right after Brando's acclaim in the film version of *A Streetcar Named Desire*. The efforts were worthwhile, even though the public did not flock to this depiction of political idealism. It accurately follows Zapata's career, from his early years as a youngster who leads a delegation to Mexico City to protest the stealing of land from his people, to his being outlawed, to his leading role in the revolution which overthrew the Diaz regime and his assassination by political rivals. Despite a certain amount of romanticizing of Zapata, the film remains a classic among political subjects and a fine example of Brando's genius as a film actor.

WAIT TILL THE SUN SHINES, NELLIE

Produced by George Jessel
Directed by Henry King
Screenplay by Allan Scott, from a novel by Ferdinand
    Reyher
Photographed in Technicolor by Leon Shamroy
Music by Alfred Newman
109 minutes

Cast: David Wayne, Jean Peters, Hugh Marlowe, Albert Dekker, Helene Stanley, Tommy Morton, Joyce MacKenzie, Alan Hale, Jr., Richard Karlan, Merry Anders, Jim Moloney, Warren Stevens, Charles Watts, David Wolfe

Richard Burton and Olivia de Havilland in *My Cousin Rachel.*

Richard Crenna and Dan Dailey in *The Pride of St. Louis.*

Tyrone Power and Penny Edwards in *Pony Soldier.*

Jeanne Crain and Farley Granger in *O. Henry's Full House.*

Richard Widmark in *Red Skies of Montana.*

Gregory Peck and Susan Hayward in *The Snows of Kilimanjaro.*

Clifton Webb in *The Stars and Stripes Forever.*

Anthony Quinn, Marlon Brando, Lou Gilbert, and Harold Gordon in *Viva Zapata!*

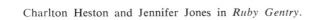
Charlton Heston and Jennifer Jones in *Ruby Gentry.*

James Cagney, Corinne Calvet, and Dan Dailey in *What Price Glory?*

A classic piece of Americana, directed by a specialist— Henry King—with a fine performance from David Wayne as a barber who loves his small town of Sevillinois. His bride (Jean Peters) doesn't share his feelings and yearns for life in the big city. She leaves him for a lover (Hugh Marlowe), but they are both killed in a railroad accident. The barber brings up his two children, but suffers great disappointment when his boy turns into a Chicago gangster and is killed in gang warfare. In time he also loses his shop in a fire, but friends help him rebuild. At the fiftieth anniversary of the town he is an honored old man, sharing his memories with old friends and doting on his granddaughter Nellie. The film contains more drama and pathos than its title implies, but it also contains beautiful images of turn-of-the-century small town life and amusing characters.

WAY OF A GAUCHO

Produced by Philip Dunne
Directed by Jacques Tourneur
Screenplay by Philip Dunne, from a novel by Herbert Childs
Photographed in Technicolor by Harry Jackson
Music by Sol Kaplan
87 minutes

Cast: Rory Calhoun, Gene Tierney, Richard Boone, Hugh Marlowe, Everett Sloane, Enrique Chiaco, Jorge Villoldo, Roland Dumas, Lidia Campos, Hugh Mancini, Nestor Yoan, Raoul Astor

Set in the Argentina of the 1870's—and filmed in that scenic country—the story is that of a likeable gaucho (Rory Calhoun) who resents the coming of civilization and its restrictions. Forced into the army rather than serve a jail sentence for manslaughter, he deserts and organizes a band of outlaws to hold back the railroad. The head of the police (Richard Boone), who was also

his commanding officer in the army, resolves to bring him in. With most of his friends gone and his men scattered, the gaucho realizes he must bend to progress and gives in. The policeman also concedes a few points and leaves him free to marry the society girl (Gene Tierney) with whom he has fallen in love. A good basic Western yarn backed up by stunning vistas of the pampas and the snow-capped Andes.

WE'RE NOT MARRIED

Produced by Nunnally Johnson
Directed by Edmund Goulding
Screenplay by Nunnally Johnson, from a story by Gina Kaus and Jay Dratler
Music by Cyril J. Mockridge
Musical direction by Lionel Newman
85 minutes

Cast: Ginger Rogers, Fred Allen, Victor Moore, Marilyn Monroe, David Wayne, Eve Arden, Paul Douglas, Eddie Bracken, Mitzi Gaynor, Louis Calhern, Zsa Zsa Gabor, James Gleason, Paul Stewart

A marital spoof about a judge (Victor Moore) who marries a number of couples before his appointment is official, with the result that a few years later they all find themselves unmarried. The results range from the poignant to the humorous. A young soldier (Eddie Bracken) is concerned about his pregnant wife (Mitzi Gaynor) and gets remarried by radio, while a tycoon (Louis Calhern) is delighted to divest himself of a fortune-hunting wife (Zsa Zsa Gabor). The news is also a relief to a pair of radio performers (Ginger Rogers and Fred Allen), who have to behave lovingly on the air but actually hate each other. Good writing and good playing make this a permanently amusing picture.

WHAT PRICE GLORY?

Produced by Sol C. Siegel
Directed by John Ford
Screenplay by Phoebe and Henry Ephron, based on a play by Maxwell Anderson and Laurence Stallings
Photographed in Technicolor by Joe MacDonald
Music by Alfred Newman
109 minutes

Cast: James Cagney, Corinne Calvet, Dan Dailey, William Demarest, Craig Hill, Robert Wagner, Marisa Pavan, Casey Adams, James Gleason, Wally Vernon, Henry Letondal, Fred Libby, Ray Hyke

A remake of the classic silent film of 1926, with James Cagney as the feisty Captain Flagg, Dan Dailey as the cocky Sergeant Quirt, and Corinne Calvet as the adorable Charmaine, the girl over whom they quarrel. In between quarrels they fight the Germans in the World War I trenches of France. The two veteran Marines drink and brawl but respect one another's courage. John Ford's direction makes this version less poignant than the original film. It plays up the knock-about comedy of the conflict between Flagg and Quirt, allowing for loudly bravura performances from Cagney and Dailey.

WITH A SONG IN MY HEART

Produced by Lamar Trotti
Directed by Walter Lang
Screenplay by Lamar Trotti
Photographed in Technicolor by Leon Shamroy
Musical direction by Alfred Newman
117 minutes

Cast: Susan Hayward, Rory Calhoun, David Wayne, Thelma Ritter, Robert Wagner, Helen Westcott, Una Merkel, Richard Allan, Max Showalter, Lyle Talbot, Leif Erickson, Stanley Logan, Eddie Firestone

The story of singer Jane Froman, with Susan Hayward giving a fine performance as the courageous lady and using her singing voice. The story is that of a St. Louis girl who makes good on the radio and marries the man (David Wayne) who activates and manages her career.

She soon feels the marriage is a mistake. Now famous, she is invited by the USO to tour the camps in the war and becomes a victim of an air crash. Another survivor of the crash is one of the pilots (Rory Calhoun). They fall in love during their time in the hospital and eventually the husband agrees to a divorce so that they can marry. The film clearly outlines the Froman determination to survive her near fatal accident and her refusal to become a cripple. It also allows for a large amount of music, including all the songs with which she became identified, and an admirable performance by Susan Hayward.

20TH CENTURY-FOX ACADEMY AWARDS FOR 1952

ANTHONY QUINN: Best supporting actor in *Viva Zapata*.
ALFRED NEWMAN: Best scoring of a musical, *With a Song in My Heart*.
A LIGHT IN THE WINDOW: Best short subject (one-reel). Produced by Art Films Production, Boris Vermont.

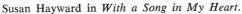
Susan Hayward in *With a Song in My Heart.*

1953

BENEATH THE 12 MILE REEF

Produced by Robert Bassler
Directed by Robert D. Webb
Screenplay by A. I. Bezzerides
Photographed in Technicolor and CinemaScope by
    Edward Cronjager
Music by Bernard Herrmann
102 minutes

Cast: Robert Wagner, Terry Moore, Gilbert Roland, J. Carrol Naish, Richard Boone, Angela Clarke, Peter Graves, Jay Novello, Jacques Aubuchon, Gloria Gordon, Harry Carey, Jr., James Harakas

Shot on location in Key West and Tarpon Springs, Florida. The title refers to the areas in which sponge fisherman ply their trade, sometimes at the risk of death. The story concerns two rival families and a Romeo-and-Juliet romance. The son (Robert Wagner) of a Greek diver (Gilbert Roland) falls in love with the daughter (Terry Moore) of a native Florida diver (Richard Boone). Members of the two families habitually thrash each other, but love conquers all. The film's main assets are the eerie music score of Bernard Herrmann and the enchanting underwater photography, in addition to Wagner's battle with an octopus.

A BLUEPRINT FOR MURDER

Produced by Michael Abel
Directed by Andrew Stone
Screenplay by Andrew Stone
Photographed by Leo Tover
Musical direction by Lionel Newman
76 minutes

Cast: Joseph Cotten, Jean Peters, Gary Merrill, Catherine McLeod, Jack Kruschen, Barney Phillips, Fred Ridgeway, Joyce McCluskey, Mae Marsh, Harry Carter, Jonathan Hole

A murder mystery concerning a man (Joseph Cotten) who admires his beautiful sister-in-law (Jean Peters) until he begins to suspect her of killing one of her stepchildren. After the child's death, an autopsy reveals strychnine poisoning. Since the husband has only recently died and there is a question of inheritance, the brother pursues his hunches. He follows her when she takes a ship to Europe and inveigles her into revealing her guilt.

CALL ME MADAM

Produced by Sol C. Siegel
Directed by Walter Lang
Screenplay by Arthur Sheekman, based on the Broadway
    musical comedy by Howard Lindsay and Russel Crouse
Songs by Irving Berlin
Photographed in Technicolor by Leon Shamroy
Musical direction by Alfred Newman
115 minutes

Cast: Ethel Merman, Donald O'Connor, Vera-Ellen, George Sanders, Billy DeWolfe, Helmut Dantine, Walter Slezak, Steven Geray, Ludwig Stossel, Lilia Skala, Charles Dingle, Emory Parnell

The Irving Berlin Broadway musical brought to the screen with full impact, together with its dynamic star Ethel Merman. Here she is the cheerful, gregarious Washington party-giver who is appointed ambassador to the tiny European country of Lichtenburg. She livens up the staid little kingdom and falls in love with its elegant foreign minister (George Sanders), while her press attaché (Donald O'Connor) woos and wins a princess (Vera-Ellen). What little political conniving comes her way is soon squelched by the big-hearted Madam Ambassador. Merman, Berlin, colorful sets and costumes, and lively dancing make the film a winner on all counts.

CITY OF BAD MEN

Produced by Leonard Goldstein
Directed by Harmon Jones
Screenplay by George W. George and George F. Slavin
Photographed in Technicolor by Charles G. Clarke
Music by Lionel Newman
82 minutes

Cast: Jeanne Crain, Dale Robertson, Richard Boone, Lloyd Bridges, Carole Mathews, Carl Betz, Whitfield Connor, Hugh Sanders, Rodolfo Acosta, Pascuala Garcia Pena, Harry Carter, Robert Adler

An offbeat Western about an adventurer (Dale Robertson) who arrives in Carson City, Nevada, in 1897 as the town is getting ready for the prizefight between Jim Corbett and Bob Fitzsimmons. He and his few friends have just left Mexico after fighting on the wrong side in a revolution and they see the opportunity to steal money. They sign on as deputies with the idea of afterwards taking the gate proceeds. But the ex-girl friend (Jeanne Crain) of the adventurer is in town and meeting her rekindles his love, with the result that he changes his mind about the robbery and helps put an end to his colleagues.

DANGEROUS CROSSING

Produced by Robert Bassler
Directed by Joseph M. Newman
Screenplay by Leo Townsend, from a story by John Dickson Carr
Photographed by Joseph La Shelle
Music by Lionel Newman
75 minutes

Cast: Jeanne Crain, Michael Rennie, Casey Adams, Carl Betz, Mary Anderson, Marjorie Hoshelle, Willis Bouchey, Yvonne Peattie, Karl Judwig Lindt, Gayne Whitman, Anthony Jochim, Charles Tannen

A bride (Jeanne Crain) happily boards a ship for a trans-Atlantic honeymoon, which soon becomes a nightmare when her husband (Carl Betz) disappears. She finds herself listed under her maiden name, with no one on board aware of the existence of the husband. The ship's doctor (Michael Rennie) sympathizes with her, thinking she is hallucinating, but comes to realize the danger she is in. His investigation solves the mystery—that the girl is the victim of a murder conspiracy engineered by the husband.

THE DESERT RATS

Produced by Robert L. Jacks
Directed by Robert Wise
Screenplay by Richard Murphy
Photographed by Lucien Ballard
Music by Leigh Harline
Musical direction by Alfred Newman
88 minutes

Cast: Richard Burton, Robert Newton, Robert Douglas, Torin Thatcher, Chips Rafferty, Charles Tingwell, Charles Davis, Ben Wright, James Mason, James Lilburn, John O'Malley, Ray Harden, John Alderson

A follow-up to the success of *The Desert Fox,* with James Mason making a brief appearance as Rommel, but concentrating on the part played by the Australian contingent of the British Eighth Army in their defense of Tobruk. An English officer (Richard Burton) is put in charge of a company of Australians and wins their dislike with his coldly formal manner of command. His qualities as a soldier gradually bring respect but never affection. He is captured and questioned by Rommel,

but escapes and later leads his small, almost exhausted group of survivors in holding a crucial hill, which controls a road on which the British forces are expected. A first-rate war adventure story, firmly directed by Robert Wise.

DESTINATION GOBI

Produced by Stanley Rubin
Directed by Robert Wise
Screenplay by Everett Freeman, from a story by Edmund G. Love
Photographed in Technicolor by Charles G. Clarke
Music by Sol Kaplan
Musical direction by Alfred Newman
89 minutes

Cast: Richard Widmark, Don Taylor, Casey Adams, Murvyn Vye, Darryl Hickman, Martin Milner, Ross Bagdasarian, Judy Dann, Rodolfo Acosta, Russell Collins, Leonard Strong, Anthony Earl Numkena

An interesting and amusing war adventure story, based on fact, about a group of Navy men assigned to Mongolia for the purpose of weather observation. A chief petty officer (Richard Widmark) takes over when their commander is killed in a Japanese air raid and he leads them 800 miles across the desert to the coast. They are there captured by the Japanese but rescued by a Mongol chieftain (Murvyn Vye), whose price for helping is sixty saddles, which he gets once the Pentagon recovers from the shock of the strange request. The Chief procures a Chinese junk for the Navy men and they make their way to Okinawa, following their triumph over a Japanese launch. The settings and the story lines make *Destination Gobi* an outstanding item in the war movie genre.

DOWN AMONG THE SHELTERING PALMS

Produced by Fred Kohlmar
Directed by Edmund Goulding
Screenplay by Claude Binyon, Albert Lewin, and Burt Styler, from a story by Edward Hope
Photographed in Technicolor by Leon Shamroy
Musical direction by Lionel Newman
73 minutes

Cast: William Lundigan, Jane Greer, Mitzi Gaynor, David Wayne, Gloria De Haven, Gene Lockhart, Jack Paar, Alvin Greenman, Billy Gilbert, Henry Kulky, Lyle Talbot, Ray Montgomery

A lightweight musical about an island in the South Pacific following the war. An army officer (William Lundigan) is assigned to occupy the island and ordered not to allow fraternization, which is a problem because his men are girl hungry and the island is populated with attractive females. The officer himself falls in love with the daughter (Jane Greer) of a missionary, but also has a lovely native (Mitzi Gaynor) presented to him as a gift by the local chief. Songs by Harold Arlen and Ralph Blane help to make it all agreeable and amusing.

THE FARMER TAKES A WIFE

Produced by Frank P. Rosenberg
Directed by Henry Levin
Screenplay by Walter Bullock, Sally Benson, and Joseph Fields, based on the play by Frank B. Elser and Marc Connelly
Photographed in Technicolor by Arthur Arling
Songs by Harold Arlen and Dorothy Fields
Musical direction by Lionel Newman
80 minutes

Cast: Betty Grable, Dale Robertson, Thelma Ritter, John Carroll, Eddie Foy, Jr., Charlotte Austin, Kathleen Crowley, Merry Anders, Donna Lee Hickey, Noreen Michaels, Ruth Hall, William Pullen, Jaunita Evers, Mort Mills, Lee Turnbull, Howard Negley, Joanne Jordan, Gene Roth, Mel Pogue, Gwyneth Verdon, Fred Graham, Jack Stoney, John Butler, Gordon Nelson

A remake of the Fox film of 1935 starring Henry Fonda and Janet Gaynor. The results are disappointing, mostly because of a misguided attempt to turn it into a musical. The screenplay is much the same, dealing with early nineteenth-century adventures on the Erie Canal. The girl friend (Betty Grable) of the toughest captain (John Carroll) on the canal hires as a boat hand a young farmer (Dale Robertson) who is eager to save up money for a farm. She falls for the farmer and he gradually brings her around to his love of the land. Grable sings and dances pleasantly, but the film is too much of a "picture postcard" to have any impact as a believable slice of Americana, as did the Fonda version.

GENTLEMEN PREFER BLONDES

Produced by Sol C. Siegei
Directed by Howard Hawks
Screenplay by Charles Lederer, based on the musical comedy by Joseph Fields and Anita Loos
Photographed in Technicolor by Harry J. Wild
Songs by Jule Styne and Leo Robin
Musical direction by Lionel Newman
91 minutes

Cast: Jane Russell, Marilyn Monroe, Charles Coburn, Elliott Reed, Tommy Noonan, George Winslow, Marcel Dalio, Taylor Holmes, Norma Varden, Howard Wendell, Steven Geray, Henri Letondal, Leo Mostovoy

Based on the Broadway musical but somewhat altered to fit the style of Marilyn Monroe as Lorelei and Jane Russell as her friend Dorothy. Lorelei's millionaire fiancé (Tommy Noonan) sends the girls to France, but his father (Tayor Holmes) also sends a detective (Elliott Reid) on the same boat to get enough evidence on the flirty, diamond-loving Lorelei to break the engagement. Instead, the detective falls in love with Dorothy. The girls, in need of cash, work in a night club in Paris and get into trouble when an old playboy (Charles Coburn) gives Lorelei a tiara and then denies it when his wife finds out. The complications evolve into a double wedding for the girls and their fellows. The film retains most of the famous songs from the original show but adds two new ones by Hoagy Carmichael and Harold Adamson. But it's Monroe singing "Diamonds Are a Girl's Best Friend" that lingers in the memory.

THE GIRL NEXT DOOR

Produced by Robert Bassler
Directed by Richard Sale
Screenplay by Isobel Lennart, from a story by L. Bus-Fekete and Mary Helen Fay
Photographed in Technicolor by Leon Shamroy
Songs by Mack Gordon and Josef Myrow
Music by Cyril J. Mockridge
Musical direction by Lionel Newman
91 minutes

Cast: Dan Dailey, June Haver, Dennis Day, Billy Gray, Cara Williams, Natalie Schafer, Clinton Sundberg, Hayden Rorke, Mary Jane Sanders, Donna Lee Hickey, Lyn Wilde, Mona Knox, Jane Wurster

A pleasant musical about a Broadway star (June Haver) who buys a house and finds her next door neighbor to be a comic strip illustrator (Dan Dailey), with a young son (Billy Gray), who objects when the two adults become romantically involved. But the boy's own girl friend (Mary Jane Saunders) points out to him that life is made up of couples, as in Noah's Ark, which gives the boy an idea for his father's strip. The idea is a success—and allows the film to have a delightful UPA cartoon sequence. The singing and dancing of Haver and Dailey provide the film's main attractions.

THE GLORY BRIGADE

Produced by William Bloom
Directed by Robert D. Webb
Screenplay by Franklin Coen
Photographed by Lucien Ballard
Musical direction by Lionel Newman
81 minutes

Cast: Victor Mature, Alexander Scourby, Lee Marvin, Richard Egan, Nick Dennis, Roy Roberts, Alvy Moore, Russell Evans, Henry Kulky, Gregg Martell, Lamont Johnson, Carleton Young, Frank Gerstle

A Korean war story about a U.S. Army lieutenant of Greek parentage (Victor Mature) who volunteers to help a Greek regiment cross a river into enemy territory. The lieutenant loses most of his platoon in the action and becomes bitter about the Greeks, particularly when he notices there is no blood on their bayonets. He later learns the Greek soldiers traditionally wipe the blood from their bayonets, and in being involved with them on a later engagement he also learns they are a crack unit.

HOW TO MARRY A MILLIONAIRE

Produced by Nunnally Johnson
Directed by Jean Negulesco
Screenplay by Nunnally Johnson, based on plays by Zoe Akins, Dale Eunson, and Katherine Albert
Photographed in Technicolor and CinemaScope by Joe MacDonald
Music by Cyril J. Mockridge and Alfred Newman
Musical direction by Alfred Newman
95 minutes

Cast: Betty Grable, Marilyn Monroe, Lauren Bacall, David Wayne, Rory Calhoun, Cameron Mitchell, Alex D'Arcy, Fred Clark, William Powell, George Dunn, Percy Helton, Robert Adler, Harry Carter

The familiar story of three girls who join forces to snare rich husbands, with Lauren Bacall, Marilyn Monroe, and Betty Grable pretending to be wealthy and renting a Manhattan penthouse as their parlor. Grable goes for a weekend in the mountains with a married man (Fred Clark), but falls for a forest ranger (Rory Calhoun). Monroe finally meets the tax-evading owner (David Wayne) of the apartment building, and Bacall throws over the proposal of a middle-aged rancher (William Powell) and marries a seemingly poor working man (Cameron Mitchell), who afterwards reveals himself as a millionaire. Brisk direction, writing, and playing make this the most amusing treatment of the oft-told tale. The film offers a bonus for film music lovers, with Alfred Newman conducting the 20th Century-Fox Orchestra in a performance of his "Street Scene."

INFERNO

Produced by William Bloom
Directed by Roy Baker
Screenplay by Francis Cockrell
Photographed in Technicolor by Lucien Ballard
Music by Paul Sawtell
Musical direction by Lionel Newman
83 minutes

Cast: Robert Ryan, Rhonda Fleming, William Lundigan, Harry Keating, Henry Hull, Carl Betz, Robert Burton, Everett Glass, Adrienne Mardin, Barbara Pepper, Dan White, Henry Carter, Robert Adler

The first 3-D production of 20th Century-Fox. A tough melodrama about a millionaire playboy (Robert Ryan) who breaks his leg while on a desert trip and is left by his wife (Rhonda Fleming) and his business associate (William Lundigan). They pretend to go for help but actually plan to leave him to die. This gradually dawns upon him and his anger gives him the determination to survive. He makes a splint and agonizingly makes his way home, where he settles the score with his wife and her lover. The film, largely filmed in rugged desert country, is an excellent study in survival, with a brilliant performance from Ryan.

INVADERS FROM MARS

Produced by Edward L. Alperson
Directed by William Cameron Menzies
Screenplay by Richard Blake
Photographed in Eastmancolor by John Seitz
Music by Raoul Kraushaar
80 minutes

Cast: Helena Carter, Arthur Franz, Jimmy Hunt, Leif Erickson, Hillary Brooke, Morris Ankrum, Max Wagner, Janine Perreau, Bill Phipps, Milburn Stone

A science fiction thriller about a space ship which burrows into the earth and then sucks in anyone passing overhead. A young boy (Jimmy Hunt) awakens in the night to see the ship land, but finds it hard to get anyone to believe him. More and more people are sucked into the space scheme and eventually the army is brought in to quell the space invasion. In the meantime a number of people undergo weird adventures in coming into contact with the space people. The film is an interesting entry in its field, largely because the veteran and highly esteemed film designer William Cameron Menzies is also its director.

MAN ON A TIGHTROPE

Produced by Robert L. Jacks
Directed by Elia Kazan
Screenplay by Robert E. Sherwood, from a story by Neil Peterson
Photographed by Georg Kraus
Music by Franz Waxman
105 minutes

Cast: Fredric March, Terry Moore, Cameron Mitchell, Gloria Grahame, Adolphe Menjou, Robert Beatty, Alex D'Arcy, Richard Boone, Hansi, Pat Henning, Paul Hartman, John Dehner, Dorothy Wieck, Edelweiss Malchin

Filmed entirely in Bavaria, *Man on a Tightrope* tells of a Czech circus company trying to crack the Iron Curtain and escape to the West. The manager (Fredric March) is long weary of being subjected to state control, of having his artists taken from him and of dealing with spies. He also suffers from the indifference of his young wife (Gloria Grahame) and worries about a wayward daughter (Terry Moore). He wins the respect of his family and his employees when he finally makes his move to cross the border, which results in freedom for his troupe but his own death. With a masterly performance by March and tight direction from Kazan, and the skillful use of locations, *Man on a Tightrope* is a film collector's item.

THE KID FROM LEFT FIELD

Produced by Leonard Goldstein
Directed by Harmon Jones
Screenplay by Jack Sher
Photographed by Harry Jackson
Music by Lionel Newman
80 minutes

Cast: Dan Dailey, Anne Bancroft, Billy Chapin, Lloyd Bridges, Ray Collins, Richard Egan, Bob Hopkins, Alex Gerry, Walter Sande, Fess Parker, George Phelps, John Gallaudet, Paul Salata, John Bernardino, Gene Thompson, Malcolm Cassell, Ike Jones

A baseball fable, about a nine-year-old (Billy Chapin) who gets to manage a big league team. His father (Dan Dailey) is an ex-player, now reduced to being a ball park salesman. He gives his son tips on playing to give to the team and those tips result in their becoming a success. With that the youngster is hired as manager, but during a spell of sickness he admits that it has been his father who has been the brains behind it all. Father gets the job as manager. A pleasing comedy and a gentle spoof on baseball fanatics.

KING OF THE KHYBER RIFLES

Produced by Frank P. Rosenberg
Directed by Henry King
Screenplay by Ivan Goff and Ben Roberts, from a story by Harry Kleiner, based on a novel by Talbot Mundy
Photographed in Technicolor and CinemaScope by Leon Shamroy
Music by Bernard Herrmann
99 minutes

Cast: Tyrone Power, Terry Moore, Michael Rennie, John Justin, Guy Rolfe, Richard Stapley, Murray Matheson, Frank de Kova, Argentina Brunetti, Sujata, Frank Lackteen, Gilchrist Stuart, Karam Dhaliwal

Adventures with the British Army in India, circa 1857. Tyrone Power is a captain in the Khyber Rifles but not quite socially acceptable because he is a half caste. His military record is first class, but when he falls in love with the daughter (Terry Moore) of his commanding officer (Michael Rennie), bias raises its head. He is sent to the Khyber Pass to quell a rebel uprising led by a boyhood friend (Guy Rolfe), and the success and bravery of his exploits bring him the approval of his fellow officers and the hand of the girl he loves. Spectacular locations and action sequences help overcome the limited plot. A remake of John Ford's *The Black Watch* (1929).

MR. SCOUTMASTER

Produced by Leonard Goldstein
Directed by Henry Levin
Screenplay by Leonard Praskins and Barney Slater, from a book by Rice E. Cochran
Photographed by Joseph La Shelle
Music by Cyril J. Mockridge
Musical direction by Lionel Newman
87 minutes

Cast: Clifton Webb, Edmund Gwenn, George Foghorn Winslow, Frances Dee, Veda Ann Borg, Orley Lindgren, Jimmy Moss, Sammy Ogg, Jimmy Hawkins, Skip Torgerson, Dee Aaker, Mickey Little, Jon Gardner

In an effort to learn more about the ways of children, a writer (Clifton Webb) joins the scout movement. His sophistication suffers some rude shocks in his conflicts with the boys, particularly a spoiled brat (Jimmy Moss), whom he crowns with a dish of ice cream. Another boy (George Winslow) brags about being the son of wealthy parents, but when it is revealed that he is a child of poverty, he runs away. The scoutmaster persuades his boys to make a search, but when the boy turns up, the scoutmaster becomes lost. By the end of the story he has indeed learned something about the ways of children.

NIAGARA

Produced by Charles Brackett
Directed by Henry Hathaway
Screenplay by Charles Brackett, Walter Reisch, and Richard Breen
Photographed in Technicolor by Joe MacDonald
Music by Sol Kaplan
Musical direction by Lionel Newman
92 minutes

Cast: Marilyn Monroe, Joseph Cotten, Jean Peters, Casey Adams, Denis O'Dea, Richard Allan, Don Wilson, Lurene Tuttle, Russell Collins, Will Wright, Lester Matthews, Carleton Young

Niagara Falls, spendidly color photographed by the ace Joe MacDonald, is the setting for this intriguing murder mystery, in which Marilyn Monroe plots to kill her husband (Joseph Cotten). The scheme goes awry and it is the co-plotter (Richard Allan) whose body is found in the river. The husband pursues the frantic wife and strangles her. He then steals a motorboat to race up the river to Buffalo, taking with him, as a hostage in order to hold off the police, a honeymooning bride (Jean Peters). The boat runs out of gas and smashes on the rocks. The fugitive saves the girl by pushing her to safety, but is himself killed when he is swept over the falls. The setting heightens the drama, but it is the image of the sexy Monroe, and her famous walk, that gives *Niagara* a special place in the movie memory.

Ethel Merman and Donald O'Connor in *Call Me Madam*.

Marilyn Monroe and Jane Russell in *Gentlemen Prefer Blondes*.

Richard Burton and Robert Newton in *The Desert Rats*.

Betty Grable and Dale Robertson in *The Farmer Takes a Wife*.

Marilyn Monrôe, Lauren Bacall and Betty Grable in *How to Marry a Millionaire*.

Marilyn Monroe and Joseph Cotten in *Niagara*.

J. Carrol Naish, Robert Wagner, and Gilbert Roland in *Beneath the Twelve Mile Reef*.

Tyrone Power and Michael Rennie in *King of the Khyber Rifles*.

Clifton Webb as *Mr. Scoutmaster*.

The p
Corne
by a
up wi
of the
whose
their
the d
malar
to his
rights
in Gu

VICI

Produ
Direc
Scree
Fisl
Phot
Music
Music
85 m

Cast:
Boon
Spelli

A re
few
into
Reid)
(Ricl
and
dead
killer
by h
the n

WH

Prod
Direc
Scree
no
Phot
Musi
95 m

Cast:
Masl
Timc
Thor
Brow

Adv
Mitc
cate
a tri
they
son

249

Jean Sir
inson, a
ton in

THE ADVENTURES OF HAJJI BABA

Produced by Walter Wanger
Directed by Don Weis
Screenplay by Richard Collins
Photographed in De Luxe Color and CinemaScope by
  Harold Lipstein
Music by Dimitri Tiomkin
92 minutes

Cast: John Derek, Elaine Stewart, Rosemarie Bowe,
Thomas Gomez, Paul Picerni, Donald Randolph, Amanda
Blake, Linda Danson

Arabian Nights nonsense, with John Derek as a barber
who helps a princess (Elaine Stewart) on her way to
marry a distant prince (Paul Picerni) against the
wishes of her father. Once they arrive at the palace
of the prince they soon discover he is a rogue, whose
plans for marriage are purely political. Hajji Baba then
defeats the prince and claims the princess for his own.
The adventures are almost slapstick but amusing.

BLACK THIRTEEN

Produced by Roger Proudlock
Directed by Ken Hughes
Screenplay by Pietro Germi
Photographed by Gerald Gibbs
Music by Carlo Rustichelli
75 minutes

Cast: Peter Reynolds, Rona Anderson, Patric Barr, Lana
Morris, Genine Graham, Michael Balfour, John Forrest,
Viola Lyel, John Le Mesurier, Martin Benson

A British melodrama, concerning the son (Peter Reynolds) of a good family who opts for a life of crime.
He starts by robbing cafes and then looks to fleece a
gambling casino of its proceeds. His sister (Rona
Anderson) falls in love with a policeman (Patric Barr),
who gradually realizes what is going on. When the
police raid the casino as it is being robbed, the young
man uses his sister as a shield, but dies when he
crashes his car in escaping. The story of a very nasty
fellow.

BLACK WIDOW

Produced and directed by Nunnally Johnson
Screenplay by Nunnally Johnson, from a story by Patrick
  Quentin
Photographed in De Luxe Color and CinemaScope by
  Charles G. Clarke
Music by Leigh Harline
Musical direction by Lionel Newman
95 minutes

Cast: Ginger Rogers, Van Heflin, Gene Tierney, George
Raft, Peggy Ann Garner, Reginald Gardiner, Virginia
Leith, Otto Kruger, Cathleen Nesbitt, Skip Homeier,
Hilda Simms, Harry Carter

The lady of the title is a celebrated Broadway actress
(Ginger Rogers), a woman of great style and wit but
heartless, who has emasculated her husband (Reginald
Gardiner). The story is a murder mystery: a calculating young girl (Peggy Ann Garner) is found dead in
the apartment of a producer (Van Heflin), whose
wife (Gene Tierney) often moves to leave him because
of his philandering ways. A detective (George Raft)
sorts his way through the complicated web to arrive
at the culprit—the black widow herself, who has
killed the pregnant girl because her husband has been
having an affair with her. The stylish acting makes this
a sophisticated whodunit.

BROKEN LANCE

Produced by Sol C. Siegel
Directed by Edward Dmytryk
Screenplay by Richard Murphy, based on material by
  Philip Yordan
Photographed in CinemaScope and De Luxe Color by
  Joe MacDonald and Anthony Newman
Music by Leigh Harline
96 minutes

Cast: Spencer Tracy, Robert Wagner, Jean Peters, Rich-
ard Widmark, Katy Jurado, Hugh O'Brian, Eduard Franz,
Earl Holliman, E. G. Marshall, Carl Benton Reid, Philip
Ober, Robert Burton, Robert Alder

Although not advertised as such, *Broken Lance* is a
remake of *House of Strangers,* the story of a powerful,

self-made man and his four sons who squabble to gain his holdings. Here the setting is Arizona and the man (Spencer Tracy) is a cattle baron who has always acted as a law unto himself and has treated his sons harshly. Only one son (Robert Wagner) has any affection for the father; the others look forward to his demise so they may take over the ranch. The old man dies of a stroke, mostly brought on by the hatred and avarice within his family, and the good son eventually inherits the property. *Broken Lance* survives its ripe melodramatics thanks largely to the dignified presence of Tracy and the beautiful settings in southern Arizona.

CARMEN JONES

Produced and directed by Otto Preminger
Screenplay by Harry Kleiner
Book and lyrics by Oscar Hammerstein II
Photographed in De Luxe Color and CinemaScope by
  Sam Leavitt
Music by Georges Bizet
Musical direction by Herschel Burke Gilbert
107 minutes

Cast: Dorothy Dandridge, Harry Belafonte, Olga James, Pearl Bailey, Diahann Carroll, Roy Glenn, Nick Stewart, Joe Adams, Brock Peters, Sandy Lewis, Mauri Lynn, DeForest Covan, and the voices of Le Vern Hutcherson, Marilyn Horne, and Marvin Hayes

Oscar Hammerstein's Americanized, all-black version of Bizet's opera *Carmen,* with his own lyrics, and the sultry Dorothy Dandridge as Carmen (dubbed by Marilyn Horne) and Harry Belafonte (dubbed by Le Vern Hutcherson) as the soldier she loves. Bizet's cigarette factory becomes a wartime parachute factory in the Deep South, the tavern becomes a nightclub, and the matadors become prize fighters. Carmen remains the petulant flirt and ends up being strangled by her soldier when she goes with a boxer. A lusty and interesting version of the old warhorse.

DEMETRIUS AND THE GLADIATORS

Produced by Frank Ross
Directed by Delmer Daves
Screenplay by Philip Dunne, based on a character created by Lloyd C. Douglas in *The Robe*
Photographed in CinemaScope and De Luxe Color by
  Milton Krasner
Music by Franz Waxman
99 minutes

Cast: Victor Mature, Susan Hayward, Michael Rennie, Debra Paget, Anne Bancroft, Jay Robinson, Barry Jones, William Marshall, Richard Egan, Ernest Borgnine, Charles Evans, Everett Glass, Karl Davis

A sequel to *The Robe,* with Victor Mature again playing Demetrius, the Greek slave and dedicated Christian. Here, because of his magnificent physique, he is forced to fight in the Roman arena for the amusement of the mad and bloodthirsty emperor Caligula (Jay Robinson), which brings him the attentions of the sensuous Messalina (Susan Hayward), wife of Claudius (Barry Jones). She seduces the virile Demetrius, causing him to lose his faith in Christianity as he becomes her lover. But Peter (Michael Rennie) manages to save him. The accent is more on spectacle and action than religion, with excellently staged combats in the arena.

DESIREE

Produced by Julian Blaustein
Directed by Henry Koster
Screenplay by Daniel Taradash, based on the novel by
  Annemarie Selinko
Photographed in CinemaScope and De Luxe Color by
  Milton Krasner
Music by Alex North
110 minutes

Cast: Marlon Brando, Jean Simmons, Merle Oberon, Michael Rennie, Cameron Mitchell, Elizabeth Sellars, Charlotte Austin, Cathleen Nesbitt, Evelyn Varden, Isobel Elsom, John Hoyt, Alan Napier, Nicolas Koster, Richard Deacon, Edith Evanson, Carolyn Jones, Sam Gilman, Larry Craine, Judy Lester

Although based on fact, this glossy account of Napoleon's love for Desiree Clary is a movie fantasy of historical romance. Marlon Brando's performance as the great French soldier-statesman gives the film its principal interest, and he is backed up with sumptuous production values. The fanciful tale begins in 1794 when young Napoleon meets seventeen-year-old Desiree (Jean Simmons) in Marseilles and falls in love with her. As his career progresses it becomes more difficult for the lovers to see each other and his offer of marriage gradually takes second place to his desire to conquer the world. Desiree marries Count Bernadotte, who becomes one of the generals who bring about the defeat of Napoleon, and it is his wife who persuades the great figure that his surrender would be in the best interests of France. If not viewed as a history lesson, *Desiree* is good entertainment and at least a point of departure for a study of Napoleon.

DEVIL'S HARBOR

Produced by Charles Deane
Directed by Montgomery Tully
Screenplay by Charles Deane
Photographed by Geoffrey Faithful
71 minutes

Cast: Richard Arlen, Greta Gynt, Donald Houston, Mary Germaine, Elspeth Gray, Vincent Ball, Howard Lang, Anthony Vicars, Edwin Richfield, Michael Balfour, Arnold Adrian, Sidney Bromley

255

A British crime yarn about an American (Richard Arlen) who skippers a small boat and is used by drug smugglers. An insurance company detective (Donald Houston) trails him, but finds the skipper knows nothing about his involvement. The two men then join forces to track down the criminals, who are in league with some of the insurance company employees.

THE EGYPTIAN

Produced by Darryl F. Zanuck
Directed by Michael Curtiz
Screenplay by Philip Dunne and Casey Robinson, based on the novel by Mika Waltari
Photographed in CinemaScope and De Luxe Color by Leon Shamroy
Music by Alfred Newman and Bernard Herrmann
138 minutes

Cast: Jean Simmons, Victor Mature, Gene Tierney, Michael Wilding, Bella Darvi, Peter Ustinov, Edmond Purdom, Judith Evelyn, Henry Daniell, John Carradine, Carl Benton Reid, Tommy Rettig, Anitra Stevens, Donna Martell, Mimi Gibson, Carmen de Lavallade, Harry Thompson, George Melford, Ian MacDonald

With Marlon Brando as its star, as originally planned, *The Egyptian* might have been a box office winner. But with the studio's decision to use contract player Edmund Purdom in the title role of this huge, expensive historical drama, the film was badly launched. Partly for reasons of casting and partly because it is slowly paced pageant, *The Egyptian* proved a loser. Its plot concerns the adventures of a young doctor (Purdom) in pre-Christian times, who through suffering and exile gains faith in the concept of one God and is gradually ennobled by it. Called to attend the epileptic Pharaoh (Michael Wilding), he also comes into contact with Babylonian courtesan Nefer (Bella Darvi), with whom he has a fling. Tiring of her wiles, he goes back to his faithful girl friend (Jean Simmons), who is later slain for her religious convictions. Hovering around the story as the doctor's servant is Peter Ustinov. Asked what it was like being involved in the film, Ustinov replied, "It was like being on a monstrously huge set of *Aida* and not being able to find the way out."

THE GAMBLER FROM NATCHEZ

Produced by Leonard Goldstein
Directed by Henry Levin
Screenplay by Gerald Drayson Adams and Irving Wallace, from a story by Gerald Drayson Adams
Photographed in Technicolor by Lloyd Ahern
Music by Lionel Newman
88 minutes

Cast: Dale Robertson, Debra Paget, Thomas Gomez, Lisa Daniels, Kevin McCarthy, Douglas Dick, John Wengraf, Donald Randolph, Henri Letondal, Jay Novello, Woody Strode, Peter Mamakos

An early nineteenth-century adventure tale about a soldier (Dale Robertson) who returns to New Orleans after fighting in Texas and finds that his gambler father has been dishonored and murdered by three of his associates. In the manner of the Count of Monte Cristo, he sets out to track down and destroy each of the villains, with time out to flirt with a society beauty (Lisa Daniels) and succumb to the advances of a lusty river girl (Debra Paget). The film has action and humor, and makes good use of its colorful Louisiana locations.

GARDEN OF EVIL

Produced by Charles Brackett
Directed by Henry Hathaway
Screenplay by Frank Fenton, based on a story by Fred Freiberger and William Tunberg
Photographed in CinemaScope and Technicolor by Milton Krasner and Jorge Stahl, Jr.
Music by Bernard Herrmann
100 minutes

Cast: Gary Cooper, Susan Hayward, Richard Widmark, Hugh Marlowe, Cameron Mitchell, Rita Moreno, Victor Manuel Mendoza, Fernando Wagner, Arturo Soto Bangel

Three American adventurers (Gary Cooper, Richard Widmark, and Cameron Mitchell) agree to help a woman (Susan Hayward) rescue her husband (Hugh Marlowe), who is injured and trapped in a gold mine deep in the wilds of Mexico. They perform the rescue, but on the way back they are harrassed by Indians, until there are only two left—the most decent of the Americans (Cooper) and the woman, who will probably find a life together after having survived the evil influence of gold. *The Garden of Evil* is thin on plot, but it contains magnificent color photography of Mexican mountains and a full-blooded symphonic score by the superb Bernard Herrmann.

GORILLA AT LARGE

Produced by Robert L. Jacks
Directed by Harmon Jones
Screenplay by Leonard Praskins and Barney Slater
Photographed in Technicolor by Lloyd Ahern
Musical direction by Lionel Newman
84 minutes

Cast: Cameron Mitchell, Anne Bancroft, Lee J. Cobb, Raymond Burr, Charlotte Austin, Peter Whitney, Lee Marvin, Warren Stevens, John G. Kellogg, Charles Tannen

A juicy melodrama, shot in 3-D, taking place in an

amusement park, where the main attraction is a ferocious gorilla. Several murders occur and the main suspect is a trapeze artist (Cameron Mitchell), who does an act as a gorilla with the wife (Anne Bancroft) of the owner (Raymond Burr). The wife is revealed as a sexy adulteress and the killer proves to be her husband. The gorilla goes wild, carries the wife to the top of a roller coaster, and has to be killed. A bizarre carnival tale and floridly amusing.

HELL AND HIGH WATER

Produced by Raymond Klune
Directed by Samuel Fuller
Screenplay by Jesse L. Lasky, Jr., from a story by David Hempstead
Photographed in Technicolor and CinemaScope by Joe MacDonald
Music by Alfred Newman
103 minutes

Cast: Richard Widmark, Bella Darvi, Victor Francen, Cameron Mitchell, Gene Evans, David Wayne, Stephen Bekassy, Richard Loo, Henry Kulky, Wong Artarne, Harry Carter, Robert Adler, Don Orlando, Rollin Moriyama, John Gifford

A far-fetched adventure tale about an attempt to stop communist atomic plans in the north Pacific. A famed French atomic scientist (Victor Francen) and his assistant-daughter (Bella Darvi) organize a group of international scientists and military men and rent a submarine with a mercenary American commander (Richard Widmark). They trail a freighter to an Arctic island and observe it delivering charges for an atomic bomb, to be dropped on Korea and blamed on the United States. The submarine load of idealists see that it is the island itself which is atomically blown up. The special effects are the true stars of the picture.

MAN CRAZY

Produced by Sidney Harman and Philip Yordan
Directed by Irving Lerner
Screenplay by Sidney Harman and Philip Yordan
Photographed by Floyd Crosby
Music by Ernest Gold
79 minutes

Cast: Neville Brand, Christine White, Irene Anders, Coleen Miller, John Brown, Joe Turkel, Karen Steele, Jack Larsen, Bill Lundmark, John Crawford, Ottola Nesmith, Charles Victor, Frances Osborne

Three young girls arrive in Hollywood, having stolen money from a druggist in their Minnesota home town —money which he has secreted in order not to pay income tax. They proceed to have a good time, but experience trouble with men as well as trying to dodge the pursuing druggist. The instigator of the trio (Christine White) marries a man (Neville Brand) who knows her money is stolen but nonetheless uses it to buy a farm. The law eventually catches up with all concerned.

MAN IN THE ATTIC

Produced by Robert L. Jacks
Directed by Hugo Fregonese
Screenplay by Robert Presnell, Jr. and Barre Lyndon, from *The Lodger,* by Mary Belloc Lowndes
Photographed by Leo Tover
Musical direction by Lionel Newman
81 minutes

Cast: Jack Palance, Constance Smith, Byron Palmer, Frances Bavier, Rhys Williams, Sean McClory, Leslie Bradley, Tita Phillips, Leslie Mathews, Harry Cording, Lillian Bond, Lisa Daniels

A remake of *The Lodger* (1944), with Jack Palance as the psychotic killer of women in the fogbound streets of London in the late 1800's. A pathologist by trade, he rents a room and an attic in a house in which the daughter (Constance Smith) is a dance hall entertainer. He falls in love with her and when she doesn't respond he becomes strangely depressed. In the meantime a Scotland Yard inspector (Byron Palmer), long on the trail of a knife-wielding killer of female entertainers, closes in on his suspect, arriving at a theatre in time to save this one. After a frantic chase, the pathologist ends his life by jumping in the Thames.

MISS ROBIN CRUSOE

Produced and directed by Eugene Frenke
Screenplay by Harold Nebenzal and Richard Yriondo, from a story by Al Zimbalist
Photographed in Eastmancolor by Virgil Miller
Music by Elmer Bernstein
74 minutes

Cast: Amanda Blake, George Nader, Rosalind Hayes

The classic Defoe tale given a twist, with the main character being a shipwrecked girl (Amanda Blake) who survives on a desert island and rescues a native girl (Rosalind Hayes) from being killed by other natives. She becomes her Friday. Later a seaman (George Nader) is washed up from another wreck and it takes a while before Robin responds to him, due to her hatred of men from previous experiences. When a vessel passes the island, they make good their escape, as Friday holds back the natives at the cost of her own life. The film is pleasing to the eye and no strain on the mind.

NEW FACES

Produced by Edward L. Alperson
Directed by Harry Horner
Photographed in Eastmancolor and CinemaScope by Lucien Ballard

257

Musical direction by Raoul Kraushaar
96 minutes

Cast: Ronny Graham, Eartha Kitt, Robert Clary, Alice Ghostley, June Carroll, Virginia DeLuce, Paul Lynde, Bill Mullikin, Rosemary O'Reilly, Elizabeth Logue, Allen Conroy, Jimmy Russell, George Smiley, Polly Ward, Carol Lawrence, Johnny Laverty, Faith Burwell, Clark Ranger

A photographed account of the 1952 smash Broadway revue, with a slight added story line, about actor-producer Ronny Graham's attempts to raise money from a rich Texan by putting his pretty daughter in the show. Graham is also seen to advantage within the actual show, particularly in a take-off on *Death of a Salesman,* also featuring Paul Lynde. The emphasis is on Eartha Kitt, who became a star because of *New Faces.* Also prominent are Alice Ghostley and her "Boston Beguine" and Robert Clary in several songs. A collector's item for music theatre buffs.

NIGHT PEOPLE

Produced and directed by Nunnally Johnson
Screenplay by Nunnally Johnson, from a story by Jed Harris and Thomas Reed
Photographed in CinemaScope and De Luxe Color by Charles G. Clarke
Music by Cyril J. Mockridge
Musical direction by Lionel Newman
93 minutes

Cast: Gregory Peck, Broderick Crawford, Anita Bjork, Rita Gam, Walter Abel, Buddy Ebsen, Casey Adams, Jill Esmond, Peter Van Eyck, Marianne Koch, Ted Avery, Hugh McDermott, Paul Carpenter

An American soldier is kidnapped by the Russians in Berlin and his influential, industrialist father (Broderick Crawford) storms into town demanding immediate action. His bombast is cut down to size by an intelligence colonel (Gregory Peck) who is working on the case. He explains to the distraught father that the price of returning his son is the handing over of an elderly German couple, formerly anti-Nazis, who will doubtlessly be killed. When the father meets them, his attitude softens. The colonel discovers that one of his chief agents (Anita Bjork) is working for the Russians and he devises a scheme whereby she is sent back in place of the soldier. *Night People* is a top-notch cold war melodrama, with Peck excellent as the tough colonel and fine work from writer-director Johnson, who filmed entirely on location in Germany.

THE OTHER WOMAN

Produced and directed by Hugo Haas
Screenplay by Hugo Haas
Photographed by Eddie Fitzgerald
Music by Ernest Gold
81 minutes

Cast: Cleo Moore, Hugo Haas, Lance Fuller, Lucille Barkley, John Qualen, Jack Macy, Jan Arvin, Karolee Kelly, Mark Lowell, Jan Englund, Steve Mitchell, Art Marshall, Sue Casey, Melinda Markey, Sharon Dexter, Ivan Haas

A Hollywood morality tale, about a director (Hugo Haas) who is lured to the apartment of a beautiful and ambitious would-be actress (Cleo Moore), who drugs him and afterwards demands $50,000 to keep quiet about their "affair." He can't remember what he has done, but as the son-in-law of a film mogul he decides to kill the girl and fix the blame on a derelict man (John Qualen). He almost gets away with it, but evidence trips him up and he lands in jail.

THE OUTLAW'S DAUGHTER

Produced and directed by Wesley Barry
Screenplay by Sam Rocca
Photographed in Eastmancolor by Gordon Avil
Music by Raoul Kraushaar
75 minutes

Cast: Bill Williams, Kelly Ryan, Jim Davis, George Cleveland, Elisha Cook, Jr., Guinn Williams, Sara Haden, Nelson Leigh, George Barrows

The girl of the title (Kelly Ryan) joins an outlaw band when its leader (Bill Williams) convinces her that the town marshall (Jim Davis) killed her father. Actually it was the leader himself, which she doesn't discover until he and his men have been wiped out by the marshall. He offers to let her go, inasmuch as he has long been in love with her, but she decides to turn herself in for legal judgment before accepting his offer of a new life.

PRINCE VALIANT

Produced by Robert L. Jacks
Directed by Henry Hathaway
Screenplay by Dudley Nichols, based on King Features Syndicate's *Prince Valiant* by Harold Foster
Photographed in Technicolor and CinemaScope by Lucien Ballard
Music by Franz Waxman
100 minutes

Cast: James Mason, Janet Leigh, Robert Wagner, Debra Paget, Sterling Hayden, Victor McLaglen, Donald Crisp, Brian Aherne, Barry Jones, Mary Philips, Howard Wendell, Tom Conway, Sammy Ogg, Neville Brand, Ben Wright

A rousing adventure story set in the England of King Arthur, as a young Viking prince (Robert Wagner) seeks to become a knight in Camelot. He is trained by Sir Gawain (Sterling Hayden) and falls in love with a princess (Janet Leigh), but runs afoul of the deadly Black Knight, who is eventually revealed as Sir Brack

(James Mason), in league with the usurpers who would overthrow not only Arthur's realm but that of the Vikings as well. Valiant returns to Scandia, leads his people in a revolt against the tyrants, and restores his family to the throne. Then he returns to England, puts an end to Sir Brack, and claims the hand of the princess. Historical nonsense, but lavishly and excitingly staged, with film photography and a sweeping music score by Franz Waxman.

PRINCESS OF THE NILE

Produced by Robert L. Jacks
Directed by Harmon Jones
Screenplay by Gerald Drayton Adams
Photographed in Technicolor by Lloyd Aherne
Music by Lionel Newman
73 minutes

Cast: Debra Paget, Jeffrey Hunter, Michael Rennie, Dona Drake, Wally Cassell, Edgar Barrier, Michael Ansara, Jack Elam, Lester Sharp, Lee Van Cleef, Billy Curtis, Robert Roark, Lisa Daniels, Merry Anders, Suzanne Alexander

A girlie-swashbuckler, with Debra Paget as a thirteenth-century, scimitar-wielding princess who rouses her people to save Egypt from the ambitions of a powerful Bedouin (Michael Rennie). She joins forces with the son (John Derek) of the Caliph of Baghdad to bring about this end—but also finds time to do a great deal of exotic dancing. The accent is not on history but on the visual pleasure of multitudes of beautiful girls in tantalizing costumes.

RACING BLOOD

Produced and directed by Wesley Barry
Screenplay by Sam Rocca, based on a story by Sam Rocca and Wesley Barry
Photographed by John Martin, in Color Corp. process
Music by Edward J. Kay
75 minutes

Cast: Bill Williams, Jean Porter, Jimmy Boyd, George Cleveland, John Eldredge, Sam Flint, Fred Kohler, Jr., George Steele, Bobby Johnson, Frankie Darro

A horse race yarn, about a stable boy (Jimmy Boyd) who comes to the aid of a colt born with a split hoof and about to be destroyed. The colt is one of twins, and the boy nurses the split-hoof and trains the animal until it wins the big race over its favored brother.

THE RAID

Produced by Robert L. Jacks
Directed by Hugo Fregonese
Screenplay by Sydney Boehm, from a story by Herbert Ravenal Sass
Photographed in Technicolor by Lucien Ballard

Music by Roy Webb
82 minutes

Cast: Van Heflin, Anne Bancroft, Richard Boone, Lee Marvin, Tommy Rettig, Peter Graves, Douglas Spencer, Paul Cavanaugh, Will Wright, James Best, John Dierkes, Helen Ford, Harry Hines

An interesting Civil War story, based on fact, about a group of Confederates who enter Vermont in 1864 from the Canadian border and proceed to the town of St. Albans. Their leader (Van Heflin) poses as a businessman and boards in a house owned by a lady (Anne Bancroft). His purpose is to scout the town in order to destroy it and thus create a diversion that will ease Union pressure on the Southern armies. He is delayed by the arrival of a Union cavalry contingent, but afterwards brings in his men and sacks the town as planned. He leaves a note for the landlady, of whom he has become fond, explaining that what he has done has been for the good of the Confederacy and not in spite.

RIVER OF NO RETURN

Produced by Stanley Rubin
Directed by Otto Preminger
Screenplay by Frank Fenton, from a story by Louis Lantz
Photographed in Technicolor and CinemaScope by Joseph La Shelle
Songs by Lionel Newman and Ken Darby
Music by Cyril J. Mockridge
Musical direction by Lionel Newman
90 minutes

Cast: Robert Mitchum, Marilyn Monroe, Rory Calhoun, Tommy Rettig, Murvyn Vye, Douglas Spencer, Don Beddoe, Will Wright, Hal Baylor

Set in northwest Canada in the gold rush days of the late nineteenth century, and handsomely filmed in the Rockies, the story is that of a farmer (Robert Mitchum) making his way to a homestead with his son (Tommy Rettig) and being bushwacked by a gambler (Rory Calhoun) in the company of a dance hall girl (Marilyn Monroe). The girl disapproves of the gambler's brutality and stays with the farmer, who is willing to settle down with her once he has caught up with the gambler and paid him back for leaving them all horseless and without supplies in savage Indian territory. The film's visual assets, of mountains and rapid rivers, add to the attraction of Monroe braving her way through the wilderness.

THE ROCKET MAN

Produced by Leonard Goldstein
Directed by Oscar Rudolph
Screenplay by Lenny Bruce and Jack Henley, from a story by George W. George and George F. Slavin

coins into the Trevi fountain and hope for romance. A secretary (Dorothy McGuire) gradually wins the love of her writer-employer (Clifton Webb). Another (Jean Peters) is romanced by a wolf (Rossano Brazzi) and tames him, and a third (Maggie McNamara) lands herself a prince (Louis Jourdan). The three sets of romances allow for a generous look at the glories of Rome, with a side trip to Venice, and they are all backed up by the fine title song by Sammy Cahn and Jule Styne, plus sumptuous color photography by Milton Krasner.

THREE YOUNG TEXANS

Produced by Leonard Goldstein
Directed by Henry Levin
Screenplay by Gerald Drayson Adams, from a story by
    William MacLeod Raine
Photographed in Technicolor by Harold Lipstein
Musical direction by Lionel Newman
77 minutes

Clifton Webb, Dorothy McGuire, Louis Jourdan, Maggie McNamara, Rossano Brazzi, and Jean Peters in *Three Coins in the Fountain.*

Cornel Wilde, June Allyson, Clifton Webb, and Arlene Dahl in *Woman's World.*

Cast: Mitzi Gaynor, Keefe Brasselle, Jeffrey Hunter, Harvey Stephens, Dan Riss, Michael Ansara, Aaron Spelling, Morris Ankrum, Frank Wilcox, Helen Wallace, John Harman, Alex Montoya

A Western morality tale about a young man (Jeffrey Hunter) who robs a train so that his father cannot comply with the blackmailers who want to force him to rob it. The father wounds a gambler and the blackmailers lie about his being dead. The young man's girl friend (Mitzi Gaynor) goes along with the plan, but once they have the money, their friend (Keefe Brasselle) takes it for himself. This costs him his life when the leader of the blackmailing group (Michael Ansara) takes the money. But the young hero shoots it out with the villain and kills him, and afterwards clears himself with the sheriff about the train robbery.

WOMAN'S WORLD

Produced by Charles Brackett
Directed by Jean Negulesco
Screenplay by Claude Binyon, Mary Loos and Richard
    Sale, from a story by Mona Williams
Photographed in Technicolor and CinemaScope by Joe
    MacDonald
Song by Sammy Cahn and Cyril J. Mockridge
Music by Cyril J. Mockridge
Musical direction by Lionel Newman
94 minutes

Cast: Clifton Webb, June Allyson, Van Heflin, Lauren Bacall, Fred MacMurray, Arlene Dahl, Cornel Wilde, Elliott Reid, Margalo Gillmore, Alan Reed, David Hoffman, George Melford, Eric Wilton

An automobile manufacturer (Clifton Webb) brings three of his top field executives to New York to choose one as his new general manager. From Philadelphia comes a workaholic (Fred MacMurray) and his caustic wife (Lauren Bacall); from Kansas City comes a man (Cornel Wilde) who would rather not take the job, whose wife (June Allyson) feels the same way; and from Texas comes a highly efficient man (Van Heflin), with a wife (Arlene Dahl) who is an eager beaver socialite. It's the Texan who gets the job, with the advice that he get rid of his conniving wife. A witty insight into business politics, with accent on the part wives play—and plenty of scope for displaying their wardrobes.

20TH CENTURY-FOX ACADEMY AWARDS FOR 1954

PHILIP YORDAN: Best motion picture story, *Broken Lance.*
MILTON KRASNER: Best cinematography, color, *Three Coins in the Fountain.*
JULE STYNE and SAMMY CAHN: Best song, "Three Coins in the Fountain."

THE ADVENTURES OF SADIE

Produced by George Minter
Directed by Noel Langley
Screenplay by Noel Langley
Photographed in Eastmancolor by Wilkie Cooper
Music by Ronald Binge
Musical direction by Muir Mathieson
88 minutes

Cast: Joan Collins, George Cole, Kenneth More, Robertson Hare, Walter Fitzgerald, Hattie Jacques, Felix Felton, Lionel Merton, Anthony Tencred, Michael Meachem, Hermione Gingold

A British comedy, largely filmed in Majorca, with Jean Collins as the only girl survivor of a shipwreck, washed up with three men: a cynical journalist (George Cole), a stuffy professor (Robertson Hare), and an Irish stoker (Kenneth More). The journalist and the professor find it hard to keep their hands off the girl, while the stoker shows little interest in her. But he's the one the girl wants. They are rescued, but again they are shipwrecked and marooned. This time with the girl happily wed to her stoker.

ANGELA

Produced by Steven Pallos
Directed by Dennis O'Keefe
Screenplay by Jonathan Rix and Edoardo Anton, from a story by Steve Carruthers
Photographed by Leonida Barboni
Music by Mario Nascimbene
81 minutes

Cast: Dennis O'Keefe, Mara Lane, Rosanno Brazzi, Arnoldo Foa, Galeazzo Benti, Enzo Fiermonte, Nino Crisman, Giovanni Fostini, Francesco Tensi, Maria Theresa Paliani

An Italian melodrama about an ex-GI (Dennis O'Keefe —who also directed), who settles in Rome after the war and gets involved with a beautiful girl (Mara Lane). She kills her boss but tells the American he died of a heart attack, which he believes, but which also causes him to become a fugitive not only from the police but from the girl's husband (Rosanno Brazzi). He kills the husband in self-defense, but finally rea-

lizes the girl is evil and lets the police take her away. The Roman backgrounds help the lurid tale along.

THE DEEP BLUE SEA

Produced and directed by Anatole Litvak
Screenplay by Terence Rattigan
Photographed in De Luxe Color and CinemaScope by Jack Hildyard
Music by Malcolm Arnold
Musical direction by Muir Mathieson
101 minutes

Cast: Vivien Leigh, Kenneth More, Eric Portman, Emlyn Williams, Moira Lister, Arthur Hill, Dandy Nichols, Jimmy Hanley, Miriam Karlin, Heather Thatcher, Bill Shine, Brian Oulton, Sidney James

The first British film in CinemaScope. A melodramatic love story about the neurotic and estranged wife (Vivien Leigh) of a judge (Emlyn Williams), who lives with a dashing but irresponsible ex-RAF pilot (Kenneth More). She refuses to return to the kindly, understanding judge and is saved from suicide, after she throws her lover out, by a disbarred doctor turned gambler (Eric Portman). He gives her the strength to face life, whether the lover comes back or not. A Sargasso sea of emotions, made fascinating by the performance of Leigh and an expert cast.

THE GIRL IN THE RED VELVET SWING

Produced by Charles Brackett
Directed by Richard Fleischer
Screenplay by Walter Reisch and Charles Brackett
Photographed in De Luxe Color and CinemaScope by Milton Krasner
Music by Leigh Harline
Musical direction by Lionel Newman
108 minutes

Cast: Ray Milland, Joan Collins, Farley Granger, Luther Adler, Cornelia Otis Skinner, Glenda Farrell, Frances Fuller, Philip Reed, Gale Robbins, James Lorimer, John Hoyt, Robert Simon, Harvey Stephens

A plush account of a celebrated scandal of 1906, with Ray Milland as the playboy-architect Stanford White, Farley Granger as the spoiled, erratic millionaire

Harry K. Thaw, and Joan Collins as Evelyn Nesbit, the beautiful showgirl over whose affections they were rivals. The insanely jealous millionaire marries Evelyn, but makes her life miserable with his constant harping upon White's love for her. His obsession leads him to kill White during a performance at the Madison Square Garden Roof. At his trial, her testimony saves Thaw from the gallows as she deliberately blackens White's character in order to give motivation for the killing. But afterwards the Thaw family ostracize her and she is left to her own devices to make a living, and ever subject to lurid offers of publicity. The screenplay somewhat softens the facts in the case but offers an interesting evocation of period.

DADDY LONG LEGS

Produced by Samuel G. Engel
Directed by Jean Negulesco
Screenplay by Phoebe and Henry Ephron, from the novel by Jean Webster
Photographed in De Luxe Color and CinemaScope by Leon Shamroy
Songs by Johnny Mercer
Music by Alex North
125 minutes

Cast: Fred Astaire, Leslie Caron, Terry Moore, Thelma Ritter, Fred Clark, Charlotte Austin, Larry Keating, Kathryn Givney, Kelly Brown, Ray Anthony and his Orchestra, Sara Shane, Numa Lapeyre, Ann Codee

A remake of the 1931 Janet Gaynor–Warner Baxter film but greatly expanded to allow for the dancing of Fred Astaire and Leslie Caron. The slim story is that of a French orphan whose schooling is sponsored by an American millionaire, on the stipulation that she will never know who he is. His secretary (Thelma Ritter) is so touched by her letters of gratitude, delivered by the school, that she persuades him to visit. He is then enchanted by the elegant, lovely girl and falls in love with her—and she with him, without knowing who he is. The film contains a wide range of music, including a jazz dance by Astaire with drums, a ballet danced by Caron, several dream sequences with Astaire imagining himself as a playboy and a rich cowboy, and Johnny Mercer's memorable song "Something's Gotta Give."

GOOD MORNING, MISS DOVE

Produced by Samuel G. Engel
Directed by Henry Koster
Screenplay by Eleanore Griffin, from the novel by Frances Gray Patton
Photographed in De Luxe Color and CinemaScope by Leon Shamroy
Music by Leigh Harline
Musical direction by Lionel Newman
107 minutes

Cast: Jennifer Jones, Robert Stack, Kipp Hamilton, Robert Douglas, Peggy Knudsen, Marshall Thompson, Chuck Connors, Biff Elliot, Jerry Paris, Mary Wickes, Ted Marc, Dick Stewart

A nostalgic story about a New England schoolteacher (Jennifer Jones) who looks back on her long career and remembers some of the many children with whom she dealt. A prim spinster, she is respected for her high standards and looked upon as a town institution with her exact habits. When she is taken ill, the townspeople take stock of what she has meant to the community and a former pupil, now a surgeon (Robert Stack), administers to her. Among her visitors are a policeman (Chuck Connors) and a playwright (Jerry Paris), both of whom were able to overcome bleak childhoods because of their teacher. A charming assessment of a life's contributions, made vital and poignant by the performance of Jennifer Jones.

HOUSE OF BAMBOO

Produced by Buddy Adler
Directed by Samuel Fuller
Screenplay by Harry Kleiner
Photographed in De Luxe Color and CinemaScope by Joe MacDonald
Music by Leigh Harline
Musical direction by Lionel Newman
103 minutes

Cast: Robert Ryan, Robert Stack, Shirley Yamaguchi, Cameron Mitchell, Brad Dexter, Sessue Hayakawa, Biff Elliot, Sandro Giglio, Elko Hanabusa, Harry Carey, Peter Gray, Robert Quarry

Crime in postwar Japan, with Robert Stack as a detective working with the American military police and the Japanese security forces to round up a group of ex-GI's who have formed a gang in Tokyo and run a number of rackets. Their leader (Robert Ryan) is a shrewd mastermind, whose skill challenges the best efforts of the police. The detective falls in love with a lovely local girl (Shirley Yamaguchi), the widow of a GI, who becomes innocently involved with the gang and who aids him in getting around her country. *House of Bamboo* is a top-notch crime caper on any ground, but its excellent use of Japanese locations gives it added fascination.

HOW TO BE VERY, VERY POPULAR

Produced and directed by Nunnally Johnson
Screenplay by Nunnally Johnson, from a play by Howard Lindsay
Photographed in De Luxe Color and CinemaScope by Milton Krasner
Song by Jule Styne and Sammy Cahn
Music by Cyril J. Mockridge
Musical direction by Lionel Newman
95 minutes

Cast: Betty Grable, Sheree North, Bob Cummings, Charles Coburn, Tommy Noonan, Orson Bean, Fred Clark, Charlotte Austin, Alice Pearce, Rhys Williams, Andrew Tombes, Noel Toy

Betty Grable's last film, with her and Sheree North as striptease girls who witness a murder and flee to a college town to escape the murderer. They become involved with college boys, who hide them in their fraternity house until the murderer is caught. Betty pairs off with a man (Robert Cummings) who has been delaying his graduation for years, in order to claim an inheritance, and Sheree settles for a genial but dim student (Orson Bean) who flunks every course. Charles Coburn steals the film as a college president who will graduate anyone with money.

THE LEFT HAND OF GOD

Produced by Buddy Adler
Directed by Edward Dmytryk
Screenplay by Alfred Hayes, based on the novel by William E. Barrett
Photographed in CinemaScope and De Luxe Color by Franz Planer
Music by Victor Young
87 minutes

Cast: Humphrey Bogart, Gene Tierney, Lee J. Cobb, Agnes Moorehead, E. G. Marshall, Jean Porter, Carl Benton Reid, Victor Sen Yung, Philip Ahn, Benson Fong, Richard Cutting, Leon Lontoc, Don Forbes

A colorful but none too credible yarn, *The Left Hand of God* tells of an American pilot (Humphrey Bogart) who, after crashing in China during the second World War, becomes a military adviser to a warlord (Lee J. Cobb)—until he becomes so disgusted with the warlord he makes his escape, dressed in the clothes of a slain priest. He arrives at a mission and introduces himself as the expected priest, and carries off the deception until the arrival of the warlord, who wishes to regain the services of his deserter. The two men agree to settle the matter with dice and the warlord loses, leaving the bogus priest to make a confession to the church and hopefully make a union with the nurse (Gene Tierney) he has come to love. Once again, the strength of Bogart helps save a doubtful piece of glossy melodrama.

THE LIEUTENANT WORE SKIRTS

Produced by Buddy Adler
Directed by Frank Tashlin
Screenplay by Albert Belch and Frank Tashlin, from a story by Albert Belch
Photographed in De Luxe Color and CinemaScope by Leo Tover
Music by Cyril J. Mockridge
Musical direction by Lionel Newman
98 minutes

Cast: Tom Ewell, Sheree North, Rita Moreno, Rick Jason, Les Tremayne, Alice Reinheart, Gregory Walcott, Joan Willes, Sylvia Lewis, Edward Platt, Jacqueline Fontaine, Arthur Q. Bryan, Marjorie Hellen

A television writer and former war hero (Tom Ewell) is called back into the Air Force against his wishes, because he doesn't want to be separated from his young bride (Sheree North). He is rejected on medical grounds, but in the meantime his wife enlists and is sent to Hawaii. He follows and becomes the only civilian husband on the base, to his embarrassment. He does everything he can to get her out, but nature comes to his aid when she gets pregnant, resulting in a discharge from the service. A knockabout comedy with Ewell excelling as the frantic husband.

LIFE IN THE BALANCE

Produced by Leonard Goldstein
Directed by Harry Horner
Screenplay by Robert Presnell, Jr. and Leo Townsend, from a story by Georges Simenon
Photographed by J. Gomez Urquiza
Music by Raul Lavista
74 minutes

Cast: Ricardo Montalban, Anne Bancroft, Lee Marvin, Jose Perez, Rodolfo Acosta, Carlos Muzquiz, George Trevino, Jose Torvay, Eva Calvo, Fanny Schiller, Tamara Garina, Pascual G. Pena, Antonio Carbajai

Filmed in Mexico City with the cooperation of its police department, the life in the balance is that of a young boy (Jose Perez) who tracks a psychopathic killer (Lee Marvin) across the city during carnival activities. His musician father (Ricardo Montalban) is arrested as a suspect in the killing of a number of young girls, but his son ingeniously smashes a series of police call boxes, thereby leaving a trail for the police —who arrive in time to save the boy's life.

LOVE IS A MANY-SPLENDORED THING

Produced by Buddy Adler
Directed by Henry King
Screenplay by John Patrick, from the novel by Han Suyin
Photographed in De Luxe Color and CinemaScope by Leon Shamroy
Song by Sammy Fain and Paul Francis Webster
Music by Alfred Newman
102 minutes

Cast: William Holden, Jennifer Jones, Torin Thatcher, Isobel Elosm, Murray Matheson, Virginia Gregg, Richard Loo, Soo Yong, Philip Ahn, Jorja Curtright, Donna Martell, Candace Lee, Kam Tong

An American newspaper correspondent (William Holden) in Hong Kong falls in love with a beautiful

Leslie Caron and Fred Astaire in *Daddy Long Legs*.

Ray Milland and Joan Collins in *The Girl in the Red Velvet Swing*.

Jennifer Jones and William Holden in *Love Is a Many-Splendored Thing*.

Eurasian doctor (Jennifer Jones), the widow of a Chinese general. The complete ardor of their love is marred by the fact that he cannot get a divorce and that her relatives disapprove. They also meet bias in Hong Kong society about interracial unions. Their happiness comes to an end when the newspaperman is killed in Korea, leaving the girl with her memories of a true love. The successful title song sets the tone of this romantic picture and the performances of Holden and Jones, in fascinating locations, make it among the best of its kind.

LOVER BOY

Produced by Paul Graetz
Directed by René Clement
Screenplay by Hugh Mills and René Clement, from a
    novel by Louis Hemon
Photographed by Osward Morris
Music by Roman Vlad
85 minutes

Cast: Gerard Philipe, Natasha Parry, Valerie Hobson, Joan Greenwood, Margaret Johnston, Germaine Montero, Percy Marmont, Diana Decker, Bill Shine, Eric Pohlmann, Mai Bacon, Margot Field

The story of a French philanderer (Gerard Philipe) and his amorous adventures in London. The handsome charmer lives off a number of ladies until he marries one of them (Valerie Hobson). Bored with her, he courts another (Natasha Parry) and when she refuses to give in, he stages a phony suicide attempt on a high balcony. But he slips and falls to his death.

THE MAGNIFICENT MATADOR

Produced by Edward L. Alperson
Directed by Budd Boetticher

266

Betty Grable and Robert Cummings in *How to Be Very, Very Popular*.

Robert Stack, Jennifer Jones, and Biff Elliot in *Good Morning, Miss Dove*.

Humphrey Bogart in *The Left Hand of God*.

Anthony Quinn, Maureen O'Hara, and Thomas Gomez in *The Magnificent Matador*.

Tom Ewell and Marilyn Monroe in *The Seven Year Itch*.

Lana Turner and Richard Burton in *The Rains of Ranchipur*.

Screenplay by Charles Lang, from a story by Budd Boetticher
Photographed in Eastman Color and CinemaScope by Lucien Ballard
Song by Paul Herrick and Edward L. Alperson, Jr.
Music by Raoul Kraushaar
90 minutes

Cast: Maureen O'Hara, Anthony Quinn, Manuel Rojas, Richard Denning, Thomas Gomez, Lola Albright, William Brooks Ching, Eduardo Noriega, Lorraine Chanel, Anthony Caruso, Joaquin Rodriguez

Anthony Quinn is the magnificent matador, an idolized veteran who fails to turn up at an event to introduce a young matador (Manuel Rojas). He has received what he believes to be an omen of death. He leaves Mexico City and is pursued by a rich American (Maureen O'Hara), with whom he has a romance, to the chagrin of her boyfriend (Richard Denning), who accuses him of being a coward. That and the persuasion of the girl help him overcome his superstition. He returns to the arena and triumphs together with the youngster, whom he reveals as his illegitimate son. The Mexican locations and the respectful coverage of the pageantry of bull fighting give the film its values.

A MAN CALLED PETER

Produced by Samuel G. Engel
Directed by Henry Koster
Screenplay by Eleanore Griffin, from the book by Catherine Marshall
Photographed in De Luxe Color and CinemaScope by Harold Lipstein
Music by Alfred Newman
117 minutes

Cast: Richard Todd, Jean Peters, Marjorie Rambeau, Jill Esmond, Les Tremayne, Robert Burton, Gladys Hurlbut, Richard Garrick, Gloria Gordon, Billy Chapin, Sally Corner, Voltaire Perkins, Marietta Canty

The story of Scottish minister Peter Marshall, who as a young man went to Washington and became the pastor of the Church of the Presidents. By the time of his death he was the chaplain to the Senate and a greatly respected man. Although a Presbyterian, the wisdom and sincerity of his sermons appealed to people of all faiths. The film distills a great deal of the substance of his sermons about the nature of life and death, without making them sound like preachments. The performance by Scottish actor Richard Todd as Marshall is masterly, and he is warmly aided by Jean Peters as his wife, on whose book the film is based. *A Man Called Peter* rates as one of the finest films dealing with religion.

PRINCE OF PLAYERS

Produced and directed by Philip Dunne

Screenplay by Moss Hart, based on a book by Eleanor Ruggles
Photographed in De Luxe Color and CinemaScope by Charles G. Clarke
Music by Bernard Herrmann
102 minutes

Cast: Richard Burton, Maggie McNamara, John Derek, Raymond Massey, Charles Bickford, Elizabeth Sellars, Eva Le Gallienne, Christopher Cook, Dayton Lummis, Ian Keith, Paul Stader, Ruth Clifford

The story of the Booths, America's first major family of actors, with Richard Burton as Edwin, John Derek as John, and Raymond Massey as their alcoholic, slightly mad genius of a father. Edwin tours the country as his father's manager and becomes an actor when his father dies. When John assassinates Lincoln, the public turns against actors as a breed. But Edwin stages a performance of *Hamlet* and receives their abuse, appearing on stage as the audience pelt him with garbage. He stands his ground unflinching. The sentiment changes and they then applaud him for his courage. For those interested in the history of the theatre, the film is a fascinating insight into the gifted but tragic family, with Burton shining in his many opportunities to perform Shakespearean passages.

THE RACERS

Produced by Julian Blaustein
Directed by Henry Hathaway
Screenplay by Charles Kaufman, based on the novel by Hans Ruesch
Photographed in CinemaScope and De Luxe Color by Joe MacDonald
Music by Alex North
112 minutes

Cast: Kirk Douglas, Bella Darvi, Gilbert Roland, Cesar Romero, Lee J. Cobb, Katy Jurado, Charles Goldner, John Hudson, George Dolenz, Agnes Laury, John Wengraf, Richard Allan, Francesco de Scaffa, Norman Schiller

In *The Racers* Kirk Douglas is an Italian bus driver burning with ambition to become a famous racing driver—and he does. He builds his own car, enters the Grand Prix de Napoli, and progresses from there to most of the famed runways of Europe. He is a man obsessed with a desire to win and he pays the price by way of antagonism from fellow drivers and estrangement from the woman (Bella Darvi) who loves him. But he finally sees the error of his ways and becomes a better man. For those interested in sports car racing and the places where it is done, *The Racers* is a film worth watching.

THE RAINS OF RANCHIPUR

Produced by Frank Ross

Directed by Jean Negulesco
Screenplay by Merle Miller, from a novel by Louis Bromfield
Photographed in De Luxe Color and CinemaScope by Milton Krasner
Music by Hugo Friedhofer
104 minutes

Cast: Lana Turner, Richard Burton, Fred MacMurray, Joan Caulfield, Michael Rennie, Eugenie Leontovich, Gladys Hurlbut, Madge Kennedy, Carlo Rizzo, Beatrice Kraft, King Calder, Argentina Brunetti

A remake of the 1939 film, with Richard Burton playing the Tyrone Power part of the Indian doctor-prince who is seduced by a wealthy lady (Lana Turner), but who realizes his duty is to his people and not to leaving the country with her. He comes to see this when a severe monsoon and earthquake devastate his city. Aiding in containing the disaster is a cynical American engineer (Fred MacMurray), who finds some spiritual value in his efforts and also in the arms of the daughter (Joan Caulfield) of missionaries. As with the original, the special effects dominate the film, together with attractive location footage shot in Pakistan.

SEVEN CITIES OF GOLD

Produced by Robert D. Webb and Barbara McLean
Directed by Robert D. Webb
Screenplay by Richard L. Breen and John C. Higgins, from a novel by Isabelle Gibson Ziegler
Photographed in De Luxe Color and CinemaScope by Lucien Ballard
Music by Hugo Friedhofer
103 minutes

Cast: Richard Egan, Anthony Quinn, Michael Rennie, Jeffrey Hunter, Rita Moreno, Eduardo Norega, Leslie Bradley, John Doucette, Victor Juncos, Julio Villareal, Miguel Inclan, Carlos Musquiz, Pedro Galvan

The Spanish Conquistadors in eighteenth-century California, looking for the seven great deposits of gold made by the Indians. The military commander (Anthiny Quinn) comes into conflict with Father Junipero Serra (Michael Rennie), the revered churchman who founded California's string of missions and who protected the Indians. One of the commander's officers (Richard Egan) trifles with an Indian girl (Rita Moreno) and sacrifices himself to their tortures in order to keep the Indians from rising against his comrades. A good adventure story and an interesting insight into early California history.

THE SEVEN YEAR ITCH

Produced by Charles K. Feldman and Billy Wilder
Directed by Billy Wilder
Screenplay by Billy Wilder and George Axelrod, from a play by George Axelrod

Photographed in De Luxe Color and CinemaScope by Milton Krasner
Music by Alfred Newman
104 minutes

Cast: Marilyn Monroe, Tom Ewell, Evelyn Keyes, Sonny Tufts, Robert Strauss, Oscar Homolka, Marguerite Chapman, Victor Moore, Roxanne, Donald McBride, Carolyn Jones, Butch Bernard, Doro Merande, Dorothy Ford

A New Yorker (Tom Ewell) takes care of himself when his wife leaves town for the summer. Lonely, he fantasizes about romantic conquests. When a gorgeous but naive blonde (Marilyn Monroe) moves into the building, his imagination runs riot. She accepts his invitation to spend a little time with him, but is completely unaware of her blatant sexiness and the effect she has on him, causing him to become ever more deluded in his imagination. The poor fellow is brought back to ordinary life when his wife returns. The film is an amiable spoof on sex, with a performance from Monroe that contains some of her most memorable lines and images.

SOLDIER OF FORTUNE

Produced by Buddy Adler
Directed by Edward Dmytryk
Screenplay by Ernest K. Gann, based on his novel
Photographed in CinemaScope and De Luxe Color by Leo Tover
Music by Hugo Friedhofer
96 minutes

Cast: Clark Gable, Susan Hayward, Michael Rennie, Gene Barry, Alex D'Arcy, Tom Tully, Anna Sten, Russell Collins, Leo Gordon, Richard Loo, Soo Yong, Frank Tang, Jack Kruschen, Mel Welles, Jack Raine, George Wallace, Alex Finlayson

A major asset in *Soldier of Fortune* is the setting. Much of it was filmed in Hong Kong and vicinity, and good use is made of the harbor and the bazaars to accent this story of an American adventurer (Clark Gable) who makes a good living as a smuggler, and whose services are engaged by a lady (Susan Hayward) trying to locate her missing photographer husband (Gene Barry). The husband is found in Red China and after many adventures he is rescued. But he soon realizes his wife and his rescuer are in love, and since he prefers to roam the world as a single man, he leaves them to find their happiness. Clark Gable was getting a little too old for these kinds of larks, but the films holds attention with its good yarn and its interesting locations.

THE TALL MEN

Produced by William A. Bacher and William B. Hawks
Directed by Raoul Walsh

Screenplay by Sydney Boehm and Frank Nugent, based on the novel by Clay Fisher
Photographed in CinemaScope and De Luxe Color by Leo Tover
Music by Victor Young
122 minutes

Cast: Clark Gable, Jane Russell, Robert Ryan, Cameron Mitchell, Juan Garcia, Harry Shannon, Emile Meyer, Steve Darrell, Will Wright, Robert Adler, J. Lewis Smith, Russell Simpson, Mae Marsh, Gertrude Graner, Tom Wilson

Two Texan brothers (Clark Gable and Cameron Mitchell), late of the Confederate Army, proceed to Montana with the idea of making a fortune in the gold fields. Instead they end up working for an unscrupulous businessman (Robert Ryan) and driving a vast herd of cattle from Texas to Montana. Along the way they fight off bandits and Indians and rescue a lusty girl (Jane Russell) from an Indian attack. Her affections flutter between the businessman and the trail boss, but eventually settle on the latter, who survives a planned doublecross by his boss. *The Tall Men* is a Class A Western, thanks largely to the direction of the veteran Raoul Walsh, an expert with action and macho humor, here backed up with fine color photography of some luscious Western landscapes.

THAT LADY

Produced by Sy Bartlett
Directed by Terence Young
Screenplay by Anthony Veiller and Sy Bartlett, from a play by Kate O'Brien
Photographed in De Luxe Color and CinemaScope by Robert Krasker
Music by John Addison
100 minutes

Cast: Olivia de Havilland, Gilbert Roland, Paul Scofield, Francoise Rosay, Dennis Price, Anthony Dawson, Robert Harris, Petter Illing, Pepe Nieto, Christopher Lee, Andy Shine, Angel Peralta

The lady is Ana de Mendoza (Olivia de Haviland), the most powerful woman in the Spain of King Philip II (Paul Scofield). Famed for her beauty and the fact that she wears an eye patch, the King asks her to help the career of a man (Gilbert Roland) he wishes to promote to high office. But when she falls in love with him, the jealous monarch has him arrested for murder, although knowing he is innocent. The lady is contained under house arrest, but her lover escapes and visits her. She asks him to leave the country and take her son with him. Later, when she receives a message that the two of them are safely overseas, she dies. A sad history lesson brightened with delightful locations in Spain.

UNTAMED

Produced by Bert E. Friedlob and William A. Bacher

Directed by Henry King
Screenplay by Talbot Jennings, Frank Fenton, and Michael Blankfort, from a novel by Helga Moray
Photographed in De Luxe Color and CinemaScope by Leo Tover
Music by Franz Waxman
111 minutes

Cast: Tyrone Power, Susan Hayward, Richard Egan, John Justin, Agnes Moorehead, Rita Moreno, Hope Emerson, Brad Dexter, Henry O'Neill, Paul Thompson, Alexander D. Havermann, Louis Mercier, Emmett Smith

A magnificently filmed African adventure, with Tyrone Power as a Boer leader struggling to build up his country while conducting a tempestuous love affair with a spirited Irish immigrant (Susan Hayward). Her husband (John Justin) is killed when Zulus attack a wagon train as it treks to the interior. A Boer cavalry unit, commanded by Power, saves the survivors, among whom is a rough Dutch farmer (Richard Egan), who claims the Irishwoman for his own. He forms his own outlaw band in order to control the diamond territory and eventually faces the authority represented by the cavalry commander, who afterwards settles down with his Irish lady. The plot lines are complicated, but the film offers beautiful scenery in South Africa and fine action sequences, particularly the Zulu attack on the wagon train.

THE VIEW FROM POMPEY'S HEAD

Produced and directed by Philip Dunne
Screenplay by Philip Dunne, from a novel by Hamilton Basso
Photographed in De Luxe Color and CinemaScope by Joe MacDonald
Music by Elmer Bernstein
97 minutes

Cast: Richard Egan, Dana Wynter, Cameron Mitchell, Sidney Blackmer, Marjorie Rambeau, Dorothy Patrick Davis, Rosemarie Bowe, Jerry Paris, Ruby Goodwin, Howard Wendell, Dayton Lummis, Bess Flowers

Pride and prejudice in the South. A lawyer (Richard Egan) leaves New York to return to his home town to investigate charges made by the wife (Marjorie Rambeau) of an aging author (Sidney Blackmer) that his royalties have been embezzled. He finds the author has been giving the money to his black mother to keep her quiet about his mixed parentage. On hearing this the wife drops the case. The lawyer also meets a former love (Dana Wynter), now married to a wealthy but uncouth man (Cameron Mitchell). Their feelings for each other are rekindled, but they finally realize they each must return to their families.

VIOLENT SATURDAY

Produced by Buddy Adler
Directed by Richard Fleischer

Screenplay by Sydney Boehm, from a novel by William L. Heath

Photographed in De Luxe Color and CinemaScope by Charles G. Clarke

Music by Hugo Friedhofer

91 minutes

Cast: Victor Mature, Richard Egan, Stephen McNally, Virginia Leith, Tommy Noonan, Lee Marvin, Margaret Hayes, J. Carrol Naish, Sylvia Sidney, Ernest Borgnine, Dorothy Patrick, Billy Chapin

Three crooks (Stephen McNally, Lee Marvin, and J. Carrol Naish) arrive in the mining town of Bisbee, Arizona, to pull off a bank robbery. Their caper affects the lives of a number of people, principally an engineer (Victor Mature) whose young son regrets that his father never served in the war and became a hero. Others are a bank manager (Tommy Noonan), a voyeur who dies in the robbery, as does an erring wife (Margaret Hayes), a librarian (Sylvia Sidney) who has stolen money to pay off her debts but who has it stolen from her, and an Amish farmer (Ernest Borgnine), who is opposed to violence until he has to use it to save his life. The engineer proves himself a hero in thwarting the robbery. An interesting study of a town, with good photographic use of its setting.

THE VIRGIN QUEEN

Produced by Charles Brackett

Directed by Henry Koster

Screenplay by Harry Brown and Mindret Lord

Photographed in CinemaScope and De Luxe Color by Charles G. Clarke

Music by Franz Waxman

92 minutes

Cast: Bette Davis, Richard Todd, Joan Collins, Jay Robinson, Herbert Marshall, Dan O'Herlihy, Robert Douglas, Romney Brent, Marjorie Hellen, Lisa Daniels, Lia Davis, Barry Bernard, Robert Adler, Noel Drayton, Ian Murray, Margery Weston, Rod Taylor

A Hollywood version of British history, *The Virgin Queen* has Queen Elizabeth I doting on Sir Walter Raleigh in the way she supposedly doted on the Earl of Essex some years previously. Which is doubtless what the producers of this film had in mind when they cast Bette Davis as the queen, allowing her to reprise her famous 1939 portrayal in which she dallied with the Essex of Errol Flynn. *The Virgin Queen* is actually a story about young Raleigh (Richard Todd) and his ambitions to sail to the New World in search of treasure. He deliberately comes to the attention of the queen—the incident of his laying down his cloak in a mud puddle for her to step on is here well staged —but he sabotages his scheme when he marries a royal lady-in-waiting (Joan Collins). The queen is irate and sentences him to execution, but later has a softening of heart about the young lovers and allows

them to sail away. It all makes for a pretty picture, but it is Davis as the proud and crafty monarch that stays in the memory.

THE WARRIORS

Produced by Walter Mirisch

Directed by Henry Levin

Screenplay by Daniel B. Ulman

Photographed in Technicolor and CinemaScope by Guy Green

Music by Cedric Thorpe Davie

Musical direction by Louis Levy

85 minutes

Cast: Errol Flynn, Joanne Dru, Peter Finch, Yvonne Furneaux, Patrick Holt, Michael Hordern, Moultrie Kelsall, Robert Urquhart, Noel Willman, Frances Rowe, Alastair Hunter, Rupert Davies

Errol Flynn in fourteenth-century France—as Edward, the Black Prince, helping his father, King Edward III of England hang on to their conquered lands in Aquitaine. The leader of the opposition, a villainous French baron (Peter Finch), wants to control the country for his own purposes. He kidnaps an English noblewoman (Joanne Dru), who is then rescued by Edward and taken to his castle. The Frenchmen raid the castle and after a loud and bloody battle lose the day, leaving Aquitaine still under the British flag. *The Warriors* (called *The Dark Avenger* for its British release) was Flynn's last swashbuckling epic—good, but far from his best.

WHITE FEATHER

Produced by Robert L. Jacks

Directed by Robert Webb

Screenplay by Delmer Daves and Leo Townsend, from a story by John Prebble

Photographed in Technicolor and CinemaScope by Lucien Ballard

Music by Hugo Friedhofer

Musical direction by Lionel Newman

100 minutes

Cast: Robert Wagner, John Lund, Debra Paget, Jeffrey Hunter, Eduard Franz, Noah Beery, Virginia Leith, Emile Meyer, Hugh O'Brien, Milburn Stone

A respectful telling of the 1877 campaign in Wyoming to contain the Indians by persuading them to leave the plains, sign treaties, and move to reservations. The colonel (John Lund) in charge is helped by a surveyor (Robert Wagner) who has made Indian friends, particularly two young bucks (Jeffrey Hunter and Hugh O'Brien). Complications arise when the girl (Debra Paget) engaged to one of the bucks falls in love with the surveyor and he with her. At the signing of the treaty the two bucks jeopardize the touchy meeting by challenging the army to fight. The surveyor saves

271

the day by offering a personal challenge to the two, and kills them. The treatment of the Indians in this picture is intelligent and good use is made of the handsome locations.

20TH CENTURY-FOX ACADEMY AWARDS FOR 1955

SAMMY FAIN and PAUL FRANCIS WEBSTER: Best song, "Love Is a Many-Splendored Thing."

ALFRED NEWMAN: Best scoring of a dramatic or comedy picture, *Love Is a Many-Splendored Thing.*

CHARLES LEMAIRE: Best costume design, color, *Love Is a Many-Splendored Thing.*

EDMUND REEK: Best one-reel short subject, *Survival City.*

CLASS III SCIENTIFIC and TECHNICAL AWARD: Combination lenses for CinemaScope photography.

CLASS III SCIENTIFIC and TECHNICAL AWARD: Spraying process creating simulated metallic surfaces.

CLASS III SCIENTIFIC and TECHNICAL AWARD: Improved spotlight to maintain fixed light over varied distance.

Clark Gable and Susan Hayward in *Soldier of Fortune.*

Robert Wagner, Jeffrey Hunter, and Debra Paget in *White Feather.*

Richard Todd, Herbert Marshall, Bette Davis, and Robert Douglas in *The Virgin Queen.*

Susan Hayward and Tyrone Power in *Untamed.*

John Derek and Richard Burton in *Prince of Players.*

Jane Russell and Clark Gable in *The Tall Men.*

Joanne Dru, Errol Flynn, and Peter Finch in *The Warriors.*

272

Jean Peters and Richard Todd in *A Man Called Peter.*

ABDULLAH'S HAREM

Produced and directed by Gregory Ratoff
Screenplay by George St. George and Boris Ingster
Photographed in Technicolor
Music by Lambert Williamson
92 minutes·

Cast: Gregory Ratoff, Kay Kendall, Marina Berti, Sydney Chaplin, Alex D'Arcy, Mary Costes, Marti Stevens

Not destined to be one of the studio's all-time hits, this supposed satirical comedy could not decide what direction to go in. The product of triple-threat Gregory Ratoff, who, in 1956, was not the best known of auteurs, *Abdullah's Harem* told the story of a dethroned Middle Eastern King, known in his heyday as Abdullah the Great. The prodigal king of Bondaria (Gregory Ratoff) uses his great wealth solely for his own selfish satisfaction. Because of his lack of devotion for the country, his army, led by a Mohammedan soldier (Sydney Chaplin), revolts and removes him from the throne. Most of the film is told in flashback, as Abdullah recounts his amorous affairs with a bevy of beauties. There was more of a harem in the ads than in the film, which did not live up to any minor expectations of audiences.

ANASTASIA

Produced by Buddy Adler
Directed by Anatole Litvak
Screenplay by Arthur Laurents, based on the play by Marcelle Maurette
Photographed in CinemaScope and De Luxe Color by Jack Hilyard
Music by Alfred Newman
105 minutes

Cast: Ingrid Bergman, Yul Brynner, Helen Hayes, Akim Tamiroff, Martita Hunt, Felix Aylmer, Sacha Pitoeff, Ivan Desny, Natalie Schaefer, Gregoire Gromoff, Karel Stepanek, Ina de la Haye

Marking Ingrid Bergman's return to American movies after a seven-year absence, *Anastasia* provided her with a superbly etched role which she developed well enough to win an Academy Award. The film was a rare combination of mystery, romance, and drama skillfully blended by director Litvak. A group of Russian exiles in Paris conspire to present someone as Anastasia, the daughter of Czar Nicholas, so they can collect the £10,000,000 held in her name by the Bank of England. General Bounin (Yul Brynner) finds a destitute girl (Ingrid Bergman) on the verge of suicide. He takes her under his care and grooms her in all of Anastasia's ways. However, the more he learns of her, the more he begins to believe that she is the real Anastasia. The mystery persists until the end of the story, when she is presented to the Empress (Helen Hayes), who will identify her as the true heiress to the money. By this time, though, Bounin has fallen in love with the girl and the money is no longer important.

THE BEST THINGS IN LIFE ARE FREE

Produced by Henry Ephron
Directed by Michael Curtiz
Screenplay by William Bowers and Phoebe Ephron
Photographed in CinemaScope and De Luxe Color by Leon Shamroy
Music supervised and conducted by Lionel Newman
104 minutes

Cast: Gordon MacRae, Dan Dailey, Ernest Borgnine, Sheree North, Tommy Noonan, Murvyn Vye, Phyllis Avery, Larry Keating, Tony Galento, Norman Brooks, Jacques d'Amboise, Roxanne Arlen, Byron Palmer, Linda Brace, Patty Lou Hudson, Julie Van Zandt, Eugene Borden, Harold Miller, Emily Belser, Paul Glass, Bill Foster

Continuing the tradition of the Hollywood "and then I wrote" biographies, *The Best Things in Life Are Free* traces the early careers of songwriters DeSylva (Gordon MacRae), Brown (Ernest Borgnine), and Henderson (Dan Dailey). It's the typical story of three men who meet, become friends, work together successfully, and then are threatened with a break-up when their ambitions grow too large for them to function as a team. When they realize that their strength and talent lies in teamwork, they finally get back together. Most of the film was spent showcasing many of the trio's best-known musical numbers, including "Button Up Your

Overcoat," "Black Bottom," "Sunnyside Up," "Birth of the Blues," and the title song. However, the most exciting aspect of the picture was an energetic portrayal of Kitty Kane by Sheree North, whom the studio had finally decided would not be another Marilyn Monroe and assigned a part on her own merit.

BETWEEN HEAVEN AND HELL

Produced by David Weisbart
Directed by Richard Fleischer
Screenplay by Harry Brown, based on the novel by Francis Gwaltney
Photographed in CinemaScope and De Luxe Color by Leo Tover
Music by Hugo Friedhofer
93 minutes

Cast: Robert Wagner, Terry Moore, Broderick Crawford, Buddy Ebsen, Robert Keith, Brad Dexter, Mark Damon, Ken Clark, Harvey Lembeck, Skip Homeier, L. Q. Jones, Tod Andrews, Biff Elliott, Bart Burns, Frank Gerstle, Carl Switzer, Gregg Martell, Frank Gorshin, Darlene Fields, Ilene Brown, Scotty Morrow, Pixie Parkhurst, Brad Morow, Scatman Crothers, Sam Edwards

Robert Wagner was being groomed as the new Tyrone Power and was assigned to many of Fox's adventure films. The results were usually good, except in cases like *Between Heaven and Hell* when the action was overtaken by dramatic intention. Wagner played a Southern landowner who had treated his sharecroppers badly, and only came to realize the error of his ways when he was put among the troops in the Pacific theater in World War II. There, he encounters a psychopathic commanding officer (Broderick Crawford) who almost breaks him, but the young man regains his resources and becomes a hero when he saves a fellow soldier (Buddy Ebsen). Probably most damaging to the film were the ads, which promised a big, action-packed story, but aside from a beachhead landing made up mainly of stock shots and the final battle with the enemy, there was a lot of talk.

BIGGER THAN LIFE

Produced by James Mason
Directed by Nicholas Ray
Screenplay by Cyril Hume and Richard Maibaum, based on an article in the *New Yorker* by Berton Roueche
Photographed in CinemaScope and De Luxe Color by Joe MacDonald
Music by David Raksin
95 minutes

Cast: James Mason, Barbara Rush, Walter Matthau, Robert Simon, Christopher Olsen, Roland Winters, Rusty Lane, Rachel Stephens, Kipp Hamilton, Betty Caulfield, Virginia Carroll, Renny McEvoy, Bill Jones, Dee Aaker, Jerry Mather, Portland Mason, Natalie Masters, Richard Collier, Lewis Charles, John Monoghan, Gus Schilling,

Alex Frazer, Mary McAdoo, Mary Carver, Eugenia Paul, Gladys Richards, David Bedell, Ann Spencer, Nan Dolan

Dealing with a subject never tackled by the movies, miracle drugs and their unpredictable side-effects, *Bigger Than Life* was almost doomed to financial failure from the beginning. It was not the type of CinemaScope entry audiences had become accustomed to. There were no battles, wide vistas, or outdoor chases. There was only some very good drama in which James Mason, as a modest schoolteacher, is prescribed cortisone for an illness which is characteristically fatal. Although the drug does him some good, it turns him into a psychotic and by the final minutes of the film, he is prepared to kill himself, his son, and his wife. Fortunately, a friend, played by a young Walter Matthau, manages to stop him just in time. The cast performed well and the film gained further critical acclaim for Nicholas Ray, but audiences were not interested in the depressingly dramatic story angle.

THE BLACK WHIP

Produced by Robert Stabler
Directed by Charles Marquis Warren
Screenplay by Orville Hampton
Photographed by RegalScope by Joseph Biroc
Music by Raoul Kraushaar
81 minutes

Cast: Hugh Marlowe, Coleen Gray, Paul Richards, Angie Dickinson, Richard Gilden, Adele Mara, Strother Martin, Dorothy Schuyler, Patrick O'Moore, Charles Gray

One of the early group of Regal Flms productions headed by "B" producer Robert L. Lippert, *The Black Whip* was an average entry for double bills. Four women (Coleen Gray, Angie Dickinson, Adele Mara, and Dorothy Schuyler) are run out of a Western town for setting free a notorious outlaw. The girls are packed onto a stagecoach, which breaks down before it gets to another town. Taken to a way station run by Hugh Marlowe, the wagon is repaired, but not before a gang of outlaws shows up to claim the girls. The meek owner of the way station has to put up with much abuse from the gang, but outsmarts them at the end and a sheriff's posse help him shoot them down.

THE BOTTOM OF THE BOTTLE

Produced by Buddy Adler
Directed by Henry Hathaway
Screenplay by Sydney Boehm, from the novel by Georges Simenon
Photographed in CinemaScope and De Luxe Color by Lee Garmes
Music by Leigh Harline
88 minutes

Cast: Van Johnson, Joseph Cotten, Ruth Roman, Jack Carson, Margaret Hayes, Bruce Bennett, Brad Dexter,

Peggy Knudsen, Jim Davis, Margaret Lindsay, Nancy Gates, Gonzalez-Gonzalez

The old chestnut about two brothers being separated and then coming together was given a new lease on life by *The Bottom of the Bottle.* An escaped convict (Van Johnson) shows up at his brother's sumptuous ranch in Arizona and needs help to get back to his wife and three children in Mexico. The brothers never got along in the first place, but to make matters worse, the rancher (Joseph Cotten) is a prominent attorney and worries about his reputation should he aid a convict. Instead, he introduces him to everyone on his ranch as a friend. The attorney's unhappy wife (Ruth Roman) finally prods him into helping the fugitive brother.

BUS STOP

Produced by Buddy Adler
Directed by Joshua Logan
Screenplay by George Axelrod, based on a play by
   William Inge
Photographed in CinemaScope and De Luxe Color by
   Milton Krasner
Music by Alfred Newman and Cyril J. Mockridge
96 minutes

Cast: Marilyn Monroe, Don Murray, Arthur O'Connell, Betty Field, Eileen Heckart, Robert Bray, Hope Lange, Hans Conreid, Casey Adams, Henry Slate, Terry Kelman, Linda Brace, Greta Thyssen, Helen Mayon, Lucille Knox

Bus Stop proved to audiences that Marilyn Monroe could act. Her energetic and warm portrayal of Cherie also exposed her vulnerability without hampering her radiance. Cherie is working her way across the country with a final goal of Hollywood and Vine Streets. After all, that is where movie stars are discovered. In Phoenix, though, she meets Don Murray, who has come to take part in a rodeo. Never were there two more unlikely types. Murray is the brash, almost obnoxious, cowboy, who has never had a fling with love, and Monroe is the woman who wants to rise above singing stints in cheap bars. Deciding that Cherie is the girl of his dreams, Murray pursues her relentlessly until she finally grows fond of him and agrees to marry. *Bus Stop* is filled with wonderful moments of humor, pathos, and drama. Monroe performs one of the hardest feats for an actress; in a tawdry nightclub, she sings a number terribly but still makes it magical, and audiences loved it.

CAROUSEL

Produced by Henry Ephron
Directed by Henry King
Screenplay by Phoebe and Henry Ephron, based on the
   play by Richard Rodgers and Oscar Hammerstein II,
   as adapted from *Liliom* by Ferenc Molnar

Photographed in CinemaScope and De Luxe Color by
   Charles G. Clarke
Music by Richard Rodgers
Lyrics by Oscar Hammerstein II
Music supervision by Alfred Newman
128 minutes

Cast: Gordon MacRae, Shirley Jones, Cameron Mitchell, Barbara Ruick, Claramae Turner, Robert Rounseville, Gene Lockhart, Audrey Christie, Susan Luckey, William Le Massena, John Dehner, Jacques D'Amboise, Frank Twedell, Sylvia Stanton, Mary Orozco, Dee Pollack

A simple fantasy set to music, *Carousel* is the tale of a young man who, in heaven, explains to the starkeeper that he must return to earth for one day to help his unhappy daughter overcome the shame she feels regarding her dead father. In telling his story, there are flashbacks to the time Billy Bigelow (Gordon MacRae) meets, courts, and marries Julie (Shirley Jones). Then come his problems holding down a job, and the final act of committing a robbery, during which he is slain. Explaining satisfactorily that his intentions were good, but he got involved with the wrong types, Billy is allowed his one day on earth. No expense was spared to make this simple piece lavishly extravagant, from the rich locations in New England, to the complex dance numbers. But as big and bubbling as *Carousel* was, it was not as successful as other Rodgers and Hammerstein screen versions and lost over $2,000,000 for the studio.

D-DAY, THE SIXTH OF JUNE

Produced by Charles Brackett
Directed by Henry Koster
Screenplay by Ivan Moffat and Harry Brown, based on
   the novel by Lionel Shapiro
Photographed in CinemaScope and De Luxe Color by
   Lee Garmes
Music by Lyn Murray
106 minutes

Cast: Robert Taylor, Richard Todd, Dana Wynter, Edmond O'Brien, John Williams, Jerry Paris, Robert Gist, Richard Stapley, Ross Elliott, Alex Finlayson, Cyril Delevanti, Marie Brown, Rama Bai, Dabbs Greer, Geoffrey Steele, George Pelling

A more adult rehashing of the love triangle found in *Crash Dive* and *A Yank in the RAF* was the sum and substance of *D-Day, the Sixth of June.* Awaiting the invasion on the coast of France, both Robert Taylor and Richard Todd remember their love for Dana Wynter. While Todd was away fighting Rommel's forces in Africa, Wynter fell in love with Taylor, in London with the American Army. Although Taylor had a wife in the United States, he started an affair with Wynter. When Todd returned from Africa, Wynter decided to give up Taylor, whom she truly loved, in order to be faithful to her first lover. But the producers provided an appropriately bittersweet ending. While walking on a beach after the D-Day invasion, Todd steps on a land mine, but Wynter, a girl of conscience, does not tell Taylor and he returns to his wife.

THE DESPERADOES ARE IN TOWN

Produced and directed by Kurt Neumann
Screenplay by Earl Snell and Kurt Neumann, based on a story by Bennett Foster
Photographed in RegalScope by John Mescall
Music by Paul Sawtell and Bert Shefter
72 minutes

Cast: Robert Arthur, Kathy Nolan, Rhys Williams, Rhodes Reason, Dave O'Brien, Kelly Thordsen, Mae Clarke, Robert Osterloh, William Challee, Carol Kelly, Frank Sully

Because the film was produced on a minuscule budget, none of the performers had a chance to show their abilities in this tale of a young man who runs away from his home in the South and joins a gang of desperadoes in the West. When the young man decides to return home to his girl friend, the gang follows him and wants him to help them rob the local bank. Before the robbery, though, the young man has a chance to kill the gang leader. The local banker finds out about the young man's past, but decides to forgive him because of his services to the town.

THE GIRL CAN'T HELP IT

Produced and directed by Frank Tashlin
Screenplay by Frank Tashlin and Herbert Baker
Photographed in CinemaScope and De Luxe Color by Leon Shamroy
Music supervised by Lionel Newman
98 minutes

Cast: Tom Ewell, Jayne Mansfield, Edmond O'Brien, Henry Jones, John Emery, Juanita Moore, Julie London, Ray Anthony, Barry Gordon, Fats Domino, The Platters, Little Richard and his Band, Gene Vincent and his Blue Caps, The Treniers, Eddie Fontaine, The Chuckles, Abbey Lincoln, Johnny Olenn, Nino Tempo, Eddie Cochran

Frank Tashlin had been an illustrator for comic books, and his film style always exhibited a kind of unreal farce. *The Girl Can't Help It* was the first big-budget rock-and-roll picture, and Tashlin built plenty of farcical satire into the story. Tom Ewell plays a down-and-out agent who is hired by a mobster (Edmond O'Brien) to make a star out of his sexpot girl friend (Jayne Mansfield). Ewell gives her a rock and roll act and introduces her at various clubs (so that there is ample opportunity to showcase the film's other high-priced acts). To add a little twist to the story, Mansfield only wants to be a housewife and mind the kitchen, and she falls in love with Ewell. It was

Mansfield's starring debut and her best lines were not the ones written.

HILDA CRANE

Produced by Herbert B. Swope Jr.
Directed by Philip Dunne
Screenplay by Philip Dunne, based on a play by Samson Raphaelson
Photographed in CinemaScope and De Luxe Color by Joe MacDonald
Music by David Raksin
Musical direction by Lionel Newman
87 minutes

Cast: Jean Simmons, Guy Madison, Jean Pierre Aumont, Judith Evelyn, Evelyn Varden, Peggy Knudsen, Gregg Palmer, Richard Garrick, Jay Jostyn, Helen Mayon, Blossom Rock

The girl of the title (Jean Simmons) returns to her small home town after having had two failed marriages and disappointing experiences in her career. Her former boyfriend (Guy Madison) asks her to marry him, against the wishes of his dominating mother (Evelyn Vardan). She fakes a heart attack, but it develops into the real thing and she dies. After they marry, the husband broods about his mother and his wife finds solace with a charming French author (Jean Pierre Aumont). The husband breaks up the affair, but has more problems when the remorseful wife tries suicide but fails. He finally comes to realize he must be a more loving man and not be concerned with the negative memory of his mother. A soap opera, given some style by the acting of Jean Simmons as the sensitive, confused Hilda.

THE KING AND I

Produced by Buddy Adler
Directed by Walter Lang
Screenplay by Ernest Lehman, based on the stage play by Richard Rodgers and Oscar Hammerstein II
Photographed in CinemaScope and De Luxe Color by Leon Shamroy
Musical direction by Alfred Newman
133 minutes

Cast: Yul Brynner, Deborah Kerr, Rita Moreno, Martin Benson, Terry Saunders, Rex Thompson, Alan Mowbray, Carlos Rivas, Patrick Adiarte, Geoffrey Toone, Yuriko, Marion Jim, Jocelyn Lew

One of Rodgers and Hammerstein's most memorable musicals, *The King and I* was gloriously brought to the wide screen as an eye-filling and ear-pleasing treat. Based on the original *Anna and the King of Siam*, it boasted excellent performances and expert direction. The tuneful retelling of Anna Leonowen's adventures as schoolteacher to the royal palace of Siam, pits her (Deborah Kerr) against the unbearably stubborn king

(Yul Brynner). The representatives of two polar opposite cultures argue about each other's ways, but finally recognize and respect their differences. Although he has brought the schoolteacher to modernize his family, he soon realizes that some customs must not change, but others cannot be maintained. Anna's greatest achievement is to convince the king that he cannot keep a young girl, Tuptim (Rita Moreno), as one of his wives, because she loves someone else. Through all the arguments and disappointments, a love develops between the widowed teacher and the cantankerous king. Songs include "Shall We Dance," "Hello Young Lovers," and "Getting to Know You."

THE LAST WAGON

Produced by William B. Hawks
Directed by Delmer Daves
Screenplay by James Edward Grant, Delmer Daves, and Gwen Bagni Gielgud
Photographed in CinemaScope and De Luxe Color by Wilfrid Cline
Music by Lionel Newman
98 minutes

Cast: Richard Widmark, Felicia Farr, Susan Kohner, Tommy Rettig, Stephanie Griffin, Ray Stricklyn, Nick Adams, Carl Benton Reid, Douglas Kennedy, George Mathews, James Drury, Ken Clark, Timothy Carey, George Ross, Juney Ellis, Abel Fernandez

Richard Widmark continued his gallery of tough roles in *The Last Wagon.* As a man who has just murdered three brothers in revenge for his wife's death, Widmark is arrested and chained to a wagon train. When the procession is attacked by Indians, there are no survivors, except some children who had been at a swimming hole, and Widmark, who has been left for dead. When the children free him, he takes control of the group and is responsible for leading them safely back to the nearest fort. *The Last Wagon* was a suspenseful and action-packed Western. Its cast was made up largely of newcomers, and it is to director Daves' credit that the picture played so well. Aside from a sugary-sweet hearing at which Widmark is exonerated of his murders, the film was tough and taut throughout.

LOVE ME TENDER

Produced by David Weisbart
Directed by Robert D. Webb
Screenplay by Robert Buckner
Photographed in CinemaScope by Leo Tover
Music by Lionel Newman
89 minutes

Cast: Richard Egan, Debra Paget, Elvis Presley, Robert Middleton, William Campbell, Neville Brand, Mildred Dunnock, Bruce Bennett, James Drury, Russ Conway, Ken Clark, Barry Coe, L. Q. Jones, Paul Burns, Jerry Sheldon

If nothing else, the black and white post-Civil War Western called *Love Me Tender* brought to the movies one of the most popular entertainers of all time, Elvis Presley. Why the studio felt that starring him in a Western would be successful is merely academic. When Elvis broke into gyrations and song, audiences were electrified. The story, as if audiences cared, was about three brothers in a band of Confederate soldiers who rob a Union Army payroll and then discover that the war is over, and their crime must be paid for. Hiding the money, they decide to use it for themselves, and return home to the family farm and their fourth brother (Presley). When the eldest of the group (Richard Egan) finds Presley has married his girl friend (Debra Paget), enmity erupts. Egan later decides that the men's best chance is to return the money. Some of the Confederates are angered and turn Presley against Egan. In the shooting that follows, Egan is wounded, but Presley is killed by one of the Confederates and dies begging for forgiveness. It was a potent ending for the millions of viewers that the film attracted.

THE MAN IN THE GRAY FLANNEL SUIT

Produced by Darryl F. Zanuck
Directed by Nunnally Johnson
Screenplay by Nunnally Johnson, based on the novel by Sloan Wilson
Photographed in De Luxe Color by Charles G. Clarke
Music by Bernard Herrmann
152 minutes

Cast: Gregory Peck, Jennifer Jones, Fredric March, Marisa Pavan, Ann Harding, Lee J. Cobb, Keenan Wynn, Gene Lockhart, Gigi Perreau, Portland Mason, Arthur O'Connell, Henry Daniell, Connie Gilchrist, Joseph Sweeney, Sandy Descher, Mickey Maga, Kenneth Tobey, Ruth Clifford, Geraldine Wall

The Man in the Gray Flannel Suit is a comment on success in big business and the balance between ambition and personal satisfaction. Tom Rath (Gregory Peck), after some distinction as a wartime army officer, lands a job as a writer with a broadcasting corporation in New York, and part of his job lies in writing speeches for its president (Frederic March). The president respects the younger man and reveals that his great success has been achieved at the sacrifice of his private life. When Rath is finally offered a major position, he turns it down in favor of a lesser one, so he can devote more time to his family. The film is a glossy critique of certain aspects of the American way of life, and made the more forceful by the fine performances of Peck and March.

THE MAN WHO NEVER WAS

Produced by Andre Hakim
Directed by Ronald Neame

Ernest Borgnine, Gordon MacRae, Sheree North, and Dan Dailey in *The Best Things in Life Are Free*.

Ingrid Bergman and Yul Brynner in *Anastasia*.

Shirley Jones, Gordon MacRae, and Cameron Mitchell in *Carousel*.

Marilyn Monroe and Don Murray in *Bus Stop*.

Elvis Presley and Debra Paget in *Love Me Tender*.

Robert Taylor in *D-Day, The Sixth of June*.

Jayne Mansfield and Tom Ewell in *The Girl Can't Help It*.

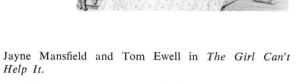

Jennifer Jones and Gregory Peck in *The Man in the Gray Flannel Suit*.

278

Yul Brynner and Deborah Kerr in *The King and I.*

Screenplay by Nigel Balchin, based on the book by Ewen Montagu
Photographed in CinemaScope and De Luxe Color by Oswald Morris
Music by Alan Rawsthorne
103 minutes

Cast: Clifton Webb, Gloria Grahame, Robert Flemyng, Josephine Griffin, Stephen Boyd, Laurence Naismith, Geoffrey Keene, Moultrie Kelsall, Cyril Cusack, Andre Morell, Michael Hordern, Allan Cuthbertson, Joan Hickson, Terrence Longden, Gibb McLaughlin, Miles Malleson, Richard Wattis

A true and intriguing account of an episode of World War II espionage, in which the British were able to dupe the Germans into believing that a Mediterranean invasion would take place in Greece rather than Sicily. The scheme is the invention of a Royal Navy officer (Clifton Webb), who plants a corpse in the Mediterranean, a corpse dressed as a British officer and carrying the plans for the phony invasion. An Irishman (Stephen Boyd), who is a German agent, arrives in London to check out the plans and finds them to be genuine. Thus the British ruse is successful. The film is skillfully written and acted, and gives a fine insight into the workings of wartime intelligence operations on the highest level.

MASSACRE

Produced by Robert L. Lippert, Jr.
Directed by Louis King
Screenplay by D. D. Beachamp, based on a story by Fred Freiberger and William Tunberg
Photographed in Ansco Color by Gilbert Warrenton
Music by Gonzalo Curiel
76 minutes

Cast: Dane Clark, James Craig, Marta Roth, Jaime Fernandez, Ferrusquilla, Miguel Torruco, Jose Munoz, Enrique Zambrano

Filmed in Mexico, with Dane Clark as a captain of mounted police assigned to locate the renegades who are selling guns to the savage Yaqui Indians and inciting them to warfare. The captain finds the smugglers and their hideout, and blows up the whole cache. But before he and his prisoners can leave, they are surrounded by the Yaquis and wiped out to the last man.

MOHAWK

Produced by Edward L. Alperson
Directed by Kurt Neumann
Screenplay by Maurice Geraghty and Milton Krims
Photographed in Eastman Color by Karl Struss
Music by Edward L. Alperson, Jr.
80 minutes

Cast: Scott Brady, Rita Gam, Neville Brand, Lori Nelson, Allison Hayes, John Hoyt, Vera Vague, Rhys Williams, Ted de Corsia, Mae Clark, John Hudson, Tommy Cook, Michael Granger, James Lilburn, Chabon Jadi

Set in the Mohawk Valley in pre-Revolutionary War times. A Boston artist (Scott Brady), assigned by the Massachusetts Society to paint pictures of landscapes and Indians, becomes involved in war between the Indians and the settlers when a greedy landowner (John Hoyt) sets the factions against each other by killing the son of a chief. The artist proves his courage by eliminating a fierce warrior (Neville Brand) and afterwards settles down to frontier life with a lovely Boston girl (Lori Nelson). A good eastern Western, with colorfully staged action sequences.

ON THE THRESHOLD OF SPACE

Produced by William Bloom
Directed by Robert Webb
Screenplay by Simon Wincelberg and Francis Cockrell

Robert Flemyng and Clifton Webb in *The Man Who Never Was.*

279

Photographed in CinemaScope and De Luxe Color by
Joe MacDonald
Music by Lyn Murray
96 minutes

Cast: Guy Madison, Virginia Leith, John Hodiak, Dean Jagger, Warren Stevens, Martin Milner, King Calder, Walter Coy, Ken Clark, Donald Murphy, Barry Coe, Richard Grant, Donald Freed, Ben Wright, Carlyle Mitchell, Robert Cornwaithe

Based upon actual research done by the Air Force in the probable problems to be encountered by space travel, the film deals with a young doctor (Guy Madison) who makes himself a guinea pig in experimenting with stress and strain in the speed and pressures of outer space. His daring leads him to take a balloon higher than anyone has been before in order to discover how the body will react. Filmed at Air Force bases in Florida and New Mexico, the picture presents fascinating information about aero-medical programs.

THE PROUD ONES

Produced by Robert L. Jacks
Directed by Robert D. Webb
Screenplay by Edmund North and Joseph Petracca, based on a novel by Verne Athanas
Photographed in CinemaScope and De Luxe Color by Lucien Ballard
Music by Lionel Newman
94 minutes

Cast: Robert Ryan, Virginia Mayo, Jeffrey Hunter, Robert Middleton, Walter Brennan, Arthur O'Connell, Ken Clark, Rodolfo Acosta, George Mathews, Fay Roope, Edward Platt, Whit Bissell, Paul Burns, Richard Deacon, Frank Gerstle

The marshall (Robert Ryan) of Flat Rock, Kansas, prepares for trouble as the first trail herd from Texas is expected. His two chief worries are a cowboy (Jeffrey Hunter), whose father the marshall killed in the line of duty, and a saloon owner (Robert Middleton), who tries to have the lawman relieved of his job in order for the town to be wide open for wild business. The young cowboy learns that his father was killed fairly and joins the marshall in controlling the town. A solid Western, with a good performance from Ryan as the uncompromising marshall.

QUEEN OF BABYLON

Produced by Nat Wachsberger
Directed by Carlo Ludovico Bragaglia
Screenplay by C. L. Bragaglia, S. Continenza, E. De Concini, and G. Mangioni, based on a story by Maria Bory
Photographed in Technicolor by Gabor Pogany
Music by Renzo Rosselini
98 minutes

Cast: Rhonda Fleming, Ricardo Montalban, Roldano Lupi, Carlo Ninchi, Tamara Lees

An Italian production. A lavishly costumed action epic set in Babylon eight centuries before Christ and concerning the campaign of a rebel leader (Ricardo Montalban) to overthrow a corrupt king (Roldano Lupi). He falls in love with a beautiful peasant girl (Rhonda Fleming), who becomes a favorite of the king and who becomes a suspect when the king is poisoned. The killer is the king's conniving advisor (Carlo Ninchi), whose schemes are ended by the rebel leader. Colorful nonsense, but with the beautiful Fleming a definite asset.

THE REVOLT OF MAMIE STOVER

Produced by Buddy Adler
Directed by Raoul Walsh
Screenplay by Sydney Boehm, based on the novel by William Bradford Huie
Photographed in CinemaScope and De Luxe Color by Leo Tover
Music by Hugo Friedhofer
93 minutes

Cast: Jane Russell, Richard Egan, Joan Leslie, Agnes Moorehead, Jorja Curtright, Michael Pate, Richard Coogan, Alan Reed, Eddie Firestone, Jean Willes, Leon Lontok, Kathy Marlowe, Margia Dean, Jack Mather, Boyd "Red" Morgan, John Halloran

The true story of a Honolulu prostitute and madam, but watered down to meet the restrictions of 1956 censorship. Mamie Stovie (Jane Russell) is forced out of San Francisco by the police as an undesirable character and on the boat to Hawaii meets an author (Richard Egan) who sympathizes with her desire to make money but advises her to avoid the dance halls of Honolulu. But Mamie sees this as her only way to acquire wealth and becomes an attraction of the town's nightlife. With the coming of war and the flooding of the islands with servicemen she builds up her wealth with the purchase of land. She believes that her success will bring her the love of the respected novelist, but it does not. Mamie gives away her money and returns to her hometown in Mississippi. The film presents an interesting view of certain aspects of Hawaiian life, but the censorship takes away its impact.

STAGECOACH TO FURY

Produced by Earle Lyon
Directed by William Claxton
Screenplay by Eric Norden, based on a story by Eric Norden and Earle Lyon
Photographed in RegalScope by Walter Strenge
Music by Paul Dunlap
75 minutes

Cast: Forrest Tucker, Mari Blanchard, Wallace Ford,

Margia Dean, Rudolfo Hoyos, Paul Fix, Rico Alaniz, Wright King, Ian MacDonald, William Phillips, Ellen Corby, Alex Montoya, Rayford Barnes, Norman Leavitt, Steven Geray

A stagecoach is held up by Mexican bandits at a relay station and the passengers become prisoners until the arrival of a gold shipment due for transfer to the stage. As they wait, the film flashes back to the past lives of several of the passengers and reveals their characters and their ability to face the present crisis. One of them, a cavalry captain (Forrest Tucker), organizes the others into a successful attempt to outwit the bandits and save the gold.

TEENAGE REBEL

Produced by Charles Brackett
Directed by Edmund Goulding
Screenplay by Walter Reisch and Charles Brackett, based on the play by Edith Sommer
Photographed in CinemaScope by Joe MacDonald
Music by Leigh Harline
94 minutes

Cast: Ginger Rogers, Michael Rennie, Mildred Natwick, Rusty Swope, Lili Gentle, Louise Beavers, Irene Hervey, John Stephenson, Betty Lou Keim, Warren Berlinger, Diane Jergens, Susan Luckey, James O'Rear, Gary Gray, Pattee Chapman, Wade Dumas, Richard Collier

The story of a fifteen-year-old girl (Betty Lou Keim), who is reunited with her mother (Ginger Rogers) after eight years with the divorced father. The girl has received little love from anyone and resents her mother and the man (Michael Rennie) who is now her husband. The couple have a small son (Rusty Swope) and he, along with several neighborhood kids, gradually manage to break through the girl's surly exterior. It takes time for the girl to realize she has come into a home where she is loved and wanted, but she finally gets the message. The film is a good depiction of teenage problems and the need for the virtues of good family life.

23 PACES TO BAKER STREET

Produced by Henry Ephron
Directed by Henry Hathaway
Screenplay by Nigel Balchin, based on the novel by Philip MacDonald
Photographed in CinemaScope and De Luxe Color by Milton Krasner
Music by Leigh Harline
103 minutes

Cast: Van Johnson, Vera Miles, Cecil Parker, Patricia Laffan, Maurice Denham, Estelle Winwood, Liam Redmond, Isobel Elsom, Martin Benson, Natalie Norwick, Terrence de Marney, Queenie Leonard, Charles Keane, Lucie Lancaster, A. Cameron Grant

The title refers to the distance from the front door of the London home of a blind writer (Van Johnson) to the street on which he lives. He overhears a conversation which reveals an intent to kidnap, but when he tells the police about it they politely decline belief. His friends humor him, but he feels so strongly about the case that he sets out to solve it himself with the aid of his fiancée (Vera Miles). He ends up grappling with the kidnapper in a dark alley and almost losing his life. A fine suspense story, made the more interesting by the clever use of London locations and Johnson's performance as the blind man struggling with the almost impossible problem of unraveling a crime he cannot see and tormented by the frustrations imposed by the lack of sight.

20TH CENTURY-FOX ACADEMY AWARDS FOR 1956

YUL BRYNNER: Best actor, *The King and I.*

INGRID BERGMAN: Best actress, *Anastasia.*

LYLE R. WHEELER and JOHN DE CUIR: Best art direction, color, *The King and I.*

WALTER M. SCOTT and PAUL S. FOX: Best set decoration, color, *The King and I.*

IRENE SHARAFF: Best costume design, color, *The King and I.*

CARL FAULKNER and 20TH CENTURY-FOX SOUND DEPARTMENT: Best sound recording, *The King and I.*

ALFRED NEWMAN and KEN DARBY: Best scoring of a musical, *The King and I.*

Richard Egan and Jane Russell in *The Revolt of Mamie Stover.*

Ginger Rogers and Betty Lou Keim in *Teenage Rebel.*

1957

THE ABDUCTORS

Produced by Ray Wander
Directed by Andrew V. McLaglen
Screenplay by Ray Wander
Photographed in RegalScope by Joseph La Shelle
Music by Paul Glass
Musical direction by Ingolf Dahl
80 minutes

Cast: Victor McLaglen, George Macready, Fay Spain, Carl Thayer, Gavin Muir, John Morley, Carlyle Mitchell, George Cisar, Jason Johnson, Pat Lawless, James Logan

A released convict (Victor McLaglen) in 1876 tries to arrange for the escape of a jailed counterfeiter, who can provide $100,000 in payment when freed, plus the plates of almost perfect replicas. With the aid of a colleague (George Macready) he abducts the daughter (Fay Spain) of the warden, but the scheme goes awry. They then think of another ruse—to steal the body of Abraham Lincoln from its tomb in Springfield. But one of their associates (Gavin Muir), when drunk, lets slip information about their intentions and the Secret Service nabs them in the act. A good yarn, based on fact.

THE ABOMINABLE SNOWMAN OF THE HIMALAYAS

Produced by Aubrey Baring
Directed by Val Guest
Screenplay from a story by Nigel Kneal
Photographed in RegalScope by Arthur Grant
Music by Humphrey Searle
Musical direction by John Hollingsworth
83 minutes

Cast: Forrest Tucker, Peter Cushing, Maureen Connell, Richard Wattis, Robert Brown, Michael Brill, Wolfe Morris, Arnold Marle, Anthony Chin

An American adventurer (Forrest Tucker) and a British scientist (Peter Cushing) lead an expedition into the Himalayas in search of the legendary, huge, half-human beasts called Yetis, who leave their footprints but are seldom seen. They are warned by a mystical priest that it is death to look upon the Yetis,

but they proceed anyway. One by one the men meet their doom, with only the scientist surviving. A good horror adventure, with its mountain footage shot in the Pyrenees.

AN AFFAIR TO REMEMBER

Produced by Jerry Wald
Directed by Leo McCarey
Screenplay by Delmer Daves and Leo McCarey, from a story by Leo McCarey and Mildred Cram
Photographed in CinemaScope and De Luxe Color by Milton Krasner
Songs by Harry Warren, Harold Adamson, and Leo McCarey
Music by Hugo Friedhofer
114 minutes

Cast: Cary Grant, Deborah Kerr, Richard Denning, Neva Patterson, Cathleen Nesbitt, Robert Q. Lewis, Charles Watts, Fortunio Bonanova, Matt Moore, Lewis Mercier, Geraldine Wall

Leo McCarey's remake of his 1939 *Love Affair,* with Cary Grant and Deborah Kerr playing the Charles Boyer and Irene Dunne roles of the lovers who meet while making an ocean voyage to Europe. Having fallen deeply in love, they test the love by agreeing to a six-months' separation, so that the wealthy man can try to prove his worth as a commercial artist. When she doesn't turn up at the meeting, he thinks she has changed her mind, when in fact she had been injured in an accident. They finally meet again through happenstance. The story works as well in the remake as the original, with winning performances by Grant and Kerr and fine melodies by Harry Warren, especially the title song.

APACHE WARRIOR

Produced by Plato Skouras
Directed by Elmo Williams
Screenplay by Carroll Young, Kurt Neumann, and Eric Norden, from a story by Carroll Young and Kurt Neumann
Photographed in RegalScope by John M. Nickolaus, Jr.
Music by Paul Dunlap
74 minutes

Cast: Keith Larsen, Jim Davis, Rodolfo Acosta, Eugenia Paul, John Milijan, Damian O'Flynn, George Keymas, Lane Bradford, Dehl Berti, Eddie Little, Michael Carr, Nick Thompson

An Indian scout known as the Apache Kid (Keith Larsen) helps the army round up his scattered brothers after the defeat of Geronimo but turns renegade when an actual brother is murdered by another Indian. Tribal law allows for revenge, but white law does not. A former colleague, a white scout (Jim Davis), is dispatched to bring him in but finally decides the Indian is within his rights and lets him go. Supposedly based on fact, the film ends with a note that the Apache Kid vanished and was never seen again.

APRIL LOVE

Produced by David Weisbart
Directed by Henry Levin
Screenplay by Winston Miller, based on a novel by
  George Agnew Chamberlain
Photographed in CinemaScope and De Luxe Color by
  Wilfred Cline
Songs by Paul Francis Webster and Sammy Fain
Musical direction by Cyril J. Mockridge and Lionel New-
  man
99 minutes

Cast: Pat Boone, Shirley Jones, Dolores Michaels, Arthur O'Connell, Matt Crowley, Jeanette Nolan, Brad Jackson

A remake of *Home in Indiana* (1944), with Pat Boone as the big city boy, with a slight theft record, who comes to the bluegrass country of Kentucky, and Shirley Jones as the local girl with whom he falls in love. At first doubtful about country life, the boy gradually changes his mind when he becomes interested in a certain horse and goes on to become a top league trotting driver. Filmed on the horse farms around Lexington, Kentucky, the film is a pleasant, bucolic musical, aided by a good title song by Fain and Webster, which turned out to be one of Boone's best-selling records.

BACK FROM THE DEAD

Produced by Robert Stabler
Directed by Charles Marquis Warren
Screenplay by Catherine Turney, based on a novel by
  Catherine Turney
Photographed in RegalScope by Ernest Haller
Music by Raoul Kraushaar
79 minutes

Cast: Peggie Castle, Arthur Franz, Marsha Hunt, Don Haggerty, Marianne Stewart, Otto Reichow, Helen Wallace, James Bell, Evelyn Scott, Jeanne Bates

The second wife (Peggy Castle) of a man (Arthur Franz) is victimized by the spirit of the dead first wife, who died because of her involvement with an evil sect of a local satanist (Otto Reichow). Together the wife's husband and sister (Marsha Hunt) fight the influence of the sect, whose activities include human sacrifice, and they break up a meeting in which a neighbor is set to die. The leader of the cult is shot by a jealous, rejected disciple (Marianne Stewart) and the wife is restored to mental health.

BADLANDS OF MONTANA

Produced and directed by Daniel B. Ullman
Screenplay by Daniel B. Ullman
Photographed in RegalScope by Frederick Gately
Music by Irving Gertz
75 minutes

Cast: Rex Reason, Margia Dean, Beverly Garland, Keith Larsen, Robert Cunningham, Emile Meyer, Russ Bender, Ralph Peters, Lee Tung Foo, Stanley Farrar, Rankin Mansfield, William Phippes, John Pickard

A candidate for mayor (Rex Reason) is run out of town when he is tricked into a gun fight in which he kills his opponent. He takes up with a gang of outlaws and takes part in robberies, during the course of which he is wounded and captured. Friends rescue him and bring him back to town, where he is elected sheriff. When the outlaw band attack the town, he cleans them up but persuades the daughter (Beverly Garland) of the leader (Emile Meyer) to come over to his side and marry him. A Western that draws a slim line between law and the lack of same.

BERNARDINE

Produced by Samuel G. Engel
Directed by Henry Levin
Screenplay by Theodore Reeves, based on a play by
  Mary Chase
Photographed in CinemaScope and De Luxe Color by
  Paul Vogel
Music by Lionel Newman
95 minutes

Cast: Pat Boone, Terry Moore, Janet Gaynor, Dean Jagger, Richard Sargent, James Drury, Ronnie Burns, Walter Abel, Natalie Schafer, Isabel Jewell, Edith Angold

The movie debut of Pat Boone, as one of a group of high school seniors who have invented a mythical girl called Bernardine, mostly to confuse telephone operators. One of the boys (Richard Sargent) falls in love with a new telephone operator (Terry Moore), but makes no move until he finishes his studies, by which time she has taken up with somebody else. He joins the army and when he returns to visit his friends half a year later, he's a wiser lad. The slight script is merely a framework for pleasant school antics and songs, and a little philosophizing about the pangs of young love.

BOY ON A DOLPHIN

Produced by Samuel G. Engel
Directed by Jean Negulesco
Screenplay by Ivan Moffat and Dwight Taylor, from a novel by David Divine
Photographed in CinemaScope and DeLuxe Color by Milton Krasner
Music by Hugo Friedhofer
Musical direction by Lionel Newman
112 minutes

Cast: Alan Ladd, Clifton Webb, Sophia Loren, Alexis Minotis, Jorge Mistral, Laurence Naismith, Piero Giagnoni, Gertrude Flynn

A visually handsome adventure story, shot among the Greek Islands and the Aegean Sea, with Sophia Loren as a Greek sponge diver who discovers a statue of a boy on a dolphin. She tells an English doctor (Laurence Naismith) about it and he realizes it is a vastly important, ancient treasure. He sends her to Athens to find a sponsor for the raising of the statue. She approaches an American archeologist (Alan Ladd), but he shows no interest, until a rich private collector (Clifton Webb) hires the girl and tries to gain the piece for his own collection. She switches her allegiance when she sees he means to keep it for himself, and the archeologist joins with her in claiming the statue for the glory of Greece. The film is a scenic delight and a great part of that scenic delight is Sophia Loren.

CHINA GATE

Produced and directed by Samuel Fuller
Screenplay by Samuel Fuller
Photographed in CinemaScope by Joseph Biroc
Song by Victor Young and Harold Adamson
Music by Victor Young and Max Steiner
93 minutes

Cast: Gene Barry, Angie Dickinson, Nat "King" Cole, Paul DuBov, Lee Van Cleef, George Givot, Gerald Milton, Neyle Morrow, Marcel Dalio, Maurice Marsac, Warren Hsieh

An American soldier of fortune (Gene Barry) in Indo-China—prior to the U.S. involvement in Vietnam—joins up with his estranged wife (Angie Dickinson), a Eurasian and political activist, to lead a party of guerrillas on an expedition to destroy a Chinese Communist ammunition dump. The trip is tough and tense, partly because of the love-hate relationship between the couple, but it ends in success, although the girl dies in the explosions. The film is a good adventure yarn, with Nat "King" Cole playing a world-weary soldier and singing the title song. Composer Victor Young died during production and his score was finished by his friend Max Steiner.

284

COPPER SKY

Produced by Robert Stabler
Directed by Charles Marquis Warren
Screenplay by Eric Norden, from a story by Robert Stabler
Photographed in RegalScope by Brydon Baker
Music by Raoul Kraushaar
77 minutes

Cast: Jeff Morrow, Coleen Gray, Strother Martin, Paul Brinegar, John Pickard, Pat O'Moore, Jack Lomas, Bill Hamel, Dorothy Schuyler

Apaches wipe out the residents of a small Western town, except for the sole resident (Jeff Morrow) of the jail. A Bostonian schoolteacher (Coleen Gray) arrives at the scene shortly after and the two set out for the nearest white settlement. The outlaw drinks a lot and the schoolteacher lectures him a lot, as they survive the trek across the desert.

COURAGE OF BLACK BEAUTY

Produced by Edward L. Alperson
Directed by Harold Schuster
Screenplay by Steve Fisher
Photographed in Pathé Color by John Snyder
Songs by Edward L. Alperson, Jr. and Paul Herrick and Dick Hughes and Richard Stapley
Music by Edward L. Alperson, Jr.
78 minutes

Cast: Johnny Crawford, Mimi Gibson, John Bryant, Diane Brewster, J. Pat O'Malley, Russell Johnson, Ziva Rodann

A film for horse lovers, about a boy (Johnny Crawford) living on a California ranch and feeling at odds with the world, especially with his widower father (John Bryant). Dad gives his son a foal, which grows up into a black beauty and gives the boy a focus in life. Together they survive several crises, including one in which it seems the horse will have to be destroyed, but pulls through, which results in a better relationship between the boy and his father.

THE DEERSLAYER

Produced and directed by Kurt Neumann
Screenplay by Carroll Young and Kurt Neumann, from the novel by James Fenimore Cooper
Photographed in CinemaScope and De Luxe Color by Karl Struss
Music by Paul Sawtell and Bert Shefter
76 minutes

Cast: Lex Barker, Rita Moreno, Forrest Tucker, Cathy O'Donnell, Jay C. Flippen, Carlos Rivas, John Halloran, Joseph Vitale, Rocky Shahan, Phil Schumacker, George Robotham, Carol Henry

A young white man (Lex Barker), reared by the Mohicans in pre-Colonial times, gets involved with an old trader (Jay C. Flippen) and his two daughters (Rita Moreno and Cathy O'Donnell), when he saves them from a Huron attack. The old man has been secretly Indian-hunting to sell their scalps for bounty. The Hurons capture the man and threaten his life unless he returns the scalps. Barker the Deerslayer fortunately arrives in time to save his life and see that the scalps are returned. A reworking of the James Fenimore Cooper classic.

DESK SET

Produced by Henry Ephron
Directed by Walter Lang
Screenplay by Phoebe and Henry Ephron, based on a
  play by Robert Fryer and Lawrence Carr
Photographed in De Luxe Color by Leon Shamroy
Music by Cyril J. Mockridge
103 minutes

Cast: Spencer Tracy, Katharine Hepburn, Gig Young, Joan Blondell, Dina Merrill, Sue Randall, Neva Patterson, Harry Ellerbe, Nicholas Joy, Diane Jergens, Merry Anders, Ida Moore, Rachel Stephens, Sammy Ogg

Into the office of a television network research expert (Katharine Hepburn) comes an esteemed efficiency expert (Spencer Tracy), with an assignment to modernize the department. This involves bringing in computers and other sophisticated mechanical devices. Since the lady in charge is conservative by nature as well as highly efficient, she resents the invader. It is a situation that can only produce sparks—of all kinds, including the eventual ones of love. With Tracy and Hepburn as its stars, *Desk Set* is a highly polished comedy and an excellent vehicle for its legendary players.

THE ENEMY BELOW

Produced and directed by Dick Powell
Screenplay by Wendell Mayes, based on a novel by
  D. A. Rayner
Photographed in CinemaScope and De Luxe Color by
  Harold Rosson
Music by Leigh Harline
Musical direction by Lionel Newman
97 minutes

Cast: Robert Mitchum, Curt Jurgens, Al Hedison, Theodore Bikel, Russell Collins, Kurt Krueger, Frank Albertson, Biff Elliot, Alan Dexter, Doug McClure, Jeff Daley, David Blair

An excellent account of naval warfare in the Atlantic in World War II, with Robert Mitchum as the captain of a U.S. destroyer and Curt Jurgens as the commander of a German U-boat. The film is basically a battle of wits between the two men, with the submarine trying to elude the pursuing destroyer, while also trying to get into a position to sink the American ship. The tense conflict ends in a draw—the two vessels fight it out on the surface and both sink. The two opposing officers finally meet after days of having played a deadly game of chess, and in respect they salute each other. *The Enemy Below* takes an impartial look at war, with both officers presented as civilized men doing a job, and the success of the film is a great credit to director-producer Dick Powell.

A FAREWELL TO ARMS

Produced by David O. Selznick
Directed by Charles Vidor
Screenplay by Ben Hecht, from the novel by Ernest
  Hemingway
Photographed in CinemaScope and De Luxe Color by
  Piero Portalupi and Oswald Morris
Music by Mario Nascimbene
152 minutes

Cast: Rock Hudson, Jennifer Jones, Vittorio de Sica, Alberto Sordi, Oscar Homolka, Mercedes McCambridge, Elaine Stritch, Kurt Kasznar, Victor Francen, Franco Interlengi, Leopoldo Trieste

The Hemingway love story was filmed in 1932 with Gary Cooper as the American serving with the Italian Army in the first World War and Helen Hayes as the nurse he loves. In this handsome David O. Selznick version, filmed in Italy, the lovers are Rock Hudson and Jennifer Jones. They are caught in the turmoil of the Italian front in the winter of 1917 and after realizing the madness and futility of the war they make their way to Switzerland, where her child is born dead and she dies a few hours later. The story is touching, but its highly personal nature is somewhat swamped by the great scope of the film. The winter mountains are awesome, as is the sight of long lines of retreating Italian soldiers making their way on the snowy slopes. Visually the film is magnificent.

FORTY GUNS

Produced and directed by Samuel Fuller
Screenplay by Samuel Fuller
Photographed in CinemaScope by Joseph Biroc
Music by Harry Sukman
85 minutes

Cast: Barbara Stanwyck, Barry Sullivan, Dean Jagger, John Ericson, Gene Barry, Eve Brent, Robert Dix, Jack "Jidge" Carroll, Paul Dubov, Gerald Milton, Ziva Rodann

The boss of Cochise County, Arizona, is a lady (Barbara Stanwyck) who rides around with her own army of forty armed men. Her command of the area around Tombstone is shaken by the appearance of a marshall (Barry Sullivan) and his two brothers. The marshall and the lady respect each other and become friendly, but the friendship is shattered by her willful, brawling young brother (John Ericson), who kills one of the marshall's brothers (Gene Barry), causing the marshall to gun down the young man. The lady retires from her aggressive local role and a degree of peacefulness falls over the territory. Writer-director-producer Samuel Fuller packs his Western with action and movement and makes it seem better than its plot.

GHOST DIVER

Produced by Richard Einfeld
Directed by Richard Einfeld and Merrill G. White
Screenplay by Richard Einfeld and Merrill G. White
Photographed in RegalScope by John M. Nickolaus, Jr.
Music by Paul Sawtell and Bert Shefter
76 minutes

Cast: James Craig, Audrey Totter, Nico Minardos, Lowell Brown, Rodolfo Hoyos, Jr., Pira Louis, George Trevino, Elena Da Vinci, Paul Stader

The star (James Craig) of a television adventure series promises his viewers he will find a long-lost treasure in South American waters, and takes with him his faithful, loving secretary (Audrey Totter) and his skin-diver son (Lowell Brown). Their dangerous forays into the depths are menaced by a local diver (Nico Minardos), who wants the treasure for himself. All the efforts end in vain, as an underwater earthquake seals off the treasure forever. But the star realizes he loves his secretary and the son brings home a lovely local girl (Pira Louis).

GOD IS MY PARTNER

Produced by Sam Hersh
Directed by William F. Claxton
Screenplay by Charles Francis Royal
Photographed in RegalScope by Walter Strenge
Music by Paul Dunlap
82 minutes

Cast: Walter Brennan, John Hoyt, Marion Ross, Jesse White, Nelton Leigh, Charles Lane, Ellen Corby, Paul Cavanaugh, Nancy Kulp, John Harmon, Charles Gray, Lyle Talbot

A respected surgeon (Walter Brennan) retires and starts to give away large portions of his savings to religious causes. His family launch a suit against him, declaring him incapable of handling his money. He is brought to trial and a niece (Marian Ross) acts as his defense attorney. Her witnesses persuade the judge that since the surgeon believes his skill and success came as the result of divine influence, he has the right to donate his money as he sees fit.

A HATFUL OF RAIN

Produced by Buddy Adler
Directed by Fred Zinnemann
Screenplay by Michael V. Gazzo and Alfred Hayes, based on the play by Michael V. Gazzo
Photographed in CinemaScope by Joe MacDonald
Music by Bernard Herrmann
108 minutes

Cast: Eva Marie Saint, Don Murray, Anthony Franciosa, Lloyd Nolan, Henry Silva, Gerald O'Laughlin, William Hickey, Albert Dannibal

One of Hollywood's first major films on the subject of drug addiction, and a sensitive, compassionate account. A young man (Don Murray) becomes hooked on narcotics and tries to keep the fact from his pregnant wife (Eva Marie Saint). His sympathetic brother (Anthony Franciosa) gives him money, but the debts pile up and a pusher (Henry Silva) starts to pressure the addict. His father (Lloyd Nolan), who left both sons in an orphanage when they were young, tries to help, but the situation is beyond his understanding. The addict attempts to keep up a normal front, but he takes a step toward cure when he finally admits to himself, his wife, and his family that he is indeed a junkie and needs outside help. Don Murray's performance is heart-rending, and the direction of Fred Zinnemann gives the film taste as well as poignancy.

HEAVEN KNOWS, MR. ALLISON

Produced by Buddy Adler and Eugene Frenke
Directed by John Huston
Screenplay by John Lee Mahin and John Huston, based on a novel by Charles Shaw
Photographed in CinemaScope and De Luxe Color by Oswald Morris
Music by Georges Auric
Musical direction by Lambert Williamson
106 minutes

Cast: Deborah Kerr, Robert Mitchum

A Roman Catholic nun (Deborah Kerr) and a tough Marine sergeant (Robert Mitchum) become isolated on a South Pacific island swarming with Japanese troops in the second World War. They hide together in a cave and although the Marine treats her with respect, he cannot help but fall in love with the attractive woman. She is compassionate, but gently explains that her life is dedicated to her faith and that she cannot return his affection. Before the two are rescued by the American landing forces, they have shared some hardships and dangers together, plus some amusement over common problems, but with never any impropriety. The adventure, beautifully filmed in the West Indies, is a touching story of unrequited love and an expert acting duet by Kerr and Mitchum.

HELL ON DEVIL'S ISLAND

Produced by Leon Chooluck and Laurence Stewart
Directed by Christian Nyby
Screenplay by Steven Ritch, from a story by Armand and Ethel Giusti
Photographed in RegalScope by Ernest Haller
Music by Irving Gertz
73 minutes

Cast: Helmut Dantine, William Talman, Donna Martell, Jean Willes, Rex Ingram, Jay Adler, Peter Adams, Edward Colmans, Mel Wells, Charles Bohbot

A convict (Helmut Dantine) is released from Devil's Island after eight years and, as a former journalist, aids the new governor of the French colony in his aim to abolish the infamous prison. The convict also investigates a local plantation and finds it is being manned by convicts who never return to the prison. The overseer of the prison (William Talman) is in league with the owners of the plantation, who are actually operating a gold mine and illegally shipping out their finds. The convict puts an end to the operation and wins the love of the governor's daughter (Donna Martell) in the process.

ISLAND IN THE SUN

Produced by Darryl F. Zanuck
Directed by Robert Rossen
Screenplay by Alfred Hayes, from the novel by Alec Waugh
Photographed in CinemaScope and De Luxe Color by F. A. Young
Music by Malcolm Arnold
120 minutes

Cast: James Mason, Joan Fontaine, Dorothy Dandridge, Joan Collins, Michael Rennie, Harry Belafonte, Diana Wynyard, John Williams, Stephen Boyd, Patricia Owens, Basil Sydney

For his first film as an independent producer releasing through 20th Century-Fox, Darryl F. Zanuck chose a spicy story of interracial love on a West Indian island. The head (James Mason) of a ruling family murders a gentlemanly English drifter (Michael Rennie) who, he believes, is having an affair with his wife (Patricia Owens). He is thereafter doggedly pursued by a police inspector (John Williams) until the suspect gives in. In the meantime, his sister-in-law almost has an affair with a handsome leader (Harry Belafonte) of the black community, who finally decides it wouldn't be good for his political future, while the governor's aide-de-camp (John Justin) resigns his commission and marries the black girl (Dorothy Dandridge) he loves. The daring (for 1957) love themes still retain their spark and the performances are fine, although it's Freddie Young's photography of the tropical paradise that really dominates the film.

Pat Boone and Richard Sargent in *Bernardine*.

Cary Grant and Deborah Kerr in *An Affair to Remember*.

Shirley Jones and Pat Boone in *April Love*.

Sophia Loren and Alan Ladd in *Boy on a Dolphin*.

Spencer Tracy and Katharine Hepburn in *Desk Set*.

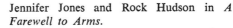

Jennifer Jones and Rock Hudson in *A Farewell to Arms*.

Robert Mitchum in *The Enemy Below*.

Eva Marie Saint and Don Murray in *A Hatful of Rain*.

KISS THEM FOR ME

Produced by Jerry Wald
Directed by Stanley Donen
Screenplay by Julius Epstein, based on the play by Luther Davis, from a novel by Frederic Wakeman
Photographed in CinemaScope and De Luxe Color by Milton Krasner
Music by Lionel Newman
103 minutes

Cast: Cary Grant, Jayne Mansfield, Suzy Parker, Leif Erickson, Ray Walston, Larry Blyden, Nathaniel Frey, Werner Klemperer, Jack Mullaney, Ben Wright, Michael Ross

Three World War II naval officers, headed by a decorated flier (Cary Grant), arrive in San Francisco for a well-deserved leave and take a suite at the Mark Hopkins Hotel. Their purpose is to have a long party and invite everyone. Among the guests is a voluptuous girl (Jayne Mansfield) whose war effort consists of being friendly to all servicemen, and a cool, elegant socialite (Suzy Parker), who is thawed out by the flier. The film is basically a party, but it gets in a few digs at people who profit on the home front, and Grant gives it a touch of class it would not otherwise have.

KRONOS

Produced and directed by Kurt Neumann
Screenplay by Lawrence Louis Goldman, from a story by Irving Block
Photographed in RegalScope by Kurt Struss
Music by Paul Sawtell and Bert Shefter
78 minutes

Cast: Jeff Morrow, Barbara Lawrence, John Emery, George O'Hanlon, Morris Ankrum, Kenneth Alton, John Parrish, José Gonzales-Gonzales, Richard Harrison, Marjorie Stapp

An accumulator, a huge metal monster from another planet, arrives on earth to capture energy and resources. It is directed by a top U.S. scientist (John Emery) whose brain has been seized and controlled by the other planet. A fellow scientist (Jeff Morrow), an expert on interplanetary forces, tracks the monster, named Kronos, after an evil Greek god, and ultimately brings about its destruction.

LURE OF THE SWAMP

Produced by Sam Hersh
Directed by Hubert Cornfield
Screenplay by William George, from a novel by Gil Brewer
Photographed in RegalScope by Walter Strenge
Music by Paul Dunlap
75 minutes

Cast: Marshall Thompson, Willard Parker, Joan Vohs, Jack Elam, Leo Gordon, Joan Lora, James Maloney

A Florida swamp guide (Marshall Thompson) is hired by a man (Willard Parker) who is a bank robber with a large sum he wants to secret in the swamp. Later, three of his cohorts turn up and vie with the guard in trying to find the spot where the robber, since killed by them, has hidden the money. In the ensuing search, the guide is wounded, the cohorts all die in the swamp, and the money sinks into the quicksands, gone forever.

NO DOWN PAYMENT

Produced by Jerry Wald
Directed by Martin Ritt
Screenplay by Philip Yordan, from a novel by John McPartland
Photographed in CinemaScope by Joseph La Shelle
Music by Leigh Harline
Musical direction by Lionel Newman
102 minutes

Cast: Joanne Woodward, Sheree North, Tony Randall, Jeffrey Hunter, Cameron Mitchell, Patricia Owen, Barbara Rush, Pat Hingle, Robert Harris, Aki Aleong, Jim Hayward

A study of a slice of suburbia called Sunrise Hills, a new upper-working-class tract, and four of its couples. They struggle to keep up with each other in their "on credit" paradise and try to hide their personal strains. One man (Cameron Mitchell) has a yen for the wife (Patricia Owens) of a neighbor (Jeffrey Hunter) and finally rapes her, which brings on a fight with the husband in which the rapist is killed. Another neighbor (Tony Randall) is a glib car salesman vainly hoping to make easy money, with a wife (Sheree North) who quietly stands by him. Another (Pat Hingle) fights against popular sentiment for the rights of a Japanese who wants to move into the area. And so on. The film is fairly candid by 1957 standards, but subsequent accounts of suburbia make it dated.

OH MEN! OH WOMEN!

Produced and directed by Nunnally Johnson
Screenplay by Nunnally Johnson, from the play by Edward Chodorov
Photographed in CinemaScope and De Luxe Color by Charles G. Clarke
Music by Cyril J. Mockridge
89 minutes

Cast: Dan Dailey, Ginger Rogers, David Niven, Barbara Rush, Tony Randall, Natalie Schafer, Rachel Stephens, John Wengraf, Cheryll Clarke, Charles Davis, Roy Glenn

A spoof on psychiatry, with David Niven as an analyst who has become intimidated by his own rationales.

His problems and those of his patients are seemingly all concerned with love, especially one (Tony Randall) whose affair with a madcap girl (Barbara Rush) has driven him almost around the bend. But this same girl is also engaged to the psychiatrist! Another patient (Ginger Rogers) suffers because her husband (Dan Dailey) is passive at home, though he has the image of a great lover in his work as an actor. The doctor prevails upon him to spread a little of the image around the home front, although the poor doctor is shaken to learn that the actor has also known his intended wife. The film is veritably a contemporary version of a Moliere comedy of manners.

PEYTON PLACE

Produced by Jerry Wald
Directed by Mark Robson
Screenplay by John Michael Hayes, from the novel by Grace Metalious
Photographed in CinemaScope and De Luxe Color by William Mellor
Music by Franz Waxman
157 minutes

Cast: Lana Turner, Hope Lange, Lee Philips, Lloyd Nolan, Diane Varsi, Arthur Kennedy, Russ Tamblyn, Terry Moore, David Nelson, Barry Coe, Betty Field, Mildred Dunnock, Leon Ames

Life, particularly love life, in a small New England town (filmed in Camden, Main) and an improvement on the book. The film avoids the trashy approach and presents its people in a compassionate light. Among the people: a shop owner (Lana Turner) bitter about a past love that produced an illegitimate daughter (Diane Varsi) but who cannot resist the attentions of the school principal (Lee Philips); a mother's boy (Russ Tamblyn) who is loved and given strength by the shop owner's daughter; and a girl (Hope Lange) who is raped by her stepfather (Arthur Kennedy) and kills him. Her trial, at which she is acquitted, helps bring the townspeople together. The photography of the town and its setting, and a beautifully sympathetic music score by Franz Waxman, make *Peyton Place* a gem of a romantic melodrama.

PLUNDER ROAD

Produced by Leo Chooluck and Laurence Stewart
Directed by Hubert Cornfield
Screenplay by Steven Ritch, from a story by Jack Charney and Steven Ritch
Photographed in RegalScope by Ernest Haller
Music by Irving Gertz
82 minutes

Cast: Gene Raymond, Jeanne Cooper, Wayne Morris, Elisha Cook, Jr., Stafford Repp, Steven Ritch, Nora Hayden, Helene Heigh, Harry Tyler, Paul Harber, Don Garrett, Michael Fox

A group of robbers, headed by a mastermind (Gene Raymond), hold up a U.S. Mint train and get away with a large gold shipment. They split into three groups, each with a truck. Two of the trucks are intercepted by police, but the other gets to Los Angeles, where the mastermind melts the gold into fittings for a Cadillac. When the car becomes involved in an accident on the freeway, the ruse is detected and the mastermind is killed trying to get away. *Plunder Road*, well scripted, acted and directed, is among the very best of all Grade-B crime pictures.

THE QUIET GUN

Produced by Earle Lyon
Directed by William Claxton
Screenplay by Eric Norden
Photographed in RegalScope by John Mescall
Music by Paul Dunlap
77 minutes

Cast: Forrest Tucker, Mara Corday, Jim Davis, Kathleen Crowley, Lee Van Cleef, Tom Brown, Lewis Martin, Hank Worden, Gerald Milton

An unusual Western, about a sheriff (Forrest Tucker) who is called upon to investigate charges that a rancher friend (Jim Davis) is carrying on with an Indian girl (Mara Corday) while his wife (Kathleen Crowley) is out of town. The scandal leads to the rancher killing the town attorney (Lewis Martin) and being lynched by the townspeople. Later he finds that two men, a saloon owner (Tom Brown) and a cohort (Lee Van Cleef) triggered the nasty affair in order to gain the rancher's property. In facing the sheriff, both men end up dead in the street.

THE RESTLESS BREED

Produced by Edward L. Alperson
Directed by Allan Dwan
Screenplay by Steve Fisher
Photographed in Eastman Color by John W. Boyle
Music by Edward L. Alperson, Jr.
Musical direction by Raoul Kraushaar
85 minutes

Cast: Scott Brady, Anne Bancroft, Jay C. Flippen, Jim Davis, Rhys Williams, Leo Gordon, Scott Marlowe, Eddy Waller, Harry Cheshire, Myron Healey, Gerald Milton, Dennis King, Jr.

A young man (Scott Brady) turns up in a tough Texas border town to avenge the killing of his agent father by gun runners. The leader of the smugglers (Jim Davis) resides on the Mexican side and when his men fail to get rid of the young man, he accepts the challenge for a showdown, which ends his career. A good, taut Western directed by the veteran Allan Dwan and notable for the acting of young Anne Bancroft as the half-breed Indian girl who wins the hero.

RIDE A VIOLENT MILE

Produced by Robert Stabler
Directed by Charles Marquis Warren
Screenplay by Eric Norden, from a story by Charles
  Marquis Warren
Photographed in RegalScope by Brydon Baker
Music by Raoul Kraushaar
80 minutes

Cast: John Agar, Penny Edwards, John Pickard, Bing
Russell, Richard Shannon, Charles Gray, Sheb Wooley,
Rush Williams, Richard Gilden, Rocky Shahan

Civil War espionage in the West, with Penny Edwards
as a Union agent, posing as a dance hall girl, who inter-
cepts a Confederate scheme to exchange a shipment
of cattle for Mexican help against the Union. With
the help of a boyfriend (John Agar) she scatters the
cattle and cleans up the Southerners. A not very convincing account.

THE RIVER'S EDGE

Produced by Benedict Bogeaus
Directed by Allan Dwan
Screenplay by Harold Jacob Smith and James Leicester,
  based on a novel by Harold Jacob Smith
Photographed in CinemaScope and De Luxe Color by
  Harold Lipstein
Music by Louis Forbes
87 minutes

Cast: Ray Milland, Anthony Quinn, Debra Paget, Harry
Carey, Jr., Chubby Johnson, Byron K. Foulger, Tom
McKee, Frank Gerstle

A thief (Ray Milland) turns up at the home of his
ex-girl friend and partner-in-crime (Debra Paget), who
is now married to a rancher (Anthony Quinn). He
hires them to get him into Mexico with the large sum
of money he has collected from his thefts. Although
he tempts her with the money, she realizes his selfish-
ness and cruelty, and the worth of her husband. Their
grueling trek across the mountains ends with the thief
falling to his death and his money scattered to the
winds, and with the couple surrendering to the police
and admitting their involvement. A good crime adventure, well shot on Mexican locations.

ROCKABILLY BABY

Produced and directed by William F. Claxton
Screenplay by Will George and William Driskill
Photographed in RegalScope by Walter Strenge
Music by Paul Dunlap
81 minutes

Cast: Virginia Field, Douglas Kennedy, Les Brown and
his Band of Renown, Irene Ryan, Ellen Corby, Lewis
Martin, Judy Busch, Marlene Willis, Gary Vinson, Norman Levitt

A lightweight musical about a former fan dancer
(Virginia Field), who moves to a small Virginia town
with her son (Gary Vinson) and daughter (Judy
Busch) to make a new life. She becomes a respected
member of the community and is romanced by the
school principal (Douglas Kennedy). Both children
do well in school. When they become friends with
the town's social leader (Ellen Corby), another socialite (Irene Ryan), acting in jealousy, finds out about
the dancer's past and exposes her. But by then the
townspeople like her so much, they don't care.

SEA WIFE

Produced by Andre Hakim
Directed by Bob McNaught
Screenplay by George K. Burke, from the novel by
  J. M. Scott
Photographed in CinemaScope and DeLuxe Color by
  Ted Schaif
Music by Kenneth V. Jones and Leonard Salzedo
81 minutes

Cast: Joan Collins, Richard Burton, Basil Sydney, Cy
Grant, Ronald Squire, Harold Goodwin, Roddy Hughes,
Gib McLaughlin, Lloyd Lamble, Ronald Adam, Nicholas
Hannen

Following the British evacuation of Singapore in 1942,
a freighter packed with refugees is sunk and four
survivors find themselves adrift in the Indian Ocean:
an RAF officer (Richard Burton), an ill-mannered
business tycoon (Basil Sydney), a black purser (Cy
Grant), and a young nun (Joan Collins), who doesn't
reveal herself because of the tycoon's harsh atheism.
After the long ordeal of exposure, and the death of
the purser to a shark, the three are picked up and
taken to England. The officer by this time is deeply in
love with the girl, who has not encouraged him and
allowed only that she is committed to someone else.
In London he searches for her in vain. He does in fact
see her, but she is dressed in full regalia and he doesn't
recognize her. A truly unrequited love story.

SHE DEVIL

Produced and directed by Kurt Neumann
Screenplay by Carrol Young and Kurt Neumann, from
  a story by John Jessel
Photographed in RegalScope by Karl Struss
Music by Paul Sawtell and Bert Shefter
77 minutes

Cast: Mari Blanchard, Jack Kelly, Albert Dekker, John
Archer, Fay Baker, Blossom Rock, Paul Cavanagh,
George Baxter, Helen Jay, Joan Bradshaw, X Brands,
Tod Griffin

An incredible science fiction tale, about a doctor (Jack
Kelly) who invents a serum that cures illness and a
girl (Mari Blanchard) dying of tuberculosis who

agrees to be a guinea pig. She not only becomes well and strong, but she develops strange characteristics and a scheming personality. She kills a woman in order to marry the wealthy husband (John Archer) and later kills him to gain his wealth. By this time the doctor and his superior (Albert Dekker) decide that something should be done. She is tricked into an operation and returned to her former dying, tubercular self.

SMILEY

Produced and directed by Anthony Kimmins
Screenplay by Moore Raymond and Anthony Kimmins
Photographed in CinemaScope and Technicolor by Ted Scaife
Music by William Alwyn
96 minutes

Cast: Sir Ralph Richardson, John McCallum, Colin Peterson, Bruce Archer, Jocelyn Hernfield, Peg Christensen, Reg Lye, Chips Rafferty, Gavin Davies, Charles Tingwell

An Australian boy called Smiley (Colin Peterson), the son of poor parents living in a small town in the Outback, teams up with a chum in order to get all the odd jobs they can, to save money to buy bicycles. Just when he has saved up enough, his father (Reg Lye), back from a long cattle drive, takes the money to make up for his own gambling losses. He survives the setback, just as he also survives getting inadvertantly mixed up with narcotics pushers when he accepts a delivery job. The film, shot entirely in Australia and making good use of the vast landscapes, is a charming Mark Twainish children's story, well acted, and with Ralph Richardson taking top billing for his portrayal of a warm-spirited parson.

STOPOVER TOKYO

Produced by Walter Reisch
Directed by Richard L. Breen
Screenplay by Richard L. Breen and Walter Reisch, from a novel by John P. Marquand
Photographed in CinemaScope and DeLuxe Color by Charles G. Clarke
Music by Paul Sawtell
100 minutes

Cast: Robert Wagner, Joan Collins, Edmond O'Brien, Ken Scott, Keiko Oyama, Larry Keating, Sarah Selby, K. J. Seijto, Solly Nakamura, Yuki Kaneko, Michei Miura

A U.S. intelligence agent (Robert Wagner) in Japan moves to block an attempt to assassinate the American ambassador (Larry Keating) and finds his job made harder by the fact that the ambassador doesn't believe in any such plot and refuses to cooperate. The plot is the work of an American communist (Edmond O'Brien), who intends to blow up the ambassador as he dedicates a peace monument. The agent manages to dispose of the bomb and foil the assassins, but he then meets disappointment when he finds the girl (Joan Collins) he has been romancing is not interested in being the wife of an espionage man and bids him goodbye. A superior film of its kind and made the more interesting because of the Japanese locations and associations.

THE STORM RIDER

Produced by Bernard Glasser
Directed by Edward Bernds
Screenplay by Edward Bernds and Don Martin, from a novel by L. L. Foreman
Photographed in RegalScope by Brydon Baker
Music by Les Baxter
72 minutes

Cast: Scott Brady, Mala Powers, Bill Williams, John Goddard, William Fawcett, Roy Engel, George Keymas, Olin Howlin, Bud Osborne, James Dobson, Rocky Lundy, Hank Patterson, Wayne Mallory

A former gunman (Scott Brady) for a ranchers' association is hired by a group of small ranchers to help them fend off a big rancher who wants their land. They are unaware that he killed their leader. The gunman falls in love with the widow (Mala Powers) and guns down a killer brought in by the big rancher, and thereby brings peace to the community. Despite his love for the widow, he rides away, knowing that the killing of the husband will always stand between them.

THE SUN ALSO RISES

Produced by Darryl F. Zanuck
Directed by Henry King
Screenplay by Peter Viertel, based on the novel by Ernest Hemingway
Photographed in CinemaScope and DeLuxe Color by Leo Tover
Music by Hugo Friedhofer
129 minutes

Cast: Tyrone Power, Ava Gardner, Mel Ferrer, Errol Flynn, Eddie Albert, Gregory Ratoff, Juliette Greco, Marcel Dalio, Henry Daniell, Bob Cunningham, Danik Patisson, Robert Evans, Eduardo Noriega, Jacqueline Evans, Carlos Muzquiz, Rebecca Iturbi, Carlos David Ostigos

The books of Ernest Hemingway have defied film-makers and *The Sun Also Rises* is no exception, although it is one of the better transfers. It benefits greatly from being filmed on locations like Paris and Biarritz and Mexico (doubling for Spain), but it is unconvincing as an account of Hemingway's lost generation of Americans living in Paris after the first World War, mostly because all the actors are too old to pass as youngsters. However, the casting of Errol Flynn as the gentlemanly roué Mike Campbell turned out to be the film's best feature and resulted in a rekindling of Flynn's faded career. He is genuinely touching and amusing, especially when he and Eddie Albert try to outrun the bulls of Pamplona. Sadly it would turn out to be the final 20th Century-Fox film for their veteran star Tyrone Power, who would die of a heart attack a year later at the age of forty-four.

THREE BRAVE MEN

Produced by Herbert B. Swope, Jr.
Directed by Philip Dunne
Screenplay Philip Dunne, based on the Pulitzer Prize articles by Charles G. Clarke
Photographed in CinemaScope by Charles G. Clarke
Music by Hans Salter
89 minutes

Cast: Ray Milland, Ernest Borgnine, Frank Lovejoy, Nina Foch, Dean Jagger, Virginia Christine, Edward Andrews, Frank Faylen, Diane Jergens, Warren Berlinger, Andrew Duggan

A veteran Navy Civil Service employee (Ernest Borgnine) is dismissed as a security risk. He is dumbfounded and hires a lawyer to help him clear himself. The lawyer (Ray Milland) finds that his client has in the past subscribed to a publication which was communist owned and that he had attended study groups which proved to be communist inspired. The lawyer balances this almost innocent flirtation with communism with the man's record as a loyal citizen and government worker. The Assistant Secretary of the Navy (Dean Jagger) agrees with the findings and the man is reinstated. An interesting peek into security problems.

THE THREE FACES OF EVE

Produced and directed by Nunnally Johnson
Screenplay by Nunnally Johnson, based on a book by Corbett H. Thigpen, M.D., and Hervey M. Cleckley, M.D.
Photographed in CinemaScope by Stanley Cortez
Music by Robert Emmett Dolan
95 minutes

Cast: Joanne Woodward, David Wayne, Lee J. Cobb, Edwin Jerome, Alena Murray, Nancy Kulp, Douglas Spencer, Terry Ann Ross, Ken Scott, Mimi Gibson

The true story of a young Georgia woman (Joanne Woodward) with a rare mental aberration—multiple personality. Basically she is an ordinary, withdrawn housewife, until she starts to have blackouts, during which she becomes two other completely different kinds of women. Her puzzled husband (David Wayne) takes her to a psychiatrist (Lee J. Cobb), who is intrigued with the case. The woman moves from her plain self to being a sexy, saucy girl, and then to being an intelligent, well balanced woman. Each guise is unrelated to the other. Through treatment, largely through hypnosis, the psychiatrist clears away the less favorable personalities and allows her to merge as a normal, mentally healthy woman. The film is of particular interest for psychologists, but the Oscar-winning performance of Woodward makes it universally understandable.

THE TRUE STORY OF JESSE JAMES

Produced by Herbert B. Swope, Jr.
Directed by Nicholas Ray
Screenplay by Walter Newman, based on a screenplay by Nunnally Johnson
Photographed in CinemaScope and DeLuxe Color by Joe MacDonald
Music by Leigh Harline
Musical direction by Lionel Newman
93 minutes

Cast: Robert Wagner, Jeffrey Hunter, Hope Lange, Agnes Moorehead, Alan Hale, Alan Baxter, John Carradine, Rachel Stephens, Barney Phillips, Biff Elliot, Frank Overton, Barry Atwater, Marion Seldes, Chubby Johnson

This version of the James story claims that the entry of Jesse (Robert Wagner) and Frank (Jeffrey Hunter) into the life of crime was due to the family being of Confederate persuasion and living among Union-sympathizing neighbors in post-Civil War Missouri. Hard put to find work, the boys tackle a robbery with the idea of getting enough money to leave, and then become addicted to the exciting life of robbing banks and trains. The film covers the eighteen years from the end of the war to Jesse's death at the hands of an assassin eager to pick up the $25,000 reward offered by the Remington Detective Agency. A good account, well paced by director Nicholas Ray and artfully using a few action clips from the 1939 version.

UNDER FIRE

Produced by Plato Skouras
Directed by James B. Clark
Screenplay by James Landis
Photographed in RegalScope by John M. Nickolaus, Jr.
Music by Paul Dunlap
76 minutes

Cast: Rex Reason, Henry Morgan, Steve Brodie, Peter Walker, Robert Levin, Jon Locke, Gregory LaFayette, Karl Lukas, William Allyn, Frank Gerstle, Tom McKee

Following World War II, four American soldiers are courtmartialed on a charge of killing a fellow soldier while on patrol in Germany and deserting. Their counsel (Rex Reason) probes until he finds that Germans dressed as Americans were responsible for the crime. The Americans are reluctant to tell their story

Joanne Woodward in *The Three Faces of Eve*.

Lana Turner and Diane Varsi in *Peyton Place*.

Jeffrey Hunter, Hope Lange, and Robert Wagner in *The True Story of Jesse James*.

Robert Mitchum and Deborah Kerr in *Heaven Knows, Mr. Allison*.

Harry Belafonte and Joan Fontaine in *Island in the Sun*.

Richard Burton and Joan Collins in *Sea Wife*.

Jayne Mansfield, Cary Grant, and Suzy Parker in *Kiss Them for Me*.

Ginger Rogers and Dan Dailey in *Oh, Men! Oh, Women!*

Ava Gardner and Tyrone Power in *The Sun Also Rises*.

293

1958

AMBUSH AT CIMARRON PASS

Produced by Herbert E. Mendelson
Directed by Jodie Copelan
Screenplay by Richard G. Taylor and John K. Butler, from a story by Roberts A. Reeds and Robert W. Woods
Photographed in RegalScope by John M. Nickolaus, Jr.
Music by Paul Sawtell and Bert Shefter
73 minutes

Cast: Scott Brady, Margia Dean, Clint Eastwood, Irving Bacon, Frank Gerstle, Dirk London, Baynes Barron, Ken Mayer, Keith Richards, William Vaughan, John Damler

A cavalry sergeant (Scott Brady) and a small troop take a prisoner to their fort through hostile Apache country. They come across a group of former Confederate soldiers and join forces, although bickering all the way. Indians drive off their horses and after seven days of walking, the handful of survivors turn up at the fort. A hard trek.

THE BARBARIAN AND THE GEISHA

Produced by Eugene Frenke
Directed by John Huston
Screenplay by Charles Grayson, based on a story by Ellis St. Joseph
Photographed in CinemaScope and DeLuxe Color by Charles G. Clarke
Music by Hugo Friedhofer
104 minutes

Cast: John Wayne, Eiko Ando, Sam Jaffe, Soh Yamamura, Norman Thomson, James Robbins, Morita, Kodaya Ichikawa

A true story, that of Townsend Harris, sent to Japan in 1856 as the first American consul. Harris (John Wayne) finds hostility as he takes up residence in the city of Shimoda and almost no interest on the part of the Japanese in the treaties offered by the United States. With great patience, and much waiting, he slowly wins the respect of local officials, who make it possible for him to proceed to Tokyo. A beautiful geisha (Eiko Ando), introduced into his residence to distract him from his mission, falls in love with him. She foils an attempt on his life and later leaves him so that she will not be a drawback in his negotiations

with her people. Beautifully staged and filmed but slowly paced and short on action, the film found little interest among the general public.

BLOOD ARROW

Produced by Robert W. Stabler
Directed by Charles Marquis Warren
Screenplay by Fred Freiberger
Photographed in RegalScope by Fleet Southcott
Music by Raoul Kraushaar
76 minutes

Cast: Scott Brady, Paul Richards, Phyllis Coates, Don Haggerty, Rock Shahan, Des Slattery, Bill McGraw, Patrick O'Moore, Jeanne Bates, Richard Gilden, John Dierkes, Diana Darrin

A Mormon girl (Phyllis Coates) transports smallpox serum through hostile Blackfoot country in order to save the remaining families in the valley where she lives. A scout (Scott Brady) decides to help her, as does a trapper (Don Haggerty), although a gambler (Paul Richards) joins the group only because he thinks there is gold in her valley. Despite the Indian attacks, they struggle through.

THE BRAVADOS

Produced by Herbert B. Swope, Jr.
Directed by Henry King
Screenplay by Philip Yordan, from the novel by Frank O'Rourke
Photographed in CinemaScope and DeLuxe Color by Leon Shamroy
Music by Lionel Newman
Musical direction by Bernard Kaun
99 minutes

Cast: Gregory Peck, Joan Collins, Stephen Boyd, Albert Salmi, Henry Silva, Kathleen Gallant, Barry Coe, George Voskovec, Herbert Rudley, Lee Van Cleef, Andrew Duggan, Ken Scott

A grim stranger (Gregory Peck) rides into a small Western town the night before the hanging of four outlaws. He has been on their trail for what he believes is the rape-murder of his wife. When the men escape from jail, he pursues them relentlessly. Coming across one of them, he kills him mercilessly, even though the man protests his innocence. He succeeds in overtaking and killing two others. The lone survivor (Henry Silva), makes his way home and when the pursuer turns up, he manages to convince him that neither he nor his comrades had anything to do with the crime. The avenger is now forced to face what he has done, that he has brutally taken the law into his own hands. Fortunately, he has a child to whom he can return and a former lady love (Joan Collins) with whom he can start a new life. A somber Western, handsomely directed by the veteran Henry King and sturdily played by Peck.

CATTLE EMPIRE

Produced by Robert Stabler
Directed by Charles Marquis Warren
Screenplay by Endre Bohem and Eric Norden, from a story by Daniel B. Ullman
Photographed in CinemaScope and DeLuxe Color by Brydon Baker
Music by Paul Sawtell and Bert Shefter
82 minutes

Cast: Joel McCrea, Gloria Talbott, Don Haggerty, Phyllis Coates, Bing Russell, Paul Brinegar, Hal K. Dawson, Duane Grey, Richard Shannon, Charles Gray, Patrick O'Moore

A trail boss (Joel McCrea) is released from prison— a term he served because his men shot up a town and killed some people—and is hired to drive cattle to a distant point. For his crew he chooses to hire a number of townspeople who have made life miserable for him because of the prior incident. The drive is hazardous but successful and his men learn that he is a tough but decent man. A better than average Western, thanks to the presence of McCrea and his aura of quiet authority.

A CERTAIN SMILE

Produced by Henry Ephron
Directed by Jean Negulesco
Screenplay by Frances Goodrich and Albert Hackett, from a novel by Francoise Sagan
Photographed in CinemaScope and DeLuxe Color by Milton Krasner
Music by Alfred Newman
Song by Sammy Fain and Paul Francis Webster
105 minutes

Cast: Rossano Brazzi, Joan Fontaine, Bradford Dillman, Christine Carere, Eduard Franz, Katherine Locke, Kathryn Givney, Steven Geray, Trude Wyler, Sandy Livingston

A young girl (Christine Carere) falls out with her boyfriend (Bradford Dillman) and accepts an invitation from his uncle (Rossano Brazzi) to spend a week on the Riviera. She accepts, even though she is ac-

quainted with his pleasant wife (Joan Fontaine). She becomes fascinated by the middle-aged lothario and follows him to Paris when he returns home. There she learns she is but one of the many romantic dalliances in his life and that his wife is understanding, although hurt. The Sagan comedy of sexual errors here gets a slick and glossy treatment, and is greatly aided by generous photography of Paris and the scenic attractions of the Riviera.

COUNT FIVE AND DIE

Produced by Ernest Gartside
Directed by Victor Vicas
Screenplay by Jack Seddon and David Pursall
Photographed in CinemaScope by Arthur Grant
Music by John Wooldridge
92 minutes

Cast: Jeffrey Hunter, Nigel Patrick, Annamarie Duringer, David Kossoff, Rolf Lefebvre, Larry Burns, Philip Bond, Beth Rogan

An Allied secret service unit in London during World War II operates a plan to fool the Germans into thinking that the invasion of Europe will take place through Holland. The head of the unit (Nigel Patrick) warns his American assistant (Jeffrey Hunter) that the Dutch agent (Annamarie Duringer) with whom he is smitten is actually a German agent. She kills the American when she is found out and is herself killed by her own people to prevent any leak of information about their side. An interesting espionage item, based on OSS files.

DESERT HELL

Produced by Robert W. Stabler
Directed by Charles Marquis Warren
Screenplay by Endre Bohem, from a story by Charles Marquis Warren
Photographed in RegalScope by John M. Nicholaus, Jr.
Music by Raoul Kraushaar
82 minutes

Cast: Brian Keith, Barbara Hale, Richard Denning, John Desmond, Phillip Pine, Richard Shannon, Duane Grey, Charles Gray, Lud Veigel, Richard Gilden, Ronald Foster, John Verros

Adventures with the French Foreign Legion in the Sahara, as they move to contain the Tuareg tribe and their intention to provoke a revolution. The captain (Brian Keith) of the company sent against the rebels is at odds with his lieutenant (John Desmond) because he found him in the arms of his wife (Barbara Hale) just before setting out on the mission. Their differences come to naught because they and all their men die in the successful attempt to quell the rebels.

DIAMOND SAFARI

Produced and directed by Gerald Mayer
Screenplay by Larry Marcus
Photographed by David Millin and Peter Lang
Music by Woolf Phillips
66 minutes

Cast: Kevin McCarthy, Andre Morrell, Betty McDowall, Bob Vice, Gert van den Berh, Patrick Simpson, John Clifford, Michael McNeile, Joel Herholdt

An American detective (Kevin McCarthy) living in Johannesburg takes on the job of investigating false murder charges made against a native and stumbles onto the activities of a diamond smuggling ring led by an American woman (Betty McDowall). Despite a sympathy between them, he is forced to turn her in. A slight story, but interesting because of the good use of South African backgrounds.

ESCAPE FROM RED ROCK

Produced by Bernard Glasser
Directed by Edward Bernds
Screenplay by Edward Bernds
Photographed in RegalScope by Brydon Baker
Music by Les Baxter
75 minutes

Cast: Brian Donlevy, Eilene Janssen, Gary Murray, Jay C. Flippen, William Phipps, Michael Healey, Nesdon Booth, Daniel White, Andre Adoree, Courtland Shepard, Tina Menard

A young ranchman (Gary Murray) is forced into involvement in a hold-up when an outlaw leader (Brian Donlevy) threatens to let his wounded brother die if he doesn't join in. The ranchman afterwards leaves town in the company of a girl (Eileen Janssen) and they get married in Mexico. They take refuge in a cabin and finds its occupants dead from an Apache attack, but that their small baby is alive. A posse sent to bring the ranchman in on a murder charge learn of his innocence and save the young couple from an Indian attack.

THE FIEND WHO WALKED THE WEST

Produced by Herbert B. Swope, Jr.
Directed by Gordon Douglas
Screenplay by Harry Brown and Philip Yordan, based on a story by Eleazar Lipsky
Photographed in CinemaScope by Joe MacDonald
Musical direction by Leon Klatzkin
103 minutes

Cast: Hugh O'Brian, Robert Evans, Dolores Michaels, Linda Cristal, Stephen McNally, June Blair, Edward Andrews, Ron Ely, Ken Scott, Emile Meyer, Gregory Morton, Shari Lee Bernath

A Western loosely based on *Kiss of Death*, with Robert Evans as a psychotic, sadistic killer, a la Richard Widmark. When first seen, he is in the same jail cell as a decent man (Hugh O'Brian), driven to robbery in desperate need, who confides in him information about a sum of money hidden with a cohort. When the psychotic is released, he goes after the cohort, kills him, gains the money, and torments his cellmate's wife (Linda Cristal). In an effort to capture him, the authorities arrange for the cellmate to escape, with the promise of a pardon if he is successful. The scheme works, after many brutal bits of byplay, and the fiend ends up dead on a barroom floor. The film lacks the credibility of the original, mostly because the Evans role, as written and played, is excessive.

THE FLY

Produced and directed by Kurt Neumann
Screenplay by James Clavell, from a story by George Langelaan
Photographed in CinemaScope and DeLuxe Color by Karl Struss
Music by Paul Sawtell
94 minutes

Cast: Al Hedison, Patricia Owens, Vincent Price, Herbert Marshall, Kathleen Freeman, Betty Lou Gerson, Charles Herbert, Eugene Borden, Torben Meyer

A science fiction masterpiece, about a research scientist (Al Hedison, who later changed his first name to David) who successfully devises a system for breaking matter into its atomic components and rematerializing it elsewhere. Flushed with his triumphs using guinea pigs, he decides to experiment on himself, not noticing that a fly has flown into his convergence chamber. As a result he emerges with the head of the fly and vice versa. He desperately tries to find the fly but as his intelligence sinks and he realizes there is no recourse, he asks his wife (Patricia Owens) to kill him, which she eventually does by crushing him in a giant press in an electronics plant, while the fly with the human head is devoured by a spider. The fantastic tale is given chilling credibility by its stylish treatment and retains its horrific impact. The film was produced as a "B" programmer but turned into the sleeper of the year for 20th Century-Fox.

FRAULEIN

Produced by Walter Reisch
Directed by Henry Koster
Screenplay by Leo Townsend, from a novel by James McGovern
Photographed in CinemaScope and DeLuxe Color by Leo Tover
Music by Daniele Amfitheatrof
100 minutes

Cast: Mel Ferrer, Dana Wynter, Dolores Michaels, Helmut Dantine, Theodore Bikel, Ivan Triesault, James Edwards, May Britt, Jack Kruschen, Luis Van Rooten, Trudy Wyler, Fred Essler, Edith Claire

The adventures of a German girl (Dana Wynter) in the last days of the second World War. A girl of gentle background, she helps an American officer (Mel Ferrer) to escape during an air raid. Later she is harassed by the Russians but manages to escape to the American sector, where she innocently registers herself as a prostitute. She meets the American officer, who falls in love with her. But her concern is with her wounded German fiancé (Helmut Dantine), until she realizes he no longer cares. Then, with the aid of a kindly corporal (James Edwards) who destroys the records that mark her as a prostitute, she is free to accept her American officer. Well shot on locations, the story benefits from the dignified performance of Dana Wynter.

FROM HELL TO TEXAS

Produced by Robert Buckner
Directed by Henry Hathaway
Screenplay by Robert Buckner and Wendell Mayes, from a book by Charles O. Locke
Photographed in CinemaScope and DeLuxe Color by Wilfrid M. Cline
Music by Daniele Amfitheatrof
99 minutes

Cast: Don Murray, Diane Varsi, Chill Wills, Dennis Hopper, R. G. Armstrong, Jay C. Flippen, Margo, John Larch, Ken Scott, Rodolfo Acosta, Salvador Baguez, Harry Carey, Jr.

An easy-going cowboy (Don Murray) accidentally kills a son of a powerful rancher (R. G. Armstrong) and is pursued as a murderer. They chase him across the wastes of New Mexico and the rancher becomes even more angry when a second son is trampled in a cattle stampede and several members of the posse die in the pursuit. The cowboy receives some help from a kindly rancher (Chill Wills) and his daughter (Diane Varsi), but the posse eventually catches up with him. The conflict comes to an end when the cowboy saves the life of the rancher's last surviving son (Dennis Hopper). An excellent Western, directed by a master hand: Henry Hathaway.

FRONTIER GUN

Produced by Richard E. Lyons
Directed by Paul Landres
Screenplay by Stephen Kandel
Photographed in Regalscope by Walter Strenge
Music by Paul Dunlap
70 minutes

Cast: John Agar, Joyce Meadows, Barton MacLane, Robert Strauss, Lyn Thomas, James Griffith, Morris Ankrum, Leslie Bradley, Doodles Weaver, Mike Ragan, Tom Daly, Sammy Ogg

A lawman (John Agar) takes on the job of town marshall when a terrorizing bad man (Robert Strauss) makes life miserable for everyone. He is slow on the draw, due to an early wrist injury, but when his father (Barton McLane) is killed by the bad man, he summons the determination to face him. Although twice shot, he takes careful aim and puts a bullet between the bad man's eyes.

GANG WAR

Produced by Harold E. Knox
Directed by Gene Fowler, Jr.
Screenplay by Louis Vittes, from a novel by Ovid Demaris
Photographed in RegalScope by John M. Nickolaus, Jr.
Music by Paul Dunlap
75 minutes

Cast: Charles Bronson, Kent Taylor, Jennifer Holden, John Doucette, Gloria Henry, Gloria Grey, Barney Phillips, Ralph Manza, George Eldredge, Billy Snyder, Lyn Guild, Jack Reynolds

A Los Angeles high school teacher (Charles Bronson) witnesses a gangland killing and although he wants nothing to do with it, he is forced into giving testimony. He is then harassed by the syndicate responsible for the killing and his wife (Gloria Henry) dies as a result of their assaults on his home. His cooperation with the police leads to the nabbing of the gang, but only after a series of chases and fights. An interesting item on the Bronson career, triggering the style that he would later develop, that of the quiet man forced into violence.

THE GIFT OF LOVE

Produced by Charles Brackett
Directed by Jean Negulesco
Screenplay by Luther Davis, from a story by Nelia Gardner White
Photographed in CinemaScope and DeLuxe Color by Milton Krasner
Music by Cyril J. Mockridge
Song by Sammy Fain and Paul Francis Webster
105 minutes

Cast: Lauren Bacall, Robert Stack, Evelyn Rudie, Lorne Greene, Anne Seymour, Edward Platt, Joseph Kearnes

A remake of *Sentimental Journey* (1946), with Lauren Bacall as the devoted, dying wife, who adopts a little girl (Evelyn Rudie), so that her husband (Robert Stack) will have someone to love him in the future. When the wife dies, the husband finds it hard to stand the child, who is a fantasist by nature while he is a physicist by trade. He returns her to the orphanage, but later, sensing she is in trouble, he rescues her from a fall into the ocean. He then realizes he wants the child with him and that she is in fact his wife's gift of love.

HARRY BLACK AND THE TIGER

Produced by John Brabourne
Directed by Hugo Fregonese
Screenplay by Sydney Boehm, from a book by David Walker
Photographed in CinemaScope and Technicolor by John Wilcox
Music by Clifton Parker
Musical direction by Muir Mathieson
106 minutes

Cast: Stewart Granger, Barbara Rush, Anthony Steel, Frank Olegario, Kamala Devi, Gladys Boot, George Curzon, Martin Stephens, I. S. Johar, John Helier, Tom Bowman, Harold Siddons, Allan McLelland

When a tiger causes several deaths in India, a famed hunter (Stewart Granger) is brought in to track and kill the animal. The hunter suffers from an artificial leg, the result of a wound received while in a German POW camp. In starting out on the hunt he meets up with a wartime acquaintance (Anthony Steel), now the manager of a tea plantation, who begs to go along, in order to impress his son (Martin Stephens) and his wife (Barbara Rush), who was once loved by the hunter. The manager's cowardice results in the hunter being badly mauled by the tiger. He is nursed back to health, but takes to drinking to compensate for not having been able to win back his old love. But when the boy is lost in the jungle, he pulls himself together, goes in, finds the boy, and kills the tiger. A good adventure yarn, with fine Indian location photography.

THE HUNTERS

Produced and directed by Dick Powell
Screenplay by Wendell Mayes, based on a novel by James Salter
Photographed in CinemaScope and DeLuxe Color by Charles G. Clarke and Tom Tutwiler
Music by Paul Sawtell
105 minutes

Cast: Robert Mitchum, Robert Wagner, Richard Egan, May Britt, Lee Phillips, John Gabriel, Stacy Harris, Victor Sen Yung, Candace Lee

The hunters of the title are American jet pilots in Korea in 1952, as they take to the skies to knock down the Russian MIGs flown by the enemy. A tough, veteran flyer, a major (Robert Mitchum) is put in charge of a squadron of much younger men, one of whom is a flip and cocky type (Robert Wagner) and one of whom is a man beset with fear (Lee Phillips). The wife (May Britt) of the fearful one asks the veteran to look out for him and help him, but the vet finds himself falling in love with the wife, with some response from her. When the husband crash lands behind enemy lines, the vet and the cocky pilot rescue him and together fight their way back to their own lines, an experience which proves to the frightened pilot that he has courage and which teaches some humility to the cocky one. Dick Powell's direction gives punch to the story, but it is the superb aviation footage which makes *The Hunters* memorable.

I, MOBSTER

Produced by Edward L. Alperson
Directed by Roger Corman
Screenplay by Steve Fisher
Photographed in CinemaScope by Floyd Crosby
Music by Gerald Fried and Edward L. Alperson, Jr.
Songs by Jerry Winn and Edward L. Alperson, Jr.
81 minutes

Cast: Steve Cochran, Lita Milan, Robert Strauss, Celia Lovsky, Lili St. Cyr, John Brinkley, Yvette Vickers, Robert Shayne, Grant Withers, Frank Gerstle, Wally Cassell, John Mylong

The story of a racketeer (Steve Cochran), tracing his rise from his early days as a neighborhood collector for bookies, to his days as a narcotics pusher and gradually becoming a businessman of crime, leading to his high position in the syndicate and finally to top rank as a crime czar. This also leads to his being called before the Senate Rackets Investigating Committee, whose evidence against him is strong enough to make him useless to the syndicate, who elect one of his long-time henchmen (Robert Strauss) to eliminate him. A cool look at the career of a gangster, well played by Cochran, and including his profoundly sad effect upon his decent parents (John Mylong and Celia Lovsky).

IN LOVE AND WAR

Produced by Jerry Wald
Directed by Philip Dunne
Screenplay by Edward Anhalt, from a novel by Anton Myrer
Photographed in CinemaScope and DeLuxe Color by Leo Tover
Music by Hugo Friedhofer
107 minutes

Cast: Robert Wagner, Dana Wynter, Jeffrey Hunter, Hope Lange, Bradford Dillman, Sheree North, France Nuyen, Mort Sahl, Steven Gant, Harvey Stephens, Paul Comi, Joe di Reda

The experiences of three young marines in the second World War. A rugged sergeant (Jeffrey Hunter) mar-

color guard go to New Orleans to be part of the Mardi Gras celebration. The cadet winner (Pat Boone) finds the young French star even more exciting than he imagined, as she indulges herself by ducking out of her commitments and having fun. Her publicity girl (Sheree North) has to impersonate her at several functions, and two other cadets (Tommy Sands and Gary Crosby) meet romance with a stripteaser (Barrie Chase) and a lovely tourist (Jennifer West). A good time is had by all, and the photography of New Orleans and Virginia, plus a great deal of singing and dancing, make it a fun trip for the audience.

NAKED EARTH

Produced by Adrian Worker
Directed by Vincent Sherman
Screenplay by Milton Helmes
Photographed in CinemaScope by Erwin Hillier
96 minutes

Cast: Richard Todd, Juliette Greco, John Kitzmiller, Finlay Currie, Laurence Naismith, Christopher Rhodes, Orlando Martins, Harold Kasket

An Irish farmer (Richard Todd) arrives in Uganda in 1895 to join a friend in a tobacco growing operation and finds the friend deceased. But the widow (Juliette Greco) likes the new arrival and suggests they get married, largely as a matter of convenience. When their natives go off on a ceremonial trip, the tobacco crop is ruined. The farmer leaves his wife and becomes a crocodile hunter, until he is double-crossed. He and his wife reconcile and decide to stay in Uganda and understand the local customs, and help the native people.

A NICE LITTLE BANK THAT SHOULD BE ROBBED

Produced by Anthony Muto
Directed by Henry Levin
Screenplay by Sydney Boehm, based on an article by Evan Wylie
Photographed in CinemaScope by Leo Tover
Music by Lionel Newman
88 minutes

Cast: Tom Ewell, Mickey Rooney, Mickey Shaughnessy, Dina Merrill, Madge Kennedy, Frances Bavier, Richard Deacon, Stanley Clements, Tom Greenway

An auto mechanic and hypochondriac (Tom Ewell) is talked into robbing a bank by a would-be horse trainer (Mickey Rooney). They manage to get $30,000 but fritter it away, partly because of the poor advice of a bookie (Mickey Shaughnessy) who angles his way into their lives. They buy a horse but need more money to enter it, so they rob another bank. This time they get caught, and to add irony to their misery,

their horse is acquired by a bank and becomes a winner. An amusing picture, but falling short of its potential.

RALLY 'ROUND THE FLAG, BOYS!

Produced and directed by Leo McCarey
Screenplay by Claude Binyon and Leo McCarey, from the novel by Max Shulman
Photographed in CinemaScope and DeLuxe Color by Leon Shamroy
Music by Cyril J. Mockridge
106 minutes

Cast: Paul Newman, Joanne Woodward, Joan Collins, Jack Carson, Dwayne Hickman, Tuesday Weld, Gale Gordon, Tom Gilson, O. Z. Whitehead, Jon Lormer, Joseph Holland, Burt Mustin, Percy Helton

A combination of bedroom farce and social satire, as the women of the town of Putnam's Landing, within commuting distance of New York, unite to prevent the Army from using their community for a missile base. They don't really know anything about the base but assume it will be bad for their children. The leader of the women (Joanne Woodward) neglects her duties as a wife and her husband (Paul Newman) finally pays attention to the neglected wife (Joan Collins) of a local business tycoon. Their affair is more comedic than amorous and the town-organizing wife comes to see where she has been derelict. The film sizzles with bright comment on the American way of life and some of its questionable values, with Newman excellent as the man trying to win the attentions of a wife while dallying with another.

THE ROOTS OF HEAVEN

Produced by Darryl F. Zanuck
Directed by John Huston
Screenplay by Romain Gary and Patrick Leigh-Fermor, based on the novel by Romain Gary
Photographed in DeLuxe Color by Oswald Morris
Music by Malcolm Arnold
131 minutes

Cast: Errol Flynn, Juliette Greco, Trevor Howard, Eddie Albert, Orson Welles, Paul Lukas, Herbert Lom, Gregoire Aslan, Andre Luguet, Friedrich Ledebur, Edric Connor, Olivier Hussenot, Pierre Dudan, Marc Doelnitz, Dan Jackson, Maurice Cannon

The story of the making of *The Roots of Heaven* is possibly more interesting than the film itself. Director John Huston took cast and crew deep into what was then French Equatorial Africa and suffered severely in heat and fever. Several crew members were shipped out, dangerously ill, and Eddie Albert spent several days in delirium because of sunstroke. The story concerns the efforts of an idealist (Trevor Howard) to

John Wayne in *The Barbarian and the Geisha*.

Gregory Peck and Joan Collins in *The Bravados*.

Robert Evans and Dolores Michaels in *The Fiend Who Walked the West*.

Joan Fontaine, Bradford Dillman, Rossano Brazzi, and Christine Carere in *A Certain Smile*.

Patricia Owens in *The Fly*.

Robert Wagner in *In Love and War*.

May Britt and Robert Mitchum in *The Hunters*.

Ingrid Bergman and Curt Jurgens in *The Inn of the Sixth Happiness*.

Robert Stack and Lauren Bacall in *The Gift of Love*.

ries his pregnant girl friend (Hope Lange) and goes off to the South Pacific, where he dies a hero's death. A recruit (Robert Wagner) is a fun lover and a coward, who is pushed into action by the sergeant and finds courage. Another (Bradford Dillman) is an intellectual who dumps his neurotic socialite (Dana Wynter), who commits suicide, and finds love with a Hawaiian nurse (France Nuyen). The film is a good account of love and war, although its attitudes are now outdated.

THE INN OF THE SIXTH HAPPINESS

Produced by Buddy Adler
Directed by Mark Robson
Screenplay by Isobel Lennart, from a novel by Alan Burgess
Photographed in CinemaScope and DeLuxe Color by F. A. Young
Music by Malcolm Arnold
156 minutes

Cast: Ingrid Bergman, Curt Jurgens, Robert Donat, Michael David, Athene Seyler, Ronald Squire, Moultrie Kelsall, Richard Wattis, Peter Chong, Tsai Chin, Edith Sharpe

China in the 1930's—with rugged north Wales doubling for the Orient—and Ingrid Bergman as a missionary who carries the Christian creed to the war-torn regions and persuades even a mandarin (Robert Donat) to declare himself a Christian. She falls in love with a Chinese army officer (Curt Jurgens), but has to leave him when it becomes necessary to lead a large party of Chinese children to safety over the mountains. The film, based on the life of Gladys Aylward, is a fine adventure story and a religious triumph, without pounding dogma. Bergman is its strength, although the final appearance of Robert Donat, who died before the film was released, is very touching inasmuch as his last line is one of farewell.

INTENT TO KILL

Produced by Adrian D. Worker
Directed by Jack Cardiff
Screenplay by Jimmy Sangster, from a novel by Michael Bryan
Photographed in CinemaScope by Desmond Dickinson
Music by Kenneth V. Jones
Musical direction by Muir Mathieson
88 minutes

Cast: Richard Todd, Betsy Drake, Herbert Lom, Warren Stevens, Carlo Justini, Paul Carpenter, Alexander Knox, Lisa Gastoni, Peter Arne, Catherine Boyle, Kay Callard, Jackie Collins

A doctor (Richard Todd) in a Montreal hospital suffers the nagging of a wife (Catherine Boyle) who wants him to take a fashionable practice in London, and tries not to fall in love with a fellow doctor (Betsy Drake). His chief concern is a South American president (Herbert Lom), whom he is treating for brain surgery and who is marked for assassination by a cunning colleague (Carlo Justini), in league with the president's wife (Lisa Gastoni). The doctor and a police detective (Paul Carpenter) fight off the assassins. A good suspense yarn, filmed during a Montreal winter.

THE LONG HOT SUMMER

Produced by Jerry Wald
Directed by Martin Ritt
Screenplay by Irving Ravetch and Harriet Frank, Jr., based on stories by William Faulkner
Photographed in CinemaScope and DeLuxe Color by Joseph La Shelle
Music by Alex North
117 minutes

Cast: Paul Newman, Joanne Woodward, Anthony Franciosa, Orson Welles, Lee Remick, Angela Lansbury, Richard Anderson, Sarah Marshall, Mabel Albertson, J. Pat O'Malley, William Walker

The amorously sultry South of William Faulkner, with Paul Newman as a virile young drifter who worms his way into the family of a Big Daddy type (Orson Welles). He wins the affection of the tycoon, while offending the sensitive daughter (Joanne Woodward) and the weakling son (Anthony Franciosa). The son has a giddy wife (Lee Remick) and the tycoon has a mistress (Angela Lansbury), all of whom bicker with each other. The intruder at first challenges them, but in time they settle down and accept him. The film gains its strength from the playing and the dialogue, with a finely realized Southern ambiance——and a music score by Alex North that gives the picture a sensual glow.

MARDI GRAS

Produced by Jerry Wald
Directed by Edmund Goulding
Screenplay by Winston Miller and Hal Kanter, from a story by Curtis Harrington
Photographed in CinemaScope and DeLuxe Color by Wilfred M. Cline
Songs by Sammy Fain and Paul Francis Webster
Musical direction by Lionel Newman
107 minutes

Cast: Pat Boone, Christine Carere, Tommy Sands, Sheree North, Gary Crosby, Fred Clark, Richard Sargent, Barrie Chase, Jennifer West, Geraldine Wall, King Calder, Robert Burton

The cadets of the Virginia Military Institute conduct a raffle to see who will win a date with a French movie star (Christine Carere) when the academy's band and

save the elephants from extinction at the hands of hunters. He enlists a dubious group of followers, among them an alcoholic ex-British Army officer (Errol Flynn) and a night club singer (Juliette Greco). They, too, suffer in the jungle, but they make the headlines of the world, mostly because of an opportunistic American commentator (Orson Welles), and a moral point is made in favor of the elephants. The film fails to communicate much passion or excitement. Sadly it is the final major film made by Errol Flynn before his death at the age of fifty.

SIERRA BARON

Produced by Plato A. Skouras
Directed by James B. Clark
Screenplay by Houston Branch, from a novel by Thomas Wakefield Blackburn
Photographed in CinemaScope and Deluxe Color by Alex Phillips
Music by Paul Sawtell and Bert Shefter
82 minutes

Cast: Brian Keith, Rick Jason, Rita Gam, Mala Powers, Steve Brodie, Carlos Musquiz, Lee Morgan, Allan Lewis, Pedro Galvan, Fernando Wagner, Tommy Riste, Reed Howes

California in the mid-nineteenth century as unscrupulous easterners move in and attempt to fleece the residents. The proprietor (Rick Jason) of a large tract, a Spanish land grant, is hassled by a land promoter (Steve Brodie), who brings in a Texas gunman (Brian Keith) to lend weight to his threats. The owner allows the exhausted members of a wagon train to rest on his land long enough to grow crops, and the grateful settlers come to his aid in fending off the attacks of the promoter. The Texan changes sides when he falls in love with the owner's sister (Rita Gam), but loses his life fighting. An interesting slice of California history, although filmed entirely in Mexico.

SHOWDOWN AT BOOT HILL

Produced by Harold E. Knox
Directed by Gene Fowler, Jr.
Screenplay by Louis Vittes
Photographed in RegalScope by John M. Nickolaus, Jr.
Music by Albert Harris
71 minutes

Cast: Charles Bronson, Robert Hutton, John Carradine, Carole Mathews, Paul Maxey, Thomas B. Henry, William Stevens, Martin Smith, Joseph McGuinn

A U.S. marshall (Charles Bronson) follows a murderer to a Western town and there kills him. But he finds the man has no local criminal record and has in fact been popular. Since there is a bounty to be collected, the townspeople refuse to identify the dead man. This gives the marshall reason to sit back and reflect on his

lifestyle and what has made him what he is. A fine little Western, with a good performance by Bronson as the soul-searching gunman.

SING, BOY, SING

Produced and directed by Henry Ephron
Screenplay by Claude Binyon, from a story by Paul Monash
Photographed in CinemaScope by William C. Mellor
Music by Lionel Newman
91 minutes

Cast: Tommy Sands, Lili Gentle, Edmond O'Brien, John McIntire, Nick Adams, Diane Jergens, Josephine Hutchinson, Jerry Paris, Tami Conner, Regis Toomey, Art Ford, Bill Randle

A successful but bewildered rock and roll star (Tommy Sands), pushed by his manager (Edmond O'Brien) and his press agent (Jerry Paris), is bothered by the fact that his grandfather (John McIntire) is a revivalist who has instilled in him a sense of sin about what he is doing. The grandfather dies and the boy's aunt (Josephine Hutchinson) assures him that the grandfather was an egocentric tyrant and that it is no sin to use the gifts given him by God. With that he goes on to further success. The film was designed to exploit the popularity of recording star Sands, and does it agreeably.

SMILEY GETS A GUN

Produced and directed by Anthony Kimmins
Screenplay by Anthony Kimmins and Rex Rienits, from a novel by Moore Raymond
Photographed in CinemaScope and DeLuxe Color by Tad Scaife
Music by Wilbur Sampson
90 minutes

Cast: Sybil Thorndike, Chips Rafferty, Keith Calvert, Bruce Archer, Margaret Christensen, Reg Lye, Grant Taylor, Verena Kimmins, Leonard Teale, Jannice Dinnen, Brian Farley

A sequel to *Smiley* but with another young actor (Keith Calvert) in the role of the likeable Aussie lad who gets into Tom Sawyer-like scrapes in the outback village of Murrumbilla. A policeman (Chips Rafferty) promises him a gun if he will improve his conduct and get good marks in school. The boy feels uneasy when locals start betting on him, and when an elderly, eccentric lady (Sybil Thorndike) is robbed, she accuses the boy. But the real thief is caught and Smiley gets his gun. A genial yarn and nicely photographed in the weirdly beautiful Aussie outback.

SOUTH PACIFIC

Produced by Buddy Adler

Directed by Joshua Logan
Screenplay by Paul Osborn, from the play by Richard Rodgers, Oscar Hammerstein II, and Joshua Logan, based on a novel by James A. Michener
Photographed in Todd-AO and Technicolor by Leon Shamroy
Songs by Richard Rodgers and Oscar Hammerstein II
Musical direction by Alfred Newman and Ken Darby
165 minutes

Cast: Rossano Brazzi, Mitzi Gaynor, John Kerr, Ray Walston, Juanita Hall, France Nuyen, Russ Brown, Jack Mullaney, Ken Clark, Floyd Simmons, Candace Lee, Warren Hsieh, Tom Laughlin

A handsome filming of the classic Rodgers and Hammerstein musical, with the spectacular Hawaiian islands doubling for those of the South Pacific. Mitzi Gaynor is a pleasing and feisty Nellie and Rossano Brazzi (with Giorgio Tozzi's singing voice) is virile as the middle-aged French planter Emile, who finally agrees that the age difference does not matter. John Kerr is the doomed young lieutenant who loves the daughter (France Nuyen) of the enterprising Bloody Mary (Juanita Hall), and Ray Walston is the seabee who leads his chums in thinking that there is nothing like a dame. The musical direction of Alfred Newman gives fresh vitality to the music and the film takes a step beyond any stage production with its brilliant photography, although the use of tints in certain scenes continues to meet with mixed reactions.

SPACEMASTER X-7

Produced by Bernard Glasser
Directed by Edward Bernds
Screenplay by George Worthin Yates and Daniel Mainwaring
Photographed in RegalScope by Brydon Baker
Music by Josef Zimanich
71 minutes

Cast: Bill Williams, Lyn Thomas, Robert Ellis, Paul Frees, Joan Barry, Thomas B. Henry, Fred Sherman, Jesse Kirkpatrick, Moe Howard, Rhoda Williams

A space ship returning from Mars brings back a strange fungus, which kills the scientist (Paul Frees) who examines it and contaminates his wife (Lyn Thomas). Two government agents (Bill Williams and Robert Ellis) are assigned to track her down. The fungus, called blood rust, is in her baggage and it kills those who touch it. The agents catch up with her en route to Hawaii and it almost devours the plane before the pilot can make a crash landing and the agents can finalize the fungus. A neat science fiction item.

TEN NORTH FREDERICK

Produced by Charles Brackett
Directed by Philip Dunne

Screenplay by Philip Dunne, based on the novel by John O'Hara
Photographed by Joe MacDonald
Music by Leigh Harline
102 minutes

Cast: Gary Cooper, Diane Varsi, Suzy Parker, Geraldine Fitzgerald, Tom Tully, Ray Stricklyn, Philip Ober, John Emery, Stuart Whitman, Linda Watkins, Barbara Nichols, Joe McGuinn, Jess Kirkpatrick, Nolan Leary, Helen Wallace

A complex plot, *Ten North Frederick* tells of a wealthy, middle-aged businessman (Gary Cooper), who is goaded into politics by his ambitious wife (Geraldine Fitzgerald), and who donates a large sum to a conniving politician in order to win a nomination. He finds no pleasure in politics, just as he has found

Orson Welles and Paul Newman in *The Long Hot Summer.*

Pat Boone and Christine Carere in *Mardi Gras.*

Juliette Greco and Errol Flynn in *The Roots of Heaven.*

Joanne Woodward and Paul Newman in *Rally 'Round the Flag, Boys!*

Geraldine Fitzgerald and Gary Cooper in *Ten North Frederick.*

Mitzi Gaynor and Rossano Brazzi in *South Pacific.*

Cast: Joan Crawford, Hope Lange, Stephen Boyd, Suzy Parker, Louis Jourdan, Martha Hyer, Diane Baker, Brian Aherne, Robert Evans, Brett Halsey, Donald Harron, Sue Carson, Linda Hutchings, Lionel Kane, Ted Otis, June Blair, Myrna Hansen, Alena Murray, Rachel Stevens

An involved, complicated soap-opera, *The Best of Everything* gives Joan Crawford yet another vehicle to portray the successful businesswoman with a frustrating love life. Here she is the editor of a magazine publishing house, taking out her frustrations on her attractive female employees, like an aspiring actress (Suzy Parker), who is involved in an unfulfilling love affair with a director (Louis Jourdan), and her secretary (Hope Lange), who is involved with an editor (Stephen Boyd). The boss lady has a fling at marriage, but finds it too tame and returns to being a tycoon. The title refers more to the production values of the film than the lives of its characters.

BLOOD AND STEEL

Produced by Gene Corman
Directed by Bernard L. Kowalski
Screenplay by Joseph C. Gillette
Photographed by Floyd D. Crosby
Music by Calvin Jackson
62 minutes

Cast: John Lupton, Ziva Rodann, Bred Halsey, James Edwards, John Brinkley, Allen Jung, Bill Saito, Clarence Lung, James Hong

A war yarn, about four sailors who are assigned to explore a Japanese-held island in the South Pacific and report on its possible use as an airfield. They find it unsuitable but manage to blow up a Japanese radio station and inflict casualties before getting back to their ship. The operation costs them one man dead, another badly wounded, and a native girl (Ziva Rodann), who has helped them, accidentally killed by one of the sailors.

THE BLUE ANGEL

Produced by Jack Cummings
Directed by Edward Dymtryk
Screenplay by Nigel Balchin, based on the screenplay by Karl Zuckmayer, Karl Vollmoeller, and Robert Liebman and the novel by Heinrich Mann
Photographed in CinemaScope and DeLuxe Color by Leon Shamroy
Music by Hugo Friedhofer
108 minutes

Cast: Curt Jurgens, May Britt, Theodore Bikel, John Banner, Fabrizzio Mioni, Ludwig Stossel, Wolfe Barzell, Ina Anders, Richard Tyler, Voytek Dolinski, Ken Wallace, Del Erickson, Edit Angold

A remake of the classic 1930 film which made a star of Marlene Dietrich but lacking the flavor and style of the original. The story is that of a respected German professor (Curt Jurgens), a man of middle age, who falls for a young singer (May Britt) in a tavern. His infatuation consumes him and he gives up his job to marry the girl and join her company of performers. The shallow girl cares little for him, particularly when his money runs out, but the manager (Theodore Bikel) sees publicity value in having the former teacher playing the role of a clown. When the young wife has affairs with men her own age, the husband is driven to murderous fury, but his school colleagues prevent him from killing her and help restore him to academic life—a happy ending at variance with that of the original. Jurgens is good as the unhappily smitten professor, but the image of Emil Jannings lingers too strongly to prevent comparison. And May Britt, pretty and alluring, suffers more so in stepping into the celebrated Dietrich role.

BLUE DENIM

Produced by Charles Brackett
Directed by Philip Dunne
Screenplay by Edith Sommer and Philip Dunne, based on the play by James Leo Herlihy and William Noble
Photographed in CinemaScope by Leo Tover
Music by Bernard Herrmann
89 minutes

Cast: Carol Lynley, Brandon de Wilde, Macdonald Carey, Marsha Hunt, Warren Berlinger, Buck Class, Nina Shipman, Vaughn Taylor, Roberta Shore, Mary Young, William Schallert, Michael Gainey, Jenny Maxwell, Juney Ellis

The problems of being a teenager, and particularly the problem of sex. A girl (Carol Lynley), eager about sex but naive, is impregnated by her boyfriend (Brandon de Wilde) and then tortured by not knowing how to tell her doting father (Vaughn Taylor). The boy has little rapport with his parents (Macdonald Carey and Marsha Hunt). With the help of a friend (Warren Berlinger) the couple raise enough money for an abortion, but the boy, in his anxiety, finally tells his parents, who stop the abortion. The boy, sacrificing his education, decides to marry the girl and leave town. The film's accent is on the lack of communication between youngsters and parents in the modern age and the need for understanding from both sides.

BOBBIKINS

Produced by Oscar Brodney
Directed by Robert Day
Screenplay by Oscar Brodney
Photographed in CinemaScope by Geoffrey Faithful
Music by Philip Green
90 minutes

Cast: Shirley Jones, Max Bygraves, Steven Stocker, Billie Whitelaw, Barbara Shelley, Dolin Gordon, Charles Tingwell, Lionel Jeffries, Charles Carson, Rupert Davies, Noel Hood, David Lodge, Murray Kash

Filmed in London, with Shirley Jones as an entertainer who marries a sailor and gives birth to a son who talks at the age of fourteen months—but only to his father (Max Bygraves), who can't get work in show business after coming out of the navy. In a park the baby becomes friendly with the British Chancellor of the Exchequer (Charles Carson), from whom he picks up tips about the financial world, which he passes on to his father, resulting in the father becoming wealthy. But when the baby sees that wealth is breaking up his happy home, he passes on some bad tips, which brings Daddy back to poverty and a job as an entertainer. And a happy home.

COMPULSION

Produced by Richard D. Zanuck
Directed by Richard Fleischer
Screenplay by Richard Murphy, based on the novel by Meyer Levin
Photographed in CinemaScope by William C. Mellor
Music by Lionel Newman
105 minutes

Cast: Orson Welles, Diane Varsi, Dean Stockwell, Bradford Dillman, E. G. Marshall, Martin Milner, Richard Anderson, Robert Simon, Edward Binns, Robert Burton, Wilton Graff, Louise Lorimer, Gavin MacLeod, Terry Becker, Russ Bender, Gerry Lock, Harry Carter, Simon Scott, Voltaire Perkins

Based upon the notorious 1924 Chicago-based murder case of Leopold and Loeb and their eloquent defense by Clarence Darrow—but with the names changed. Here the two upper-class boys who murder just for the fun of committing a perfect crime are a bossy, compulsively evil but mother-dominated type (Bradford Dillman) and his sensitive, introverted, pliable friend (Dean Stockwell). The boys' crime is detected and they are brought to trial—a trial which commands full journalistic coverage—and they are found guilty, despite the brilliant, theatrical performance of their lawyer (Orson Welles), who loses to the quietly patient State's Attorney (E. G. Marshall). *Compulsion* is a fascinating excursion into a psychotic crime, excellently acted, written and directed. But dominated by the bravura performance of Welles as the crafty, florid lawyer.

THE DIARY OF ANNE FRANK

Produced and directed by George Stevens
Screenplay by Frances Goodrich and Albert Hackett, based on their play, using Anne Frank's diary
Photographed in CinemaScope by William C. Mellor and Jack Cardiff
Music by Alfred Newman
170 minutes

Cast: Millie Perkins, Joseph Schildkraut, Shelley Winters, Richard Beymer, Gusti Huber, Lou Jacobi, Diane Baker, Ed Wynn, Douglas Spencer, Dody Heath

Despite its epic length, the film is an intimate account of the survival of a Jewish family in an Amsterdam attic for two years during the German occupation. With the aid of Dutch friends, the father (Joseph Schildkraut) is able to hide his daughter Anne (Millie Perkins), her sister (Diane Baker), and their mother (Shelley Winters) in the attic, along with another family. Their confined lives are made bearable by their discipline and their imagination, as if they were carrying on under normal conditions. Anne, thirteen at the start of the confinement, falls in love with the boy (Richard Beymer) of the other family and they imagine their first date, with Anne dressing for the occasion. Then, in August of 1944, they are discovered and taken away to concentration camps. Only the father survived. With the exteriors filmed in Amsterdam, but largely shot on studio sets with fluid camera work, Stevens was able to communicate the muted horror of the long confinement and its tragic conclusion. Critics in general found that his casting of the pretty but inexperienced Millie Perkins was a factor against arriving at the total poignancy that might have been achieved in telling this story of an extraordinary and beautifully spiritual young girl.

A DOG OF FLANDERS

Produced by Robert D. Radnitz
Directed by James B. Clark
Screenplay by Ted Sherdeman, based on a story by Ouida
Photographed in CinemaScope and DeLuxe Color by Otto Heller
Music by Paul Sawtell and Bert Shefter
97 minutes

Cast: David Ladd, Donald Crisp, Theodore Bikel, Max Croiset, Gibst Tersteeg, Monique Ahrens, John Soer, Lo van Hernsbergen, Slobhan Taylor, Katherine Holland

The classic tale (written in 1872 and twice filmed during the silent era) is about a Dutch boy (David Ladd) who lives with his wise old grandfather (Donald Crisp) in a little house on the great Flanders Plain. They make their living collecting milk from nearby farms and delivering it to Antwerp in a hand cart. They save an abandoned dog and nurse it back to health—the grandfather realizing it will be a good companion for the boy when he is gone. When the grandfather dies, the boy has a hard time until he is adopted by a painter (Theodore Bikel). The film

Gregory Peck and Deborah Kerr in *Beloved Infidel*.

Hope Lange, Suzy Parker, and Joan Crawford in *The Best of Everything*.

tells its simple story in a straightforward and winning manner, and benefits from fine location shooting in Belgium and the Netherlands.

FIVE GATES TO HELL

Produced and directed by James Clavell
Screenplay by James Clavell
Photographed in CinemaScope by Sam Leavitt
Music by Paul Dunlap
98 minutes

Cast: Dolores Michaels, Patricia Owens, Neville Brand, Ken Scott, Nobu McCarthy, Benson Fong, Nancy Culp, John Morley, Gerry Gaylor, Shirley Knight, Greta Chi, Linda Wong, Irish McCalla

In the Vietnam of the 1950's, a Communist warrior (Neville Brand) raids a French hospital and abducts two doctors and seven nurses. His purpose is to have them tend his ailing warlord and then turn the women over to his men as spoils of war. But when the garrison is away on a raid, the captives stage an uprising, during which the two doctors, several of the women, and most of the remaining soldiers are killed. The film is something of a tribute to women, suggesting that they are better organized and more capable of survival than men. James Clavell spent five years as a prisoner of the Japanese during the second World War and his film shows a sympathetic insight into Oriental customs and thinking.

HERE COME THE JETS

Produced by Richard Einfeld
Directed by Gene Fowler, Jr.
Screenplay by Lou Vittes
Photographed in CinemaScope by Karl Struss
Music by Paul Dunlap
72 minutes

Cast: Steve Brodie, Lyn Thomas, Mark Dana, John Doucette, Jean Carson, Carleton Young, Joseph Turkel, Gloria Moreland, Vikki Dougen, I. Stanford Jolley, Joseph Hamilton, Glenn Morgan, B. B. Hughes, Walter Maslow

An alcoholic Korean War veteran (Steve Brodie) is hired as a test pilot by a jet aircraft executive (John Doucette), who believes the daring, ace veteran is the best man for the job and that it will straighten him out. This proves to be the case. After some setbacks the veteran gets to test the big, new jetliner that is the executive's proud creation. In the meantime the film allows for an interesting look at jet plane production and testing devices.

HOLIDAY FOR LOVERS

Produced by David Weisbart
Directed by Henry Levin
Screenplay by Luther Davis, based on the play by Ronald Alexander
Photographed in CinemaScope and DeLuxe Color by Charles G. Clarke
Music by Leigh Harline
103 minutes

Cast: Clifton Webb, Jane Wyman, Jill St. John, Carol Lynley, Paul Henreid, Gary Crosby, Nico Minardos, Wally Brown, Henry Backus, Nora O'Mahoney, Buck Class, Al Austin, José Greco, Nestor Amaral and his Orchestra

A Boston psychiatrist (Clifton Webb) and his wife (Jane Wyman) take their daughters (Jill St. John and Carol Lynley) on a trip to South America and find all their time is spent keeping the attractive young girls away from men. Father objects to the elder daughter (St. John) falling for an architect (Paul Henreid) and is then more concerned when he finds that it is the architect's beatnik son (Nico Minardos) who is the actual light of love. The other daughter takes up with a burly Air Force sergeant (Gary Crosby). Gradually the learned psychiatrist realizes that all his esteemed knowledge means little in dealing with his daughters' love life. As he learns this, the film spins some fancy footage of Rio de Janeiro and São Paulo, Brazil, and Lima, Peru, and its bullfights.

HOUND-DOG MAN

Produced by Jerry Wald
Directed by Don Siegel
Screenplay by Fred Gipson and Winston Miller, based on the novel by Fred Gipson
Photographed in CinemaScope and DeLuxe Color by Charles G. Clarke
Music by Cyril Mockridge
Songs by Ken Darby, Frankie Avalon and Sol Ponti, Robert Marcucci and Pete De Angelis, Doc Pomus and Mort Shuman
87 minutes

Cast: Fabian, Carol Lynley, Stuart Whitman, Arthur O'Connell, Dodie Stevens, Betty Field, Royal Dano, Margo Moore, Claude Akins, Edgar Buchanan, Jane Darwell, L. Q. Jones, Virginia Gregg, Dennis Holmes, Rachel Stephens, Jim Beck, Hope Summers, Harry Carter

Fabian, at sixteen, makes his movie debut in a slice of rural Americana, circa 1912, dealing with nothing much more than the activities of youngsters as they run counter to their parents' wishes. A lusty lad (Stuart Whitman) takes Fabian hunting when he should be tending the farm. Fabian falls for a pretty hillbilly blonde (Carol Lynley), until he comes across an attractive married lady (Margo Moore). And so on. The pleasant rustic settings mainly form a backdrop for a string of songs designed for young ears.

JOURNEY TO THE CENTER OF THE EARTH

Produced by Charles Brackett
Directed by Henry Levin
Screenplay by Walter Reisch and Charles Brackett, based on the novel by Jules Verne
Photographed in CinemaScope and DeLuxe Color by Leo Tover
Music by Bernard Herrmann
129 minutes

Cast: Pat Boone, James Mason, Arlene Dahl, Diane Baker, Thayer David, Peter Ronson, Robert Adler, Alan Napier, Alex Finlayson, Ben Wright, Mary Brady, Frederick Halliday, Alan Caillou

Relying on more than just special effects, *Journey to the Center of the Earth* is one of the few science-fiction adventures which has the advantage of a humorous and literate script by two of Billy Wilder's ex collaborators, Reisch and Brackett. At Edinburgh University around the turn of the century, Professor Oliver Lindenbrook (James Mason) is brought a lump of lava by student Alec McEwen (Pat Boone). Because it feels very heavy for its type of lava, the geology professor melts it down and finds, to everyone's surprise, a plumb-bob on which are inscribed the directions to the center of the earth. The voyage which follows is both exciting and exhilarating, and the special effects wizards provide huge dimetrodons, giant mushrooms, crystalline caverns, and an underworld ocean. Bernard Herrmann's musical score contributes to the wonderment of the marvelous visual effects.

THE LITTLE SAVAGE

Produced by Jack Leewood
Directed by Byron Haskin
Screenplay by Eric Norden, based on a story by Frederick Marryat
Photographed by George Stahl, Jr.
Music by Paul Lavista
72 minutes

Cast: Pedro Armendariz, Christiane Martel, Rodolfo Hoyos, Terry Rangno, Robert Palmer

A Treasure Island-type adventure yarn, filmed in Mexico, with Pedro Armendariz as a pirate left for dead by his captain (Rodolfo Hoyos) after they have buried their treasure. The pirate is nursed to health by a shipwrecked young boy (Terry Rangno) and they spend the next ten years together. When the captain returns to the island, he and the old pirate kill each other, and the boy, now a man (Robert Palmer), sails off to England with the girl (Christiane Martel) they rescued from warlike natives some years previously.

LONE TEXAN

Produced by Jack Leewood
Directed by Paul Landres
Screenplay by James Landis and Jack Thomas, based on the novel by Landis
Photographed in RegalScope by Walter Strenge
Music by Paul Dunlap
71 minutes

Cast: Willard Parker, Grant Williams, Audrey Dalton, Douglas Kennedy, June Blair, Dabbs Greer, Barbara Heller, Rayford Barnes, Tyler McVey, Lee Far, Jimmy Murphy, Dick Monahan, Robert Dix, Gregg Barton, I. Stanford Jolley, Sid Melton

In the aftermath of the Civil War, a Texan (Willard Parker) who has fought for the North returns to his home and finds himself at odds with local sentiment. His young brother (Grant Williams) runs the town to his own advantage and when a lawyer (Douglas Kennedy) is murdered trying to stop the organized crimes, the older brother steps in, resulting in the death of the younger one and a return to law and order.

THE MAN WHO UNDERSTOOD WOMEN

Produced and directed by Nunnally Johnson
Screenplay by Nunnally Johnson, based on the novel *The Colors of the Day* by Romain Gary
Photographed in CinemaScope and DeLuxe Color by Milton Krasner
Music by Robert Emmett Dolan
105 minutes

Cast: Leslie Caron, Henry Fonda, Cesare Danova, Myron McCormick, Marcel Dalio, Conrad Nagel, Edwin Jerome, Harry Ellerbe, Frank Cady, Bern Hoffman, Ben Astor

A satire on Hollywood, with Henry Fonda as an aging wonder boy, a producer-director-writer whose films win Oscars but never make money. He claims to understand women, when in fact he does not, being much too wrapped up in making pictures to pay them the attention they need. He marries a lovely French girl (Leslie Caron) and sets out to make her a star.

He does, but his inattention causes her to take off with a French aviator (Cesare Danova) when they vacation on the Riviera. The frantic husband tries desperate measures to get her back, but it's the aviator who decides that she should return. The film is diffuse in making its satiric points, but the Johnson wit sparks it and allows Fonda some good lines as the genius who at one point admits, "Beneath this gaudy haberdashery there beats the sterling heart of a Methodist."

MASTERS OF THE CONGO JUNGLE

Produced by Henri Storck
Directed by Heinz Sielmann and Henry Brandt
Screenplay by Joe Wills, from a story by Sam Hill
Photographed in CinemaScope and DeLuxe Color
Narrated by Orson Welles and William Warfield
Music by Richard Cornu
90 minutes

A documentary made by the International Scientific Foundation dealing with the stone-age natives of the northeastern Belgian Congo and filmed by a number of uncredited cameramen. The film explores the dense vegetation of the West African jungles, with their Pygmy villages, wildlife, birds, and animals. The photography is superb, as is the narration and editing.

THE MIRACLE OF THE HILLS

Produced by Richard E. Lyons
Directed by Paul Landres
Screenplay by Charles Hoffman
Photographed in CinemaScope by Floyd Crosby
Music by Paul Sawtell and Bert Shefter
73 minutes

Cast: Rex Reason, Nan Leslie, Betty Lou Gerson, Charles Arnt, Jay North, June Vincent, Paul Wexler, Ken Mayer, Kelton Garwood, Claire Carleton, Tom Daly, Tracy Stratford, Gil Smith, I. Stanford Jolley, Gene Roth, Gene Collins

A Western with religious overtones, about an Episcopal minister (Rex Reason) who takes over a rundown church in a Western town in the 1880's. He comes into conflict with the town's dominant citizen, a lady (Betty Lou Gerson), once a prostitute but now the owner of a prosperous coal mine and bitter about the townspeople. Her attitude softens and she becomes more generous when three children trapped in a flooded mine are saved by a miracle—an earth tremor that unjams an opening, allowing for the water to subside.

THE OREGON TRAIL

Produced by Richard Einfeld
Directed by Gene Fowler, Jr.
Screenplay by Louis Vittes and Gene Fowler, Jr.
Photographed in CinemaScope and DeLuxe Color by Kay Norton
Music by Paul Dunlap
86 minutes

Cast: Fred MacMurray, William Bishop, Nina Shipman, Gloria Talbot, Henry Hull, John Carradine, John Dierkes, Elizabeth Patterson, James Bell, Ralph Sanford, Tex Terry, Arvo Ojala, Roxene Wells, Gene N. Fowler

A New York reporter (Fred MacMurray) is sent West in 1846 to cover the opening up of the Oregon territory by pioneers, some of whom are soldiers dressed as pioneers and sent by President Polk to secure the British-held area for the United States. The reporter joins the wagon train in Missouri and undergoes the long and arduous trek; by the time they get to Fort Laramie, Wyoming, the territorial dispute has been settled, and by this time he has decided to give up journalism and settle down in the West with a pretty Indian girl (Gloria Talbot). The film wins few points for historical accuracy but offers nice scenery and some spirited Indian attacks.

A PRIVATE'S AFFAIR

Produced by David Weisbart
Directed by Raoul Walsh
Screenplay by Winston Miller, based on a story by Ray Livingston Murphy
Photographed in CinemaScope and DeLuxe Color by Charles G. Clarke
Music by Cyril J. Mockridge
93 minutes

Cast: Sal Mineo, Christine Carere, Barry Coe, Barbara Eden, Gary Crosby, Terry Moore, Jim Backus, Jessie Royce Landis, Robert Burton, Alan Hewitt, Robert Denver, Tige Andrews, Ray Montgomery, Rudolph Anders, Debbie Joyce

A wacky comedy in an army setting, mostly concerning the foul-up brought on by a private (Barry Coe), under sedation in a hospital, accidentally finding himself married to the female Assistant Secretary of the Army (Jessie Royce Landis). With his buddies (Sal Mineo and Gary Crosby) they find themselves put in detention, but because they have talent they also get invited to represent the army on a television variety show. The spirited playing of the young actors helps overcome the involved and farcical script.

THE REMARKABLE MR. PENNYPACKER

Produced by Charles Brackett
Directed by Henry Levin
Screenplay by Walter Reisch, based on the play by Liam O'Brien
Photographed in CinemaScope and DeLuxe Color by Milton Krasner
Music by Leigh Harline
87 minutes

May Britt in *The Blue Angel*.

Millie Perkins in *The Diary of Anne Frank*.

Dorothy McGuire and Clifton Webb in *The Remarkable Mr. Pennypacker*.

Bradford Dillman and Dean Stockwell in *Compulsion*.

Vincent Price in *The Return of the Fly*.

Arlene Dahl, James Mason, and Pat Boone in *Journey to the Center of the Earth*.

Henry Fonda and Leslie Caron in *The Man Who Understood Women*.

313

Cast: Clifton Webb, Dorothy McGuire, Charles Coburn, Jill St. John, Ron Ely, Ray Stricklyn, David Nelson, Dorothy Stickney, Larry Gates, Richard Deacon, Mary Jane Saunders, Mimi Gibson, Donald Losby, Chris Van Scoyk, Jon Van Scoyk, Terry Rango, Nora O'Mahoney, Harvey B. Brown

Mr. Pennypacker (Clifton Webb) is remarkable because he is a bigamist in the Pennsylvania of the 1890's—with one family in Philadelphia and another in Harrisburg. He is also a successful businessman, a free-thinker, a Darwinist, and the father of a total of seventeen children. When found out, he admits that the Philadelphia wife has been dead for some years—much to the relief of the Harrisburg wife (Dorothy McGuire). The film shows obvious signs of its stage origins, but the fine decor and the suave playing of Webb give the dated material its lift.

RETURN OF THE FLY

Produced by Bernard Glasser
Directed by Edward L. Bernds
Screenplay by Edward L. Bernds
Photographed in CinemaScope by Brydon Baker
Music by Paul Sawtell and Bert Shefter
78 minutes

Cast: Vincent Price, Brett Halsey, David Frankham, John Sutton, Dan Seymour, Danielle De Metz, Janine Grandel, Richard Flato, Barry Bernard, Pat O'Hara, Jack Daly, Michael Mark, Gregg Martell, Francisco Villalobas

An obvious sequel to *The Fly*, concerning a young scientist (Brett Halsey) who continues the experiments of his father, despite the warnings of his uncle (Vincent Price). Like his father, the scientist's body becomes scrambled with that of a fly, with the result that he becomes murderous and kills an assistant (David Frankham), who has been selling secrets of the experiment to another party. Ultimately the uncle and a policeman (John Sutton) succeed in unscrambling the formula and restoring the scientist to his original form. Not as good as the original, but still a fascinating item in the horror genre.

THE ROOKIE

Produced by Tommy Noonan
Directed by George O'Hanlon
Screenplay by Tommy Noonan and George O'Hanlan
Photographed in CinemaScope by Floyd Crosby
Music by Paul Dunlap
84 minutes

Cast: Tommy Noonan, Pete Marshall, Julie Newmar, Jerry Lester, Claude Stroud, Norman Leavitt, Joe Besser, Vince Barnett, Herb Armstrong, Richard Reeves, Don Corey, Rodney Bell

A military farce, featuring Tommy Noonan as an eager beaver who is inducted into the army as the war ends and insists that he receive basic training, even though the army would rather pass up on his enlistment. Through a Pentagon misunderstanding, an army camp is kept in operation simply to train this one soldier. The starlet girl friend (Julie Newmar) of his sergeant (Pete Marshall) sees it as a good opportunity for publicity. A fair amusement, with Noonan and Marshall repeating some of their nightclub material.

THE SAD HORSE

Produced by Richard E. Lyons
Directed by James B. Clarke
Screenplay by Charles Hoffman
Photographed in CinemaScope and DeLuxe Color by Karl Struss
Music by Paul Sawtell and Bert Shefter
77 minutes

Cast: David Ladd, Chill Wills, Rex Reason, Patrice Wymore, Gregg Palmer, Eve Brent, Leslie Bradley, William Yip, Dave De Paul

A ten-year-old boy (David Ladd) spends his summer vacation with his grandfather (Chill Wills) on his horse ranch and becomes acquainted with a horse that is depressed because it has lost its dog-mascot. Since the boy has a dog and the horse reacts favorably to it, the horse owner (Patrice Wymore) tries to buy it. The boy at first refuses, but eventually sees how strong the friendship is between the horse and the dog and lets him go. A pleasing film for animal lovers.

SAY ONE FOR ME

Produced and directed by Frank Tashlin
Screenplay by Robert O'Brien
Photographed in CinemaScope and DeLuxe Color by Leo Tover
Songs by Sammy Cahn and James Van Heusen
Musical direction by Lionel Newman
119 minutes

Cast: Bing Crosby, Debbie Reynolds, Robert Wagner, Ray Walston, Les Tremayne, Connie Gilchrist, Frank McHugh, Joe Besser, Alena Murray, Stella Stevens, Nina Shipman, Sebastian Cabot, Judy Harriet, Dick Whittington, Robert Montgomery, Jr.

A musical comedy combining show business with religion, with Bing Crosby as a priest whose parish is just off Broadway and who ministers to sundry theatrical types—occasionally saving them from their sinful ways. He guides a talented parishioner (Debbie Reynolds) as she seeks a career as an entertainer and tries to save her from the clutches of a wolfish young nightclub operator (Robert Wagner), a task made difficult by the fact that she loves him. The slick operator sees the light and promises to settle down with the girl. The picture is a genial and knowing account of

Broadway life, with Crosby and Reynolds singing and dancing in their usual agreeable manner.

THE SHERIFF OF FRACTURED JAW

Produced by Daniel M. Angel
Directed by Raoul Walsh
Screenplay by Arthur Dales, from a story by Jacob Hay
Photographed in CinemaScope and Technicolor by Otto Heller
Music by Robert Farnon
102 minutes

Cast: Kenneth More, Jayne Mansfield, Henry Hull, Bruce Cabot, Ronald Squire, William Campbell, Sidney James, Reed de Rouen, Charles Irwin, Donald Stewart, Clancy Cooper, Gordon Tanner, Robert Morley, David Horne, Eynon Evans

A British spoof on Westerns, with exteriors filmed in Spain, with Kenneth More as a gentlemanly English firearms salesman in frontier Texas and Jayne Mansfield as a saloon singer. He is appointed sheriff after winning a poker game against the mayor of a wild town and enforces law and order with a derringer in his sleeve. He is also adopted into a Sioux tribe and has the tribe out as his aids in stopping feuding whites in a range war. The film rests on the amusing performance of More as the staunch Briton imposing his manners and concepts on the wild Westerners.

SON OF ROBIN HOOD

Produced and directed by George Sherman
Screenplay by George George and George Slavin
Photographed in CinemaScope and color by Arthur Grant
Music by Leighton Lucas
81 minutes

Stephen Boyd and Susan Hayward in *Woman Obsessed.*

Dorothy Malone, Anthony Quinn, and Henry Fonda in *Warlock.*

Joanne Woodward and Yul Brynner in *The Sound and the Fury.*

315

Cast: David Hedison, June Laverick, David Farrar, Marius Goring, Philip Friend, Delphi Lawrence, George Coulouris, George Woodbridge, Humphrey Lestocq, Noel Wood, Shelagh Fraser

A crusader (David Hedison) returns to England and finds it in danger of being taken over by an ambitious nobleman (David Farrar). In order to lead the people in rebellion, he assumes the guise of the son of Robin Hood, but then finds that Robin's only child is a girl (June Laverick). She shares his views and joins him in his plans to squelch the villain, who is finally dispatched in the usual man-to-man sword fight. Filmed in England, with good action and location values.

THE SOUND AND THE FURY

Produced by Jerry Wald
Directed by Martin Ritt
Screenplay by Irving Ravetch and Harriet Frank, Jr., based on the novel by William Faulkner
Photographed in CinemaScope and DeLuxe Color by Charles G. Clarke
Music by Alex North
115 minutes

Cast: Yul Brynner, Joanne Woodward, Margaret Leighton, Stuart Whitman, Ethel Waters, Jack Warden, Francoise Rosay, John Beal, Albert Dekker, Stephen Perry, William Gunn, Roy Glenn

The melodramatically murky South of William Faulkner, with Yul Brynner as the head of a Mississippi family, which includes among its problems alcoholism, nymphomania, and idiocy. Foremost in the tangled web of frustrated emotions is the out-of-wedlock daughter (Joanne Woodward) of the nympho (Margaret Leighton). The daughter searches for the love she has never known and finds solace in the arms of a lusty circus roustabout (Stuart Whitman). He leaves her, but his leaving brings out the strength in her character, which pleases the head of the house—that at least one of the family has the strength to face the world. The film, backed by a pulsing Alex North score, captures the ambiance of the locale but offers little reason to spend much time with its characters.

THE STORY ON PAGE ONE

Produced by Jerry Wald
Directed by Clifford Odets
Screenplay by Clifford Odets
Photographed in CinemaScope by James Wong Howe
Music by Elmer Bernstein
122 minutes

Cast: Rita Hayworth, Anthony Franciosa, Gig Young, Margaret Dunnock, Hugh Griffith, Sanford Meisner, Robert Burton, Alfred Ryder, Katherine Squire, Raymond Greenleaf, Myrna Fahey, Leo Penn, Sheridan Comerate, Biff Elliot, Tom Greenway, Jay Adler, Carol Seflinger, Theodore Newton

An exciting courtroom drama, finely scripted and directed by Clifford Odets, about a man (Gig Young) and a woman (Rita Hayworth) who kill her husband (Alfred Ryder), a brutish fellow, and whose love holds them together through their ordeal at the trial. The fact that they care so much for each other brings them the defense of an attorney (Anthony Franciosa) who sympathizes with them, despite being aware that he is going up against a tough, veteran prosecutor (Robert Burton). The trial brings out the fact that the killing was accidental, and also reveals the lives of the people involved. The dialogue is brilliant and well performed.

THESE THOUSAND HILLS

Produced by David Weisbart
Directed by Richard Fleischer
Screenplay by Alfred Hayes, based on the novel by A. B. Guthrie, Jr.
Photographed in CinemaScope and DeLuxe Color by Charles G. Clarke
Music by Leigh Harline
96 minutes

Cast: Don Murray, Richard Egan, Lee Remick, Patricia Owens, Stuart Whitman, Albert Dekker, Harold J. Stone, Royal Dano, Jean Willes, Douglas Fowley, Fuzzy Knight, Robert Adler, Barbara Morrison, Ned Weaver, Ken Renard

The story of an ambitious cowboy (Don Murray), who saves his money and buys a ranch with a loan from a dance hall girl (Lee Remick). He marries the niece (Patricia Owens) of a banker (Albert Dekker) and becomes a political candidate. He is forced to join a posse led by a rancher (Richard Egan), which tracks down and hangs a former buddy (Stuart Whitman) of the cowboy-turned-leading citizen, who is unable to do anything about saving his friend. But when the rancher beats up the dance hall girl, he steps in to fight the bully. Just as the bully is about to kill him, he is shot by the dance hall girl. Murray is fine as the cowboy who learns about life and the script contains more incident and character than most Westerns.

WARLOCK

Produced and directed by Edward Dymtryk
Screenplay by Robert Alan Aurthur, based on the novel by Oakley Hall
Photographed in CinemaScope and DeLuxe Color by Joe MacDonald
Music by Leigh Harline
122 minutes

Cast: Henry Fonda, Richard Widmark, Anthony Quinn, Dorothy Malone, Dolores Michaels, Wallace Ford, Tom Drake, Richard Arlen, De Forest Kelley, Regis Toomey, Vaughn Taylor, Don Beddoe, Whit Bissell, Bartlett

Robinson, J. Anthony Hughes, Donald Barry, Frank Gorshin, Ian MacDonald

A darkly hued and dramatic Western, with Henry Fonda as a top frontier marshall who comes to the town of Warlock to protect it from a gang of outlaws, but who also expects graft and privileges. The town deputy (Richard Widmark) is himself a reformed outlaw now dedicated to the peaceful life, and the townspeople finally back him in cleaning up the lawless elements, which includes getting rid of the strutting marshal and his neurotic gambler-sidekick (Anthony Quinn). *Warlock,* partly filmed in Utah, contains many interesting characters in its multileveled plot and delves deeper into frontier life than the majority of Westerns.

WOMAN OBSESSED

Produced by Sydney Boehm
Directed by Henry Hathaway
Screenplay by Sydney Boehm, based on a novel by John Mantley
Photographed in CinemaScope and DeLuxe Color by William C. Mellor
Music by Hugo Friedhofer
103 minutes

Cast: Susan Hayward, Stephen Boyd, Barbara Nichols, Dennis Holmes, Theodore Bikel, Ken Scott, James Philbrook, Florence MacMichael, Jack Raine, Mary Carroll, Fred Graham, Mike Lally

A young widow (Susan Hayward), living in the wilds of the Canadian Northwest with her eight-year-old son (Dennis Holmes), has a hard time keeping her farm going and takes on a rough young man (Stephen Boyd) as a helper. They fall in love and marry, but the boy doesn't like the quick-tempered new father, who sometimes slaps his mother. His temper causes him to be jailed for a month, during which time his wife finds she is pregnant. In searching for her missing son in a violent storm she has a miscarriage. The husband continues the search, which causes him to fall into a quagmire, from which he is rescued by the boy. The trials bring the family members together in a resolve for better understanding. The blizzards and the rains and the forest fires contribute to the desperately difficult life of the lady of the title.

20TH CENTURY-FOX ACADEMY AWARDS FOR 1959

SHELLEY WINTERS: Best supporting actress, *The Diary of Anne Frank.*

WILLIAM C. MELLOR: Best cinematography, black and white, *The Diary of Anne Frank.*

LYLE R. WHEELER, GEORGE W. DAVIS: Best art direction, black and white, *The Diary of Anne Frank.*

WALTER M. SCOTT, STUART A. REISS: Best set decoration, black and white, *The Diary of Anne Frank.*

CAN-CAN

Produced by Jack Cummings
Directed by Walter Lang
Screenplay by Dorothy Kingsley and Charles Lederer, based on the stage musical by Abe Burrows
Photographed in Todd-AO and Technicolor by William H. Daniels
Songs by Cole Porter
Musical direction by Nelson Riddle
131 minutes

Cast: Frank Sinatra, Shirley MacLaine, Maurice Chevalier, Louis Jourdan, Juliet Prowse, Marcel Dalio, Leon Belasco, Nestor Paiva, John A. Neris, Jean Del Val, Eugene Borden, Jonathan Kidd, Ann Codee, Marc Wilder, Lili Valenty

The rowdy Cole Porter Broadway musical brought to the screen with the same story lines, but with three Porter standards added to make it more appealing to a wider audience. The story takes its cue from the fact that the can-can was banned as lewd in the Paris of the late nineteenth century. Shirley MacLaine is the owner of a nightclub where the dance is performed and she is frequently hauled into court to pay fines. Her lawyer-boyfriend (Frank Sinatra) always comes to her aid but never gets around to marrying her, so she accepts a proposal from a judge (Louis Jourdan), which rouses jealousy and a resolve to marry from the lawyer. The story is thus lightly strung together to allow for a procession of Porter songs and dances, with Maurice Chevalier as a knowing old judge enjoying the banned dance and helping to get it sanctioned by the law. The choreography of Hermes Pan helps audiences understand why the wild dance was an eyebrow-raiser in its day.

CRACK IN THE MIRROR

Produced by Darryl F. Zanuck
Directed by Richard Fleischer
Screenplay by Mark Canfield, based on the novel *Drama in the Mirror* by Marcel Haedrich
Photographed in CinemaScope by William C. Mellor
Music by Maurice Jarré
97 minutes

Cast: Orson Welles, Juliette Greco, Bradford Dillman, Alexander Knox, Catherine Lacey, William Lucas, Maurice Teynac, Austin Willis, Cec Linder, Eugene Deckers, Yves Brainville, Vivian Matalon, Jacques Marin, Martine Alexis

A tricky courtroom drama, with Orson Welles, Juliette Greco, and Bradford Dillman each playing two roles in similar dramatic circumstances—that of an older man with a mistress and a business associate, with the latter killing the first. The film cuts back and forth between the two levels of society—the one grubby and the other elegant—and allows viewers to draw comparisons between the justice afforded in each case. Filmed in Paris and capturing the character of the city, the film suffers from its involved devices but retains interesting insights into French jurisprudence.

DESIRE IN THE DUST

Produced and directed by William F. Claxton
Screenplay by Charles Lang, based on a novel by Harry Whittington
Photographed in CinemaScope by Lucien Ballard
Music by Paul Dunlap
105 minutes

Cast: Raymond Burr, Martha Hyer, Joan Bennett, Ken Scott, Brett Halsey, Anne Helm, Jack Ging, Edward Binns, Maggie Mahoney, Douglas Fowley, Kelly Thordsen, Rex Ingram, Irene Ryan, Paul Baxley, Robert Earle, Patricia Snow

Drama in the Deep South, with Raymond Burr as the head of a wealthy family, who welcomes home a convict (Ken Scott) after he has served a sentence for the car accident killing of a family son. The actual accident was caused by the father and his daughter (Martha Hyer), who promise to take care of the convict on his return provided he will take the blame. Since he loves the daughter, he does as asked. But the shifty family do not live up to their promises and the convict has to clear himself in order to be free of their machinations.

ESTHER AND THE KING

Produced and directed by Raoul Walsh
Screenplay by Raoul Walsh and Michael Elkins

Photographed in CinemaScope and Technicolor by Mario
  Bava
Music by Francesco Lavagnino and Roberto Nicolosi
110 minutes

Cast: Joan Collins, Richard Egan, Denis O'Dea, Sergio
Fantoni, Rick Battaglia, Renato Baldini, Danielle Rocca,
Folco Lulli, Gabriele Tinti, Rosalba Neri, Robert
Buchanan

A biblical epic made in Italy, with the accent more on
spectacle than the scriptures. Esther (Joan Collins)
marries King Ahasuerus (Richard Egan) because she
believes that as a Jew she can help her people under
the anti-Semitic rule of Persia, a policy advocated by
the king's wicked minister (Sergio Fantoni). Her faith
helps bring peace to the king and the country. A
more enlightening account may be found in the Bible.

FLAMING STAR

Produced by David Weisbart
Directed by Don Siegel
Screenplay by Clair Huffaker and Nunnally Johnson,
  based on a novel by Clair Huffaker
Photographed in CinemaScope and DeLuxe Color by
  Charles G. Clarke
Music by Cyril J. Mockridge
92 minutes

Cast: Elvis Presley, Steve Forrest, Barbara Eden, Dolores
Del Rio, John McIntire, Rudolph Acosta, Karl Swenson,
Ford Rainey, Richard Jaeckel, Anne Benton, L. Q.
Jones, Douglas Dick, Tom Reese, Marian Goldina

An interesting Western, with Elvis Presley—and just
two songs—as an Indian half-breed caught up in
racial tensions in frontier Texas. His loyalties are torn
between his white father (John McIntire) and his
Kiowa mother (Dolores Del Rio). His settler father
is a champion for tolerance, but raids by Kiowas
make his position impossible and finally bring death
to his son. It remains for the all-white brother (Steve
Forrest) to carry on the message for understanding
between the races and peace for all. A solid script and
a good, quiet performance by Presley make the film a
respectable item in the genre and something quite removed from most of Presley's pictures.

FOR THE LOVE OF MIKE

Produced and directed by George Sherman
Screenplay by D. D. Beauchamp
Photographed in CinemaScope and DeLuxe Color by
  Alex Philips
Music by Paul La Vista
87 minutes

Cast: Richard Basehart, Stuart Erwin, Arthur Shields,
Danny Zaidivar, Armando Silvestre, Elsa Cardenas,
Michael Steckler, Rex Allen, Danny Bravo

A genial Western with religious overtones, about two
priests (Richard Basehart and Arthur Shields) trying
to raise money for a new church in a small Mexican
town. One of their wards, a homeless boy (Danny
Zaldivar) who loves and cares for animals, enters a
horse he has nursed back to health in a race sponsored
by Western star Rex Allen (playing himself) and wins.
He turns over the cash prize to the priests to help
them get their church.

FRECKLES

Produced by Harry Spalding
Directed by Andrew V. McLaglen
Screenplay by Harry Spalding, based on the novel by
  Gene Stratton Porter
Photographed in CinemaScope and DeLuxe Color by
  Floyd Crosby
Music by Henry Vars
83 minutes

Cast: Martin West, Carol Christensen, Jack Lambert,
Steven Peck, Roy Barcroft, Lorna Thayer, Ken Curtis,
John Eldredge

A timber Western, filmed in the Big Bear Lake area of
California, about a shy, freckled-faced young man
(Martin West), who falls in love with the daughter
(Carol Christensen) of his timber-baron boss (Roy
Barcroft) and proves himself a hero when he helps
halt the bandits who are stealing timber. His courage
is a moral pointer in view of the fact that the boy
has only one hand. In this fourth filming of the 1903
Porter novel, the accent is again on sentiment.

FROM THE TERRACE

Produced and directed by Mark Robson
Screenplay by Ernest Lehman, based on a novel by John
  O'Hara
Photographed in CinemaScope and DeLuxe Color by
  Leo Tover
Music by Elmer Bernstein
144 minutes

Cast: Paul Newman, Joanne Woodward, Myrna Loy,
Ina Balin, Leon Ames, Elizabeth Allen, Barbara Eden,
George Grizzard, Patrick O'Neal, Felix Aylmer, Raymond
Greenleaf, Malcolm Attesbury, Raymond Bailey, Ted de
Corsia

John O'Hara's raunchy novel, somewhat mellowed for
the 1960 screen, but still stinging with sexual tensions.
A Wall Street financial adviser (Paul Newman) is
unhappy in his marriage; his wife (Joanne Woodward)
is promiscuous, but largely because he has shown her
little love, just as his father (Leon Ames) had shut
aside his wife (Myrna Loy), causing her to become
alcoholic and adulterous. The father has loved only
one member of his family, a boy killed in childhood.
The surviving son tries to win his father's respect by

becoming even more successful in business than him, but eventually sees the folly of such striving and settles down with a decent young girl (Ina Balin) who loves him. Long and loquacious, the film nevertheless contains some fine dialogue and insights into its complex characters.

THE HIGH-POWERED RIFLE

Produced and directed by Maury Dexter
Screenplay by Joseph Fritz
Photographed by Floyd Crosby
Music by Albert Glasser
62 minutes

Cast: Willard Parker, Allison Hayes, Dan Simmons, John Holland, Shirley O'Hara, Terrea Lea, Lennie Geer, Clark Howat, A. G. Vitanza

A private detective (Willard Parker) survives a number of attempts on his life by an unknown assailant. His investigation leads him into a romance with the girl friend (Allison Hayes) of a crime boss, until he finds that she is the would-be killer and why she wants him out of the way.

HIGH TIME

Produced by Charles Brackett
Directed by Blake Edwards
Screenplay by Tom and Frank Waldman, based on a story by Garson Kanin
Photographed in CinemaScope and DeLuxe Color by Ellsworth Fredericks
Songs by Sammy Cahn and James Van Heusen
Music by Henry Mancini
102 minutes

Cast: Bing Crosby, Fabian, Tuesday Weld, Nicole Maurey, Richard Beymer, Patrick Adiarte, Yvonne Craig, Jimmy Boyd, Gavin MacLeod, Kenneth MacKenna, Nina Shipman, Paul Schreiber, Angus Duncan, Dick Crockett

Bing Crosby at college—as a millionaire widower who decides to get the education he never had when he was a youngster, despite his great success in business. He enrolls for the whole four, live-in years and endears himself to the fellow students with his willingness to go through the throes of initiation, which includes appearing at a dance as Scarlett O'Hara. He does everything but chase after young girls; instead he sets his sights on a faculty member (Nicole Maurey). A pleasant comedy, resting largely on Bing's talents, and containing a memorable song by Sammy Cahn and Jimmy Van Heusen, "The Second Time Around."

LEGIONS OF THE NILE

Produced by Virgile De Blasi and Italo Zingarelli
Directed by Vittorio Cottafavi

Screenplay by Vittorio Cottafavi, Giorgio Cristallini, Arnoldo Marrousu, and Ennio de Concini
Photographed in CinemaScope and DeLuxe Color by Mario Pacheco
Music by Renzo Rossellini
87 minutes

Cast: Linda Cristal, Georges Marchal, Ettore Manni, Maria Mahor, Conrado Sammartin, Alfredo Mayo, Daniela Rocca, Mino Doro, Juan Majan, Andrea Aureli, Stefano Terra, Stefano Oppedisano

An Italian production about Cleopatra and acquired by 20th Century-Fox so that it would not conflict with their ultra-plush film about the same famous lady. Here she appears in the guise of Linda Cristal, with Georges Marchal as Antony and Conrado Sanmartin as Caesar, together with the familiar plot.

LET'S MAKE LOVE

Produced by Jerry Wald
Directed by George Cukor
Screenplay by Norman Krasna, with additional material by Hal Kanter
Photographed in CinemaScope and DeLuxe Color by Daniel L. Fapp
Music direction by Lionel Newman
Songs by Sammy Cahn and Jimmy Van Heusen
118 minutes

Cast: Marilyn Monroe, Yves Montand, Tony Randall, Frankie Vaughan, Wilfred-Hyde White. David Burns, Michael David, Mara Lynn, Dennis King, Jr., Joe Besser, Madge Kennedy
Guest stars: Milton Berle, Bing Crosby, Gene Kelly

The main character of *Let's Make Love* is an international tycoon (Yves Montand) who falls in love with a Broadway star (Marilyn Monroe) but refrains from telling her who he is because he is the satirical subject of the show in which she is appearing. Instead he lets her think he is a struggling actor—and hires the likes of Milton Berle, Bing Crosby, and Gene Kelly to give him lessons in comedy, singing, and dancing. Eventually he confesses his ruse and manages to persuade her that he is not the ogre her show paints him as being. For all the talent involved, *Let's Make Love* is an uneven and unconvincing package. But it contains many fine moments and serves as a generous reminder of the marvelous Marilyn.

THE LOST WORLD

Produced and directed by Irwin Allen
Screenplay by Charles Bennett and Irwin Allen, based on a story by Arthur Conan Doyle
Photographed in CinemaScope and DeLuxe Color by Winton Hoch
Music by Paul Sawtell and Bert Shefter
97 minutes

Cast: Michael Rennie, Jill St. John, David Hedison, Claude Rains, Fernando Lamas, Richard Haydn, Ray Stricklyn, Jay Novello, Vitina Marcus, Ian Wolfe, John Graham, Colin Campbell

The 1925 filming of the Conan Doyle science-fiction classic was a trailblazer of its kind. This version offers visual improvements on the original, with splendid special effects, such as actual lizards photographed to appear huge and fearsome. The story is that of an expedition led by a famous scientist (Claude Rains) to a remote area of the Amazon, where he believes life has not changed since prehistoric times. The fierce monsters and wild terrain exceed even his expectations. Among the group are a nobleman-sportsman (Michael Rennie), his girl friend (Jill St. John), who falls in love with the covering reporter (David Hedison), and a dour fellow zoologist (Richard Haydn). Several of the party lose their lives before the expedition returns to tell its exotic story.

THE MILLIONAIRESS

Produced by Pierre Rouve
Directed by Anthony Asquith
Screenplay by Wolf Mankowitz, based on the play by George Bernard Shaw
Photographed in CinemaScope and DeLuxe Color by Jack Hildyard
Music by Georges van Parys
90 minutes

Cast: Sophia Loren, Peter Sellers, Alistair Sim, Vittorio de Sica, Dennis Price, Gard Raymond, Alfie Bass, Miriam Karlin, Noel Purcell, Virginia Vernon, Basil Hoskins, Diana Coupland, Graham Stark, Pauline Johnson

A spoiled and greatly wealthy girl (Sophia Loren), who believes money can buy anything, runs up against a challenge when she meets a Hindu doctor (Peter Sellers) working in a clinic in the slums of London. He is totally dedicated to his work and is a socialist politically. She falls in love with him, but fails to make any impression with her beauty or her money. He tries to evade marriage by inventing a clause in his mother's creed which stipulates that a wife must set out with only five dollars and make her own living for three months. The feisty beauty goes to work in a sweatshop and turns it into a factory within weeks. Her wily lawyer (Alistair Sim), fearing for her mental well being, devises a scheme to win her the modest doctor she loves. The film is a pleasant blending of the wit and social commentary of Shaw, the lusty beauty of Loren, and the comedic acting of Sellers. A fine brew.

MURDER INC.

Produced by Burt Balaban
Directed by Burt Balaban and Stuart Rosenberg
Screenplay by Irv Tunick and Mel Barr, from a book by Burton Turkus and Sid Feder
Photographed in CinemaScope by Gayne Rescher
Music by Frank De Vol
104 minutes

Cast: Stuart Whitman, May Britt, Henry Morgan, Peter Falk, David J. Stewart, Simon Oakland, Morey Amsterdam, Joseph Benard, Warren Fennerty, Joseph Elic, Vincent Gardenia, Eli Mintz, Helen Waters, Sarah Vaughn

Brooklyn in the early Thirties, as a crime syndicate flourishes and controls numerous businesses. A young singer (Stuart Whitman) and his dancer girl friend (May Britt) are drawn into the ring when he borrows money from a bad source—a wily, repulsive killer named Abe Reles (Peter Falk), who works for syndicate leader Louis "Lepke" Buchalter (David J. Stewart). The film lacks excitement, but presents the facts about the infamous organization that once made Brooklyn a center of commercialized murder. Actual locations are valuable assets and Falk's performance as the hood who turned state's evidence—at the cost of his life—is chillingly memorable.

NORTH TO ALASKA

Produced and directed by Henry Hathaway
Screenplay by John Lee Mahin, Martin Rackin, and Claude Binyon, based on a play *Birthday Gift* by Laszlo Fodor and an idea by John Kafka
Photographed in CinemaScope and DeLuxe Color by Leon Shamroy
Songs by Russell Faith, Robert P. Marcucci, and Peter de Angelis
Musical direction by Lionel Newman
122 minutes

Cast: John Wayne, Stewart Granger, Ernie Kovacs, Fabian, Capucine, Mickey Shaughnessy, Karl Swenson, Joe Sawyer, Kathleen Freeman, John Qualen, Stanley Adams, Stephen Courtleigh, Douglas Dick, Jerry O'Sullivan, Ollie O'Toole, Frank Faylen, Fred Graham, Alan Carney, Peter Bourne

A roisterous north-Western, with John Wayne and Stewart Granger as gold mining partners striking it lucky in the Alaska of the 1890's. Granger asks Wayne to go to Seattle and bring back his fiancée (Capucine), but Wayne falls in love with the spirited girl himself and eventually gets her, with Granger accepting the fact as he looks for other girls and other brawls. In the meantime a con man (Ernie Kovacs) manages to get both men involved in bizarre schemes. *North to Alaska* fills its two hours with a stream of action and a vast amount of fist fights, including one of the most elaborately staged barroom brawls in Hollywood history.

ONE FOOT IN HELL

Produced by Sydney Boehm
Directed by James B. Clark
Screenplay by Aaron Spelling and Sydney Boehm, from a story by Aaron Spelling
Photographed in CinemaScope and DeLuxe Color by William C. Mellor
Music by Dominic Frontiere
89 minutes

Cast: Alan Ladd, Don Murray, Dan O'Herlihy, Dolores Michaels, Barry Coe, Larry Gates, Karl Swenson, John Alexander, Rachel Stephens, Henry Norrell, Harry Carter, Ann Morriss, Stanley Adams

A Western with a theme of revenge. A townsman (Alan Ladd) resents his fellow citizens when his pregnant wife dies because of their failure to provide a small sum for medicine. The town is contrite, but he quietly prepares to cripple their economy. He becomes the sheriff and plans to rob the bank when all the returns are in from the cattle season. He recruits an alcoholic artist (Don Murray) and a mean young gunslinger (Barry Coe), but when the artist falls in love with a girl (Dolores Michaels), he decides to go straight, which includes putting an end to the sheriff's scheme. An unusual Western, with a strong strain of morality, although not wholly plausible.

SECRET OF THE PURPLE REEF

Produced by Gene Corman
Directed by William Witney
Screenplay by Harold Yablonsky, based on a novel by Dorothy Cottrell
Photographed in CinemaScope and DeLuxe Color by Kay Norton
Music by Buddy Bregman
81 minutes

Cast: Jeff Richards, Margia Dean, Peter Falk, Richard Chamberlain, Terence de Marney, Gina Petrushka, Phil Rosen, Robert Earl, Larry Markow, Frank Ricco, Jerry Mitchell

A mystery set in the Caribbean, concerning a young man (Jeff Richards) out to solve the loss of a family fishing ship during calm weather. He and his brother (Richard Chamberlain) receive some help from the girl friend (Margia Dean) of a vice lord (Peter Falk) who is at the bottom of the dirty work. A conventional crime yarn considerably helped by the colorful scenery and waters of the West Indies.

SEPTEMBER STORM

Produced by Edward L. Alperson
Directed by Byron Haskin
Screenplay by Paul Stader, based on a story by Steve Fisher
Photographed in StereoVision, CinemaScope, and DeLuxe Color by Jorge Stahl, Jr., and Lamar Boren

Songs by Edward L. Alperson, Jr., and Jerry Winn
Music by Edward L. Alperson, Jr., and Raoul Kraushaar
99 minutes

Cast: Joanne Dru, Mark Stevens, Robert Strauss, Asher Dann, Jean Pierre Kerien, Claude Ivry, Vera Valmont, Charito Leon, Ernesto Lapena

A New York model (Joanne Dru) on vacation in Majorca meets a handsome local boy (Asher Dann), who passes himself off as a yacht owner, although he merely works for one. An American adventurer (Mark Stevens) and his surly partner (Robert Strauss) persuade the boy to take them and the girl out to the site of sunken treasure. After surviving a storm and underwater mishaps, they find the treasure, and the adventurer and the model find romance together. Originally shot in 3-D, the film takes advantage of the colorful Majorca scenery and contains some fine underwater filming.

SEVEN THIEVES

Produced by Sydney Boehm
Directed by Henry Hathaway
Screenplay by Sydney Boehm, from a novel by Max Catto
Photographed in CinemaScope by Sam Leavitt
Music by Dominic Frontiere
102 minutes

Cast: Edward G. Robinson, Rod Steiger, Joan Collins, Eli Wallach, Alexander Scourby, Michael Dante, Berry Kroeger, Sebastian Cabot, Marcel Hillaire, John Berardino, Alphonse Martell, Jonathan Kidd

A group of skillful crooks, led by a discredited professor (Edward G. Robinson), plan an intricate, bold scheme to rob four million dollars from the vaults beneath the casino at Monte Carlo. They move against impossible odds, circumvent the Casino's elaborate security devices, and achieve their objective. But the excitement of success proves too much for the professor, who succumbs to a heart attack. The survivors then find that their loot is in such high denominations they cannot get rid of it. The film is an expert exercise in heisting, with a fine cast and tight direction from Henry Hathaway.

SINK THE BISMARCK

Produced by John Brabourne
Directed by Lewis Gilbert
Screenplay and story by Edmund H. North, from a book by C. S. Forester
Photographed in CinemaScope by Christopher Challis
Music by Clifton Parker
Musical direction by Muir Mathieson
97 minutes

Cast: Kenneth More, Dana Wynter, Carl Mohner, Laurence Naismith, Geoffrey Keene, Karel Stepanek, Michael

Frank Sinatra, Shirley MacLaine, and Maurice Chevalier in *Can-Can*.

Orson Welles and Juliette Greco in *Crack in the Mirror*.

Tom Tryon and Elana Eden in *The Story of Ruth*.

Rick Battaglia and Joan Collins in *Esther and the King*.

Elvis Presley and Dolores Del Rio in *Flaming Star*.

Capucine and John Wayne in *North to Alaska*.

Yves Montand and Marilyn Monroe in *Let's Make Love*.

Joanne Woodward and Paul Newman in *From the Terrace*.

Jay Novello, Claude Rains, Michael Rennie, Fernando Lamas, Richard Haydn, David Hedison, Jill St. John, Ray Stricklyn, and Vitina Marcus in *The Lost World*.

Bing Crosby and Nicole Maurey in *High Time*.

Sophia Loren and Peter Sellers in *The Millionairess*.

Dean Stockwell and Wendy Hiller in *Sons and Lovers*.

Hordern, Maurice Denham, Michael Goodliffe, Edmund Knight, Jack Watling, Jack Gwillam, Mark Dignam, Ernest Clarke, John Horsley, Peter Burton

A fascinating account of the career of the German battleship, from its launching (using German newsreel footage) to its end in the Spring of 1941, when it was surrounded and sunk by British warships. The central figure is a stern intelligence captain (Kenneth More), who has lost his wife in an air raid and whose son is a naval pilot in the engagement against the *Bismarck*. He directs a brilliant campaign from the naval headquarters in London, finding, tracking, and deploying his forces against the almost invincible German ship. His job is made somewhat more bearable by the sympathetic help of a young lady naval officer (Dana Wynter). The film is a clever explanation of the decisive battle, using models as well as actual footage to give a sense of drama to the difficult task of sinking the great battleship.

SONS AND LOVERS

Produced by Jerry Wald
Directed by Jack Cardiff
Screenplay by Gavin Lambert and T. E. B. Clarke, from a novel by D. H. Lawrence
Photographed in CinemaScope by Freddie Francis
Music by Mario Nascimbene
103 minutes

Cast: Trevor Howard, Dean Stockwell, Wendy Hiller, Mary Ure, Heather Sears, William Lucas, Conrad Phillips, Donald Pleasance, Ernest Thesiger, Rosalie Crutchely, Elizabeth Begley, Sean Barrett

The D. H. Lawrence story of the complexities of love here receives a respectable treatment, although somewhat lessening the son's fondness for his mother. The story is set in a grimy English mining town in the early years of the century, and centers on a young man (Dean Stockwell) who is the product of a rough,

miner-father (Trevor Howard) and his mismatched, gentle wife (Wendy Hiller). The boy wants to be an artist, which offends his father but which gains every support from his mother—and later from local girls. His strong attachment to his mother inhibits him emotionally, but with her death he finds the release and resolve to leave home and pursue his interests in the world. A good cast helps overcome the limiting subject matter, as does the direction of former photographer Jack Cardiff, whose visual instincts supply sensitive extra dimensions.

THE STORY OF RUTH

Produced by Samuel G. Engel
Directed by Henry Koster
Screenplay by Norman Corwin
Photographed in CinemaScope and DeLuxe Color by Arthur E. Arling
Music by Franz Waxman
132 minutes

Cast: Stuart Whitman, Tom Tryon, Peggy Wood, Viveca Lindfors, Jeff Morrow, Elana Eden, Thayer David, Les Tremayne, Eduard Franz, Leo Fuchs, Lili Valenty, John Gabriel, Ziva Rodann, Basil Ruysdael, John Banner, Adelina Pedroza, Daphne Einhorn

Norman Corwin's treatment of the biblical tale makes Ruth (Elana Eden) a Moabite priestess who renounces the graven gods for the God of Israel. Her dedication takes time to find acceptance because she is a foreigner and suspect. Eventually her rights are upheld by the Jewish courts and she marries Boaz (Stuart Whitman), which helps her in her resolve to be a force in the religious life of her adopted country. The film is sincere but rather turgid and requires a degree of religious knowledge to be fully appreciated. Interesting decor and a refined score by Franz Waxman are plus factors.

THE THIRD VOICE

Produced by Maury Dexter and Hubert Cornfield
Directed by Hubert Cornfield
Screenplay by Hubert Cornfield, from a novel by Charles Williams
Photographed in CinemaScope by Ernest Haller
Music by Johnny Mandel
80 minutes

Cast: Edmond O'Brien, Julie London, Laraine Day, Olga San Juan, George Eldredge, Tom Hernandez, Abel Franco, Edward Colmans, Tom Daly, Ralph Brooks, Lucile Curtis, Shirley O'Hara, Raoul De Leon, Sylvia Rey

The ex-secretary and mistress (Laraine Day) of a wealthy businessman plans to murder him and gain some of his wealth. She hires a man (Edmond O'Brien) to help her kill the man when he arrives in Mexico City and then assume his identity. But the cohort is a

Kenneth More and Dana Wynter in *Sink the Bismarck.*

Ernie Kovacs and Dick Shawn in *Wake Me When It's Over.*

Montgomery Clift and Lee Remick in *Wild River.*

greedy type and schemes to acquire all of the wealth for himself. He almost kills the girl, but another girl (Julie London), who has allowed herself to be picked up by the cohort and who is actually the murdered man's fiancée, arrives with the police in time to save the plotter and arrest the pair.

13 FIGHTING MEN

Produced by Jack Leewood
Directed by Harry Gerstad
Screenplay by Robert Hamer and Jack Thomas
Photographed in CinemaScope by Walter Strenge
Music by Irving Gertz
71 minutes

Cast: Grant Williams, Brad Dexter, Carole Mathews, Robert Dix, Richard Garland, Richard Crane, Rayford Barnes, John Erwin, Bob Palmer, Rex Holman, John Merrick, Mark Hickman, Dick Monahan

At the end of the Civil War, a group of returning Confederates take the opportunity to seize a Union gold shipment, with the rationale that things will be hard for them and that this will make their return home easier. Their leader (Brad Dexter) has problems keeping them from turning into bandits and the Union commander (Grant Withers) finds that the presence of gold has a demoralizing effect on his men, too.

TRAPPED IN TANGIERS

Produced by Antonio Cervi
Directed by Ricardo Freda
Screenplay by Alessandro Continenza, Vittorio Petrilli, Paolo Spinola, and Ricardo Freda
Photographed in Supercinescope by Gabor Pogany
77 minutes

Cast: Edmund Purdom, Genevieve Page, Gino Cervi, José Guardiola, Felix De Franco, Antonio Molino, Enrique Relayo, Mario Moreno, Amparo Rivelles

A minor crime melodrama, about an American agent (Edmund Purdom) working in Tangiers to trace a ring of narcotics smugglers. He falls in love with the adopted daughter (Genevieve Page) of a prominent citizen (Gino Cervi), who turns out to be the leader of the ring, whose death leaves the way clear for the lovers. The film is an inferior sample of the kind of material 20th Century-Fox was acquiring for distribution at this time.

TWELVE HOURS TO KILL

Produced by John Healy
Directed by Edward L. Cahn
Screenplay by Jerry Sohl, based on a serial by Richard Stern
Photographed in CinemaScope by Floyd Crosby
Music by Paul Dunlap
83 minutes

Cast: Nico Minardos, Barbara Eden, Grant Richards, Russ Conway, Art Baker, Gavin MacLeod, Cece Whitney, Richard Reeves, Byron Foulger, Barbara Mansell, Ted Knight, Shep Sanders, Charles Meredith

A young Greek engineer (Nico Minardos) becomes an eyewitness to a murder and is taken into custody by the police for safekeeping. But it turns out that the police are in cahoots with the murderers and the Greek then has to flee for his life from both sets before a solution is found. In the meantime he is subjected to a great amount of pursuit in this very complicated crime yarn.

VALLEY OF THE REDWOODS

Produced by Gene Corman
Directed by William Witney
Screenplay by Leo Gordon and Daniel Madison, from a story by Gene Corman
Photographed in CinemaScope by Kay Norton
Music by Buddy Bregman
63 minutes

Cast: John Hudson, Lynn Bernay, Ed Nelson, Michael Forest, Robert Shayne, John Brinkley, Bruno De Soto, Hal Torey, Chris Miller

Yet another crime caper, as three colleagues (John Hudson, Lynn Bernay, and Ed Nelson) plan a payroll robbery, carry it out, and make their getaway. Their perfect plan turns out to be less foolproof than they thought. Things go wrong and the culprits end up either dead or captured.

WAKE ME WHEN IT'S OVER

Produced and directed by Mervyn LeRoy
Screenplay by Richard Breen, from a novel by Howard Singer
Photographed in CinemaScope and DeLuxe Color by Leon Shamroy
Music by Cyril J. Mockridge
Musical direction by Lionel Newman
126 minutes

Cast: Ernie Kovacs, Margo Moore, Jack Warden, Nobu McCarthy, Dick Shawn, Don Knotts, Robert Strauss, Noreen Nash, Parley Baer, Robert Emhardt, Marvin Kaplan, Tommy Nishimura, Raymond Bailey, Robert Burton

A wacky service comedy, about a veteran (Dick Shawn), who is redrafted by mistake and sent to a small, lonely island off Japan. The commander is a captain (Ernie Kovacs) who is bored, as are his men. To perk up morale, the veteran—a talented fix-it operator—puts together a hotel from surplus materials and hires local girls as servants. The hotel becomes popular and soon leads to a service investigation and a court-martial of the veteran. His captain puts up a good defense, but the veteran gets out by the same fluke under which he was reenlisted. An amusing concoction, more than a little short on credibility, but a fond reminder of the genially lunatic Ernie Kovacs.

WHEN COMEDY WAS KING

Produced by Robert Youngson
Written by Robert Youngson
Music by Ted Royal
Musical direction by Herman Fuchs and Louis Turchen
Narrated by Dwight Weist
90 minutes

Cast: The Keystone Cops, Harry Langdon, Laurel and Hardy, Charlie Chase, Buster Keaton, Edgar Kennedy, Fatty Arbuckle, Wallace Beery, Charlie Chaplin, Billy Bevan, Andy Clyde, Chester Conklin, Vernon Dent, Gloria Swanson, Ben Turpin, Mabel Normand, The Sennett Girls, Snub Pollard, Madeline Hurlock

A superb compilation of clips from the early days of the silent screen, concentrating on the great slapstick performers, like the Keystone Kops and Fatty Arbuckle, Ben Turpin and Buster Keaton, etc. The fact that much of the original material has been lost or deteriorated makes this film an ever more valuable collection.

WILD RIVER

Produced and directed by Elia Kazan
Screenplay by Paul Osborn, from two novels, *Mud on the Stars* by William Bradford Huie and *Dunbar's Cove* by Borden Deal
Photographed in CinemaScope and DeLuxe Color by Ellsworth Fredericks
Music by Kenyon Hopkins
115 minutes

Cast: Montgomery Clift, Lee Remick, Jo Van Fleet, Albert Salmi, Jay C. Flippen, James Westerfield, Barbara Loden, Frank Overton, Malcolm Atterbury, Robert Earl Jones, Bruce Dern

A drama of the Tennessee Valley Authority in the early 1930's, with Montgomery Clift as a sensitive TVA agent representing progress and coming into conflict with local residents who object to the progress inflicted by the government. In particular he clashes with an old lady (Jo Van Fleet) who refuses to give up the tract of land the TVA needs to complete its project on the Tennessee River. She dies when finally evicted. The agent also receives opposition from local bigots, who resent his liberal views toward blacks. His success is hard won but helped by the love of the old lady's granddaughter (Lee Remick). *Wild River* suffers from the too poetic image of Clift as the agent—a more practical image would have been better—but

Elia Kazan's direction and attention to detail makes this an interesting piece of little-heralded Americana.

THE WIZARD OF BAGHDAD

Produced by Sam Katzman
Directed by George Sherman
Screenplay by Jesse L. Lasky, Jr. and Pat Silver, from a story by Samuel Newman
Photographed in CinemaScope and DeLuxe Color by Ellis W. Carter
Music by Irving Gertz
92 minutes

Cast: Dick Shawn, Diane Baker, Barry Coe, John Van Dreelen, Robert F. Simon, Vaughn Taylor, Michael David, Stanley Adams, William Edmonson, Leslie Wenner, Michael Burns, Don Beddoe, Kim Hamilton, Joey Faye

An incompetent genie (Dick Shawn) tries to straighten out things in old Baghdad. A wicked sultan (John Van Dreelen) aims to take over the throne and keep the prince (Barry Coe) and the princess (Diane Baker) from assuming their rightful places, but the bumbling genie sees to it that the sultan loses. As a spoof on oriental fantasies, the film is amusing but falls short of its marks.

YOUNG JESSE JAMES

Produced by Jack Leewood
Directed by William Claxton
Screenplay by Orville H. Hampton and Jerry Sackheim
Photographed in CinemaScope by Carl Berger
Music by Irving Gertz
73 minutes

Cast: Ray Stricklyn, Willard Parker, Merry Anders, Robert Dix, Emile Myer, Jacklyn O'Donnell, Rayford Barnes, Rex Holman, Bob Palmer, Sheila Bromley, Johnny O'Neill, Leslie Bradley, Norman Leavitt

Another version of the celebrated Missouri outlaw, with Ray Stricklyn as Jesse and Robert Dix as brother Frank, finding it hard to adjust to postwar problems. They join the raiders of Quantrell (Emile Meyer) and meet Cole Younger (Willard Parker) and Belle Starr (Merry Anders)—all of whom have been depicted with greater interest in many other films. The main advantage of this version is its suggestion that Jesse was possibly a meaner and more complicated fellow than that essayed by Tyrone Power in the glamorous 1939 treatment.

20TH CENTURY-FOX ACADEMY AWARDS FOR 1960

FREDDIE FRANCIS: Best cinematography, black and white, *Sons and Lovers*.
CLASS III SCIENTIFIC and TECHNICAL AWARD: Mechanical effects.

ALL HANDS ON DECK

Produced by Oscar Brodney
Directed by Norman Taurog
Screenplay by Jay Sommers, from a novel by Donald R. Morris
Photographed in CinemaScope and DeLuxe Color by Leo Tover
Songs by Ray Evans and Jay Livingston
Music by Cyril J. Mockridge
98 minutes

Cast: Pat Boone, Buddy Hackett, Dennis O'Keefe, Barbara Eden, Warren Berlinger, Gale Gordon, David Brandon, Joe E. Ross, Bartlett Robinson, Paul Von Schriber, Ann B. Davis, Jody McCrea, Louise Glenn, Paul London

A lightweight naval comedy with Pat Boone as a lieutenant who falls in love with a reporter (Barbara Eden) but whose ship sails for the Aleutian Islands before he can marry her. The anxious lieutenant has other problems on board, mainly that of an Indian seaman (Buddy Hackett) who has brought along his pet turkey, which takes a great liking to the captain (Dennis O'Keefe). The lieutenant solves the love problem by bringing a pelican on board, which results in a turkey-pelican egg. When the ship gets back to Long Beach, the egg has to be kept out of the way of an inspecting admiral (Gale Gordon), as does the reporter, who has slipped on board to see her lieutenant. But it seems that the reporter is a friend of a senator who is in charge of naval appropriations. The admiral turns a blind eye to the goings-on on board. Boy gets girl. Navy stays intact.

BATTLE AT BLOODY BEACH

Produced by Richard Maibaum
Directed by Herbert Coleman
Screenplay by Richard Maibaum and Willard Willingham, from a story by Richard Maibaum
Photographed in CinemaScope by Kenneth Peach
Music by Sonny Burke
83 minutes

Cast: Audie Murphy, Gary Crosby, Dolores Michaels, Alejandro Rey, Marjorie Stapp, Barry Atwater, E. J. Andre, Dale Isimoto, Lillian Bronson, Miriam Colon, Pilar Seurat, William Mims, Ivan Dixon

The Philippines in the second World War, with Audie Murphy as a civilian working with the guerrillas but intent on locating the wife (Dolores Michaels) from whom he became separated while honeymooning in Manila when the Japanese struck. He does find her, but in the meantime he becomes convinced of the cause of the guerrillas in fighting for their country. She, thinking him long dead, has become enamored of the underground forces leader (Alejandro Rey), who honorably steps aside for the girl to be united with her husband. An offbeat war romance, made interesting because of its Philippine setting.

THE BIG GAMBLE

Produced by Darryl F. Zanuck
Directed by Richard Fleischer
Screenplay by Irwin Shaw
Photographed in Eastmancolor and CinemaScope by William Mellor
Music by Maurice Jarré
100 minutes

Cast: Stephen Boyd, Juliette Greco, David Wayne, Sybil Thorndike, Gregory Ratoff, Harold Goldblatt, Philip O'Flynn, Maureen O'Dea, Mary Kean, Alain Saury, Fergal Stanley, Fernand Ledoux, J. G. Devlin

An Irishman (Stephen Boyd) sets off with his French bride (Juliette Greco) and his shy cousin (David Wayne) to open a trucking business in Africa. The trio find the terrain of the Dark Continent far more severe than they had bargained for, with all kinds of obstacles as they drive a ten-ton truck from the west coast into the interior, where its value will be tremendous in helping build a new life. The story lines are slight, but the photography of the treacherous landscapes and the rigors of the trip make the film a diverting experience.

THE BIG SHOW

Produced by Ted Sherdeman and James B. Clark
Directed by James B. Clark
Screenplay by Ted Sherdeman
Photographed in CinemaScope and DeLuxe Color by Otto Heller

Music by Paul Sawtell and Bert Shefter
103 minutes

Cast: Cliff Robertson, Esther Williams, Nehemiah Persoff, Robert Vaughn, Margia Dean, David Nelson, Carol Christensen, Kurt Pecher, Renata Mannhardt, Franco Andrei, Peter Capell, Stephen Schnabel, Carleton Young, Philo Hauser, Mariza Tomic

An unofficial remake of *Broken Lance* (1954), which was a remake of *House of Strangers* (1949). Here the brutal self-made man with a family business is Nehemiah Persoff. The business is the circus. The good son is Cliff Robertson and the evil son trying to take over the business is Robert Vaughn. When the father's harsh management causes the death of several performers, the good son is blamed and jailed. Later he forgives the father and carries on the family business in fine style. The film benefits from having been filmed in Munich, taking advantage of a number of top-notch European circus acts.

THE CANADIANS

Produced by Herman E. Webber
Directed by Burt Kennedy
Screenplay by Burt Kennedy
Photographed in CinemaScope and DeLuxe Color by
    Arthur Ibbetson
Songs by Ken Darby
Music by Muir Mathieson
85 minutes

Cast: Robert Ryan, John Dehner, Torin Thatcher, Burt Metcalfe, John Sutton, Jack Creley, Scott Peters, Richard Alden, Teresa Stratas, Michael Pate

Following the Custer massacre in 1876, three members of the Canadian Mounted Police meet the Sioux as they leave Montana and enter Canada. They are told they must be peaceful and not use guns, which is difficult when a tough American rancher (John Dehner) and his men kill Indians as they move to reclaim horses. The leader of the Mounties (Robert Ryan) takes the cowboys into custody for their crimes, but the Indians get rid of them before he can bring them to justice. Filmed in Canada and based on fact, the film lacks excitement in telling what might have been a more interesting story.

A CIRCLE OF DECEPTION

Produced by Tom Monahan
Directed by Jack Lee
Screenplay by Nigel Balchin and Robert Musel, from a
    story by Alec Waugh
Photographed in CinemaScope by Gordon Dines
Music by Clifton Parker
101 minutes

Cast: Bradford Dillman, Suzy Parker, Harry Andrews, Robert Stephens, Paul Rogers, John Welsh, Ronald Allen,

A. J. Brown, Martin Boddey, Charles Lloyd Pack, Jacques Cey, John Dearth, Norman Coburn, Basil Peale

A British agent (Bradford Dillman) is parachuted into German-occupied France. He has been fed misinformation because his superiors believe he will break under interrogation. But he resolves to be brave when captured and not reveal any facts—until he realizes that he has been betrayed by his own people. During his moments in confinement he thinks about his girl (Suzy Parker) and his suave boss (Harry Andrews), and mulls over the irony of what has happened to him. An unusual espionage tale, with a good performance by Dillman as the cheated spy.

THE COMANCHEROS

Produced by George Sherman
Directed by Michael Curtiz
Screenplay by James Edward Grant and Clair Huffaker,
    based on a novel by Paul I. Wellman
Photographed in CinemaScope and DeLuxe Color by
    William H. Clothier
Music by Elmer Bernstein
107 minutes

Cast: John Wayne, Stuart Whitman, Ina Balin, Nehemiah Persoff, Lee Marvin, Michael Ansara, Pat Wayne, Bruce Cabot, Joan O'Brien, Edgar Buchanan, Henry Daniel, Richard Devon, Steve Baylor, John Dierkes, Roger Mobley

The last film directed by the remarkable Michael Curtiz and well in the tradition of his fluid, action-packed adventure yarns. Set in Texas prior to its statehood, with John Wayne as a Texas Ranger teaming up with a gambler (Stuart Whitman) to control the comancheros (renegade whites) who join with Indians to run guns and whisky and anything else to make money. They find the headquarters of the renegades, attack it, and wipe it out, with their own demise being prevented by the timely arrival of a band of Rangers. The gambler falls for the daughter (Ina Balin) of the renegade chieftain (Nehemiah Persoff), but the Ranger gives his blessing and rides off. The story is predictable, but the Wayne image, a rousing Elmer Bernstein score, and Curtiz's flair for action makes the film an essential in any listing of superior Westerns.

DAYS OF THRILLS AND LAUGHTER

Produced and written by Robert Youngson
Music by Jack Shaindlin
Narration by Jay Jackson
93 minutes

Cast: Charlie Chaplin, Douglas Fairbanks, Stan Laurel, Oliver Hardy, Houdini, Pearl White, Harry Langdon, Ben Turpin, Charlie Chase, Snub Pollard, Mack Sennett, Fatty Arbuckle, Mabel Normand, Ford Sterling, Boris

Karloff, Warner Oland, Ruth Roland, Monty Banks, Al St. John, Keystone Kops

The third of Robert Youngson's compilations of film clips from Hollywood's early days, this one accenting the laughter derived from the action sequences, such as runaway cars barely missing trams and trains and people ending up hanging off cliffs. The athletic Douglas Fairbanks is in evidence, as is Charlie Chaplin and the inventive slapstick antics of Mack Sennett.

THE FIERCEST HEART

Produced and directed by George Sherman
Screenplay by Edmund H. North, based on a novel by
    Stuart Cloete
Photographed in CinemaScope and DeLuxe Color by
    Ellis W. Carter
Music by Irving Gertz
91 minutes

Cast: Stuart Whitman, Juliet Prowse, Ken Scott, Raymond Massey, Geraldine Fitzgerald, Rafer Johnson, Michael David, Eduard Franz, Rachel Stevens, Dennis Holmes, Edward Platt, Alan Caillou, Hari Rhodes

A Western set in South Africa, with the Boers trekking through wild terrain in 1837 and being attacked by Zulus. An escapee (Stuart Whitman) from a British Army stockade throws in with a group of Boers as they seek the promised land and gradually learns to be less cynical and more trusting, partly because of falling in love with the daughter (Juliet Prowse) of the trek leader (Raymond Massey). Scenic values compensate for the overly familiar tale.

FRANCIS OF ASSISI

Produced by Plato A. Skouras
Directed by Michael Curtiz
Screenplay by Eugene Vale, James Forsyth, and Jack
    Thomas, based on a novel by Louis de Wohl
Photographed in CinemaScope and DeLuxe Color by
    Piero Portalupi
Music by Mario Nascimbene
105 minutes

Cast: Bradford Dillman, Dolores Hart, Stuart Whitman, Pedro Armendariz, Cecil Kellaway, Eduard Franz, Athene Seyler, Finlay Currie, Mervyn Johns, Russell Napier, John Welsh, Harold Goldblatt, Edith Sharpe, Jack Lambert

A tasteful and respectful, although not stimulating, account of the life of the revered thirteenth-century saint, with Bradford Dillman giving some virility to his portrayal of the man who befriended animals and expressed his love of God by his veneration of them. The film ranges from his early years as a lusty youngster to his final days when he had reformed and become a questing philosopher, and also managed after much travail to found his own order. The production

values are lavish, even to the use of Giotto frescoes in the titles.

THE GODDESS OF LOVE

Produced by Gian Paolo Bigazzi
Directed by Victor von Tourjansky
Screenplay by Damiano Damiani
Photographed in CinemaScope and DeLuxe Color
68 minutes

Cast: Belinda Lee, Jacques Sernas, Massimo Girotti, Maria Frau, Luigi, Claudio Gora, Elli Parvo, Camillo Pilotto, Enzo Fermonte

An Italian-French coproduction, set in Greece in the fourth century, concerning a great sculptor (Massimo Girotti) who fashions likenesses of Aphrodite but fails to appreciate the beauty of his model (Belinda Lee) until she is loved by a Macedonian soldier (Jacques Sernas). The sculptor turns the Macedonian in to the Greek soldiers, but is rejected by the model for so doing. She leaves him and becomes a courtesan, until her Macedonian, now a returning conqueror, finds her, saves her from suicide, and pledges his love.

THE HUSTLER

Produced and directed by Robert Rossen
Screenplay by Robert Rossen and Sidney Carroll, based
    on a novel by Walter S. Tevis
Photographed in CinemaScope by Eugen Shuftan
Music by Kenyon Hopkins
134 minutes

Cast: Paul Newman, Jackie Gleason, Piper Laurie, George C. Scott, Myron McCormick, Murray Hamilton, Michael Constantine, Stefan Gierasch, Jake LaMotta, Gordon B. Clarke, Alexander Ross, Carolyn Coates, Carl York, Vincent Gardenia

An intense, realistic study of the world of the pool shark, with Paul Newman as the title character, a crack pool player who makes his living hustling other players and dead set on becoming the best in the business. The grubby, scrounging lifestyle of these men is held under a microscope by writer-director Rossen. Newman is the pupil of a brilliant but evil gambler (George C. Scott) as he resolves to take on and beat the uncrowned champ of the game (Jackie Gleason). He wins, but finds the success less than he imagined. The long film is largely confined to a single, dingy back room and one contest, but the dialogue, the acting, the detail, and the tension make this a masterpiece of its kind.

THE INNOCENTS

Produced and directed by Jack Clayton
Screenplay by William Archibald and Truman Capote,
    based on *The Turn of the Screw* by Henry James

Photographed in CinemaScope by Freddie Francis
Music by Georges Auric
100 minutes

Cast: Deborah Kerr, Peter Wyngarde, Megs Jenkins, Michael Redgrave, Pamela Franklin, Martin Stephens, Isla Cameron, Clytie Jessop

A major item in the fantasy genre and an admirable treatment of Henry James' famous ghost story. The Victorian story is that of a governess (Deborah Kerr) who takes on the teaching of two orphans in a wealthy English home and gradually discovers that there is something strangely amiss in the eerie mansion. The children (Pamela Franklin and Martin Stephens) appear to be angelic, but are in fact quite evil, with some kind of force affecting them. From the housekeeper (Megs Jenkins) she learns that the previous governess and a valet had had a passionate but doomed love affair. It occurs to her that the dead lovers have possessed the souls of the children and she tries to protect them, but with frightening results. The chilling atmosphere and the mounting tension of the disturbing picture are a credit to producer-director Clayton, and Deborah Kerr is superb as the nice, compassionate lady caught up in the evil vortex.

LITTLE SHEPHERD OF KINGDOM COME

Produced by Maury Dexter
Directed by Andrew McLaglen
Screenplay by Barre Lyndon, based on the novel by John Fox, Jr.
Photographed in CinemaScope and DeLuxe Color
108 minutes

Cast: Jimmie Rodgers, Luana Patten, Chill Wills, Linda Hutchings, Robert Dix, George Kennedy, Shirley O'Hara, Ken Miller, Neil Hamilton, Lois January

An orphaned Kentucky teenager (Jimmie Rodgers) takes off from the home of his mean guardian (George Kennedy) and finds a more pleasant one with the family of a schoolteacher (Robert Dix) in the town of Kingdom Come. He also builds up a growing love for the young daughter (Luana Patten). With the outbreak of the Civil War he joins the Union Army and learns the anguish of fighting among former friends and acquaintances. The experiences mature him and he returns to face a promising future with the schoolteacher's daughter. A pleasant rural tale, designed for young audiences.

THE LONG ROPE

Produced by Margia Dean
Directed by William Witney
Screenplay by Robert Hamner
Photographed by Kay Norton

Music by Paul Sawtell and Bert Shefter
61 minutes

Cast: Hugh Marlowe, Alan Hale, Robert Wilkie, Chris Robinson, Jeffrey Morris, Lisa Montell, David Renard, Madeleine Holmes, John Alonzo, Jack Powers, Kathryn Harte, Jack Carlin

A circuit judge (Hugh Marlowe) in the old West rides into a town that is largely a one-family enterprise. His job is to defend a Mexican (John Alonzo) accused of murdering the brother of an influential citizen. It turns out that his mad mother-in-law (Madeleine Holmes) is the killer—because she wanted her daughter (Lisa Montell) to marry into the controlling family. A new twist in an old genre.

MARINES, LET'S GO

Produced and directed by Raoul Walsh
Screenplay by John Twist, from a story by Raoul Walsh
Photographed in CinemaScope and DeLuxe Color by Lucien Ballard
Music by Irving Gertz
103 minutes

Cast: Tom Tyron, David Hedison, Tom Reese, Linda Hutchins, William Tyler, Barbara Stuart, David Brandon, Steve Baylor, Peter Miller, Adoree Evans, Hideo Inamura

Set in the Korean War but basically a conventional service adventure involving a squad of Marines as they fight fiercely on the battlefield and playfully among themselves. The usual cross-section of types, ranging from the quiet, brainy officer (Tom Tyron) to the roughneck sergeant (Tom Reese) and the Boston aristocrat (David Hedison)—and with some good action sequences under the direction of the macho veteran Walsh.

THE MARRIAGE-GO-ROUND

Produced by Leslie Stevens
Directed by Walter Lang
Screenplay by Leslie Stevens
Photographed in CinemaScope and DeLuxe Color by Leo Tover
Music by Dominic Frontiere
98 minutes

Cast: Susan Hayward, James Mason, Julie Newmar, Robert Paige, June Clayworth, Joe Kirkwood, Jr., Mary Patton, Trax Colton, Everett Glass, Ben Astar

A frivolous sex comedy, about a conservative college professor (James Mason) whose loving wife (Susan Hayward) starts to feel edgy when a beautiful, athletic Swedish girl (Julie Newmar) becomes their house guest. The pragmatic Swede admires the professor's mind and suggests that she would like to have a child by him, since it would have perfect parentage, combining his brains with her splendid physique. He manfully, after a certain amount of consideration, resists the offer, with a great deal of help from his wife, who ejects the lusty Swede. Leslie Stevens, both producing and scripting from his own stage play, invests the film with some good lines attacking conventional views on sexual conduct.

MR. TOPAZE

Produced by Pierre Rouve
Directed by Peter Sellers
Screenplay by Pierre Rouve, from a play by Marcel Pagnol
Photographed in CinemaScope and DeLuxe Color by John Wilcox
Music by Georges Van Parys
95 minutes

Cast: Peter Sellers, Joan Sims, John Le Mesurier, Nadia Gray, Herbert Lom, Leo McKern, Martita Hunt, John Neville, Billie Whitelaw, Michael Gough

Peter Sellers, directing himself, in a role played with great style by John Barrymore in 1933, but falling short of the Barrymore standard. The title character is a college teacher in a French town, a man of such honesty and integrity that he will not compromise on any issue. When he refuses to alter a paper in order to make a pupil look better, an influential parent gets him fired. He is then hired as a front man for a crooked businessman (Herbet Lom) and once he is exposed to the ways of crime he decides to become a success as a crook, combining his brains with unscrupulous methods. The film was also released a year later with the title *I Like Money*, but in neither case did it win Sellers much favorable reaction.

PIRATES OF TORTUGA

Produced by Sam Katzman
Directed by Robert D. Webb
Screenplay by Melvin Levy, Jesse L. Lasky, Jr., and Pat Silver, based on a story by Melvin Levy
Photographed in CinemaScope and DeLuxe Color by Ellis W. Carter
Music by Paul Sawtell and Bert Shefter
97 minutes

Cast: Ken Scott, Leticia Roman, Dave King, John Richardson, Rafer Johnson, Robert Stephens, Rachel Stephens, Stanley Adams, Edgar Barrier, James Forrest, Patrick Saxon, Arthur Gould-Porter

A minor swashbuckling item concerning the British government's plans to halt the activities of the bold buccaneer Henry Morgan. A privateer (Ken Scott) is instructed to pose as a pirate and undermine Morgan's operations, which he does—but with little flair.

THE PURPLE HILLS

Produced and directed by Maury Dexter

Screenplay by Edith Cash Pearl and Russ Bender
Photographed in CinemaScope and DeLuxe Color by Floyd Crosby
Music by Richard LaSalle
60 minutes

Cast: Gene Nelson, Kent Taylor, Danny Zapien, Medford Salway, Russ Bender, Joanna Barnes, Jerry Summers, John Carr

Two bounty hunters in the old West argue over which one killed a wanted man. The actual killer (Gene Nelson) buries the body, but when the pretender (Kent Taylor) makes his claim, they ride to the grave with a sheriff (Russ Bender) to settle the claim. The victim's young brother (Jerry Summers) is frustrated in his plan to kill the killer, but attacking Apaches cause the death of the pretender and the other bounty hunter decides he doesn't want the reward money after all. Instead he rides off with the kid brother and his attractive guardian (Joanna Barnes).

RETURN TO PEYTON PLACE

Produced by Jerry Wald
Directed by José Ferrer
Screenplay by Ronald Alexander, based on a book by Grace Metalious
Photographed in CinemaScope and DeLuxe Color by Charles G. Clarke
Music by Franz Waxman
123 minutes

Cast: Carol Lynley, Jeff Chandler, Eleanor Parker, Mary Astor, Robert Sterling, Luciana Paluzzi, Brett Halsey, Gunnar Hellstrom, Tuesday Weld, Kenneth MacDonald, Bob Crane, Bill Bradley

A sequel to *Peyton Place*, which examines the impact on the small New England town the book supposedly made. The young author (Carol Lynley) finds an eager publisher (Jeff Chandler) in New York, but he encourages her to be even more frank about the loves and scandals of the town, which ends up in a trial brought on by several inhabitants who feel they have been maligned but which is actually a discussion about free speech. Less interesting than the original, but still a good soap opera, set in a pretty town brimming over with lusty people. Outstanding is Mary Astor as a mean and selfish mother.

THE RIGHT APPROACH

Produced by Oscar Brodney
Directed by David Butler
Screenplay by Fay and Michael Kanin, based on a play by Garson Kanin
Photographed in CinemaScope by Sam Leavitt
Music by Dominic Frontiere
92 minutes

Cast: Martha Hyer, Frankie Vaughan, Juliet Prowse, Gary Crosby, David McLean, Jesse White, Jane Withers, Rachel Stephens, Steve Harris, Paul von Schreiber, Robert Casper

A show-biz yarn, with several songs, about a group of young men bent on success as entertainers. They band together and live in dormitory style, but one of them (Frankie Vaughan) is selfish and unscrupulous and brings discord into the group. He achieves his success, but learns a little humility in the process.

SANCTUARY

Produced by Richard D. Zanuck
Directed by Tony Richardson
Screenplay by James Poe, based on works by William Faulkner
Photographed in CinemaScope by Ellsworth Fredericks
Music by Alex North
90 minutes

Cast: Lee Remick, Yves Montand, Bradford Dillman, Harry Townes, Odetta, Howard St. John, Jean Carson, Reta Shaw, Strother Martin, William Mims, Marge Redmond, Jean Bartel, Hope Du Bois

Based on Faulkner stories and set in the South of the late 1920's, the unpleasant story is about a pretty young woman (Lee Remick) with a masochistic streak who has enjoyed the abuse of a virile macho type (Yves Montand). She settles down to domestic life with a nice husband (Bradford Dillman), but lapses back into her dissolute ways when the lover drifts back into her life. Her servant (Odetta) then kills the woman's young daughter, presumably to save her from the influence of the amoral mother. The dark shades of Greek tragedy are interesting, but the ingredients of the film fail to come together convincingly.

THE SECOND TIME AROUND

Produced by Jack Cummings
Directed by Vincent Sherman
Screenplay by Oscar Saul and Cecil Dan Hansen, based on a novel by Richard Emery Roberts
Photographed in CinemaScope and DeLuxe Color by Ellis W. Carter
Music by Gerald Fried
98 minutes

Cast: Debbie Reynolds, Steve Forrest, Andy Griffith, Juliet Prowse, Thelma Ritter, Ken Scott, Isobel Elsom, Rudolph Acosta, Timothy Carey, Tom Greenway, Eleanor Audley

A young widow (Debbie Reynolds) and her two children arrive in an Arizona town in 1912 to start a new life and find it a life greatly different from anything they have ever known. The wild and booming town meets its match in the temper and spirit of the lady, especially when she becomes sheriff and starts to clean things up. And she gets a fine second husband (Steve Forrest). The film borders on farce and gets most of its lift from the lively presence of Reynolds.

SEVEN WOMEN FROM HELL

Produced by Harry Spaulding
Directed by Robert D. Webb
Screenplay by Jesse L. Lasky, Jr., and Pat Silver
Photographed in CinemaScope by Floyd Crosby
Music by Paul Dunlap
88 minutes

Cast: Patricia Owens, Denise Darcel, Cesar Romero, John Kerr, Margia Dean, Yvonne Craig, Pilar Seurat, Sylvia Daneel, Richard Loo, Evadene Baker, Bob Okazaki, Yuki Shimoda

Seven women escape from the hell of a Japanese prison camp in New Guinea in the early days of the second World War, among them a British ornithologist (Patricia Owens) and a French thief (Denise Darcel). Several die before reaching safety and several others undergo various adventures. A German-Argentine plantation owner (Cesar Romero) who collaborates with the Japanese pays with his life when one of the girls finds out about him, and a wounded American pilot (John Kerr) dies in the arms of another. A purely Hollywood version of the war.

THE SILENT CALL

Produced by Leonard A. Schwartz
Directed by John Bushelman
Screenplay by Tom Maruzzi
Photographed by Kay Norton
Music by Richard D. Aurandt
63 minutes

Cast: Roger Mobley, David McLean, Gail Russell, Joe Besser, Rusty Wescoatt, Roscoe Ates, Sherwood Keith, Milton Parsons, Dal McKennon, Jack Younger

The story of a dog's love for his young master and the dog's trekking over a thousand miles, when the poor parents move from Nevada to Los Angeles, to find the boy (Roger Mobley). Left behind when they move, the dog breaks away from its new keeper and somehow, after many adventures, turns up at the new home, to the great joy of the heart-broken boy and to the relief of his parents (David McLean and Gail Russell).

SNIPER'S RIDGE

Produced and directed by John Bushelman
Screenplay by Tom Maruzzi
Photographed in CinemaScope by Ken Peach
Music by Richard LaSalle
61 minutes

Cast: Jack Ging, Stanley Clements, John Goddard, Douglas Henderson, Gabe Castle, Allan Marvin, Anton Van Stralen, Al Freeman, Jr., Mason Curry, Henry Delgado, Mark Douglas, Thomas A. Sweet, Scott Randall, Joe Cawthon

In the final hours before the cease fire in Korea, a neurotic captain (John Goddard) orders his weary men to undertake one more mission. The mission never takes place because he steps on a mine and freezes on the spot, knowing that to move will mean death. He is rescued by his most rebellious corporal (Jack Ging), who is injured in so doing. A modest war picture, but a tautly made one and a good insight into battle fatigue.

SNOW WHITE AND THE THREE STOOGES

Produced by Charles Wick
Directed by Walter Lang
Screenplay by Noel Langley and Elwood Ullman, based on a story by Charles Wick
Photographed in CinemaScope and DeLuxe Color by Leon Shamroy
Songs by Harry Harris and Earl Brent
Musical direction by Lyn Murray
107 minutes

Cast: Three Stooges, Carol Heiss, Edson Stroll, Patricia Medina, Guy Rolfe, Buddy Baer

The screen debut of champion figure skater Carol Heiss, with Moe, Curly, and Larry substituting preposterously, for the Seven Dwarfs. The basics of the fairy tale are retained, although with great liberties. Patricia Medina is the wicked queen, Edson Stroll is Prince Charming, Guy Rolfe the evil adviser to the queen, and Buddy Baer is the huntsman torn between duty and compassion. But the film's appeal rests entirely on the skating of Heiss and the antics of the Stooges.

SQUAD CAR

Produced and directed by Ed Leftwich
Screenplay by E. M. Parsons and Scott Flohr
Photographed by Henry Cronjager
62 minutes

Cast: Vici Raaf, Paul Bryar, Don Marlow, Lynn Moore, Jack Harris, Norman MacDonald

A Phoenix, Arizona, night club singer (Vici Raaf) becomes part of a counterfeiting ring and brings on the investigation of a police lieutenant (Paul Bryar) when an aviation mechanic (Norman MacDonald) is murdered. The mechanic's boss (Don Marlow) is drawn into the nefarious business, but with the aid of his girl friend (Lynn Moore) is able to extricate himself and help the police bring the crooks to a halt.

TESS OF THE STORM COUNTRY

Produced by Everett Chambers
Directed by Paul Guilfoyle
Screenplay by Charles Lang, based on a novel by Grace Miller White
Photographed in CinemaScope and DeLuxe Color by James Wong Howe
Music by Paul Sawtell and Bert Shefter
84 minutes

Cast: Diane Baker, Lee Philips, Wallace Ford, Jack Ging, Robert F. Simon, Archie Duncan, Bert Remsen, Grandon Rhodes, Nancy Valentine

A popular Mary Pickford film of 1922, and remade ten years later with Janet Gaynor, this version has Diane Baker as the Scottish girl who arrives in the Pennsylvania Dutch country to find her intended husband dead. She is loved by a Mennonite lad (Jack Ging) and they overcome the local prejudices against the sect, which is further complicated by the Mennonites having sold land to a chemical company which is polluting the streams, to the despair of farmers. Still an old-fashioned tale, but made interesting by the photography of James Wong Howe in the area around Sonora, California.

THE TRAPP FAMILY

Produced by Wolfgang Reinhardt
Directed by Wolfgang Liebeneiner
Screenplay by George Hurdalek, based on material by Baroness Maria Trapp
Photographed in Eastmancolor by Werner Krien
Music by Franz Grothe
104 minutes

Cast: Ruth Leuwerik, Hans Holt, Maria Holst, Josef Meinrad, Friedrich Domin, Hilde von Stolz, Agnes Windeck, Leisl Karstadt, Alfred Balthoff, Hans Schumm, Gretl Theimer

The story of the family made famous a few years later by *The Sound of Music.* The basic plot is the same as the Julie Andrews musical—that of a nun who is hired by a baron as a tutor to his seven motherless children and whom he marries. She encourages their talent as singers and they leave Austria in 1938 to make their home in the United States, where they become popular as a singing family. The German film, acquired by 20th Century-Fox, is a strong and sunny telling of the tale.

20,000 EYES

Produced and directed by Jack Leewood
Screenplay by Jack Thomas
Photographed in CinemaScope by Bryden Baker
Music by Albert Glasser
61 minutes

Cast: Gene Nelson, Merry Anders, James Brown, John Banner, Judith Rawlins, Robert Shayne, Paul Maxley, Rex Holman, Barbara Parkins, Ollie O'Toole, Bruno Ve Sota, Rusty Westcoatt

A man (Gene Nelson) swindles a retired mobster out of some stock in order to cover a loan and is then threatened with his life to get the funds back. He devises a scheme to pilfer diamonds from an art museum and replace them with cheap duplicates, but the scheme goes awry and costs him his life. The film is a good example of the B product being turned out at this time by Associated Producers Inc., in cooperation with Fox, for small budgets (of around $100,000) and often shot within six days.

VOYAGE TO THE BOTTOM OF THE SEA

Produced and directed by Irwin Allen
Screenplay by Irwin Allen and Charles Bennett, based on a story by Irwin Allen
Photographed in CinemaScope and DeLuxe Color by Winton Hoch
Music by Paul Sawtell and Bert Shefter
105 minutes

Dennis O'Keefe and Pat Boone in *All Hands on Deck*.

Deborah Kerr in *The Innocents*.

Bradford Dillman and Dolores Hart in *Francis of Assisi*.

Yves Montand and Lee Remick in *Sanctuary*.

Stuart Whitman and John Wayne in *The Comancheros*.

George C. Scott and Paul Newman in *The Hustler*.

Cast: Walter Pidgeon, Joan Fontaine, Barbara Eden, Peter Lorre, Robert Sterling, Michael Ansara, Frankie Avalon, Regis Toomey, John Litel, Howard McNear, Henry Daniell, Skip Ward

A science fiction classic—and the mother feature of a long-running TV series—about a futuristic atomic submarine, sent to the depths to heal a fissure in the surface of the earth likely to cause the planet to burst into fire. The commander (Walter Pidgeon) of the huge sub takes it upon himself to quell the fire, despite the negative advice of the United Nations. Fortunately his theories prove right. Among his passengers are several scientists and doctors (Joan Fontaine, Peter Lorre, etc.) who vary in their opinions about what is to be done. But it is the underwater photography and the special effects that really matter on this outing.

WALK TALL

Produced and directed by Maury Dexter
Screenplay by Joseph Fritz

Photographed in CinemaScope and DeLuxe Color by
  Floyd Crosby
Music by Richard D. Aurandt
60 minutes

Cast: Willard Parker, Joy Meadows, Kent Taylor, Russ
Bender, Ron Soble, Bill Mims, Alberto Monte, Felix
Locher, Dave De Paul

A small-scaled Western about an army captain (Willard Parker) bringing in a cocky gunman and Indian
killer (Kent Taylor), whose irresponsible acts are
likely to cause an Indian uprising. The killer's gang
pursue the pair and catch up, but a band of Shoshones
arrive in time and help the captain complete his
mission.

WILD IN THE COUNTRY

Produced by Jerry Wald
Directed by Philip Dunne
Screenplay by Clifford Odets, based on a novel by
  J. R. Salamanca
Photographed in CinemaScope and DeLuxe Color by
  William C. Mellor
Music by Kenyon Hopkins
112 minutes

Cast: Elvis Presley, Hope Lange, Tuesday Weld, Millie
Perkins, Rafer Johnson, John Ireland, Gary Lockwood,
William Mims, Raymond Greenleaf, Christina Crawford,
Robin Raymond, Doreen Lang

Set in the Shenandoah Valley of Virginia but actually
filmed in the Napa Valley of California, the story is
that of a young delinquent (Elvis Presley) who is
saved from his erring ways by a pretty widow and
counselor (Hope Lange), who discovers the boy has
writing talent. He also has an innocent girl friend
(Millie Perkins) and a more earthy one (Tuesday
Weld), but once he has settled down and got the wildness out of him, he goes off to college to study writing,
with the implication that the counselor will wait for
him. Not entirely convincing, but a good vehicle for
Presley, who croons several songs, which doubtlessely
please the fans but make it harder to accept his characterization as a potential literary giant.

20TH CENTURY-FOX ACADEMY AWARDS
FOR 1961

EUGEN SHUFTAN: Best cinematography, black and
  white, *The Hustler.*
HARRY HORNER: Best art direction, black and white,
  The Hustler.
GENE CALLAHAN: Best set decoration, black and white,
  The Hustler.
CLASS II SCIENTIFIC and TECHNICAL AWARD: System
  of decompressing and recomposing CinemaScope
  pictures for conventional aspect ratios.

Tuesday Weld and Elvis Presley in *Wild
in the Country.*

Walter Pidgeon and Joan Fontaine
in *Voyage to the Bottom
of the Sea.*

Jeff Chandler and Carol Lynley in
Return to Peyton Place.

James Mason, Julie Newmar, and Susan Hayward in *Marriage-Go-Round.*

Thelma Ritter and Debbie Reynolds in *The Second Time
Around.*

335

1962

ADVENTURES OF A YOUNG MAN

Produced by Jerry Wald
Directed by Martin Ritt
Screenplay by A. E. Hotchner, based on stories by
Ernest Hemingway
Photographed in CinemaScope and DeLuxe Color by
Lee Garmes
Music by Franz Waxman
145 minutes

Cast: Richard Beymer, Diane Baker, Corinne Calvet, Fred
Clark, Dan Dailey, James Dunn, Juano Hernandez,
Arthur Kennedy, Ricardo Montalban, Paul Newman,
Susan Strasberg, Jessica Tandy

The young man of the title is actually Hemingway himself, although using the name Nick Adams (Richard Beymer) to make the adventures more applicable to a general observation about life. The young man leaves his backwoods Michigan home in search of knowledge about the world. He starts as a hobo and as such comes to know a punchdrunk fighter (Paul Newman). He tackles New York and then goes on to Europe, where he serves in the Italian Army in the first World War and where he experiences a doomed love affair with a nurse (Susan Strasberg). By the time he reaches home he realizes that there is no returning to his old life and that he must find his success elsewhere and on different terms. The long film sags in places and suffers from an inadequate performance from Beymer, but it offers some interesting people and places and a superior score by Franz Waxman.

AIR PATROL

Produced and directed by Maury Dexter
Screenplay by Henry Cross
Photographed in CinemaScope by John M. Nicholaus, Jr.
Music by Albert Glasser
62 minutes

Cast: Willard Parker, Merry Anders, Robert Dix, John
Holland, Russ Bender, Douglas Dumbrille, George Eldredge, Jack Younger, Lee Patterson

A crime yarn about the robbery of art treasures, with the bandits getting away in a helicopter. They issue a ransom note, but a pair of detectives (Williard Parker and Robert Dix) track them, also by the use of helicopter, and eventually put an end to their schemes.

BACHELOR FLAT

Produced by Jack Cummings
Directed by Frank Tashlin
Screenplay by Frank Tashlin and Budd Grossman, based
on a play by Budd Grossman
Photographed in CinemaScope and DeLuxe Color by
Daniel L. Fapp
Music by Johnny Williams
92 minutes

Cast: Tuesday Weld, Richard Beymer, Terry-Thomas,
Celeste Holm, Francesca Bellini, Howard McNear, Ann
Del Guercio, Roxanne Arlen, Alice Reinheart, Stephen
Bekassy, Margo Moore, George Bruggeman

An English archaeologist (Terry-Thomas) lives in a beach house and runs into emotional complications when a young girl (Tuesday Weld) moves in on him without telling him she is the daughter of his fiancée (Celeste Holm). Other lively teenagers, from the campus where he is lecturing, casually drop in on the reserved Briton and one of them (Richard Beymer) brings his dachshund, which keeps burying the professor's prize dinosaur bone in the sands. The film amuses, but doesn't quite manage to blend British and American styles of humor, although Terry-Thomas struggles manfully with the material.

THE BROKEN LAND

Produced by Leonard Schwartz
Directed by John Bushelman
Screenplay by Edward Lakso
Photographed in CinemaScope and DeLuxe Color
60 minutes

Cast: Kent Taylor, Dianna Darrin, Jody McCrea, Robert
Sampson, Jack Nicholson

A sheriff (Kent Taylor) in a small Western town after the Civil War grows more and more bitter and becomes involved in crime. His honest young deputy (Jody McCrea) tries to halt the crooked ways of his boss but loses his life in the attempt. A minor entry in the Western catalog.

THE CABINET OF CALIGARI

Produced and directed by Roger Kay
Screenplay by Robert Bloch
Photographed in CinemaScope by John Russell
Music by Gerald Fried
105 minutes

Cast: Glynis Johns, Dan O'Herlihy, Dick Davalos, Lawrence Dobkin, Constance Ford, J. Pat O'Malley, Vicki Trickett, Estelle Winwood, Doreen Lang, Charles Fredericks, Phyllis Teagarden

Bearing little relationship with the celebrated silent film of the same title, the story here is that of a distraught woman (Glynis Johns) who seeks help at a mansion when her car breaks down. The owner, Caligari (Dan O'Herlihy), takes her in but subjects her to humiliations, as he does other guests. Her experiences with him are nightmarish—and then she wakes up and find that it is all a dream. She is in a sanitarium, and she is much older than in her dream, and Caligari is her psychiatrist.

THE DAY MARS INVADED EARTH

Produced and directed by Maury Dexter
Screenplay by Harry Spaulding
70 minutes

Cast: Kent Taylor, Marie Windsor, William Mims, Betty Beall, Lowell Brown, Gregg Shank

A scientist (Kent Taylor) who has been responsible for an earth-to-Mars racket brings on the wrath of the far planet. When taking a vacation to California to visit his estranged wife (Marie Windsor), he meets people he knows, but gradually realizes they are doubles. They are actually invaders from Mars who have taken on human guises, and they succeed in their invasion of earth—killing the scientist and everyone else.

THE FIREBRAND

Produced and directed by Maury Dexter
Screenplay by Harry Spaulding
61 minutes

Cast: Kent Taylor, Valentin De Vargas, Lisa Montell, Chubby Johnson, Barbara Mansell

In the years of the California gold rush, a Mexican bandit (Valentin De Vargas) of the Robin Hood kind steals from the gold-hungry settlers. A California ranger (Kent Taylor) sets about bringing him to justice with some mean tricks, but it's the ranger who loses and the bandit who rides off into the sunset.

FIVE WEEKS IN A BALLOON

Produced and directed by Irwin Allen
Screenplay by Charles Bennett, Irwin Allen, and Albert Gail, based on a story by Jules Verne
Photographed in CinemaScope and DeLuxe Color by Winton Hoch
Music by Paul Sawtell
101 minutes

Cast: Red Buttons, Fabian, Barbara Eden, Cedric Hardwicke, Peter Lorre, Richard Haydn, Barbara Luna, Billy Gilbert, Herbert Marshall, Reginald Owen, Henry Daniell, Mike Mazurki

A Jules Verne fantasy but done somewhat as a comedy adventure, relating the tribulations of a party of mid-nineteenth-century Britons as they cross four thousand miles of Africa for the purpose of planting the British flag on unclaimed land before others get there. The leader of the expedition (Cedric Hardwicke) is a crusty old explorer; also on board are a reporter (Red Buttons), whose curiosity gets the party into various scrapes, a fussy scientist (Richard Haydn), and a young assistant (Fabian) who falls in love with a slave girl (Barbara Luna). The reporter pairs off with a schoolteacher (Barbara Eden) and a good time is had by all—especially Peter Lorre in a florid portrayal of a slave trader.

GIGOT

Produced by Kenneth Hyman
Directed by Gene Kelly
Screenplay by John Patrick, based on a story by Jackie Gleason
Photographed in DeLuxe Color by Jean Bourgoin
Music by Jackie Gleason
104 minutes

Cast: Jackie Gleason, Katherine Kath, Gabrielle Dorziat, Jean Lefebvre, Jacques Marin, Albert Remy, Yvonne Constant, Germaine Delbat, Albert Dinan, Diane Gardner

Gigot is entirely the creation of Jackie Gleason. It was his idea to do a film about a warm-hearted, mute French simpleton, and it is his story, performance, and musical score. He was enthusiastically supported by Gene Kelly as his director, and the decision was made to shoot the entire picture in Paris. But the end result about this gentle but pathetic figure, so loving by nature and so badly treated by others, is too special a piece of material to find a large audience. Gleason and Kelly also claim that the film was edited without their approval and ruined in the process.

HAND OF DEATH

Produced by Eugene Ling
Directed by Gene Nelson
Screenplay by Eugene Ling

337

Photographed by Floyd Crosby
Music by Sonny Burke
60 minutes

Cast: John Agar, Paul Raymond, Steve Dunne, Roy Gordon, John Alonzo

A research chemist (John Agar) who works with poisonous gases is turned into a hideous monster when one of his experiments goes awry. The shock and the pain get worse and worse until he goes on the rampage and has to be destroyed. A minor entry in the horror genre.

IT HAPPENED IN ATHENS

Produced by James S. Elliott
Directed by Andrew Marton
Screenplay by Laslo Vadnay
Photographed in CinemaScope and DeLuxe Color by Curtis Courant
Music by Manos Hadjidakis
105 minutes

Cast: Jayne Mansfield, Trax Colton, Nico Minardos, Bob Mathias, Maria Zenia, Ivan Triesault, Marion Silva, Roger Fradet, Ben Bennett, Lili Valenty, Jean Murat, Denton De Gray, Todd Windsor

Based on a true incident—the participation in 1896 of an untrained young Greek (Trax Colton), a shepherd, in the Olympic Games of that year and how he defeated all the track contestants, including some acclaimed runners. The film is interesting when focusing on the events, especially in the final marathon, but sags in credibility when Jayne Mansfield appears as a Greek movie star ready to marry the winner as a publicity stunt. He prefers to marry his true love (Maria Zenia).

THE LION

Produced by Samuel G. Engel
Directed by Jack Cardiff
Screenplay by Irene Kamp and Louis Kamp, based on a novel by Joseph Kessel
Photographed in CinemaScope and DeLuxe Color by Ted Scaife
Music by Malcolm Arnold
96 minutes

Cast: William Holden, Trevor Howard, Capucine, Pamela Franklin, Makara Kwaiha Ramahadi, Paul Oduor, Christopher Agunda

A New York attorney (William Holden) arrives at the Kirinyaga Game Reserve in Kenya at the request of his ex-wife (Capucine), who is worried about their daughter (Pamela Franklin). The girl is growing up with an attachment to the jungle life and its animals, particularly with a lion she has raised from a cub. The stepfather (Trevor Howard) is a hunter and game warden and he senses that his wife and the ex-husband still have a yen for one another. In time he comes to realize that he cannot hold the wife and that it is best to let her, the girl, and the lawyer return to a more normal way of life in America. The film's main assets are its location shots of landscapes and animal life, and especially its footage of the magnificent, well-trained title beast.

LISA

Produced by Mark Robson
Directed by Philip Dunne
Screenplay by Nelson Gidding, based on the novel by Jan de Hartog
Photographed in CinemaScope and DeLuxe Color by Arthur Ibbetson
Music by Malcolm Arnold
112 minutes

Cast: Stephen Boyd, Dolores Hart, Leo McKern, Hugh Griffith, Donald Pleasance, Harry Andrews, Robert Stephens, Marius Goring, Finlay Currie, Harold Goldblatt, Neil McCallum, Geoffrey Keen, Jean Anderson, Jane Jordan, Jack Gwillim

Largely filmed in Holland and taking advantage of its quaint scenery, the story concerns a Dutch Jewish girl (Dolores Hart) who is aided in her quest to leave Holland and reach Israel by a Dutch police official (Stephen Boyd). He feels moved to atone for cowardice shown toward the Jews during the war. The girl is a psychologically scarred survivor of Auschwitz and terrified at the prospect of going through interrogations in order to reach the new Jewish state. She flees from country to country before succeeding, providing the audience with scenes of many places as well as an interesting story.

THE LONGEST DAY

Produced by Darryl F. Zanuck
Directed by Ken Annakin, Andrew Marton, and Bernard Wicki
Screenplay by Cornelius Ryan, based on his book
Photographed in CinemaScope by Henri Persin, Walter Wottitz, Pierre Levent, and Jean Bourgoin
Music by Maurice Jarré
180 minutes

Darryl Zanuck's masterly war film, requiring almost as much preparation as the actual campaign it depicts. In order to make the film as authentic as possible, Zanuck employed the locations called for in Ryan's screenplay, such as the command posts occupied by the Germans, the French underground network, Omaha Beach, Ste. Mere Eglise, and Utah Beach, as well as sites in England. The film is a clear examination of D-Day looked at from almost every viewpoint, particularly from that of the Germans, who are overwhelmed by the forces brought against them. It is in fact a German officer, at the start of the day, who gives the story its title, as he looks at the approaching armada and says, "This will be the longest day." In three hours Zanuck and his staff give meaning to the scope of the day, with a huge cast of name players, such as John Wayne, Henry Fonda, Richard Burton, and Robert Mitchum playing small roles and blending with, literally, an army of extras. All the characters speak in their own languages, with subtitles, and add to the documentary feeling of this gigantic and fascinating film.

MADISON AVENUE

Produced and directed by Bruce Humberstone
Screenplay by Norman Corwin, based on the novel *The Build-Up Boys* by Jeremy Kirk
Photographed in CinemaScope by Charles G. Clarke
Music by Harry Sukman
94 minutes

Cast: Dana Andrews, Eleanor Parker, Jeanne Crain, Eddie Albert, Howard St. John, Henry Daniell, Kathleen Freeman, David White, Bettie Andrews, Jack Orrison, Yvonne Pattie, Arlene Hunter

The machinations of the advertising business, with Dana Andrews as a tough, shrewd, and clever account executive who is fired by his boss (Howard St. John) when he starts getting too big for his job. He takes his talents elsewhere, which proves to the ex-boss that he has lost a valuable man, so he hires him back. In the meantime he makes and sacrifices friends according to his objectives, although he finally realizes the love of his girl (Jeanne Crain) is more valuable than all his accounts. A good coverage, if not appealing, of its subject matter.

MR. HOBBS TAKES A VACATION

Produced by Jerry Wald
Directed by Henry Koster
Screenplay by Nunnally Johnson, based on a novel by Edward Streeter
Photographed in DeLuxe Color and CinemaScope by William C. Mellor
Music by Henry Mancini
116 minutes

Cast: James Stewart, Maureen O'Hara, Fabian, John Saxon, Marie Wilson, Reginald Gardiner, Lauri Peters, Valerie Varda, Lili Gentle, John McGiver, Natalie Trundy, Josh Peine, Minerva Urecal, Michael Burns

Like many family men, Mr. Hobbs (James Stewart) takes a vacation somewhat against his own desires and ends up in a weird old house on the Pacific Coast, with his wife (Maureen O'Hara) and their children and grandchildren. The plumbing is bad, the children misbehave, and some of the local people are strange. Mr. Hobbs finds himself even more harassed on his holiday than during the rest of his year. The substance of the film is slight, but the witty script of Nunnally Johnson and the skillful playing of Stewart make the vacation amusing, at least for the viewer.

SATAN NEVER SLEEPS

Produced and directed by Leo McCarey
Screenplay by Claude Binyon and Leo McCarey, based on a novel by Pearl S. Buck
Photographed in CinemaScope and DeLuxe Color by Oswald Morris
Music by Richard Rodney Bennett
126 minutes

Cast: William Holden, Clifton Webb, France Nuyen, Athene Seyler, Martin Benson, Edith Sharpe, Robert Lee, Marie Yang, Andy Ho, Burt Kwouk, Weaver Lee, Lin Chen

Leo McCarey seems to have taken his own *Going My Way* and put it into a darkly political setting in order to make this film. A priest (William Holden) arrives in China in 1949 as the Communists are taking over and proceeds to the mission long administered by an aging but brave cleric (Clifton Webb). The drama comes from the growing persecution of the white missionaries by the new regime, with some redemption of a Communist officer (Weaver Lee) after he has raped a lovely local girl (France Nuyen), who harbors a love for the younger priest. The officer returns to Christianity after the birth of his child. The theme of spirituality versus materialism is interesting but not successfully realized in this lengthy treatise.

STATE FAIR

Produced by Charles Brackett
Directed by José Ferrer
Screenplay by Richard Breen, based on a novel by Phil Srong
Photographed in CinemaScope and DeLuxe Color by William C. Mellor
Songs by Richard Rodgers and Oscar Hammerstein II
Musical direction by Alfred Newman
118 minutes

Cast: Pat Boone, Bobby Darin, Pamela Tiffin, Ann-Margret, Tom Ewell, Alice Faye, Wally Cox, David Brandon, Clem Harvey, Robert Foulk, Linda Henrich, Edward "Tap" Canutt, Margaret Deramee

A remake of the 1945 musical, but moving the story from Iowa to Texas, with location filming at the fairgrounds in Dallas. Most of the Rodgers and Hammerstein songs remain, with three new ones penned by Rodgers. The story is the same, with the Frake family—father (Tom Ewell), mother (Alice Faye), daughter (Pamela Tiffin), and son (Pat Boone)

—finding success and love at the fair. The success comes in the form of a promoter (Bobby Darin) and an entertainer (Ann-Margret). The picture is pleasing but lacks the style of the 1945 version. Alice Faye fans were happy to have her return to the screen after a seventeen-year absence.

SWINGIN' ALONG

Produced by Jack Leewood
Directed by Charles Barton
Screenplay by Jameson Brewer
Photographed in CinemaScope and DeLuxe Color by Arthur E. Arling
Music by Arthur Morton
74 minutes

Cast: Tommy Noonan, Pete Marshall, Barbara Eden, Ray Charles, Roger Williams, Bobby Vee, Connie Gilchrist, Carol Christensen, Alan Carney, Mike Mazurki, Tommy Farrell, Lennie Bremen

The original title for this slight musical comedy was *The Schnook,* which perfectly describes its main character (Tommy Noonan), a composer who takes his tunes from bird calls and door bell chimes. He falls in with a glib promoter (Pete Marshall), who needs money badly to pay off his gambling debts. He enters his bumbling friend in a contest, which he fortunately wins. Guests stars like Ray Charles and Roger Williams lend their helpful talents.

TENDER IS THE NIGHT

Produced by Henry T. Weinstein
Directed by Henry King
Screenplay by Ivan Moffatt, based on the novel by F. Scott Fitzgerald
Photographed in CinemaScope and DeLuxe Color by Leon Shamroy
Music by Bernard Herrmann
146 minutes

Cast: Jennifer Jones, Jason Robards, Jr., Joan Fontaine, Tom Ewell, Cesare Danova, Jill St. John, Paul Lukas, Bea Benadaret, Charles Fredericks, Sanford Meisner, Mac McWhorter, Albert Carrier

A long and visually beautiful account of F. Scott Fitzgerald's story about a group of wealthy Americans living in Europe in the 1920's. A rich but neurotic girl (Jennifer Jones) undergoes psychiatric treatment in Zurich and falls in love with her doctor (Jason Robards, Jr.). He marries her and goes to live on her Riviera estate, but the easy idle life gradually dissipates his abilities. He grows weaker as his patient-wife grows stronger. Also on hand are an American composer (Tom Ewell) drowning in alcohol, and a mercenary sister (Joan Fontaine) who truly believes that money is everything. Thus the film contrasts physical ease with spiritual anguish, as Fitz-gerald juggles life's values. Somewhat too long for its material, but a pleasure to watch because of its gorgeous locations.

THE 300 SPARTANS

Produced by Rudolph Mate and George St. George
Directed by Rudolph Mate
Screenplay by George St. George, based on a story by Ugo Liberatori, Remigio Del Grosso, Giovanni D'Eramo, and Gian Paolo Callegari
Photographed in CinemaScope and DeLuxe Color by Geoffrey Unsworth
Music by Manos Hajidakis
108 minutes

Cast: Richard Egan, Ralph Richardson, Diane Baker, Barry Coe, David Farrar, Donald Houston, Anna Synodinou, Kieron Moore, John Crawford, Robert Brown, Laurence Naismith

A better-than-average historical adventure, filmed in Greece and dealing with the defense of Greece by the Spartans of Thermopylae in 480 B.C. The small group of Spartans wage a hopeless battle against the immense Persian armies, but their example serves as an inspiration to Greeks on other fronts. The film is at its best when dealing with the fighting and at its least convincing when engaged in dialogue. The Greek locations are a major asset.

YOUNG GUNS OF TEXAS

Produced by Robert L. Lippert and Maury Dexter
Directed by Maury Dexter
Screenplay by Henry Cross
Photographed in DeLuxe Color and CinemaScope by John Nickolaus, Jr.
Music by Paul Sawtell and Bert Shefter
78 minutes

Cast: James Mitchum, Alana Ladd, Jody McCrea, Chill Wills, Gary Conway, Barbara Mansell, Robert Lowery, Troy Melton, Fred Krone, Alex Sharp

A minor Western, of interest to film students because of the casting of the three leads, all of them offspring of famous stars. James Mitchum is an outlaw brought up by Comanches, who falls in love with the daughter (Alana Ladd) of a mean rancher. Also in the band is a young man (Jody McCrea) who has stolen army funds and whose brother (Gary Conway) sets out to find him to discover the truth. The matters are settled when most of the characters die in a battle with Apaches.

20TH CENTURY-FOX ACADEMY AWARDS FOR 1962

JEAN BOURGOIN, WALTER WOTTITZ: Best cinematography, black and white, *The Longest Day*.

ROBERT MACDONALD, JACQUES MAUMONT: Best special effects, *The Longest Day*.

Richard Beymer and Diane Baker in *Adventures of a Young Man*.

Sir Cedric Hardwicke, Peter Lorre, Richard Haydn, Fabian, and Barbara Eden in *Five Weeks in a Balloon*.

William Holden and Pamela Franklin in *The Lion*.

Jackie Gleason and Diane Gardner in *Gigot*.

James Stewart in *Mr. Hobbs Takes a Vacation*.

Jennifer Jones and Jason Robards, Jr. in *Tender Is the Night*.

John Wayne, Tom Tryon, and Stuart Whitman in *The Longest Day*.

Ann-Margret and Pat Boone in *State Fair*.

Weaver Lee, William Holden, and Clifton Webb in *Satan Never Sleeps*.

CLEOPATRA

Produced by Walter Wanger
Directed by Joseph L. Mankiewicz
Screenplay by Joseph L. Mankiewicz, Ranald MacDougall, and Sidney Buchman, based on Plutarch, Suetonius, Appian, and C. M. Franzero
Photographed in Todd-AO and DeLuxe Color by Leon Shamroy
Music by Alex North
254 minutes

Cast: Elizabeth Taylor, Richard Burton, Rex Harrison, Pamela Brown, George Cole, Hume Cronyn, Cesare Danova, Kenneth Haigh, Andrew Keir, Martin Landau, Roddy McDowall, Robert Stephens, Francesca Annis, Gregoire Aslan, Martin Benson

The most costly—to date—film ever made, and a splendid telling of the celebrated Queen and her doomed love for Mark Antony. The brilliant script by Mankiewicz covers the eighteen years leading up to the formation of the Roman Empire, starting with Cleopatra (Elizabeth Taylor) meeting Julius Caesar (Rex Harrison) in Egypt, when he arrives as conqueror, and ending with her suicide when defeated by Rome and when her Roman general and lover (Richard Burton) also ends his life. The visual content of the film is stunning, especially Cleopatra's entry into Rome, carried on a vast throne-platform and bringing with her the son sired by Caesar. Also impressive is her barge as it sails into Tarsus, and the vast battle of Actium. The sets and costumes are among the finest ever created for the screen, but it is the literacy of Mankiewicz's script and the strength of his direction that give *Cleopatra* distinctions of great importance.

THE CONDEMNED OF ALTONA

Produced by Carlo Ponti
Directed by Vittorio de Sica
Screenplay by Abby Mann and Cesare Zavattini, based on a play by Jean-Paul Sartre
Photographed in CinemaScope by Roberto Girardi
Music derived from Symphony No. 11 by Dimitri Shostakovich
114 minutes

Cast: Sophia Loren, Maximilian Schell, Fredric March, Robert Wagner, Francoise Prevost, Alfredo Franchi, Lucia Pelella, Roberto Massa, Carlo Antonini

A pretentious critique of postwar Germany, *The Condemned of Altona* failed to win either critical approval or public interest. Its story is that of an industrial tycoon (Fredric March), patterned on Krupp, with one son who is demented (Maximilian Schell) and another who is decent-minded (Robert Wagner). The politically amoral father is stricken with cancer—as if to symbolize the corruptness of his life and enterprises. The gloom and the muddle make this a dreary picture.

HOUSE OF THE DAMNED

Produced and directed by Maury Dexter
Screenplay by Harry Spaulding
Photographed by John Nickolaus, Jr.
Music by Henry Vars
62 minutes

Cast: Ronald Foster, Merry Anders, Richard Crane, Erika Peters, Georgia Schmidt, Dal McKennon

A minor effort in the horror catalog, about an architect (Ronald Foster) who visits a large, gloomy house for business reasons and experiences a raft of frightening happenings, which are meant to scare him off but don't.

THE LEOPARD

Produced by Goffredo Lombardo
Directed by Luchino Visconti
Screenplay by Suso Cecchi D'Amico, Pasquale Festa Campanile, Enrico Medioli, Massimo Franciosa, and Luchino Visconti, based on a novel by Giuseppe Tomasi Di Lampedusa
Photographed in DeLuxe Color by Giuseppe Rotunno
Music by Nino Rota
165 minutes

Cast: Burt Lancaster, Claudia Cardinale, Alain Delon, Rina Morelli, Paolo Stoppa, Romolo Valli, Lucilla Moralacchi, Serge Reggiani, Leslie French, Ivo Garrani, Lola Braccini, Mario Gerotti

Set in Italy in the 1860's, when Garibaldi was moving to unite the Italian provinces, the story concerns a prince (Burt Lancaster), an aristocrat intent on holding together his way of life in the face of changing times. He sees the rise of the business class as a threat, but is astute enough to arrange the marriage of his handsome nephew (Alain Delon) to the daughter (Claudia Cardinale) of his wealthy estate manager. The proud prince succeeds in not letting the values of the old world sink beneath the waves of the new. The film is visually impressive, well shot on Sicilian locations, and gives a richly detailed account of a vanished era. Lancaster is a pillar of strength as the prince, but Visconti's style is a little too leisurely for the mass audience. The long ball sequence is a masterpiece of decor and elegance.

LOVES OF SALAMMBO

Produced by Fides-Stella
Directed by Sergio Grieco
Screenplay by John Blamy and Barbara Schmers, based on a story by Gustave Flaubert
Photographed in DeLuxe Color and CinemaScope
Music by Alexandre Derenevsky
74 minutes

Cast: Jeanne Valeric, Jacques Sernas, Edmund Purdom, Arnolda Foa, Ricardo Garrone, Kamala Devi, Charles Fawcett

An Italian-made historical yarn about Salammbo (Jeanne Valeric), the daughter of Hamilcar, the defender of Carthage, and her love for a mercenary (Jacques Sernas) employed by her father. Trouble arises when the mercenaries are not paid and they revolt against Carthage, with a wily politician (Edmund Purdom) using the situation to seize control of the city. The lovers refuse to part, even though the mercenary has been condemned to death by Hamilcar. But in the face of true love he relents.

MARILYN

Narration written by Don Medford
Narration delivered by Rock Hudson
86 minutes

A documentary composed largely of clips from Marilyn Monroe's films for 20th Century-Fox and including a few shots from *Something's Got to Give*, the film she was making at the time of her death in 1962. The first film represented is the 1949 *A Ticket to Tomahawk*, in which she did a bit as a chorus girl. Also included are characteristic samples from *Niagara*, *Gentlemen Prefer Blondes*, *The Seven-Year Itch*, *Bus Stop*, and others. With a warmly delivered narration by her friend Rock Hudson, the film is direct in its tribute and presents no deep analysis of her personality or her problems.

MOVE OVER, DARLING

Produced by Aaron Rosenberg and Martin Melcher
Directed by Michael Gordon
Screenplay by Hal Kanter and Jack Sher, based on a screenplay by Bella Spewack and Samuel Spewack, from a story by Bella Spewack, Samuel Spewack, and Leo McCarey
Photographed in CinemaScope and DeLuxe Color by Daniel L. Fapp
Music by Lionel Newman
103 minutes

Cast: Doris Day, James Garner, Polly Bergen, Chuck Connors, Thelma Ritter, Fred Clark, Don Knotts, Elliott Reid, Edgar Buchanan, John Astin, Pat Harrington, Jr., Eddie Quillan

A remake of *My Favorite Wife* (1940), a remake that was in production as a Marilyn Monroe vehicle at the time of her death. Here Doris Day is the wife who returns after five years and finds her husband (James Garner) with a new bride (Polly Bergen). Although thought killed in a plane crash, she is very much alive and desirous of resuming her marriage and getting to know her two children. The second wife eventually surrenders to this, but only after putting up a fight, with a good deal of confusion for the husband. The solid basic comedy still works.

NINE HOURS TO RAMA

Produced and directed by Mark Robson
Screenplay by Nelson Gidding, based on the book by Stanley Wolpert
Photographed in CinemaScope and DeLuxe Color by Arthur Ibbetson
Music by Malcolm Arnold
125 minutes

Cast: Horst Buchholz, José Ferrer, J. S. Casshyap, Valerie Gearon, Don Borisenko, Robert Morley, Diane Baker, Harry Andrews, Jairaj, David Abraham, Achla Sachdev, Marne Maidland, Harold Goldblatt

The story of the assassination of Mahatma Gandhi, with Indian actor J. S. Casshyap in a remarkably exact portrayal of the great religious leader. A fanatic (Horst Buchholz) within Gandhi's own Hindu party, who blames the leader's policy of nonviolence for their failures against the Moslems, sets out to kill him. The police become aware of this, as does Gandhi, who will not cooperate in any plan of protection for himself. This gives the police a double problem—how to protect him and how to find the assassin before he can strike. They fail at the last moment. The film, mostly shot in India, succeeds in presenting the strange, complex factors of Indian life and in giving some understanding of the great and doomed pundit.

OF LOVE AND DESIRE

Produced by Victor Stoloff
Directed by Richard Rush
Screenplay by Laszlo Gorog and Richard Rush, from a
 story by Victor Stoloff and Jacquine Delessert
Photographed in CinemaScope and DeLuxe Color by
 Alex Phillips
Music by Ronald Stein
97 minutes

Cast: Merle Oberon, Steve Cochran, Curt Jurgens, John
Agar, Steve Brody, Edward Noriega, Rebecca Iturbide,
Elsa Cardenas, Tony Carbajal, Aurora Munoz, Felix
Gonzalez, Felipe Flores

Filmed in Mexico and taking advantage of striking
settings (including Merle Oberon's own elegant
home), the story is that of a socialite (Oberon) given
to nymphomania. An American engineer (Steve Cochran) comes into her life and helps free her from her
trauma—her attachment to her half-brother (Curt
Jurgens). Oberon and the scenery are appealing, but
the material is too exotic to accept.

POLICE NURSE

Produced and directed by Maury Dexter
Screenplay by Harry Spaulding
Photographed by John Nickolaus, Jr.
Music by Richard La Salle
64 minutes

Cast: Ken Scott, Merry Anders, Oscar Beregi, Barbara
Mansell, John Holland, Byron Morrow, Ivan Bonar,
Merry Murray, Justin Smith, Carol Brewster

A police nurse (Merry Anders) enlists the aid of a
police sergeant (Ken Scott) to find out why her sister
committed suicide. They find out that the girl had
given birth to a child, which had been taken from her
and given to a childless couple. The culprit is an evil
drug addict (Oscar Beregi) who runs his own hospital.
By locking him in a room and denying the addict his
drugs, the policeman wrings from him the facts about
his illegal operation.

SODOM AND GOMORRAH

Produced by Goffredo Lombardo
Directed by Robert Aldrich
Screenplay by Robert Aldrich and Giorgio Prosperi
Photographed in DeLuxe Color by Mario Montuori
Music by Miklos Rozsa
155 minutes

Cast: Stewart Granger, Pier Angeli, Stanley Baker, Rosanna Podesta, Anouk Aimee, Claudia Mori, Rik Battaglia, Giacomo Rossi Stuart, Feodor Chaliapin, Aldo
Silvani

A lavish Italian production, with American director
Robert Aldrich also partly responsible for the script

and keeping it from becoming a sensual spectacle. Lot
(Stewart Granger) leads his nomadic band of Jews
across the desert into the twin cities of Sodom and
Gomorrah, whose ruler is a power-hungry hedonist
(Anouk Aimee). Some of the Jews succumb to the
pleasures of the wicked cities, but divine intercession
causes Lot to lead his people away. His wife (Pier
Angeli) defies the command not to look back and is
turned into a pillar of salt. The film contains some
good action, but lumbers in its length and discussions.
The score by Miklos Rozsa lends some distinction.

THE STRIPPER

Produced by Jerry Wald
Directed by Franklin Schaffner
Screenplay by Meade Roberts, based on a play by Wil-
 liam Inge
Photographed in CinemaScope by Ellsworth Fredericks
Music by Jerry Goldsmith
95 minutes

Cast: Joanne Woodward, Richard Beymer, Claire Trevor,
Carol Lynley, Robert Webber, Louis Nye, Gypsy Rose
Lee, Michael J. Pollard, Sondra Kerr, Susan Brown,
Marlene De Lamater, Gary Pagett

The last production of Jerry Wald and an unsuccessful
attempt to make something of the flop Inge play about
a would-be actress (Joanne Woodward) who returns
to her Kansas home town after being dumped by a
theatrical act. She moves in with an old friend (Claire
Trevor), whose son (Richard Beymer) falls in love
with her. She responds to him and they give hope to
each other—despite her being able to find work only
as a stripper at a convention. He persuades her that
she is capable of better things and she helps him reach
a sense of maturity. Woodward works hard at the role,
but her obvious intelligence is greater than that of the
pathetic character.

TAKE HER, SHE'S MINE

Produced and directed by Henry Koster
Screenplay by Nunnally Johnson, based on a play by
 Phoebe and Henry Ephron
Photographed in CinemaScope and DeLuxe Color by
 Lucien Ballard
Music by Jerry Goldsmith
98 minutes

Cast: James Stewart, Sandra Dee, Audrey Meadows,
Robert Morley, Philippe Forquet, John McGiver, Robert
Denver, Monica Moran, Cynthia Pepper, Jenny Maxwell,
Maurice Marsac, Irene Tsu

A comedy about a father's adjustments to his daughter's growing up. Father (James Stewart), very much
of the old school, is constantly perplexed by his pretty,
lively daughter (Sandra Dee) and her fleeting involve-
ments in social fads and far-out politics. When she

goes to art school in Paris and poses for weird paintings, he follows to check up on her and manages to get himself in a house of ill repute as well as a fancy dress ball. The comedy fails to really take off, although Stewart's presence gives it some appeal, even when he is constantly being mistaken for the movie star James Stewart.

THUNDER ISLAND

Produced and directed by Jack Leewood
Screenplay by Don Devlin and Jack Nicholson
Photographed in CinemaScope by John Nickolaus
Music by Paul Sawtell and Bert Shefter
65 minutes

Cast: Gene Nelson, Fay Spain, Brian Kelly, Miriam Colon, Art Bedard, Antonio Torres Martino, Esther Sandoval, José de San Anton, Evelyn Kaufman, Stephanie Rifkinson

A suspense adventure filmed in Puerto Rico, dealing with a cold-blooded American assassin (Gene Nelson) hired by a group of political idealists to kill an out-of-power dictator, whom they fear is trying to get back into power. The film is largely a chase as the hit man tries to get near his target. He fails to do the job.

THE YELLOW CANARY

Produced by Maury Dexter
Directed by Buzz Kulik
Screenplay by Rod Serling, based on *Evil Come, Evil Go,* by Whit Masterson
Photographed in CinemaScope by Floyd Crosby
Music by Kenyon Hopkins
93 minutes

Cast: Pat Boone, Barbara Eden, Steve Forrest, Jack Klugman, Jesse White, Steve Harris, Milton Selzer, John Banner, Jeff Corey, Jo Helton, Vici Raff, Harold Gould, Joe Turkey

A murder mystery, with Pat Boone as a popular singer who despises his public and generally behaves in an obnoxious manner. When his infant son is kidnapped and three innocent people are killed by the kidnapper, the singer finds strength of character and becomes more humane, but also determined to track down the villain, who turns out to be his own psychotic bodyguard (Steve Forrest). The recovery of the child also brings him together with his estranged wife (Barbara Eden).

20TH CENTURY-FOX ACADEMY AWARDS FOR 1963

LEON SHAMROY: Best cinematography, color, *Cleopatra.*

JOHN DE CUIR, JACK MARTIN SMITH, HILYARD BROWN, HERMAN BLUMENTHAL, ELVEN WEBB, MAURICE PELLING, BORIS JURAGA: Best art direction, color, *Cleopatra.*

WALTER M. SCOTT, PAUL S. FOX, RAY MOYER: Best set decoration, color, *Cleopatra.*

IRENE SHARAFF, VITTORIO NINO NOVARESE, RENIE: Best costume design, color, *Cleopatra.*

EMIL KOSA, JR.: Best special visual effects, *Cleopatra.*

Richard Burton, Rex Harrison, and Elizabeth Taylor in *Cleopatra.*

Rina Morelli and Burt Lancaster in *The Leopard.*

Pier Angeli and Stewart Granger in *Sodom and Gomorrah.*

Doris Day and James Garner in *Move Over, Darling.*

Joanne Woodward in *The Stripper.*

James Stewart and Sandra Dee in *Take Her, She's Mine.*

1964

THE CURSE OF THE LIVING CORPSE

Produced and directed by Del Tenney
Screenplay by Del Tenney
Photographed by Richard Hilliard
84 minutes

Cast: Helen Warren, Roy Scheider, Margot Hartman, Robert Milli, Hugh Franklin

A dying man is afraid of being buried alive, because he suffers from seizures that give him the appearance of death. He threatens in his will to come back and kill the members of his family if he is buried when not dead. They make the mistake of doing so and he slays them in a series of dreadful acts.

THE EARTH DIES SCREAMING

Produced by Robert Lippert and Jack Parsons
Directed by Terence Fisher
Screenplay by Henry Cross
Photographed by Arthur Lavis
62 minutes

Cast: Willard Parker, Virginia Field, Dennis Price, Vanda Godsell, Thorley Walters, David Spenser

A science fiction yarn, about a crack space pilot (Willard Parker) who returns to earth and finds the planet has been devastated by some unknown forces. But there are a few survivors and he organizes them in a plan to ward off control by a group of killer robots.

FATE IS THE HUNTER

Produced by Aaron Rosenberg
Directed by Ralph Nelson
Screenplay by Harold Medford, based on a book by Ernest K. Gann
Photographed in CinemaScope by Milton Krasner
Music by Jerry Goldsmith
106 minutes

Cast: Glenn Ford, Nancy Kwan, Rod Taylor, Suzanne Pleshette, Jane Russell, Wally Cox, Nehemiah Persoff, Mark Stevens, Max Showalter, Constance Towers, Howard St. John, Robert Wilkie

The flight director (Glenn Ford) of an airline undertakes to make his own investigation of a crash which took the lives of fifty-three people, because the dead pilot (Rod Taylor) was a wartime buddy and a man he knew to be reliable. With the aid of the one survivor, the stewardess (Suzanne Pleschette), he recreates the flight and finds that the crash was caused by a short circuit. In making this discovery he saves the reputation of his late friend. The film fascinates with its detail of what goes into a crash inquiry and uses many flashbacks to establish the character of the pilot and his adventures. In one of the wartime sequences Jane Russell appears as herself, doing a spot of troop entertaining.

GOODBYE CHARLIE

Produced by David Weisbart
Directed by Vincente Minnelli
Screenplay by Harry Kurnitz, based on the play by George Axelrod
Photographed in CinemaScope and DeLuxe Color by Milton Krasner
Music by Andre Previn
116 minutes

Cast: Tony Curtis, Debbie Reynolds, Pat Boone, Walter Matthau, Joanna Barnes, Ellen McRae, Laura Devon, Martin Gabel, Roger Carmel, Harry Madden, Myrna Hansen, Michael Romanoff

A comedy with an incredible premise: a ladies' man is murdered by a jealous husband, a movie producer (Walter Matthau), and returns to life in the form of a beautiful girl (Debbie Reynolds), who moves in with his/her old friend (Tony Curtis), who is understandably dumbfounded. And confused to have a lovely girl on hand who doesn't seem to realize she is a lovely girl, but still acts like her former self. As such she decides to cash in on some of the inside information about film affairs, including those of her murderer. The film has some amusing moments, especially when Matthau is on screen as the wild, amoral Hungarian producer, but the premise is too fragile to sustain the whole.

GUNS AT BATASI

Produced by George Brown
Directed by John Guillermin
Screenplay by Robert Holles, based on a novel by Robert Holles
Photographed in CinemaScope by Douglas Slocombe
Music by John Addison
105 minutes

Cast: Richard Attenborough, Flora Robson, John Leyton, Jack Hawkins, Mia Farrow, Errol John, Earl Cameron, Percy Herbert, David Lodge, Graham Stark, John Meillon, Bernard Horsfall

A melodrama pitting politics against the military, as the members of a British army post try to maintain order when an African country moves from colonialism to independence. The soldiers find themselves on difficult ground when an African officer (Errol John) heads a movement to take control of the newly emerging country, in opposition to the people approved by the British government. The film offers a gripping study of the predicament, the theme of which seems to be that soldiering and politicking never mix well, and it contains a masterly account of a ramrod-stiff, by-the-book sergeant major played by Richard Attenborough. Proud and honest, the sergeant major is at a loss to understand why his values do not apply in the new situation.

HARBOR LIGHTS

Produced and directed by Maury Dexter
Screenplay by Henry Cross
Photographed by John Nickolaus, Jr.
Music by Paul Sawtell and Bert Shefter
68 minutes

Cast: Kent Taylor, Miriam Colon, Jeff Morrow, Antonio Torres Martino, Jose de San Anton, Braulio Castillo, Ralphie Rodriguez, Allan Sague

An American gambler (Kent Taylor) arrives in Puerto Rico to visit his brother and finds him murdered as the result of being involved with a stolen diamond. He is questioned by a police detective (Antonio Torres Martino) and pursued by an underworld figure (Jeff Morrow) who thinks the brother has the diamond. The brother ferrets his way around Puerto Rico until he finds the diamond and the killers, who are also smugglers.

THE HORROR OF IT ALL

Produced by Robert L. Lippert
Directed by Terence Fisher
Screenplay by Ray Russell
Photographed by Arthur Lavis
Musical direction by Philip Martell
75 minutes

Cast: Pat Boone, Erica Rogers, Dennis Price, Andre Melly, Valentine Dyall, Jack Bligh, Erik Chitty, Archie Duncan

An American (Pat Boone) in England pursues his fiancée (Erica Rogers) to her family home and finds them to be a strange lot. One member is a mad inventor, another is kept locked in a padded cell, yet another has Dracula leanings, etc., and one by one they are killed. The film fails to either frighten or amuse.

THE HORROR OF PARTY BEACH

Produced and directed by Del Tenney
Screenplay by Richard L. Hilliard
Photographed by Richard Hilliard
Music by The Del Aires
82 minutes

Cast: John Scott, Alice Lyon, Allen Laurel, Eulabelle Mode, Marilyn Clark

Radioactive material in the ocean turns skeletons into living monsters, which come up on the beach and kill teenagers as they hold parties. A number of kids die before a scientist devises the solution of pouring sodium over the monsters and dissolving them. The thin yarn is spaced out by a half dozen rock and roll members.

HUSH . . . HUSH, SWEET CHARLOTTE

Produced and directed by Robert Aldrich
Screenplay by Henry Farrell and Lukas Heller
Photographed by Joseph Biroc
Music by Frank DeVol
134 minutes

Cast: Bette Davis, Olivia de Havilland, Joseph Cotten, Agnes Moorehead, Cecil Kellaway, Victor Buono, Mary Astor, William Campbell, Wesley Addy, Bruce Dern, George Kennedy, Dave Willock, John Megna, Ellen Corby, Helen Kleeb, Marianne Stewart, Frank Ferguson, Mary Henderson

Bette Davis' great success in the 1961 *grande guignol* exercise *Whatever Happened to Baby Jane?* made a further entry almost inevitable. *Hush . . . Hush, Sweet Charlotte* does not have quite the same impact, but it is still a fascinating item of *film noir*. Here Davis is an elderly Southern recluse, almost demented by horrible recollections, and fearful that her home might be demolished by the state (to make way for a road), exposing evidence that her father murdered her husband-to-be. She is encouraged in these dreadful delusions by her cousin (Olivia de Havilland) and a doctor (Joseph Cotten), who are actually in cahoots to drive her insane and acquire all of her properties and inheritances. They do not succeed.

MAN IN THE MIDDLE

Produced by Walter Seltzer
Directed by Guy Hamilton
Screenplay by Keith Waterhouse and Willis Hall, based
   on a novel by Howart Fast
Photographed in CinemaScope by Wilkie Cooper
Music by Lionel Bart and John Barry
94 minutes

Cast: Robert Mitchum, France Nuyen, Barry Sullivan,
Trevor Howard, Keenan Wynn, Sam Wanamaker, Alexander Knox, Gary Cockrell, Robert Nichols, Michael
Goodliffe, Errol John

A military courtroom melodrama, set in India during
the second World War, with Robert Mitchum as an
army lawyer assigned to defend an American lieutenant (Keenan Wynn) who has killed a British sergeant
and strained the already tense U.S.-British relationship
in the area. The army wants the officer convicted and
the case disposed of as fast as possible, but the lawyer
finds the officer to be mentally unstable and deserving
of more sympathy and justice than the given facts
would seem. He is thus at odds with the service in
arriving at a fair trial for his client—the point being
that the sick are also entitled to justice.

NIGHT TRAIN TO PARIS

Produced by Robert L. Lippert and Jack Parsons
Directed by Robert Douglas
Screenplay by Henry Cross
Photographed by Arthur Lavis
Songs by Brian Potter and Graham Dee
Music by Kenny Graham
65 minutes

Cast: Leslie Nielsen, Alizia Gur, Dorinda Stevens, Eric
Pohlman, Edina Ronay, Louis Vernay, Cyril Raymond,
Stanley Morgan

A former OSS agent (Leslie Nielsen), now in public
relations work, agrees to help a girl (Alizia Gur) get
some tapes to Paris. He realizes the importance of the
tapes when a friend who has encouraged him to help
the girl is killed. And he dodges the opposition until he
makes the delivery. A neat little espionage tale and
made the more interesting by the train trip from
London and across the channel to Paris.

THE PLEASURE SEEKERS

Produced by David Weisbart
Directed by Jean Negulesco
Screenplay by Edith Sommer, based on a book by John
   H. Secondari
Photographed in CinemaScope and DeLuxe Color by
   Daniel L. Fapp
Songs by Sammy Cahn and James Van Heusen
Music by Lionel Newman
107 minutes

Cast: Ann-Margret, Tony Franciosa, Carol Lynley, Gardner McKay, Pamela Tiffin, Andre Lawrence, Gene Tierney, Brian Keith, Vito Scotti, Isobel Elsom, Maurice
Marsac, Shelby Grant

Three American girls in Madrid—a singer-dancer
(Ann-Margret), a secretary (Carol Lynley), and an
art student (Pamela Tiffin)—seek husbands and find
them in, respectively, the forms of a young Spanish
doctor (Andre Lawrence), an American newsman
(Gardner McKay), and a nobleman (Tony Franciosa).
In the meantime the audience is treated to some beautiful shots of Madrid and Toledo, and close-ups of
famed art treasures, such as those of Goya and El
Greco. Aside from the agreeable travelogue, the film
sports four Cahn-Van Heusen songs sung and danced
by the fetching Ann-Margret.

RIO CONCHOS

Produced by David Weisbart
Directed by Gordon Douglas
Screenplay by Joseph Landon and Clair Huffaker, based
   on a novel by Clair Huffaker
Photographed in CinemaScope and DeLuxe Color by
   Joe MacDonald
Music by Jerry Goldsmith
107 minutes

Cast: Richard Boone, Stuart Whitman, Tony Franciosa,
Wende Wagner, Jim Brown, Warner Anderson, Rodolfo
Acosta, Barry Kelley, Vita Scotti, House Peters, Jr.,
Edmond O'Brien

A superb Western, set in Texas soon after the Civil
War, dealing with the Army's attempts to keep guns
out of the hands of warlike Indians. A sadistic Indian-killer (Richard Boone) and a Mexican bandit (Tony
Franciosa) are released from jail in the company of a
captain (Stuart Whitman), with the proviso that they
will find the source of the gun supply. The trail leads
them to the camp of a grandiose but demented ex-Confederate general (Edmond O'Brien), who turns
out to be the supplier and who is building himself a
mansion on the banks of the Rio Conchos, where he
expects to retire in luxury. Instead, his dream is blown
sky high. The acting of Boone and Franciosa, the
pacing and the action, and the music of Jerry Goldsmith make this a top item in its drawer.

SHOCK TREATMENT

Produced by Aaron Rosenberg
Directed by Denis Sanders
Screenplay by Sydney Boehm, based on a novel by
   Winfred Van Atta
Photographed in CinemaScope by Sam Leavitt
Music by Jerry Goldsmith
94 minutes

Cast: Stuart Whitman, Carol Lynley, Roddy McDowall,

Lauren Bacall, Olive Deering, Ossie Davis, Donald Buka, Pauline Myers, Evadne Baker, Robert Wilke, Bert Freed, Judith De Hart, Judson Laire

An adventure in psychopathology, as an actor (Stuart Whitman) is hired to feign mental illness in order to gain entry to a sanitarium, where the murderer (Roddy McDowall) of an elderly philanthropist has been placed. The killer may or may not have burned a million dollars in cash or stashed it away, and he may be in cahoots with a psychiatrist (Lauren Bacall). It turns out he isn't, but the psychiatrist goes mad anyway. Part of the actor's ordeal is to undergo electro-shock therapy and hypodermic needles before finding the truth from the killer, who is a rose gardener by hobby and likes to use his pruning shears on people.

SURF PARTY

Produced and directed by Maury Dexter
Screenplay by Harry Spaulding
Photographed by Kay Norton
Music by Jimmy Haskell
68 minutes

Cast: Bobby Vinton, Patricia Morrow, Jackie DeShannon, Kenny Miller, Lory Patrick, Richard Crane, Jerry Summers

The flaming youth of 1964, having a wild time on the beach with parties, and singing and dancing the music of the day. The boys and girls love each other with free abandon and risk their necks surfing the mighty waves. Wild stuff at the time, but now rather quaint.

THE THIRD SECRET

Produced by Robert L. Joseph
Directed by Charles Crichton
Screenplay by Robert L. Joseph
Photographed in CinemaScope by Douglas Slocombe
Music by Richard Arnell
103 minutes

Cast: Stephen Boyd, Jack Hawkins, Richard Attenborough, Diane Cilento, Pamela Franklin, Paul Rogers, Alan Webb, Rachel Kempson, Peter Sallis, Patience Collier, Freda Jackson

A London psychiatrist apparently commits suicide, contrary to his strong character, and one of his patients, a newscaster (Stephen Boyd) sets out to discover if the man was murdered. He talks to the three other patients: a judge (Jack Hawkins), a secretary (Diane Cilento), and an art gallery owner (Richard Attenborough), but eventually he finds the murderer —the psychiatrist's own disturbed daughter (Pamela Franklin).

THE VISIT

Produced by Julien Derode and Anthony Quinn
Directed by Bernhard Wicki
Screenplay by Ben Barzman, based on the play by Friedrich Duerrenmatt
Photographed in CinemaScope by Armando Nannuzzi
Music by Hans-Martin Majewski
101 minutes

Cast: Ingrid Bergman, Anthony Quinn, Irina Demich, Paolo Stoppa, Hans-Christian Blech, Romolo Valli, Valentina Cortese, Claude Dauphin, Eduardo Ciannelli, Marco Guglielmi

A woman of great wealth (Ingrid Bergman) returns to the small town where she was ruined when young and driven into prostitution. She has already reaped her revenge by gradually undermining the town's economy by purchasing its resources. Now she seeks the final payment—the death of her original seducer (Anthony Quinn), who had her run out of town. She offers the town a huge amount of money and return to prosperity if the citizens will kill him. At first outraged, they gradually turn against him and prepare to do as she asks. But she relents and satisfies herself that he will have to continue living among people who might have killed him. The film is well played but lacking in appeal, with Bergman cast too far against image to be really acceptable.

WHAT A WAY TO GO

Produced by Arthur P. Jacobs
Directed by J. Lee Thompson
Screenplay by Betty Comden and Adolph Green, based on a story by Gwen Davis
Photographed in CinemaScope and DeLuxe Color by Leon Shamroy
Music by Nelson Riddle
111 minutes

Cast: Shirley MacLaine, Paul Newman, Robert Mitchum, Dean Martin, Gene Kelly, Robert Cummings, Dick Van Dyke, Reginald Gardiner, Margaret Dumont, Lou Nova, Fifi D'Orsay, Maurice Marsac, Wally Vernon, Jane Wald, Lenny Kent

The theme of *What a Way to Go* is that of wry humor, dealing as it does with a lady (Shirley MacLaine) who has the Midas touch for the men she marries, except that great wealth also brings death to each man in turn: a storekeeper (Dick Van Dyke), a painter (Paul Newman), an industrialist (Robert Mitchum), and an entertainer (Gene Kelly). Finally she marries the man she originally spurned (Dean Martin), once wealthy but now penniless. They, presumably, live happily ever after. The film is ruined by its excesses, and the humor derived from death is forced. But it has fine moments, especially the satire, "Musical Extravaganza," by Kelly and MacLaine, on the lavish Busby Berkeley-like routines.

Olivia de Havilland and Bette Davis in *Hush . . . Hush, Sweet Charlotte.*

Tony Curtis and Debbie Reynolds in *Goodbye Charlie.*

Suzanne Pleshette and Glenn Ford in *Fate Is the Hunter.*

Ingrid Bergman and Anthony Quinn in *The Visit.*

Carol Lynley, Ann-Margret, and Pamela Tiffin in *The Pleasure Seekers.*

Shirley MacLaine and Gene Kelly in *What a Way to Go.*

350

Anthony Quinn and Alan Bates in *Zorba the Greek*.

WITCHCRAFT

Produced by Robert Lippert and Jack Parsons
Directed by Don Sharp
Screenplay by Harry Spaulding
Photographed by Arthur Lavis
Music by Carlo Martelli
79 minutes

Cast: Lon Chaney, Jack Hedley, Jill Dixon, Viola Keats, Marie Ney, Yvette Rees, David Weston, Diane Clare, Barry Lineham, Victor Brooks, Marianne Stone, John Dunbar, Hilda Fennemore

A coven of witches come to life when housing developers level an old graveyard in England. The head of a local family (Lon Chaney) tries to stop them, since he is himself a member, but the builder (Jack Hedley) pays no attention until his aunt and a partner die mysteriously. His wife (Jill Dixon) is kidnapped and subjected to a witches' sabbath, and in rescuing her there is a fire which destroys the coven and its crew—hopefully forever. *Witchcraft* is a typical example of the good grade "B" horror movies produced in England in quantity throughout the Sixties.

THE YOUNG SWINGERS

Produced and directed by Maury Dexter
Screenplay by Harry Spaulding
71 minutes

Cast: Rod Lauren, Molly Bee, Gene McDaniels, Jack Larson, Karen Gunderson, John Merritt, Jo Helton, Justin Smith, Jerry Summers, Jack Younger

When a real estate developer (Jo Helton) moves to demolish a teen clubhouse to make way for a high rise building, the members kick up a fuss. A romancing pair of singer-dancers (Molly Bee and Rod Lauren) create problems, which end with the developer compromising and building them a club on another location, with the kids putting on a benefit show.

ZORBA THE GREEK

Produced and directed by Michael Cacoyannis
Screenplay by Michael Cacoyannis, based on a book by Nikos Kazantzakis
Photographed by Walter Lassally
Music by Mikis Theodorakis
146 minutes

Cast: Anthony Quinn, Alan Bates, Irene Papas, Lila Kedrova, George Foundas, Eleni Anousaki, Sotris Moustakas, Takis Emmanuel, George Voyadjis, Anna Kyriakou

A young English writer (Alan Bates) arrives in Crete with the idea of sorting out his values and musing, but comes into contact with a loud and lusty Greek (Anthony Quinn), who takes it upon himself to be the young man's mentor. He introduces him to a lovely widow (Irene Papas), coveted, but never possessed, by all the local men, and their love results in her being killed by the islanders for adultery. The Englishman then observes his Greek friend accepting the charms of an aging courtesan (Lila Kedrova), who dies in his arms, and whose house is ransacked by the locals even before her body is cold. Next he is inveigled into a business scheme which turns into a disaster. But the deaths and the failures are only part of the experiences—the young man is also exposed to great humor and enjoyment as the Greek encourages him to open up his heart and his mind. Zorba is a man who cannot be beaten by life and as acted by Anthony Quinn he remains a tower in the movie memory.

20TH CENTURY-FOX ACADEMY AWARDS FOR 1964

LILA KEDROVA: Best supporting actress, *Zorba the Greek.*

WALTER LASSALLY: Best cinematography, black and white, *Zorba the Greek.*

VASSILIS FOTOPOULOS: Best art direction, black and white, *Zorba the Greek.*

CLASS III SCIENTIFIC and TECHNICAL AWARD: Mechanical effects.

Richard Boone, Stuart Whitman, and James Brown in *Rio Conchos.*

1965

THE AGONY AND THE ECSTASY

Produced and directed by Carol Reed
Screenplay and story by Philip Dunne, based on the
   novel by Irving Stone
Photographed in Todd-AO and DeLuxe Color by Leon
   Shamroy
Music by Alex North
138 minutes

Cast: Charlton Heston, Rex Harrison, Diane Cilento,
Harry Andrews, Alberto Lupo, Adolfo Celi, Venantino
Venantini, John Stacy, Fausto Tozzi, Maxine Audley,
Thomas Millian

The story of the painting of the ceiling of the Sistine
Chapel by Michelangelo (Charlton Heston) and his
commission to do it by Pope Julius II (Rex Harrison).
The film brings out the fact that the artist was not
greatly interested in doing the job, but was goaded
into it by the ambitious Pope, eager to leave creations
by which he would be remembered. It also points up
the fervor of early sixteenth-century Italian history,
with the Pope leading his armies on the battlefield to
unite the country in the name of the church. For the
most part it focuses on the slow and painful work of
Michelangelo lying on his back on a scaffold, creating
the divine frescoes and being nagged by his employer
to hurry up with the job. As drama the film suffers
from tedium, but for its decor and its study of the
work of a genius it is a fascinating history lesson.

APACHE RIFLES

Produced by Grant Whytock
Directed by William H. Witney
Screenplay by Charles B. Smith
Photographed in DeLuxe Color by Arch R. Dalzell
93 minutes

Cast: Audie Murphy, Michael Dante, Linda Lawson,
L. Q. Jones, Ken Lynch, Joseph Vitale, Robert Brubaker

The commander (Audie Murphy) of an army post in
Arizona finds his attitudes toward the Apaches mel-
lowing when he falls in love with a half-Indian missionary (Linda Lawson). He proposes more honorable
treatment of the Indians, but he is opposed by white
miners who are seeking gold on Apache lands. They

manage to get him replaced by another officer, but
in the ensuing battle between the whites and the
Apaches, his views are vindicated.

BACK DOOR TO HELL

Produced by Fred Roos
Directed by Monte Hellman
Screenplay by Richard A. Guttman and John Hackett
Photographed by Mars Rasca
Music by Mike Velarde
68 minutes

Cast: Jimmie Rogers, Jack Nicholson, John Hackett,
Annabelle Huggins, Conrad Maga, Johnny Monteiro

Guerrilla warfare in the Philippines, as a party of
three American soldiers led by an intelligence officer
(Jimmie Rogers) seek information from the guerrillas
prior to the American invasion. With their own radio
transmitter destroyed, the soldiers take a Japanese
post in order to send messages back to their headquarters to tell them to proceed with the invasion.
A conventional war picture, shot in the Philippines
on a limited budget.

THE CAVERN

Produced and directed by Edgar G. Ulmer
Screenplay and story by Michael Pertwee and Jack Davis
Photographed by Gabor Pogany
Music by Carlo Rustichelli and Gene di Novi
83 minutes

Cast: John Saxon, Rosanna Schiaffino, Larry Hagman,
Peter L. Marshall, Brian Aherne, Nino Castelnuovo,
Hans von Borody, Joachim Hansen

As the result of an aerial bombardment, six soldiers
and a woman (Rosanna Schiaffino) become trapped
in a cave in the Italian mountains in the last days of
the second World War. The cave, which contains ammunition and supplies, is covered by Italian partisans
and two of the trapped party are shot trying to get
out. They wear on each other's nerves and finally a
British general (Brian Aherne) shoots himself, and
in so doing sets off an explosion which enables the
survivors to get out.

CONVICT STAGE

Produced by Hal Klein
Directed by Leslie Selander
Screenplay by Daniel Mainwaring
Photographed by Gordon Avil
71 minutes

Cast: Harry Lauter, Donald Barry, Hanna Landy, Jodi Mitchell, Joseph Partridge, Eric Matthews

A Westerner (Harry Lauter) sets out to revenge the vicious killing of his sister by a gang led by a woman (Hanna Landy) but it's a veteran lawman (Donald Barry) who brings the gang to justice, while teaching the bitter avenger about working within the limits of the law.

THE CURSE OF THE FLY

Produced by Robert L. Lippert and Jack Parsons
Directed by Don Sharp
Screenplay by Harry Spaulding
Photographed by Basil Emmott
86 minutes

Cast: Brian Donlevy, George Baker, Carole Gray, Michael Graham, Jeremy Wilkins, Charles Carson, Bert Kwouk, Yvette Rees, Rachel Kempson, Mary Manson, Warren Stanhope, Arnold Bell

A horror item about teleportation—the transference of humans from one place to another electronically. A Canadian scientist (Brian Donlevy) has perfected this means of travel, but runs into problems when his son (George Baker) marries a girl (Carole Gray) without explaining that he has a badly disfigured wife hidden away—a victim of experimenting with teleportation. The hideous wife escapes and attacks the bride, which results in the police finding the family home. To save them, the father moves to teleport them, but something goes wrong and he is lost in transit forever. Critics suggested a similar fate should meet this film.

DEAR BRIGITTE

Produced and directed by Henry Koster
Screenplay by Hal Kanter, based on a book by John Haase
Photographed in CinemaScope and DeLuxe Color by Lucien Ballard
Music by George Duning
100 minutes

Cast: James Stewart, Fabian, Glynis Johns, Cindy Carol, Billy Mumy, John Williams, Jack Kruschen, Ed Wynn, Charles Robinson, Howard Freeman, Jane Wald, Alice Pearce, Jesse White, Brigitte Bardot

A college professor (James Stewart), devoted to the arts rather than the sciences, find that his ten-year-old son (Billy Mumy) is a mathematical wizard, with a brain that works as fast as a computer. A race track tout discovers that the boy can also, when fed the facts, predict winners. His father agrees to let him be so used provided the winnings are turned over to a foundation for the arts. But the boy has his own condition: before he goes to work as a horse handicapper he wants to go to France to meet his idol, Brigitte Bardot. He does, and she gives him a puppy.

DEVILS OF DARKNESS

Produced by Tom Blakely
Directed by Lance Comfort
Screenplay by Lyn Fairhurst
Photographed in DeLuxe Color by Reg Wyer
Music by Bernie Fenton
88 minutes

Cast: William Sylvester, Hubert Noel, Tracy Reed, Carole Gray, Diana Decker, Rona Anderson, Peter Illing, Gerard Heinz, Victor Brooks, Avril Angers, Brian Oulton, Marie Burke

An Englishman (William Sylvester) takes a vacation in Brittany and comes across an evil cult, whose leader (Hubert Noel) has found the secret of everlasting life, which requires the sacrifice of other human lives. When two of his friends are killed, the Englishman moves to bring the cult to an end, especially when he learns that his girl friend (Tracy Reed) is their next scheduled victim.

DO NOT DISTURB

Produced by Aaron Rosenberg and Martin Melcher
Directed by Ralph Levy
Screenplay by Milt Rosen and Richard Breen
Photographed in CinemaScope and DeLuxe Color by Leon Shamroy
Music by Lionel Newman
102 minutes

Cast: Doris Day, Rod Taylor, Hermione Baddeley, Sergio Fantoni, Reginald Gardiner, Maura McGiveney, Aram Katcher, Leon Askin, Lisa Pera, Michael Romanoff, Albert Carrier, Barbara Morrison

An American wool executive (Rod Taylor) and his wife (Doris Day) proceed to his new appointment in London, but the wife spends so much time fixing up their home that he feels neglected and starts to pay attention to his secretary (Maura McGiveney). But his jealousies are aroused when the wife pays a visit to Paris and spends time with a handsome antique dealer (Sergio Fantoni). She has too much to drink and can't remember whether or not she spent the night with the dealer. She didn't, of course, but she does help swing a big deal for her husband with a Viennese wool tycoon (Leon Askin). Lightweight comedy, but stylishly done, which includes good use of its London and Paris locations.

FLIGHT OF THE PHOENIX

Produced and directed by Robert Aldrich
Screenplay by Lucas Heller, based on a novel by Elleston Trevor
Photographed in DeLuxe Color by Joseph Biroc
Music by Frank De Vol
149 minutes

Cast: James Stewart, Richard Attenborough, Peter Finch, Hardy Kruger, Ernest Borgnine, Ian Bannen, Ronald Fraser, Christian Marquand, Dan Duryea, George Kennedy, Gabriele Tinti, Alex Montoya

A study of survival, as a group of oil men and passengers await death or rescue in the Sahara desert when their plane has to force land. The veteran pilot (James Stewart) takes the blame, but his navigator (Richard Attenborough) is largely at fault because of his drinking. As the days pass, the strengths and weaknesses of the various men begin to show up. One of them comes up with a plan which seems hardly likely to work, but the men reason that it is their only chance. He is a German designer (Hardy Kruger) and he designs a single-engined aircraft from the wreckage of their plane. Exhausted by lack of food and water and with some already dead, the survivors do indeed build the plane and fly out. Sadly, in actual fact, the veteran film pilot and stuntman Paul Mantz lost his life in the making of this film.

FORT COURAGEOUS

Produced by Hal Klein
Directed by Leslie Selander
Screenplay by Richard Landau
Music by Richard LaSalle
72 minutes

Cast: Fred Bier, Kent Taylor, Harry Lauter, Donald Barry, Hanna Landy

A Cavalry patrol proceeds to Fort Courageous with an unjustly court-martialed sergeant (Fred Bier), who takes over the patrol when the captain is wounded in an Indian attack. When they get to the fort, they find only one survivor, a major (Donald Barry). Their heroic defense of the fort finally wins the admiration of the Indians, who allow them to leave in peace.

A HIGH WIND IN JAMAICA

Produced by John Croydon
Directed by Alexander Mackendrick
Screenplay by Ronald Harwood, Denis Cannon, and Stanley Mann, based on the book by Richard Hughes
Photographed in CinemaScope and DeLuxe Color by Douglas Slocombe

Music by Larry Adler
100 minutes

Cast: Anthony Quinn, James Coburn, Dennis Price, Gert Frobe, Lila Kedrova, Deborah Baxter, Martin Amis, Karen Flack, Henry Beltran, Roberta Tovey, Jeffrey Chandler, Viviane Ventura, Kenneth J. Warren

In 1870 a group of children depart Jamaica for England but become the captives of pirates when their ship is seized. The captain (Anthony Quinn) is puzzled by what to do with the children, since he is too soft-hearted to do away with them. He attempts to set them aboard a Dutch ship, but brings on a mutiny from his men when he refuses to pillage the vessel. One of the children, a girl, kills the Dutch captain (Gert Frobe) when she thinks her life is in danger. Later, when the pirates are captured and put on trial in England, the little girl blames the captain for the killing of the Dutchman and he, not able to turn on a child, accepts the penalty. The unusual story points up the strange rationale of children when placed in bizarre circumstances.

JOHN GOLDFARB, PLEASE COME HOME

Produced by Steve Parker
Directed by J. Lee Thompson
Screenplay by William Peter Blatty
Photographed in CinemaScope and DeLuxe Color by Leon Shamroy
Music by Johnny Williams
96 minutes

Cast: Shirley MacLaine, Peter Ustinov, Richard Crenna, Jim Backus, Scott Brady, Fred Clark, Harry Morgan, Wilfrid Hyde-White, Patrick Adiarte, Richard Deacon, Jerome Cowan, Leon Askin

A U-2 pilot (Richard Crenna) crash lands in the Arabian country of Fawz, governed by an amiable simpleton of a king (Peter Ustinov), who plays with toy trains and dreams of having a football team that will beat Notre Dame. The U.S. State Department wants the pilot to come home, but the king wants him to coach his team, or be turned over to the Russians. Also on hand is an American reporter (Shirley MacLaine), pretending to be a member of the harem in order to get an inside story, while eluding the hands of the king. The film ends with a wacky football game but falls short of its intention to satirize international politics. But with Ustinov as the playful monarch, all is not lost.

MORITURI

Produced by Aaron Rosenberg
Directed by Bernard Wicki
Screenplay by Daniel Taradash, based on the novel by Werner Joerg Luedecke
Photographed by Conrad Hall

Music by Jerry Goldsmith
128 minutes

Cast: Marlon Brando, Yul Brynner, Janet Margolin, Trevor Howard, Martin Benrath, Hans Christian Blech, Wally Cox, Max Haufler, Rainer Penkert, William Redfield, Oscar Beregi, Martin Brandt, Gary Crosby, Charles De Vries, Carl Esmond, Martin Kosleck, Norbert Schiller

Marlon Brando again played a spiritually tormented German, but with far less success than in *The Young Lions*. Here he is a spy in the employ of the British, sailing on a German freighter from Japan to Germany and striving to turn the ship over to the enemy. The voyage turns into a series of moral equations regarding Nazism and anti-Nazism and tension between the various factions, with the captain finally siding with the spy. *Morituri* is admirable in concept but dull in execution and proved to be one of Brando's least successful films.

MORO WITCH DOCTOR

Produced and directed by Eddie Romero
Screenplay by Eddie Romero
Photographed by Felipe Sacdalan
Music by Ariston Avelinc
61 minutes

Cast: Jock Mahoney, Margia Dean, Pancho Magalona, Paraluman, Mike Parsons, Vic Diaz

An Interpol agent (Jock Mahoney) in the Philippines investigates a dope smuggling ring and finds the Moros are involved. An American co-owner of a plantation is killed by the Moros, which leads the agent to believe that the other owner is involved with the ring. He is, and ends up dead after battling the agent, who consoles himself with the sister (Margia Dean) of the murdered owner.

THE NANNY

Produced by Jimmy Sangster
Directed by Seth Holt
Screenplay by Jimmy Sangster, based on the novel by Evelyn Piper
Photographed by Harry Waxman
Music by Richard Rodney Bennett
93 minutes

Cast: Bette Davis, Wendy Craig, Jill Bennett, James Villiers, William Dix, Pamela Franklin, Jack Watling, Maurice Denham, Alfred Burke, Nora Gordon, Sandra Power, Harry Fowler, Angharad Aubrey

Less frightening than Bette Davis' previous forays into horror, *The Nanny* is perhaps more disturbing because the character is a credible one. The veteran nursemaid of the title is in conflict with a ten-year-old charge (William Dix), who is thought to have been responsible for the death by drowning of his sister. The boy claims the Nanny did it. And he is right, although it was an accident. It seems the Nanny gave away her own daughter when she was six months old, and years later found that she had died from an abortion. These facts have gradually made the Nanny psychotic and unsafe to be around children. She almost kills the boy in her care, but regains sanity in time—enough to retire from her profession.

RAIDERS FROM BENEATH THE SEA

Produced and directed by Maury Dexter
Screenplay by Harry Spaulding, based on a story by F. Paul Hall
Photographed by Floyd Crosby
Music by Hank Levine
73 minutes

Cast: Ken Scott, Merry Anders, Russ Bender, Booth Colman, Garth Benton, Bruce Anson, Walter Maslow, Stacy Winters, Ray Dannis, Larry Barton, Roger Creed

Four men attempt to rob a bank on Catalina Island by emerging from the sea in diving suits and then attaching the proceeds to the bottom of a ferry boat. Things starts to go wrong when the wife (Merry Anders) objects to her husband-ringleader (Ken Scott) being involved in crime and when he brings in his brother (Garth Benton), who has a yen for his sister-in-law. The crime ends in disaster for the culprits.

RAPTURE

Produced by Christian Ferry
Directed by John Guillermin
Screenplay by Stanley Mann, based on the book *Rapture in Rags* by Patricia Hastings
Photographed in CinemaScope by Marcel Grignon
Music by Georges Delerue
104 minutes

Cast: Patricia Gozzi, Melvyn Douglas, Dean Stockwell, Gunnel Lindblom, Leslie Sands, Murray Evans, Sylvia Kane, Peter Sallis

A lonely, retarded girl (Patricia Gozzi) lives with her bitter father (Melvyn Douglas) in Brittany and hovers in her fantasies until a young man (Dean Stockwell) comes along. He is a fugitive from the law, but he falls in love with the pretty recluse and helps her find happiness, taking her with him to Paris and enjoying their times together until the law catches up with him and he is killed. An unusual and very tragic romance.

THE RETURN OF MR. MOTO

Produced by Robert L. Lippert and Jack Parsons
Directed by Ernest Morris
Screenplay by Fred Eggers
Photographed by Basil Emmott
Music by Douglas Gamley
71 minutes

Cast: Henry Silva, Terence Longdon, Suzanne Lloyd, Marne Maitland, Martin Widdeck, Manley Morgan, Peter Zander, Harold Kasket, Gordon Tanner

Mr. Moto (Henry Silva) returns, not in his native Hawaii but in foggy London and working for Interpol. While walking with an oil executive, the two are attacked—the executive is killed and Moto survives. In investigating the attack he finds an espionage plot to eradicate a number of Middle East oilmen and take over their fields. As always, Moto sees to it that such plans do not materialize.

THE REWARD

Produced by Aaron Rosenberg
Directed by Serge Bourguignon
Screenplay by Serge Bourguignon and Oscar Millard, based on a novel by Michael Barrett
Photographed in CinemaScope and DeLuxe Color by Joe MacDonald
Music by Elmer Bernstein
94 minutes

Cast: Max Von Sydow, Yvette Mimieux, Efrem Zimbalist, Jr., Gilbert Roland, Emilio Fernandez, Nina Castelnuovo, Henry Silva, Rodolfo Acosta

An American (Efrem Zimbalist, Jr.) on the run in Mexico because of a murder charge and a price of $50,000 on his head—and accompanied by his girl friend (Yvette Mimieux)—is chased and caught by a police chief (Gilbert Roland) and his men. The reward causes dissension among the men, rousing their greed and superstitions, until most of them are destroyed.

THE SOUND OF MUSIC

Produced and directed by Robert Wise
Screenplay by Ernest Lehman, based on the stage musical by Howard Lindsay and Russel Crouse
Photographed in Todd-AO and DeLuxe Color by Ted McCord
Songs by Richard Rodgers and Oscar Hammerstein II
Musical direction by Irwin Kostal
176 minutes

Cast: Julie Andrews, Christopher Plummer, Eleanor Parker, Richard Haydn, Peggy Wood, Charmian Carr, Heather Menzies, Nicholas Hammond, Duane Chase, Angela Cartwright, Debbie Turner, Kym Karath, Anna Lee, Portia Nelson

The most successful film musical ever made and a joyous celebration of life, as it tells the story of the Austrian family, the Trapps, who decided to leave their homeland when the Nazis took over and proceed to America. The Rodgers and Hammerstein stage production here benefits enormously from being filmed in handsome Austrian mountains and in Salzburg, and from a spirited performance by Julie Andrews as the young governess who was hired by Admiral Von

Trapp (Christopher Plummer) to manage his seven children and later becomes his wife. With her guidance they become a group of singers and as such they elude the Nazis and slip into Switzerland. The film is a winner on every count, with its score, its performances, and perhaps most of all its visually stunning setting.

SPACE FLIGHT IC-I

Produced by Robert L. Lippert and Jack Parsons
Directed by Bernard Knowles
Screenplay by Harry Spaulding
Photographed by Geoffrey Faithfull
Music by Elizabeth Lutyens
65 minutes

Cast: Bill Williams, Kathleen Breck, John Cairney, Donald Churchill, Jeremy Longhurst, Linda Marlow, Margo Mayne, Norma West, Tony Doonan, Andrew Downie

A futuristic science fiction yarn, made in England, concerning the computerized, emotionless life to come. A spaceship is sent to colonize a new planet and the people are selected because of health and brains, in specifications laid down by a universal government. But human feelings cause unrest and mutiny on the trip and the implication is that life in the new colony cannot be simply coldly calculated but must include human values.

THANK HEAVEN FOR SMALL FAVORS

Produced by Henri Diamant-Berger and Jerome Goulven
Directed by Jean-Pierre Mocky
Screenplay by Michel Servin, Alain Moury, and Jean-Pierre Mocky
Photographed by L. H. Burel
84 minutes

Cast: Bourvil, Francis Blanche, Jean Poiret, Jean Yonnell

An impoverished French aristocrat (Bourvil), who will do anything except work, goes to church to ask for divine guidance. The rattle of a collection box leads him to think that God is inviting him to help himself. He does, and goes on to rob church boxes all over the place, causing a furor with church security. Eventually he returns the fortune he has filched and flees the country. Good Gallic humor, with Bourvil at his best.

THOSE MAGNIFICENT MEN
IN THEIR FLYING MACHINES

Produced by Stan Margulies
Directed by Ken Annakin
Screenplay by Jack Davies and Ken Annakin
Photographed in Todd-AO and DeLuxe Color by Christopher Challis
Music by Ron Goodwin
133 minutes

Cast: Stuart Whitman, Sarah Miles, James Fox, Alberto Sordi, Robert Morley, Gert Frobe, Jean-Pierre Cassel, Eric Sykes, Terry-Thomas, Red Skelton, Irina Demich, Benny Hill, Yujiro Ishihara, Flora Robson, Karl Michael Vogler

A magnificent comic adventure, as pioneer aviators compete in the 1910 London-to-Paris air race in a variety of weird planes, mostly with honest sportsmanship, but with a few cads, such as Terry-Thomas, trying to win by any means. Chief among them are an Arizona cowboy (Stuart Whitman) and a British Guards officer (James Fox), who vie for the attentions of the daughter (Sarah Miles) of the blustering publisher (Robert Morley) who is the sponsor of the race. Along the way the film manages to poke gentle fun at European types, such as the German, the French, and the Italian with burlesqued characteristics. But its real triumph is the re-creation of the prototype airplanes and the sight of them making their peculiar way through the skies, ably backed up by the good-natured music of Ron Goodwin.

UP FROM THE BEACH

Produced by Paul Graetz
Directed by Robert Parrish
Screenplay by Stanley Mann and Claude Brule, based on a novel by George Barr
Photographed in CinemaScope by Walter Wottitz
Music by Edgar Cosma
99 minutes

Cast: Cliff Robertson, Red Buttons, Irina Demich, Marius Goring, Slim Pickens, James Robertson-Justice, Broderick Crawford, George Chamarat, Françoise Rosay

The day after D Day, as a patrol of American soldiers led by a sergeant (Cliff Robertson) liberate a French village and rescue a group of French hostages held by the Germans. The sergeant evacuates the civilians from the war area and is then told to take them in some other direction. He finds himself in the role of a confused shepherd. The film is a comment on the plight of civilans in war and is made interesting by the actual Normandy locations and the acting of some distinguished French performers, notably Françoise Rosay as a dignified, elderly lady.

VON RYAN'S EXPRESS

Produced by Saul David
Directed by Mark Robson
Screenplay by Wendell Mayes, based on the novel by Joseph Westheimer
Photographed in CinemaScope and DeLuxe Color by William H. Daniels
Music by Jerry Goldsmith
117 minutes

Cast: Frank Sinatra, Trevor Howard, Raffaella Carra, Brad Dexter, Sergio Fantoni, John Leyton, Edward Mul-

James Stewart, Billy Mumy, and Brigitte Bardot in *Dear Brigitte.*

Charlton Heston and Rex Harrison in *The Agony and the Ecstasy.*

Anthony Quinn and James Coburn in *A High Wind in Jamaica.*

Richard Crenna and Shirley MacLaine in *John Goldfarb, Please Come Home.*

Yul Brynner and Marlon Brando in *Morituri.*

Richard Attenborough, James Stewart, and Hardy Kruger in *The Flight of the Phoenix.*

The Sound of Music, with Julie Andrews, Christopher Plummer, and a slew of Trapps.

Photographed by Bob Hike
Music by Stanley Black
89 minutes

Cast: Ray Charles, Tom Bell, Mary Peach, Dawn Addams, Piers Bishop, Betty McDowell, Lucy Appleby, Joe Adams, Robert Lee Ross, Anne Padwick, Monika Henreid, the Ray Charles Orchestra

The acting debut of blind jazz singer-pianist Ray Charles, playing himself in a story set in London, with Charles befriending a recently blinded English boy (Piers Bishop) and trying to persuade his mother (Mary Peach) not to be overprotective. Her boyfriend (Tom Bell) is a composer who sides with Charles and talks her into letting them take the boy to Paris, while they do a concert, and have him see a specialist who might save the boy's sight. The film is a cheerful yarn, perked up with a lot of performances by Ray Charles and his musicians.

DRACULA—PRINCE OF DARKNESS

Produced by Anthony Nelson Keyes
Directed by Terence Fisher
Screenplay by John Sanson
Photographed in Technicolor and Techniscope by Michael Reed
Music by James Bernard
90 minutes

Cast: Christopher Lee, Barbara Shelley, Andrew Keir, Francis Matthes, Suzan Farmer, Charles Tingwell, Thorley Walters, Walter Brown, Philip Latham, George Woodbridge

A party of Britons, two brothers and their wives, become stranded in the Carpathian Mountains and receive hospitality from the butler of a strange mansion. One of the brothers (Charles Tingwell) is killed and his blood is used to revive the body of Count Dracula (Christopher Lee). The Count sinks his teeth into the widow (Barbara Shelley) and turns her into a vampire. It remains for the other brother (Francis Matthews), with the help of a knowledgeable friar (Andrew Keir), to save his wife and put an end to Dracula, which he does by drowning. For the time being.

FANTASTIC VOYAGE

Produced by Saul David
Directed by Richard Fleischer
Screenplay by Harry Kleiner, based on a story by Otto Klement and Jay Lewis Bixby
Photographed in CinemaScope and DeLuxe Color by Ernest Laszlo
Music by Leonard Rosenman
100 minutes

Cast: Stephen Boyd, Raquel Welch, Edmond O'Brien, Donald Pleasance, Arthur O'Connell, William Redfield, Arthur Kennedy, Jean Del Val, Barry Coe, Ken Scott, Shelby Grant, James Brolin

A science fiction masterpiece. A team of scientists, one of them a woman (Raquel Welch), are miniaturized, placed in a tiny capsule, and injected into the body of a scientist. Their job is to proceed to his brain and relieve a blood clot, a mission of great risk, since the scientist is a man of vast importance who has been injured by the enemy so that his secrets will not fall into American hands. The trip through his arterial system is a success, despite one of the team being an enemy agent. The film is a triumph for its special effects crew and photographer Ernest Laszlo, with incredible passages through the human blood stream and into the lungs, coated with huge blobs of tar, and with the body's natural functions making the trip entirely rough and hazardous.

HOW TO STEAL A MILLION

Produced by Fred Kohlmar
Directed by William Wyler
Screenplay by Harry Kurnitz, based on a story by George Bradshaw
Photographed in Panavision and DeLuxe Color by Charles Lang
Music by Johnny Williams
127 minutes

Cast: Audrey Hepburn, Peter O'Toole, Eli Wallach, Hugh Griffith, Charles Boyer, Fernand Gravet, Marcel Dalio, Jacques Marin, Moustache, Roger Treville, Eddie Malin, Bert Bertram

A stylish crime caper, short on crime but happily brimming over with chic style. A Parisian (Hugh Griffith) amuses himself in his plush retirement by copying masterpiece paintings and objets d'art, but when his copy of a Cellini statuette gets into a museum and is likely to be examined by experts, he is anxious to retrieve it. His daughter (Audrey Hepburn) hires a man (Peter O'Toole) whom she believes to be a burglar but is in fact a detective. The two of them invade the museum to pull off the strange theft. The acting, particularly that of the elegant Hugh Griffiith as the compulsive forger, is delightful, as is the Kurnitz script, the Wyler direction, and the Parisian locations.

I DEAL IN DANGER

Produced by Buck Houghton
Directed by Walter Grauman
Screenplay by Larry Cohen
Photographed in DeLuxe Color by Sam Leavitt and Kurt Grigoleit
Music by Lalo Schifrin
90 minutes

Cast: Robert Goulet, Christine Carere, Horst Frank, Donald Harron, Werner Peters, Eva Pflug, Christine Schmidtmer, John van Dreelen, Hans Reiser

A feature film spin-off of the television series *Blue Light*, with Robert Goulet as an American spy operating in Germany during World War II. He pretends to be a traitor to his own country and as such worms his way into the confidence of the Nazis. Helping him and providing a little romance is a French agent (Christine Carere) and a German scientist (Eva Pflug), who aid him in his objective—to blow up an underground factory producing secret weapons.

MODESTY BLAISE

Produced by Joseph Janni
Directed by Joseph Losey
Screenplay by Evan Jones, based on the comic strip by Peter O'Donnell
Photographed in DeLuxe Color by Jack Hildyard
Music by John Dankworth
120 minutes

Cast: Monica Vitti, Terence Stamp, Dirk Bogarde, Harry Andrews, Michael Craig, Scilla Gabel, Alexander Knox, Tina Marquand, Clive Revill, Rossella Falk, Joe Melia, Lex Schoorel

The title refers to a superspy, a kind of female James Bond, played with sultry panache by Monica Vitti. The film is derived from a popular British comic strip and retains comic strip style. When the British government want a vast sum of money transferred to an oil rich sheik, they employ Modesty to supervise and keep away the powerful thieves. The most powerful is Gabriel (Dirk Bogarde), who lives in great splendor and maintains exotic habits. His agents cause her all kinds of bizarre problems and dangers, but Gabriel is outwitted. The film is so lavishly and outrageously camp that it borders on surrealism.

THE MURDER GAME

Produced by Robert L. Lippert and Jack Parsons
Directed by Sidney Salkow
Screenplay by Harry Spaulding, from a story by Irving Yergin
Photographed by Geoffrey Faithfull
Music by Carlo Martelli
77 minutes

Cast: Ken Scott, Marla Landi, Trader Faulkner, Conrad Phillips, Gerald Sim, Rosamund Greenwood, Victor Brooks

A British-made melodrama about an Englishman (Trader Faulkner) who realizes that the bride (Marla Landi) with whom he is sharing a honeymoon is actually plotting with an ex-husband (Ken Scott) to murder him and gain his wealth. He gradually turns the tables on them with his own plot, which consists of setting up his own murder and neatly implicating the other two as the murderers.

OUR MAN FLINT

Produced by Saul David
Directed by Daniel Mann
Screenplay by Hal Fimberg and Ben Starr, from a story by Hal Fimberg
Photographed in CinemaScope and Technicolor by Daniel L. Fapp
Music by Jerry Goldsmith
107 minutes

Cast: James Coburn, Lee J. Cobb, Gila Golan, Edward Mulhare, Benson Fong, Shelby Grant, Sigrid Valdis, Gianna Serra, Helen Funai, Michael St. Clair, Rhys Williams, Russ Conway

James Coburn as Flint, an American James Bond and every bit as pleasingly preposterous in his super abilities at defeating villains and winning multitudes of beautiful girls. The head of U.S. espionage (Lee J. Cobb) calls in the cool Flint when it seems a group of enemy agents are out to control the world with secret weapons that control the weather. Their top agent is a lovely girl (Gila Golan), but she melts in Flint's arms and helps him locate the enemy headquarters, which are blown to smithereens. The film's tone is one of parody, but its rich production values put it on the same level as the material it sends up.

THE PLAGUE OF THE ZOMBIES

Produced by Anthony Nelson Keys
Directed by John Gilling
Screenplay by Peter Bryan
Photographed in DeLuxe Color by Arthur Grant
Music by James Bernard
90 minutes

Cast: Andre Morell, Diane Clare, John Carson, Brook Williams, Alexander Davion, Jacqueline Pearce, Michael Ripper, Marcus Hammond, Roy Royston

A number of people die mysteriously in a Cornish town of a hundred years ago. The local doctor cannot understand the deaths and calls in an expert (Andre Morell), who becomes suspicious when the squire (John Carson) refuses to permit autopsies. It seems the squire is having people killed and then turned into zombies in order to work in his tin mine. The expert puts an end to this weird method of labor recruitment.

THE QUILLER MEMORANDUM

Produced by Ivan Foxwell
Directed by Michael Anderson
Screenplay by Harold Pinter, based on a novel by Adam Hall
Photographed in Panavision and DeLuxe Color by Erwin Hiller
Music by John Barry
103 minutes

Cast: George Segal, Alec Guinness, Max Von Sydow, Senta Berger, George Sanders, Robert Helpmann, Robert Flemyng, Peter Carsten, Edith Schneider, Gunther Meisner, Robert Stass, Ernst Walder

A spy film along serious lines, with no gunplay or gimmicks. Instead it offers a chilling account of just what espionage is all about, as an American agent (George Segal) roams around Berlin trying to get a grip on a group of neo-Nazis and their aristocratic leader (Max Von Sydow). They actually get a firm grip on him, from which he eventually and painfully extricates himself. Most painful of all is the fact that the lovely schoolteacher (Senta Berger) who has seemingly been helping him and loving him is also a Nazi who has escaped detection. The film is a superior exercise in playing the spy game, with good use of Berlin locations and a subtle script by Harold Pinter.

RASPUTIN—THE MAD MONK

Produced by Anthony Nelson Keys
Directed by Don Sharp
Screenplay by John Elder
Photographed in CinemaScope and DeLuxe Color by Michael Reed
Music by Don Banks
92 minutes

Cast: Christopher Lee, Barbara Shelley, Richard Pasco, Francis Matthews, Susan Farmer, Nicholas Pennell, Renee Asherson

A fanciful account of Rasputin (Christopher Lee) and his hypnotic powers over the Russian royal family prior to the revolution. He insinuates himself into the palace by seducing a lady-in-waiting (Barbara Shelley), which causes her fiancé (Nicholas Pennell) to plot with others for the death of the powerful monk. Rasputin is finally disposed of, although it takes great efforts to end his life. A stylish horror item, with Lee indulging himself as the lusty, sexy, brutal Rasputin.

THE REPTILE

Produced by Anthony Nelson Keys
Directed by John Gilling
Screenplay by John Elder
Photographed in DeLuxe Color by Michael Reed
Music by Don Banks
90 minutes

Cast: Ray Barrett, Noel Willman, Jennifer Daniels, Jacqueline Pearce, Michael Ripper, John Laurie, Marne Maitland, David Baron, Charles Lloyd Pack, Harold Goldblatt, George Woodbridge

The people in a Cornish village live in fear as a number of them start to die from a mysterious disease which causes the victims to turn black. The brother (Ray Barrett) of one of the victims come to live in his brother's home and starts to investigate. He exhumes some of the bodies and finds punctures on their necks. His trail leads him to the home of a clergyman (Noel Willman), whose daughter (Jacqueline Pearce) lives with a curse picked up in Borneo. At certain times she turns into a reptile and bites people, but her tragedy, and that of the village, ends when she dies in a fire.

THE SAND PEBBLES

Produced and directed by Robert Wise
Screenplay by Robert Anderson, based on the novel by Richard McKenna
Photographed in Panavision 70 and DeLuxe Color by Joseph MacDonald
Music by Jerry Goldsmith
188 minutes

Cast: Steve McQueen, Richard Attenborough, Richard Crenna, Candice Bergen, Marayat Andriane, Mako, Larry Gates, Charles Robinson, Simon Oakland, Ford Rainey, Joe Turkel, Gavin MacLeod

The adventures of a U.S. Navy gunboat on the Yangtze River of China in 1926, as foreign powers strive to maintain their interests in the restive country. The boat's captain (Richard Crenna) has the difficult job of controlling his men through long months on the river and justifying their presence. They rescue American missionaries who do not seem to realize the danger they are in as China is convulsed with political turmoil. One of them (Candice Bergen) falls in love with a tough, independent sailor-engineer (Steve McQueen), who is willing to desert and run away with her, but who loses his life in an action with Chinese rebels. The film is long and rambling, but offers an intriguing account of a forgotten episode in naval history, as well as touching upon the issues of foreign intervention.

SMOKY

Produced by Aaron Rosenberg
Directed by George Sherman
Screenplay by Harold Medford, based on a novel by Will James
Photographed in DeLuxe Color by Jack Swain
Songs by Hoyt Axton, Ernie Sheldon, and Leith Stevens
103 minutes

Cast: Fess Parker, Diana Hyland, Katy Jurado, Hoyt Axton, Robert Wilke, Armando Silvestre, Jose Hector Galindo, Jorge Martinez de Hoyos, Ted White

A remake of the 1946 film, with Fess Parker playing the Fred MacMurray part of the cowboy who becomes attached to a beautiful wild stallion. He tames the horse for his personal use but realizes its nature is that of an independent, free animal. He loses track of the horse, which becomes abused in rodeos and ends up as a junkman's nag, but they are finally brought together and the cowboy releases Smoky to run free in the wilds.

STAGECOACH

Produced by Martin Rackin
Directed by Gordon Douglas
Screenplay by Joseph Landon, based on Dudley Nichol's screenplay and the story by Ernest Haycox
Photographed in CinemaScope and DeLuxe Color by William H. Clothier
Music by Jerry Goldsmith
115 minutes

Cast: Ann Margret, Red Buttons, Michael Connors, Alex Cord, Bing Crosby, Robert Cummings, Van Heflin, Slim Pickens, Stefanie Powers, Keenan Wynn, Brad Weston, Joseph Hoover, John Gabriel, Oliver McGowen

A remake of John Ford's classic western of 1939, with Alex Cord in the John Wayne part of the outlaw Ringo and Ann-Margret in the Claire Trevor role of the prostitute who finds love with Ringo. The plot lines are the same, telling the story of a disparate group of people traveling in a stagecoach across dangerous Indian territory and being savagely attacked. Their characters are revealed in the action, including an absconding bank manager (Robert Cummings) and an alcoholic doctor (Bing Crosby). The film is an exciting Western, but not the equal of the original, although its spectacular photography by William H. Clothier, partly shot in Colorado, is a major asset. The main chase, as the Indians furiously pursue the coach through rugged mountain terrain, is deserving of full marks for its stunt work and filming.

THAT TENNESSEE BEAT

Produced and directed by Richard Brill
Screenplay by Paul Schneider
Photographed by Jack Steeley
Musical direction by Tommy Hill
84 minutes

Cast: Sharon DeBord, Earl Richards, Dolores Faith, Minnie Pearl, Merle Travis, Jim Reader, Cecil Scaife, Rink Hardin, Lightnin Chance, Sam Tarpley, Buddy Mize, Ed Livingston

A rebellious, sullen youth (Earl Richards) steals money in order to get to Nashville and fulfill his dreams of becoming a country star. On the way he is relieved of his ill-gotten gains by thugs, but is befriended by a brother-and-sister country music team (Jim Reader and Sharon DeBord), who help him achieve his ambitions. With success he becomes a nicer boy and shows remorse for his old ways. A film for country music fans, with a number of Nashville guest stars lending support.

Burt Ward and Adam West in *Batman.*

George Peppard receives *The Blue Max.*

Fantastic Voyage.

Peter O'Toole and Audrey Hepburn in *How to Steal a Million.*

Lee J. Cobb and James Coburn in *Our Man Flint*.

Max Von Sydow and George Segal in *The Quiller Memorandum*.

Ann-Margret, Robert Cummings, Alex Cord, Van Heflin, Slim Pickens, Red Buttons, and Bing Crosby in *Stagecoach*.

WAY . . . WAY OUT

Produced by Malcolm Stuart
Directed by Gordon Douglas
Screenplay by William Bowers and Laslo Vadnay
Photographed in CinemaScope and DeLuxe Color by
  William H. Clothier
Music by Lalo Schifrin
101 minutes

Cast: Jerry Lewis, Connie Stevens, Robert Morley, Dennis Weaver, Howard Morris, Brian Keith, Dick Shawn, Anita Ekberg, William O'Connell, Bobo Lewis

Jerry Lewis in Outer Space. In the year 1994, Jerry qualifies as a space weatherman when he marries a space lady (Connie Stevens), since the government wants a married couple on the space station, rather than the bachelors who are paying attention to lady Russian astronauts. Once up there they meet a Russian couple (Dick Shawn and Anita Ekberg), with whom they get quickly drunk on vodka and whom they persuade to get married. The material is not as amusing as it might be, but Robert Morley perks things up with his nutty portrayal of the head of the weather service. The accent seems to be on sex in outer space rather than weather problems.

WEEKEND AT DUNKIRK

Produced by Robert Hakim and Raymond Hakim
Directed by Henri Verneuil
Screenplay by Francois Boyer, from a novel by Robert
  Merle
Photographed in CinemaScope and DeLuxe Color by
  Henri Decae
Music by Maurice Jarre
101 minutes

Cast: Jean-Paul Belmondo, Catherine Spaak, George Geret, Jean-Pierre Marielle, Pierre Mondy, Marie Dubois

A French account of the Allied evacuation in June of 1940, focusing on a handful of French soldiers led by a sergeant (Jean-Paul Belmondo). He has trouble keeping his dispirited men in line and he has to kill two of them for trying to rape a beautiful girl (Catherine Spaak), who does not want to leave her home. He finally persuades her, but he is killed as he goes to leave the beach. The film benefits from the use of actual war locations and from well-staged action scenes of masses of soldiers making their way to the boats and being harassed by German aircraft.

20TH CENTURY-FOX ACADEMY AWARDS FOR 1966

JACK MARTIN SMITH, DALE HENNESY: Best art direction, color, *Fantastic Voyage*.

WALTER M. SCOTT, STUART A. REISS: Best set decoration, color, *Fantastic Voyage*.

ART CRUICKSHANK: Best special visual effects, *Fantastic Voyage*.

Richard Attenborough, Charles Robinson, and Steve McQueen in *The Sand Pebbles*.

THE FLIM-FLAM N

Produced by Lawrence T
Directed by Irvin Kershn
Screenplay by William R
   Owen
Photographed in Panavisi
   Lang
Music by Jerry Goldsmith
104 minutes

Cast: George C. Scott,
Harry Morgan, Jack Alt
Salmi, Slim Pickens, Stro

George C. Scott is the b
old codger who charm
chance and promotes g
his victims. He recru
(Michael Sarrazin) as h
the job until he falls in
and begins to have some
work. He ends up surr
before getting his crafty
him escape. The film is
at human frailties and
in which the two con

FRANKENSTEIN (

Produced by Anthony Ne
Directed by Terrence Fis
Screenplay by John Elde
Photographed in DeLuxe
Music by James Bernard
Musical direction by Phi
92 minutes

Cast: Peter Cushing, Su
Robert Morris, Peter Blyt
Alan MacNaughton, Pe
Duncan Lamont

The title is somewhat
doesn't so much create
fanatic doctor (Peter (
transmigration of souls
executed young man a
disfigured young woma
juvenates her into a be
soul causes her to set
brought about the exec

A GUIDE FOR TH

Produced by Frank McC
Directed by Gene Kelly
Screenplay by Frank Ta
Photographed in Panavis
   Joe MacDonald
Music by John Williams
89 minutes

BEDAZZLED

Produced and directed by Stanley Donen
Screenplay by Peter Cook and Dudley Moore, from a
   story by Peter Cook
Photographed in Panavision and DeLuxe Color by Austin
   Dempster
Music by Peter Cook
104 minutes

Cast: Peter Cook, Dudley Moore, Eleanor Bron, Raquel
Welch, Alba, Robert Russell, Barry Noel, Howard Goor-
ney, Michael Bates, Bernard Spear, Robin Hawdon,
Michael Trubshawe, Evelyn Moore

A Mephistophelean comedy-fantasy set in London,
dealing with the misadventures of a short-order cook
(Dudley Moore) who longs for the love of a certain
waitress (Eleanor Bron). His despair sinks to the
suicide level, but he is saved by the sudden appearance
in his apartment of the devil, in very ordinary guise
(Peter Cook), who grants him seven wishes, all involving love and wealth, but all of which go wrong.
At the end he is stuck with having turned into a nun
in a cloister. The film is stylish humor, albeit along
very British lines, and brightened at one point with
the appearance of Raquel Welch, materlializing in
one of the cook's wishes as Lillian Lust.

CAPRICE

Produced by Aaron Rosenberg and Martin Melcher
Directed by Frank Tashlin
Screenplay by Jay Jayson and Frank Tashlin
Photographed in CinemaScope and DeLuxe Color by
   Leon Shamroy
Music by Frank DeVol
97 minutes

Cast: Doris Day, Richard Harris, Ray Walston, Jack
Kruschen, Edward Mulhare, Lilia Skala, Irene Tsu, Larry
D. Mann, Maurice Marsac, Michael J. Pollard, Michael
Romanoff, Lisa Seagram

A comedy-fantasy of international intrigue, with Doris
Day as an espionage agent of the cosmetics industry,
whose job includes killing other agents, who may be
involved in narcotics. Doris at one point is rescued
while skiing—a photographically fine sequence—from
a would-be assassin, and made love to by a charming

agent (Richard Harris), who may work for a rival
company or even be a member of Interpol. The script
satirizes the cosmetics trade, who seemingly carry on
like spies in global politics. The film fails with its
confused plot lines, but wins with stylish modes and
settings, and Doris being her sexy self.

COME SPY WITH ME

Produced by Paul M. Heller
Directed by Marshall Stone
Screenplay by Cherney Berg, based on a story by Stuart
   James
Photographed in DeLuxe Color by Zoli Vidor
Music by Bob Bowers
85 minutes

Cast: Troy Donahue, Andrea Dromm, Albert Dekker,
Mart Hulswit, Valerie Allen, Dan Ferrone, Howard Schell,
Chance Gentry, Louis Edmonds, Kate Aldrich, Lucienne
Bridou

Spies and counterspies cavorting through the lush
settings of the Caribbean, with an underworld villain
(Albert Dekker) setting out to sabotage a scheme for
world peace and being foiled by a dashing scuba
diving expert (Troy Donahue). A minor entry in the
genre, perked up with some good location shooting
in Bermuda and Jamaica.

THE DAY THE FISH CAME OUT

Produced and directed by Michael Cacoyannis
Screenplay by Michael Cacoyannis
Photographed in DeLuxe Color by Walter Lassally
Music by Mikis Theodorakis
109 minutes

Cast: Tom Courtenay, Sam Wanamaker, Colin Blakely,
Candice Bergen, Ian Ogilvy, Patricia Burke, Dimitris
Nicolaidis, Paris Alexander, Nicolaos Alexiou, Arthur
Mitchell

A melodrama, bordering on the surrealistic, about two
American Air Force men (Tom Courtenay and Colin
Blakely) dropping radioactive containers on a small
Greek island and then ditching their plane in the sea.
Hoping to prevent an international incident, a secret
agent (Sam Wanamaker) and his team arrive on the

island disguise
containers. Re
beautiful arch
vain. The islar

THE DEVIL

Produced by A
Directed by Cy
Screenplay by
  Curtis
Photographed i
Music by Richa
91 minutes

Cast: Joan Fon
Bell, Ingrid Br
Ffrangcon-Davis
Martin Stephen:

An occult susp
woman who su
doctors in Afri
in a quiet Engl
the pretty villa
they seem. Stra
stricken with il
stuck in them
experiences in
in under the s]
a ritual orgy, b
survive. A supe

DOCTOR D

Produced by A
Directed by Ricl
Screenplay by L
  Lofting
Photographed in
  Surtees
Songs by Leslie
Music direction
152 minutes

Cast: Rex Harri
Richard Attenbo
liam Dix, Geoffr

A large-scale m
of Hugh Loftir
doctor of Victo
on humans and
welfare—and co
the help of hi
animal languag
them and learn
to be arrested
sails off to the
Sea Snail. With
and his assista

366

Cast: Tony Musante, Martin Sheen, Beau Bridges, Bob Bannard, Ed McMahon, Diana Van der Vlis, Victor Arnold, Donna Mills, Jack Gilford, Thelma Ritter, Mike Kellin, Jan Sterling, Gary Merrill, Brock Peters, Ruby Dee

Two hoodlums (Tony Musante and Martin Sheen) menace a group of people traveling on a New York subway train. Among the passengers: a black power advocate (Brock Peters) who enjoys seeing the whites humiliated until he himself breaks down, an elderly Jewish couple (Jack Gilford and Thelma Ritter), and a soldier (Beau Bridges) with a broken arm, who finally lashes out and fells the murderous punks. He then rails against the apathy of the cowed, abused passengers, who have been revealed during the incident as cowardly, unhappy, and compromised people. An arresting and brutal comment on society.

IN LIKE FLINT

Produced by Saul David
Directed by Gordon Douglas
Screenplay by Hal Fimberg
Photographed in CinemaScope and DeLuxe Color by
  William Daniels
Music by Jerry Goldsmith
110 minutes

Cast: James Coburn, Lee J. Cobb, Jean Hale, Andrew Duggan, Anna Lee, Hanna Landy, Totty Ames, Steve Ihnat, Yvonne Craig, Diane Bond, Mary Michael, Jacki Ray

The head of U.S. espionage (Lee J. Cobb) sends for super agent Flint (James Coburn) when he learns that a group of women, who run a health spa in the Virgin Islands, are planning a take-over of the world. The ladies, who are cosmetics experts, replace the U.S. president with a substitute they can control, and they stock a space station with nuclear bombs as a threat to the world. But all is in vain once Flint gets into action. Despite the preposterous plot and the antics, the film is a superior spoof of the genre with excellent production values.

THE MUMMY'S SHROUD

Produced by Anthony Nelson Keys
Directed by John Gilling
Screenplay by John Gilling
Photographed in DeLuxe Color by Arthur Grant
Music by Don Banks
90 minutes

Cast: Andre Morell, John Phillips, David Buck, Elizabeth Sellars, Maggie Kimberley, Michael Ripper, Tim Barrett, Roger Delgado, Catherine Lacey

In the 1920's a British team of archeologists headed by an arrogant financier (John Phillips) excavate a

368

---

mummy in Egypt and bring on an ancient curse. It seems the mummy is that of a murdered prince, the victim of a palace coup of four thousand years ago, and the unhappy diggers receive the pent-up resentment in full force.

ONE MILLION YEARS B.C.

Produced by Michael Carreras
Directed by Don Chaffey
Screenplay by Michael Carreras, from a story by Mickell
  Novak, George Baker, and Joseph Frickert
Photographed in Technicolor by Wilkie Cooper
100 minutes

Cast: Raquel Welch, John Richardson, Percy Herbert, Martine Beswick, Jean Waldon, Lisa Thomas, Malya Nappi, Richard James, William Lyon Brown, Terence Maidment

A vivid impression of prehistoric life, with no dialogue but a lot of grunting, some of it in anger and some in satisfaction. The humans are divided into two groups —the Rock People, who are mean and primitive, and the Shell People, who are more kind and gentle. A Rock man (John Richardson) is banished from his tribe, wanders the land, and finds himself among the Shell types, one of whom (Raquel Welch) is beautiful and loving. They decide to face the cruel world together, which means fighting off a variety of huge and hideous beasts, and surviving an earthquake. Since the beasts are the creation of special effects wizard Ray Harryhausen, the film is a notable item in the science-fiction league.

PREHISTORIC WOMEN

Produced and directed by Michael Carreras
Screenplay by Henry Younger
Photographed in CinemaScope and DeLuxe Color by
  Michael Reed
Music by Carlo Martelli
95 minutes

Cast: Martine Beswick, Michael Latimer, Edina Ronay, Stephanie Randell, Sally Calclough, Louis Mahoney

While on safari in Africa, a white hunter (Michael Latimer) stumbles into a strange community of female amazons, whose queen (Martine Beswick) imprisons him in order to satisfy her lust. He leads a revolt among the other captive men and manages to struggle to freedom. The film implies that it was all perhaps a dream. Or nightmare.

THE ST. VALENTINE'S DAY MASSACRE

Produced and directed by Roger Corman
Screenplay by Howard Browne
Photographed in Panavision and DeLuxe Color by Milton
  Krasner

Music by Fred Steiner
Musical direction by Lionel Newman
100 minutes

Cast: Jason Robards, George Segal, Ralph Meeker, Jean Hale, Clint Richie, Frank Silvera, Joseph Campanella, Richard Bakalyan, David Canary, Bruce Dern, Harold J. Stone, Kurt Kreuger, Paul Richards

A vividly bloody recounting of the infamous Chicago gangland slaying in 1929, with Jason Robards as Al Capone, the underworld dictator of the south side of the city and Ralph Meeker as Bugs Moran, the commander of the north side. The script by Howard Browne, a student of the era, clearly points up the public apathy at the hundreds of gangland murders and the millions of dollars extracted by the gangs in supplying liquor and other commodities of the years of prohibition. But the slaying of seven Moran hoods in a garage on February 14, 1929, did indeed provoke public cries of outrage and an eventual backing of the police in their campaign to halt the widespread crime. Corman's film makes a clear and exciting examination of the times.

TONY ROME

Produced by Aaron Rosenberg
Directed by Gordon Douglas
Screenplay by Richard Breen, based on a novel by Marvin H. Albert
Photographed in Panavision and DeLuxe Color by Joseph Biroc
Music by Billy May
110 minutes

Cast: Frank Sinatra, Jill St. John, Richard Conte, Gena Rowlands, Simon Oakland, Jeffrey Lynn, Lloyd Bochner, Robert J. Wilke, Virginia Vincent, Sue Lyon, Joan Shawlee, Richard Krishner, Lloyd Gough, Babe Hart

Frank Sinatra is the detective of the title, a tough, swinging bachelor living alone on a cruiser in Florida's Biscayne Bay. He runs into trouble when he does a friend a favor and takes home the drunk daughter (Sue Lyon) of a wealthy businessman (Simon Oakland) and finds she is missing a valuable diamond. Before he is able to track it down and return it, he is chased, cheated, made love to, cut up and shot at. All of which enables the audience to savor a tour of Miami from its sleaziest levels to its ornate rich pads, plus a number of hotels, night clubs, and weirdo hang-outs. Sinatra—Bogart-like—is well cast as the amorous, flip sleuth.

TWO FOR THE ROAD

Produced and directed by Stanley Donen
Screenplay by Frederic Raphael
Photographed in Panavision and DeLuxe Color by Chris Challis

Dudley Moore and Raquel Welch in *Bedazzled.*

Richard Harris and Doris Day in *Caprice.*

Samantha Eggar and Rex Harrison in *Doctor Doolittle.*

George C. Scott and Michael Sarrazin in *The Flim-Flam Man.*

Robert Morse and Walter Matthau in *A Guide for the Married Man.*

Paul Newman in *Hombre.*

John Richardson and Raquel Welch in *One Million Years, B.C.*

369

James Coburn in *In Like Flint*.

Albert Finney and Audrey Hepburn in *Two for the Road*.

Music by Henry Mancini
112 minutes

Cast: Audrey Hepburn, Albert Finney, William Daniels, Eleanor Bron, Claude Dauphin, Gabrielle Middleton, Cathy Jones, Carol Van Dyke, Karyn Balm

The road is marriage and the two are an English architect (Albert Finney) and his music student bride (Audrey Hepburn). The film follows them through five years of marriage, with them making basically the same trip, from London to the Riviera, three times at two-year intervals. The husband remains much the same, always gruffly cheerful, but the wife goes from enthusiastic young girl to mother to slightly bored wife. The views on marriage are amusing, perceptive, sometimes cynical and bitter, as the young couple move up and down the scales of understanding. Since they also do a lot of moving across France, the audience is treated to some delightful photography. The writing, the acting, and the direction makes this one of the most sophisticated and knowing looks at marriage, and the score by Henry Mancini is a major plus.

VALLEY OF THE DOLLS

Produced by David Weisbart
Directed by Mark Robson
Screenplay by Helen Deutsch and Dorothy Kingsley, based on the novel by Jacqueline Susann

Jason Robards, Jr., in *St. Valentine's Day Massacre*.

Frank Sinatra and Gena Rowlands in *Tony Rome*.

Photographed in Panavision and DeLuxe Color by William Daniels
Music by John Williams
123 minutes

Cast: Barbara Parkins, Patty Duke, Paul Burke, Sharon Tate, Tony Scotti, Martin Milner, Charles Drake, Alex Davion, Lee Grant, Susan Hayward, Naomi Stevens, Robert H. Harris

A splashy soap opera about show business and three girls who weather its storms, with one of them (Sharon Tate) ending up a suicide when she realizes she has cancer and will no longer be able to work in porno pictures. Another is an ambitious singer (Patty Duke) who finds success hard to take and becomes an addict of pills. The other is a prim New Englander (Barbara Parkins) who is lured into television advertising. Despite the money, she also takes to pills, but gets hold of herself and goes home. Also on hand is Susan Hayward as a tough survivor, a star who needs no pills to continue her career. All in all, not an inducement for a life in the world of entertainment. But as a piece of juicy yarn spinning it all works.

20TH CENTURY-FOX ACADEMY AWARDS FOR 1967

L. B. ABBOTT: Best visual effects, *Doctor Dolittle*.
LESLIE BRICUSSE: Best song, "Talk to the Animals," *Doctor Dolittle*.

Sharon Tate, Patty Duke, and Barbara Parkins in *Valley of the Dolls*.

370

THE ANNIVERSARY

Produced by Jimmy Sangster
Directed by Roy Ward Baker
Screenplay by Jimmy Sangster. from a play by Bill MacIlwraith
Photographed in DeLuxe Color by Harry Waxman
Music by Philip Martell
95 minutes

Cast: Bette Davis, Sheila Hancock, Jack Hedley, James Cossins, Elaine Taylor, Christian Roberts

The action takes place during the course of a single day as a horrendous mother (Bette Davis) brings her three children together to celebrate her wedding anniversary to the deceased husband she hated. One son (James Cossins) is a transvestite, with mother's approval, another (Jack Hedley) has five children (supported by mother, although he finally summons up the courage to leave the country, and the third (Christian Roberts) spites mother by bringing home his already pregnant girl friend. Despite their resolve to turn their backs on her forever, she sets about plans that will bring them home next year. A very black comedy.

BANDOLERO

Produced by Robert L. Jacks
Directed by Andrew V. McLaglen
Screenplay by James Lee Barrett, based on a story by Stanley Hough
Photographed in Panavision and DeLuxe Color by William Clothier
Music by Jerry Goldsmith
106 minutes

Cast: James Stewart, Dean Martin, Raquel Welch, George Kennedy, Andrew Prine, Will Geer, Clint Ritchie, Tom Heaton, Denver Pyle, Rudy Diaz, Sean McClory, Harry Carey, Donald Barry

A hangman (James Stewart) rides into a Texas town to despatch a group of badmen. But he isn't really a hangman, just an imposter who succeeds in freeing his brother (Dean Martin) and his gang from the death sentence. The bandit brothers take off for Mexico, pursued by the sheriff (George Kennedy), who has a yen for a Mexican widow (Raquel Welch), who has a yen for the younger brother. The older brother urges the younger to quit the life of crime and settle down, but before this decision can be realized they are surrounded by Mexican bandits. The sheriff and the brothers join forces to fight off the Mexicans, but both brothers are mortally wounded, leaving the widow and the sheriff to ride back to their town and return the money. A stylish Western, but much rougher and bloodier than usual.

THE BOSTON STRANGLER

Produced by Robert Fryer
Directed by Richard Fleischer
Screenplay by Edward Anhalt, based on the book by Gerold Frank
Photographed in Panavision and DeLuxe Color
Music by Lionel Newman
120 minutes

Cast: Tony Curtis, Henry Fonda, George Kennedy, Mike Kellin, Hurd Hatfield, Murray Hamilton, Jeff Corey, Sally Kellerman, William Marshall, George Voskovec, Leora Dana

A semidocumentary account of the dozen murders, all of women, which took place in Boston between 1962 and 1964 and all the work of a schizophrenic named Albert De Salvo (Tony Curtis). A plumber by trade and a normal, happily married man under most conditions, he lapses into comas during which he commits sex-strangulation killings. The police, headed by a state appointed officer (Henry Fonda), arrest a number of men before accidentally stumbling upon evidence that leads them to the killer. When apprehended, the killer is unaware of his crimes and under interrogation he breaks down mentally. The film is an intriguing examination of a complex case and is made visually the more interesting by the use of split-screen devices and multiple panels.

A CHALLENGE FOR ROBIN HOOD

Produced by Clifford Parkes
Directed by C. M. Pennington-Richards
Screenplay by Peter Bryan
Photographed in DeLuxe Color by Arthur Grant
Music by Gary Hughes
85 minutes

Cast: Barrie Ingham, James Hayter, Leon Greene, Peter Blythe, Gay Hamilton, Alfie Bass, John Arnatt

A minor entry in the Robin Hood filmography, made in England and dealing with Robin (Barrie Ingham) opposing his cousin Roger (Peter Blythe), who has assumed dictatorship over Sherwood Forest. Once again Robin and his Merry Men attack Nottingham Castle, rescue Maid Marian, and put an end to the villains.

DEADFALL

Produced by Paul Monash
Directed by Bryan Forbes
Screenplay by Bryan Forbes, based on the novel by Desmond Cory
Photographed in Eastmancolor by Gerry Turpin
Music by John Barry
122 minutes

Cast: Michael Caine, Giovanna Ralli, Eric Portman, Nanette Newman, David Buck, Carlos Pierre, Leonard Rossiter, Emilio Rodriguez, Vladek Sheybal, George Ghent, Carmen Dene

A crime caper with psychological overtones, strikingly filmed in Majorca and Spain, about a trio of jewel thieves who attempt to rob the home of a rich but sadistic man (David Buck). He almost welcomes thieves in order that he can enjoy his own games of detection and torture. A crack jewel thief (Michael Caine) teams up with a mastermind (Eric Portman) and his pretty young wife (Giovanna Ralli), who is used as bait. The thief falls in love with the bait himself, which leads to eventual disaster. The film is long and complex and suffers from confusion. Of particular interest is the music score by John Barry, which includes a guitar concerto against which some of the robbery is performed.

THE DETECTIVE

Produced by Aaron Rosenberg
Directed by Gordon Douglas
Screenplay by Abby Mann, based on a novel by Roderick Thorp
Photographed in Panavision and DeLuxe Color by Joseph Biroc
Music by Jerry Goldsmith
114 minutes

Cast: Frank Sinatra, Lee Remick, Ralph Meeker, Jack Klugman, Horace McMahon, Lloyd Bochner, William Windom, Tony Musante, Al Freeman, Jr., Robert Duvall, Jacqueline Bisset, James Inman

A tough, realistic look at the life of New York police detectives, with Frank Sinatra as one whose personal problems spill over into his work. His pretty wife (Lee Remick) is a nymphomaniac from whom he eventually parts. At the same time he is assigned to find the killer of a homosexual (James Inman) and in his disgust he railroads the wrong man (Tony Musante) into the electric chair. This costs him his job. Filmed in New York and making use of actual police precinct stations, the film takes a candid tack in dealing with corruption and brutality, and a sympathetic stand on the unfair attitudes toward homosexuals.

THE DEVIL'S BRIDE

Producel by Anthony Nelson Keys
Directed by Terence Fisher
Screenplay by Richard Matheson, from a novel by Dennis Wheatley
Photographed in DeLuxe Color by Arthur Grant
Music by James Bernard
95 minutes

Cast: Christopher Lee, Charles Gray, Patrick Mower, Sarah Lawson, Gwen Ffrangcon-Davies, Nike Arrighi, Leon Greene, Paul Eddington, Rosalyn Landor, Russell Waters

The evils of black magic and the lure of the Devil. A good nobleman (Christopher Lee) strives to save the soul of a friend (Patrick Mower), who has been possessed by an apostle (Charles Gray) of evil. The nobleman's daughter (Rosalyn Landor) is seized in spite, but saved from the sacrificial altar in the breath of time. For devotees of this brand of whimsy, a superior item.

FIVE MILLION YEARS TO EARTH

Produced by Anthony Nelson Keys
Directed by Roy Ward Baker
Screenplay by Nigel Kneale
Protographed in DeLuxe Color by Arthur Grant
Music by Tristram Cary
98 minutes

Cast: Andrew Keir, Barbara Shelley, James Donald, Maurice Good, James Guilliford, Robert Morris, Bee Duffell, Kenneth Ives, Simon Brent, Peter Bennett, Sheila Steafel, Hugh Morton

A London anthropologist (James Donald) unearths skeletons during an excavation which suggest the presence of life on earth five million years ago. Adjacent to this discovery is a missile, which contains decomposed bodies of creatures resembling demons. The missile also gives off a strange force, which the scientists deduce is something left over from the dead planet Mars. The news causes panic before the scientists find their solutions.

A FLEA IN HER EAR

Produced by Fred Kohlmar
Directed by Jacques Charon

Screenplay by John Mortimer, based on a play by Georges Feydeau
Photographed in Panavision and DeLuxe Color by Charles Lang
Music by Bronislau Kaper
95 minutes

Cast: Rex Harrison, Rosemary Harris, Louis Jourdan, Rachel Roberts, John Williams, Gregoire Aslan, Edward Hardwicke, Georges Descrieres, Isla Blari, Frank Thornton, Victor Sen-Yung

A classic French farce, but played in the British manner and losing something in the transmigration of style. A popular attorney (Rex Harrison) is accused of infidelity by his wife (Rosemary Harris), who is convinced that his lack of vitality at home is due to his dallying with numerous females elsewhere. To trap him, she arranges a rendezvous with him at a hotel used for affairs of this kind—a place brimming over with lovers, jealous husbands, and strange characters. The husband manages to satisfy his wife, although it is assumed nothing has really changed. The sets and costumes are delightful, as is the cheerful musical score by Bronislau Kaper, but the film fails to reach its potential.

THE FURTHER PERILS OF LAUREL AND HARDY

Produced and written by Robert Youngson
Music by John Parker
99 minutes

Cast: Stan Laurel, Oliver Hardy, Charlie Chase, Jean Harlow, Edgar Kennedy, James Finlayson, Snub Pollard, Billy West, Charlie Hall, Tom Kennedy, Noah Young, Charlotte Mineau

A must for students of Laurel and Hardy, lovingly put together by Robert Youngson and concentrating on the pair's earliest pictures made at Pathé and MGM in 1927, '28 and '29. It also includes footage of the work done by Laurel and Hardy as solo artists before their teaming.

JOANNA

Produced by Michael S. Laughlin
Directed and written by Michael Sarne
Photographed in Panavision and DeLuxe Color by Walter Lassaly
Songs by Rod McKuen
115 minutes

Cast: Genevieve Waite, Christian Doermer, Calvin Lockhart, Donald Sutherland, Glenna Forster-Jones, David Scheuer, Michelle Cook, David Collings

A flip, almost surrealistic musical set in London and concerning the doings of a cheerfully amoral art student, Joanna (Genevieve Waite), who flits from affair to affair, sometimes in imagination and other times in reality. Her boyfriends include a rich playboy (Donald Sutherland), who takes her on a trip to North Africa before dying of leukemia. She later becomes pregnant by a black boyfriend. The film ends with Joanna at Paddington station being serenaded by the whole cast and crew, and Joanna telling all that she will be back. She never has.

LADY IN CEMENT

Produced by Aaron Rosenberg
Directed by Gordon Douglas
Screenplay by Marvin H. Albert and Jack Guss, based on a novel by Marvin H. Albert
Photographed in Panavision and DeLuxe Color by Joseph Biroc
Music by Hugo Montenegro
94 minutes

Cast: Frank Sinatra, Raquel Welch, Richard Conte, Martin Gabel, Lainie Kazan, Pat Henry, Dan Blocker, Steve Peck, Virginia Wood, Richard Deacon, Frank Raiter

Frank Sinatra back in Miami as private eye Tony Rome and hired by a small-time hood (Dan Blocker) to find his missing girl friend, who is the lady of the title—dead at the bottom of Biscayne Bay. In finding out why she is dead he runs across a variety of shady characters, including a Mafia chieftain (Martin Gabel) and a beautiful alcoholic (Raquel Welch), who is at first thought to be the killer. The film is flip and crude, but makes good use of its colorful settings as its characters fight, cheat, swim, chase, and make love.

THE LOST CONTINENT

Produced and directed by Michael Carreras
Screenplay by Michael Nash, based on the novel by Dennis Wheatley
Photographed in DeLuxe Color by Paul Benson
Music by Gerard Schurmann
89 minutes

Cast: Eric Porter, Hildegard Knef, Suzanna Leigh, Tony Beckley, Nigel Stock, Neil McCallum, Benito Carruthers, Jimmy Hanley, James Cossins, Dana Gillespie, Victor Maddern

A motley group of characters abandon ship when a storm threatens to capsize them, but later they rediscover the vessel, hardly the worse for wear, and reboard her. They then sail into a weird world of monsters, including a 30-foot-long squid, massive crabs, and prehistoric sharks. The cast, and survivors of other wrecks, come to a grisly end in fire and explosions.

THE MAGUS

Produced by Jud Kinberg and John Kohn

Directed by Guy Green
Screenplay by John Fowles, based on his novel
Photographed in Panavision and DeLuxe Color by Billy Williams
Music by John Dankworth
117 minutes

Cast: Michael Caine, Anthony Quinn, Candice Bergen, Anna Karina, Paul Stassino, Julian Glover, Takis Emmanuel, George Pastell, Daniele Noel, Jerome Willis, Ethel Farrugia, Andreas Melandrinos

An English schoolteacher (Michael Caine) arrives on a Greek island to fill a position and is drawn to visit a villa in a remote part of the island. The villa is owned by a man (Anthony Quinn) who is a genius with cards and games and introduces him to a beautiful girl (Candice Bergen) he claims is a ghost. Later he says she is a schizophrenic being treated by him, but finally admits she is an actress in a film he wanted to make about his life, and that the schoolteacher has been drawn into the scheme to play a part. It seems the host is a man with a very troubled past. The teacher is relieved to escape the mad atmosphere and seek out his former girl friend (Anna Karina), to whom he resolves to behave more lovingly. An ambitious film, metaphysical in its thesis but ultimately confusing.

PLANET OF THE APES

Produced by Arthur P. Jacobs
Directed by Franklin J. Schaffner
Screenplay by Michael Wilson and Rod Serling, based on a novel by Pierre Boulle
Photographed in Panavision and DeLuxe Color by Leon Shamroy
Music by Jerry Goldsmith
112 minutes

Cast: Charlton Heston, Roddy McDowall, Kim Hunter, Maurice Evans, James Whitmore, James Daly, Linda Harrison, Robert Gunner, Lou Wagner, Woodrow Parfrey, Jeff Burton, Buck Kartalian, Norman Burton, Wright King

A science fiction masterpiece and a superb exercise in fantasy-adventure filmmaking. An astrounaut (Charlton Heston) and his crew land on a far planet and find it inhabited by a race of Neanderthal beings. After being imprisoned and treated as beasts of a lower order, they gradually come to realize that this society is complex. It includes beings ranging from barbarians to those of refinement. Among the latter are two chimpanzee scientists (Roddy McDowall and Kim Hunter) who help the astronauts escape the excesses of those who would destroy them. The film is a fine suspense adventure, but it also satirizes human life with its allusions to social and political matters. Strikingly filmed in the Lake Powell area of Utah and Arizona. Credit is due make-up designer John Chambers for his marvelous simian masks.

374

PRETTY POISON

Produced by Marshall Backlar and Noel Black
Directed by Noel Black
Screenplay by Lorenzo Semple, Jr., based on a novel by Stephen Geller
Photgrophed in DeLuxe Color by David Quaid
Music by Johnny Mandel
89 minutes

Cast: Anthony Perkins, Tuesday Weld, Beverly Garland, John Randolph, Dick O'Neill, Clarice Blackburn, Joseph Bova, George Ryan's High-Steppers

A pleasant but psychotic young man (Anthony Perkins), who has served a jail sentence for complicity in a death, meets a cute girl, a model student in school (Tuesday Weld), and amuses her with his tales about being an espionage agent. Despite her innocent appearance, she is a vicious, coldly manipulative girl, who kills the mother she hates and persuades the boy to indulge in other crimes. When caught, she reverts to being cutely innocent and the boy takes all the blame. *Pretty Poison* is a gem of a psychological crime tale, tightly scripted and written—a frightening account of madness in a mundane setting—with a fascinating performance from Tuesday Weld.

PRUDENCE AND THE PILL

Produced by Kenneth Harper and Ronald J. Kahn
Directed by Fielder Cook
Screenplay by Hugh Mills, based on a novel by Hugh Mills
Photographed in Color by DeLuxe by Ted Moore
Music by Bernard Ebbinghouse
92 minutes

Cast: Deborah Kerr, David Niven, Robert Coote, Irina Demich, Judy Geeson, Keith Mitchell, Edith Evans, Joyce Redman, Vikery Turner, David Dundas

A sex comedy of dubious taste, about a wealthy Briton (David Niven) who has a mistress (Irina Demich) as well as a wife (Deborah Kerr). He exchanges his wife's birth control pills for aspirins in the hope she will become pregnant by her doctor lover (Keith Mitchell), but a visiting niece (Judy Geeson) also switches pills in order to indulge in her own love life and causes her parents (Robert Coote and Joyce Redman) to become expectant parents. The mistress also becomes pregnant—and so on. The adult material is well played by a deft cast and stylishly photographed amid pleasant settings in London.

THE SECRET LIFE OF AN AMERICAN WIFE

Produced and directed by George Axelrod
Screenplay and story by George Axelrod
Photographed in DeLuxe Color by Leon Shamroy

Music by Billy May
93 minutes

Cast: Walter Matthau, Anne Jackson, Patrick O'Neal, Edy Williams, Richard Bull, Paul Napier, Gary Brown

A thirtyish, bored wife (Anne Jackson), tired of her dull, unloving husband (Patrick O'Neal), who is the press agent of a movie star (Walter Matthau), decides to have a fling at being a call girl, to see if she has any sex appeal left. Her first client turns out to be the movie star, who is a nice, lonely man in need of love himself. The husband arrives on the scene, loses his temper at seeing his wife with the star, hits the star, and takes his wife home to a renewed sense of her worth. An amusing concept, well played by Matthau and Jackson, but somewhat lacking in conviction.

STAR

Produced by Saul Chaplin
Directed by Robert Wise
Screenplay by William Fairchild
Photographed in Todd-AO and DeLuxe Color by Ernest Laszlo
Musical direction by Lennie Hayton
172 minutes

Cast: Julie Andrews, Richard Crenna, Michael Craig, Daniel Massey, Robert Reed, Bruce Forsyth, Beryl Reed, John Collins, Alan Oppenheimer, Richard Anthony Eisley, Jock Livingston, J. Pat O'Malley, Lester Matthews, Murray Matheson, Bernard Fox

The life and career of Gertrude Lawrence, with Julie Andrews as the fabled musical comedy star of the London and Broadway stages. The film lovingly traces her adventures from an ambitious bit player in English music halls to her triumphs as the lead in many famous musicals, especially those of her friend Noel Coward (Daniel Massey). It also shows her climb to success in British society, due to the love of a nobleman (Michael Craig) and her gradual acceptance in social circles. Her private life is frenetic, but she eventually finds personal happiness with an understanding American banker-producer (Richard Crenna). The film suffers from being overblown, but allows lovers of theatre music a wide range of material by Coward, Gershwin, Porter, Weill, and others, well performed by Julie Andrews. It has top-notch production values.

THE SWEET RIDE

Produced by Joe Pasternak
Directed by Harvey Hart
Screenplay by Tom Mankiewicz, based on a novel by William Murray
Photographed in Panavision and DeLuxe Color by Robert B. Hauser
Music by Pete Rugolo
109 minutes

Cast: Tony Franciosa, Michael Sarrazin, Jacqueline Bisset, Bob Denver, Michael Wilding, Michele Carey, Lara Lindsay, Norma Crane, Percy Rodriquez, Warren Stevens, Pat Buttram, Michael Forest, Lloyd Gough

A sardonic melodrama which refutes its title. The sweet ride is the easy, sunny lifestyle of the beach dwellers at California's Malibu coast—people holding off growing up but finally realizing the futility. Among

Charlton Heston in *Planet of the Apes.*

Dean Martin and James Stewart in *Bandolero.*

Tony Curtis and Henry Fonda in *The Boston Strangler.*

Frank Sinatra and Jacqueline Bisset in *The Detective.*

Frank Sinatra and Raquel Welch in *The Lady in Cement.*

Michael Caine and Eric Portman in *Deadfall.*

them is an aging tennis star (Tony Franciosa), a surfer (Michael Sarrazin), and an actress (Jacqueline Bisset), who is raped and killed by motorcyclists. The sleazy characters are a bittersweet contrast with the pleasant settings.

THE TOUCHABLES

Produced by John Bryan
Directed by Robert Freeman
Screenplay by Ian La Frenais, based on a story by Robert Freeman and David Cammell

Rachel Roberts and Rex Harrison in *A Flea in Her Ear.*

Anthony Perkins and Tuesday Weld in *Pretty Poison.*

Anne Jackson and Walter Matthau in *The Secret Life of an American Wife.*

Donald Sutherland and Genevieve Waite in *Joanna.*

Deborah Kerr and David Niven in *Prudence and the Pill.*

Julie Andrews and Daniel Massey in *Star!*

Photographed in DeLuxe Color by Alan Pudney
Music by Ken Thorne

Cast: Judy Huxtable, Esther Anderson, Marilyn Rickard, Kathy Simmonds, David Anthony, Ricky Starr, Harry Baird, Michael Chow, John Ronane, James Villiers, Fuzzo Kay

A British melodrama about four young girls, out for kicks, who kidnap a rock singer (David Anthony) and have their way with him. After various humiliations, he is rescued by his friends, which is something that will never happen to this unpleasant little movie.

THE VENGEANCE OF SHE

Produced by Aida Young
Direcetd by Cliff Owen
Screenplay by Peter O'Donnell, based on characters created by H. Rider Haggard
Photographed in color by Wolf Suschitzky
Music by Mario Nascimbene
101 minutes

Cast: John Richardson, Olinka Berova, Edward Judd, Colin Blakely, George Sewell, Andre Morell, Noel Willman, Derek Godfrey, Jill Melford, Danielle Noel, Gerald Lawson

In the lost city of Kuma, the ruler Killikrates (John Richardson) awaits the return of Queen Ayesha so that he may immortalize her. His ambitious high priest (Noel Willman) lures a look-alike (Olinka Berova) from the south of France, but the plot is foiled by her doctor lover (Edward Judd) and the city of Kuma ends up in flames. This sequel to *She* fails to make a satisfying yarn.

THE VIKING QUEEN

Produced by John Temple-Smith
Directed by Don Chaffey
Screenplay by Clarke Reynolds, from a story by John Temple-Smith
Photographed in Technicolor by Stephen Dade
Music by Philip Martell
90 minutes

Cast: Don Murray, Carita, Donald Houston, Andrew Keir, Niall MacGinnis, Adrienne Corri, Wilfrid Lawson, Sean Caffrey, Nicola Pagett, Percy Herbert, Patrick Troughton, Bryan Marshall

An adventure spectacle filmed in Ireland but dealing with ancient England under the domination of the Roman Empire. The Roman governor (Don Murray) falls in love with the queen of the local tribes (Carita) and she with him. Despite his efforts to keep peace among the invaders and the conquered people, a Druid priest (Donald Huston) leads them in a rebellion, causing the queen to take to the battlefield against the governor, and ending with her brave, inevitable death.

THE BOYS OF PAUL STREET

Produced by Endre Bohem
Directed by Zoltan Fabri
Screenplay by Zoltan Fabri and Endre Bohem, based on a novel by Ferenc Molnar
Photographed in Agfascope and Eastmancolor by Gyorgy Illes
Music by Emil Petrovics
105 minutes

Cast: Anthony Kemp, William Burleigh, John Moulder-Brown, Julien Holdaway, Mari Toroscik, Sandor Pecsi

A Hungarian film, acquired by 20th Century-Fox for distribution, about street warfare among gangs of boys in Budapest. One gang claims territorial rights over a vacant lot and another gang challenges them, although in the end the ground is taken over by the city for building. The film is a clever and touching allegory, pointing up the futility of actual war.

BUTCH CASSIDY AND THE SUNDANCE KID

Produced by John Foreman
Directed by George Roy Hill
Screenplay by William Goldman
Photographed in Panavision and DeLuxe Color by Conrad Hall
Music by Burt Bacharach
112 minutes

Cast: Paul Newman, Robert Redford, Katharine Ross, Strother Martin, Henry Jones, Jeff Corey, George Furth, Cloris Leachman, Ted Cassidy, Kenneth Mars, Donnelly Rhodes, Jody Gilbert, Timothy Scott

The most successful Western ever made, although actually far more than a Western. It's an adventure story, romance, and a comedy all rolled into one and dealing, mostly light-heartedly, with the exploits of a pair of legendary robbers in the west of the 1890's—quick-witted Butch Cassidy (Paul Newman) and quiet, quick-drawing Sundance (Robert Redford). The amiable couple, who steal from banks and trains with casual ease, finally get tired of being chased by the law and take off for Bolivia, where the language difficulties make their trade somewhat harder and where

they find the opposition tougher. They now find it necessary to kill, which eventually brings their own deaths when surrounded by a company of Bolivian soldiers. The film is a masterpiece of photographic inventiveness and deft direction, with appealing performances from Newman and Redford—and Kathryn Ross as the cheerful girl friend of Sundance who is also a chum to Butch, and manages to maintain a decent *ménage à trois*. A model of stylish filmmaking.

THE CHAIRMAN

Produced by Mort Abrahams
Directed by J. Lee Thompson
Screenplay by Ben Maddow, from a novel by Jay Richard Kennedy
Photographed in Panavision and DeLuxe Color by John Wilcox
Music by Jerry Goldsmith
99 minutes

Cast: Gregory Peck, Anne Heywood, Arthur Hill, Alan Dobie, Conrad Yama, Zienia Merton, Ori Levy, Eric Young, Burt Kwouk, Alan White, Keye Luke, Francisca Tu, Mai Ling, Janet Key

An espionage thriller with political overtones, mostly set in Red China, but filmed in North Wales, concerning a U.S. agent (Gregory Peck) who goes to see Mao (Conrad Yama). He is a bio-scientist who is sent to China for the covert purpose of learning about an enzyme the Communists have developed to speed the growth of food. The Chinese want to keep the secret for themselves, although they welcome the distinguished scientist. What they don't know is that he has a minute transmitter imbedded in his head, with which they can monitor his conversations. Only he knows that it also contains an explosive, with which his people can kill him if necessary. The inventor (Keye Luke) of the enzyme admits that he is alarmed about his countrymen keeping the discovery for themselves, which admission costs him his life and causes the American to be imprisoned. But he manages to escape and crosses the border with Russian help. An interesting yarn, but far removed from the popular espionage image of Bond and company.

William Dysart, Thorley Walters, Joan Young, Lionel Murton, Helen Horton, John Nettleton, John Wentworth, Alistair Williamson

A famed marriage counselor (Hugh Marlowe) in London neglects his wife (Patricia Haines) and declines to give her a divorce so she can marry her lover (William Dysart). The lover kills the husband and fakes it as the work of a burglar, but the husband's seceretary (Zena Walker), also given scant attention by her employers, comes in on the plot for a price. A minor item in the movie murder league.

100 RIFLES

Produced by Marvin Schwartz
Directed by Tom Gries
Screenplay by Clair Huffaker and Tom Gries, based on a novel by Robert MacLeod
Photographed in DeLuxe Color by Cecilio Paniagua
Music by Jerry Goldsmith
110 minutes

Cast: Jim Brown, Raquel Welch, Burt Reynolds, Fernando Lamas, Dan O'Herlihy, Hans Gudegast, Michael Forest, Aldo Sambrell, Soledad Miranda, Alberto Dalbes, Carlos Bravo

Adventures in Mexico, circa 1912, as a black sheriff (Jim Brown) pursues an outlaw (Burt Reynolds) below the border and gets involved in warfare between the opposed locals and the military regime of a greedy general (Fernando Lamas). A major force in the uprising is a beautiful Yaqui Indian (Raquel Welch), whose father has been hanged by the general. Despite the general's expert German adviser (Hans Gudegast—later known as Eric Braeden), he loses his regime and his life when the revolutionaries, with the help of the Americans, outmaneuver him. The film is a slam-bang action epic, with loads of explosions and gory fighting, making little sense but a lot of amusing noise.

THE PRIME OF MISS JEAN BRODIE

Produced by Robert Fryer
Directed by Ronald Neame
Screenplay by Jay Presson Allen, from a novel by Muriel Spark
Photographed in DeLuxe Color by Ted Moore
Music by Rod McKuen
Musical direction by Arthur Greenslade
116 minutes

Cast: Maggie Smith, Robert Stephens, Pamela Franklin, Gordon Jackson, Celia Johnson, Jane Carr, Diane Grayson, Shirley Steedman, Margo Cunningham, Ann Way, Isla Cameron, Helena Gloag, Molly Weir, Lavinia Lang

A teacher (Maggie Smith) at an exclusive Edinburgh school for girls inspires her students with her idealism and her personal convictions, but misleads them with her nonconformist views on politics, such as her infatuation with Mussolini and Franco, and her discussions of her private life. She is dedicated but conceited as she proudly turns out prize pupils, but her unorthodox ways eventually lose her her job. Partly responsible for the loss is a student (Pamela Franklin) who becomes as worldly wise as, and something of a threat to, the teacher. Maggie Smith is a triumph as the irrepressible but slightly mad teacher, spouting her dedication to the arts, to love, and the pursuit of truth.

SECRET WORLD

Produced by Jacques Strauss
Directed by Robert Freeman
Screenplay by Gerard Brach
Photographed in DeLuxe Color by Peter Biziou
Music by Antonie Duhamel
95 minutes

Cast: Jacqueline Bisset, Giselle Pascal, Pierre Zimmer, Marc Porel, Jean-Francois Maurin, Paul Bonifas, Guy D'Avout, Jacques Riberolles, Judith Magre

A strange, introspective drama about a beautiful English girl (Jacqueline Bisset), a product of swinging London, who visits the owner (Pierre Zimmer) of an elegant chateau in France. She has previously been his mistress and her presence causes some stirring in the household—from the owner, his frustrated wife (Giselle Pascal), their twenty-year-old son (Marc Porel), who vainly tries to woo the visitor, and from their eleven-year-old nephew (Jean-Francois Maurin). The boy, whose parents have been killed in a car crash, is reclusive and sullen, but the kindness of the English girl awakens sexual fantasies in him. She leaves the chateau, having made changes in the lives of its people, and especially in the boy, who fondly remembers her.

STAIRCASE

Produced and directed by Stanley Donen
Screenplay by Charles Dyer, based on a play by Charles Dyer
Photographed in Panavision and DeLuxe Color by Christopher Challis
Music by Dudley Moore
100 minutes

Cast: Richard Burton, Rex Harrison, Cathleen Nesbitt, Pat Heywood, Avril Angers, Beatrix Lehmann, Gordon Heath, Shelagh Fraser, Stephen Lewis, Jake Kavanaugh, Gwen Nelson

Richard Burton and Rex Harrison as two aging homosexuals, living over their barber shop in London and bickering. Burton is the maternal one, worrying about losing his hair, who coddles the bitchy Harrison, a man with lost pretensions about the theatre, who is stinging with his arrest as a transvestite. They take out their frustrations on one another but ultimately realize that they are dependent and needing of each other. *Staircase* does not pander to sensationalism or dwell on any facets of homosexuality. It is a study of two men of a certain kind, although the casting of Burton and Harrison, despite their skill as actors, is too much against image to be completely successful.

THE UNDEFEATED

Produced by Robert L. Jacks
Directed by Andrew V. McLaglen
Screenplay by James Lee Barrett, based on a story by Stanley L. Hough
Photographed in Panavision and DeLuxe Color by William Clothier
Music by Hugo Montenegro
118 minutes

Cast: John Wayne, Rock Hudson, Tony Aguilar, Roman Gabriel, Marian McCargo, Lee Meriwither, Merlin Olsen, Melissa Newman, Bruce Cabot, Michael Vincent, Ben Johnson, Edward Faulkner

A Confederate colonel (Rock Hudson) sets fire to his plantation house at the end of the Civil War, rather than let it fall into the hands of carpetbaggers, and sets off for Mexico with his family and a group of followers to set up a new home for themselves. They are saved from the attacks of Mexican bandits by a former Union colonel (John Wayne), who has decided to drive his herd of three thousand horses into Mexico rather than be tricked by crooked army agents. The two former enemies join forces in fighting off the soldiers of Emperor Maximilian and those of the rebel leader Juarez. When the rebels take the Confederate party prisoners, the Union man ends up sacrificing his horses to free the Southerners. A conventional Western, beefed up by big production values and good Mexican scenery.

James Coburn and Lee Remick in *Hard Contract*.

Omar Sharif in *Che*.

Barbra Streisand in *Hello, Dolly!*

James Brown, Burt Reynolds, and Raquel Welch in *100 Rifles*.

Dustin Hoffman and Mia Farrow as *John and Mary*.

Michael York and Anouk Aimee in *Justine*.

Robert Redford and Paul Newman in *Butch Cassidy and the Sundance Kid*.

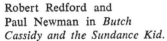

Gregory Peck in *The Chairman*.

Robert Stephens and Maggie Smith in *The Prime of Miss Jean Brodie.*

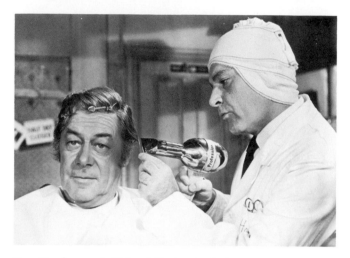

Rex Harrison and Richard Burton in *Staircase.*

John Wayne and Rock Hudson in *The Undefeated.*

A WALK WITH LOVE AND DEATH

Produced by Carter De Haven
Directed by John Huston
Screenplay by Dale Wasserman, from a novel by Hans Koningsberger
Photographed in DeLuxe Color by Ted Scaife
Music by Georges Delerue
90 minutes

Cast: Anjelica Huston, Assaf Dayan, Anthony Corlan, John Hallam, Robert Lang, Guy Deghy, Michael Gough, George Murcell, Eileen Murphy, Anthony Nicholls, Joseph O'Connor, John Franklyn

During the Hundred Years War of the Middle Ages in France, a student (Assaf Dayan) wanders the countryside and comes across the daughter (Anjelica Huston, the daughter of the director) of a nobleman and falls in love with her. They devote themselves to each other and move to flee the country. But there is no escape. Carnage is everywhere and they lose their lives along with many others. The film is slowly paced and introspective, but offering lovely photography and a delicate musical score by Georges Delerue. It does not spare the audience the savagery of the times in which it deals, although it makes an antiwar statement that applies to all ages.

20TH CENTURY-FOX ACADEMY AWARDS FOR 1969

MAGGIE SMITH: Best actress, *The Prime of Miss Jean Brodie.*

WILLIAM GOLDMAN: Best original screenplay, *Butch Cassidy and the Sundance Kid.*

CONRAD HALL: Best cinematography, *Butch Cassidy and the Sundance Kid.*

JOHN DE CUIR, JACK MARTIN SMITH, HERMAN BLUMENTHAL: Best art direction, *Hello, Dolly.*

WALTER M. SCOTT, GEORGE HOPKINS, RAPHAEL BRETTON: Best set decoration, *Hello, Dolly.*

JACK SOLOMON, MURRAY SPIVACK: Best sound, *Hello, Dolly.*

WILLIAM REYNOLDS: Best editing, *Hello, Dolly.*

BURT BACHARACH, HAL DAVID: Best song, "Raindrops Keep Falling on My Head," *Butch Cassidy and the Sundance Kid.*

BURT BACHARACH: Best original score, *Butch Cassidy and the Sundance Kid.*

LENNIE HAYTON, LIONEL NEWMAN: Best scoring of a musical, *Hello, Dolly.*

Assaf Dayan and Angelica Huston in *A Walk with Love and Death.*

BENEATH THE PLANET OF THE APES

Produced by Arthur P. Jacobs
Directed by Ted Post
Screenplay by Paul Dehn, from a story by Paul Dehn and Mort Abrahams based on characters created by Pierre Boulle
Photographed in Panavision and DeLuxe Color by Milton Krasner
Music by Leonard Rosenman
94 minutes

Cast: James Franciscus, Kim Hunter, Maurice Evans, Linda Harrison, Paul Richards, Victor Buono, James Gregory, Jeff Corey, Natalie Trundy, Thomas Gomez, David Watson

A good sequel to *The Planet of the Apes*, although lacking the impact of the original. An astronaut (James Franciscus) is assigned to seek out the missing leader (Charlton Heston) of the first mission. With the aid of a mute human (Linda Harrison), he seeks the leader in the forbidden zone and runs afoul of a militaristic group of strange mutants who worship a nuclear bomb, which they use as a threat to their enemies. The astronaut discovers the ruins of Manhattan in the grown-over shambles of former destruction before rescuing the missing leader and making their escape from the mutants. A juicy item for science fiction buffs.

BEYOND THE VALLEY OF THE DOLLS

Produced and directed by Russ Meyer
Screenplay by Robert Ebert, based on a story by Roger Ebert and Russ Meyer
Photographed in Panavision and DeLuxe Color by Fred J. Koenekamp
Music by the Strawberry Alarm Clock
109 minutes

Cast: Dolly Read, Cynthia Myers, Marcia McBroom, John LaZar, Michael Blodgett, David Gurian, Edy Williams, Erica Gavin, Phillis Davis, Harrison Page, Duncan McLeod, Jim Iglehart, Charles Napier

A three-girl rock group called the Carrie Nations search for success in the teeming, scheming music community of Los Angeles and find a little success and a lot of depravity. They attend parties at which people smoke marijuana and make love, sometimes to those of the same sex, and get involved in affairs which lead to heartbreaks and even killing. A product of porno specialist Russ Meyer, the film is a raunchy outing and too bizarre and comic strip to be really offensive, despite its restricted rating. And despite its title it has nothing to do with the Jacqueline Susann novel.

COVER ME BABE

Produced by Lester Linsk
Directed by Noel Black
Screenplay by George Wells
Photographed in DeLuxe Color by Michel Hugo
Music by Fred Karlin
89 minutes

Cast: Robert Forster, Sondra Locke, Susanne Benton, Robert S. Fields, Ken Kercheval, Sam Waterston, Michael Margotta, Floyd Mutrux, Maggie Thrett, Jeff Corey, Regis Toomey, Mitzi Hoag

A weird montage of a film, about a student filmmaker (Robert Forster) with a craving for filming reality, which causes him to go around with a camera and shoot people in the act of doing things like making love, committing suicide, and being derelict. His cinema arts professor (Robert Fields) finally points out to him what is reality to one man may not be reality to another. When last seen, the filmmaker is jogging along the beach, presumably mulling it all over.

FOUR CLOWNS

Produced by Robert Youngson
Written by Robert Youngson
Narration by Jay Jackson
Music by Manny Albam
Musical direction by Angelo Ross
97 minutes

Another of Robert Youngson's excellent compilation films, using rare footage of the early years of the cinema, in this case concentrating on the careers of classic movie comedians Buster Keaton, Charley

Chase, and Laurel and Hardy. With Youngson having covered the best of Laurel and Hardy in previous assemblies, the value here is in his tribute to the somewhat forgotten Charlie Chase, and the classic chase sequence from Keaton's *Seven Chances* (1925).

THE GAMES

Produced by Lester Linsk
Directed by Michael Winner
Screenplay by Erich Segal, from a book by Hugh Atkinson
Photographed in Panavision and DeLuxe Color by Robert Paynter
Music by Francis Lai
95 minutes

Cast: Michael Crawford, Stanley Baker, Ryan O'Neal, Charles Aznavour, Jeremy Kemp, Elaine Taylor, Athol Compton, Kent Smith, Sam Elliot

Erich Segal's screenplay focuses on the training of four young men from different countries as they prepare for the 26-mile marathon race at the Olympics in Rome. A former British track star (Stanley Baker) coaches a young milkman (Michael Crawford); a Yale student (Ryan O'Neal) trains despite his weak heart; a 41-year-old Czech (Charles Aznavour) is forced by his government to enter for national honor; and an Australian aborigine (Athol Compton), given short shrift because of his color, distinguishes himself. A fine coverage of its subject, partly due to writer Segal's himself being an amateur marathon runner.

THE GREAT WHITE HOPE

Produced by Lawrence Turman
Directed by Martin Ritt
Screenplay by Howard Sackler, based on his play
Photographed in Panavision and DeLuxe Color by Burnett Guffey
Musical direction by Lionel Newman
102 minutes

Cast: James Earl Jones, Jane Alexander, Lou Gilbert, Joel Fuellen, Chester Morris, Robert Webber, Marlene Warfield, R. G. Armstrong, Hal Holbrook, Beah Richards

The story of Jack Johnson, the first black heavyweight boxing champion, crowned in 1908, with James Earl Jones repeating the portrayal that won him great acclaim on the stage. Despite his talents, Jackson (called Jefferson in the film) is subjected to the humiliations of a white society, particularly with regard to his having a white mistress (Jane Alexander). The final humiliation in his having to feign defeat in favor of a white fighter whom he could easily beat. The film graphically reveals the blood lust of the fans, the scheming promoters and journalists, and strongly implies that the prejudices of the past are not entirely

384

gone. The performance of Jones is a milestone in the annals of black American art.

HELLO—GOODBYE

Produced by Andre Hakim
Directed by Jean Negulesco
Screenplay by Roger Marshall
Photographed in DeLuxe Color by Henri Decae
Music by Francis Lai
102 minutes

Cast: Michael Crawford, Curt Jurgens, Genevieve Gilles. Ira Furstenberg, Lon Satton, Peter Myers, Mike Marshall. Didier Haudepin, Vivien Pickles, Agathe Natanson. Georges Bever

An English car salesman (Michael Crawford), on a buying excursion in France, meets a seemingly lonely girl (Genevieve Gilles) who rambles around the country by herself. She is, however, the wife of a baron (Curt Jurgens), who understands her rambling ways and hires the Englishman to coach his son (by a former marriage) about cars. The Englishman, whose policy is "love 'em and leave 'em," finds himself deeply in love with the wife and unable to leave her. The baron, who himself has a roving eye, agrees to let them go their way. An amiable comedy-romance in nice settings.

THE KREMLIN LETTER

Produced by Carter De Haven and Sam Weisenthal
Directed by John Huston
Screenplay by John Huston and Gladys Hill, from a novel by Noel Behn
Photographed in Panavision and DeLuxe Color by Ted Scaife
Music by Robert Drasnin
123 minutes

Cast: Bibi Andersson, Richard Boone, Nigel Green, Dean Jagger, Lila Kedrova, Michael MacLiammoir, Patrick O'Neal, Barbara Parkins, Ronald Rodd, George Sanders, Raf Vallone, Max Von Sydow

An elaborate espionage tale, visually intriguing but somewhat too involved. An American naval officer (Patrick O'Neal) is cashiered and recruited into the spy trade. His mission is to circumvent a letter written by a U.S. official to Russia which proposes an attack on China. Before he and his fellow spies achieve their purpose, several die, one (Barbara Parkins) almost commits suicide because of her love for the ex-Navy man, and another (Richard Boone) turns out to be an agent for the other side. All the spies, of no matter what allegiance, are people of sadness and duplicity and strife. An interesting view, but hardly conducive to espionage recruitment.

M*A*S*H

Produced by Ingo Preminger
Directed by Robert Altman
Screenplay by Ring Lardner, Jr., based on the novel by
  Richard Hooker
Photographed in DeLuxe Color by Harold E. Stine
Music by Johnny Mandel
116 minutes

Cast: Donald Sutherland, Elliott Gould, Tom Skeritt,
Sally Kellerman, Robert Duvall, Jo Ann Pflug, Rene
Auberjonois, Roger Brown, Gary Burghoff, David Arkin,
Fred Williamson, Michael Murphy, Kim Atwood

A triumph of black humor, combining farcical humor
with a searing comment on the bloody horror of war
—certainly bloody from the point of view of the
Mobile Army Surgical Hospital crews trying to keep
up with the overwhelming flow of wounded and dying
men in Korea. The doctors and the nurses and the
orderlies have become inured not only to war but to
military routines. Two among them (Donald Sutherland and Elliott Gould) offend their superiors with
their lack of respect for rank and rules, but perform
trojan service to the needy. The film mixes slapstick
with the tragedy of carnage and pokes merciless fun at
military pomposity, empty religion, and incompetence.
It sticks its tongue out at hypocrisy—the same attitudes
which have made the spin-off television series highly
successful.

MOVE

Produced by Pandro S. Berman
Directed by Stuart Rosenberg
Screenplay by Joel Lieber and Stanley Hart, based on a
  novel by Joel Lieber
Photographed in Panavision and DeLuxe Color by Wil-
  liam Daniels
Music by Marvin Hamlisch
90 minutes

Cast: Elliott Gould, Paula Prentiss, Genevieve Waite,
John Larch, Joe Silver, Graham Jarvis, Ron O'Neal,
Garrie Beau, David Burns, Richard Bull, Mae Questal,
Aly Wassil, John Wheeler, Rudy Bond

A frustrated, would-be playwright (Elliot Gould), who
makes most of his income writing pornographic novels,
and his wife (Paula Prentiss) move from one apartment to a larger one, in the hope that it will have a
better atmosphere and be more conducive to his
artistry. The film takes place in the course of a weekend and hovers between the reality of their harsh lifestyle in New York and the fantasies of the writer's
frenetic mind. He is a contemporary Walter Mitty, although more neurotic, and the comedy of his life contains much comment on the social traumas of 1970
American life.

MYRA BRECKINRIDGE

Produced by Robert Fryer
Directed by Michael Sarne
Screenplay by Michael Sarne and David Giler, based on
  a novel by Gore Vidal
Photographed in Panavision and DeLuxe Color by Rich-
  ard Moore
Musical direction by Lionel Newman
94 minutes

Cast: Mae West, John Huston, Raquel Welch, Rex Reed,
Farrah Fawcett, Roger C. Carmel, Roger Herren, George
Furth, Calvin Lockhardt, Jim Backus, John Carradine,
Andy Devine

The first 20th Century-Fox film to receive an "X"
rating. A sex fantasy, about a young man who undergoes a change and turns into a beautiful girl (Raquel
Welch) in the Hollywood of the 1940's. She finds her
uncle (John Huston) has a talent school, she barges
in on it, and uses it to fight her way to success. The
film flits back and forth between Myra and her old
self, Myron (Rex Reed), and the fantasy is hyped
with clips from famous Fox films, including the images
of Marilyn Monroe, Laurel and Hardy, Shirley Temple,
et al. Heavily criticized for its lack of dramatic co-
hesion, it is also sabotaged by a staggering lack of
taste.

THE ONLY GAME IN TOWN

Produced by Fred Kohlmar
Directed by George Stevens
Screenplay by Frank D. Gilroy, based on a play by
  Frank D. Gilroy
Photographed in DeLuxe Color by Henri Decae
Music by Maurice Jarre
113 minutes

Cast: Elizabeth Taylor, Warren Beatty, Charles Braswell,
Hank Henry

Basically a two-character story, about a Las Vegas
showgirl (Elizabeth Taylor) and a cocktail bar pianist (Warren Beatty). Her affair with a married man
(Charles Braswell) falls through after five years and
she takes up with the pianist, who is desperately trying
to save money in order to get to New York and a
hopeful upswing in his career. He moves in with
her on a "no strings" basis. Both are emotional waifs,
who find it hard to admit their growing dependence
on one another. He tries to follow his plan and leave,
but he gambles away the money and returns to her.
With that they realize they are in love and a team.
Thin material, but helped by the playing of the glamorous stars.

PATTON

Produced by Frank McCarthy
Directed by Franklin J. Schaffner

Screenplay by Francis Ford Coppola and Edmund H. North, based on factual material from *Patton: Ordeal and Triumph,* by Ladislas Farago, and *A Soldier's Story* by Omar Bradley
Photographed in Dimension 150 and DeLuxe Color by Fred Koenekamp
Music by Jerry Goldsmith
170 minutes

Cast: George C. Scott, Karl Malden, Stephen Young, Michael Strong, Cary Loftin, Albert Dumortier, Frank Latimore, Morgan Paull, Karl Michael Vogler, Bill Hickman, Patrick J. Zurica

A magnificent portrait by George C. Scott of the flamboyant warrior general of the second World War, which reveals him in all his glory as well as his vanity and compulsive drive to fulfill what he believes to be his destiny as a hero. The story starts with his arrival in North Africa in 1943 and his promotion to Lieutenant General. He successfully tackles the forces of Rommel, then proceeds to the campaign in Sicily, which he regards as a contest to beat the efforts of the British Field Marshall Montgomery (Michael Bates). Later in Italy he is relieved of his command, because of the bad publicity resulting from his slapping of a sick soldier. He cools his heels in England until given command of the U.S. Third Army, which he brilliantly leads across Europe. The film presents war as a ghastly business, largely conducted by wily tacticians like Omar Bradley (Karl Malden), but aware that colorful, fearless cavaliers like Patton fill a vital function. Scott's Oscar-winning performance is the steel spine of this superb film.

THE SICILIAN CLAN

Produced by Jacques Strauss
Directed by Henri Verneuil
Screenplay by Henri Verneuil, Jose Giovanni, and Pierre Pellegri, from a novel by Auguste Le Breton
Photographed in Panavision and Eastmancolor by Henri Decae
Music by Ennio Morricone
119 minutes

Cast: Jean Gabin, Alain Delon, Lino Ventura, Irina Demich, Amedeo Nazzari, Sydney Chaplin, Elise Cegani, Karen Blanguernon, Marc Porel, Yves Lefebvre

A top-notch crime caper filmed in France and dealing with a family who indulge in robberies. The father (Jean Gabin) arranges for a condemned man (Alain Delon) to escape en route to the guillotine and hires him to help plan a jewel heist, the proceeds from which will enable him to return to his Sicilian birthplace and live out his life in ease. With the aid of an old colleague in America (Amedeo Nazzari) they rob a shipment of jewels being sent from Rome to New York. The heist is a complete success, but later a member of the family finds the hired man making

love to one of the wives (Irina Demich), which prompts retaliation from the clan. The lovers end up dead and the family ends up arrested. Expertly directed and acted, the film is a classy sample of its kind.

TORA! TORA! TORA!

Produced by Elmo Williams
Directed by Toshio Masuda, Kinji Fukasaka, and Richard Fleischer
Screenplay by Larry Forrester, Hideo Oguni, and Ryuzko Kikushima
Photographed in Panavision and DeLuxe Color by Charles Wheeler, Sinsaku Himeda, Masamichi Satoh, and Osami Furuya
Music by Jerry Goldsmith
143 minutes

Cast: Martin Balsam, Soh Yamamura, Joseph Cotten, Tatsuya Mihashi, E. G. Marshall, Takahiro Tamura, James Whitmore, Eijoro Tono, Wesley Addy, Frank Aletter, Leon Ames, Richard Anderson

A detailed and expensive examination of the events leading up to the Japanese attack on Pearl Harbor, revealing their carefully prepared plans and the almost total American unawareness. The film does for Pearl Harbor what Zanuck's *The Longest Day* did for D-Day. The Japanese segments are the work of Japanese directors and lend some respect to the attackers and their operation, infamous though it is, and the American portions are the work of Richard Fleischer, with almost the whole second half of the film devoted to the destruction of the fleet and bases at Pearl. Many famous historical personalities are accurately portrayed and actual locations are utilized as much as possible to convey a documentary style. But the real stars of the film are the special effects men, who created the means to restage the terrible day in all its spectacular agony.

20TH CENTURY-FOX ACADEMY AWARDS FOR 1970

PATTON: Best picture.

GEORGE C. SCOTT: Best actor, *Patton.*

FRANKLIN J. SCHAFFNER: Best director, *Patton.*

RING LARDNER, JR.: Best adapted screenplay, *M*A*S*H.*

FRANCIS FORD COPPOLA, EDMUND H. NORTH: Best original screenplay, *Patton.*

URIE MCCLEARY, GIL PARRONDO: Best art direction, *Patton.*

ANTONIO MATEOS, PIERRE-LOUIS THEVENET: Best set decoration, *Patton.*

DOUGLAS WILLIAMS, DON BASSMAN: Best sound, *Patton.*

HUGH S. FOWLER: Best editing, *Patton.*

A. D. FLOWERS, L. B. ABBOTT: Best visual effects, *Tora! Tora! Tora!.*

Beneath the Planet of the Apes.

Elliott Gould, Tom Skerritt, and Donald Sutherland in *M*A*S*H*.

Dolly Read and Michael Blodgett in *Beyond the Valley of the Dolls*.

George C. Scott as *Patton*.

Jane Alexander and James Earl Jones in *The Great White Hope*.

Mae West and Raquel Welch in *Myra Breckinridge*.

Barbara Parkins and Patrick O'Neal in *The Kremlin Letter*.

Tora! Tora! Tora!

Elizabeth Taylor and Warren Beatty in *The Only Game in Town*.

387

1971

B.S. I LOVE YOU

Produced by Arthur M. Broidy
Directed and written by Steven Hillard Stern
Photographed in DeLuxe Color by David Dans
Music by Jimmy Dale and Mark Shekter
99 minutes

Cast: Peter Kastner, JoAnna Cameron, Louis Sorel, Gary Burghoff, Richard B. Schull, Joanna Barnes, John Gerstad, Mary Lou Mellace, Jeanne Sorel, Joe Kotter, Tom Ruisinger

A comedy, heavily laced with sex, spoofing the lifestyle of New York advertising people. A television ad man (Peter Kastner) promotes his career by his ability as a lover, especially with his beautiful boss (Joanna Barnes), but encounters problems when he finds that an eighteen-year-old (JoAnna Cameron) with whom he has also been having an affair is her daughter. He thinks things over and decides to go back to his girl friend (Louise Sorel) in Connecticut, arriving in time to stop her marrying someone else. The film is a hit-and-miss affair, sometimes funny in its barbs and situations and somewhat hampered by its hero not being very believable as an ambitious Don Juan.

CELEBRATION AT BIG SUR

Produced by Carl Gottlieb
Directed by Baird Bryant and Johanna Demetrakas
Photographed in DeLuxe Color by Baird Bryant, Bill Kaplan, Gary Weis, Peter Smokler, and Joan Churchill
82 minutes

Cast: Joan Baez, Carol Ann Cisneros, David Crosby, Chris Ethridge, Mimi Farina, Joni Mitchell, Dorothy Morrison, Graham Nash, Julie Payne, Greg Reeves, John Sebastian

Filmed in September of 1969, during the three-day, annual Big Sur Folk Festival at Esalen, California, and presenting a large number of the performers, edited and intercut with audience reactions and shots of the spectacular coastal setting. Foremost among the acts are those of Joan Baez, Joni Mitchell, and John Sebastian.

ESCAPE FROM THE PLANET OF APES

Produced by Arthur P. Jacobs
Directed by Don Taylor
Screenplay by Paul Dehn
Photographed in Panavision and DeLuxe Color by Joseph Biroc
Music by Jerry Goldsmith
97 minutes

Cast: Roddy McDowall, Kim Hunter, Bradford Dillman, Natalie Trundy, Eric Braeden, William Windom, Sal Mineo, Albert Salmi, Jason Evers, John Randolph, Harry Lauter

The third in the simian science fiction series, with Roddy McDowall and Kim Hunter reprising their roles as sensitive, cultured apes. They, and another (Sal Mineo), escape the holocaust dealt with in the previous film and splash down in a capsule off the California coast. They then become the objects of curiosity, amusement, and resentment that the humans were on the ape planet. Among the enemies is a presidential adviser (Eric Braeden), who wants the chimps exterminated before they can breed and a kindly circus owner (Ricardo Montalban), who gives them a place to hide. An entertaining adventure yarn, with some pertinent comments on our civilization.

THE FRENCH CONNECTION

Produced by Philip D'Antoni
Directed by William Friedkin
Screenplay by Ernest Tidyman, based on a book by Robin Moore
Photographed in DeLuxe Color by Owen Roizman
Music by Don Ellis
104 minutes

Cast: Gene Hackman, Fernando Rey, Roy Scheider, Tony LoBianco, Marcel Bozzuffi, Frederic De Pasquale, Bill Hickman, Ann Rebbot, Harold Gary, Arlene Farber, Eddie Egan, Andre Ernotte, Sonny Grosso

The story of the police operations against heroin smugglers in New York, with some shots of the point of origin of the drugs (Marseilles) and two of the acutal detectives involved in the 1961 breaking of the case (Eddie Egan and Sonny Grosso) playing small parts in the film. The principal cop (Gene Hackman) is a tough, hard-driving fanatical hater of narcotics crooks, who brings the big smuggler (Fernando Rey) and his operation to a halt. The film is a masterpiece of editing and suspense, with a classic chase as its highlight. The cop takes out after a killer (Marcel Bozzuffi), who boards an elevated train to escape and holds a gun to the driver to keep going. But the cop follows in a car under the train, crashing, skidding, and bouncing off obstacles, until he catches up with the stalled train. Possibly the best filmed chase in movie history—and the climax of an engrossing foray into the world of drug smuggling.

LITTLE MURDERS

Produced by Jack Brodsky
Directed by Alan Arkin
Screenplay by Jules Feiffer, based on his play
Photographed in DeLuxe Color by Gordon Willis
Music by Fred Kaz
110 minutes

Cast: Elliott Gould, Marcia Rodd, Vincent Gardenia, Elizabeth Wilson, Jon Korkes, John Randolph, Doris Roberts, Donald Sutherland, Lou Jacobi, Alan Arkin

A satire, more biting than comedic, about the break-up of life in New York as crime and violence grip the city. Into the middle-class home of the Newquists comes a photographer (Elliott Gould), who claims to be nothing but apathetic. But his spirits pick up a little when he falls in love with the daughter (Marcia Rodd). They are married by a freaked-out minister (Donald Sutherland), but their happiness is cut short when the girl is killed by an anonymous sniper. Then apathy turns to militancy; the husband and the family arm themselves, armor plate their apartment, and prepare to ward off the evil hordes coming off the streets of the city. The Jules Feiffer script gets its points across, but suffers in not knowing whether to invite the audience to laugh or recoil in horror.

MADE FOR EACH OTHER

Produced by Roy Townshend
Directed by Robert B. Bean
Screenplay by Renee Taylor and Joseph Bologna
Photographed in DeLuxe Color by William Storz
Music by Trade Martin
103 minutes

Cast: Renee Taylor, Joseph Bologna, Paul Sorvino, Olympia Dukakis, Helen Verbit, Louis Zorich, Ron Carey, Peggy Pope, Susan Brockman, Michael Brockman, Art Levy, Freeda Wexler

The husband-and-wife writing team of Renee Taylor and Joseph Bologna here appear as the stars of their own script about a pair of New Yorkers, both describable as losers, who meet at a group-therapy session and fall in love. The script is semi-autobiographical and full of amusing, touching, and revealing incidents about ordinary people struggling to keep afloat in a mad society, or as the girl herself says, "Two self-destructives confronting the life force." One of the highlights is the girl doing an excruciatingly bad cabaret act. Energetic, poignant, and funny.

MAKING IT

Produced by Albert S. Ruddy
Directed by John Erman
Screenplay by Peter Bart, based on a novel by James Leigh
Photographed in DeLuxe Color by Richard C. Glounder
Music by Charles Fox
97 minutes

Cast: Kristoffer Tabori, Marlyn Mason, Bob Balaban, Lawrence Pressman, Louise Latham, John Fiedler, Sherry Miles, Denny Miller, Doro Merande, Maxine Stuart, Tom Troupe, Joyce Van Patten

A study of adolescence, ranging from comedic to poignant, and touching on the use of drugs, the publishing of underground newspapers, and especially the preoccupation with sex. The leading character (Kristoffer Tabori) is sex mad and goes after students as well as the wives of teachers. The self-assured young cynic gets by on charm but receives a few emotional kicks, as when his widowed mother (Joyce Van Patten) loses a prospective husband in a car crash, and when he has to borrow money for an abortion. The film is true to its title—attempting to hold the mirror up to contemporary life, and making it.

THE MARRIAGE OF A YOUNG STOCKBROKER

Produced and directed by Lawrence Turman
Screenplay by Lorenzo Semple, Jr., based on a novel by Charles Webb
Photographed in DeLuxe Color by Laszlo Kovacs
Music by Fred Karlin
95 minutes

Cast: Richard Benjamin, Joanna Shimkus, Elizabeth Ashley, Adam West, Patricia Barry, Tiffany Bolling, Ed Prentiss, William Forrest, Johnny Scott Lee, Bill McConnell

The gentleman (Richard Benjamin) of the title is successful but bored, and amuses himself by girl watching and seeing porno movies. His passive wife (Joanna Shimkus) is encouraged by her liberated sister (Elizabeth Ashley) to swing free, just as she has done with her own, alcoholic husband (Adam West). But she is not the type and instead chooses to remain with her voyeuristic husband. One of his fantasies, that of Tiffany Bolling, is a highlight of the film, which ends with a group-therapy session that suggests the couple might solve their problems. Amusing but drifting in its pertinence.

389

THE MEPHISTO WALTZ

Produced by Quinn Martin
Directed by Paul Wendkos
Screenplay by Ben Maddow, based on a novel by Fred
  Mustard Stewart
Photographed in DeLuxe Color by William W. Spencer
Music by Jerry Goldsmith
115 minutes

Cast: Alan Alda, Jacqueline Bisset, Barbara Parkins,
Bradford Dillman, William Windom, Kathleen Widdoes,
Pamelyn Ferdin, Curt Lowens, Gregory Morton, Berry
Kroeger, Curt Jurgens

A stylish, occult mystery about a famed concert pianist (Curt Jurgens) who is dying of cancer and who
grants a rare interview to a music journalist (Alan
Alda). The journalist comes under the spell of the
pianist and his beautiful daughter (Barbara Parkins),
but the journalist's wife is bothered by the changes
she detects in her husband. And for good reason. He is
being possessed by the pianist, who is a satanist eager
to take over a new body so as to continue his own
life. The daughter is also a satanist, and eventually the
journalist and his wife are killed and absorbed.
Chilling and fascinating, and backed up by a fine
Jerry Goldsmith score.

PANIC IN NEEDLE PARK

Produced by Dominick Dunne
Directed by Jerry Schatzberg
Screenplay by Joan Didion and John Gregory Dunne,
  based on a book by James Mills
Photographed in DeLuxe Color by Adam Holender
110 minutes

Cast: Al Pacino, Kitty Winn, Alan Vint, Richard Bright,
Kiel Martin, Michael McClanathan, Warren Finnerty,
Marcia Jean Kurtz, Raul Julia, Angie Ortega, Larry
Marshall

The lives of drug addicts in New York, particularly in
the city's upper west side area, and photographed in
bleak reality. A street boy (Al Pacino) encourages his
girl friend (Kitty Winn) to try narcotics, which results
in her being drawn into his world of pushers, pimps,
prostitutes, and thieves. Their love for each other grows
as they also become more dependent on drugs, until
death seems like the best trip to take. A tragic love
story and a chilling film, but an accurate coverage of
its shocking subject matter.

THE SEVEN MINUTES

Produced and directed by Russ Meyer
Screenplay by Richard Warren Lewis, based on a novel
  by Irving Wallace
Photographed in DeLuxe Color by Fred Mandl
Music by Stu Phillips
115 minutes

Cast: Wayne Maunder, Marianne McAndrew, Yvonne
DeCarlo, Philip Carey, Jay C. Flippen, Edy Williams,
Lyle Bettger, Jackie Gayle, Ron Randell, Charles Drake,
John Carradine

A case against censorship, as a movie star (Yvonne
De Carlo) is brought to trial for writing an allegedly
pornographic novel. Her lawyer is a forceful defender
of freedom (Wayne Maunder), while the district attorney (Philip Carey) is a conservative representing
the establishment. Producer-director Russ Meyer, himself a porno expert, defeats his film by loading the
favor all to one side. Those in favor of censorship are
squares and those against it are with-it swingers.

VANISHING POINT

Produced by Norman Spencer
Directed by Richard C. Sarafian
Screenplay by Guillermo Colin, from a story outline by
  Malcolm Hart
Photographed in DeLuxe Color by John A. Alonzo
Music by Jimmy Bowen
107 minutes

Cast: Barry Newman, Cleavon Little, Dean Jagger, Victoria Medlin, Paul Koslo, Bob Donner, Timothy Scott,
Gilda Texter, Anthony James, Arthur Malet

A war veteran, also a failed policeman and sometimes
stock car racer (Barry Newman), sets out to drive
from Denver to San Francisco at top speed, keeping
himself awake on pills and defying the law. He is
chased by various policemen, but keeps tuned to a
radio station playing rock music, with a DJ (Cleavon
Little), a blind black man, warning him about police
signals. Finally the driver dies in a furious crash. The
film fails to make much sense, although presumably a
symbolic comment on contemporary life, and is notable only for its car stunt work.

WALKABOUT

Produced by Si Litvinoff
Directed by Nicholas Roeg
Screenplay by Edward Bond, from a novel by James
  Vance Marshall
Photographed in Eastmancolor by Nicholar Roeg
Music by John Barry
95 minutes

Cast: Jenny Agutter, Lucien John, David Gumpilil, John
Meillon, Peter Carver, John Illingsworth, Barry Donnelly,
Noelene Brown, Carlo Manchini

An Australian adventure, with social overtones, about
a girl (Jenny Agutter) and her small brother (Lucien
John), who are stranded in the Outback when their
father (John Meillon) loses his mind and shoots himself. They have nothing except a small transistor radio,
but they come across a young aborigine (David Gum-

pilil) who guides them and shows them how to live off the land. The girl flirts with the aborigine, but when he finally makes an advance toward her she rebuffs him, which results in his taking his own life. Later, in the city and in removed comfort, she remembers the ordeal in a much more rosy version. The film is exquisitely photographed in the stark Aussie wastelands. The gentle music score by John Barry helps make it an unusual film.

20TH CENTURY-FOX ACADEMY AWARDS FOR 1971

THE FRENCH CONNECTION: Best picture.

GENE HACKMAN: Best actor, *The French Connection*.

WILLIAM FRIEDKIN: Best director, *The French Connection*.

ERNEST TIDYMAN: Best adapted screenplay, *The French Connection*.

JERRY GREENBERG: Best editing, *The French Connection*.

Curt Jurgens and Alan Alda in *The Mephisto Waltz*.

Escape from the Planet of the Apes.

Marianne McAndrew in *The Seven Minutes*.

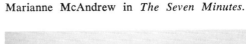

Joanna Shimkus and Richard Benjamin in *The Marriage of a Young Stockbroker*.

Gene Hackman in *The French Connection*.

Elliott Gould in *Little Murders*.

David Gumpilil, Lucien John, and Jenny Agutter, in *Walkabout*.

Kitty Winn and Al Pacino in *Panic in Needle Park*.

391

1972

AND HOPE TO DIE

Produced by Serge Silberman
Directed by René Clément
Screenplay by Sébastien Japrisot
Photographed in Eastmancolor by Edmond Richard
Music by Francis Lai
104 minutes

Cast: Robert Ryan, Aldo Ray, Tisa Farrow, Jean-Louis Trintignant, Lea Massari, Jean Gaven, Nadine Nabokov, Andre Lawrence, Daniel Breton

A fugitive Frenchman (Jean-Louis Trintignant) flees to Canada and runs afoul of a band of gypsies and a group of criminals planning a big robbery. The leader (Robert Ryan) of the group decides to take the man into their group, but it ends in their deaths, with the fugitive dying at the hands of the gypsies. It seems he had been responsible for the death of some gypsy children, albeit accidentally. The Canadian landscapes and the Montreal backgrounds give some interest to a confusing melodrama.

BLINDMAN

Produced by Tony Anthony and Saul Swimmer
Directed by Ferdinando Baldi
Screenplay by Vincenzo Cerami, Piero Anchisi, and Tony Anthony
Photographed in Techniscope and Technicolor by Riccardo Pallotini
Music by Stelvio Cipriani
105 minutes

Cast: Tony Anthony, Ringo Starr, Agneta Eckemyr, Lloyd Batista, Magda Konopka, Raf Baldassarie

An absurd Western, nominally a put-on, filmed in Spain with Tony Anthony as a blind sharpshooter, who takes on the job of delivering fifty brides to Texas clients. The girls are stolen by Mexican bandits, who also beat up the blind gunman, who manages to trail them to their hideaway with the aid of an apparently seeing eye horse. The bandits are wiped out, but the girls remain in Mexico. The film fails to be even a spoof.

THE CONCERT FOR BANGLADESH

Produced by George Harrison and Allen Klein
Directed by Saul Swimmer
Photographed in Technicolor by Saul Negrin, Richard Brooks, Fred Hoffman, and Tohru Nakamura
100 minutes

Cast: Eric Clapton, Bob Dylan, George Harrison, Billy Preston, Leon Russell, Ravi Shankar, Ringo Starr, Klaus Voorman, Badfinger, Jesse Davis, Jim Horn, Jim Keltner, Claudia Linnear

A film record of the historic benefit concert given at Madison Square Garden in New York in August of 1971, in aid of Bangladesh, with straightforward performances, and little camera trickery, of such people as Ravi Shankar, George Harrison, Ringo Starr, and especially Bob Dylan, doing their specialties to a highly appreciative audience.

CONQUEST OF THE PLANET OF THE APES

Produced by Arthur P. Jacobs
Directed by J. Lee Thompson
Screenplay by Paul Dehn, based upon characters created by Pierre Boulle
Photographed in Panavision and DeLuxe Color by Bruce Surtees
88 minutes

Cast: Ricardo Montalban, Roddy McDowall, Don Murray, Natalie Trundy, Hari Rhodes, Severn Darden, Lou Wagner, John Randolph, Asa Maynor, H. M. Wynand, David Show

Number Four in the ape series picks up the story left by Number Three, as the son (Roddy McDowall) of the apes who came to earth rallies his kind against human oppression. In the year 1990 apes have replaced dogs and cats as house pets, and they are also being used as servants. The governor (Don Murray) of the state has assumed Big Brother proportions and urges complete subjugation of apes. The ape leader organizes a revolution and wipes out the bad humans. A fine entry in the series, offering scenic adventure and a goodly dash of searing social comment on the human species.

COUNTESS DRACULA

Produced by Alexander Paal
Directed by Peter Sasdy

Screenplay by Jeremy Paul, from a story by Alexander Paal and Peter Sasdy
Photographed in Color by Ken Talbot
94 minutes

Cast: Ingrid Pitt, Nigel Green, Sandor Eles, Patience Collier, Maurice Denham, Peter Jeffrey, Lesley-Anne Down

An elderly countess (Ingrid Pitt) finds that by bathing in the blood of young virgins she can restore herself to her youth, when she was beautiful. Her faithful servant (Nigel Green) keeps her supplied. As a young beauty she makes love to a handsome fellow (Sandor Eles) by passing herself off as her own daughter. But the treatments need to become more and more frequent, à la Dr. Jekyll and Mr. Hyde, and finally catch up with her. An unusual and good entry in the horror genre.

THE CULPEPPER CATTLE CO.

Produced by Paul A. Helmick
Directed by Dick Richards
Photographed in DeLuxe Color by Lawrence Edward Williams and Ralph Woolsey
Music by Tom Scott
92 minutes

Cast: Gary Grimes, Billy (Green) Bush, Luke Askew, Bo Hopkins, Geoffrey Lewis, Wayne Sutherlin, John McLiam, Matt Clark, Raymond Guth, Anthony James, Charlie Martin Smith, Larry Finley, Bob Morgan, Jan Burrell

A Western along conventional lines, dealing with a cattle drive from Texas to Colorado, headed by a tough trail boss (Billy "Green" Bush) and attended by a young boy (Gary Grimes) bent on becoming a cowboy and hired as a cook's helper. The drive is harrassed by bandits and ends with a battle in which all of the bandits and many of the cowboys lose their lives. What makes the film unconventional is the realistic treatment of the characters, who look like the kind of men pictured in actual photographs of the West. They are rugged and grimy and not the kind usually seen in Hollywood's version of the West, and the hard, grueling job of trailing cattle is presented for what it is. Not a glamour Western, but an interesting item for students of the West.

THE DARWIN ADVENTURE

Produced by Joseph Strick
Directed by Jack Couffer
Screenplay by William Fairchild, from a story by Jack Couffer and Max Bella
Photographed in DeLuxe Color by Denys Coop, Jack Couffer, Robert Crandall, and Ken Middleman
Music by Marc Wilkinson
91 minutes

Cast: Nicholas Clay, Susan Macready, Ian Richardson, Robert Flemyng, Christopher Martin, Philip Brack

The story of the famed British naturalist Charles Darwin (Nicholas Clay), who shocked Victorian England with his theories that man was a descendant of the ape family and not the product defined in the Bible. The film shows him from youth to old age, with a goodly amount of footage on nature, and presents his gradual success against the great odds of religious prejudice, although without much excitement.

THE EFFECT OF GAMMA RAYS ON MAN-IN-THE-MOON MARIGOLDS

Produced and directed by Paul Newman
Screenplay by Alvin Sargent, based on the play by Paul Zindel
Photographed in DeLuxe Color by Adam Holender
Music by Maurice Jarre
101 minutes

Cast: Joanne Woodward, Nell Potts, Roberta Wallach, Judith Lowry, Richard Venture, Carolyn Coates, Will Hare, Estelle Omens, Jess Osuna, David Spielberg, Ellen Dano, Lynn Rogers

An embittered mother and widow (Joanne Woodward) tries to bring up her daughters as best she can, although they are greatly dissimilar girls. Ruth (Roberta Wallach) is outgoing and high-strung, Matilda (Nell Potts, the daughter of director Paul Newman) is introverted and shy. Mother ekes out a living boarding elderly people and making telephone solicitations for a dance studio, and she is at odds with most men with whom she comes into contact, including a teacher (David Spielberg), who is accused of endangering Matilda's life for his encouragement of her growing of marigolds requiring cobalt exposure. The flowers are Matilda's entry in the school's Science Fair and they dramatically serve as a symbolic metaphor for the life force, surviving amid the trauma of the film's characters. Filmed in Bridgeport, Connecticut, the film is a touching study of ordinary but troubled family life.

THE HEARTBREAK KID

Produced by Edgar J. Scherick
Directed by Elaine May
Screenplay by Neil Simon, based on a story by Bruce J. Friedman
Photographed in DeLuxe Color by Owen Roizman
107 minutes

Cast: Charles Grodin, Cybill Shepherd, Jeannie Berlin, Eddie Albert, Audra Lindley, William Prince, Augusta Dabney, Michell Jason, Art Metrano, Marilyn Putnam, Jack Housman

A New York salesman (Charles Grodin) finds that

393

his bride (Jeannie Berlin) has irritating mannerisms as they drive on their honeymoon to Florida. His sense of mistake and regret are highly accented when he meets a beautiful blonde (Cybill Shepherd) on the beach. She is a cool, elegant product of The Establishment, who accepts his advances, causing him to divorce his bride and follow the girl to her Minneapolis home, where her wealthy father (Eddie Albert) does what he can to dissuade her intention to marry the glib, somewhat shifty salesman. But to no avail. All the father can hope is that the marriage will eventually run a swift course. The Neil Simon script and the Elaine May direction make this a keenly felt satire on American mores.

THE HOT ROCK

Produced by Hal Landers and Bobby Roberts
Directed by Peter Yates
Screenplay by William Goldman, based on a novel by Donald E. Westlake
Photographed in Panavision and DeLuxe Color by Ed Brown
Music by Quincy Jones
101 minutes

Cast: Robert Redford, George Segal, Ron Leibman, Paul Sand, Moses Gunn, William Redfield, Topo Swope, Charlotte Rae, Graham P. Jarvis, Harry Bellaver, Seth Allen, Robert Levine, Zero Mostel

A comedy crime caper, with Robert Redford as a safecracker just out of jail and George Segal as the friend who picks him up and persuades him to "do a job" right away. The two are hired to steal a diamond, which they do, but they lose it almost immediately and scramble to get it back from other thieves. In the process of so doing, they careen around a large area of New York, providing the audience with breathtaking photography of swift trips in cars and helicopters. The bungling burglars make it an amusing outing.

THE OTHER

Produced and directed by Robert Mulligan
Screenplay by Thomas Tyron, based on a novel by Thomas Tyron
Photographed in DeLuxe Color by Robert L. Surtees
Music by Jerry Goldsmith
100 minutes

Cast: Uta Hagen, Diana Muldaur, Chris Udvarnoky, Martin Udvarnoky, Norma Connolly, Victor French, Loretta Leversee, Lou Frizzell, Portia Nelson, Jenny Sullivan, John Ritter, Jack Collins, Ed Bakey

Thomas Tryon's best-selling Gothic novel, in a fine screen treatment and with his own scripting. The story takes place during a hot summer in New England in the 1930's, as a pair of twins (Chris and Martin Udvarnoky) cavort around a farmhouse. Strange things happen, including several deaths and injuries. A newborn baby is found floating in a wine cask. It seems the boys are possessed by evil and at the end it also seems that evil may not have been fully exorcised. A splendid tale of horror with a fine, visual sense of period.

THE POSEIDON ADVENTURE

Produced by Irwin Allen
Directed by Ronald Neame
Screenplay by Stirling Silliphant and Wendell Mayes, based on a novel by Paul Gallico
Photographed in Panavision and DeLuxe Color by Harold E. Stine
Music by John Williams
117 minutes

Cast: Gene Hackman, Ernest Borgnine, Red Buttons, Carol Lynley, Roddy McDowall, Stella Stevens, Shelley Winters, Jack Albertson, Pamela Sue Martin, Arthur O'Connell, Eric Shea, Fred Sadoff

An adventure indeed, as an ocean liner the size of the *Queen Mary* is bowled over by a gigantic wave and turned upside down. Most of the passengers, caught in the main dining room during New Year's Eve celebrations, are killed. But ten survive and with the leadership of a tough-talking minister (Gene Hackman) make their way through the inverted ship, proceeding to the bottom, which projects above the water. The going is rough and only four manage to get to the point where they can tap on the bottom and bring the attention of a rescue team, who cut through the metal plates. The film is a triumph for its special effects team and gives a gripping account of an incredible disaster.

THE SALZBURG CONNECTION

Produced by Ingo Preminger
Directed by Lee H. Katzin
Screenplay by Oscar Millard, based on a novel by Helen MacInnes
Photographed in DeLuxe Color by Wolfgang Treu
Musical direction by Lionel Newman
94 minutes

Cast: Barry Newman, Anna Karina, Klaus-Maria Brandauer, Karen Jensen, Joe Moross, Wolfgang Preiss, Helmut Schmid, Udo Kier, Michael Hauserman, Whit Bissell, Raoul Retzer

Espionage agents from a number of countries converge on Austria when it is discovered that a chest has been recovered from the bottom of a lake and that it contains a list of Nazi collaborators. A vacationing American lawyer (Barry Newman) is pressed into service by the CIA, as agents chase agents and several change their minds about whether the list should be revealed or destroyed. A beautiful setting for a very confusing yarn.

SLEUTH

Produced by Morton Gottlieb
Directed by Joseph L. Mankiewicz
Screenplay by Anthony Shaffer, based on a play by Anthony Shaffer
Photographed in DeLuxe Color by Oswald Morris
Music by John Addison
137 minutes

Cast: Laurence Olivier, Michael Caine, Alec Cawthorne, Margo Channing, John Matthews, Teddy Martin

An elegant battle of wits between a successful gentleman of English literature (Laurence Olivier) and a not-quite gentleman of London commerce (Michael Caine) over the author's wife, who is being loved by the Londoner. The eccentric author invites the lover to his country home and while pretending to be civilized about the whole thing, sets the lover up in a trap that will make him look like a burglar and hence a likely subject to be killed. But it's a trick to make the lover feel like a coward—a trick that provokes revenge that makes the author feel like a fool. Tragically, it provokes another response. The film is a two-character study, brilliantly acted by Olivier and Caine, and stylishly directed by Mankiewicz. A film in a class of its own.

SOUNDER

Produced by Robert B. Radnitz
Directed by Martin Ritt
Screenplay by Lonnie Elder III, from a novel by William H. Armstrong
Photographed in DeLuxe Color by John Alonzo
Music by Taj Mahal
105 minutes

Cast: Cicely Tyson, Paul Winfield, Kevin Hooks, Carmen Mathews, Taj Mahal, James Best, Yvonne Jarrell, Eric Hooks, Sylvia "Kuumba" Williams, Janet MacLachlan, Teddy Airhart

A family of black sharecroppers in the Louisiana of the 1930's struggle to survive not only poverty but the white supremacy of the times and the prejudice that relegates them to the lowest level of society. The father (Paul Winfield) is jailed for stealing food to feed his family and his wife (Cicely Tyson) maintains her home despite the privations. Their son (Kevin Hooks) and his dog Sounder make a trip to see the father and on the way he learns about the bewildering difference in the lifestyle of blacks and whites. The film, beautifully filmed on location, is perhaps the most compassionate look yet taken at the plight of the blacks of this period, and in Cicely Tyson it receives a superb depiction of strength and pride under heart-breaking conditions.

THE STRANGE VENGEANCE OF ROSALIE

Directed by Jack Starrett
Screenplay by Anthony Greville-Bell and John Kohn
Photographed in color by Ray Parslow
107 minutes

Cast: Bonnie Bedelia, Ken Howard, Anthony Zerbe

A lonely young Indian girl in New Mexico (Bonnie Bedelia) hitches a ride with a traveling salesman (Ken Howard) and takes him to her cabin. There she breaks his leg in order that he cannot leave and so she can care for him. A lustful motorcyclist (Anthony Zerbe) drops by to rob, but the girl kills him. Despite her violent actions, the girl expresses genuine concern for her captive, who makes several painful attempts to escape. A disturbing look at a very odd couple.

TROUBLE MAN

Produced by Joel D. Freeman
Directed by Ivan Dixon
Screenplay by John Black
Photographed in DeLuxe Color by Michael Hugo
Music by Marvin Gaye
99 minutes

Cast: Robert Hooks, Paul Winfield, Ralph Waite, William Smithers, Paula Kelly, Julius Harris, Bill Henderson, Vince Howard, Larry Cook, Aliki Jones

A crime yarn, with Robert Hooks as a slick operator who hovers between the law and the lack of it. He is concerned with righting the wrongs of the black ghettoes of Los Angeles, but makes his money working for gambling czars. He is hired by a pair of crooks (Paul Winfield and Ralph Waite) to hassle a rival ganglander (Julius Harris), a deadly villain with a sensitive sense of humor. The hero, or rather the anti-hero, confuses the police lieutenant (William Smithers) assigned to bring in the crooks, but helps eradicate the bad types. An unrealistic crime picture that makes good use of Los Angeles locations.

VAMPIRE CIRCUS

Produced by Wilbur Stark
Directed by Robert Young
Screenplay by Judson Kinberg
Photographed in color by Walter Byatt
87 minutes

Cast: Adrienne Corri, Laurence Payne, Thorley Walters, John Moulder-Brown, Lynne Frederick, Elizabeth Seal, Anthony Corlan

The story of a murdered count-vampire's revenge on a Serbian village. In 1810 a circus troupe make their way to the village and entertain the residents—before attacking them with their fangs. The circus is made up of the count's vampire relatives and they drink their fill.

R:
M
qu

ACE ELI AND RODGER OF THE SKIES

Produced by Boris Wilson
Directed by Bill Sampson
Screenplay by Chips Rosen, based on a story by Steven Spielberg
Photographed in Panavision and DeLuxe Color by David M. Walsh
Music by Jerry Goldsmith
92 minutes

Cast: Cliff Robertson, Eric Shea, Pamela Franklin, Rosemary Murphy, Bernadette Peters, Alice Ghostley, Kelly Jean Peters, Don Keefer, Patricia Smith, Royal Dano, Robert Hamm

The story of a World War I pilot (Cliff Robertson) who becomes a barnstorming pilot in Kansas during the 1920's and takes his eleven-year-old son around with him. This doesn't stop him from being a great hit with the ladies everywhere he goes. The period settings and the aerial photography are impressive, but the plot is thin. The film is in fact a flop, so much so that the names of the producer, director, and writer are fictitious.

BATTLE FOR THE PLANET OF THE APES

Produced by Arthur P. Jacobs
Directed by J. Lee Thompson
Screenplay by John William Corrington and Joyce Hooper Corrington, from a story by Paul Dehn, based on characters created by Pierre Boulle
Photographed in Panavision and DeLuxe Color by Richard H. Kline
Music by Leonard Rosenman
86 minutes

Cast: Roddy McDowall, Claude Akins, Natalie Trundy, Severn Darden, Lew Ayres, Paul Williams, Austin Stoker, Noah Keen, Richard Eastham, France Nuyen, Paul Stevens

The fifth and final in the ape series, with Roddy McDowall again appearing as Caesar, the civilized leader of the simians. It concentrates on the growth of ape culture in the wake of the defeat of the humans and their oppression, and it draws parallels with the history of human society. Various factions in the ape culture move to establish their own policies, including an aggressive military one, partly brought on by the attacks of human mutants who live in the ruins of their former cities. The film presents the same stylish mastery of special effects presented in the previous entries, although with a certain sense of straining to maintain credible story lines.

CINDERELLA LIBERTY

Produced and directed by Mark Rydell
Screenplay from his novel by Darryl Ponicsan
Photographed in Panavision and DeLuxe Color by Vilmos Zsigmond
Music by John Williams
117 minutes

Cast: James Caan, Marsha Mason, Kirk Calloway, Eli Wallach, Burt Young, Bruce Kirby, Jr., Allyn Ann McLerie, Dabney Coleman, Fred Sadoff, Allan Arbus, Jon Korkes, Don Calfa, Paul Jackson, David Proval, Ted D'Arms

The title refers to the Navy slang for a pass which ends at midnight. The story is that of a good-natured sailor (James Caan) who meets a pleasant but complicated prostitute in a Seattle dive. He beats her at a game of pool, which entitles him to her favors for the evening, but he is dismayed to find she has an eleven-year-old mulatto son (Kirk Calloway), obviously in need of fatherly care. He feels compelled to enter their lives and even marries the girl, despite her expecting a child by another man. The child dies and her sense of guilt sabotages the attempt of the sailor to provide a good family life. She runs away and the film ends with the sailor going AWOL in an attempt to find her. A dark and ugly study, but made with compassion and expertly acted by Caan and Mason.

THE EMPEROR OF THE NORTH POLE

Produced by Stan Hough
Directed by Robert Aldrich
Screenplay by Christopher Knopf
Photographed in DeLuxe Color by Joe Biroc
Music by Frank DeVol
132 minutes

398

Cast: Lee Marvin, Ernest Borgnine, Keith Carradine, Charles Tyner, Malcolm Atterbury, Simon Oakland, Harry Caesar, Hal Baylor, Matt Clark, Elisha Cook, Joe di Reda

The Pacific Northwest in 1933 and the story of hobos who ride the rails—in particular the story of one (Lee Marvin) who is regarded with respect in his league because he outwits the railroad men and even tackles the vicious conductor (Ernest Borgnine) who kills hobos who defy him. A young drifter (Keith Carradine) challenges No. One but fails to measure up, and the veteran train-jumper has the last laugh. The subject matter is brutal, but director Aldrich makes it exciting as he stages his fights on fast-moving trains. The film also focuses on the now forgotten hobo jungles of the Depression and suggests that even among the lowly there is a certain code of conduct—such as being No. One train-jumper and winning the title Emperor of the North Pole.

GORDON'S WAR

Produced by Robert L. Schaffel
Directed by Ossie Davis
Screenplay by Howard Friedlander and Ed Spielman
Photographed in DeLuxe Color by Victor J. Kemper
Music by Andy Badale and Al Elias
89 minutes

Cast: Paul Winfield, Carl Lee, David Downing, Tony King, Gilbert Lewis, Carl Gordon, Nathan C. Heard, Grace Jones, Jackie Page, Charles Bergansky, Adam Wade, Hansford Rowe

A Green Beret veteran (Paul Winfield) returns from Vietnam and finds his wife has died as the result of being mixed up with a heroin pusher (Nathan C. Heard). He rounds up some of his army friends and takes out after the drug dealers of Harlem, blasting them with weaponry with which they are experts. The film, knowingly directed by Ossie Davis with a keen eye for characters and locations, provides excitement in its moral crusade against vicious elements, but fails in presenting a truly credible story.

THE GOSPEL ROAD

Produced by June and Johnny Cash
Directed by Robert Elfstrom
Screenplay by Johnny Cash and Larry Murray
Photographed in Color by Robert Elfstrom and Tom McDonough
Music by Larry Butler
86 minutes

Cast: Johnny Cash, Robert Elfstrom, June Carter Cash, Larry Lee, Paul Smith, Alan Dater, Robert Elfstrom, Jr., Gillis LaBlanc, Terrance Winston Mannock, Thomas Leventhal

A semidocumentary about Jesus Christ, with Johnny Cash in Jerusalem pointing out historic sites and triggering dramatized incidents in which the director, Robert Elfstrom, plays Christ. Modestly scaled and laced with many songs, the film gives a somewhat folksy version of the epic tale while avoiding any epic movie techniques.

KID BLUE

Produced by Marvin Schwartz
Directed by James Frawley
Screenplay by Edwin Shrake
Photographed in Panavision and DeLuxe Color by Billy Williams
Music by Tim McIntire
100 minutes

Cast: Dennis Hopper, Warren Oates, Peter Boyle, Ben Johnson, Lee Purcell, Janice Rule, Ralph Waite, Clifton James, Jose Torvay, Mary Jackson, Jay Varela, Claude Ennis Starrett, Jr., Warren Finnerty

In a small Texas town in 1902, a young delinquent (Dennis Hopper) with a record as a train robber, decides to go straight. He takes a series of menial jobs and receives little encouragement, least of all from the sheriff (Ben Johnson), a ramrod law-and-order man. Eventually the boy feels he will never fit the straight mold, which makes no allowance for his free-wheeling ways, and steals the Christmas payroll of a local factory. With the help of some Indian friends he makes off successfully. The film sets itself up as a comedy but manages to forward a number of comments on puritanism and the American devotion to work.

THE LAST AMERICAN HERO

Produced by William Roberts and John Cutts
Directed by Lamont Johnson
Screenplay by William Roberts, based on articles by Tom Wolfe
Photographed in Panavision and DeLuxe Color by George Silano
Music by Charles Fox
95 minutes

Cast: Jeff Bridges, Valerie Perrine, Geraldine Fitzgerald, Ned Beatty, Gary Busey, Art Lund, Ed Lauter, William Smith II, Tom Ligon, Gregory Walcott, Ernie Orsatti, Erica Hagen, James Murphy

A perceptive look at a certain slice of Americana—the stock car races and its milieu, with Jeff Bridges as the son of a North Carolina moonshiner (Art Lund) who is jailed for his illicit work. The son, also adept at running whiskey past the police, takes to racing as a means of raising money to help his father out of jail. He wins a demolition derby and goes on to success in stock racing. A promoter (Ed Lauter) bankrolls him into the big leagues and a groupie (Valerie Perrine) lends her loving support. Aside from its excellent footage of car racing and good location photography, the film is an incisive commentary on certain kinds of human values, such as those of sports promoters, drivers possessed by a need to succeed, and women in need of reflected glory.

THE LAUGHING POLICEMAN

Produced and directed by Stuart Rosenberg
Screenplay by Thomas Rickman, based on a novel by Per Wahloo and Maj Sjowall
Photographed in DeLuxe Color by David Walsh
Music by Charles Fox
111 minutes

Cast: Walter Matthau, Bruce Dern, Lou Gossett, Albert Paulsen, Anthony Zerbe, Val Avery, Cathy Lee Crosby, Mario Gallo, Joanna Cassidy, Shirley Ballard, William Hansen, Jonas Wolfe

When a San Francisco police detective is among those slaughtered on a bus, another (Walter Matthau) is assigned to investigate. He is a fussy kind of man, and irritated to have as his partner an abrasive, cocky cop (Bruce Dern). They gradually pick up clues that establish the policeman was killed because he was on the trail of a sex criminal, who turns out to be a closet gay (Albert Paulsen), a rich man with a taste for violent sex. The film gives a graphic look at San Francisco's gay community and contains much humor, but blunts its appeal with an abundance of violence.

THE LEGEND OF HELL HOUSE

Produced by Albert Fennell and Norman T. Herman
Directed by John Hough
Screenplay by Richard Matheson
Photographed in DeLuxe Color by Alan Hume
Music by Brian Hodgson and Delia Derbyshire
94 minutes

Cast: Pamela Franklin, Roddy McDowall, Clive Revill, Gayle Hunnicutt, Roland Culver, Peter Bowles

Four people are hired by an eccentric millionaire (Roland Culver) to see if a supposedly haunted house actually is. An idealistic medium (Pamela Franklin) feels she can communicate with a trapped spirit; a physical medium (Roddy McDowall) joins in because of an unsuccessful prior attempt; and a skeptical physicist (Clive Revill) brings his wife (Gayle Hunnicutt). They experience shocking moments as poltergeists and evil forces shake the house and take possession of them, particularly the wife, who becomes lascivious. It seems the house was once owned by an evil munitions tycoon, who filled it with psychic phenomena. A good, chilling item in the ghost movie league.

THE NEPTUNE FACTOR

Produced by Sanford Howard
Directed by Daniel Petrie
Screenplay by Jack DeWitt
Photographed in Panavision and DeLuxe Color by Harry Makin
Music by William McCauley
100 minutes

Cast: Ben Gazzara, Yvette Mimieux, Walter Pidgeon, Ernest Borgnine, Chris Wiggins, Donnelly Rhodes, Ed McGibbon, Michael J. Reynolds, David Yorston, Stuart Gillard, Mark Walker

An underwater adventure. When a laboratory on the ocean floor collapses because of an earthquake, a pressurized vessel is sent down to rescue the aquanauts. When they reach the depths, huge tropical fish attack. But despite all, the rescue is a success. The film fails to excite, because of poor scripting and muddled direction. Soft on characterizations, but enlivened by good underwater special effects.

THE PAPER CHASE

Produced by Robert C. Thompson and Rodrick Paul
Directed by James Bridges
Screenplay by James Bridges, based on a novel by John Jay Osborn, Jr.
Photographed in Panavision and DeLuxe Color by Gordon Willis
Music by John Williams
111 minutes

Cast: Timothy Bottoms, Lindsay Wagner, John Houseman, Graham Beckel, Edward Herrmann, Boy Lydiard, Craig Richard Nelson, James Naughton, Regina Baff, David Clennon

A young Minnesotan (Timothy Bottoms), intent on a career in law, enrolls in the Harvard Law School and struggles to keep up with his studies, while becoming almost transfixed by his awesome professor (John Houseman) and also falling in love with the professor's daughter (Lindsay Wagner). The film gives an excellent account of college life and especially the tough, famed law school. But it is essentially a study of two characters—an innocent, intelligent boy battling his way through sophisticated surroundings and overcoming his doubts and fears, and an intellectual giant of a teacher, compassionate at heart but uncompromising in his standards and maintaining a balance between academic pomposity and genuine wisdom. A film about brains—and the inspiration for the TV series.

THE SEVEN UPS

Produced and directed by Philip D'Antoni
Screenplay by Albert Ruben and Alexander Jacobs, based on a story by Sonny Grosso
Photographed in DeLuxe Color by Urs Furrer

Music by Don Ellis
103 minutes

Cast: Roy Scheider, Tony LoBianco, Larry Haines, Victor Arnold, Jerry Leon, Ken Kercheval, Richard Lynch, Bill Hickman, Ed Jordan, David Wilson, Robert Burr, Rex Everhart, Matt Russo

Crime in New York, and in particular the pursuit of criminals whose deeds merit at least seven years in jail. An undercover detective (Roy Scheider) uses disguises and trickery to nab his felons, and uses a boyhood friend (Tony Lo Bianco), a member of the underground, to feed him information that leads to arrests. The friend also uses, without the detective's knowing it, police secrets to run a ring which specializes in kidnapping mobsters for ransom. The betrayal of friendship builds to a final confrontation. The film is an exciting coverage of its material and draws particular excitement from director D'Antoni's staging of a car chase through midtown Manhattan, across the George Washington Bridge, and onto the Palisades Parkway.

20TH CENTURY-FOX ACADEMY AWARDS FOR 1973

JOHN HOUSEMAN: Best supporting actor, *The Paper Chase*.

James Caan and Marsha Mason in *Cinderella Liberty*.

Battle for the Planet of the Apes.

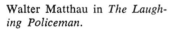

Jeff Bridges and Valerie Perrine in *The Last American Hero.*

Walter Matthau in *The Laughing Policeman.*

The Seven Ups, with Larry Haines and Roy Scheider.

Timothy Bottoms in *The Paper Chase.*

Ernest Borgnine, Yvette Mimieux, and Ben Gazzara in *The Neptune Factor.*

1974

CLAUDINE

Produced by Hannah Weinstein
Directed by John Berry
Screenplay by Tina and Lester Pine
Photographed in DeLuxe Color by Gayne Rescher
Music by Curtis Mayfield
92 minutes

Cast: Diahann Carroll, James Earl Jones, Lawrence Hilton-Jacobs, Tamu, David Kruger, Yvette Curtis, Eric Jones, Socorro Stephens, Adam Wade, Harrison Avery

A husbandless Harlem mother of six (Diahann Carroll) secretly works as a maid to supplement her welfare checks and falls for a charming, macho garbageman (James Earl Jones). Her children at first object to him but gradually come to like him. When love seems lasting and likely to lead to marriage, the footloose garbageman loses his nerve and takes off. But the kids track him down and persuade him to return to them and to their mother. A study of life in the black ghettoes, the film touches upon the sex roles in them, especially that of the dominant mother figure. As such it gets its power from the strong performance of Diahann Carroll as the spirited leader of her family, who is well backed by Jones as the seemingly strong man who has to find the strength to accept a real relationship.

CONRACK

Produced by Martin Ritt and Harriet Frank, Jr.
Directed by Martin Ritt
Screenplay by Irving Ravetch and Harriet Frank, Jr., based on a book by Pat Conroy
Photographed in Panavision and DeLuxe Color by John Alonzo
Music by John Williams
107 minutes

Cast: Jon Voight, Paul Winfield, Hume Cronyn, Madge Sinclair, Tina Andrews, Antonio Fargas, Ruth Attaway, James O'Reare

The true story of a schoolteacher named Pat Conroy (Jon Voight) who goes to an island off the coast of South Carolina to teach a group of deprived black children. They have no knowledge of any kind and have difficulty pronouncing his name, calling him "Conrack." His teaching policies are new and liberal and meet opposition from the stuffy superintendent (Hume Cronyn) and the narrow-minded principal (Madge Sinclair). He is compassionate toward the children and wins their love with his stories and his antics, but eventually he receives his dismissal. However, the influence he has had on the children doubtlessly remains with them. A touching film, with a persuasive performance from Voight and good use of the children on St. Simons Island, Georgia.

THE CRAZY WORLD OF JULIUS VROODER

Produced by Edward Rissien and Arthur Hiller
Directed by Arthur Hiller
Screenplay by Daryl Henry
Photographed in Panavision and DeLuxe Color by David Walsh
Music by Bob Alcivar
101 minutes

Cast: Timothy Bottoms, Barbara Seagull, Lawrence Pressman, Albert Salmi, George Marshall, Richard A. Dysart, Dena Dietrich, Debralee Scott, Lou Frizzell, Jack Murdock

Julius Vrooder (Timothy Bottoms) is crazy because of his experiences in Vietnam. He is a patient in a hospital for veterans of wars going back to the one of 1914–1918 and he defies all attempts to bring him into line. He digs himself a booby-trapped hiding place and fixes it up with electricity, water and telephone. He plans to marry his nurse (Barbara Seagull) and flee to Canada, but The System prevents him going out into the real world. The film's point is that the real world is possibly crazier than his own. The point here receives amusing but not conclusive treatment.

DIRTY MARY, CRAZY LARRY

Produced by Norman H. Herman
Directed by John Hough
Screenplay by Leigh Chapman and Antonio Santean, based on a novel by Richard Unekis
Photographed in color by Mike Margulies

Music by Jimmy Haskell
93 minutes

Cast: Peter Fonda, Susan George, Adam Roarke, Vic Morrow, Fred Daniels, Roddy McDowall, Lynn Borden, Adrian Herman, Janear Hines

A small-time racing driver (Peter Fonda) and his buddy (Adam Roarke) extort $150,000 from a supermarket manager (Roddy McDowall), with the object of buying an expensive car in which to race. As they leave the market they find a girl (Susan George) waiting in their car. She is a parolee and she insists on going with them. The police, led by a tough sheriff (Vic Morrow) soon latch on to them and for the better part of a day chase them all over northern California with a helicopter and a fleet of cars. The cocky racing driver gives them a run for their money —until he runs headlong into a train. The film is an almost continuous chase, with not very likeable people, but a tribute to the stunt drivers responsible.

11 HARROWHOUSE

Produced by Elliott Kastner
Directed by Aram Avakian
Screenplay by Jeffrey Bloom, based on a novel by Gerald A. Browne
Photographed in Panavision and DeLuxe Color by Arthur Ibbetson
Music by Michael J. Lewis
95 minutes

Cast: Charles Grodin, Candice Bergen, John Gielgud, Trevor Howard, James Mason, Helen Cherry

An eccentric English millionaire (Trevor Howard) commissions a mild-mannered diamond salesman (Charles Grodin) to rob the vaults of a diamond clearing house in London. He is egged on by his feisty, rich girl friend (Candice Bergen), and together they devise an ingenious method of doing the job—by leading a vacuum line into the vault and sucking out the vast fortune in stones. In this they are aided by a clerk (James Mason), who is peeved over his employer's (John Gielgud) intention to dismiss him with a small pension. With the job done, the young robbers are then pursued by the millionaire's henchmen with the object of killing them. In an extended chase across the millionaire's estate, involving horses as well as cars, most of the henchmen are eliminated and with the help of the millionaire's lady friend (Helen Cherry) the robbers escape. Not a likely caper, but an amusing one, with a splendid romp finale.

HARRY AND TONTO

Produced and directed by Paul Mazursky
Screenplay by Paul Mazursky and Josh Greenfield
Photographed in DeLuxe Color by Michael Butler

Music by Bill Conti
110 minutes

Cast: Art Carney, Ellen Burstyn, Chief Dan George, Geraldine Fitzgerald, Larry Hagman, Arthur Hunnicut, Phil Bruns, Joshua Mostel, Melanie Mayron, Dolly Jonah, Herbert Berghof

A seventy-two-year-old New York widower (Art Carney) is forced out of his comfortable retirement when his apartment building is torn down. Rather than look for another place, he decides to take a trip to Los Angeles, taking with him his cat Tonto. In making the odyssey he is awakened to all that is going on in life today, much of which seems to be unhappy, but none of which dismays the old man. He visits his children in New Jersey and Chicago and meets a variety of people as he makes his way across the nation by bus and by hitchhiking. When he gets to Los Angeles, he rejects the plastic lifestyle of his son (Larry Hagman) and finds his own place in the sun. A genial look at contemporary America and its strange levels of culture, with a beguiling performance from Carney as a man undaunted by life.

THE HOUSE ON SKULL MOUNTAIN

Produced by Ray Storey
Directed by Ron Honthaner
Screenplay by Mildred Pares
Photographed in DeLuxe Color by Monroe Askins
Music by Jerrold Immel
85 minutes

Cast: Victor French, Janee Michelle, Jean Durand, Mike Evans, Xernona Clayton, Lloyd Nelton, Ella Woods, Mary J. Todd McKenzie, Don Devendorf

Four distant relatives arrive at the creepy old house of a dying woman (Mary J. Todd McKenzie) to hear her will and come under the influence of the voodoo-practicing butler (Jean Durand). After several deaths, the strongest of the relatives (Victor French), a white man who learns he has black blood, banishes the butler and saves a beautiful black girl (Janee Michelle) with whom he is in love. A routine horror item.

LACOMBE, LUCIEN

Produced and directed by Louis Malle
Screenplay by Louis Malle and Patrick Modiano
Photographed in Eastmancolor by Tonino Delli Colli
Music by Django Reinhardt and the Quintet from the Hot Club of France, Andre Cleveau, and Irene de Trebert
141 minutes

Cast: Pierre Blaise, Aurore Clement, Holger Lowenadler, Therese Gieshe, Stephane Bouy, Loumi Iazobesco, Rene Bouloc, Pierre Decazes, Jean Rougherie

Louis Malle's powerful indictment of French collaborators during the Nazi occupation. A teenage farmboy (Pierre Blaise) is rejected by the Resistance as too young, but is recruited by the Gestapo, who build up his ego and supply him with liquor and whatever he wants. He enjoys his new-found rank, his police pass, and his gun. He betrays a teacher and becomes used to the tortures meted out to his countrymen. His fortunes take a turn for the worse when he falls in love with a Jewish girl (Aurore Clement), which causes her father to be deported. With the girl and her mother, he sets out for Spain, but the Resistance have him marked for execution. The film pulls no punches in dealing with the underside of French life during the German occupation.

THE MAD ADVENTURES OF RABBI JACOB

Produced by Bertrand Javal
Directed by Gerard Oury
Screenplay by Gerard Oury, Danielle Thompson, and Josy Eisenberg
Photographed in Panavision and color by Henri Decae
Music by Vladimir Cosma
95 minutes

Cast: Louis De Funes, Susy Delair, Marcel Dalio, Claude Giraud, Claude Pieplu, Renzo Montagnani, Henry Gutbert, Janet Brandt

An almost Chaplinesque French comedy about a bigot, a middle-aged businessman (Louis De Funes), who has no use for civil rights or tolerance and would prefer to fire his Jewish chauffeur rather than give him Saturday off. He unwittingly helps a political figure (Claude Giraud) escape his Moslem pursuers and the French police, but then comes to be pursued by them himself. To escape capture at Orly airport, the two men disguise themselves as rabbis, which causes them to be mistaken for a pair who are being met by an awaiting family preparing for the Bar Mitzvah of their son. By the time his adventures are through, the bigot has learned something about human understanding. A hilarious romp, made special by the comedic talents of Louis De Funes.

99 AND 44/100% DEAD

Produced by Joe Wizan
Directed by John Frankenheimer
Screenplay by Robert Dillon
Photographed in Panavision and DeLuxe Color by Ralph Woolsey
Music by Henry Mancini
97 minutes

Cast: Richard Harris, Edmond O'Brien, Bradford Dillman, Ann Turkel, Constance Ford, David Hall, Kathrine Baumann, Janice Heiden, Max Kleven, Karl Lukas, Anthony Brubaker

A mock-gangster saga, blending comic-strip antics and pop art with a certain liberal cyncism. A professional killer (Richard Harris) is hired by a gangster (Edmond O'Brien) to fight a rival gangster (Bradford Dillman) and stop him from taking over control of a city. The film is almost a montage of car chases and killings in bizarre locations as the killer hunts down his quarry and the quarry's men try to ward him off. It achieves a stunning measure of visual style, but the confusing story and the lack of sympathetic figures defeat the picture.

THE PHANTOM OF LIBERTY

Produced by Serge Silberman
Directed by Luis Buñuel
Screenplay by Luis Buñuel and Jean-Claude Carriere
Photographed in Eastmancolor by Edmond Richard
104 minutes

Cast: Jean-Claude Brialy, Monica Vitti, Milena Vukotic, Michael Lonsdale, Claude Pieplu, Michel Piccoli, Julien Bertheau, Adriana Asti, Paul Frankeur, Paul Leperson

An absurdist look at the world by Luis Buñuel, in which he reverses standards and concepts and defies logic. It begins with Spanish soldiers being shot by the firing squads of Napoleon, as the men cry "Down with liberty." It soon switches to the future, in a Paris park as a woman reads about what the audience has just seen. A sinister man sells postcards to young girls, warning them not to show their parents, but they are simply pictures of tourist spots. Later a nurse seeks refuge from a storm and finds herself among monks, playing poker with religious medallions as chips. And at a dinner party, guests sit on toilets and ask permission to go to the dining room. The film is a mad, almost surrealistic, look at human activities, but made arresting by the cinematic genius of Buñuel.

PHANTOM OF THE PARADISE

Produced by Edward R. Pressman
Directed by Brian De Palma
Screenplay by Brian De Palma
Photographed in Movielab Color by Larry Pizer
Music by Paul Williams and George Aliceson Tipton
91 minutes

Cast: Paul Williams, William Finley, Jessica Harper, George Memmoli, Gerrit Graham, Jeffrey Comanor, Archie Hahn, Harold Oblong

A kind of pop-rock version of *The Phantom of the Opera,* with Paul Williams as a rock mogul who rips off a songwriter (William Finley) and causes him to be jailed. While in jail the songwriter suffers an accident which disfigures him. Later, having fallen in love with a singer (Jessica Harper), he promotes her career by electrocuting the mogul's star (Gerrit

Graham) and causing him to use the girl, who becomes a smash. The mogul tries to romance his new star, but the scarred songwriter aborts the effort. In the end the poor fellow dies in the arms of the girl he adores. The film is a comedy with horror overtones and is made appealing to the young audiences by the presence and the music of Paul Williams.

S*P*Y*S

Produced by Irwin Winkler and Robert Chartoff
Directed by Irvin Kershner
Screenplay by Mal Marmorstein, Laurence J. Cohen, and Fred Freedman
Photographed in DeLuxe Color by Gerry Fisher
Music by Jerry Goldsmith
87 minutes

Cast: Elliott Gould, Donald Sutherland, Zouzou, Joss Ackland, Kenneth Griffith, Vladek Sheybal, Kenneth J. Warren, Yuri Borienko, Michael Petrovitch, Pierre Oudry

A satire on international espionage, with Donald Sutherland and Elliott Gould as a pair of bumbling agents whom the CIA wish to get rid of. When the pair bungle the defection of a Russian dancer (Michael Petrovitch), they are marked for extinction by both the CIA and the Russians. They take refuge with a group of French anarchists, which has its own hazards. Eventually the boys survive, but only after torture, being shot at and chased, and running into a stream of weird characters. The film misses the total mark, but scores a lot of comedic hits as it careens along.

THE THREE MUSKETEERS

Produced by Michael Alexander and Ilya Salkind
Directed by Richard Lester
Screenplay by George MacDonald Fraser, from the book by Alexander Dumas
Photographed in Technicolor by David Watkin
Music by Michel Legrand
105 minutes

Cast: Oliver Reed, Charlton Heston, Raquel Welch, Faye Dunaway, Richard Chamberlain, Michael York, Frank Finlay, Geraldine Chaplin, Christopher Lee, Simon Ward, Jean-Pierre Cassell

Another version of the Dumas classic and possibly the most accurate, certainly in costume and set details, but bordering on farce, with Michael York as a youthful, eager but bumbling D'Artagnan and not a cavalier of Fairbanksian proportions. Richard Lester's direction propels the story at a swift clip, as the musketeers aid the queen (Geraldine Chaplin) when Cardinal Richelieu (Charlton Heston) seeks to compromise her and seize power. The film is true to Dumas' story lines, but beneath its dash and humor, with the musketeers behaving like fun-loving boy scouts, is plenty of impli-

cation about the desperate politics of the time and the poverty and squalor of the masses.

TOGETHER BROTHERS

Produced by Robert L. Rosen
Directed by William A. Graham
Screenplay by Jack De Witt and Joe Greene, from a story by Jack De Witt
Photographed in DeLuxe Color by Philip Lathrop and Charles Rosher
Music by Barry White
94 minutes

Cast: Ahmad Nurradin, Anthony Wilson, Nelson Sims, Kenneth Bell, Owen Pace, Kim Dorsey, Ed Bernard, Lincoln Kilpatrick, Glynn Turman, Richard Yniguez, Angela Gibbs, Mwako Cumbuka

A realistic crime drama, filmed in the run-down sections of Galveston, Texas, about a fifteen-year-old boy (Ahmad Nurradin), who rounds up his gang of black and Chicano kids to hunt down the killer of a black policeman (Ed Bernard) they all respect. The boy's five-year-old brother (Anthony Wilson) is the only witness to the murder and the experience has traumatized him into silence. The killer, a homosexual paranoid (Lincoln Kilpatrick), stalks the little boy, but he is caught before he can kill him.

THE TOWERING INFERNO

Produced by Irwin Allen
Directed by John Guillermin
Screenplay by Stirling Silliphant, based on novels by Richard Martin Stern and Thomas Scortia
Photographed in Panavision and DeLuxe Color by Fred Koenekamp and Joseph Biroc
Music by John Williams
165 minutes

Cast: Steve McQueen, Paul Newman, William Holden, Faye Dunaway, Fred Astaire, Susan Blakely, Richard Chamberlain, Jennifer Jones, O. J. Simpson, Robert Vaughn, Robert Wagner, Susan Flannery, Sheila Mathews

A 138-story San Francisco skyscraper catches fire during its gala dedication ceremonies and many people are trapped in the upper floors. Among those directly involved in the fierce drama are the architect (Paul Newman), the head of the fire-fighting department (Steve McQueen), the builder (William Holden), and the subcontractor who has cut corners on his job (Richard Chamberlain). Many of the trapped die in the awesome fire or in falls from the building, but the firefighter manages to save others with his bold plans. As the film's title makes plain, it is a gigantic disaster story, the work of a specialist in this form—Irwin Allen—and employs a team of greatly skilled designers and stuntmen. Movie technology is the real star of the picture, with the drama resting on the blame

James Earl Jones and Diahann Carroll in *Claudine*.

Jon Voight in *Conrack*.

Elliott Gould and Donald Sutherland in *S*P*Y*S*.

406

laid upon human greed—the payoffs and kickbacks in the building of the mammoth tower. The film is dedicated to firemen, as well it might be.

YOUNG FRANKENSTEIN

Produced by Michael Gruskoff
Directed by Mel Brooks
Screenplay by Gene Wilder and Mel Brooks
Photographed by Gerald Hirschfeld
Music by John Morris
109 minutes

Cast: Gene Wilder, Peter Boyle, Marty Feldman, Madeline Kahn, Cloris Leachman, Teri Garr, Kenneth Mars, Richard Haydn, Liam Dunn, Danny Goldman, Oscar Beregi

A loving spoof on Hollywood's version of the Frankenstein legend invented by Mary Shelley, with Gene Wilder as the grandson of the infamous baron. In visiting his family home in Transylvania he gets the idea of creating a human being on his own, which turns out to be a big dolt (Peter Boyle) not unlike the original. His hunchbacked helper Igor (Marty Feldman) delights in being a part of the invention, as does a sex-starved nurse (Teri Garr). Director Mel Brooks fills his picture with a torrent of sight gags and references that have meaning to all lovers of the old Frankenstein films, and even approximates the black-and-white style and the sets of the early years. The music score by John Morris follows suit.

ZARDOZ

Produced and directed by John Boorman
Screenplay by John Boorman
Photographed in Panavision and DeLuxe Color by Geoffrey Unsworth
Music by David Munrow
102 minutes

Cast: Sean Connery, Charlotte Rampling, Sara Kestelman, John Alderton, Sally Ann Newton, Niall Buggy, Bosco Hogan, Jessica Swift, Bairbre Dowling, Christopher Casson, Reginald Jarman

A futuristic melodrama, set in the year 2293 and taking place on a planet which has long descended into a dark age of human division. The elite live in tranquil splendor and the mass of deprived live outside the select areas. The masses worship a huge Zeus-like head called Zardoz, which gives forth weapons to a chosen few, who hold the rest of the populace in submission. One of the chosen (Sean Connery) decides to invade the select regions and destroy their controlling devices. He finds their world to be a failing paradise, and with the love of an elite girl (Charlotte Rampling) survives on his own terms. Writer-director John Boorman fails to make a totally convincing statement and

Candice Bergen and Charles Grodin in *11 Harrowhouse*.

his vision of the future is confusing, but the film contains admirable sets by designer Anthony Pratt and some superb photographic imagery by Geoffrey Unsworth.

20TH CENTURY-FOX ACADEMY AWARDS FOR 1974

ART CARNEY: Best actor, *Harry and Tonto.*

FRED KOENEKAMP, JOSEPH BIROC: Best cinematography, *The Towering Inferno.*

HAROLD F. KRESS, CARL KRESS: Best editing, *The Towering Inferno.*

AL KASHA, JOEL HIRSCHORN: Best song, "We May Never Love Like This Again," *The Towering Inferno.*

Peter Fonda and Susan George in *Dirty Mary, Crazy Larry.*

Paul Williams and William Finley in *Phantom of the Paradise.*

Michael York, Raquel Welch, and Simon Ward in *The Three Musketeers.*

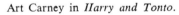

Art Carney in *Harry and Tonto.*

Paul Newman and Steve McQueen in *The Towering Inferno.*

Gene Wilder and Peter Boyle in *Young Frankenstein.*

1975

THE ADVENTURE OF SHERLOCK HOLMES' SMARTER BROTHER

Produced by Richard A. Roth
Directed by Gene Wilder
Screenplay by Gene Wilder
Photographed in Color by Gerry Fisher
Music by John Morris
91 minutes

Cast: Gene Wilder, Madeline Kahn, Marty Feldman, Dom DeLuise, Leo McKern, Roy Kinnear, John Le Mesurier, Douglas Wilmer, Thorley Walters

A manic comedy by writer-director-star Gene Wilder as the title character, who tackles his brother Sherlock's archenemy, Professor Moriarty (Leo McKern) when Sherlock (Douglas Wilmer) is out of the country. The insanely jealous younger brother, furious about always living in the shadow of the celebrated sleuth, is actually being used by Sherlock, who is trying to retrieve state papers stolen by Moriarty. Helping the kid brother is a policeman (Marty Feldman) with a photographic memory but not much sense. That they succeed is hardly important; what is important here is the comedic antics of Wilder and the throbbing presence of Madeline Kahn as the singing lady of mystery.

AT LONG LAST LOVE

Produced and directed by Peter Bogdanovich
Screenplay by Peter Bogdanovich
Photographed in Technicolor by Laszlo Kovacs
Music and lyrics by Cole Porter
Musical direction by Artie Butler and Lionel Newman
115 minutes

Cast: Burt Reynolds, Cybill Shepherd, Madeline Kahn, Duilio Del Prete, Eileen Brennan, John Hillerman, Mildred Natwick, Elvin Moon, M. Emmet Walsh, Burton Gilliam, Albert Lantieri, Tanis Van Kirk, Ned Wettimer

An attempt by Peter Bogdanovich to create a 1930's style musical, complete with striking art deco sets and the nonsensical story lines. Using sixteen Cole Porter songs, he spins a gossamer plot around idle, young rich types who play amorous games with one another and seemingly have nothing else to do. The attempt fails because the slight material is stretched over too long a playing time and because the stars, Burt Reynolds and Cybill Shepherd, while appealing, are not genuine song-and-dance people.

BLACK MOON

Produced by Claude Nedjar
Directed by Louis Malle
Screenplay by Louis Malle, Ghislain Uhry, and Joyce Bunuel
Photographed in color by Sven Nykvist
Music by Diego Masson
92 minutes

Cast: Cathryn Harrison, Theresa Giehse, Alexandra Stewart, Joe Dallesandro

A surrealistic Alice in Wonderland story, about a young girl (Cathryn Harrison) who drives across the countryside and comes across a war in which men are fighting women. She flees the site and enters a remote house, in which she finds an old lady in bed (Theresa Giehse). In the garden is a unicorn and children who play with a pig. A young couple in the house (Alexandra Stewart and Joe Dallesandro) have nothing to say, except when they sing. *Black Moon*, beautifully photographed by Sven Nykvist, is a puzzle—too much of one for its own good.

CAPONE

Produced by Roger Corman
Directed by Steve Carver
Screenplay by Howard Browne
Photographed in DeLuxe Color by Villis Lapenieks
Music by David Grisman
101 minutes

Cast: Ben Gazzara, Susan Blakely, Harry Guardino, John Cassavetes, Sylvester Stallone, Peter Maloney, Frank Campanella, Royal Dano, Dick Miller, John D. Chandler, John Orchard

The story of the Chicago ganglord of the 1920's, with Ben Gazzara giving a cool portrayal of the arrogant megalomaniac. The film charts his rise from a neighborhood punk to a czar of the booze and gambling rackets, seeking to control his rivals. He is finally turned in by one of his own men (Sylvester Stallone) and jailed on a charge of income tax evasion. A great deal of gunfire and killing intensifies the brutal account.

THE DEVIL IS A WOMAN

Produced by Annis Nohra
Directed by Damiano Damiani
Screenplay by Damiano Damiani, Fabrizio Onofri, and Audrey Nohra, from a story by Damiano Damiani
Photographed in color by Mario Vulpiani
Music by Ennio Morricone
105 minutes

Cast: Glenda Jackson, Claudio Cassinelli, Lisa Harrow, Adolfo Celi, Arnoldo Foa, Rolf Tasna, Duilio Del Prete, Gabriele Lavia, Francis Rabal

Into a Roman hostel-convent comes a writer (Claudio Cassinelli) to do a book on one of the residents, a Polish priest (Adolfo Celi) who collaborated with the Nazis. The priest is like all the other residents—people with great guilt, trying to cleanse their souls under the guidance of Sister Geraldine (Glenda Jackson), who rules with an iron hand. One of them is a beautiful girl (Lisa Harrow), whose political betrayal of her husband caused his death. She falls in love with the writer and leaves with him, and several of the others are moved to rebel. But in the end they all return to the strict care of the Sister. A strange, introverted drama, which ultimately fails to convince.

THE DRAGON FLIES

Produced by Raymond Chow and John Fraser
Directed by Brian Trenchard Smith
Screenplay by Brian Trenchard Smith
Photographed in color by Russell Boyd
Music by Noel Quinlan
102 minutes

Cast: Jimmy Wang Yu, George Lazenby, Frank Thring, Hugh Keays-Bryne, Roger Ward, Ros Speirs, Rebecca Grilling, Hung Kam Po, Deryk Barnes, Bill Hunter, Ian Jamieson

A kung fu adventure, filmed in Australia and dealing with a narcotics dealer (George Lazenby) in Sydney, who is a kung fu expert. To tackle him the Aussie police assign one of their men (Jimmy Wang Yu) who is also an expert. After a large number of physical encounters, including the smashing up of property and people, the agent brings in his man. For kung fu addicts—a trip.

THE FOUR MUSKETEERS

Produced by Alexander Salkind

Directed by Richard Lester
Screenplay by George MacDonald Fraser, based on a novel by Alexander Dumas
Photographed in Technicolor by David Watkin
Music by Lalo Schifrin
105 minutes

Cast: Oliver Reed, Raquel Welch, Richard Chamberlain, Michael York, Frank Finlay, Christopher Lee, Jean-Pierre Cassell, Geraldine Chaplin, Simon Ward, Spike Milligan, Roy Kinnear, Nicole Calfan, Faye Dunaway, Charlton Heston

A continuation of Richard Lester's *The Three Musketeers,* with much the same cast and mostly filmed at the same time as the previous film. It begins with a reprise of the famous plot and then follows the musketeers and D'Artagnan as they continue to help the royal family in their plight as Cardinal Richelieu (Charlton Heston) plans to assume more and more power. Lester's film contains an endless stream of action, some of it bordering on slapstick, but contrasts the raucous humor of the musketeers with tragedy as the conniving Milady (Faye Dunaway) kills Constance (Raquel Welch) and is then condemned by the musketeers to execution. Again the costumes and settings give added dimensions to the familiar action.

FRENCH CONNECTION II

Produced by Robert L. Rosen
Directed by John Frankenheimer
Screenplay by Robert and Laurie Dillon and Alexander Jacobs, based on a story by Laurie Dillon
Photographed in DeLuxe Color by Claude Renoir
Music by Don Ellis
119 minutes

Cast: Gene Hackman, Fernando Rey, Bernard Fresson, Jean-Pierre Castaldi, Charles Millot, Cathleen Nesbitt, Pierre Collet, Alexandre Fabre, Phillippe Leotard, Ed Lauter

Narcotics cop Popeye Doyle (Gene Hackman) continues his pursuit of heroin czar Frog One (Fernando Rey), who slipped away at the end of the previous film. He follows him to Marseilles, the drug capital of Europe, where his aggressive methods spoil the local police campaign. As the only man who can identify Frog One, Popeye is captured by the narcotics ring and shot full of cocaine, which turns him into a junkie, but from which desperate condition he manages to retrieve himself. He then sets out to capture his man, which he does after chasing him around the harbor of Marseilles and surviving the gang's attempts to drown him in a flooded dry dock. The film offers the same excitement as the original, but with a fascinating look at the French city and some fearful insights into the effects of drugs on humankind.

LUCKY LADY

Produced by Michael Gruskoff
Directed by Stanley Donen
Screenplay by Willard Huyck and Gloria Katz
Photographed in DeLuxe Color by Geoffrey Unsworth
Music by Ralph Burns
Songs by Fred Ebb and John Kander
117 minutes

Cast: Gene Hackman, Liza Minnelli, Burt Reynolds, Geoffrey Lewis, John Hillerman, Robby Benson, Michael Hordern, Anthony Holland, John McLiam, Val Avery, Louis Guss

An expensive but muddled adventure comedy, largely filmed in Mexico, about three liquor smugglers in the Prohibition era. The two men (Gene Hackman and Burt Reynolds) team up with a nightclub singer (Liza Minnelli) to expand their operation, but form an uneasy ménage à trois, since both men are in love with her. Aside from actually hauling liquor, their problems come in eluding both the U.S. Coast Guard and an organized gang who want no competition. The two men pose as Coast Guard officers and bring on a lavish sea battle in which the hoods are wiped out—a visually impressive sequence, although quite improbable. The film has many pleasing moments, but suffers from a wavering serio-comic attitude.

THE NICKEL RIDE

Produced and directed by Robert Mulligan
Screenplay by Eric Roth
Photographed in DeLuxe Color by Jordon Croenweth
Music by Dave Grusin
106 minutes

Cast: Jason Miller, Linda Haynes, Victor French, John Hillerman, Bo Hopkins, Richard Evans, Brendan Burns, Lou Frizzell, Jeanne Lange, Bart Burns, Harvey Gold

A searing, nightmarish look at crime in downtown Los Angeles, with Jason Miller as a wheeler-dealer acting as a middleman between crooked city hall officials and big-money racketeers. He operates in the black marketing of all kinds of merchandise, shipping it directly from warehouses, but he is fighting a losing battle to maintain his contacts. Other and younger middlemen are taking over and he finally learns he is set up for elimination. Robert Mulligan's film is a black look at its subject matter, reflecting the worst aspects of big city crime and giving little reason to look for improvements.

PEEPER

Produced by Irwin Winkler and Robert Chartoff
Directed by Peter Hyams
Screenplay by W. D. Richter, based on a novel by Keith Laumer
Photographed in Panavision and DeLuxe Color by Earl Rath
Music by Richard Clements
88 minutes

Cast: Michael Caine, Natalie Wood, Kitty Winn, Thayer David, Liam Dunn, Dorothy Adams, Timothy Agoglia Carey, Don Calfa, Michael Constantine, Gary Combs, Robert Ito, Buffy Dee

A spoof of the private eye movies of the forties—including a Bogart impressionist introducing the film—with Michael Caine in the role of a Philip Marlowe type in the Los Angeles of 1947. He is hired by a rich man (Michael Constantine) to find his long-lost daughter so that she will inherit his fortunes. Along the way, the not-very-good sleuth stumbles upon a family of eccentrics, one of whose daughters (Natalie Wood) engages his affections. By the time he completes his job he has undergone the usual quota of beatings, chases, and doublecrosses. The film sadly misses its satiric mark.

RACE WITH THE DEVIL

Produced by Wes Bishop
Directed by Jack Starrett
Screenplay by Wes Bishop and Lee Frost
Photographed in color by Robert Jessup
Music by Leonard Rosenman
88 minutes

Cast: Peter Fonda, Warren Oates, Loretta Swit, Lara Parker, R. G. Armstrong, Clay Tanner, Carol Blodgett, Bob Jutson, Peggy Kokernot, Carol Cannon, James Harrell

Two married couples in Texas go on vacation in a large camper and during the first night out they unwittingly come across a group around a campfire. The group are satanists and they sacrifice a girl. The vacationers try to slip away undetected, but they are noticed. From then on it's a chase, as the satanists assault the camper, try to break into, and slip poisonous snakes into it. When the camper moves off, it is pursued—and furiously. The occupants fight off the attackers and eventually succeed, but only after the audience has been treated to some of the most incredible car stunt work yet filmed.

THE ROCKY HORROR PICTURE SHOW

Produced by Michael White and Lou Adler
Directed by Jim Sharman
Screenplay by Jim Sharman and Richard O'Brien
Photographed in Eastmancolor by Peter Suschitzky
Music and lyrics by Richard O'Brien
100 minutes

Cast: Tim Curry, Susan Sarandon, Barry Bostwick, Richard O'Brien, Jonathan Adams, Nell Campbell, Peter Hinwood, Meatloaf, Patricia Quinn, Charles Grey

A fantasy spoof of Hollywood's old horror movies, with contemporary music and weird sexual overtones. A young engaged couple (Susan Sarandon and Barry Bostwick) seek refuge from a storm and enter a forbidding old house. They find it to be the lair of a strange group from the planet Transylvania, whose leader (Tim Curry) seduces both the boy and the girl. Also on hand is the leader's monster creation called Rocky (Peter Hinwood) and a variety of freaky types. Eventually the couple escape and the house and its fearful people are consumed in fire and explosions. The film—a "way out" piece of camp—has become a cult item with the younger generation.

ROYAL FLASH

Produced by David V. Picker and Denis O'Dell
Directed by Richard Lester
Screenplay by George MacDonald Fraser, based on his novel
Photographed in DeLuxe Color by Geoffrey Unsworth
Music by Ken Thorne
98 minutes

Cast: Malcolm McDowell, Alan Bates, Florinda Bolkan, Oliver Reed, Britt Eklund, Lionel Jeffries, Tom Bell, Joss Ackland, Christopher Cazenove, Leon Green, Richard Hurndall

A farcical swashbuckling epic, about a Victorian Englishman (Malcolm McDowell) who struts as a hero while actually being a coward and cons his way into the upper strata of European society. He comes into contact with courtesan Lola Montez (Florinda Balken), which alienates him with ambitious young statesman Otto von Bismarck (Oliver Reed), who nevertheless uses him to pose as a German prince, in order to marry a duchess (Britt Eklund) for political purposes. After that he has to save himself from the intended elimination. The film, largely photographed in Germany, is visually impressive, but the main character is a scoundrel of such little charm that it undermines the impact of the story.

SCENT OF A WOMAN

Produced by Pio Angeletti and Adriano De Micheli
Directed by Dino Risi
Screenplay by Ruggero Maccari and Dino Risi
Photographed in Technicolor by Claudio Cirillo
Music by Armando Trovaioli
100 minutes

Cast: Vittorio Gassman, Alessandro Momo, Agostina Belli, Moira Orsei

An Italian comedy-drama about a blinded army officer (Vittorio Gassman) injured in war maneuvers and bitterly resentful of the humiliation. He sets out on a trip with his seeing-eye private (Alessandro Momo) to keep a rendezvous with a fellow officer and their dual suicide. But the trip proves enjoyable as he senses the life force in such cities as Turin, Naples, and Rome, with all the admiring girls they have to offer, and he changes his mind about death. The film is a tour de force for Gassman as the cynical but basically warm-hearted officer, and a visual delight to the audience in its close look at various Italian points.

TAKE A HARD RIDE

Produced by Harry Bernsen
Directed by Anthony M. Dawson
Screenplay by Eric Bercovici and Jerry Ludwig
Photographed in DeLuxe Color by Riccardo Pallotini
Music by Jerry Goldsmith
109 minutes

Cast: Jim Brown, Lee Van Cleef, Fred Williamson, Catherine Spaak, Jim Kelly, Barry Sullivan, Harry Carey, Jr., Robert Donner, Ronald Howard, Dana Andrews

A Western (shot in the Canary Islands) about a black cowboy (Jim Brown) who promises his dying boss (Dana Andrews) that he will deliver the boss's profits on his last cattle drive to his wife in Mexico. The cowboy sets out to do so and is joined by a slick gambler (Fred Williamson), who has other ideas about the money. He helps the cowboy fend off numerous attempts to trap and kill them, until the final face-to-face at the end of the trail. A conventional Western, with a great deal of violence and pretty scenery.

THE TERRORISTS

Produced by Peter Rawley
Directed by Casper Wrede
Screenplay by Paul Wheeler
Photographed in DeLuxe Color by Sven Nykvist
Music by Jerry Goldsmith
97 minutes

Cast: Sean Connery, Ian McShane, Norman Bristow, John Cording, Isabel Dean, William Fox, Richard Hampton, Robert Harris, Harry Landis, Preston Lockwood, James Maxwell, John Quentin, Jeffry Wickham

When a British ambassador and his staff are held hostage by terrorists in Norway, a Norwegian security officer (Sean Connery) is assigned to the case. The British government complies with the demand to free jailed terrorists in London, but the Norwegian government is reluctant to provide safe conduct for the culprits out of Norway. The security officer is instructed to bring the terrorists in but to avoid bloodshed. He finds it impossible to obey the order and ends up killing all the terrorists. Good location work, but a muddled telling of the tale.

Madeleine Kahn and Gene Wilder in *The Adventures of Sherlock Holmes' Smarter Brother*.

Burt Reynolds and Cybill Shepherd in *At Long Last Love*.

Bobby Benson, Burt Reynolds, Liza Minnelli, and Gene Hackman in *Lucky Lady*.

Oliver Reed, Richard Chamberlain, Michael York, and Frank Finlay in *The Four Musketeers*.

Gene Hackman and Bernard Fresson (right) in *French Connection II*.

Ben Gazzara as *Capone*.

Warren Oates and Peter Fonda, with Lara Parker at the window, in *Race With the Devil*.

Tim Curry, Little Nell, Patricia Quinn, and Richard O'Brien in *The Rocky Horror Picture Show*. Curry is the one with the garter belt.

Burt Reynolds in *W. W. and the Dixie Dancekings,* introducing Jerry Reed, Don Williams, James Hampton, Conny Van Dyke, and Richard Hurst.

W. W. AND THE DIXIE DANCEKINGS

Produced by Stanley S. Canter
Directed by John G. Avildsen
Screenplay by Thomas Richman
Photographed in Color by Jim Crabe
Music by Dave Grusin
94 minutes

Cast: Burt Reynolds, Conny Van Dyke, Jerry Reed, Ned Beatty, James Hampton, Don Williams, Richard D. Hurst, Mel Tillis, Furry Lewis, Sherman G. Lloyd, Mort Marshall

A charmingly glib Southern con man (Burt Reynolds) of the 1950's takes over a third-rate country music act, headed by a girl named Dixie (Conny Van Dyke) and hustles them into becoming good enough to crack the Grand Old Opry in Nashville. The con man also robs gasoline stations to spite an oil company that once treated him badly, and usually hands back a part of the take to the station attendants. He's a Dixie Robin Hood—and the role fits Burt Reynolds like a glove. The film also benefits from a number of top country stars playing parts, particularly Jerry Reid as Dixie's top performer, and the 82-year-old Beale Street blues singer Furry Lewis. Adding to the amusement is Ned Beatty's portrait of a country superstar who has slickly managed himself into a corporation.

WHIFFS

Produced by George Barrie
Direcetd by Ted Post
Screenplay by Malcolm Marmorstein
Photographed in DeLuxe Color by David Walsh
Songs by Sammy Cahn
Music by John Cameron
90 minutes

Cast: Elliott Gould, Eddie Albert, Harry Guardino, Godfrey Cambridge, Jennifer O'Neill, Alan Manson, Donald Barry, Richard Masur, Howard Hesseman

A service comedy, attempting to satirize the army's Chemical Corps experiments, with Elliot Gould as a willing guinea pig. After suffering the side effects of the tests, one of which is impotency, he gets his revenge by joining a crooked friend (Harry Guardino) and using gas to help them carry out robberies. They even gas a whole town in order to steal from two banks. The comedy fails to amuse because the subject matter, the use of chemical warfare, is too frightful to allow much laughter.

ALEX AND THE GYPSY

Produced by Richard Shepherd
Directed by John Korty
Screenplay by Lawrence B. Marcus, based on a novella by Stanley Elkins
Photographed in DeLuxe Color by Bill Butler
Music by Henry Mancini
106 minutes

Cast: Jack Lemmon, Genevieve Bujold, James Woods, Gino Ardito, Robert Emhardt, Tito Vandis, Bill Cort, Todd Martin, Frank Doubleday, Joseph X. Flaherty

An embittered and aging bailbondsman (Jack Lemmon) bails out a gypsy girl (Genevieve Bujold) for assaulting her lover. He is motivated by the fact that she had jilted him in the past and that he still has a yen for her, even though they are temperamentally mismatched and quarrel when together. He takes her home and makes love to her, while also keeping her prisoner so she will not jump bail. She tries hard to escape because she knows that prison will crush her. He lets her escape only after meeting her lout of a lover, knowing that it will ruin his job, but that perhaps they will meet again. A sordid affair and none too convincing.

ALL THIS AND WORLD WAR II

Produced by Sandy Lieberson and Martin J. Machat
Directed by Susan Winslow
Research by Tony Palmer
Songs by John Lennon and Paul McCartney
Musical direction by Low Reizner
91 minutes

Artists: Ambrosia, Peter Gabriel, Helen Reddy, Boyd Wood, Leo Sayer, the Bee Gees, Henry Gross, Tina Turner, Frankie Laine, Bryan Ferry, David Essex, Elton John, Status Quo, the Brothers Johnson

An entertainment documentary, balancing a montage of clips from war films and newsreels with a great many songs of more recent vintage, particularly those of the Beatles. The images are edited to fit the music, with the lyrics forming a commentary, sometimes humorous and often touching. Not altogether successful, but an interesting venture.

THE BLUE BIRD

Produced by Paul Maslansky
Directed by George Cukor
Screenplay by Hugh Whitemore and Alfred Hayes, based on a novel by Maurice Maeterlinck
Photographed in DeLuxe Color by Freddie Young and Ionas Gritzus
Songs by Andrei Petrov and Tony Harrison
Musical direction by Irwin Kostal
99 minutes

Cast: Elizabeth Taylor, Jane Fonda, Ava Gardner, Cicely Tyson, Robert Morley, Harry Andrews, Todd Lookinland, Patsy Kensit, Will Geer, Mona Washbourne, George Cole, Richard Pearson

A reworking of Maeterlinck's fantasy, filmed as a Shirley Temple feature in 1940 without great success and done here as an American-Russian production with even less success. Taylor appears in two roles, principally as the mother of the children looking for the bluebird of happiness. On their trip the children visit the worlds of the Dead, the Night, the Forest, Luxury, and the Future. The visuals are impressive, but the telling is muddled and heavy-handed, rather than the light fantastic the story needs.

BREAKING POINT

Produced by Claude Heroux and Bob Clark
Directed by Bob Clark
Screenplay by Roger E. Swaybill and Stanley Mann
Photographed in DeLuxe Color by Marc Champion
Music by David McLey
92 minutes

Cast: Bo Svenson, Robert Culp, John Colicos, Belinda J. Montgomery, Stephen Young, Linda Sorenson, Jeffrey Lynas, Gerry Salsberg, Richard M. Davidson, Jonathan White, Alan McRae

A witness (Bo Svenson) to a gangland killing in Philadelphia does not get the police protection he was promised and moves his family to Toronto. But the villains still pursue him and draw him out into the open by shooting the boyfriend of his sister. Despite the attempts of a friendly police officer (Robert Culp) to help, the witness takes the law into his own hands to eradicate the opposition. Lots of car chases and much violence, and not much encouragement to those citizens thinking of vigilante action.

THE DUCHESS AND THE DIRTWATER FOX

Produced and directed by Melvin Frank
Screenplay by Melvin Frank, Barry Sandler, and Jack
   Rose, based on a story by Barry Sandler
Photographed in Panavision and DeLuxe Color by Joseph
   Biroc
Songs by Sammy Cahn and Melvin Frank
Music by Charles Fox
103 minutes

Cast: George Segal, Goldie Hawn, Conrad Janis, Thayer David, Jennifer Lee, Sid Gould, Pat Ast, E. J. Andre, Dick Farnsworth, Roy Jenson, Boy Hoy, Bennie Dobbins

The Duchess (Goldie Hawn) is a dance hall girl in the Wild West and the Dirtwater Fox (George Segal) is a gambler operating on more luck than skill. Although drawn to one another, they mostly bicker when together. They get involved with a group of Mormons making a trek, as well as stumbling into a Jewish wedding, and they undergo some rough adventures when they tie in with a band of outlaws. A knockabout comedy, pleasingly vulgar, with Hawn and Segal carrying the picture, and backed up with some fine Colorado scenery.

END OF THE GAME

Produced by Maximilian Schell and Arlene Sellers
Directed by Maximilian Schell
Screenplay by Friedrich Duerrenmatt, based on a novel by
   Friedrich Duerrenmatt
Photographed in DeLuxe Color by Ennio Guarnieri,
   Roberto Gerardi, and Klaus Koenig
Music by Ennio Morricone
103 minutes

Cast: Jon Voight, Jacqueline Bisset, Martin Ritt, Robert Shaw, Helmut Qualtinger, Gabriele Ferzetti, Rita Calderoni, Friedrich Duerrenmatt, Donald Sutherland

An existentialist murder mystery, mostly filmed during a Swiss winter, about a veteran police inspector (Martin Ritt) who never gives up in his attempts to nail a rich, crooked industrialist (Robert Shaw), who thirty years previously coolly killed the girl they both loved. The veteran's new assistant (Jon Voight) brings fresh enthusiasm and newer methods to the case. His previous assistant (Donald Sutherland) may also have been murdered by the industrialist, and the dead man's girl friend (Jacqueline Bisset) confuses everyone with her own attempts to solve the crime. Eventually the veteran gets his man on his own terms. A strange film, with the playing almost like that of a chess game.

FIGHTING MAD

Produced by Roger Corman
Directed by Jonathan Demme
Screenplay by Jonathan Demme
Photographed in DeLuxe Color by Michael Watkins
Music by Bruce Langharne
90 minutes

Cast: Peter Fonda, Lynn Lowry, John Doucette, Philip Carey, Scott Glen, Kathleen Miller, Harry Northup

A Southerner (Peter Fonda) living in the coal mining country becomes militant when a mining magnate (Philip Carey) buys up the land adjacent to that of his family and tries to get the family to sell. When they refuse, the magnate arranges for a brother and his wife to be killed in a car accident. The sheriff's office chooses not to take action, so the Southerner does. He conducts his own campaign to bring about the death of the magnate. The film is a good pitch for ecology, but wavers in its stand about the taking of the law into one's own hands.

I WILL . . . I WILL . . . FOR NOW

Produced by George Barrie
Directed by Norman Panama
Screenplay by Norman Panama and Albert E. Lewin
Photographed in Panavision and Technicolor by John A.
   Alonzo
Music by John Cameron
108 minutes

Cast: Elliott Gould, Diane Keaton, Paul Sorvino, Victoria Principal, Robert Alda, Warren Berlinger, Candy Clark, Madge Sinclair, Carmen Zapata

A comedy of contemporary (and confused) mores, about a man (Elliott Gould) trying to win back his liberated wife (Diane Keaton), and managing to get some agreement from her because of new, contract-type marriages. The couple are unhappy in their divorce, so another attempt is likely, except that their lawyer (Paul Sorvino), who draws up the contract, would like to have the ex-wife for himself. To iron out their problems, the couple go to a sex research institute in Santa Barbara, where, after multiple mix-ups, they agree to try marriage again. The comedic onslaught on marriage fails to allow any helpful conclusions, but contains enough pertinent comment on the man-woman war to draw a few laughs, albeit painful ones.

THE LAST HARD MEN

Produced by Walter Seltzer and Russell Thacher
Directed by Andrew V. McLaglen
Screenplay by Guerdon Trueblood, from a novel by
   Brian Garfield
Photographed in Panavision and DeLuxe Color by Duke
   Callaghan

Music by Jerry Goldsmith
103 minutes

Cast: Charlton Heston, James Coburn, Barbara Hershey, Jorge Rivero, Michael Parks, Larry Wilcox, Morgan Paull, Thalmus Rasulala, Bon Donner, John Quade

An outlaw (James Coburn) escapes from a chain gang in Arizona in 1909, takes six men with him, and goes after the retired sheriff (Charlton Heston) who was responsible for the death of his wife in the gun battle in which he was captured. The gang kidnap the man's daughter (Barbara Hershey) and use her, on the threat of gang rape, to draw him out into the open. The current sheriff (Michael Parks) subscribes to newer methods of criminology and it is the older methods of the veteran, who realizes his opponent has been in jail for a dozen years and knows only the old ways, who brings an end to the brutal adventure. An interesting Western, dealing with the last years of the vanishing Wild West and not giving in to any attempt to glamorize it.

MOTHER, JUGS AND SPEED

Produced by Peter Yates and Tom Mankiewicz
Directed by Peter Yates
Screenplay by Tom Mankiewicz, from a story by Stephen Manes and Tom Mankiewicz
Photographed in Panavision and DeLuxe Color by Ralph Woolsey
97 minutes

Cast: Bill Cosby, Raquel Welch, Harvey Keitel, Allen Garfield, Dick Butkus, L. Q. Jones, Bruce Davison, Larry Hagman, Milt Kamen

The adventure of an ambulance company in a big city, spotlighting three of the employees—the chief driver known as Mother (Bill Cosby), a beautiful nurse called, against her wishes, Jugs (Raquel Welch), and a slick operator known as Speed (Harvey Keitel). These hardboiled paramedics dash all over town, often careening at breakneck speed through traffic, and they come into contact with lots of weird characters as well as people in desperate need. Some of their encounters are comic, a few are tragic. The film wisely starts off with a warning that the company featured in the story bears no resemblance to any actual ambulance company. It is a reassuring piece of information.

MOVING VIOLATION

Produced by Julie Corman
Directed by Charles S. Dubin
Screenplay by David R. Osterhout and William Norton, from a story by David R. Osterhout
Photographed in DeLuxe Color by Charles Correll
Music by Don Peake
91 minutes

Cast: Stephen McHattie, Kay Lenz, Eddie Albert, Lonny Chapman, Will Geer, Jack Murdock, John S. Ragin, Dennis Redfield, Michael Ross Verona

A young couple (Stephen McHattie and Kay Lenz) accidentally witness a sheriff (Lonnie Chapman) murdering his deputy, at the behest of the town's most powerful citizen, an oil czar (Will Geer). To keep them moving, the sheriff lets it be known that the youngsters are underground terrorists and that they killed the deputy. From then until the time the youngsters can establish their innocence, the film is a marathon chase, with some amazing car stunt work, including collisions with buildings and oil derricks, and multiple flips and rolls. The drama is second to the superb unit direction of Barbara Peeters, with stunt coordination by Conrad Palmisano. In a film like this they deserve star billing.

NEXT STOP, GREENWICH VILLAGE

Produced by Paul Mazursky and Tony Ray
Directed by Paul Mazursky
Screenplay by Paul Mazursky
Photographed in color by Arthur Ornitz
Music by Bill Conti
109 minutes

Cast: Lenny Baker, Shelley Winters, Ellen Green, Lois Smith, Christopher Walken, Dori Brenner, Antonio Fargas, Lou Jacobi, Mike Kellin

An almost autobiographical trip by Paul Mazursky, detailing the adventures of a young Brooklyn man and his ambition to get into the theater. Mazursky calls him Larry Lapinsky (Lenny Baker) and among his other steps forward he manages to break away from his overly protective mother (Shelley Winters). Larry picks up money doing odds jobs, including working in a health bar, while studying acting in an off-Broadway theater. Eventually Larry gets a break when a Hollywood director chooses him for a small part in a picture. Mazursky's film is a loving look-back to Greenwich Village in the early Fifties, to a seemingly less cynical and more generous time, and his recollection takes in a wide variety of people, some amusing and a few desperate. An excellent evocation of a time and place.

THE OMEN

Produced by Harvey Bernhard
Directed by Richard Donner
Screenplay by David Seltzer
Photographed in Panavision and DeLuxe Color by Gil Taylor
Music by Jerry Goldsmith
111 minutes

Cast: Gregory Peck, Lee Remick, David Warner, Billie Whitelaw, Leo McKern, Harvey Stephens, Patrick

Jack Lemmon and Genevieve Bujold in *Alex and the Gypsy*.

Dom DeLuise, Marty Feldman, and Mel Brooks in *Silent Movie*.

Todd Lookinland, Elizabeth Taylor, and Patsy Kensit in *The Blue Bird*.

I Will, I Will . . . For Now, with Diane Keaton and Elliott Gould.

Charlton Heston and Michael Parks in *The Last Hard Men*.

Bill Cosby, Raquel Welch and Harvey Keitel in *Mother, Jugs and Speed*.

Lenny Baker and Ellen Greene in *Next Stop, Greenwich Village*.

Troughton, Anthony Nicholls, Martin Benson, Sheila Raynor, Holly Palance

The American ambassador to Great Britain (Gregory Peck) and his wife (Lee Remick) are beset by strange happenings as their five-year-old son Damien (Harvey Stephens) becomes more difficult to handle. He is, in fact, not their child, but a substitute made when their own died at birth. His nanny hangs herself and a replacement (Billie Whitelaw) turns out to be an agent of the devil. A photographer friend (David Warner) sees things in his photos which the eye cannot and it gradually becomes apparent that the boy is himself a devil's manifestation, an anti-Christ. The father seeks advice from a learned exorcist (Leo McKern), who tells him he must kill the boy. But the boy is rescued by the police and it is the father who dies. The slight smile on the face of the boy at the funeral implies that there is more to come. A superb entry in the fantasy-horror genre, with a score by Jerry Goldsmith that chillingly adds to the disturbing ambiance of the film.

SILENT MOVIE

Produced by Michael Hertzberg
Directed by Mel Brooks
Screenplay by Mel Brooks, Ron Clark, Rudy DeLuca, and Barry Levinson, from a story by Ron Clark
Photographed in DeLuxe Color by Paul Lohmann
Music by John Morris
86 minutes

Cast: Mel Brooks, Marty Feldman, Dom DeLuise, Bernadette Peters, Sid Caesar, Harold Gould, Ron Carey, Carol Arthur, Liam Dunn, Fritz Feld, Chuck McCann, Valerie Curtin, Yvonne Wilder, Anne Bancroft

As its title tells—a silent movie, except for a delightful musical score by John Morris which carries the picture from start to finish. Director Mel Brooks plays a has-been contemporary director who goes to the head of a studio (Sid Caesar) with what he thinks is a brilliant idea for a movie—to make it silent. This he feels will save the studio from being taken over by a conglomerate. Incredibly it does, but only after a barrage of sight gags and comic misadventures. Among the highlights: a sequence with Paul Newman being chased in a wheelchair, and Anne Bancroft doing a wild tango with Brooks in a nightclub. Plus some antics that may remind movie buffs of The Three Stooges.

SILVER STREAK

Produced by Thomas L. Miller and Edward K. Milkis
Directed by Arthur Hiller
Screenplay by Colin Higgins
Photographed in DeLuxe Color by David Walsh
Music by Henry Mancini
113 minutes

Cast: Gene Wilder, Jill Clayburgh, Richard Pryor, Patrick McGoohan, Ned Beatty, Clifton James, Ray Walston, Stefan Gierasch, Len Birman, Valerie Curtin, Richard Kiel

A mild-mannered book executive (Gene Wilder) boards the train for Chicago in Los Angeles, looking forward to a restful trip—and gets anything but. He romances a secretary (Jill Clayburgh) to an art specialist, but is appalled to see the specialist drop from the train. It seems the gentleman carried evidence that would expose a gang of art forgers, led by a smooth crook (Patrick McGoohan), who sets about eliminating the book executive once he realizes he is a witness. The executive is several times dumped from the train, but chases it either by car or plane. By the time the train crashes in the terminal in Chicago, the villains have been accounted for and the audience has enjoyed a frantic and amusing trip, largely because of Wilder's ability to convey a comically manic sense of frustration.

SKY RIDERS

Produced by Terry Morse, Jr.
Directed by Douglas Hickox
Screenplay by Jack DeWitt, Stanley Mann, and Garry Michael Whit
Phtographed in Todd-AO and DeLuxe Color by Ousama Rawi, Greg McGillivray, and Jim Freeman
Music by Lalo Schifrin
91 minutes

Cast: James Coburn, Susannah York, Robert Culp, Charles Aznavour, Werner Pochath, Zou Zou, Kenneth Griffith, Harry Andrews, John Beck, Ernie Orsatti, Steven Keats, Henry Brown

An American pilot (James Coburn) living in Athens agrees to undertake a rescue mission when he learns that his ex-wife (Susannah York) and her two children by her rich American industrialist husband (Robert Culp) have been captured by terrorists. They are being held in an abandoned monastery, high atop a mountain peak in Greece. The pilot organizes a team of hang glider experts, raids the monastery, and carries off the wife and children, with himself clinging to one of the enemy's helicopters. Almost a third of the running time of the film is concerned with the rescue operation, spectacularly filmed in the Greek mountains and involving beautiful shots of the hang gliders. This fine sequence was under the supervision of Bob Wills and Chris Wills and it alone is worth the price of admission.

20TH CENTURY-FOX ACADEMY AWARDS FOR 1976

JERRY GOLDSMITH: Best original score, *The Omen.*

Goldie Hawn and George Segal in *The Duchess and the Dirtwater Fox.*

Gregory Peck, Harvey Stephens, and Lee Remick in *The Omen.*

James Coburn in *Sky Riders.*

Jill Clayburgh, Gene Wilder, and Richard Pryor in *Silver Streak.*

417

DAMNATION ALLEY

Produced by Jerome M. Zeitman and Paul Maslansky
Directed by Jack Smight
Screenplay by Alan Sharp and Lukas Heller
Photographed in color by Harry Stradling, Jr.
Music by Jerry Goldsmith
95 minutes

Cast: Jan-Michael Vincent, George Peppard, Dominique Sanda, Paul Winfield, Jackie Earle Haley, Kip Niven, Robert Donner, Seamon Glass, Trent Dolan, Mark L. Taylor, Bob Hackman

A frightening look into the future—assuming that the future will lead to a war of apocalyptic, atomic proportions. When the enemy forces blast America, they destroy almost everything about the country, wiping out most of the population and leaving only a few straggling survivors. The nuclear ravages of the earth upset the balance of nature and a wandering group (Jan-Michael Vincent, George Peppard, Dominique Sanda, and Paul Winfield) come across cockroaches grown to giant proportions and eager for human flesh. One of the party (Winfield) becomes a meal for the cockroaches. The film presents a slim plot, but excels in its technical effects of the awesome atomic explosions and devastation and the special microphotography of Ken Middlesham of the monstrous insects, which should give pause for any possible use of atomic weapons.

DOWN THE ANCIENT STAIRS

Produced by Fulvio Lucisano
Directed by Mauro Bolognini
Screenplay by Raffaele Andreassi, Mario Arosio, Tullio Pinelli, and Bernardion Zapponi, based on the novel by Mario Tobino
Photographed by Ennio Guarnieri
109 minutes

Cast: Marcello Mastroianni, Francoise Fabian, Marthe Keller, Barbara Bouchet, Pierre Blaise, Lucia Bose, Adriana Asti, Silvano Tranquilli, Charles Fawcett

The setting is an insane asylum in Tuscany in 1930, and Marcello Mastroianni is a dedicated doctor, so wrapped up in his studies of mental disorders that he has not left the premises in eight years. The doctor lives in fear of his own sanity, but makes life agreeable for himself by having affairs with his assistant (Marthe Keller), the wife (Lucia Bose) of the superintendent, and the wife (Barbara Bouchet) of a colleague. When another lady doctor (Francoise Fabian) comes to the asylum to further her studies, the amorous Marcello is dismayed to find that she is not interested in joining his harem. The film proffers the familiar question: are those in an asylum any more mad than those in the world at large?

FIRE SALE

Produced by Marvin Worth
Directed by Alan Arkin
Screenplay by Robert Klane
Photographed in DeLuxe Color by Ralph Woolsey
Music by Dave Grusin
87 minutes

Cast: Alan Arkin, Rob Reiner, Vincent Gardenia, Anjanette Comer, Kay Medford, Barbara Dana, Sid Caesar, Alex Rocco, Byron Stewart, Oliver Clark, Bill Bogert, Richard Libertini, MacIntyre Dixon, John Batiste

A wildly black comedy about an eccentric family who own a down-at-heels department store. Father (Vincent Gardenia) runs the place, as his wife (Kay Medford) brings her nagging presence to bear, and a son (Rob Reiner) tries his lame best to act as his father's assistant. Another son (Alan Arkin) is a not very successful basketball coach, who adopts a black teenager (Byron Stewart), partly because he needs him on his team and partly because his wife (Anjanette Comer) wants a child. Finally the family bring in a war-demented uncle (Sir Caesar) to burn down the store for the insurance money, telling him that the place is a Nazi headquarters. The film has its moments, but the direction, and intent, wavers.

HIGH ANXIETY

Produced and directed by Mel Brooks
Screenplay by Mel Brooks, Ron Clark, Rudy DeLuca, and Barry Levinson

Photographed in DeLuxe Color by Paul Lohmann
Music by John Morris
94 minutes

Cast: Mel Brooks, Madeline Kahn, Cloris Leachman, Harvey Korman, Ron Carey, Howard Morris, Dick Van Patten, Jack Riley, Ron Clark, Rudy DeLuca, Barry Levinson

An affectionate Hitchcockian send-up, with producer-director-writer-star Mel Brooks as a psychiatrist (with a great fear of heights), who takes over as head of the Psycho-Neurotic Institute for the Very, Very Nervous after the previous director is found dead under strange circumstances. His presence is resented by the assistant director (Harvey Korman) and the head nurse (Cloris Leachman) because he may find out about their business in capitalizing on their patients and bilking their families. The film parodies a raft of Hitchcock sequences, even the shower scene from *Psycho,* with Brooks doing a role that Cary Grant would have done had the film not been a spoof. A delight for students of Hitchcock and everybody else.

JULIA

Produced by Richard Roth
Directed by Fred Zinnemann
Screenplay by Alvin Sargent, based on a story by Lillian Hellman
Photographed in Technicolor by Douglas Slocombe
Music by Georges Delerue
124 minutes

Cast: Jane Fonda, Vanessa Redgrave, Jason Robards, Maximilian Schell, Hal Holbrook, Rosemary Murphy, Meryl Streep, Dora Doll, Elisabeth Mortensen, John Glover

The story of two friends—based upon author Lillian Hellman's own experiences—a daughter (Vanessa Redgrave) of wealthy circumstances, who rejects her background in order to be a political activist in the Europe of the 1930's, and a writer (Jane Fonda), who is coached by her lover, Dashiell Hammett (Jason Robards), and who learns about life in the wake of her friend. When the writer visits Julia (Redgrave) in Germany, she sees that Julia has selflessly devoted herself to fighting Nazism, causing herself bodily harm and eventually costing her her life. As she observes the heroism she also recalls their idyllic times together as children. A fascinating study of two remarkable women, beautifully played by Fonda and Redgrave and directed with great style and taste by Fred Zinnemann.

MR. BILLION

Produced by Steven Bach and Ken Friedman
Directed by Jonathan Kaplan
Screenplay by Ken Friedman and Jonathan Kaplan

Photographed in DeLuxe Color by Matthew F. Leonetti
Music by Dave Grusin
94 minutes

Cast: Terence Hill, Valerie Perrine, Jackie Gleason, Slim Pickens, William Redfield, Chill Wills, Dick Miller, R. G. Armstrong, Dave Cass, Sam Laws, Johnny Ray McGhee

An Italian auto mechanic (Terence Hill) inherits a billion-dollar fortune from his uncle in San Francisco, with the stipulation that he must turn up in the city within a certain time to make his claim. A smooth operator of the uncle's estate (Jackie Gleason) moves to keep the nephew from making the date, in order that he can acquire the fortune himself. He hires a number of people to intercept the Italian as he makes his way across he U.S., including a lovely blonde (Valerie Perrine), who falls in love with him. Together they survive the hurdles, including a fine chase sequence in the Grand Canyon, and once the young man receives his money, he decides to turn over the assets to the people who have helped him—à la Frank Capra's Mr. Deeds. An amusing trip, with some fine scenery along the way.

THE OTHER SIDE OF MIDNIGHT

Produced by Frank Yablans
Directed by Charles Jarrott
Screenplay by Herman Raucher and Daniel Taradash, based on a novel by Sidney Sheldon
Photographed in DeLuxe Color and Panavision by Fred J. Koenekamp
Music by Michel Legrand
165 minutes

Cast: Marie France Pisier, John Beck, Susan Sarandon, Raf Vallone, Clu Gulager, Christian Marquand, Michael Lerner, Sorrell Booke, Antony Ponzini, Louis Zorich

A lush and glossy melodrama of passion, betrayal, and revenge, spanning the years 1939 to 1947, and tracing the lives of a wartime aviator (John Beck) and the Parisian girl (Marie France Pisier) he loves and abandons. Enraptured with him, she is bitterly hurt when he does not return. He goes on to success as a war hero and afterwards as a commercial pilot, and she becomes a top French movie star and marries a greatly wealthy Greek (Raf Vallone). She degrades her ex-lover by causing him to lose all his jobs and then hires him as her personal pilot, which causes growing resentment from his wife (Susan Sarandon). The pilot and the star fall in love all over again and plan the murder of the wife. But the wife and the Greek husband have their own plans. The film is soap opera, but given rich treatment.

RAGGEDY ANN AND ANDY

Produced by Richard Horner and Lester Osterman

419

Directed by Richard Williams
Screenplay by Patricia Thackray and Max Wilk, based
   on original stories by Johnny Gruelle
Photographed in Panavision and color by Al Rezek
Songs by Joe Rapos
85 minutes

Cast: Claire Williams. *Voices:* Didi Conn, Mark Baker,
Fred Stuthman, Niki Flacks, George S. Irving, Arnold
Stang, Joe Silver, Alan Sues, Marty Brill, Paul Dooley

An animated film, with Claire Williams as the only
human figure and as the six-year-old girl whose play-
room comes alive when she reads stories and her dolls
become involved in adventures. Chief among the dolls
are Raggedy Ann and Andy. Also on hand are the
Loony Knight, the Camel with Wrinkled Knees, and
a greedy monster that eats anything. A cheerful and
charming film for children.

STAR WARS

Produced by Gary Kurtz
Directed and written by George Lucas
Photographed in Panavision and Technicolor by Gilbert
   Taylor
Music by John Williams
125 minutes

Cast: Mark Hamill, Harrison Ford, Carrie Fisher, Peter
Cushing, Alec Guinness, Anthony Daniels, Kenny Baker,
Peter Mayhew, David Prowse, Phil Brown, Shelagh
Fraser, Jack Purvis

Star Wars made movie history when it became the
biggest-grossing film of all time and launched a myriad
of merchandising possibilities. Aside from the staggering statistics, the film was an updated science-fiction
adventure serial, greatly helped by astounding special
effects and a warm affection for the old movies. Luke
Sykwalker (Mark Hamill) hankers to break away
from the everyday chores of his uncle's farm on the
planet Tatooine. A robot, Artoo Detoo (Kenny Baker),
accidentally plays back a videotaped message from
Princess Leia (Carrie Fisher) which is important to
the rebel forces fighting the malevolent Imperial Forces,
who want to control the galaxy. Luke meets an old
Jeddi warrior, Ben (Obi-Wan) Kenobi (Alec Guinness) who leads him off into the galaxies far, far
away. On their way to rescue Princess Leia, who is
held hostage by the evil Grand Moff Tarkin (Peter
Cushing), they join forces with mercenary Han Solo
(Harrison Ford) and his hirsute, grunting partner,
Chewbacca, a Wookie (Peter Mayhew). After a thrill-
ing rescue from the Death Star, Luke falls in love with
Leia. Although Obi-Wan is killed in a laser-sword fight
with the dark-helmeted Darth Vader (David Prowse
and the voice of James Earl Jones), he imparts the concept of "the Force" to Luke, who uses it to overcome
all evil and finally destroy the Death Star along with

the ambitions of the Imperial Forces. Darth Vader,
though, hurtles off into space to be heard from again
in *Star Wars II*. Not only did the film open up new
vistas for science-fiction fans, its success meant that
many producers would follow in a genre that had
been all but forgotten by the studios.

SUSPIRIA

Produced by Claudio Argento
Directed by Dario Argento
Screenplay by Dario Argento
Photographed in Technicolor by Luciano Tovoli
Music by The Goblins and Dario Argento
93 minutes

Cast: Jessica Harper, Stefania Casini, Joan Bennett, Alida
Valli, Flavio Bucci, Miguel Bose, Barbara Magnolfi,
Susanna Javicoli, Eva Axen, Rudolf Schundler, Udo Kier

A Grand Guignol entry, about an American girl
(Jessica Harper) who enrolls in a German dancing
academy and finds it to be a weird place. On the stormy
night that she arrives, two students are brutally murdered, and as time goes by it appears that the academy
is the home of a coven of witches. The story is ludicrous, but the visual effects are shockingly good. A
nightmare for those who enjoy them.

3 WOMEN

Produced and directed by Robert Altman
Screenplay by Robert Altman
Photographed in Panavision and DeLuxe Color by Chuck
   Rosher
Music by Gerald Busby
124 minutes

Cast: Shelley Duvall, Cissy Spacek, Janice Rule, Robert
Fortier, Ruth Nelson, John Cromwell, Sierra Pecheur,
Craig Richard Nelson

The women of the title are an attendant (Shelley
Duvall) in an old folks sanitarium in the desert, a
new member of the staff (Cissy Spacek), and a painter
(Janice Rule), who never speaks but puts her thoughts
into her murals, while also being pregnant and married
to a philandering ex-stuntman (Robert Fortier). Altman's film is a study, somewhat Ingmar Bergman-like,
of these woman, and especially of the first two, as the
newcomer develops a crush on the attendant and tries
to emulate her in every way. Eventually she comes to
believe she is the girl. A story of psychological dependence and transference, with much fascinating
imagery, the film requires patience and absorption to
understand its meanings.

THUNDER AND LIGHTNING

Produced by Roger Corman
Directed by Corey Allen

Screenplay by William Hjortsberg
Photographed in DeLuxe Color by James Pergola
Music by Andy Stein
94 minutes

Cast: David Carradine, Kate Jackson, Roger C. Carmel, Stirling Holloway, Ed Barth, Ron Feinberg, George Murdock, Pat Cranshaw, Charles Napier, Hope Pomerance

Once again the cameras focus on the Deep South and the conflict between the law and the manufacturers of illegal whiskey. The law gets short shrift as a young man (David Carradine) enthusiastically competes with his girl friend's father (Roger C. Carmel) to see which one can produce the most and get it by the revenue men, and also stay out of the clutches of the syndicate. The girl friend (Kate Jackson) enjoys sticking by her man as they are chased by the cops. The plot is familiar. What gives the film its kicks is the daring stunt work, in which cars hurtle along streets and speed boats flash across the surfaces of the Everglades. A stunt man's dream.

THE TURNING POINT

Produced by Herbert Ross and Arthur Laurents
Directed by Herbert Ross
Screenplay by Arthur Laurents
Photographed in DeLuxe Color by Robert Surtees
Music by John Lanchbery
119 minutes

Cast: Anne Bancroft, Shirley MacLaine, Tom Skerritt, Mikhail Baryshnikov, Leslie Browne, Martha Scott, Antoinette Sibley, Alexandra Danilova, Marshall Thompson, Anthony Zerbe

A study of two women, both ballet colleagues when young, who elect to go different ways. One (Shirley MacLaine) gives it all up and becomes a wife and mother in a small town. The other (Anne Bancroft) goes on to become a major ballerina. They meet after years of not seeing each other and mentally compare notes: the ballerina regrets her aging and her lack of family, and the mother regrets missing the chance at artistic satisfaction she might have had. The subtle conflict between the two women builds up when the daughter (Leslie Browne) decides on a career in ballet and the ballerina takes a motherly interest in her. But the daughter can take care of herself, including having a romance with a virile young Russian dancer (Mikhail Baryshnikov). The tension between the two women finally leads to a fight, in which they pound each other but end up in laughter as they realize how ridiculous it all is. *The Turning Point* is a double winner—as an appealing look at the world of ballet and as a look at the human comedy, particularly from the female side.

Mel Brooks in *High Anxiety*.

Damnation Alley, with Jackie Earle Haley, Dominique Sanda, Jan-Michael Vincent, and George Peppard.

Jane Fonda and Vanessa Redgrave in *Julia*.

John Beck, Charles Cioffi, and Marie-France Pisier in *The Other Side of Midnight*.

Shirley MacLaine and Anne Bancroft in *The Turning Point*.

WIZARDS

Produced and directed by Ralph Bakshi
Screenplay by Ralph Bakshi
Photographed in DeLuxe Color by Ted C. Bemiller
Music by Andrew Belling
80 minutes

Cast: (voices) Bob Holt, Jesse Wells, Richard Romanus, David Proval, James Connell, Steve Gravers, Barbara Slone, Angelo Grisanti, Hyman Wien, Christopher Tayback

Gene Wilder and Carol Kane in *The World's Greatest Lover.*

Mark Hamill, Carrie Fisher, and Harrison Ford, with Chewbacca, in *Star Wars.*

An animated fantasy-adventure, set in the future, dealing with the conflict between technology and the spirit. The conflict concerns a genial old wizard who tries to halt the warlike schemes of his evil brother. The wizard's side consists of elves and goblins and the brother's mad war figures are those of Hitler and the Nazis. Ralph Bakshi's visual fable is enjoyable, but somewhat lacking the punch the allegory needs.

THE WORLD'S GREATEST LOVER

Produced and directed by Gene Wilder
Screenplay by Gene Wilder
Photographed in DeLuxe Color by Gerald Hirschfeld
Music by John Morris
89 minutes

Cast: Gene Wilder, Carol Kane, Dom DeLuise, Fritz Feld, Carl Balantine, Matt Collins, Josip Elic, James Gleason, Ronny Graham, David Huddleston, Billy Sands, Gustaf Unger

A spoof on the Hollywood of the 1920's, with Gene Wilder as a fellow named Rudy Valentine, who comes to the Rainbow Studio—and its manic head of production (Dom DeLuise)—to compete in a Rudolph Valentino look-alike contest. His wife (Carol Kane) is a Valentino fan and goes to Paramount in the hope of seeing the great lover. Rudy, eager to please his wife, actually meets Valentino and gets some tips from him —and impersonates him on the set of *The Sheik*. The wife is enthralled, but poor Rudy can't go through with his own screen test because he is so tense and confused. Gene Wilder's film is too diffused in its attitudes, with its fantasy not really defined, but it has some fine moments, particularly the screen test sequence, with Ronny Graham as a director on the verge of madness after doing hundreds of the same test in order to find another Valentino.

20TH CENTURY-FOX ACADEMY AWARDS FOR 1977

ALVIN SARGENT: Best adapted screenplay, *Julia*.

JOHN BARRY, NORMAN REYNOLDS, LESLIE DILLEY: Best art direction, *Star Wars*.

ROGER CHRISTIAN: Best set decoration, *Star Wars*.

JOHN MOLLO: Best costume design, *Star Wars*.

DON MACDOUGALL, RAY WEST, BOB MINKLER, DEREK BALL: Best sound, *Star Wars*.

PAUL HIRSCH, MARCIA LUCAS, RICHARD CHEW: Best editing, *Star Wars*.

JOHN STEARS, JOHN DYKSTRA, RICHARD EDLUND, GRANT MCCUNE, ROBERT BLALACK: Best visual effects, *Star Wars*.

JOHN WILLIAMS: Best original score, *Star Wars*.

BENJAMIN BURTT, JR.: Special achievement award for sound effects creation, *Star Wars*.

AN UNMARRIED WOMAN

Produced by Paul Mazursky and Tony Ray
Directed by Paul Mazursky
Screenplay by Paul Mazursky
Photographed in Movielab/Color by Arthur Ornitz
Music by Bill Conti
124 minutes

Cast: Jill Clayburgh, Alan Bates, Michael Murphy, Cliff Gorman, Pat Quinn, Kelly Bishop, Lisa Lucas, Linda Miller, Andrew Duncan, Daniel Seltzer, Penelope Russianoff, Paul Mazursky, Ultra Violet

An uncompromising look at the problems of contemporary women, with Jill Clayburgh as a wife who believes she is happy with her lot until her husband (Michael Murphy) tells her he has another girl and wants a divorce. Her comfortable Manhattan life with a fifteen-year-old daughter (Lisa Lucas) undergoes rough transitions. At first turned off by men, her loneliness leads her to date, and then to an affair with an English painter (Alan Bates). He is a tender and loving man, but there is no doubt that his work is foremost in his life and that the girl is secondary. She knows that she must go on alone, but by now she is stronger in her confidence. Paul Mazursky's film is an honest account of a common dilemma and Clayburgh's grasp of the role conveys all the pain and confusion and growing awareness of a woman being forced to find a new lifestyle.

THE BOYS FROM BRAZIL

Produced by Martin Richards and Stanley O'Toole
Directed by Franklin J. Schaffner
Screenplay by Heywood Gould, from a novel by Ira Levin
Photographed in DeLuxe Color by Henri Decae
Music by Jerry Goldsmith
123 minutes

Cast: Gregory Peck, Laurence Olivier, James Mason, Lilli Palmer, Uta Hagen, Steven Guttenberg, Denholm Elliott, Rosemary Harris, John Dehner, John Rubinstein, Anne Meara, Jeremy Black

From his home in the jungle of Paraguay, a doctor (Gregory Peck) who was once an infamous experimentalist at Auschwitz, works on his plans to perfect human duplication, or cloning. He is a leader in a Fourth Reich scheme to clone Hitlers throughout the world. News of this plan comes to the attention of a dedicated Nazi hunter, an elderly Jew (Laurence Olivier) living in Vienna, who pieces together the neo-Nazi plot, which requires the death of ninety-four men of the same age. He travels around and interviews the widows of several men who have been killed and finds that each has a son (Jeremy Black) who is identical to the others. Each is, in fact, a clone of Hitler. The Nazi hunter probes until he causes the scheme to go awry, and brings about a meeting between himself and the doctor. The doctor meets a ghastly end. The film is a brilliant and bizarre espionage story, with riveting performances from Peck and Olivier, and excellent use of European and American locations.

DAMIEN—OMEN II

Produced by Harvey Bernhard
Directed by Don Taylor
Screenplay by Stanley Mann and Michael Hodges
Photographed in Panavision and DeLuxe Color by Bill Butler
Music by Jerry Goldsmith
109 minutes

Cast: William Holden, Lee Grant, Jonathan Scott-Taylor, Robert Foxworth, Nicholas Pryor, Lew Ayres, Sylvia Sidney, Lance Henriksen, Elizabeth Shepherd, Lucas Donat, Alan Arbus

In this sequel to *The Omen,* Damien (Jonathan Scott-Taylor) is a thirteen-year-old cadet at a military academy when not at the home of his rich uncle (William Holden) and aunt (Lee Grant). Damien's protector is a large raven and when an elderly aunt (Sylvia Sidney) begins to suspect that the boy is abnormal, the raven scares her to death. It also picks out the eyes of a reporter (Elizabeth Shepherd) who knows that Damien is an anti-Christ. Several others die ghastly deaths, until even his uncle and aunt have to be gotten rid of, leaving the way for an evil businessman (Robert Foxworth) to take over the uncle's industrial empire and help the Devil's work. The film is far less disturbing than the original, but potent enough in

Lee Grant, William Holden, Jonathan Scott-Taylor, and Lucas Donat in *Damien—Omen II*.

Alan Bates and Jill Clayburgh in *An Unmarried Woman*.

Sir Laurence Olivier and Gregory Peck in *The Boys From Brazil*.

its grisly impact to suggest that Damien's story has not yet ended.

THE DRIVER

Produced by Lawrence Gordon
Directed by Walter Hill
Screenplay by Walter Hill
Photographed in DeLuxe Color by Philip Lathrop
Music by Michael Small
91 minutes

Cast: Ryan O'Neal, Bruce Dern, Isabelle Adjani, Ronee Blakeley, Matt Clark, Felice Orlandi, Joseph Walsh

Perhaps the finest film yet to feature stunt car driving, with a great deal of footage given to incredible feats on wheels (and a vast amount of burned rubber), but containing only a skimpy plot. The Driver is Ryan O'Neal and he is referred to only as such in the film —no one has names, only references, such as The Detective (Bruce Dern), a manic obsessive who is out to get The Driver at all costs. The Driver is a skilled getaway man for a group of big-time crooks and he enjoys taunting the police, even to the point of leaving bits of evidence that will cause them to chase him. His girl friend is called The Player (Isabelle Adjani), because she's adept with cards, and his contact, who sets him up with his jobs, is The Connection (Ronee Blakeley). *The Driver* is really *The Big Chase*.

THE FURY

Produced by Frank Yablans
Directed by Brian DePalma
Screenplay by John Farris, based on his novel
Photographed in Panavision and DeLuxe Color by Richard H. Kline
Music by John Williams
118 minutes

Cast: Kirk Douglas, John Cassavetes, Carrie Snodgrass, Charles Durning, Amy Irving, Fiona Lewis, Andrew Stevens, Carol Rossen, William Finley, Rutanya Alda, Joyce Easton, Jane Lambert, Eleanor Merriam

While vacationing in Israel, the son (Andrew Stevens) of a U.S. government secret service agent (Kirk Douglas) is kidnapped by a former colleague (John Cassavetes), now working for some mysterious organization. The son has strange powers. He has psychokinesis and can cause physical objects to do his bidding by mind control. The enemy want his talents and in order to find him, the father recruits the services of a girl (Amy Irving) with similar powers, who takes him to an institute in Chicago where such powers are studied, and where the boy is being held prisoner. Since the boy is also being programmed for elimination, he causes horrible happenings to the people responsible. The film blends espionage with horror-fantasy, with splendid

Ryan O'Neal and Bruce Dern in *The Driver*.

photographic effects and a richly descriptive score by John Williams.

MAGIC

Produced by Joseph E. Levine and Richard P. Levine
Directed by Richard Attenborough
Screenplay by William Goldman
Photographed in Technicolor by Victor J. Kemper
Music by Jerry Goldsmith
106 minutes

Cast: Anthony Hopkins, Ann-Margret, Burgess Meredith, Ed Lauter, E. J. Andre, Jerry Hauser

A psychological thriller, about a failed magician (Anthony Hopkins), who finds he has a great talent for ventriloquism and with his dummy, called Fats, becomes a star. But he is a man with an insecure personality and the dummy gradually becomes the dominant member of the act. The dummy takes over the personality of the master. When he is offered a lucrative television contract, he declines because his insecurity has caused him to break down. His agent (Burgess Meredith) tries to persuade him and is murdered by his client when he discovers the extent of his psychosis. Master and dummy flee to his upstate New York home, where he romances a former childhood sweetheart (Ann-Margret), to the objection of her husband (Ed Lauter), which drives them all to disaster. *Magic* fails to completely convince in its bizarre story, but it has a fascinating aura of evil and an extraordinary performance from Hopkins.

A WEDDING

Produced and directed by Robert Altman
Screenplay by John Considine, Patricia Resnick, Alan Nicholls, and Robert Altman
Photograped in Panavision and DeLuxe Color by Charles Rosher
Musical direction by Tom Walls
124 minutes

Cast: Carol Burnett, Paul Dooley, Amy Stryker, Mia Farrow, Dennis Christopher, Gerald Busby, Peggy Ann Garner, Lillian Gish, Nina Van Pallandt, Vittorio Gassman, Desi Arnaz, Jr., Dina Merrill

The wedding is between the daughter (Amy Stryker) of a newly rich Southern family and the son (Desi Arnaz, Jr.) of an old-line wealthy Midwestern family. And it is a day of stress and strain and neurosis. Robert Altman's film is a tough satire on the ritualistic marriage ceremony in America, exposing its darker ingredients, such as greed, social climbing, hypocrisy, and sexual lust. The film has much humor and some pertinent criticism of certain aspects of contemporary life, but the view is perhaps too cynical and too indulgent on the part of Altman.

Kirk Douglas and Amy Irving in *The Fury.*

Vittorio Gassman, Desi Arnaz, Jr., and Carol Burnett in *A Wedding.*

Ann-Margret and Anthony Hopkins in *Magic.*

1979

ALIEN

Directed by Ridley Scott
Produced by Gordon Carroll, David Giler, and Walter Hill
Screenplay by Dan O'Bannon, from a story by Dan O'Bannon and Ronald Shusett
Photographed in Panavision and DeLuxe Color by Derek Vanlint
Music by Jerry Goldsmith
117 minutes

Cast: Tom Skerritt, Sigourney Weaver, Veronica Cartwright, Harry Dean Stanton, John Hurt, Ian Holm, Yaphet Kotto

In the far reaches of an outer galaxy, the space tug *Nostromo* is heading back to earth after gathering raw materials on foreign planets. The crew, commanded by Captain Dallas (Tom Skerritt), is in a state of interplanetary hibernation until a wake-up signal is given by the ship's computer system. A distress code, emanating from a nearby planet, brings a landing party down on a frozen and unfriendly environment. The search for the signal brings the explorers to a huge alien space ship inside which podlike creatures are being incubated. An overly anxious crew member, Kane (John Hurt), gets too close to the pods and one immediately attaches itself to his face, burning through the helmet. Brought back to the *Nostromo*, Kane lies comatose while the ship's scientist tries to remove the parasitic grip of the alien. However, the slimy, multi-limbed creature proves to be an almost insuperable foe. Through the bizarre and violently exciting events that follow, the alien develops in various stages and terrorizes the crew. Superb special effects and brilliantly effective outer world sets marked *Alien* as a diversion from the glut of benign science fiction movies. It provided audiences with a truly horrible and frightening embodiment of what might be found in outer space.

AVALANCHE EXPRESS

Produced and directed by Mark Robson
Screenplay by Abraham Polonsky, based on the novel by Colin Forbes
Photographed in Panavision and DeLuxe Color by Jack Cardiff
Music by Allyn Ferguson
88 minutes

Cast: Lee Marvin, Robert Shaw, Linda Evans, Maximillian Schell, Joe Namath, Horst Bucholz, Mike Connors, Claudia Cassinelli, David Hess

When the head of the KGB (Robert Shaw) defects, an American courier (Lee Marvin) is entrusted with bringing him safely to the West. The American's team (Linda Evans, Mike Connors, Joe Namath) is a part of his plan to take the Russian across Europe by train. A former aide of the defector (Maximillian Schell) sends out a network of agents to stop the train. However, the Americans use the opportunity to flush out all the Soviet operatives, even at risk to the defector's life. Fighting off attacks by snipers, terrorists, an avalanche and then the aide himself, the Americans succeed in getting the Russian onto a plane to Washington. Sadly, this was the last movie for Robert Shaw and director Mark Robson, both of whom died suddenly after filming.

BREAKING AWAY

Produced and directed by Peter Yates
Screenplay by Steve Tesich
Photographed in DeLuxe Color by Matthew F. Leonetti
Music adapted by Patrick Williams
100 minutes

Cast: Dennis Christopher, Dennis Quaid, Daniel Stern, Jackie Earle Haley, Barbara Barrie, Paul Dooley, Robyn Douglass, Hart Bochner, Amy Wright, Peter Maloney, John Ashton, Lisa Shure, Jennifer K. Mickel, Pamela Jayne Soles

A contemporary comedy centering on the lives of four male teenagers in Bloomington, Indiana, one of whom (Dennis Christopher) dreams of becoming an Italian motorcycle champion and annoys his family by assuming Italian mannerisms. Much of the film was shot on and around the campus of Indiana University. The four boys are in their first year of high school and drifting aimlessly, knowing only that they don't want to be separated. They begin to "break away" when the would-be Italian falls in love with sorority beauty (Robyn Douglass). This also infuriates the college crowd, which traditionally looks down on the local youths, whom they call "cutters." A tremendous brawl in the Student Union ensues. The film is highlighted by the staging of the famous Little 500 Bicycle Race, the social and sporting event of the academic year at Indiana University, which is won by the "cutters." Produced on a modest budget, *Breaking Away* proved to be a box-office surprise for the studio. The critics and the public responded warmly to its amusing and sympathetic depiction of the spirit and frustrations of modern youth.

BUTCH AND SUNDANCE: THE EARLY DAYS

Produced by Gabriel Katzka and Steven Bach
Directed by Richard Lester
Screenplay by Allan Burns, based on characters created by
    William Goldman
Photographed in DeLuxe Color by Laszlo Kovacs
Music by Patrick Williams
110 minutes

Cast: William Katt, Tom Berenger, Jeff Corey, John Schuck, Michael C. Gwynne, Peter Weller, Brian Dennehy, Chris Lloyd, Jill Eikenberry, Arthur Hill

Lee Marvin, Linda Evans and Mike Connors in *Avalanche Express.*

A scene from *Alien.*

Dennis Christopher, Jackie Earle Haley, Daniel Stern, and Dennis Quaid in *Breaking Away*.

A decade after Paul Newman and Robert Redford bit the dust at the end of the hugely successful *Butch Cassidy and the Sundance Kid,* the idea of a "prequel" seemed a viable project, and so, *Butch and Sundance: The Early Days.* Horse thief Cassidy (Tom Berenger) is paroled from a Wyoming prison, agreeing to commit no further crimes in that state. During his wanderings, he meets the Sundance Kid (William Katt) during a shootout in a saloon. The pair become immediate friends and make the saloon their first venture into crime together. However, a disgruntled member of their gang (Brian Dennehy) pursues them everywhere and seriously wounds Sundance. Then Butch tries to go straight and takes a job as a butcher, but the same man comes after him. The pair realize they will have to leave town, and they set out to rob a train. Although the heist is pulled off, the money boxes burst open and most of it is lost. Then they head off to further adventures. A gently satirical view of the old west which punctures the myths of heroism, but the biggest problem is how do you live up to Newman and Redford?

DREAMER

Produced by Michael Lobell
Directed by Noel Nosseck
Screenplay by James Proctor and Larry Bischof
Photographed in DeLuxe Color by Bruce Surtees
Music by Bill Conti
90 minutes

Cast: Tim Matheson, Susan Blakely, Jack Warden, Richard B. Shull, Barbara Stuart, Owen Bush, Marya Small, Matt Clark, John Crawford, Chris Schenkel

An assistant manager of a bowling alley in the midwest (Tim Matheson) dreams of entering the Tournament of Champions and is encouraged by an aging ex-pro bowler (Jack Warden). The dreamer's girlfriend (Susan Blakely) is more interested in settling down than touring, and thinks the old man is pushing to make the dreamer the champion he never was. After winning a preliminary match, the young man finds out that his friend is dying of a heart attack and presents his trophy to him. The girlfriend becomes more understanding and travels with the dreamer to support him and help him achieve his goals. After a gruelling championship match, he finally wins the $25,000 top prize and they buy a bowling alley, which they name for the old man. An unpretentious movie which aspires to be another *Rocky* but never quite knocks down all the pins.

LUNA

Produced by Giovanni Bertolucci
Directed by Bernardo Bertolucci
Screenplay by Giuseppe Bertolucci, Clare Peploe, Bernardo Bertolucci, English adaptation by George Malko
Photographed in color by Vittorio Storaro
139 minutes

428

Cast: Jill Clayburgh, Matthew Barry, Veronica Lazar, Renato Salvatori, Fred Gwynne, Alida Valli, Elisabetta Campeti, Franco Citti

An opera star (Jill Clayburgh), whose husband has just died, takes her 14-year-old son (Matthew Barry) with her on an engagement in Italy. There, without the proper attention from his mother, the son turns to drugs and becomes a heroin addict. The mother confronts the boy about it, then hugs him protectively, turning the moment into an incestuous romantic interlude. When she learns he has returned to drugs, she determines to find the Italian man who is the boy's real father. After the teenager meets the genial schoolteacher (Tomas Milian), he gets along well with him. The teacher sees the mother once more, who tells him what has happened to their child. Although the man strikes his son in rage, the boy is glad to have the confirmation of a father figure. A difficult and controversial subject, handled with care, but not totally successful—or appealing to general audiences.

NORMA RAE

Produced by Tamara Asseyev and Alex Rose
Directed by Martin Ritt
Screenplay by Irving Ravetch and Harriet Frank, Jr.
Photographed in Panavision and DeLuxe Color by John A. Alonzo
Music by David Shire
113 minutes

Cast: Sally Field, Beau Bridges, Ron Leibman, Pat Hingle, Barbara Baxley, Gail Strickland, Morgan Paull, Robert Broyles, John Calvin, Booth Colman

Norma Rae (Sally Field) is one of the most overworked and underpaid laborers at a Southern cotton mill. Her father (Pat Hingle) dies at the mill because of a lack of proper medical attention and her mother (Barbara Barrie) is going deaf from the clattering machinery. When a big-city labor organizer (Ron Leibman) arrives to convince the mill workers to unionize, none will co-operate under threats from management. Norma Rae, however, realizing the injustices, joins with the organizer and works selflessly to help unionize the mill. The late nights and spare-time planning cause problems with her husband (Beau Bridges), and there are reprisals by the mill manager, but the proud and independent Norma Rae persists. When she convinces the workers that they can achieve more livable working conditions through a union, they finally stand up to management and shut down production. Although the college-educated easterner and the small-town Norma Rae initially feel animosity towards each other, they part with great respect, their lives enriched by the relationship. Sally Field earned an Oscar for her superb portrayal.

NOSFERATU, THE VAMPYRE

Produced, directed and written by Werner Herzog
Photographed in color by Jorg Schmidt-Reitwein

Music by Popl Vuh/Florian Fricke
96 minutes

Cast: Klaus Kinski, Isabelle Adjani, Bruno Ganz, Roland Topor, Walter Ladengast, Dan Van Husen, Jan Groth, Carsten Bodinus

Another go-around of the vampire legend, this one stylishly done and very entertaining. German filmmaker Werner Herzog remakes the 1922 F.W. Murnau classic with an agile Klaus Kinski as the decadent Count Dracula. Jonathan Harker (Bruno Ganz) goes to the Dracula castle in Transylvania and acquires the tell-tale bite marks on the neck. He discovers the truth about the Count and is taken to safety in a convent. Meanwhile, Dracula boards a ship for Bremen and wreaks havoc on that town with a plague of rats. When Harker returns to Bremen, he introduces his wife (Isabelle Adjani) to the Count. Although repelled by the vampire, she realizes he has a hold over her husband and is responsible for the plague. She lures Dracula to her bedroom and keeps him there until daybreak, when the sun's rays turn him to ashes.

Jill Clayburgh and Matthew Barry in *Luna*.

William Katt and Tom Berenger in *Butch and Sundance: The Early Days*.

Sally Field as *Norma Rae*.

Tim Matheson and Susan Blakely in *Dreamer*.

Isabelle Adjani and Klaus Kinski in *Nosferatu, the Vampyre*.

A PERFECT COUPLE

Produced and directed by Robert Altman
Screenplay by Robert Altman and Allan Nicholls
Photographed in Panavision and DeLuxe Color by Edmond L.
  Koons
Music by Allan Nicholls
110 minutes

Cast: Paul Dooley, Marta Heflin, Titos Vandis, Belita Moreno,
Henry Gibson, Dimitra Arliss, Allan Nicholls, Ann Ryerson

Robert Altman uses his off-center perspective to examine
the question of compatibility and comes up with a tangibly
entertaining romantic comedy. Alex (Paul Dooley), a
gourmet cook, devotee of classical music, and antique
dealer is computer matched to Sheila (Marta Heflin), a non-
eater who manages a struggling rock group. Although they
develop a romantic attraction for each other, they feel that
the way they met is not conducive to a long-lasting
relationship. This leads to problems in their romance, as
they look for an excuse to confirm their suspicions. After a
series of disastrous dates, they separate. Soon, they find
themselves meeting, totally by chance, and discover they
are more compatible than they thought. Finally, they realize
they would have met by chance anyway and that the
computer brought them together a little earlier. Paul Dooley,
as always, turned in a human, touching performance.

QUINTET

Produced and directed by Robert Altman
Screenplay by Frank Barhydt, Robert Altman and Patricia Resnick, based on a Story by Robert Altman, Lionel Chetwynd,
  and Patricia Resnick
Photographed in DeLuxe Color by Jean Boffety
Music by Tom Pierson
110 minutes

Cast: Paul Newman, Vittorio Gassman, Fernando Rey, Bibi
Anderson, Brigitte Fossey, Nina van Pallandt

Robert Altman totally confused critics and alienated audiences with this murky, bleak look at the future. In a
society which has totally degenerated, people take part in a
game which involves seeking out and killing other players.
When Paul Newman's pregnant mate (Brigette Fossey) and
his brother (Tom Hill) are killed in an explosion, he realizes
that this was part of the game. Because his mate was killed
too, he sets out on a course for revenge. He finds that the
killer has been murdered himself, so he tracks down *his*
murderer (Vittorio Gassman). Newman has a brief interlude
with another player (Bibi Andersson), but ends up killing
her. In a chase over the ice, he finally does in the murderer's
murderer, then heads north as dogs chew on the corpses.
The chilly Montreal winter locations added visually to the
movie, but few could figure out what it all meant.

430

THE ROSE

Directed by Mark Rydell
Produced by Marvin Worth and Aaron Russo
Screenplay by Bo Goldman, Michael Cimino, and
  William Kerby, from a story by Marvin Worth and
  Michael Cimino
Photographed in DeLuxe Color by Vilmos Zsigmond

Cast: Bette Midler, Alan Bates, Frederic Forrest, Barry
Primus, Sandra McCabe

Living in a world of booze, drugs, and endless standing ovations, the Rose (Bette Midler) is a late-sixties
rock star at the height of her career. But for all her
wealth, fame, and talent, the hard-living, sometimes
vulgar singer finds no real happiness. Deciding that
she wants to take a year's leave from the concert and
recording cycle which has so totally filled the months
and years, she finds great resistance in her manager/
creator, Rudge (Alan Bates). Tied down by contractual
obligations, Rose feels trapped in a self-created hell.
To find some release, she picks up a young chauffeur,
Houston Dyer (Frederic Forrest), a Midwestern drifter
who has gone AWOL. In Dyer, she finds innocence
and warmth, and someone she can love. However,
Dyer does not enjoy the excesses which come with the
fame of a rock star and eventually leaves Rose. With
very little left in life, Rose looks forward to a concert
she is to give in her Florida home town. Returning as
a victorious star, though, is as empty an experience
as can be. To add to Rose's depression, Rudge threatens to call off the concert unless she agrees to abandon
any plans of a year off. Confused, Rose resorts to
liquor and pills which propel her to give the greatest
performance of her career—and her last. *The Rose*
presents a stark and horrifying portrayal of the last
frantic gyrations of a woman who could climb no
higher or fall no farther.

THE RUNNER STUMBLES

Produced and directed by Stanley Kramer
Screenplay by Milan Stitt, based on his play
Photographed in color by Laszlo Kovacs
Music by Ernest Gold
110 minutes

Cast: Dick Van Dyke, Kathleen Quinlan, Maureen Stapleton, Ray
Bolger, Tammy Grimes, Beau Bridges, Allen Nause

A priest (Dick Van Dyke) is on trial for the brutal murder of
a nun in 1927, and most of the story is told in flashback to
an attorney (Beau Bridges). The priest is assigned to a poor
parish where a nun of incredible energy (Kathleen Quinlan)
works. Attracted to her, he takes advantage of an outbreak
of consumption at the convent where she lives to offer her

residence at the rectory with him and his housekeeper (Maureen Stapleton). Gossip of a virulent nature passes among the parishoners due to their closeness, and it is later learned that the priest lied about getting the permission of the Monsignor (Ray Bolger) to have the guest. The priest soon realizes that they must stop speaking, but after the terror of a convent fire, they argue about their silence. Their love for each other becomes evident, and it is an appalled housekeeper who kills the young nun, a fact which is finally revealed during the priest's trial. Negative reaction to the film came not due to controversy, but to the story, which was considered to be lacking in direction, good scripting and acting.

SAVAGE HARVEST

Produced by Ralph Heifer, Sandy Howard and Lamar Card
Directed by Robert Collins
Screenplay by Robert Blees and Robert Collins, based on a story by Ralph Heifer
Photographed in DeLuxe Color by Ronnie Taylor
Music by Robert Falk
87 minutes

Cast: Tom Skerritt, Michelle Phillips, Shawn Stevens, Anne-Marie Martin, Derek Partridge, Arthur Malet, Tana Heifer

Set in Kenya, *Savage Harvest* deals with hordes of lions whom a severe drought turns into man hunters. They attack a plantation the way Indians used to attack wagon trains in old westerns, and use frightening skill in their strategy. A guide (Tom Skerritt) finds himself in the odd position of coming to the rescue of his ex-wife (Michele Phillips) and sundry other worried Kenyans. All of them narrowly miss becoming lion fodder, but the film itself misses being really exciting.

SCAVENGER HUNT

A Melvin Simon Production
Produced by Steven A. Vail and Paul Maslansky
Directed by Michael Schultz
Screenplay by Steven A. Vail and Henry Harper, from a story by Vail adapted by John Thompson and Gerry Woolery
Photographed in color by Ken Lamkin
Music by Billy Goldenberg
116 minutes

Cast: Richard Benjamin, James Coco, Scatman Crothers, Cloris Leachman, Cleavon Little, Roddy McDowall, Robert Morley, Richard Mulligan, Tony Randall, Dirk Benedict, Willie Aames, Stephanie Faracy, Richard Masur, Avery Schreiber, Stuart Pankin, Maureen Teefy, Hal Linden, Jr., Vincent Price

From a mere scanning of its cast list, *Scavenger Hunt* might seem impressive. Sadly, the many veteran actors here assembled were given feeble lines and comedically labored

Bette Midler
in *The Rose.*

Paul Dooley and Marta Heflin in *Perfect Couple.*

Paul Newman and Brigitte Fossey in *Quintet.*

431

Kathleen Quinlan, Tammy Grimes and Dick Van Dyke in *The Runner Stumbles*.

Shawn Stevens, Anne-Marie Martin, Michelle Phillips, Tana Helfer and Tom Skerritt in *Savage Harvest*.

situations in this attempt to find humor in the greedier aspects of human nature. Vincent Price appears at the beginning as a games manufacturer who wills the sum of two hundred million dollars, a legacy which requires his heirs and acquaintances to become contestants in a scavenger hunt in order to win the money. What is mostly required of the contestants is to survive the embarrassing situations in which·the script places them, a script that also leans heavily on such dubious humorous devices as physical deformities and belonging to racial minorities. In this film the real hunt is for comedy. Little is found.

20TH CENTURY-FOX ACADEMY AWARDS FOR 1979

SALLY FIELD: Best actress, *Norma Rae*.

ALAN HEIM: Best film editing, *All That Jazz*.

RALPH BURNS: Best music score (adaptation), *All That Jazz*.

"IT GOES LIKE IT GOES," MUSIC BY DAVID SHIRE, LYRICS BY NORMAN GIMBEL: Best original song, *Norma Rae*.

ALBERT WOLSKY: Best costume design, *All That Jazz*.

PHILIP ROSENBERG, TONY WALTON: Best art direction, *All That Jazz*.

EDWARD STEWART, GARY BRINK: Best set decoration, *All That Jazz*.

H.R. GEIGER, CARLO RAMBALDI, BRIAN JOHNSON, NICK ALDER, DENYS AYLING: Best visual effects, *Alien*.

(NOTE: *All That Jazz* had a special showing in the last week of 1979 to make it eligible for that year's Academy Awards. Its general release was in 1980.)

Richard Benjamin in *Scavenger Hunt*.

ALL THAT JAZZ

Produced by Robert Alan Aurthur
Directed by Bob Fosse
Screenplay by Robert Alan Aurthur and Bob Fosse
Photographed in Technicolor by Giuseppe Rotunno
Music by Ralph Burns
123 minutes

Cast: Roy Scheider, Jessica Lange, Ann Reinking, Leland Palmer, Cliff Gorman, Ben Vereen, Erzsebet Foldi, Michael Tolan

Thoroughly dazzling and energetic, this is not your typical musical. Bob Fosse has taken elements of his own life and fused them with fantasy for a candid look at himself. Joe Gideon (Roy Scheider) is a brilliant stage and film director, driven by perfectionism. His is a life of constant rehearsals, hours in the editing room, and little time for his daughter (Erzsebet Foldi) and girlfriend (Ann Reinking). He is under constant pressure from preparations for a Broadway show starring his ex-wife (Leland Palmer), and the backers are a constant irritation. Chain-smoking, skipping sleep and meals, leading an irregular life, Joe has a massive heart attack. While he undergoes open-heart surgery, he fantasizes the true worth of his life, complete with a glittery TV host (Ben Vereen) and an audience composed of friends, relatives, and fellow workers. He conducts a conversation with the beautiful angel of death (Jessica Lange). The ending is non-fantasy: Joe Gideon dies. Fosse has crafted a movie that may not satisfy everyone, but has such brilliant moments and extraordinary dancing that it deserves to be seen.

BRUBAKER

Produced by Ron Silverman
Directed by Stuart Rosenberg
Screenplay by W.D. Richter, based on a story by W.D. Richter and Arthur Ross
Photographed in DeLuxe Color by Bruno Nuytten
Music by Lalo Schifrin
131 minutes

Cast: Robert Redford, Yaphet Kotto, Jane Alexander, Murray Hamilton, David Keith, Morgan Freeman, Matt Clark, Tim McIntyre, Richard Ward

When Brubaker (Robert Redford) arrives at a Southern prison in uniform and manacles, he is thrown in with the other inmates. However, he turns out to be the new warden who wanted to see things "from the inside." This liberal approach wins friends as Brubaker tries to reform an institution rife with corruption, but his trustee (Yaphet Kotto) cynically disbelieves the changes will help. The warden, with the support of a reform-minded Governor's assistant (Jane Alexander), puts an end to townspeople using the prisoners for slave labor, and provides enough food for them without bribes. He even eats with the prisoners. His reforms bring down the enmity of the prison commissioner (Murry Hamilton), who is more concerned with status quo than change. Finally, when Brubaker leaves the prison, he has made a believer of his trustee and has earned the respect of even the most hardened criminals. A grim and gruelling portrayal of Southern prison life.

A CHANGE OF SEASONS

Produced by Martin Ransohoff
Directed by Richard Lang
Screenplay by Erich Segal, Ronni Kern, Fred Segal, based on a story by Erich Segal and Martin Ransohoff
Photographed in color by Philip Lathrop
Music by Henry Mancini
102 minutes

Cast: Shirley MacLaine, Anthony Hopkins, Bo Derek, Michael Brandon, Mary Beth Hurt, Ed Winter, Paul Regina, K. Callan

When the wife (Shirley MacLaine) of a New England professor (Anthony Hopkins) finds out her husband is having an affair with one of his students (Bo Derek), she gets involved with the young campus carpenter (Michael Brandon). The couple's daughter (Mary Beth Hurt) arrives home from college and is appalled by her parents' behavior. The professor follows his girlfriend back to Boston, and so do the others. They all end up on a ski weekend, at which the girlfriend's father (Ed Winter) becomes interested in the wife and proposes marriage. The professor's jealousy convinces the student that he is still interested in his wife, and she ends the affair. The wife, however, after considering the situation, decides to reject her husband and accept the other man's proposal. The professor and the carpenter go off together as new-found friends. An entertaining look at a midlife marital crisis.

433

Ben Vereen and Roy Scheider in *All That Jazz*.

Robert Redford as *Brubaker*, with Yaphet Kotto.

Anthony Hopkins and Bo Derek in *A Change of Seasons*.

THE EMPIRE STRIKES BACK

Executive Producer, George Lucas
Produced by Gary Kurtz
Directed by Irvin Kershner
Screenplay by Leigh Brackett and Lawrence Kasdan, from a story
  by George Lucas
Photographed in Panavision and DeLuxe Color by Peter
  Suschitzky
Music by John Williams
124 minutes

Cast: Mark Hamill, Harrison Ford, Carrie Fisher, Billy Dee
Williams, Anthony Daniels, Frank Oz, David Prowse, Peter
Mayhew, Kenny Baker, Alec Guinness

The second part of the *Star Wars* trilogy, in which Luke
Skywalker and friends once more battle the evil forces of
Darth Vader. Having blown up Vader's Death Star, the
rebels have moved to the ice planet of Hoth. However, Vader
tracks them down and destroys the base with huge mechanical creatures, called AT-ATs. Han Solo (Harrison Ford) and
Princess Leia (Carrie Fisher) escape and fly to Cloud City,
run by a scoundrel friend of Solo's, Lando Calrissian (Billy
Dee Williams). Luke (Mark Hamill), meanwhile, journeys
to Dagobah, where an elfin Yoda teaches him to master the
Force. Loads of adventures, thrills and special effects
follow, culminating in Han Solo being placed in carbon-
freezing hibernation, and Luke coming face-to-face in a
laser battle with Darth Vader, who turns out to be his father.
Audiences loved this one almost as much as the first,
making it one of the biggest boxoffice attractions of all
time.

FATSO

Produced by Stuart Cornfeld
Directed and written by Anne Bancroft
Photographed in DeLuxe Color by Brianne Murphy
Music by Joe Renzetti
94 minutes

Cast: Dom DeLuise, Anne Bancroft, Ron Carey, Candice Azzara,
Michael Lombard, Sal Viscuso, Delia Salvi, Robert Costanzo,
Estelle Reiner, Richard Karron

Dominic Dinapoli (Dom DeLuise) has a weight problem
due to his love of eating. When his overweight cousin dies
of a heart attack, he decides he must lose weight. His sister
(Anne Bancroft) helps as much as she can, and he goes to
diet doctors and Eaters Anonymous, but he still overeats.
Finally, he meets a young woman (Candice Azzara) and
suddenly finds he doesn't need to eat as much. When he
feels secure with her, he stays away from food, but when
things go badly in their romance, he returns to the table.
When they grow closer, he determines he will slim down
and is set to propose to her. On the evening of their date, she
disappears and he drowns his misery in glutting himself on
Chinese food. However, he learns that she could not make
the date because her brother was in an accident. Reassured
of her love, he knows a slimmer future is in the cards.

Mark Hamill in *The Empire Strikes Back*.

Anne Bancroft and Dom DeLuise in *Fatso*.

Rex Smith, Terri Treas, Vivian Reed and Paul Carafotes in *Headin' for Broadway*.

HEADIN' FOR BROADWAY

Produced and Directed by Joseph Brooks
Screenplay by Joseph Brooks, Hillary Henkin, and Larry Gross
Photographed in color by Eric Saarinen
Music by Joseph Brooks
93 minutes

Cast: Rex Smith, Terri Treas, Vivian Reed, Paul Carafotes, Gene Foote, Gary Gendell, Benjamin Rayson, Richard Boccelli

Four young people who think they have the talent to succeed on Broadway leave their homes to make it big. One is a Los Angeles songwriter/singer (Rex Smith), and the others an Ohio farmgirl (Terri Treas), a street-wise Philadelphian (Paul Carafotes), and a Harlem dancer (Vivian Reed). They meet and get to know each other. Only the dancer initially gets a job in a chorus line, but the street-wise Philadelphian gets a miraculous call-back to try out for a lead. In a *Rocky* - like training period, he gets into shape for the audition and gets the part. He also has a brief romance with the farmgirl after she is put off by the songwriter. The Philadelphian is the only one of the group to become a success after all. A syrupy look at a tough business, the highlight of which is Gene Foote as a choreographer, and the dancing scenes. The dramatic scenes in between, though, slow the film down.

HEALTH

Produced and directed by Robert Altman
Screenplay by Frank Barhydt, Paul Dooley and Robert Altman
Photographed in DeLuxe Color by Edmond L. Koons
Music by Joseph Byrd
102 minutes

Cast: Glenda Jackson, Carol Burnett, James Garner, Lauren Bacall, Dick Cavett, Paul Dooley, Donald Maffat, Henry Gibson, Diane Stilwell, MacIntyre Dixon, Alfred Woodard, Ann Ryerson, Allan Nicholls, Margery Bond

Despite Robert Altman's reputation and a strong cast of name players, *Health* proved to be a film with very little

Lauren Bacall, Dick Cavett, Carol Burnett and Glenda Jackson in *Health*.

health. It is probably the least seen of any of the Altman films. Here he attempts to spoof the health-food industry, setting his story in Florida, in and around a garish hotel, and presents Lauren Bacall as an 87-year-old who runs for office as the president of a health food organization. Her chief opposition is an equally bizarre lady (Glenda Jackson) who smokes cigars and tapes her conversations. It all takes place during a convention of health food nuts, including a sexually frustrated emissary (Carol Burnett) from the White House, who runs into her ex-husband (James Garner), a public relations man working for Bacall. Covering the weird goings-on for television is Dick Cavett. Altman's satire gets in some good barbs, but the end result is a picture without any true focus.

KAGEMUSHA

Executive Producers of international version, Franics Ford Coppola and George Lucas
Directed by Akira Kurosawa
Screenplay by Akira Kurosawa and Masato Ide
Photographed in color by Takao Saito and Shoji Ueda
Music by Shinichio Ikebe
159 minutes

Cast: Tatsuya Nakadai, Tsutomu Yamazaki, Kenichi Hagiwara, Jinpachi Nezu, Shuji Otaki, Daisuke Ryu, Masayuki Yui

A visually rich and fascinating portrayal of medieval Japanese politics and warfare in Kurosawa's unique filmmaking style. A powerful nobleman (Tatsuya Nakadai) saves a thief (also played by Nakadai) from death because he looks

Ken Hagiwara (middle foreground) in *Kagemusha*.

Stephen Collins, Shirley MacLaine, James Coburn and Susan Sarandon in *Loving Couples*.

like the lord. When the nobleman is killed in battle, his aides decide to preserve the army's strength and morale by substituting the look-alike thief. At first unwilling, the double soon enjoys playing the role of powerful master. A complication arises when the Lord's son (Tsutomu Yamazaki) wants to take power. He does so when the double is accidentally exposed, but he is not the skillful ruler his father was. The son leads the army to death and ruin, and the double, no longer thief and no longer Lord, marches off with the troops to share their fate. American producers George Lucas and Francis Ford Coppola used their financial muscle to help fund Kurosawa's artistry.

LOVING COUPLES

Produced by Renee Valente
Directed by Jack Smight
Screenplay by Martin Donovan
Photographed in color by Philip Lathrop
Music by Fred Karlin
97 minutes

Cast: Shirley MacLaine, James Coburn, Susan Sarandon, Stephen Collins, Sally Kellerman, Nan Martin, Shelly Batt, Bernard Behrens

The doctor wife (Shirley MacLaine) of a successful surgeon (James Coburn) feels neglected by her husband and has an affair with a young patient (Stephen Collins). When the young man's girlfriend (Susan Sarandon), a TV weather announcer, confronts the surgeon with this revelation, they begin an affair. Meanwhile, the young man cheats on the doctor and beds an unstable client (Sally Kellerman), who pursues him. The surgeon and the TV announcer are having their problems too, and are unhappy with the arrangement. At a medical benefit dance, all the characters meet. The unstable woman tells the doctor about the young man's unfaithfulness, which ends the affair. The surgeon ends his as well and pursues his wife once more, but she turns him down. The young man is rejected by his girlfriend as well. Finally, the surgeon follows his wife to Tahiti and wins her back. Another of the mix-and-match contemporary bedroom comedies.

THE MAN WITH BOGART'S FACE

Produced by Andrew J. Fenady
Directed by Robert Day
Screenplay by Andrew J. Fenady, based on his novel
Photographed in color by Richard C. Glouner
Music by George Duning
111 minutes

Cast: Robert Sacchi, Franco Nero, Michelle Phillips, Olivia Hussey, Misty Rowe, Victor Buono, Herbert Lom, Sybil Danning

A man (Robert Sacchi) has his face surgically altered so that he will look like Humphrey Bogart, his movie hero. He even opens a detective agency and almost immediately becomes embroiled in a Raymond Chandleresque intrigue. A lady of mystery (Michelle Phillips) wants him to find the Eyes of Alexander, legendary jewels stolen from an ancient statue. Then an attractive innocent (Olivia Hussey) shows up looking for the same quarry, as do other clients. Juggling the clients and fighting their hired thugs, he finally finds the jewels. He confronts all the clients aboard a yacht anchored offshore and tells them why each one wanted the jewels. Each tries to steal the treasure, and they fight among themselves. The detective escapes with the real jewels to return them to their true owner. Robert Sacchi steals the show as the Bogart look-alike, and adds plenty of charm to this entertaining film.

MIDDLE AGE CRAZY

Produced by Robert Cooper and Ronald Cohen
Directed by John Trent
Screenplay by Carl Kleinschmitt
Photographed in DeLuxe Color by Reginald H. Morris
Music by Matthew McCauley
95 minutes

Cast: Bruce Dern, Ann-Margret, Graham Jarvis, Eric Christmas, Helen Hughes, Geoffrey Bowes, Michael Kane, Diane Dewey, Vivan Reis, Patricia Hamilton, Deborah Wakeham

A successful architect of taco restaurants (Bruce Dern) is happily married and satisfied with life until his wife (Ann-Margret) throws a surprise fortieth birthday party for him. After the festivities, the realities and responsibilities of approaching middle age begin to set in. His father dies, leaving him the family patriarch, and his son wants to drop out of college to marry a girl he has made pregnant. Under the pressure, the architect suddenly shucks his lifestyle, buys a sports car and takes up with a Dallas Cowboys cheerleader (Deborah Wakeham). His dreams of keeping his youth, though, dissolve with his new life, which is less stable and pleasurable than the one he left. He returns to find that his wife has been unfaithful, but resolves to make the marriage work and attempts to find happiness again. A sometimes funny, sometimes tragic account of modern marriage.

MY BODYGUARD

Produced by Don Devlin
Directed by Tony Bill
Screenplay by Alan Ormsby
Photographed in color by Michael D. Margulies
Music by Dave Grusin
96 minutes

Cast: Chris Makepeace, Adam Baldwin, Matt Dillon, Paul Quandt, Joan Cusack, Dean R. Miller, Tim Reyna, Richard Bradley

A brainy 11-year-old boy (Chris Makepeace) enters Junior High School and finds it to be a particularly traumatic experience, especially when the class bully (Matt Dillon) makes him give up his lunch money for "protection." A tall, withdrawn kid (Adam Baldwin), who reputedly killed another boy, is the reason for protection. The youngster decides to pay directly to the source and bypass the bully. In doing so, he learns that the bully's extortion scheme is just a ruse. The tall boy is annoyed over the scheme, but the bright young student convinces him not to beat the bully up but to get the money back from him and become a hero to everyone. As a result, the small boy gets an imposing bodyguard whom the bully cannot intimidate. The bodyguard, in turn, learns to better his grades. They become close friends and the 11-year-old learns that the reason for his new friend's withdrawn nature is guilt over his younger brother's death when they were handling their father's gun. A sentimental and charming story about brains taming brawn which somehow got lost in the audiences' rush to the blockbusters.

NINE TO FIVE

Produced by Bruce Gilbert
Directed by Colin Higgins
Screenplay by Colin Higgins and Patricia Resnick, from a story by Patricia Resnick
Photographed in DeLuxe Color by Reynaldo Villalobos

Music by Charles Fox
109 minutes

Cast: Jane Fonda, Lily Tomlin, Dolly Parton, Dabney Coleman, Sterling Hayden, Elizabeth Wilson, Henry Jones, Lawrence Pressman, Marian Mercer, Ren Woods

A recently divorced woman (Jane Fonda) takes an office job and befriends two other secretaries. Violet (Lily Tomlin), a widow, and a buxom Doralee (Dolly Parton) show her the ropes and warn her of their male chauvinistic boss (Dabney Coleman), who constantly lusts after Doralee and harasses the women. After Violet thinks she's accidentally poisoned the boss, she and the others go to the hospital and mistakenly steal the corpse of another man. When the confusion is sorted out, they return the body and find their boss back at work and as nasty as ever. The women arrange to kidnap him, and then chain him to his bedroom ceiling and force him to watch television soap operas. Meanwhile, the women turn the office into the place they always hoped it would be. It becomes an efficient and pleasant environment. When the boss is finally released, the company president (Sterling Hayden) makes a surprise visit and is so impressed that he decides to transfer the boss to South America. A hilarious cautionary comedy about male chauvinism, the highlight of which is an animated "Snow White"-like sequence with Lily Tomlin. It was a blockbuster smash, and became a television series.

OH, HEAVENLY DOG

Produced and directed by Joe Camp
Screenplay by Rod Browning
Photographed in DeLuxe Color by Don Reddy
Music by Evel Box
Songs by Elton John, Gary Osbourne and Paul McCartney
103 minutes

Cast: Chevy Chase, Benji, Jane Seymour, Omar Sharif, Robert Morley, Alan Sues, Donnelly Rhodes, Stuart Germain, John Stride, Barbara Leigh-Hunt, Margaret Courtney, Frank Williams, Albin Pahernik, Susan Kellerman, Lorenzo Music, Marguerite Corriveau

Considered by dog fanciers as one of the most appealing mutts ever to grace the screen, Benji turned up for a third time in this aptly titled picture. Whereas the two previous entries found their markets either with the very young or the older set, producer-director Joe Camp here attempted to widen the box office appeal by bringing in the comedic Chevy Chase, the glamorous Jane Seymour and a somewhat racier script. Said script has Chase as a private detective reincarnated as a dog after being slain while investigating a sex-and-politics scandal in London. In the guise of the lovable Benji, Chase is thereby enabled to snuggle up to reporter Seymour in a matter she might otherwise find overly familiar in a suitor. The humor failed to impress sufficiently any sector of the market. Benji lovers could only hope the heavenly dog might find his way back to less salacious settings.

437

THE STUNT MAN

Produced and directed by Richard Rush
Screenplay by Lawrence B. Marcus, adapted by Richard Rush
    from a novel by Paul Brodeur
Photographed in color by Mario Tosi
Music by Dominic Frontiere
131 minutes

Cast: Peter O'Toole, Steve Railsback, Barbara Hershey, Allen
Goorwitz, Alex Rocco, Sharon Farrell, Adam Roarke, Philip
Bruns, Chuck Bail, John Garwood, Jim Hess, John B. Pierce,
Michael Railsback, George D. Wallace, Dee Carroll, Leslie
Winograde

Peter O'Toole, after several years of appearing in mediocre
movies, made a striking comeback as a rather devilish
movie director in *The Stunt Man.* This is a director who will
stoop to almost any means to get the scene right, even if it
means risking the lives of his actors. When his main stunt
man is killed in the making of a film about the First World
War, the director seizes upon a young army deserter (Steven
Railsback) and persuades him to assume the man's identity.
The deserter jumps at the opportunity, but gradually comes
to think the director deliberately killed the stunt man for the
sake of realism and is willing to do the same with his
replacement. He survives the gruelling stunts required of
him and realizes, as does the audience after seeing this film,
that the picture business is no bed of roses. Beautifully
filmed on location in San Diego, *The Stunt Man* covers its
subject matter knowingly, yet indulges in a little too much
paranoia for its own good. Are movie makers really this
devious and dangerous?

TERROR TRAIN

Produced by Harold Greenberg
Executive producer Lamar Card
Directed by Roger Spottiswoode
Screenplay by T. Y. Drake
Photographed in DeLuxe Color by John Alcott
Music by John Mills-Cockell
97 minutes

Cast: Ben Johnson, Jamie Lee Curtis, Hart Bochner, David
Copperfield, Derek MacKinnon, Sandee Currie, Timothy Webber,
Anthony Sherwood, Howard Busgang, Steve Michaels, Greg
Swanson, D. D. Winters, Joy Boushel, Victor Knight

Filmed in Canada, *Terror Train* continued Jamie Lee
Curtis's track record as the modern young women in peril.
As she had done in such films as *Halloween* and *The Fog,*
Jamie continues to survive the hideous, gory capers of
vengeful psychotics. Here the action takes place on a train
that a group of medical students have taken on a trip to
celebrate their graduation, having long forgotten a monstrous practical joke they once played on someone. The
victim, however, has not forgotten, and now sets out to
restore his pride, depriving the world of a few prospective
doctors in the process. *Terror Train* proved, if nothing else,
that a well packaged, modestly budgeted horror trip was one
of 1980s' best ways of recouping a film investment, plus
making a profit.

WILLIE AND PHIL

Produced by Paul Mazursky and Tony Ray
Directed and written by Paul Mazursky
Photographed in color by Sven Nykvist
Music by Claude Bolling
116 minutes

Cast: Michael Ontkean, Margot Kidder, Ray Sharkey, Jan Miner,
Tom Brennan, Julie Bovasso, Louis Guss, Kathleen Maguire,
Kaki Hunter, Kristine DeBell, Allison Cass Shurpin, Christine
Varnai, Lawrence Fishburne III

Willie and Phil is a film bearing the unmistakable stamp of
Paul Mazursky, set in the Greenwich Village area of
Manhattan and dealing with characters who are his spiritual
kin. Beyond that it is a deliberate American version of the
Francois Truffaut minor classic *Jules et Jim,* even to having
Mazursky's title characters profess an admiration of Truffaut
and a gradual realization of how his film has affected their
lives. Phil (Ontkean) is a Jewish photographer and Willie
(Sharkey) is an Italian teacher, and both are very much
working-class New Yorkers. When they meet a loving,
earthy, liberal-minded girl from Kentucky (Kidder), they
both fall in love with her. And they both eventually realize
they must give her up and let her go her way. As with all
Mazursky films, the plot is secondary to characterization
and human incident, and it succeeds in poignantly digging
below the surface of contemporary American life.

Bruce Dern and Ann-Margret in *Middle Age Crazy.*

Robert Sacchi, *The Man With Bogart's Face*, with Michelle Phillips.

Jane Fonda, Lily Tomlin and Dolly Parton in *Nine to Five*.

Chevy Chase and Benji in *Oh, Heavenly Dog*.

20TH CENTURY-FOX ACADEMY AWARDS FOR 1980

BRIAN JOHNSON, RICHARD EDLUND, DENNIS MURREN, BRUCE NICHOLSON: Special achievement award for special effects, *The Empire Strikes Back*.

Michael Ontkean, Margot Kidder and Ray Sharkey in *Willie and Phil*.

Peter O'Toole and Steve Railsback in *The Stunt Man*.

1981

THE AMATEUR

Produced by Joel B. Michaels and Garth H. Drabinsky
Directed by Charles Jarrott
Screenplay by Robert Littell and Diana Maddox, based on a novel by Littell
Photographed in color by John Coquillon
Music by Ken Wanneberg
111 minutes

Cast: John Savage, Christopher Plummer, Marthe Keller, Arthur Hill, Nicholas Campbell, George Coe, John Marley, Jan Rubes, Ed Lauter, Miguel Fernandez, Jan Triska, Graham Jarvis, Chapelle Jaffe, Lynne Griffin, Vladimir Valenta, Vlaste Vrana, Neil Dainard, Lee Broker, Tedde Moore

Produced by Canadians, *The Amateur,* a title which seems to have no bearing upon the story, gives the CIA such a rough going-over that the viewer might assume that some of the financing might have come from the Kremlin. The hero (John Savage) is a computer technologist, working for the CIA in Washington, who takes it upon himself to avenge the slaying of his girlfriend by terrorists when they raided the American Consulate in Munich. He tracks them down all over Europe and uses his lethal skill so well that the CIA decides he must be eliminated. As in all films dealing with modern espionage, the plot lines and characters in *The Amateur* are as devious as they are sinister. As a warning to those who might be drawn to this way of life, the film makes its points clearly and excitingly.

THE CANNONBALL RUN

Produced by Albert S. Ruddy
Directed by Hal Needham
Screenplay by Brock Yates
Photographed in Panavision and Technicolor by Michael Butler
Music supervision by Snuff Garrett
95 minutes

Cast: Burt Reynolds, Roger Moore, Farrah Fawcett, Dom De-Luise, Dean Martin, Sammy Davis, Jr., Jack Elam, Adrienne Barbeau, Terry Bradshaw, Jackie Chan, Bert Convy, Peter Fonda, George Furth, Michael Hui, Bianca Jagger

The owner of a delivery service (Burt Reynolds) who is a terrific driver decides to enter a no-holds-barred cross-country race where the drivers choose whatever vehicles they wish. He and his zany mechanic (Dom DeLuise) decide on using an ambulance to avoid any interference by the Highway Patrol. While in a bar, the two meet a dithery, ecology-minded blonde (Farrah Fawcett) whom they convince to join them as a "patient." A stoned-out proctologist (Jack Elam) is brought along for "credibility." Also in the race are various guest stars, including Sammy Davis, Jr., and Dean Martin as a pair of con-men disguised as priests, Peter Fonda as a biker, oriental Karate expert Jackie Chan, and Roger Moore as a man in an Aston Martin who tells everyone he's James Bond. Although the gold ol' boy ambulance driver loses to "James Bond," he strikes up a romance with the blonde who turns out to be his consolation prize. The thin plot is only there to provide a thread for the wild gags, chases and demolition derbies.

CHU CHU AND THE PHILLY FLASH

Produced by Jay Weston
Executive producer Melvin Simon
Directed by David Lowell Rich
Screenplay by Barbara Dana, from a story by Henry Barrow
Photographed in DeLuxe Color by Victor J. Kemper
Music by Pete Rugolo
100 minutes

Cast: Alan Arkin, Carol Burnett, Jack Warden, Danny Aiello, Adam Arkin, Danny Glover, Sid Haig, Vincent Schiavelli, Ruth Buzzi, Vito Scotti, Lou Jacobi

Basically the story of two rather pitiful people who find some strength in each other, *Chu Chu and the Philly Flash* tends to prove that movies with outlandish titles have a hard time at the box office. This one did. The parts are better than the whole. The title characters are street people—Alan Arkin an ex-baseball player, long sodden with alcohol, and Carol Burnett a down-on-her-luck entertainer, who takes to the streets as a one-woman band dressed as Carmen Miranda. They meet when they both spot a briefcase on the sidewalk and hope it contains money, enough for them to take a little and return the rest. The antics involved are amusing, but Arkin and Burnett are at their best in revealing the humanity in their characters and hinting that this meeting will change their lives for the better. The film deserved more attention than it received.

John Savage and Ed Lauter in *The Amateur*.

Carol Burnett and Alan Arkin in *Chu Chu and the Philly Flash*.

DEATH HUNT

Produced by Murray Shostak
Executive producers Albert S. Ruddy and Raymond Chow
Directed by Peter Hunt
Screenplay by Michael Grais and Mark Victor
Photographed in Technicolor by James Devis
Music by Jerold Immel
96 minutes

Cast: Charles Bronson, Lee Marvin, Andrew Stevens, Carl Weathers, Ed Lauter, Scott Hylands, Angie Dickinson, Henry Beckman, William Sanderson, Jon Cedar, James O'Connell, Len Lesser, Dick Davalos, Maury Chaykin, August Schellenberg

The Royal Canadian Mounted Police, a favorite subject of B movies in Hollywood's Golden Age, reappear in this lusty adventure movie in the form of rugged Lee Marvin, on the trail of equally rugged outlaw Charles Bronson. The time is 1931 and the two adversaries, who have apparently enjoyed hunting and dodging each other for years, seem to be leftovers from the Wild West, throwing sticks of dynamite at each other and blasting away with bear guns. Marvin has a girl (Angie Dickinson) back at headquarters, but he seems to gain more pleasure from tracking Bronson through the snows. Since the so-called hero and villain are so similar in character, *Death Hunt* is somewhat vague in its moral point of view. It is certainly light years removed from the black-and-white values of *Renfrew of the Royal Mounted*.

Dean Martin, Jamie Farr, Roger Moore, Burt Reynolds, Tara Buckman, Rick Aviles, Farrah Fawcett and Bert Convy in *The Cannonball Run*.

Charles Bronson and Lee Marvin in *Death Hunt*.

EYEWITNESS

Produced and Directed by Peter Yates
Screenplay by Steve Tesich
Photographed in Technicolor by Matthew F. Leonetti
Music by Stanley Silverman
102 minutes

Cast: William Hurt, Sigourney Weaver, Christopher Plummer, James Woods, Irene Worth, Kenneth McMillan, Pamela Reed, Albert Paulsen

When a janitor (William Hurt) finds the body of a murdered Vietnamese jeweler, he makes an ambitious TV news-

William Hurt and Sigourney Weaver in *Eyewitness*.

woman (Sigourney Weaver) believe he knows more about the story then he really does. Since he has fallen in love with her watching her news broadcasts, he wants to do whatever he can to get to know her. In doing so, he brings the killers after him. The newswoman's boyfriend (Christopher Plummer) is a mysterious figure who appears to be having an affair with her, but in reality is an Israeli who is involved in the jeweler's murder for political reasons. He uses the newswoman to set the janitor up for the kill, but she realizes what is happening and goes to the police. The Israeli is killed and the janitor has won her love.

THE FINAL CONFLICT

Produced by Harvey Bernhard
Directed by Graham Baker
Screenplay by Andrew Birkin, based on characters created by David Seltzer
Photographed in Panavision and DeLuxe Color by Robert Paynter and Phil Meheux
Music by Jerry Goldsmith
108 minutes

Cast: Sam Neill, Rossano Brazzi, Don Gordon, Lisa Harrow, Barnaby Holm, Mason Adams, Robert Arden, Tommy Duggan, Leueen Willoughby, Louis Mahoney

In the third and final episode of the *Omen* trilogy, Damien Thorn (Sam Neill) is thirty-three and Ambassador to England. He is also on an all-out mission to find and destroy the newly born Nazarene. Eliminating all possible newborns creates a wave of infanticide across the country which brings a television newswoman (Lisa Harrow) to Damien. The two have an affair and she never suspects him. Meanwhile, an Italian monk (Rosanno Brazzi) knows Damien's true identity and plans to kill him. Amidst his failed attempts, Damien learns that his assistant (Don Gordon) is really the Nazarene's father and has been hiding the truth. Using his evil powers, Damien has the mother murder her son. The Italian monk locates Damien and convinces the newswoman that he is really a devil. In a cave, she stabs Damien with one of the daggers of Megiddo, putting an end to Satan's messenger, and to the series.

FORT APACHE, THE BRONX

Produced by Martin Richards and Tom Fiorello
Directed by Daniel Petrie
Screenplay by Heywood Gould
Photographed in DeLuxe Color by John Alcott
Music by Jonathan Tunick
125 minutes

Cast: Paul Newman, Edward Asner, Ken Wahl, Danny Aiello, Rachel Ticotin, Pam Grier, Kathleen Beller, Tito Goya

Paul Newman plays an honest cop in the inner city precinct of South Bronx, New York, trying to maintain his integrity and his will to fight crime. The job becomes harder when the precinct gets a by-the-book chief (Ed Asner) who orders a crackdown on crime which only inflames the neighborhood. While this is being played out, a drug-crazed hooker (Pam Grier) is going around killing cops whenever the opportunity arises. The honest cop and his partner (Ken Wahl) witness a fellow officer (Danny Aiello) throwing a young man to his death from an apartment roof. The pressure is on the honest cop to not rat on a fellow police officer, but his conscience and sense of right make him turn to the Chief who promises justice. After the cop's girlfriend (Rachel Ticotin) dies from a drug overdose, he is ready to turn in his badge, but the Chief convinces him that the criminal element can be controlled and it's their job to do it. An ironic ending brings the cop-killing hooker into the hands of a crazed drug pusher who does her in. A gritty and unrelentingly depressing subject.

HARDLY WORKING

Produced by James J. McNamara and Igo Kantor
Directed by Jerry Lewis
Screenplay by Michael Janover and Jerry Lewis, from a story by Jerry Lewis
Photographed in color by James Pergola
Music by Morton Stevens
91 minutes

Cast: Jerry Lewis, Susan Oliver, Roger C. Carmel, Deanna Lund, Harold J. Stone, Steve Franken, Buddy Lester, Leonard Stone, Jerry Lester, Billy Barty

As a clown thrust into unemployment by a closing circus, Jerry Lewis returns to his career-long role of the maladjusted bungler. He goes to live with his sister (Susan Oliver) and attempts to find a steady job. In the process, he wreaks havoc on the U.S. Postal Service, a bar, a Japanese restaurant, and a gas station. The role even permits him an opportunity to disguise himself as an old Jewish lady. For the romantic interest, there's a young woman (Deanna Lund) he meets during his stint as a gas station jockey. Her kindness and willingness to put up with his shenanigans give him the encouragement to keep on trying. Critics and audiences alike agreed that this was not up to Lewis's previous efforts, but it was a mild boxoffice success.

HISTORY OF THE WORLD—PART I

Produced, directed and written by Mel Brooks
Photographed in Panavision and DeLuxe Color by Woody Omens
Music by John Morris
Narrated by Orson Welles
93 minutes

Cast: Mel Brooks, Dom DeLuise, Madeline Kahn, Harvey Korman, Cloris Leachman, Ron Carey, Gregory Hines, Pamela Stephenson, Andreas Voutsinas, Shecky Greene, Sid Ceasar, Howard Morris, Rudy DeLuca

Mel Brooks spoofs history and the movies this time out with

Sam Neill, Lisa Harrow and Barnaby Holm in *The Final Conflict*.

Paul Newman and Ed Asner in *Fort Apache, the Bronx*.

Jerry Lewis, Susan Oliver and Roger C. Carmel in *Hardly Working*.

hit-and-miss results. Starting at the beginning of time, a caveman (Sid Ceasar) provides insight into how slapstick comedy evolved—by getting hit on the head with a club. Then Moses (Mel Brooks) delivers the Fifteen Commandments, but drops one of the tablets and is left with ten. In ancient Rome, Brooks plays Comicus, an out-of-work comedian, who teams up with Gregory Hines and plays the palace, where Empress Nympho (Madeline Kahn) gets them into trouble. Then the Spanish Inquisition turns into a vehicle for an Esther Williamsish musical number with nuns disrobing for the swim. Finally, Brooks plays a French aristocrat in a spoof on the revolution. Ending on a more contemporary note, there is a preview of a coming science-fiction attraction, "Jews in Space." Like most of Brooks' movies, not all for all tastes.

MODERN PROBLEMS

Produced by Alan Greisman and Michael Shamberg
Directed by Ken Shapiro
Screenplay by Ken Shapiro, Tom Sherohman, and Arthur Sellers
Photographed in DeLuxe color by Edmond Koons
Music by Dominic Frontiere
92 minutes

Cast: Chevy Chase, Patti D'Arbanville, Mary Kay Place, Nell Carter, Brian Doyle-Murray, Mitch Kreindel, Dabney Coleman, Arthur Sellers, Sandy Helberg, Neil Thompson

A harried air traffic controller (Chevy Chase), distraught because his girlfriend (Patti d'Arbanville) walked out on him, is driving behind a tanker truck when some nuclear waste sloshes through his sunroof. Returning home, he discovers he has acquired a green haze and telekinetic powers. He learns how to use these powers by giving his girlfriend's obnoxious dinner date a bloody nose. He takes her home and makes her think he is a great lover. Finally, the couple spend a weekend at a friend's (Brian Doyle-Murray) beach house. Also in attendance are a previous wife (Mary Kay Place), a voodoo maid (Nell Carter), and a loudmouth, lusting writer of self-help bestsellers (Dabney Coleman). The telekinetic powers make the weekend an ordeal for the guests and a cathartic for Chase, but it is fun with a nasty streak. Although recut for a general audience rating, and considerably disjointed as a result, there are still some funny moments.

Dabney Coleman (face in mashed Potatoes), Patti D'Arbanville and Chevy Chase in *Modern Problems*.

443

Gregory Hines and Mel Brooks in *History of the World, Part I.*

and the latter by a group who wish to buy up the academy, raze it and use the grounds to build condominiums. The dilemma finds its focus in a single cadet (Tim Hutton), who leads the more militant cadets in a revolt, seizes the armory and the control of the academy, and holds off the regular army contingent sent to quell the movement. Tempers and judgment get out of hand and result in combat and the death of severl cadets before they are forced to give in. Some critics found *Taps* too dramatically exaggerated to be convincing. But no viewer could escape its painful questioning of contemporary values.

TRIBUTE

Produced by Joel B. Michaels and Garth Drabinsky
Directed by Bob Clark
Screenplay by Bernard Slade, based on his play
Photographed in color by Reginald H. Morris
Music by Ken Wannberg
121 minutes

Cast: Jack Lemmon, Robby Benson, Lee Remick, Colleen Dewhurst, John Marley, Kim Cattrall, Gale Garnett, Teri Keane

Jack Lemmon repeats his successful stage role as Scottie Templeton, a Broadway press agent who is dying of leukemia but won't seek help. The wisecracking Scottie learns of the illness just as his son (Robby Benson) from a split marriage shows up. Their personalities clash as the serious young man questions his father's frivolity. Since Scottie's ex-wife (Lee Remick) knows of his illness, she tries to bring about a reconciliation between father and son. Acting as an intermediary, she makes the boy realize how much like his father he really is, which produces a loving relationship between them. Scottie finally decides to listen to his partner (John Marley) and his doctor (Colleen Dewhurst) and seek treatment to prolong his life so that he will have more precious time to spend with his son. Lemmon's acting was a little too overdone and undercontrolled by director Bob Clark to make this the poignant study it should have been.

ZORRO, THE GAY BLADE

Produced by George Hamilton and C. O. Erickson
Executive producer Melvin Simon
Directed by Peter Medak
Screenplay by Hal Dresner, based on a story by Dresner, Greg Alt, Don Moriarty and Bob Randall
Photographed in DeLuxe Color by John A. Alonzo
Music direction by Ian Fraser
93 minutes

Cast: George Hamilton, Lauren Hutton, Brenda Vaccaro, Ron Leibman, Donovan Scott, James Booth, Helen Burns, Clive Revill, Eduardo Noriega

It took a strong-minded reviewer to resist referring to *Zorro, the Gay Blade* as a *swishbuckler.* This spoof of the classic

Jack Lemmon and Robby Benson in *Tribute.*

The Mark of Zorro (1939) overplays the limp wristed prissy side of Don Diego Vega (George Hamilton) to an embarrassing degree. As in the original, Vega returns from Spain to usurp the military dictator (Ron Leibman) who has gained control of Vega's native California. Vega horrifies his family by pretending to be a simpering dandy, while donning the mask of the avenger at other times, some of which are needed to fight off the amorous assaults of the dictator's wife (Brenda Vaccaro). Unfortunately the spoof sags with its own excesses and what was meant to be funny becomes offensive. Co-producer Hamilton obviously bit off more scenery than he could chew.

George Hamilton as *Zorro, the Gay Blade.*

AUTHOR! AUTHOR!

Produced by Irwin Winkler
Directed by Arthur Hiller
Screenplay by Israel Horovitz
Photographed in Color by Victor J. Kemper
Music by Dave Grusin
110 minutes

Cast: Al Pacino, Dyan Cannon, Tuesday Weld, Alan King, Bob Dishy, Bob Elliott, Ray Goulding, Eric Gurry

A successful dramatist (Al Pacino) is getting ready to open a new play when his wife (Tuesday Weld) walks out, leaving behind her four children from three previous marriages. Caring for his own son from another marriage in addition to the others, he finds little time to devote to rewriting his second act. Tension builds in the household with everyday problems, but the children and father somehow manage to survive and thrive. A brief affair with the play's leading lady (Dyan Cannon) provides a romantic interlude, but she realizes she cannot handle such a brood. Finally, the family grows to love one another and the father has to fight off attempts by step-parents who try to reclaim the children. They are together again by the time the play opens and gleefully celebrate its success.

THE CHOSEN

Produced by Edie and Ely Landau
Directed by Jeremy Paul Kagan
Screenplay by Edwin Gordon, based on the novel by Chaim Potok
Photographed in color by Arthur Ornitz
Music by Elmer Bernstein
107 minutes

Cast: Maximillian Schell, Rod Steiger, Robby Benson, Barry Miller, Kaethe Fine, Hildy Brooks, Ron Rifkin, Robert Burke, Lonny Price

A fine, touching movie about the friendship of two young men just after World War II. Danny (Robby Benson) is a devout Jew who meets an assimilated teenager, Reuven (Barry Miller), while playing baseball. When Reuven is injured, Danny visits him in the hospital and they become friends. Danny, who has lived a stifling existence under his stern Rabbi father (Rod Steiger), is shown what life is like outside of the confines of his religion. When the formation of Israel becomes imminent, the Rabbi forbids his son to see Reuven because his professor father (Maximillian Schell) is a Zionist, and according to Biblical law, the founding of Israel would not be permitted until the coming of the Messiah. After the establishment of Israel, the Rabbi relents and allows his son to attend Columbia College with Reuven instead of the religious seminary. Steiger and Schell turn in two of their best performances and the rest of the cast is exemplary.

I OUGHT TO BE IN PICTURES

Produced by Herbert Ross and Neil Simon
Directed by Herbert Ross
Screenplay by Neil Simon
Photographed in DeLuxe Color by David M. Walsh
Music by Marvin Hamlisch
108 minutes

Cast: Walter Matthau, Ann-Margret, Dinah Manoff, Lance Guest, Lewis Smith, Martin Ferrero, Eugene Butler, Samantha Harper, Santos Morales, David Faustino

Neil Simon strikes again, this time with varying results. A lazy screenwriter (Walter Matthau) has his life complicated when a nineteen-year-old daughter (Dinah Manoff) from his first marriage shows up on his doorstep. Since they haven't spoken in sixteen years, there is considerable awkwardness. She has decided she wants to become an actress, but her overwhelming need is a relationship with the father she never had. Though the two argue in typically humorous Simonesque style, the sparks lead to mutual respect and love. The father finally realizes he must give more of himself, especially where his sometime girlfriend (Ann-Margret) is concerned, and the daughter decides she doesn't want to be an actress after all. Unfortunately, the movie lacks the punch and poignancy of Simon's *The Goodbye Girl,* or the success.

I, THE JURY

Produced by Robert Solo
Directed by Richard T. Heffron
Screenplay by Larry Cohen, based on a novel by Mickey Spillane

Al Pacino (center) and Ben Carlin, B. J. Barie, Eric Gurry, Ari Meyers and Elva Leff in *Author! Author!*

Robby Benson and Barry Miller in *The Chosen*.

Dinah Manoff and Walter Matthau in *I Ought to Be in Pictures*.

Armand Assante in *I, the Jury*.

Photographed in color by Andrew Lazslo
Music by Bill Conti
109 minutes

Cast: Armand Assante, Barbara Carrera, Laurene Landon, Alan King, Geoffrey Lewis, Paul Sorvino, Judson Scott, Barry Snider, Julia Barr, Jessica James, Frederick Downs, Lee Anne Harris, Lynette Harris

Mickey Spillane's spicy detective yarn *I, The Jury,* was filmed in 3-D in 1953 but, in line with the censorship of the day, much of the spice was diluted. No such stricture hampered the 1982 version, replete as it is with realistic gore and sizzling sex scenes. Spillane's tough wit and sardonic style here receive unbridled treatment. Macho private eye Mike Hammer (Armand Assante) avenges the murder of a Vietnam war buddy and finds plenty of time for sexual dalliance with various uninhibited ladies, especially one (Barbara Carrera) who operates a sex therapy clinic, while engaged in more criminal activities. The principal among many villains is a former CIA man (Barry Snider), whose computerized fortress is ripped apart by Hammer. In short, *I, The Jury* is everything Spillane addicts could ask for.

KISS ME GOODBYE

Produced and directed by Robert Mulligan
Screenplay by Charlie Peters, based on material by Jorge Amado and Bruno Barreto
Photographed in DeLuxe Color by Donald Peterman
Music by Ralph Burns
101 minutes

Cast: Sally Field, James Caan, Jeff Bridges, Paul Dooley, Claire Trevor, Mildred Natwick, Dorothy Fielding, William Prince, Maryedith Burrell, Alan Haufrect, Stephen Elliott, Michael Ensign

Romantic features were a staple of Hollywood's Golden Age. *Kiss Me Goodbye* suggests that this is a genre in which Hollywood has lost its touch. A remake of the 1977 Brazilian film *Dona Flor and Her Two Husbands*, the lady in this version is the beguiling Sally Fields, who sets about starting a new life for herself after the death of her husband (James Caan) by picking herself a new one, an Egyptologist (Jeff Bridges). She chooses to remain living in her old apartment, a sumptuous place, which turns into a problem because the spirit of the deceased husband also wants to remain in residence. The spirit is visible and audible only to the wife and, until the time when the spirit has the decency to depart, life for the wife and all those in contact with her is disturbing. Had it been made in 1936 with the likes of Cary Grant and Irene Dunne, *Kiss Me Goodbye* might have been charming. In the harsh world of 1982 it seemed only mildly amusing.

Jeff Bridges, Sally Field and James Caan in *Kiss Me Goodbye*.

MAKING LOVE

Produced by Allen Adler and Daniel Melnick
Directed by Arthur Hiller
Screenplay by Barry Sandler, from a story by A. Scott Berg
Photographed in DeLuxe Color by David M. Walsh
Music by Leonard Rosenman
111 minutes

Cast: Michael Ontkean, Kate Jackson, Harry Hamlin, Wendy Hiller, Arthur Hill, Nancy Olson, John Dukakis, Terry Kiser, Dennis Howard, Asher Brauner

A successful doctor (Michael Ontkean) and his pretty wife (Kate Jackson), who is a rising television network executive, move into a new home. Soon after, although their marriage seems solid, the young man begins exploring his homosexual leanings. He meets a novelist (Harry Hamlin) and has a one-night fling, and although he wants to continue the affair, the writer is not one for making commitments. Seeing other men, the doctor fully realizes his sexual alignment and tells his wife. She reacts with complete revulsion and sends him packing. She later decides to help him, but he now knows it would not be fair to live between two worlds. They get a divorce, but when they meet again, four years later, their respect for each other continues.

Harry Hamlin, Michael Ontkean and Kate Jackson in *Making Love*.

THE MAN FROM SNOWY RIVER

Produced by Geoff Burrowes
Directed by George Miller
Screenplay by John Dixon and Fred Cullen
Photographed in Panavision and Eastman Color by Keith Wagstaff
Music by Bruce Rowland
102 minutes

Cast: Kirk Douglas, Jack Thompson, Tom Burlinson, Sigrid Thornton, Lorraine Bayly, Chris Haywood, Tony Bonner, Gus Mercutio, Terrence Donovan, David Bradshaw

Continuing a winning stream of Australian movies, *The Man From Snowy River* showed Hollywood that it was still possible to make a gloriously old-fashioned western. Filmed in the spectacular terrain of the Great Dividing Ranges in the state of Victoria, the movie is based on a familiar Aussie poem of the same name by A. B. (Banjo) Patterson, who is briefly portrayed in the film by David Bradshaw. It is the story of a pair of brothers (both played by Kirk Douglas), one a rich rancher and the other a hermit, neither of whom have spoken for years because of their rivalry over a woman. The rancher's spunky young daughter (Sigrid Thornton) falls in love with a youngster (Tom Burlinson), who has been befriended by the cheery hermit, and who wants to be nothing more than a rancher himself. The father hopes for something more socially elevated, but he has to learn that love finds its own way, no matter what. The simple story lines of *Snowy River* are secondary to its interesting insights into Australian ranch life and its spendidly photographed scenery. It also has some of the most exciting horse action sequences ever filmed, anywhere.

MEGAFORCE

Produced by Albert S. Ruddy
Directed by Hal Needham
Screenplay be James Whittaker, Albert S. Ruddy, Hal Needham and Andre Morgan
Photographed in Technicolor by Michael Butler
Music by Jerold Immel
99 minutes

Cast: Barry Bostwick, Persis Khambatta, Michael Beck, Edward Mulhare, George Furth, Henry Silva, Michael Kulcsar, Ralph Wilcox

Megaforce is a military strategist's dream come true, concerning as it does a group of elite, highly trained fighter-technicians who operate from an underground fortress containing, and at their disposal, the most scientifically advanced weaponry their designer-genius (George Furth) can devise. When a mercenary bandit (Henry Silva) leads his forces in attacking the small country of Sardoun, Megaforce commander Ace Hunter (Barry Bostwick) agrees to come to their aid. The result is a great deal of cinematic special effects, rather like *Star Wars* confined to the planet earth, and director Hal Needham, a former ace

449

stuntman, gets a dazzling amount of movement on the screen. The results at the box office, however, suggested that the public was not particularly moved by all this confusing mayhem.

MONSIGNOR

Produced by Frank Yablans and David Niven, Jr.
Directed by Frank Perry
Screenplay by Abraham Polonsky and Wendell Mayes, based on the novel by Jack Alain Leger
Photographed in DeLuxe Color by Billy Williams
Music by John Williams
122 minutes

Cast: Christopher Reeve, Genevieve Bujold, Fernando Rey, Jason Miller, Joe Cortese, Adolfo Celi, Leonard Cimino, Tomas Milian, Robert J. Prosky, Joe Pantoliano

During World War II, a young American priest (Christopher Reeve) stationed in Italy is introduced to the profits of black marketeering. He also meets and has an affair with a young novice (Genevieve Bujold) who is unaware he is a priest. During a papal mass, she sees him and discovers his true identity. In a fury, she later ends their relationship. After the war, the priest's business mind and ability to bring money into the church's coffers lead him to manage the Vatican's finances and receive the title, Monsignore. Throughout his career, there is always the scent of scandal about his dealings with organized crime, but his is protected by a Cardinal (Fernando Rey) who is close to the Pope. Finally, in later years, the Cardinal's opposition in the Vatican demand an investigation into the allegations of corruption. Once again, the Cardinal comes to the rescue and convinces the Pope (Leonard Cimino) that the church's best interests are being served.

NATIONAL LAMPOON'S CLASS REUNION

Produced by Matty Simmons
Directed by Michael Miller
Screenplay by John Hughes
Photographed in Metrocolor by Phil Lathrop
Music by Peter Bernstein and Mark Goldenberg
84 minutes

Cast: Gerrit Graham, Michael Lerner, Fred McCarren, Miriam Flynn, Stephen Furst, Marya Small, Shelley Smith, Zane Buzby, Jacklyn Zeman, Blackie Dammett, Barry Diamond, Art Evans, Maria Pennington, Randolph Powell, Misty Rowe, Jim Staahl, Garry Hibbard, Anne Ramsay, Steve Tracy, Isabel West

The enormous success of *Animal House* made similar forays by National Lampoon into the habits of young Americans, their customs, ways and interests, inevitable. Since the previous picture had made its mark by dwelling on the more gross aspects of U. S. youth, *Class Reunion* focussed even more closely on the raunchy and the bizarre, and failed to amuse. The 1972 grads who turn up for their high school reunion all appear to be either unpleasant or unbalanced. Among them is a snooty yacht salesman (Gerrit Graham), a dull do-gooder (Fred McCarren), a handicapped person in need of an exorcist (Zane Buzby) and a blind nymphomaniac (Marya Small). All of them are threatened by the antics of a deadly lunatic. An audience can be forgiven for believing that nothing could be too bad a fate for the characters in this film.

THE PIRATE MOVIE

Produced by David Joseph
Directed by Ken Annakin
Screenplay by Trevor Farrant
Photographed in color by Robin Copping
Songs by Terry Britten, Kit Hain, Sue Shifren, Brian Robertson, and Gilbert and Sullivan
99 minutes

Cast: Kristy McNichol, Christopher Atkins, Ted Hamilton, Bill Kerr, Garry McDonald, Maggie Kirkpatrick, Linda Nagle, Kate Ferguson, Rhonda Burchmore, Cathrine Lynch, Chuck McKinney, Marc Colombani, John Allansu, Pamela Jones

The Pirate Movie has an unfortunate title, since it obviously pirates some of the plot and six of the songs from *The Pirates of Penzance* and adds ideas seemingly lifted from such films as *The Princess and the Pirate,* several Beatles pictures, and *The Blue Lagoon,* whose star, Christopher Atkins, here seems to resume segments of his former role. Added to the Gilbert and Sullivan songs are a slew of youth-orientated new ones, all of which mix with G&S as oil mixes with water. Filmed in Australia, *The Pirate Movie* begins at an amusement park as a dreamy teenager (Kristy McNichol) drools over a lusty young actor (Atkins), who performs in a Pirate Day sideshow. Later rendered unconscious in an accident, she fantasizes about being Mable in the G&S operetta, finding true love with an apprentice pirate (again Atkins). The resultant confusion of styles found favor with neither G&S fans nor the youth market.

QUEST FOR FIRE

Produced by John Kemeny and Denis Heroux
Directed by Jean-Jacques Annaud
Screenplay by Gerard Brach
Special languages created by Anthony Burgess
Body language and gestures by Desmond Morris
Photographed in Panavision and Color by Claude Agostini
Music by Philippe Sarde
97 minutes

Cast: Everett McGill, Ron Perlman, Nameer El-Kadi, Rae Dawn Chong, Gary Schwartz, Naseer El-Kadi, Frank Olivier Bonnet, Jean-Michel Kindt, Kurt Schiegl

A marvellous speculation of what "life may have been like 80,000 years ago." The pleasant, sociable Ulam tribe is attacked by the savage Wagabous. In their escape, the fire-bearer loses the tribe's precious flame, so vital to their existence. As a matter of survival, three brave men set out on a quest for fire. Along the way, they battle fierce prehistoric bears, unfriendly tribes, and encounter a herd of mastodons. They also come in contact with the very sophisticated Ivaka, who educate them in the making of fire. A young female of this tribe takes a liking to one of the men and decides to run off with him. She brings to the more primitive cave-dwelling Ulams a new and important element in civilization. A wonderfully conceived and thought-provoking story with plenty of excitement, humor and tenderness, all without a single word in English.

Ron Perlman, Everett McGill and Nameer Elkadi in *Quest for Fire*.

SIX PACK

Produced by Michael Trikilis
Directed by Daniel Petrie
Screenplay by Mike Marvin and Alex Matter
Photographed in DeLuxe Color by Mario Tosi
Music by Charles Fox
110 minutes

Cast: Kenny Rogers, Diane Lane, Erin Gray, Barry Corbin, Terry Kiser, Bob Hannah, Tom Abernathy, Robbie Fleming, Anthony Michael Hall, Robby Still, Benji Wilhaite

The title refers not to a carton of beer but to a group of orphaned children of criminal inclination who are led into the better life through the loving care of a stock car driver (Kenny Rogers). The kids strip his car, but when he catches up with them he wins them over with his warm nature and soon has them working for him as he tries to make a comeback on the racing circuit. Their mechanical skill is a boon to the driver and a deterrent to the opposition. A serviceable but not remarkable film debut for the affable country singer Kenny Rogers, the story is set in the South and leans a little too heavily on Southern clichés, including the corrupt sheriff, but it happily points up the possibilities of redemption among the morally deprived younger set, even to the extent of persuading them to cut down on their cussing. As a genial crusader, Rogers may have a lot of work ahead of him.

Kristy McNichol and Christopher Atkins in *The Pirate Movie*.

Kenny Rogers and the kids: Tommy Abernathy, Ronny Still, Anthony Michael Hall, Benji Wilhoite, Robbie Fleming and Diane Ladd in *Six Pack*.

Fernando Rey and Christopher Reeve in *Monsignor*.

National Lampoon's Class Reunion.

Barry Bostwick, Ralph Wilcox and Michael Beck in *Megaforce*.

451

Paul Newman
in *The Verdict*.

THE VERDICT

Produced by Richard D. Zanuck and David Brown
Directed by Sidney Lumet
Screenplay by David Mamet, based on the novel by Barry Reed
Photographed in DeLuxe Color by Andrzej Bartowiak
Music by Johnny Mandel
126 minutes

Cast: Paul Newman, Charlotte Rampling, Jack Warden, James Mason, Milo O'Shea, Edward Binns, Julie Bovasso, Lindsay Crouse

Paul Newman gives another bravura performance as the once-idealistic, but now down-and-out attorney, Frank Galvin. A fellow lawyer and friend (Jack Warden) gives Galvin a handout case to keep him going, an open-and-shut matter of medical malpractice. Galvin, however, refuses a settlement from the hospital as a matter of principle and pursues the case in court. The hospital, run by the Boston archdiocese, hires a top but unscrupulous attorney (James Mason) to defend them. He has an attractive woman (Charlotte Rampling) infiltrate Galvin's camp and inform him of the prosecution's progress. When it looks like all is lost for Galvin, he doggedly tracks down a young nurse (Lindsay Crouse) who finally agrees to testify against the doctors. Her testimony turns the case and Galvin comes up the hero. A thoroughly entertaining movie, even though the story was assailed by lawyers as being unrealistic.

VISITING HOURS

Produced by Claude Heroux
Directed by Jean Claude Lord
Screenplay by Brian Taggert
Photographed in color by Rene Verzier
Music by Jonathan Goldsmith
105 minutes

Cast: Lee Grant, William Shatner, Michael Ironside, Linda Purl,

Michael Ironside and Lee Grant in *Visiting Hours*.

Leonore Zann, Harvey Atkin, Helen Hughes, Michael J. Reynolds, Kirsten Bishopric, Debra Kirschenbaum, Elizabeth Leigh Milne, Maureen McRae, Dustin Waln

Made in Montreal, *Visiting Hours* is an above-average entry in the psycho-suspense league, telling the harrowing tale of a TV journalist (Lee Grant) who is victimized by a lunatic (Michael Ironside) who loathes women and takes particular exception to the journalist's stand on women's rights. He not only rapes and kills women but he likes to photograph them in their death throes. The journalist survives his attack, but he follows her to the hospital in which she is placed. In attempting to catch up with her, he also wreaks considerable havoc on other patients and on the staff. With a good cast and script, director Lord generates a goodly amount of chilling tension, and inadvertently calls for greater security measures in hospitals. The one in this film is alarmingly under-policed.

YOUNG DOCTORS IN LOVE

Produced by Jerry Buckheimer
Directed by Garry Marshall
Screenplay by Michael Elias and Rich Eustis
Photographed in Metrocolor by Don Peterman
Music by Maurice Jarre
95 minutes

Cast: Michael McKean, Sean Young, Hector Elizondo, Harry Dean Stanton, Patrick Macnee, Dabney Coleman, Pamela Reed, Taylor Negron, Saul Rubinek, Patrick Collins, Ted McGinley, George Furth, John Beradino, Emily McLaughlin, Michael Damian, Steven Ford, Chris Robinson, Stuart Damon, Jaime Lee Bauer, Tom Ligon, Kin Shriner, Janine Turner, Mr. T.

Films which attempt to spoof the medical profession and hospitals seem doomed not to rise above a certain level of bedpan humor. *Young Doctors in Love* steadfastly maintains the tradition. Directed by TV veteran Garry Marshall, and peopled by TV actors well employed in sitcoms, the film barely makes the transition to the big screen. The characters include a hospital administrator (Dabney Coleman) being driven to distraction by his job, a boozy pathologist (Harry Dean Stanton), a doctor (Taylor Negron) addicted to pills, and a gangster (Hector Alizondo) who has trouble fighting off the attentions of an amorous old doctor (Patrick Macnee). As in all films of this kind, the producers try to find humor in the predicaments and embarrassments of illness. To what extent they succeed is left to the judgment and taste of the viewer.

20TH CENTURY-FOX ACADEMY AWARDS FOR 1982

SARAH MONZAI, MICHELE BURKE: Best Make-up, *Quest for Fire*.

Dabney Coleman and Michael McKean (center) in *Young Doctors in Love*.

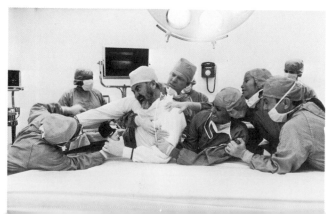

ALL THE RIGHT MOVES

Produced by Stephen Deutsch
Directed by Michael Chapman
Screenplay by Michael Kane
Photographed in DeLuxe Color

Cast: Tom Cruise, Craig T. Nelson, Lea Thompson, Charles Cioffi, Sandy Faison, Paul Carafotes, Chris Penn, Leon Robinson, Keith Ford, Walter Briggs, Jonas Miller

In a dying steel mill town in Pennsylvania, the local high school football games are taken seriously. For the students, it is a way to escape the town. The team's defensive end (Tom Cruise) wants to become an architect and a football scholarship is his ticket. The team's coach (Craig T. Nelson) also wants out and pushes the team brutally to impress scouts from a big college. When the team loses the game, the coach blames it on the young man who stands up for his rights and is kicked out. When the young man graduates, he has no choice but to work in a steel mill. Soon, when all looks bleak, he gets a coaching job at a small college in Arizona with the chance to later transfer to the state university. Following the surprise success created by the sleeper *Breaking Away,* this is another in the long line of attempts to emulate and equal the charm and excitement of its predecessor. It's old-fashioned Americana, but played a little too straight for its own good.

THE ENTITY

Produced by Harold Schneider
Directed by Sidney J. Furie
Screenplay by Frank DeFelitta, based on his novel
Photographed in Panavision and Technicolor by Stephen H. Burum
Music by Charles Bernstein
125 minutes

Cast: Barbara Hershey, Ron Silver, David Labisoa, George Coe, Margaret Blye, Jacqueline Brooks, Richard Brestoff, Michael Alldredge, Raymond Singer, Allan Rich, Natasha Ryan, Melanie Gaffin, Alex Rocco, Sully Bayar, Tom Stern, Curt Lowens

The problem with *The Entity* lies in trying to find out what it is. This is the story of a Los Angeles woman (Barbara Hershey), a single parent with three children, who is tormented by some strange, unseen entity from another level of existence. It rapes her and almost causes her death in a car accident. On the verge of cracking up from the strain, she agrees to examination by a psychiatrist (Ron Silver) and experiments by a team of parapsychologists at a university. The frightening phenomena in her life, the flickering lights and damaged objects, are all confirmed by the team, who attempt to lure the entity into an environment in which it can be trapped. But the entity into an environment in which it can be trapped. But the entity is not to be contained. This bizarre foray into the supernatural falls short of credibility, but fascinates with its probability, as well as providing some startling special effects.

HEART LIKE A WHEEL

Produced by Charles Roven
Directed by Jonathan Kaplan
Screenplay by Ken Friedman
Photographed in DeLuxe Color by Tak Fujimato
Music by Lawrence Rosenthal
113 minutes

Cast: Bonnie Bedelia, Beau Bridges, Leo Rossi, Hoyt Axton, Bill McKenney, Anthony Edwards, Dean Paul Martin, Paul Bartel, Missy Basile, Michael Cavanaugh, Ellen Geer, Nora Heflin, Bryon Thames, Tiny Wells, Brandon Brent Williams

The true story of America's first professional racing car driver, Shirley Muldowney (Bonnie Bedelia), *Heart Like a Wheel* benefits from having Muldowney herself as technical adviser. Her career began as a teenager hot-rod driver, winning every drag race in which she appeared, and then, despite being married and with a child, she was compelled to enter professional racing in 1966. The film traces her triumph over sexist prejudice, the collapse of her marriage and her affair with a champion driver (Beau Bridges) who helps her scale the heights while proving emotionally unreliable. The film's coverage of the car racing world cannot be faulted, and Bonnie Bedelia gives a creditable account of a lady surviving the trials of her personal and professional life.

KIDCO

Produced by Frank Yablans and David Niven, Jr.
Directed by Ronald F. Maxwell

Screenplay by Bennett Tramer
Photographed in DeLuxe Color by Paul Lohmann
Music by Michael Small
104 minutes

Cast: Scott Schwartz, Cinnamon Idles, Tristine Skyler, Elizabeth Gorcey

Business success by youthful entrepreneurs is the theme of this lighthearted comedy based on a true incident. An enterprising group of children from the Cessna family, headed by sixth-grader Dickie (Scott Schwartz), set up a business in fertilizers. Through hard work and sheer ingenuity, they become competition for a large established company. When the management of that company tries to buy out Kidco, Dickie refuses and corporate war is declared. As well, television publicity leads to interest by the Internal Revenue Service, which tries to collect back taxes on the family's earnings. Dickie decides to fight the case in court and gets a kindly judge who is running for public office. The kids win everyone over but end up with a huge fine, which fortunately will be paid for by Kidco T-shirts, which are selling like hotcakes. A family film which combines the elements of old movies with the contemporary drive for money, making it timely for audiences of all ages.

THE KING OF COMEDY

Produced by Arnon Milchan
Directed by Martin Scorsese
Screenplay by Paul D. Zimmerman
Photographed in color by Fred Schuler
Music direction by Robbie Robertson
108 minutes

Cast: Robert De Niro, Jerry Lewis, Diahnne Abbott, Sandra Bernhard, Ed Herlihy, Lo Brown, Shelley Hack, Doc Lawless, Margo Winkler, Katherine Scorsese. Guest stars: Tony Randall, Liza Minnelli, Joyce Brothers

The pitfalls of fame are closely examined by Martin Scorsese in this too-true-to-be-funny comedy about a hugely popular TV talk-show host (Jerry Lewis) and his super fan Rupert Pupkin (Robert De Niro), who believes that with a little luck he too can scale the heights of success in television. With skill born of cunning, Rupert inveigles himself into the life of the host. Worn down by persistence, the host advises Rupert to see his secretary for a possible audition. It proves to be an error that eventually causes the host to fear for his life as Rupert and his equally determined girlfriend (Sandra Bernhard) kidnap the host and demand, and get, him a spot on the host's show. Having achieved this dream-come-true, Rupert cheerfully goes to jail for a period—but comes out with a contract for his autobiography. Scorsese's comments on the plight of being a celebrity tend toward the glib, but he nonetheless makes some painful points and draws superb performances from De Niro and Lewis.

454

Barbara Hershey in *The Entity.*

Tom Cruise and Lea Thompson in *All the Right Moves.*

Bonnie Bedelia and Beau Bridges in *Heart Like a Wheel.*

Scott Schwartz, Tristine Skyler, Cinnamon Idles, and Elizabeth Gorcey in *Kidco.*

Jerry Lewis and Robert De Niro in *The King of Comedy*.

Marsha Mason, Jason Robards and Matthew Broderick in *Max Dugan Returns*.

MAX DUGAN RETURNS

Produced by Herbert Ross and Neil Simon
Directed by Herbert Ross
Screenplay by Neil Simon
Photographed in DeLuxe Color by David M. Walsh
Music by David Shire
98 minutes

Cast: Marsha Mason, Jason Robards, Donald Sutherland, Matthew Broderick, Dody Goodman, Sal Viscuso, Panchito Gomez

Modern family life is again the focal point of Neil Simon's humor as he asks us to consider the plight of a teacher (Marsha Mason), who can barely get by in running a home for herself and her fifteen-year-old son (Matthew Broderick). When her decrepit car is stolen she receives the warm attentions of a civilized detective (Donald Sutherland). His attention turns serious when she apparently takes in an aging lodger (Jason Robards) and quickly acquires such signs of wealth as a Mercedes-Benz sportscar, a houseful of modern appliances and a complete renovation of her modern little home. The lodger turns out to be the father who had deserted her when she was nine and who now, because he hasn't long to live, wants to make it up to her and get to know his grandson, who is delighted by the sudden wealth. The charming old scoundrel has his way, and finally departs in order not to bring any more attention from the police and the gangsters from whom he probably acquired his wealth. The question of morality takes a bit of a beating, but the film is almost as hard to resist as Max Dugan himself.

MR. MOM

Produced by Lynn Loring and Laurne Shuler
Executive producer: Aaron Spelling
Directed by Stan Dragoti
Screenplay by John Hughes
Photographed in color by Victor J. Kemper
Music by Lee Holdridge
91 minutes

Cast: Michael Keaton, Teri Garr, Frederick Koehler, Taliesin Jaffe, Courtney and Brittany White, Martin Mull, Ann Jillian, Jeffrey Tambor, Christopher Lloyd, Tom Leopold, Graham Jarvis, Carolyn Seymour, Michael Alaimo, Valri Bronfield, Charles Woolf, Mirriam Flynn

Mr. Mom places its finger squarely on one of the problems of contemporary American life—unemployment among middle-class professionals, and in particular the problems caused when the husband cannot find work and the wife has to assume the role of breadwinner. The situation has been dealt with many times on television, and the problem of this film is that it seems little more than an expensively produced version of a TV sitcom. Here a Detroit auto engineer (Michael Keaton) is laid off and his capable wife (Teri Garr) gets a job at which she shines. The comedy comes from the predictable circumstances of sex-role reversals. Hubby has to play Mommy, do housework and fight off the advances of local wives, while the wife faces and overcomes similar problems at the office. The film is amusing, mostly because of the comedic skill of Keaton and Garr.

THE OSTERMAN WEEKEND

Produced by Peter S. Davis and William N. Panzer
Directed by Sam Peckinpah
Screenplay by Alan Sharp
Photographed in color by John Coquillon
Music by Lalo Schifrin
102 minutes

Cast: Rutger Hauer, John Hurt, Craig T. Nelson, Dennis Hopper, Chris Sarandon, Meg Foster, Helen Shaver, Burt Lancaster, Cassie Yates, Sandy McPeak, Christopher Starr

Espionage—dark, convoluted and brutal. John Tanner (Rutger Hauer), the news director of a TV network in New York, lives with his wife and children in a posh, well-policed suburb. His life takes a turn for the violent worse when he agrees to cooperate with the CIA in uncovering Soviet agents, some of whom, to Tanner's horror, are among his closest friends. Some of those friends come to spend the weekend with the Tanners and suspense and impending disaster mount by the hour. Finally it is revealed that none of the friends are really agents. The real culprits are those CIA traitors who devised the scheme in order to deflect suspicion. As with all films about contemporary espionage, *The Osterman Weekend* suggests that it is a business to avoid at all costs, except perhaps for a couple of vicarious hours in a cinema.

PORKY'S II: THE NEXT DAY

Produced by Don Carmody and Bob Clark
Executive producers: Melvin Simon, Harold Greenberg and Alan
    Landsberg
Directed by Bob Clark
Screenplay by Roger E. Swaybill, Alan Ormsby and Bob Clark
Photographed in DeLuxe Color by Reginald H. Morris
Music by Carl Zittrer
95 minutes

Cast: Don Monahan, Wyatt Knight, Mark Herrier, Roger Wilson,
Cyril O'Reilly, Tony Ganios, Kaki Hunter, Scott Colomby, Nancy
Parsons, Joseph Running Fox, Eric Christmas, Bill Wiley, Edward
Winter, Cisse Cameron, Else Earl

When a film aimed at the youth movie market grosses over
fifty million dollars it is inevitable that that market is likely
to have a sequel aimed in its direction. The sequel to *Porky's*
is quite literally more of the same, including much of the
same cast and more of the same kind of raunchy, adolescent
humor. The focus this time is upon school activities, mostly
on the drama class and their plans to do a modern, lewd
version of a Shakespearean play, over the objections of the
hyper-moralistic school board. In this film old Puritanism
stands about as much chance of surviving against the
onslaught of new Liberalism as does a snowman in a heat
wave. But for all its bold vulgarity, *Porky's II: The Next Day*
did not do as well at the box office as the first trip.

RETURN OF THE JEDI

Executive Producer George Lucas
Produced by Howard Kazanjian
Directed by Richard Marquand
Screenplay by Lawrence Kasdan and George Lucas, based on a
    story by George Lucas
Photographed in Panavision and Color by Alan Hume
Music by John Williams
133 minutes

Cast: Mark Hamill, Harrison Ford, Carrie Fisher, Billy Dee
Williams, Anthony Daniels, Peter Mayhew, Sebastian Shaw, Ian
McDiarmid, Frank Oz, David Prowse, Alec Guinness

The third installment in the *"Star Wars"* series picks up
where *The Empire Strikes Back* left off. Luke Skywalker
(Mark Hamill) and friends Lando Calrissian (Billy Dee
Williams) and Princess Leia (Carrie Fisher) rescue Han
Solo (Harrison Ford) from his carbon-frozen imprisonment
at Jabba the Hutt's fortress. Luke is then off to Dagobah
once more to complete his Jedi training. Yoda, his aged
instructor, tells him he must do battle with evil Darth Vader.
As Yoda dies, Luke goes off to fulfill his destiny. Meanwhile, the Rebel forces are massing for an attack on Vader
(David Prowse) and the Emperor (Ian McDiarmid). Luke
prevents a slaughter of his comrades by using "The Force"
against the evil emperor and Vader. This is a spectacular
conclusion to George Lucas's trilogy with some nice twists:

Darth Vader is indeed Luke's father and turns back to the
good side of "The Force" as he dies; Princess Leia is
revealed as Luke's long-lost sister; the three-way romance is
resolved with Leia and Han ending as lovers. All in all, a
satisfying and terrifically entertaining wind-up to the most
successful series in movie history.

SILKWOOD

Produced by Mike Nichols and Michael Hausman
Directed by Mike Nichols
Screenplay by Nora Ephron and Alice Arlen
Photographed in color by Miroslav Ondricek
Music by Georges Delerue
128 minutes

Cast: Meryl Streep, Kurt Russell, Cher, Craig T. Nelson, Diana
Scarwid, Fred Ward, Ron Silver, Charles Hallahan, Josef Sommer

In 1983 Meryl Streep continued her remarkable track record
by portraying a courageous young lady named Karen
Silkwood, an employee of a plutonium plant in Oklahoma,
who suspects that her employers are not nearly as careful as
they should be in the handling of plutonium and are
needlessly endangering the lives of workers. With the aid of
her union she collects evidence to present her case that
faulty equipment has been used in order to speed up
production, and that records have been falsified. Karen is on
her way to a meeting with a New York reporter when she is
involved in a car crash and killed. The evidence she was
carrying is never found. *Silkwood* plays with the public's
fear of chemical and nuclear developments but loses some
of its impact by presenting the leading character as a rather
strange and undisciplined lady. For all that, both Streep and
the plot make some riveting points.

THE STAR CHAMBER

Produced by Frank Yablans
Directed by Peter Hyams
Screenplay by Roderick Taylor and Peter Hyams
Photographed in DeLuxe Color by Richard Hannah
Music by Michael Small
109 minutes

Cast: Michael Douglas, Hal Holbrook, Yaphet Kotto, Sharon
Gless, James B. Sikking, Joe Regalbuto, Don Calfa, John DiSanti,
DeWayne Jessie, Jack Kehoe, Larry Hankin, Dick Anthony
Williams

A decent conscientious judge (Michael Douglas), presiding
over a trial of the suspected murderers of a young boy, has to
set the men free even though he is convinced of their guilt.
He is urged by another judge (Hal Holbrook) to join a secret
society of vigilante judges who send a killer after those they
deem guilty but have escaped imprisonment due to legal
loopholes. Coming before the "Star Chamber," he tells the

others of the murderers' guilt and they agree to send their hit man after them. However, it is soon discovered that the two suspects are indeed innocent and the judge has to try to convince them to leave town. Failing in his efforts, he realizes they will be killed and must stop the hit man. Unfortunately, he does not prevent the murders and is almost killed himself but for a detective (Yaphet Kotto) who realizes what is going on and catches up with the hit man before he murders the judge. Interesting and thought-provoking, but the script did not hold up throughout, and neither did audience support.

TO BE OR NOT TO BE

Produced by Mel Brooks
Directed by Alan Johnson
Screenplay by Thomas Meehan and Ronny Graham
Photographed in DeLuxe Color by Gerald Hirshfeld
Music by John Morris
108 minutes

Cast: Mel Brooks, Anne Bancroft, Tim Matheson, Charles Durning, Jose Ferrer, George Gaynes, George Wyner, Lewis Stadlen

When Ernst Lubitsch's *To Be or Not to Be* was released in 1942, it was castigated as being in terrible taste. After all, Hitler was invading Europe and a story about a group of Polish actors fooling and eventually foiling the Nazis was not a gagfest for wartime audiences. Mel Brooks's remake does not have the burden of war's horrors and goes for the laughs. Brooks plays the Jack Benny part of Bronski, who considers himself the greatest Shakespearean actor in Poland but is really just a side of ham, and Anne Bancroft plays his truly talented and lovely wife, Anna. Through Anna's affair with a young flyer (Tim Matheson), the Bronskis get caught up in a Nazi spy plot and have to play-act their way through various disguises in order to infiltrate and secure a list of Polish underground fighters from an evil German (Jose Ferrer). The twists and turns are fast and furious and the ensemble injects pathos and character development not often found in a Mel Brooks movie. Certainly his finest work since *Young Frankenstein*.

TOUGH ENOUGH

Produced by William F. Gilmore
Directed by Richard Fleischer
Screenplay by John Leone
Photographed in Technicolor and Panavision by James A. Contner
Music by Michael Lloyd and Steve Wax
106 minutes

Cast: Dennis Quaid, Carlene Watkins, Stan Shaw, Pam Grier, Warren Oates, Bruce McGill, Wilford Brimley, Fran Ryan, Christopher Norris, Terra Perry, Big John Hamilton

Tough Enough is a first. It is the first film to present a hero as a song writer who abets his career by becoming a

Teri Garr and Michael Keaton in *Mr. Mom.*

Rutger Hauer and Craig T. Nelson in *The Osterman Weekend.*

Cyril O'Reilly, Scott Colomby, Dan Mohahan, Rod Ball, Mark Herrier, Wyatt Knight and Tony Ganios in *Porky's II: The Next Day.*

Carrie Fisher in *The Return of the Jedi.*

Hal Holbrook and Michael Douglas in *The Star Chamber.*

Anne Bancroft and Mel Brooks in *To Be or Not to Be.*

Meryl Streep in *Silkwood.*   Dennis Quaid in *Tough Enough.*

prizefighter. Art Long (Dennis Quaid) sings his country-western songs in small clubs at night but can't make enough to keep his wife (Carlene Watkins) and baby son in any kind of security, so he uses his skill as a boxer to enter amateur contests and soon becomes known as The Country Western Warrior. In charting his success, the film makes good points about the need to be adaptable and tenacious in the competitive world of today, especially as it applies to young people.

TWO OF A KIND

Produced by Roger M. Rothstein
Written and Directed by John Herzfeld
Photographed in DeLuxe Color by Fred Koenekamp
Music adaptation by Patrick Williams
87 minutes

Cast: John Travolta, Olivia Newton-John, Oliver Reed, Beatrice Straight, Scatman Crother, Castulo Guerra

A wild mixture of fantasy and religious parable, *Two of a Kind* presents a couple of characters who would have trouble getting by at any point in history. In the frenetic world of today, a boy named Zack (John Travolta) owes money to a loan shark and, in order to meet the loan, robs a bank, where a slick and pretty teller named Debra (Olivia Newton-John) tricks him and keeps the money for herself. They are both killed in a freak accident. In the meantime, God has become increasingly angry about the state of the world and tells his angels he wants to start again from scratch. The angels try to talk him out of it and reach a compromise when they promise to come up with a miracle. This involves proving that under different circumstances

Zack and Debbie could love and sacrifice themselves for each other. They do. Never was the fate of the world in less secure hands.

WITHOUT A TRACE

Produced and directed by Stanley R. Jaffe
Screenplay by Beth Gutcheon, based on her novel *Still Missing*
Photographed in DeLuxe Color by John Bailey
Music by Jack Nitzsche
120 minutes

Cast: Kate Nelligan, Judd Hirsch, David Dukes, Stockard Channing, Jacqueline Brooks, Keith McDermott, Kathleen Widdoes, Daniel Bryan Corkill, Cheryl Giannini, David Simon, William Duell, Joan McManagle, Louise Stubbs

The strength of *Without a Trace* lies in the restrained performance of the dignified Kate Nelligan as a woman caused extreme anguish by the disappearance of her six-year-old son one day as he walks to his school in Brooklyn. Her plight is made worse by having recently lost her husband (David Dukes) to a younger woman, and by the invasion of her life by the media, who seize upon this as a top-notch news item. The only strong suspect is a young homosexual with a history of child molestation, but he proves to be innocent. All leads seem hopeless—until the surprise ending of the story. Much credit is due producer-director Jaffe for his cool handling of the material, for not letting it become overly sentimental or emotional. He keeps the distraught mother at arm's length from the audience; she does not reunite with her husband and neither does she fall in love with the helpful investigating detective (Judd Hirsch). Jaffe's cool handling gives *Without a Trace* its chill.

Judd Hirsch and Kate Nelligan in *Without a Trace.*

Olivia Newton-John and John Travolta in *Two of a Kind.*

THE ADVENTURES OF BUCKAROO BANZAI

Produced by Neil Canton and W. D. Richter
Executive Producer Sidney Beckerman
Directed by W. D. Richter
Screenplay by Earl Mac Rauch
Photographed in Panavision and Metrocolor by Fred J. Koenekamp
Music by Michael Boddicker
103 minutes

Cast: Peter Weller, John Lithgow, Ellen Barkin, Jeff Goldblum, Christopher Lloyd, Lewis Smith, Rosalind Cash, Robert Ito, Pepe Serna, Ronald Lacey, Matt Clark, Clancy Brown, William Traylor, Carl Lumbly, Vincent Schiavelli, Dan Hedaya

With someone like Buckaroo Banzai (Peter Weller), it becomes difficult to take seriously a man the screenplay presents as a physicist and neuro-surgeon, especially when he claims to have discovered an eighth dimension and drives his jet car straight through a mountain. It is all science-fiction, but of a most fantastic kind and bordering upon parody all the way. Buckaroo takes upon himself the task of saving the planet earth from an invasion by aliens from outer space, led by a lunatic doctor (John Lithgow), who has escaped from an asylum for the criminally insane in New Jersey. The film is best enjoyed by those with some knowledge of Orson Welles's dramatization of *War of the Worlds*, which clearly inspired the scripters of this overly complicated fantasy comedy. As is often the case with movies of this genre, the special effects come off better than the players.

BACHELOR PARTY

Produced by Ron Moler and Bob Israel
Directed by Neal Israel
Screenplay by Neal Israel and Pat Proft, from a story by Bo Israel
Photographed in DeLuxe Color by Hal Trussel
Music by Robert Folk
106 minutes

Cast: Tom Hanks, Tawny Kitaen, Adrian Zmed, George Grizzard, Barbara Stuart, Robert Prescott, William Tepper, Wendy Jo Sperber, Barry Diamond, Gary Grossman

Outrageous comedy strikes again. A free-and-easy school bus driver (Tom Hanks) decides to take the plunge and settle down with his pretty girlfriend (Tawny Kitaen) over the strong objections of her father (George Grizzard). But first, the young man's friends decide to throw a wild bachelor party as a farewell to his single life. When the fiancée learns about the party, she's concerned her husband-to-be might be unfaithful. This prompts her to disguise herself as a prostitute to spy on him and to have a girl's-night-out at a male strip joint. Meanwhile, the irate father tries to get his daughter's previous boyfriend (Robert Prescott) to win her away from the bus driver. However, happy endings prevail when all the lunacy is over. A scattershot youth comedy with such inanities as cooking meatballs with a blowtorch, a suicide attempt with an electric razor, and a donkey snorting cocaine.

BLAME IT ON RIO

Produced and Directed by Stanley Donen
Screenplay by Charlie Peters and Larry Gelbart
Photographed in DeLuxe Color by Reynaldo Villalobos
Music by Ken Wannberg
102 minutes

Cast: Michael Caine, Joseph Bologna, Valerie Harper, Michelle Johnson, Demi Moore, Jose Lewgoy

A middle-aged businessman (Michael Caine) takes a vacation in Rio with his best friend (Joseph Bologna) and their teen-aged daughters. Amidst the sun and sand, the businessman is lured into an affair by his friend's daughter (Michelle Johnson). Suffering from terrible guilt, he tries to explain to the girl that he's too old for her. It does little good. The affair continues with many of the comic complications of bedroom farce until the girl's father learns of the affair. Finally, the businessman's wife (Valerie Harper) shows up and is distraught when she learns what's going on. In the subsequent mud-slinging, it becomes obvious that the wife has been carrying on an affair with the girl's father. When the vacation ends, the businessman and his wife leave on a note of reconciliation, the seductive teen finds a young man her own age, and the best friend angrily gnashes his teeth. A funny movie, but in dubious taste.

THE BUDDY SYSTEM

Produced by Alain Chammas
Directed by Glenn Jordan
Screenplay by Mary Agnes Donoghue
Photographed in DeLuxe Color by Matthew F. Leonetti
Music by Patrick Williams
110 minutes

Cast: Richard Dreyfuss, Susan Sarandon, Nancy Allen, Jean Stapleton, Wil Wheaton

The mother (Susan Sarandon) of a precocious 11-year-old boy (Wil Wheaton), whose father left them many years before, has a difficult time bringing up her son. Living with an overpowering mother (Jean Stapleton), necessary due to lack of funds, does little to help. The child becomes friendly with a security guard (Richard Dreyfuss) at school, but the mother instantly dislikes him. When the son invites the guard to a Thanksgiving play, he and the mother get to know each other a little better. They shed their current lovers for each other, and the child is delighted. The guard, a struggling inventor, endears himself to them until his ex-girlfriend comes back into his life. Mother and guard remain apart for some time, but both realize they are miserable that way. Finally, one year after the first Thanksgiving play, the guard shows up again and the trio are united. A somewhat charming, but obvious attempt to duplicate Dreyfuss's success in *The Goodbye Girl*.

DREAMSCAPE

Produced by Bruce Cohn Curtis
Directed by Joseph Ruben
Screenplay by David Loughery, Chuck Russell and Joseph Ruben
Photographed in color by Brian Tufano
Music by Maurice Jarre
95 minutes

Cast: Dennis Quaid, Max Von Sydow, Christopher Plummer, Eddie Albert, Kate Capshaw, David Patrick Kelly, George Wendt, Larry Gelman, Cory "Bumper" Yothers, Redmond Gleeson, Peter Jason, Chris Mulkey, Jana Taylor, Madison Mason, Kendall Carly Brown, Larry Cedar

Makers of science-fiction movies are always looking for new twists. *Dreamscape* looks into the phenomenon of dream research and the possibility of scientists being able to enter dreams and manipulate the dreamer. The central character is a young man (Dennis Quaid) who has a psychic talent but no serious interest in using it, until he comes under the influence of a scientist (Max Von Sydow) who operates a center for the study of dreams. The doctor's beautiful assistant (Kate Capshaw) helps the young man take his talent more seriously, especially when it is needed to defeat the evil political plans of the doctor's backer (Christopher Plummer), who has managed to tap into the nuclear nightmares of the President of the United States (Eddie Albert). *Dreamscape*, perhaps a little too bizarre for its own good, touches with good effect upon a disquieting topic but leaves the door open for better forays.

THE FLAMINGO KID

Produced by Michael Phillips
Directed by Garry Marshall
Screenplay by Neal Marshall and Garry Marshall
Photographed in Panavision and DeLuxe Color by James A. Contner
Music editor Kurt Sobel
100 minutes

Cast: Matt Dillon, Hector Elizondo, Molly McCarthy, Martha Gehman, Richard Crenna, Jessica Walter, Carole R. Davis, Janet Jones, Brian McNamara, Fisher Stevens, Leon Robinson, Bronson Pinchot

More about life among the teen-aged, circa 1963, and in particular about Jeffrey Willis (Matt Dillon), a plumber's son whose access to the higher levels of social life comes when he visits the El Flamingo Beach Club, Far Rockaway, New York, an island of leisure in a sea of upward mobility. Jeffrey gets a job at the club as a car parker during the summer after his graduation. His charm and good looks soon lead to better jobs in the club and lots of chances for leisure, including girls. The club's glibly impressive social director (Richard Crenna) tries to persuade Jeffrey to forget about college and enjoy the good life, to the horror of his honest, hard-working father (Hector Elizondo). With a sound track loaded with songs of the day, the film is about the choice the young man must make—the fun way or the hard way. Dillon turns in a good performance as the lad in a quandary who finally gets the better of his teen-age impressionability.

GIVE MY REGARDS TO BROAD STREET

Produced by Andros Epaminondas
Directed by Peter Webb
Screenplay by Paul McCartney
Photographed in Rank Color by Ian McMillan
Music by Paul McCartney
108 minutes

Cast: Paul McCartney, Bryan Brown, Ringo Starr, Barbara Bach, Linda McCartney, Tracey Ullman, Ralph Richardson, Ian Hastings

Paul McCartney, probably one of the most successful figures in the entertainment world, tries his hand at moviemaking. Starring in, writing, and composing *Broad Street* prove a bit much for even his talents. A thin story line involves McCartney trying to find the master tapes for a new album which have disappeared with an associate who has a criminal record. He's in danger of losing his music company if he can't produce the tapes by midnight. It's all nothing more than a way of getting in some old and new McCartney numbers, which in themselves would be worth the cost of admission. Unfortunately, it's the scenes between the music that do the film in. Guest appearances by Ringo Starr and Linda McCartney are of some interest to Beatles fans.

Tawny Kitane and Tom Hanks in *Bachelor Party*.

Michael Caine and Michelle Johnson in *Blame It On Rio*.

Susan Sarandon, Wil Wheaton and Richard Dreyfuss in *The Buddy System*.

The Adventures of Buckaroo Banzai, with Peter Weller as the title character.

Kate Capshaw and Dennis Quaid in *Dreamscape*.

Janet Jones and Matt Dillon in *The Flamingo Kid*.

Tracey Ullman and Paul McCartney in *Give My Regards to Broad Street*.

461

IMPULSE

Produced by Tim Zinnemann
Directed by Graham Baker
Screenplay by Bart Davis and Don Carlos Dunaway
Photographed in Panavision and DeLuxe Color by Thomas Del
  Ruth
Music by Paul Chihara
91 minutes

Cast: Tim Matheson, Meg Tilly, Hume Cronyn, John Karlen, Bill
Paxton, Amy Stryker, Claude Earl Jones, Robert Wightman,
Lorinne Vozoff, Peter Jason, Adam Baumgarten, Abigail
Booraem, Leonard Burns, Mary Celio, Jack T. Collis

Strange doings in the little farming community of Sutcliffe,
where, until this film descends upon it, life is pure, simple
and honest. Then the transformation. People begin to act
with mean spirit and malice. Restraint and inhibition
disappear. A young lady (Meg Tilly) returns to Sutcliffe
when she receives an abusive phone call from her formerly
nice mother and discovers, in the company of her boyfriend
(Tim Matheson), that the town appears to have gone mad.
What they eventually find, after witnessing a good deal of
violent behavior, is that the madness stems from a toxic
substance in the water drunk by cows, which is passed on in
their milk. In an age in which chemical mistakes are not
uncommon, *Impulse* is a well produced but uncomfortable
vicarious adventure.

JOHNNY DANGEROUSLY

Produced by Michael Hertzberg
Directed by Amy Heckerling
Screenplay by Norman Steinberg, Bernie Kukoff, Harry Colomby,
  Jeff Harris
Photographed in DeLuxe Color by David M. Walsh
Music by John Morris
90 minutes

Cast: Michael Keaton, Joe Piscopo, Marilu Henner, Maureen
Stapleton, Peter Boyle, Griffin Dunne, Glynnis O'Connor, Dom
DeLuise, Richard Dimitri, Danny DeVito, Ron Carey, Ray
Walston, Dick Butkus

A hit-and-miss spoof of the old Warner Brothers gangster
pictures of the 30s about a young man (Michael Keaton)
who was forced to turn to a life of crime to help pay for the
operations for his ill mother (Maureen Stapleton). Among
his colorful exploits are his rise to power, a stint in prison,
and his eventual downfall at the hands of a crusading district
attorney (Griffin Dunne), who just happens to be the
gangster's younger brother. Keaton does a good job spoofing
the old Cagney roles and mannerisms, playing a gang boss
with a heart of gold, an open pocket, and a taste for
feminine pulchritude. But somehow the whole venture fails
to hold together due to misfired jokes or general taste-
lessness. A strong supporting cast, though, makes it worth
watching.

PHAR LAP

Produced by John Sexton
Directed by Simon Wincer
Screenplay by David Williamson
Photographed in Panavision and color by Russell Boyd
Music by Bruce Rowland
107 minutes

Cast: Tom Burlinson, Ron Leibman, Martin Vaughan, Judy
Morris, Celia De Burgh, Richard Morgan, Robert Grubb, Georgia
Carr, James Steele, Vincent Ball, Peter Whitford, John Stanton,
Roger Newcombe, Len Wasserman, Tom Woodcock

The title refers to a legendary Australian race horse that was
actually born in New Zealand but became an Aussie symbol
of triumph during the depressed years of the Thirties. Phar
Lap's story was notably inspirational, in that the horse was
considered a loser in the early years and yet went on to
become a champion of champions. The horse was on the
verge of becoming the biggest money maker in racing
history when it died under mysterious circumstances after
winning its greatest victory at Agua Caliente Mexico, in
April of 1932. As with so many films of this kind, it is a tale
of affection between a horse and a youngster, in this case
Tommy Woodcock (Tom Burlinson), the stableboy who was
the only person Phar Lap would tolerate. Kindness is the
unfailing message, and one which the boy constantly
promotes in conflict with the severe trainer (Martin
Vaughan). Splendidly filmed in Australia, *Phar Lap* suffers
somewhat from an overdose of Aussie pride, but it is a film
irresistible to all animal lovers.

REVENGE OF THE NERDS

Produced by Ted Field and Peter Samuelson
Directed by Jeff Kanew
Screenplay by Steve Zacharias and Jeff Buhai, from a story by
  Tim Metcalfe, Miguel Tejada-Flores, Steve Zacharias, Jeff
  Bugai
Photographed in DeLuxe Color by King Baggot
Music by Thomas Newman
90 minutes

Cast: Robert Carradine, Anthony Edwards, Tim Busfield, Andrew Cassese, Curtis Armstrong, Larry B. Scott, Brian Tochi,
Julie Montgomery

Another in the *Animal House* free-for-all comedy vein.
When a group of "nerds," who are more adept at handling
computers than real life, are put out of their campus
quarters because of an accidental fire, they look for frater-
nities to join. Since they are nerds, no one is willing to
accept them. However, with the help of two freshmen
(Robert Carradine and Anthony Edwards), they manage to
form their own house, sponsored by an all-black fraternity.
Of course, there is a rival group of students who don't like
the nerds and try to make life difficult for them; but through
their combination of cleverness and sheer perseverence, the
nerds finally gain respect on campus. College pranks galore
in a funny and extremely successful movie.

RHINESTONE

Produced by Howard Smith and Marvin Worth
Directed by Bob Clark
Screenplay by Phil Alden Robinson and Sylvester Stallone
Photographed in Panavision and DeLuxe Color by Timothy Galfas
Songs by Dolly Parton
Music direction by Mike Post
111 minutes

Cast: Sylvester Stallone, Dolly Parton, Richard Farnsworth, Ron Leibman, Tim Thomerson, Steven Apostle Pec, Penny Santon, Russell Buchanan, Ritch Brinkley, Perry Potter, Jesse Welles, Phil Rubenstein, Thomas Ikeda, Christal Kim, Arline Miyazaki, Tony Munafo

Michael Keaton as *Johnny Dangerously.*

The pairing of Sylvester Stallone and Dolly Parton, two of Hollywood's most physically potent stars, should have resulted in a blockbuster picture. *Rhinestone* turned out to be a rowdy and glitzy entertainment, but one strangely lacking in box office punch. It is strictly a two-star vehicle: Parton is the leading light of a New York nightclub who bets her obnoxious boss (Ron Leibman) that she can turn anyone into an acceptable singer of current pop music, and Stallone is the taxi-driver object of her bet. This cheerful, *Rocky*-like oaf hates her kind of music, but gamefully picks up the challenge and manages, once love sets in between this improbable pair, to come up with a performance as a country singer. *Rhinestone* is fun for fans of Stallone and Parton, but for others it seems that the two stars are straining to make funny a comedy that probably seemed hilarious in the planning stages. Its major asset is the genial Parton, gloriously obvious in her appeal, belting out some of her own songs.

Robert Carradine and Anthony Edwards in *Revenge of the Nerds.*

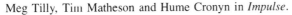
Sylvester Stallone and Dolly Parton in *Rhinestone.*

Meg Tilly, Tim Matheson and Hume Cronyn in *Impulse.*

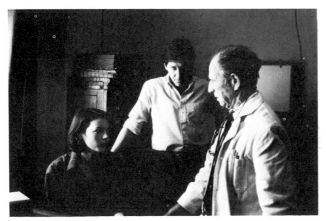

Tom Burlinson and the horse called *Phar Lap.*

463

RAGGED PRINCESS, THE
Dir. John G. Adolfi
Star June Caprice

ROMEO AND JULIET
Dir. Marwell Karger
Star Theda Bara

SERPENT, THE
Dir. Raoul Walsh
Star Theda Bara

SINS OF HER PARENT
Dir. Frank Lloyd

SINS OF MEN
Dir. James Vincent

SLANDER
Dir. Will S. Davis
Star Bertha Kalich

SPIDER AND THE FLY, THE
Dir. J. Gordon Edwards
Star Robert B. Mantell

SPORTING BLOOD
Dir. Bertram Bracken
Star Dorothy Bernard

STRAIGHT WAY, THE
Dir. Will S. Davis
Star Valeska Suratt

TORTURED HEART, THE
Dir. Will S. Davis
Star Virginia Pearson

UNDER TWO FLAGS
Dir. J. Gordon Edwards
Star Theda Bara

UNWELCOME MOTHER, THE
Dir. James Vincent
Star Walter Law

VICTIM, THE
Dir. Will S. Davis
Star Valeska Suratt

VIXEN, THE
Dir. J. Gordon Edwards
Star Theda Bara

WAR BRIDE'S SECRET, THE
Dir. Kenean Buel
Star Virginia Pearson

WHERE LOVE LEADS
Dir. Frank C. Griffin
Star Ormi Hawley

WIFE'S SACRIFICE, A
Dir. J. Gordon Edwards
Star Robert B. Mantell

WITCH, THE
Dir. Frank Powell
Star Nance O'Neill

WOMAN'S HONOR, A
Dir. Roland West
Star Jose Collins

1917

ALADDIN AND THE
WONDERFUL LAMP
Dir. C. M. and S. A. Franklin
Star Francis Carpenter

ALL FOR A HUSBAND
Dir. Carl Harbaugh
Star Virginia Pearson

AMERICAN METHODS
Dir. Frank Lloyd
Star William Farnum

BABES IN THE WOODS
Dir. C. M. and S. A. Franklin
Star Francis Carpenter

BETRAYED
Dir. R. A. Walsh
Star Miriam Cooper

BITTER TRUTH, THE
Dir. Kenean Buel
Star Virginia Pearson

BLUE STREAK, THE
Dir. William Nigh
Star Violet Palmer

BOOK AGENT, THE
Dir. Otis Turner
Star George Walsh

BRANDED SOUL, A
Dir. Bertram Bracken
Star Gladys Brockwell

BROADWAY SPORT, THE
Dir. Carl Harbaugh
Star Stuart Holmes

CAMILLE
Dir. J. Gordon Edwards
Star Theda Bara

CHILD OF THE WILD, A
Dir. John G. Adolfi
Star June Caprice

CONQUEROR, THE
Dir. Raoul Walsh
Star William Farnum

CONSCIENCE
Dir. Bertram Bracken
Star Glady Brockwell

DARLING OF PARIS, THE
Dir. J. Gordon Edwards
Star Theda Bara

DAUGHTER OF THE GODS, A
Dir. J. Gordon Edwards
Star Annette Kellerman

DERELICT, THE
Dir. Carl Harbaugh
Star Stuart Holmes

DURAND OF THE BAD LANDS
Dir. Richard Stanton

EVERY GIRL'S DREAM
Dir. Harry Millarde

FINAL PAYMENT, THE
Dir. Frank Powell
Star Nance O'Neill

FOR LIBERTY
Dir. Bertram Bracken
Star Gladys Brockwell

HEART AND SOUL
Dir. J. Gordon Edwards
Star Theda Bara

HEART OF A LION
Dir. Frank Lloyd
Star William Farnum

HER GREATEST LOVE
Dir. J. Gordon Edwards
Star Theda Bara

HER TEMPTATION
Dir. Richard Stanton
Star Gladys Brockwell

HIGH FINANCE
Dir. Otis Turner
Star George Walsh

HONOR SYSTEM, THE
Dir. R. A. Walsh
Star George Walsh

INNOCENT SINNER, THE
Dir. R. A. Walsh
Star Miriam Cooper

ISLAND OF DESIRE, THE
Dir. Otis Turner
Star George Walsh

JACK AND THE BEANSTOCK
Dir. C. M. and S. A. Franklin
Star Francis Carpenter

KINGDOM OF LOVE, THE
Dir. Frank Lloyd
Star Jewel Carmen

LOVE'S LAW
Dir. Tefft Johnson
Star Joan Sawyer

MADAME DU BARRY
Dir. J. Gordon Edwards
Star Theda Bara

MELTING MILLIONS
Dir. Otis Turner
Star George Walsh

MISS U.S.A.
Dir. Harry Millarde
Star June Caprice

MODERN CINDERELLA, A
Dir. John G. Adolfi
Star June Caprice

NEW YORK PEACOCK, THE
Dir. Kenean Buel
Star Valeska Surratt

NORTH OF FIFTY THREE
Dir. William D. Taylor
Star Dustin Farnum

ONE TOUCH OF SIN
Dir. Richard Stanton
Star Gladys Brockwell

PAINTED MADONNA, THE
Dir. O. A. C. Lund
Star Sonia Markova

PATSY
Dir. John G. Adolfi
Star June Caprice

PRICE OF HER SOUL, THE
Star Gladys Brockwell

PRICE OF SILENCE, THE
Dir. Frank Lloyd
Star William Farnum

PRIDE OF NEW YORK, THE
Dir. R. A. Walsh
Star George Walsh

PRIMITIVE CALL, THE
Dir. Bertram Bracken
Star Gladys Coburn

RICH MAN'S PLAYTHING, A
Dir. Carl Harbaugh
Star Valeska Surratt

ROSE OF BLOOD, THE
Dir. J. Gordon Edwards
Star Theda Bara

ROYAL ROMANCE, A
Dir. James Vincent
Star Virginia Pearson

SCARLET LETTER, THE
Dir. Carl Harbaugh
Star Virginia Pearson

SCARLET PIMPERNEL, THE
Dir. Richard Stanton
Star Dustin Farnum

SHE
Dir. Kenean Buel
Star Valeska Surratt

SILENT LIE, THE
Dir. R. A. Walsh
Star Miriam Cooper

SIREN, THE
Dir. Roland West
Star Valeska Surratt

SISTER AGAINST SISTER
Dir. James Vincent
Star Virginia Pearson

SLAVE, THE
Dir. William Nigh
Star Valeska Surratt

SMALL TOWN GIRL, THE
Dir. John G. Adolfi
Star June Caprice

SOME BOY
Dir. Otis Turner
Star George Walsh

SPY, THE
Dir. Richard Stanton
Star Dustin Farnum

TALE OF TWO CITIES, A
Dir. Frank Lloyd
Star William Farnum

TANGLED LIVES
Dir. J. Gordon Edwards
Star Genevieve Hamper

THIS IS THE LIFE
Dir. R. A. Walsh
Star George Walsh

THOU SHALT NOT STEAL
Dir. William Nigh
Star Virginia Pearson

TIGER WOMAN, THE
Dir. J. Gordon Edwards
Star Theda Bara

TO HONOR AND OBEY
Dir. Otis Turner
Star Gladys Brockwell

TROUBLE MAKERS
Dir. Kenean Buel
Star Jane and Katherine Lee

TWO LITTLE IMPS
Dir. Kenean Buel
Star Jane and Katherine Lee

UNKNOWN 274
Dir. Harry Millarde
Star June Caprice

WHEN A MAN SEES RED
Dir. Frank Lloyd
Star William Farnum

WHEN FALSE TONGUES SPEAK
Dir. Carl Harbaugh
Star Virginia Pearson

WIFE NUMBER TWO
Dir. William Nigh
Star Valeska Suratt

YANKEE WAY, THE
Dir. Richard Stanton
Star George Walsh

1918

ACE HIGH
Dir. Lynn Reynolds
Star Tom Mix

ALI BABA AND THE FORTY THIEVES
Dir. S. A. Franklin
Star George Stone

AMERICAN BUDS
Dir. Kenean Buel
Star Jane and Katherine Lee

BIRD OF PREY, THE
Dir. E. J. LeSaint
Star Gladys Brockwell

BLINDNESS OF DIVORCE, THE
Dir. Frank Lloyd
Star Bertha Mann

BLUE-EYED MARY
Dir. Harry Millarde
Star June Caprice

BONNIE ANNIE LAURIE
Dir. Harry Millarde
Star Peggy Hyland

BRAVE AND BOLD
Dir. Carl Harbaugh
Star George Walsh

BRIDE OF FEAR, THE
Dir. S. A. Franklin
Star Jewel Carmen

BUCHANAN'S WIFE
Dir. Charles J. Brabin
Star Virginia Pearson

CAILLAUX CASE, THE
Dir. Richard Stanton
Star Madlaine Traverse

CAMOUFLAGE KISS, THE
Dir. Harry Millarde
Star June Caprice

CAUGHT IN THE ACT
Dir. Harry Millarde
Star Peggy Hyland

CHEATING THE PUBLIC
Dir. Richard Stanton
Star Enid Markey

CLEOPATRA
Dir. J. Gordon Edwards
Star Theda Bara

CONFESSION
Dir. S. A. Franklin
Star Jewel Carmen

CUPID'S ROUNDUP
Dir. E. J. LeSaint
Star Tom Mix

DAUGHTER OF FRANCE, A
Dir. Edmund Lawrence
Star Virginia Pearson

DEBT OF HONOR
Dir. O. A. C. Lund
Star Peggy Hyland

DEVIL'S WHEEL, THE
Dir. E. J. LeSaint
Star Gladys Brockwell

DOING THEIR BIT
Dir. Kenean Buel
Star Jane and Katherine Lee

FALLEN ANGEL
Dir. Robert Thornby
Star Jewel Carmen

FAME AND FORTUNE
Dir. Lynn Reynolds
Star Tom Mix

FAN FAN
Dir. S. A. Franklin
Star Francis Carpenter

FIREBRAND, THE
Dir. Edmund Lawrence
Star Virginia Pearson

FOR FREEDOM
Dir. Frank Lloyd
Star William Farnum

FORBIDDEN PATH, THE
Dir. J. Gordon Edwards
Star Theda Bara

GIRL WITH THE CHAMPAGNE EYES, THE
Dir. C. M. Franklin
Star Jewel Carmen

HEART'S REVENGE, A
Dir. O. A. C. Lund
Star Sonia Markova

HER ONE MISTAKE
Dir. E. J. LeSaint
Star Gladys Brockwell

HER PRICE
Dir. Edmund Lawrence
Star Virginia Pearson

I WANT TO FORGET
Dir. James Kirkwood
Star Evelyn Nesbit

I'LL SAY SO
Dir. Raoul Walsh
Star George Walsh

JACK SPURLOCK, PRODIGAL
Dir. Carl Harbaugh
Star George Walsh

KID IS CLEVER, THE
Dir. Paul Powell
Star George Walsh

KULTUR
Dir. E. J. LeSaint
Star Gladys Brockwell

LAWLESS LOVE
Dir. Robert Thornby
Star Jewel Carmen

LES MISERABLES
Dir. Frank Lloyd
Star William Farnum

LIAR, THE
Dir. Edmund Lawrence
Star Virginia Pearson

MARRIAGES ARE MADE
Dir. Carl Harbaugh
Star Peggy Hyland

MISS INNOCENCE
Dir. Harry Millarde
Star June Caprice

MR. LOGAN, U.S.A.
Dir. Lynn F. Reynolds
Star Tom Mix

MORAL LAW
Dir. Bertram Bracken
Star Gladys Brockwell

ON THE JUMP
Dir. R. A. Walsh
Star George Walsh

OTHER MEN'S DAUGHTERS
Dir. Carl Harbaugh
Star Peggy Hyland

PEG O' THE PIRATES
Dir. O. A. C. Lund
Star Peggy Hyland

PRUSSIAN CUR, THE
Dir. R. A. Walsh
Star H. Von Der Goltz

QUEEN OF HEARTS
Dir. Edmund Lawrence
Star Virginia Pearson

QUEEN OF THE SEA, A
Dir. John Adolfi
Star Annette Kellerman

RAINBOW TRAIL, THE
Dir. Frank Lloyd
Star William Farnum

RIDERS OF THE PURPLE SAGE
Dir. Frank Lloyd
Star William Farnum

ROUGH AND READY
Dir. Richard Stanton
Star William Farnum

SCARLET ROAD, THE
Dir. E. J. LeSaint
Star Gladys Brockwell

SHE DEVIL, THE
Dir. J. Gordon Edwards
Star Theda Bara

SIX SHOOTER ANDY
Dir. S. A. Franklin
Star Tom Mix

SOUL OF BUDDHA, THE
Dir. J. Gordon Edwards
Star Theda Bara

STOLEN HONOR
Dir. Richard Stanton
Star Virginia Pearson

STRANGE WOMAN, THE
Dir. E. J. LeSaint
Star Gladys Brockwell

SWAT THE SPY
Dir. Arvid E. Gillstrom
Star Jane and Katherine Lee

TELL IT TO THE MARINES
Dir. Arvid E. Gillstrom
Star Jane and Katherine Lee

TREASURE ISLAND
Dir. C. M. and S. A. Franklin
Star Francis Carpenter

TRUE BLUE
Dir. Frank Lloyd
Star William Farnum

UNDER THE YOKE
Dir. J. Gordon Edwards
Star Theda Bara

WE SHOULD WORRY
Dir. Kenean Buel
Star Jane and Katherine Lee

WESTERN BLOOD
Dir. Lynn R. Reynolds
Star Tom Mix

WHEN A WOMAN SINS
Dir. J. G. Edwards
Star Theda Bara

WHY I SHOULD NOT MARRY
Dir. Richard Stanton
Star Lucy Fox

WOMAN AND THE LAW
Dir. R. A. Walsh
Star Miriam Cooper

WOMAN WHO GAVE, THE
Dir. Kenean Buel
Star Evelyn Nesbit

WHY AMERICA WILL WIN
Dir. Richard Stanton
Star Frank McGlynn

1919

BE A LITTLE SPORT
Dir. Scott Dunlap
Star Albert Ray

BROKEN COMMANDMENTS
Dir. Frank Beal
Star Gladys Brockwell

CALL OF THE SOUL
Dir. Edward J. LeSaint
Star Gladys Brockwell

CHASING RAINBOWS
Dir. Frank Beal
Star Gladys Brockwell

CHEATING HERSELF
Dir. Edmund Lawrence
Star Peggy Hyland

CHECKERS
Dir. Richard Stanton
Star All-star cast

COMING OF THE LAW
Dir. Arthur Rosson
Star Tom Mix

COWARDICE COURT
Dir. William Dowlan
Star Peggy Hyland

DANGER ZONE
Dir. Frank Beal
Star Madlaine Traverse

DAREDEVIL, THE
Dir. Edward J. LeSaint
Star Tom Mix

DEVIL'S RIDDLE, THE
Dir. Frank Beal
Star Gladys Brockwell

DIVORCE TRAP, THE
Dir. Frank Beal
Star Gladys Brockwell

EVANGELINE
Dir. Raoul Walsh
Star Miriam Cooper

EVERY MOTHER'S SON
Dir. Raoul Walsh
Star Charlotte Walker

FALLEN IDOL, THE
Dir. Kenean Buel
Star Evelyn Nesbit

FIGHTING FOR GOLD
Dir. Edward J. LeSaint
Star Tom Mix

FORBIDDEN ROOM, THE
Dir. Lynn Reynolds
Star Gladys Brockwell

GAMBLING IN SOULS
Dir. Frank Beal
Star Madlaine Traverse

GIRL IN BOHEMIA, A
Dir. Howard Mitchell
Star Peggy Hyland

GIRL WITH NO REGRETS, THE
Dir. Harry Millarde
Star Peggy Hyland

HELL ROARIN' REFORM
Dir. Edward J. LeSaint
Star Tom Mix

HELP HELP POLICE
Dir. Edward Dillon
Star George Walsh

JUNGLE TRAIL
Dir. Richard Stanton
Star William Farnum

KATHLEEN MAVOUREEN
Dir. Charles J. Brabin
Star Theda Bara

LA BELLE RUSSE
Dir. Charles J. Brabin
Star Theda Bara

LAST OF THE DUANES, THE
Dir. J. Gordon Edwards
Star William Farnum

LIGHT, THE
Dir. J. Gordon Edwards
Star Theda Bara

LINCOLN HIGHWAYMAN, THE
Dir. Emmett J. Flynn
Star William Russell

LONE STAR RANGER, THE
Dir. J. Gordon Edwards
Star William Farnum

LOST MONEY
Dir. Edmund Lawrence
Star Madlaine Traverse

LOST PRINCESS, THE
Dir. Scott Dunlap
Star Elinor Fair

LOVE AUCTION, THE
Dir. Edmund Lawrence
Star Virginia Pearson

LOVE IS LOVE
Dir. Scott Dunlap
Star Albert Ray

LOVE THAT DARES, THE
Dir. Harry Millarde
Star Madlaine Traverse

LUCK AND PLUCK
Dir. Edward Dillon
Star George Walsh

LURE OF AMBITION, THE
Dir. Edmund Lawrence
Star Theda Bara

MAN HUNTER, THE
Dir. Frank Lloyd
Star William Farnum

MARRIED IN HASTE
Dir. Arthur Rosson
Star Albert Ray

MERRY-GO-ROUND
Dir. Edmund Lawrence
Star Peggy Hyland

MISS ADVENTURE
Dir. Lynn R. Reynolds
Star Peggy Hyland

MY LITTLE SISTER
Dir. Kenean Buel
Star Evelyn Nesbit

NEVER SAY QUIT
Dir. Edward Dillon
Star George Walsh

PITFALLS OF A BIG CITY
Dir. Frank Lloyd
Star Gladys Brockwell

PUTTING ONE OVER
Dir. Edward Dillon
Star George Walsh

REBELLIOUS BRIDE, THE
Dir. Lynn Reynolds
Star Peggy Hyland

ROSE OF THE WEST
Dir. Harry Millarde
Star Madlaine Traverse

ROUGH RIDING ROMANCE
Dir. Arthur Rosson
Star Tom Mix

SACRED SILENCE
Dir. Harry Millarde
Star William Russell

SALOME
Dir. J. G. Edwards
Star Theda Bara

SEVENTH PERSON
Star George Walsh

SHOULD A HUSBAND FORGIVE
Dir. R. A. Walsh
Star Miriam Cooper

SIREN'S SONG, A
Dir. J. Gordon Edwards
Star Theda Bara

SMILES
Dir. Arvid E. Gillstrom
Star Jane and Katherine Lee

SNARES OF PARIS
Dir. Howard Mitchell
Star Madlaine Traverse

SNEAK, THE
Dir. Edward J. LeSaint
Star Gladys Brockwell

SPEED MANIAC, THE
Dir. Edward J. LeSaint
Star Tom Mix

SPLENDID SIN, THE
Dir. Howard Mitchell
Star Madlaine Traverse

THIEVES
Dir. Frank Beal
Star Gladys Brockwell

THOU SHALT NOT
Dir. Charles J. Brabin
Star Evelyn Nesbit

TIN PAN ALLEY
Dir. Frank Beal
Star Elinor Fair
  Albert Ray

TREAT 'EM ROUGH
Dir. Lynn Reynolds
Star Tom Mix

VAGABOND LUCK
Dir. Scott Dunlap
Star Elinor Fair
  Albert Ray

WEB OF CHANCE
Dir. Alfred E. Green
Star Peggy Hyland

WHEN FATE DECIDES
Dir. Harry Millarde
Star Madlaine Traverse

WHEN MEN DESIRE
Dir. J. Gordon Edwards
Star Theda Bara

WILDERNESS TRAIL, THE
Dir. Edward J. LeSaint
Star Tom Mix

WINGS OF THE MORNING
Dir. J. Gordon Edwards
Star William Farnum

WINNING STROKE, THE
Dir. Edward Dillon
Star George Walsh

WOLVES OF THE NIGHT
Dir. J. Gordon Edwards
Star William Farnum

WOMAN THERE WAS, A
Dir. J. Gordon Edwards
Star Theda Bara

WOMAN, WOMAN
Dir. Kenean Buell
Star Evelyn Nesbit

1920

ADVENTURER, THE
Dir. J. Gordon Edwards
Star William Farnum

BEWARE OF THE BRIDE
Dir. Howard Mitchell
Star Eileen Percy

BLACK SHADOWS
Dir. Howard Mitchell
Star Peggy Hyland

BLIND WIVES
Dir. Charles J. Brabin

BRIDE 13
(Serial)
Star Jack O'Brien

CHALLENGE OF THE LAW
Dir. Scott Dunlap
Star William Russell

CYCLONE, THE
Dir. Cliff Smith
Star Tom Mix

DEAD LINE, THE
Dir. Dell Henderson
Star George Walsh

DESERT LOVE
Dir. Jacques Jaccard
Star Tom Mix

DRAG HARLAN
Dir. J. Gordon Edwards
Star William Farnum

EASTWARD HO
Dir. Emmett Flynn
Star William Russell

FACE AT YOUR WINDOW
Dir. Richard Stanton
Star Earl Metcalfe

FAITH
Dir. Howard Mitchell
Star Peggy Hyland

FEUD, THE
Dir. Edward J. LeSaint
Star Tom Mix

FIREBRAND TREVISION
Dir. Thomas Heffron
Star Buck Jones

FLAME OF YOUTH
Dir. Howard Mitchell
Star Shirley Mason

FLAMES OF THE FLESH
Dir. Edward J. LeSaint
Star Gladys Brockwell

FORBIDDEN TRAILS
Dir. Scott Dunlap
Star Buck Jones

FROM NOW ON
Dir. Raoul Walsh
Star George Walsh

GIRL OF MY HEART
Dir. Edward J. LeSaint
Star Shirley Mason

HEART STRINGS
Dir. J. Gordon Edwards
Star William Farnum

HEARTS OF YOUTH
Dir. Thomas N. Miranda &
  Millard Webb
Star Harold Goodwin

HELL SHIP, THE
Dir. Scott Dunlap
Star Madlaine Traverse

HER ELEPHANT MAN
Dir. Scott Dunlap
Star Shirley Mason

HER HONOR THE MAYOR
Dir. Paul Cazeneuve
Star Eileen Percy

HUSBAND HUNTER, THE
Dir. Howard Mitchell
Star Eileen Percy

IF I WERE KING
Dir. J. Gordon Edwards
Star William Farnum

IRON HEART, THE
Dir. Denison Clift
Star Madlaine Traverse

IRON RIDER, THE
Dir. Scott Dunlap
Star William Russell

JOYOUS TROUBLEMAKER, THE
Dir. J. Gordon Edwards
Star William Farnum

JUST PALS
Dir. John Ford
Star Buck Jones

LAND OF JAZZ
Dir. Jules Furthman
Star Eileen Percy

LAST STRAW, THE
Dir. Denison Clift
Star Buck Jones

LEAVE IT TO ME
Dir. Emmett Flynn
Star William Russell

LITTLE GREY MOUSE, THE
Dir. James P. Hogan
Star Louise Lovely

LITTLE WANDERER, THE
Dir. Howard Mitchell
Star Shirley Mason

LOVE'S HARVEST
Dir. Howard Mitchell
Star Shirley Mason

MANHATTAN KNIGHT
Dir. George Beranger
Star George Walsh

MAN WHO DARED, THE
Dir. Emmett Flynn
Star William Russell

MERELY MARY ANN
Dir. Edward J. LeSaint
Star Shirley Mason

MOLLY AND I
Dir. Howard Mitchell
Star Shirley Mason

MOTHER OF HIS CHIDREN,
THE
Dir. Edward J. LeSaint
Star Gladys Brockwell

NUMBER 17
Dir. George Beranger
Star George Walsh

ORPHAN, THE
Dir. J. Gordon Edwards
Star William Farnum

PLUNGER, THE
Dir. Dell Henderson
Star George Walsh

PRAIRIE TRAILS
Dir. George Marshall
Star Tom Mix

ROSE OF NOME
Dir. Edward J. LeSaint
Star Gladys Brockwell

SCUTTLERS, THE
Dir. J. Gordon Edwards
Star William Farnum

SHARK, THE
Dir. Dell Henderson
Star George Walsh

SHOD WITH FIRE
Dir. Emmett Flynn
Star William Russell

SISTER TO SALOME, A
Dir. Edward J. LeSaint
Star Gladys Brockwell

SKYWAYMAN, THE
Dir. James P. Hogan
Star Ormer Locklear

SPIRIT OF GOD, THE
Dir. Paul Cazeneuve
Star Buck Jones

SQUARE SHOOTER
Dir. Paul Cazeneuve
Star Buck Jones

STRONGEST, THE
Dir. Raoul Walsh
Star Renee Adoree

SUNSET SPRAGUE
Dir. Paul Cazeneuve & Thomas
      Heffron
Star Buck Jones

TATTLERS, THE
Dir. Howard Mitchell
Star Madlaine Traverse

TERROR, THE
Dir. Jacques Jaccard
Star Tom Mix

TEXAN, THE
Dir. Lynn Reynolds
Star Tom Mix

THIEF, THE
Dir. Charles Giblyn
Star Pearl White

THREE GOLD COINS
Dir. Cliff Smith
Star Tom Mix

TIGER'S CUB, THE
Dir. Charles Giblyn
Star Pearl White

TWINS OF SUFFERING CREEK,
THE
Dir. Scott Dunlap
Star William Russell

TWO MOONS
Dir. Edward J. LeSaint
Star Buck Jones

UNTAMED, THE
Dir. Emmett Flynn
Star Tom Mix

WHAT WOULD YOU DO
Dir. Denison Clift
Star Madlaine Traverse

WHILE NEW YORK SLEEPS
Dir. Charles J. Brabin
Star Estelle Taylor

WHITE LIES
Dir. Edward J. LeSaint
Star Gladys Brockwell

WHITE MOLL
Dir. Harry Millarde
Star Pearl White

WORLD OF FOLLY
Dir. Frank Beal
Star Vivian Rich

WOULD YOU FORGIVE
Dir. Scott Dunlap
Star Vivian Rich

1921

AFTER YOUR OWN HEART
Dir. George Marshall
Star Tom Mix

BAR NOTHIN'
Dir. Edward Sedgwick
Star Buck Jones

BARE KNUCKLES
Dir. James Patrick Hogan
Star William Russell

BEYOND PRICE
Dir. J. Searle Dawley
Star Pearl White

BIG PUNCH, THE
Dir. John Ford
Star Buck Jones

BIG TOWN IDEAS
Dir. Carl Harbaugh
Star Eileen Percy

BIG TOWN ROUNDUP
Dir. Lynn F. Reynolds
Star Tom Mix

BLUSHING BRIDE, THE
Dir. Jules G. Furthman
Star Eileen Percy

BUCKING THE LINE
Dir. Carl Harbaugh
Star Maurice Flynn

CHEATER REFORMED, THE
Dir. Scott Dunlap
Star William Russell

CHILDREN OF THE NIGHT
Dir. Jack Dillon
Star William Russell

CINDERELLA OF THE HILLS
Dir. H. M. Mitchell
Star Barbara Bedford

COLORADO PLUCK
Dir. Jules G. Furthman
Star William Russell

CONNECTICUT YANKEE IN
KING ARTHUR'S COURT, A
Dir. Emmett Flynn
Star Harry Myers

DEVIL WITHIN, THE
Dir. Bernard Durning
Star Dustin Farnum

DYNAMITE ALLEN
Dir. Dell Henderson
Star George Walsh

EVER SINCE EVE
Dir. H. M. Mitchell
Star Shirley Mason

FOOTFALLS
Dir. Charles J. Brabin
Star Tyrone Power, Sr.

GET YOUR MAN
Dir. George W. Hill
Star Buck Jones

HANDS OFF
Dir. George Marshall
Star Tom Mix

HICKVILLE TO BROADWAY
Dir. Carl Harbaugh
Star Eileen Percy

HIS GREATEST SACRIFICE
Dir. J. Gordon Edwards
Star William Farnum

JACKIE
Dir. Jack Ford
Star Shirley Mason

JOLT, THE
Dir. George Marshall
Star Edna Murphy

KNOW YOUR MAN
Dir. Charles Giblyn
Star Pearl White

LADY FROM LONGACRE, THE
Dir. George Marshall
Star William Russell

LAMPLIGHTER, THE
Dir. Howard Mitchell
Star Shirley Mason

LAST TRAIL, THE
Dir. Emmett J. Flynn
Star Maurice Flynn

LITTLE MISS HAWKSHAW
Dir. Carl Harbaugh
Star Eileen Percy

LIVE WIRES
Dir. Edward Sedgwick
Star Edna Murphy

LOVETIME
Dir. Howard Mitchell
Star Shirley Mason

MAID OF THE WEST
Dir. Philo McCullough
Star Eileen Percy

MOTHER HEART, THE
Dir. Howard Mitchell
Star Shirley Mason

MOUNTAIN WOMAN, THE
Dir. Charles Giblyn
Star Pearl White

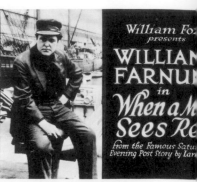

William Farnum in *When a Man Sees Red.* (1917)

Theda Bara. (1914)

Theda Bara.

Tom Mix in *Rough Riding Romance.* (1919)

William Farnum in *When a Man Sees Red* (1917)

Theda Bara in *Cleopatra.* (1918)

Annette Kellermann in *Queen of the Seas.* (1918)

Theda Bara in *Salome.* (1919)

George Walsh in *Pluck and Luck.* (1919)

Tom Mix in *The Coming of the Law.* (1919)

Pearl White in *The Broadway Peacock.* (1922)

William Farnum in *Shackles of Gold.* (1922)

NIGHT HORSEMAN, THE
Dir. Lynn Reynolds
Star Tom Mix

OLIVER TWIST, JR.
Dir. Millard Webb
Star Harold Goodwin

ONE MAN TRAIL
Dir. Bernard Durning
Star Buck Jones

OVER THE HILL
Dir. Harry Millarde

PARTNERS OF FATE
Dir. Bernard Durning
Star Louise Lovely

PERJURY
Dir. Harry Millarde
Star William Farnum

PLAY SQUARE
Dir. William K. Howard
Star Edna Murphy

PRIMAL LAW, THE
Dir. Bernard Durning
Star Dustin Farnum

QUEEN OF SHEBA, THE
Dir. J. Gordon Edwards
Star Betty Blythe

QUEENIE
Dir. Howard Mitchell
Star Shirley Mason

RIDING WITH DEATH
Dir. Jacques Jaccard
Star Charles Jones

RIDIN' ROMEO, A
Dir. George Marshall
Star Tom Mix

ROAD DEMON, THE
Dir. Lynn Reynolds
Star Tom Mix

ROOF TREE, THE
Dir. Jack Dillon
Star William Russell

ROUGH DIAMOND, THE
Dir. Edward Sedgwick
Star Tom Mix

SHAME
Dir. Emmett Flynn
Star John Gilbert

SINGING RIVER
Dir. Charles Giblyn
Star William Russell

SKIRTS
Dir. Hampton Del Ruth
Star Buster Keaton

STRAIGHT FROM THE
SHOULDER
Dir. Bernard Durning
Star Buck Jones

THUNDERCLAP
Dir. Richard Stanton
Star Mary Carr

TO A FINISH
Dir. Bernard Durning
Star Buck Jones

TOMBOY, THE
Dir. Carl Harbaugh
Star Eileen Percy

TRAILIN'
Dir. Lynn F. Reynolds
Star Tom Mix

VIRGIN PARADISE, A
Dir. J. Searle Dawley
Star Pearl White

WHATEVER SHE WANTS
Dir. C. R. Wallace
Star Eileen Percy

WHAT LOVE WILL DO
Dir. William K. Howard
Star Edna Murphy

WHILE THE DEVIL LAUGHS
Dir. George W. Hill
Star Louise Lovely

WHY TRUST YOUR HUSBAND
Dir. George Marshall
Star Eileen Percy

WING TOY
Dir. Howard Mitchell
Star Shirley Mason

WINNING WITH WITS
Dir. Howard Mitchell
Star Barbara Bedford

1922

ANY WIFE
Dir. Herbert Brenon
Star Pearl White

ARABIA
Dir. Lynn Reynolds
Star Tom Mix

ARABIAN LOVE
Dir. Jerome Storm
Star John Gilbert

BELLS OF SAN JUAN
Dir. Scott Dunlap
Star Buck Jones

BOSS OF CAMP FOUR, THE
Dir. W. S. Van Dyck
Star Buck Jones

BROADWAY PEACOCK, THE
Dir. Charles J. Brabin
Star Pearl White

CALVERT'S VALLEY
Dir. Jack Dillon
Star John Gilbert

CHASING THE MOON
Dir. Edward Sedgwick
Star Tom Mix

DESERT BLOSSOMS
Dir. Arthur Rosson
Star William Russell

DO AND DARE
Dir. Edward Sedgwick
Star Tom Mix

ELOPE IF YOU MUST
Dir. C. R. Wallace
Star Eileen Percy

EXTRA, EXTRA
Dir. William K. Howard
Star Edna Walker

FAST MAIL, THE
Dir. Bernard Durning
Star Buck Jones

FIGHTING STREAK, THE
Dir. Arthur Rosson
Star Tom Mix

FOR BIG STAKES
Dir. Lynn Reynolds
Star Tom Mix

GLEAM O'DAWN
Dir. Jack Dillon
Star John Gilbert

GREAT NIGHT, THE
Dir. Howard M. Mitchell
Star William Russell

HONOR FIRST
Dir. Jerome Storm
Star John Gilbert

IRON TO GOLD
Dir. Bernard Durning
Star Dustin Farnum

JUST TONY
Dir. Lynn Reynolds
Star Tom Mix

LIGHTS OF THE DESERT
Dir. Harry Beaumont
Star Shirley Mason

LITTLE MISS SMILES
Dir. Jack Ford
Star Shirley Mason

LOVE GAMBLER, THE
Dir. Joseph Franz
Star John Gilbert

MEN OF ZANZIBAR, THE
Dir. Rowland V. Lee
Star William Russell

MIXED FACES
Dir. Rowland V. Lee
Star William Russell

MONEY TO BURN
Dir. Rowland V. Lee
Star William Russell

MONTE CRISTO
Dir. Emmett J. Flynn
Star John Gilbert

MOONSHINE VALLEY
Dir. Herbert Brenon
Star William Farnum

MY FRIEND THE DEVIL
Dir. Harry Millarde
Star Charles Richman

NERO
Dir. J. Gordon Edwards
Star Jacques Gretillat

NEW TEACHER, THE
Dir. Joseph Franz
Star Shirley Mason

OATHBOUND
Dir. Bernard Durning
Star Dustin Farnum

PARDON MY NERVE
Dir. Reeves Eason
Star Buck Jones

RAGGED HEIRESS, THE
Dir. Harry Beaumont
Star Shirley Mason

ROUGHSHOD
Dir. Reeves Eason
Star Buck Jones

SELF MADE MAN, A
Dir. Rowland V. Lee
Star William Russell

SHACKLES OF GOLD
Dir. Herbert Brenon
Star William Farnum

SHIRLEY OF THE CIRCUS
Dir. Rowland V. Lee
Star Shirley Mason

SILVER WINGS
Dir. Jack Ford & Edwin Carewe
Star Mary Carr

SKY HIGH
Dir. Lynn Reynolds
Star Tom Mix

SMILES ARE TRUMPS
Dir. George Marshall
Star Maurice Flynn

STAGE ROMANCE, A
Dir. Herbert Brenon
Star William Farnum

STRANGE IDOLS
Dir. Bernard Durning
Star Dustin Farnum

STRENGTH OF THE PINES
Dir. Edgar Lewis
Star William Russell

TROOPER O'NEILL
Dir. C. R. Wallace & Scott Dunlap
Star Buck Jones

UP AND GOING
Dir. Lynn Reynolds
Star Tom Mix

VERY TRULY YOURS
Dir. Harry Beaumont
Star Shirley Mason

WEST OF CHICAGO
Dir. Scott Dunlap
Star Buck Jones

WESTERN SPEED
Dir. William Wallace & Scott
Dunlap
Star Buck Jones

WHILE JUSTICE WAITS
Dir. Bernard Durning
Star Dustin Farnum

WHO ARE MY PARENTS?
Dir. J. Searle Dawley
Star Roger Lytton

WITHOUT COMPROMISE
Dir. Emmett J. Flynn
Star William Farnum

WITHOUT FEAR
Dir. Kenneth Webb
Star Pearl White

YELLOW STAIN, THE
Dir. Jack Dillon
Star John Gilbert

YOSEMITE TRAIL, THE
Dir. Bernard Durning
Star Dustin Farnum

YOUTH MUST HAVE LOVE
Dir. Joseph Franz
Star Shirley Mason

1923

ALIAS THE NIGHT WIND
Dir. Joseph Vance
Star William Russell

BIG DAN
Dir. William Wellman
Star Buck Jones

BOSTON BLACKIE
Dir. Scott Dunlap
Star William Russell

BRASS COMMANDMENTS
Dir. Lynn Reynolds
Star William Farnum

BUCKING THE BARRIER
Dir. Colin Campbell
Star Dustin Farnum

BUSTER, THE
Dir. Colin Campbell
Star Dustin Farnum

CALIFORNIA ROMANCE, A
Dir. Jerome Storm
Star John Gilbert

CAMEO KIRBY
Dir. John Ford
Star John Gilbert

CATCH MY SMOKE
Dir. William Beaudine
Star Tom Mix

CRUSADER, THE
Dir. Howard M. Mitchell
Star William Russell

CUSTARD CUP
Dir. Herbert Brenon
Star Mary Carr

DOES IT PAY
Dir. Charles Horan
Star Hope Hampton

ELEVENTH HOUR, THE
Dir. Bernard Durning
Star Shirley Mason

EXILES, THE
Dir. Edward Mortimer
Star John Gilbert

FACE ON THE BARROOM
FLOOR, THE
Dir. John Ford
Star Henry B. Walthall

FOOTLIGHT RANGER, THE
Dir. Scott Dunlap
Star Buck Jones

FRIENDLY HUSBAND, A
Dir. John Blystone
Star Lupino Lane

GOODBYE GIRLS
Dir. Jerome Stern
Star William Russell

GOVERNOR'S LADY, THE
Dir. Harry Millarde
Star Robert T. Haines

GRAIL, THE
Dir. Colin Campbell
Star Dustin Farnum

GUNFIGHTER, THE
Dir. Lynn Reynolds
Star William Farnum

HELL'S HOLE
Dir. Emmett Flynn
Star Buck Jones

IF WINTER COMES
Dir. Harry Millarde
Star Percy Marmont

LIGHTS OF NEW YORK
Dir. Charles J. Brabin
Star Clarence Nordstrom

LONE STAR RANGER, THE
Dir. Lambert Hillyer
Star Tom Mix

LOVEBOUND
Dir. Henry Otto
Star Shirley Mason

MADNESS OF YOUTH
Dir. Jerome Storm
Star John Gilbert

MAN WHO WON, THE
Dir. William Wellman
Star Dustin Farnum

MAN'S SIZE, A
Dir. Howard Mitchell
Star William Russell

MILE A MINUTE ROMEO
Dir. Lambert Hillyer
Star Tom Mix

MONNA VANNA
Dir. R. Eichberg

PAWN TICKET 210
Dir. Scott Dunlap
Star Shirley Mason

RED RUSSIA REVEALED
(Documentary)

ROMANCE LAND
Dir. Edward Sedgwick
Star Tom Mix

ST. ELMO
Dir. Jerome Storm
Star John Gilbert

SECOND HAND LOVE
Dir. William Wellman
Star Buck Jones

SILENT COMMAND
Dir. J. Gordon Edwards
Star Edmund Lowe

SIX CYLINDER LOVE
Dir. Elmer Clifton
Star Ernest Truex

SKID-PROOF
Dir. Scott Dunlap
Star Buck Jones

SNOWDRIFT
Dir. Scott Dunlap
Star Buck Jones

SOFT BOILED
Dir. John Blystone
Star Tom Mix

SOUTH SEA LOVE
Dir. David Solomon
Star Shirley Mason

STEPPING FAST
Dir. Joseph Franz
Star Tom Mix

TEMPLE OF VENUS, THE
Dir. Henry Otto
Star William Walling

THREE JUMPS AHEAD
Dir. John Ford
Star Tom Mix

THREE WHO PAID
Dir. Colin Campbell
Star Dustin Farnum

TIMES HAVE CHANGED
Dir. James Flood
Star William Russell

TOWN THAT GOD FORGOT,
THE
Dir. Harry Millarde
Star Bunny Grauer

TRUXTEN KING
Dir. Jerome Storm
Star John Gilbert

VILLAGE BLACKSMITH, THE
Dir. Jack Ford
Star William Walling

WHEN ODDS ARE EVEN
Dir. James Flood
Star William Russell

YOU CAN'T GET AWAY
WITH IT
Dir. Rowland V. Lee
Star Percy Marmont

1924

AGAINST ALL ODDS
Dir. Edmund Mortimer
Star Buck Jones

ARIZONA EXPRESS
Dir. Thomas Buckingham
Star Pauline Starke

BLIZZARD, THE
Dir. Mauritz Miller

BRASS BOWL, THE
Dir. Jerome Storm
Star Edmund Lowe

CIRCUS COWBOY, THE
Dir. William Wellman
Star Buck Jones

CUPID'S FIREMAN
Dir. William Wellman
Star Buck Jones

CYCLONE RIDER, THE
Dir. Thomas Buckingham
Star Reed Howes

DANTE'S INFERNO
Dir. Henry Otto
Star Lawson Butt

DARWIN WAS RIGHT
Dir. Lewis Seiler
Star Nell Brantley

DAUGHTERS OF THE NIGHT
Dir. Elmer Clifton
Star Orville Caldwell

DESERT OUTLAW, THE
Dir. Edmund Mortimer
Star Buck Jones

EYES OF THE FOREST
Dir. Lambert Hillyer
Star Tom Mix

GENTLE JULIA
Dir. Rowland V. Lee
Star Bessie Love

GREAT DIAMOND MYSTERY
Dir. Denison Clift
Star Shirley Mason

HEART BUSTERS, THE
Dir. Jack Conway
Star Tom Mix

HEARTS OF OAK
Dir. John Ford
Star Hobart Bosworth

HONOR AMONG MEN
Dir. Denison Clift
Star Edmund Lowe

HOODMAN BLIND
Dir. John Ford
Star David Butler

IRON HORSE, THE
Dir. John Ford
Star George O'Brien

IT IS THE LAW
Dir. J. Gordon Edwards
Star Arthur Hohl

JUST OFF BROADWAY
Dir. Edmund Mortimer
Star John Gilbert

KENTUCKY DAYS
Dir. David Solomon
Star Dustin Farnum

LADIES TO BOARD
Dir. John Blystone
Star Tom Mix

LAST OF THE DUANES
Dir. Lynn Reynolds
Star Tom Mix

LONE CHANCE, THE
Dir. Howard Mitchell
Star John Gilbert

LOVE LETTERS
Dir. David Solomon
Star Shirley Mason

MAN'S MATE, A
Dir. Edmund Mortimer
Star John Gilbert

MAN WHO CAME BACK, THE
Dir. Emmett Flynn
Star George O'Brien

NET, THE
Dir. J. Gordon Edwards
Star Barbara Castleton

NO MOTHER TO GUIDE HER
Dir. Charles Horan
Star Genevieve Tobin

NORTH OF HUDSON BAY
Dir. John Ford
Star Tom Mix

NOT A DRUM WAS HEARD
Dir. William Wellman
Star Buck Jones

OH YOU TONY
Dir. John Blystone
Star Tom Mix

PAINTED LADY, THE
Dir. Chester Bennett
Star George O'Brien

PLUNDERER, THE
Dir. George Archainbaud
Star Frank Mayo

ROMANCE RANCH
Dir. Howard Mitchell
Star John Gilbert

SHADOW OF THE EAST
Dir. George Archainbaud
Star Frank Mayo

SHEPHERD KING, THE
Dir. J. Gordon Edwards
Star Violet Mensereau

TEETH
Dir. John Blystone
Star Tom Mix

THAT FRENCH LADY
Dir. Edmund Mortimer
Star Shirley Mason

THIS FREEDOM
Dir. Denison Clift

TROUBLE SHOOTER, THE
Dir. Jack Conway
Star Tom Mix

VAGABOND TRAIL, THE
Dir. William Wellman
Star Buck Jones

WARRENS OF VIRGINIA, THE
Dir. Elmer Clifton
Star George Backus

WESTERN LUCK
Dir. George Beranger
Star Buck Jones

WINNER TAKE ALL
Dir. W. S. Van Dyke
Star John Gilbert

WOLF MAN, THE
Dir. Edmund Mortimer
Star John Gilbert

1925

ANCIENT MARINER, THE
Dir. Chester Bennett & Henry Otto
Star Clara Bow

ARIZONA ROMEO
Dir. Edmund Mortimer
Star Buck Jones

AS NO MAN HAS LOVED
Dir. Rowland V. Lee
Star Edward Hearn

BEST BAD MAN, THE
Dir. John Blystone
Star Tom Mix

CHAMPION OF LOST CAUSES, THE
Dir. Chester Bennett
Star Edmund Lowe

CURLYTOP
Dir. Maurice Elvey
Star Shirley Mason

DANCERS, THE
Dir. Emmett Flynn
Star George O'Brien

DEADWOOD COACH, THE
Dir. Lynn Reynolds
Star Tom Mix

DESERT'S PRICE, THE
Dir. W. S. Van Dyke
Star Buck Jones

DICK TURPIN
Dir. John Blystone
Star Tom Mix

DURAND OF THE BAD LANDS
Dir. Lynn Reynolds
Star Buck Jones

EAST LYNNE
Dir. Emmett Flynn
Star Alma Rubens

EVERLASTING WHISPER, THE
Dir. John Blystone
Star Tom Mix

EVERYMAN'S WIFE
Dir. Maurice Elvey
Star Elaine Hammerstein

FIGHTING HEART, THE
Dir. John Ford
Star George O'Brien

FLAMES OF DESIRE
Dir. Denison Clift
Star Wyndham Standing

FOLLY OF VANITY
Dir. Maurice Elvey & Henry Otto
Star Billie Dove

FOOL, THE
Dir. Harry Millarde
Star Edmund Lowe

GERALD CRANSTON'S LADY
Dir. Emmett Flynn
Star James Kirkwood

GOLD AND THE GIRL
Dir. Edmund Mortimer
Star Buck Jones

GOLD HEELS
Dir. W. S. Van Dyke
Star Robert Agnew

GREATER THAN A CROWN
Dir. R. William Neill
Star Edmund Lowe

HAVOC
Dir. Rowland V. Lee
Star Madge Bellamy

HEARTS AND SPURS
Dir. W. S. Van Dyke
Star Buck Jones

HUNTED WOMAN, THE
Dir. Jack Conway
Star Seena Owen

IN LOVE WITH LOVE
Dir. Rowland V. Lee
Star Marguerite De La Motte

KENTUCKY PRIDE
Dir. John Ford
Star Henry B. Walthall

KISS BARRIER
Dir. R. William Neill
Star Edmund Lowe

LAST MAN ON EARTH, THE
Dir. John Blystone
Star Earle Foxe

LAZYBONES
Dir. Frank Borzage
Star Buck Jones

LIGHTNIN'
Dir. John Ford
Star Madge Bellamy

LUCKY HORSESHOE
Dir. John Blystone
Star Tom Mix

MAN WHO PLAYED SQUARE, THE
Dir. Alfred Santell
Star Buck Jones

MARRIAGE IN TRANSIT
Dir. R. William Neill
Star Edmund Lowe

MY HUSBAND'S WIVES
Dir. Maurice Elvey
Star Shirley Mason

PORTS OF CALL
Dir. Denison Clift
Star Edmund Lowe

RAINBOW TRAIL, THE
Dir. Lynn Reynolds
Star Tom Mix

RIDERS OF THE PURPLE SAGE
Dir. Lynn Reynolds
Star Tom Mix

ROUGHNECK, THE
Dir. Jack Conway
Star George O'Brien

SCANDAL PROOF
Dir. Edmund Mortimer
Star Shirley Mason

SCARLET HONEYMOON, THE
Dir. Alan Hale
Star Shirley Mason

SHE WOLVES
Dir. Maurice Elvey
Star Alma Rubens

STARDUST TRAIL
Dir. Edmund Mortimer
Star Shirley Mason

THANK YOU
Dir. John Ford
Star George O'Brien

THUNDER MOUNTAIN
Dir. Victor Schertzinger
Star Madge Bellamy

TIMBER WOLF
Dir. W. S. Van Dyke
Star Buck Jones

TRAIL RIDER, THE
Dir. W. S. Van Dyke
Star Buck Jones

TROUBLES OF A BRIDE
Dir. Thomas Buckingham
Star Robert Agnew

WAGES FOR WIVES
Dir. Frank Borzage
Star Jacqueline Logan

WHEEL, THE
Dir. Victor Schertzinger
Star Margaret Livingston

WHEN THE DOOR OPENED
Dir. Reginald Barker
Star Jacqueline Logan

WINDING STAIR, THE
Dir. John Griffith Wray
Star Alma Rubens

WINGS OF YOUTH, THE
Dir. Emmett Flynn
Star Madge Bellamy

1926

BLACK PARADISE
Dir. R. William Neill
Cast Madge Bellamy
Leslie Fenton
Edmund Lowe

BLUE EAGLE, THE
Dir. John Ford
Cast William Russell
George O'Brien
Margaret Livingston

CANYON OF LIGHT, THE
Dir. Benjamin Stoloff
Cast Tom Mix
Dorothy Dwan

CITY, THE
Dir. R. William Neill
Cast Walter McGrail
Robert Fraser
Nancy Nash
May Allison

COUNTRY BEYOND, THE
Dir. Irving Cummings
Cast Olive Borden
Ralph Graves
J. Farrell MacDonald
Evelyn Selbie

COWBOY AND THE COUNTESS, THE
Dir. R. William Neill
Cast Buck Jones

DESERT VALLEY
Dir. Scott Dunlap
Cast Buck Jones

DIXIE MERCHANT, THE
Dir. Frank Borzage
Cast Madge Bellamy
Jack Mulhall
J. Farrell MacDonald
Claire McDowell

EARLY TO WED
Dir. Frank Borzage
Cast Matt Moore
Kathryn Perry
Zasu Pitts
Arthur Housman

FAMILY UPSTAIRS, THE
Dir. John Blystone
Cast Virginia Valli
Allan Simpson
J. Farrell MacDonald
Jacqueline Wells

FIG LEAVES
Dir. Howard Hawks
Cast George O'Brien
Olive Borden
Phyllis Haver
William Austin

FIGHTING BUCKAROO, THE
Dir. R. William Neill
Cast Buck Jones
Sally Long

473

FIRST YEAR, THE
Dir. Frank Borzage
Cast Matt Moore
Kathryn Perry
John Patrick
J. Farrell MacDonald

FLYING HORSEMAN, THE
Dir. Orville Dull
Cast Buck Jones
Gladys McConnell
Bruce Covington

GENTLE CYCLONE, THE
Dir. W. S. Van Dyke
Cast Buck Jones

GILDED BUTTERFLY, THE
Dir. John Griffith Wray
Cast Alma Rubens
Frank Keenan
Robert Rawlinson
Bert Lytell

GOING CROOKED
Dir. George Melford
Cast Bessie Love
Oscar Shaw

GOLDEN STRAIN, THE
Dir. Victor Schertzinger

GREAT A AND K TRAIN ROBBERY, THE
Dir. Lewis Seiler
Cast Tom Mix
Dorothy Dwan

HARDBOILED
Dir. John Blystone
Cast Tom Mix
Helene Chadwick
Phyllis Haver

HELL'S 400
Dir. John Griffith Wray
Cast Margaret Livingston
Harrison Ford
Henry Kolker
Marceline Day

HONESTY—THE BEST POLICY
Dir. Chester Bennett
Cast Radcliffe Fellows

JOHNSTOWN FLOOD, THE
Dir. Irving Cummings
Cast Janet Gaynor
George O'Brien
Florence Gilbert
Anders Randolf

LILY, THE
Dir. Victor Schertzinger
Cast Belle Bennett
Ian Keith
Richard Tucker

MAN FOUR-SQUARE, A
Dir. R. William Neill
Cast Buck Jones

MARRIAGE LICENSE
Dir. Frank Borzage
Cast Alma Rubens
Walter Pidgeon
Walter McGrail
Richard Walling

MIDNIGHT KISS, THE
Dir. Irving Cummings
Cast Janet Gaynor
Richard Walling
Arthur Housman
Doris Lloyd

MORE PAY—LESS WORK
Dir. Albert Ray
Cast Albert Gran
Mary Brian
E. J. Radcliffe
Charles "Buddy" Rogers

MY OWN PAL
Dir. John Blystone
Cast Tom Mix
Olive Borden
Virginia Marshall

NO MAN'S GOLD
Dir. Lewis Seiler
Cast Tom Mix
Eva Novak

OUTSIDER, THE
Dir. Rowland V. Lee
Cast Walter Pidgeon
Lou Tellegen

PALACE OF PLEASURE, THE
Dir. Emmett Flynn
Cast Edmund Lowe
Betty Compson
Francis MacDonald

RETURN OF PETER GRIMM, THE
Dir. Victor Schertzinger
Cast Janet Gaynor
Richard Walling
Alec B. Francis
John Roche

ROAD TO GLORY, THE
Dir. Howard Hawks
Cast May McAvoy
Leslie Fenton
Ford Sterling

RUSTLING FOR CUPID
Dir. Irving Cummings
Cast George O'Brien
Anita Stewart
Russell Simpson
Edith York

SANDY
Dir. Harry Beaumont
Cast Madge Bellamy
Leslie Fenton
Gloria Hope
Charles Farrell

SHAMROCK HANDICAP, THE
Dir. John Ford
Cast Janet Gaynor
J. Farrell MacDonald
Claire McDowell
Leslie Fenton

SIBERIA
Dir. Victor Schertzinger
Cast Alma Rubens
Edmund Lowe
Lou Tellegen
Lilyan Tashman

SILVER TREASURE, THE
Dir. Rowland V. Lee
Cast George O'Brien
Jack Rollins
Helena D'Algy
Joan Renee

SUMMER BACHELORS
Dir. Allan Dwan
Cast Madge Bellamy
Alan Forrest
Leila Hyams
Matt Moore

Neil Hamilton
Charles Winninger

30 BELOW ZERO
Dir. Robert T. Kerr
Cast Buck Jones
Eva Novak
E. J. Ratcliffe

THREE BAD MEN
Dir. John Ford
Cast George O'Brien
Olive Borden
Lou Tellegen
Phyllis Haver

TONY RUNS WILD
Dir. Thomas Buckingham
Cast Tom Mix
Jacqueline Logan
Lawford Davidson

TRIP TO CHINATOWN, A
Dir. Robert T. Kerr
Cast Margaret Livingston
J. Farrell MacDonald
Earle Foxe

WHAT PRICE GLORY?
Dir. Raoul Walsh
Cast Edmund Lowe
Victor McLaglen
Dolores Del Rio
Leslie Fenton
Sammy Cohen

WHISPERING WIRES
Dir. Albert Ray
Cast Anita Stewart
Edmund Burns
Charles Clary
Arthur Housman

WINGS OF THE STORM
Dir. John Blystone
Cast William Russell
Virginia Brown Faire
Reed Howe
Thunder (Dog)

WOMANPOWER
Dir. Harry Beaumont
Cast Ralph Graves
Kathryn Perry
Ralph Sipperly
Margaret Livingston
David Butler

YANKEE SEÑOR, THE
Dir. Emmett Flynn
Cast Tom Mix
Olive Borden
Alec B. Francis
Francis MacDonald

YELLOW FINGERS
Dir. Emmett Flynn
Cast Olive Borden
Ralph Ince
Claire Adams
Edward Piel

1927

ANKLES PREFERRED
Dir. John Blystone
Cast Madge Bellamy
Lawrence Gray
Barry Norton
Allan Forrest

ARIZONA WILDCAT, THE

Dir. R. William Neill
Cast Tom Mix
Dorothy Sebastian
Virginia Marshall
Ben Bard

AUCTIONEER, THE
Dir. Alfred E. Green
Cast George Sydney
Gareth Hughes
Marian Nixon
Sammy Cohen

BERTHA THE SEWING MACHINE GIRL
Dir. Irving Cummings
Cast Madge Bellamy
Allen Simpson
Sally Phipps
Paul Nicholson

BLACKJACK
Dir. Orville Dull
Cast Buck Jones

BLOOD WILL TELL
Dir. Ray Flynn
Cast Buck Jones

BRONCHO TWISTER, THE
Dir. Orville Dull
Cast Tom Mix
Helene Costello
George Irving
Doris Lloyd

CHAIN LIGHTNING
Dir. Lambert Hillyer
Cast Buck Jones
Gene Cameron
Dione Ellis
Jack Baston

CIRCUS ACE, THE
Dir. Benjamin Stoloff
Cast Tom Mix
Natalie Joyce
Jack Baston

COLLEEN
Dir. Frank O'Connor
Cast Madge Bellamy
Charles Morton
J. Farrell MacDonald
Sammy Cohen

COME TO MY HOUSE
Dir. Alfred E. Green
Cast Olive Borden
Antonio Moreno
Ben Bard
Doris Lloyd

CRADLE SNATCHERS, THE
Dir. Howard Hawks
Cast Louise Fazenda
Dione Ellis
Nick Stuart
Arthur Lake

EAST SIDE WEST SIDE
Dir. Allan Dwan
Cast George O'Brien
Virginia Valli
J. Farrell MacDonald
June Collyer

GAY RETREAT, THE
Dir. Benjamin Stoloff
Cast Sammy Cohen
Ted McNamara
Gene Cameron
Betty Francisco

GOOD AS GOLD
Dir. Scott Dunlap
Cast Buck Jones
Frances Lee
Carl Miller
Charles French

HEART OF SALOME
Dir. Victor Schertzinger
Cast Alma Rubens
Walter Pidgeon
Holmes Herbert
Robert Agnew

HIGH SCHOOL HERO
Dir. David Butler
Cast Nick Stuart
Sally Phipps
John Darrow
Charlie Paddock

HILLS OF PERIL
Dir. Lambert Hillyer
Cast Buck Jones
Georgia Hale

IS ZAT SO
Dir. Alfred E. Green
Cast George O'Brien
Edmund Lowe
Katherine Lowe
Douglas Fairbanks, Jr.
Dione Ellis

JOY GIRL
Dir. Allan Dwan
Cast Olive Borden
Neil Hamilton
Marie Dressler
Helen Chandler

LADIES MUST DRESS
Dir. Victor Heerman
Cast Virginia Valli
Lawrence Gray
Nancy Carroll
Earle Foxe

LAST TRAIL, THE
Dir. Lewis Seiler
Cast Tom Mix
Carmelita Geraghty
William Davidson
Lee Shumway

LOVE MAKES 'EM WILD
Dir. Albert Ray
Cast Johnnie Harron
Natalie Kingston
Arthur Housman
Sally Phipps

LOVES OF CARMEN, THE
Dir. Raoul Walsh
Cast Dolores Del Rio
Don Alvarado
Victor McLaglen
Nancy Nash

MADAME WANTS NO CHILDREN
(Made in Germany)
Dir. Alexander Korda
Cast Maria Corda
Harry Liedke
Trude Hesterberg
Dina Gralla

MARRIAGE
Dir. R. William Neill
Cast Virginia Valli
Allan Durant

Edward David
Billie Bennett

MARRIED ALIVE
Dir. Emmett Flynn
Cast Margaret Livingston
Matt Moore

MONKEY TALKS, THE
Dir. Raoul Walsh
Cast Olive Borden
Jacques Lerner
Don Alvarado
Malcolm Waite

MUSIC MASTER
Dir. Allan Dwan
Cast Alec B. Francis
Lois Moran
Neil Hamilton
Norman Trevor

ONE INCREASING PURPOSE
Dir. Harry Beaumont
Cast Edmund Lowe
Lila Lee

OUTLAWS OF RED RIVER
Dir. Lewis Seiler
Cast Tom Mix
Margery Daw
Arthur Clayton
William Conklin

PAID TO LOVE
Dir. Howard Hawks
Cast George O'Brien
Virginia Valli
J. Farrell MacDonald
William Powell

PAJAMAS
Dir. John Blystone
Cast Olive Borden
Lawrence Gray
John J. Clark
Jerry Miley

PUBLICITY MADNESS
Dir. Albert Ray
Cast Lois Moran
Edmund Lowe
E. J. Ratcliffe
James Gordon

RICH BUT HONEST
Dir. Albert Ray
Cast Nancy Nash
Charles Morton
Majorie Beebe
J. Farrell MacDonald

SECRET STUDIO
Dir. Victor Schertzinger
Cast Olive Borden
Clifford Holland
Ben Bard
Noreen Phillips

SEVENTH HEAVEN
Dir. Frank Borzage
Cast Janet Gaynor
Charles Farrell
Albert Gram
David Butler

SILK LEGS
Dir. Arthur Rosson
Cast Madge Bellamy
James Hall
Joseph Cawthorne
Maude Fulton

SILVER VALLEY
Dir. Benjamin Stoloff
Cast Tom Mix
Dorothy Dwan
Phil McCullough

SINGED
Dir. John Griffith Wray
Cast Blanche Sweet
Warner Baxter
Mary McAllister
Ida Darling

SLAVES OF BEAUTY
Dir. John Bystone
Cast Holmes Herbert
Olive Tell
Sue Carol
Earle Foxe

STAGE MADNESS
Dir. Victor Schertzinger
Cast Virginia Valli
Tulio Carmenati
Lou Tellegen
Richard Walling
Virginia Bradford

SUNRISE
Dir. F. W. Murnau
Cast George O'Brien
Janet Gaynor
Margaret Livingston
J. Farrell MacDonald

TUMBLING RIVER
Dir. Lewis Seiler
Cast Tom Mix
Dorothy Dwan

TWO GIRLS WANTED
Dir. Alfred E. Green
Cast Janet Gaynor
Glenn Tryon
Ben Bard
Joseph Cawthorne

UPSTREAM
Dir. John Ford
Cast Earle Foxe
Nancy Nash
Raymond Hitchcock
Sammy Cohen

VERY CONFIDENTIAL
Dir. James Tinling
Cast Madge Bellamy
Patrick Cunning
Mary Duncan
Majorie Beebe

WAR HORSE, THE
Dir. Lambert Hillyer
Cast Buck Jones
Lola Todd
Lloyd Whitlock
Yola D'Avril

WHISPERING SAGE
Dir. Scott Dunlap
Cast Buck Jones
Natalie Joyce
Carl Miller

WIZARD, THE
Dir. Richard Rosson
Cast Edmund Lowe
Leila Hyams
Gustav Von Seyffertitz
Barry Norton

WOLF'S FANGS, THE
Dir. Lewis Seiler

Cast Thunder (Dog)
Charles Morton
Caryl Lincoln
James Gordon

1928

AIR CIRCUS, THE
Dir. Lewis Seiler
Howard Hawks
Cast Arthur Lake
Sue Carol
David Rollins
Louise Dresser

BLINDFOLD
Dir. Charles Klein
Cast Lois Moran
George O'Brien
Earle Foxe
Fritz Feld

BRANDED SOMBRERO
Dir. Lambert Hillyer
Cast Buck Jones
Leila Hyams
Jack Baston
Josephine Ford

CHICKEN A LA KING
Dir. Henry Lehrman
Cast Nancy Carroll
George Meeker
Arthur Stone
Ford Sterling

COWBOY KID, THE
Dir. Clyde Carruth
Cast Rex Bell
Mary Jane Temple
Brooks Benedict

DAREDEVIL'S REWARD
Dir. Eugene Forde
Cast Tom Mix
Natalie Joyce
Lawford Davidson

DON'T MARRY
Dir. James Tinling
Cast Lois Moran
Neil Hamilton
Henry Kolker
Claire McDowell

DRESSED TO KILL
Dir. Irving Cummings
Cast Mary Astor
Edmund Lowe
Ben Bard

DRY MARTINI
Dir. Harry A. D'arrast
Cast Mary Astor
Matt Moore
Joycelyn Lee
Sally Eilers

ESCAPE, THE
Dir. Richard Rosson
Cast William Russell
Virginia Valli
Nancy Drexel
William Demarest
George Meeker

FARMER'S DAUGHTER, THE
Dir. Arthur Rosson
Cast Marjorie Beebe
Warren Burke
Arthur Stone
Lincoln Steadman

FAZIL
Dir. Howard Hawks
Cast Charles Farrell
   Greta Nissen
   Mae Busch
   John Boles

FLEETWING
Dir. Lambert Hillyer
Cast Barry Norton

FOUR SONS
Dir. John Ford
Cast Margaret Mann
   James Hall
   Francis X. Bushman, Jr.
   June Collyer

GATEWAY OF THE MOON
Dir. John Griffith Wray
Cast Dolores Del Rio
   Walter Pidgeon
   Anders Randolf
   Leslie Fenton

GIRL IN EVERY PORT, A
Dir. Howard Hawks
Cast Victor McLaglen
   Robert Armstrong
   Louise Brooks
   Natalie Joyce

GIRL-SHY COWBOY
Dir. R. L. Hough
Cast Rex Bell
   George Meeker

HANGMAN'S HOUSE
Dir. John Ford
Cast Victor McLaglen
   June Collyer
   Larry Kent
   Earle Foxe
   Hobart Bosworth

HELLO CHEYENNE
Dir. Eugene Forde
Cast Tom Mix
   Garyl Lincoln
   Jack Baston
   Al St. John

HOMESICK
Dir. Henry Lehrman
Cast Sammy Cohen
   Harry Sweet
   Marjorie Beebe
   Henry Armetta

HONOR BOUND
Dir. Alfred E. Green
Cast George O'Brien
   Estelle Taylor
   Leila Hyams
   Tom Santschi

HORSEMAN OF THE PLAINS
Dir. Benjamin Stoloff
Cast Tom Mix
   Sally Blane
   Heinie Conklin

LOST IN THE ARCTIC
(*Documentary*)
(GREAT WHITE NORTH, THE)
Dir. H. A. Snow
   Sidney Snow
Narrator Vilhajalmur Stefansson

LOVE HUNGRY
Dir. Victor Heerman
Cast Lois Moran
   Lawrence Gray

   Marjorie Beebe
   Edythe Chapman

ME, GANGSTER
Dir. Raoul Walsh
Cast June Collyer
   Don Terry
   Anders Randolf
   Carole Lombard

MOTHER KNOWS BEST
Dir. John Blystone
Cast Barry Norton
   Madge Bellamy
   Louise Dresser
   Lucien Littlefield

MOTHER MACHREE
Dir. John Ford
Cast Belle Bennett
   Phillippe De Lacy
   Victor McLaglen
   Neil Hamilton
   Constance Howard

NEWS PARADE
Dir. David Butler
Cast Nick Stuart
   Sally Phipps
   Earle Foxe
   Truman H. Talley

NO OTHER WOMAN
Dir. Lou Tellegen
Cast Dolores Del Rio
   Don Alvarado
   Ben Bard

NONE BUT THE BRAVE
Dir. Albert Ray
Cast Charles Morton
   Sally Phipps
   J. Farrell MacDonald
   Sharon Lynn

PAINTED POST
Dir. Eugene Forde
Cast Tom Mix
   Natalie Kingston
   Al St. John

PLASTERED IN PARIS
Dir. Benjamin Stoloff
Cast Sammy Cohen
   Jack Pennick
   Lola Salvi
   Albert Conti

PLAY GIRL
Dir. Arthur Rosson
Cast Madge Bellamy
   Johnny Mack Brown
   Walter McGrail

PREP AND PEP
Dir. David Butler
Cast David Rollins
   Nancy Drexel
   John Darrow
   Frank Albertson

RED DANCE
Dir. Raoul Walsh
Cast Dolores Del Rio
   Charles Farrell
   Ivan Linow
   Dorothy Revier

RILEY THE COP
Dir. John Ford
Cast J. Farrell MacDonald
   Louise Fazenda

   Nancy Drexel
   David Rollins

RIVER PIRATE
Dir. William K. Howard
Cast Victor McLaglen
   Lois Moran
   Nick Stuart
   Donald Crisp

ROAD HOUSE
Dir. Richard Rosson
Cast Lionel Barrymore
   Warren Burke
   Maria Alba
   Kay Bryant

ROMANCE OF THE UNDERWORLD
Dir. Irving Cummings
Cast Mary Astor
   Ben Bard
   Robert Elliott
   John Boles

SHARP SHOOTERS
Dir. John Blystone
Cast George O'Brien
   Lois Moran
   Noah Young
   Tom Dugan

SOFT LIVING
Dir. James Tinling
Cast Madge Bellamy
   Johnny Mack Brown
   Mary Duncan
   Joyce Compton

SQUARE CROOKS
Dir. Lewis Seiler
Cast Robert Armstrong
   Johnny Mack Brown
   Dorothy Appleby
   Dorothy Dwan

STREET ANGEL
Dir. Frank Borzage
Cast Janet Gaynor
   Charles Farrell
   Natalie Kingston
   Guido Trento

THIEF IN THE DARK
Dir. Albert Ray
Cast George Meeker
   Doris Hill
   Gwen Lee
   Marjorie Beebe

UNEASY MONEY
(*Made in Germany*)
Dir. Berthold Viertel
Cast Mary Nolan
   Werner Fuetterer
   Oscar Homolka

WHY SAILORS GO WRONG
Dir. Henry Lehrman
Cast Sammy Cohen
   Ted McNamara
   Sally Phipps
   Nick Stuart

WILD WEST ROMANCE
Dir. R. L. Hough
Cast Rex Bell

WIN THAT GIRL
Dir. David Butler
Cast David Rollins
   Sue Carol

   Tom Elliott
   Roscoe Karns

WOMAN WISE
Dir. Albert Ray
Cast William Russell
   June Collyer
   Walter Pidgeon
   Theodore Kosloff

1929

BEHIND THAT CURTAIN
Dir. Irving Cummings
Cast Warner Baxter
   Lois Moran
   Boris Karloff
   Gilbert Emery

BIG TIME
Dir. Kenneth Hawks
Cast Lee Tracy
   Mae Clarke
   Daphne Pollard
   Stepin Fetchit

BLACK MAGIC
Dir. George B. Seitz
Cast Josephine Dunn
   John Holland
   Dorothy Jordan
   Henry B. Walthall

BLACK WATCH, THE
Dir. John Ford
Cast Victor McLaglen
   Myrna Loy
   Claude King
   David Rollins

BLUE SKIES, THE
Dir. Alfred Werker
Cast Helen Twelvetrees
   Frank Albertson
   Ethel Wales
   Adele Watson

CAPTAIN LASH
Dir. John Blystone
Cast Victor McLaglen
   Claire Windsor
   Jane Winton
   Clyde Cook

CHASING THROUGH EUROPE
Dir. Alfred Werker
   David Butler
Cast Nick Stuart
   Sue Carol
   Gustav Von Seyffertitz

CHRISTINA
Dir. William K. Howard
Cast Janet Gaynor
   Charles Morton
   Lucy Dorraine
   Rudolph Schildkraut

COCK-EYED WORLD, THE
Dir. Raoul Walsh
Cast Victor McLaglen
   Edmund Lowe
   Lily Damita
   El Brendel

EXALTED FLAPPER, THE
Dir. James Tinling
Cast Sue Carol
   Barry Norton
   Irene Rich
   Stuart Erwin

476

FAR CALL, THE
Dir. Allan Dwan
Cast Charles Morton
Leila Hyams
Warner Baxter
Arthur Stone

FOUR DEVILS
Dir. F. W. Murnau
Cast Anders Randolf
Barry Norton
Charles Morton
Janet Gaynor

FOX MOVIETONE FOLLIES
OF 1929
Dir. David Butler
Cast Sue Carol
Sharon Lynn
Dixie Lee
Lola Lane

FROZEN JUSTICE
Dir. Allan Dwan
Cast Lenore Ulric
Robert Frazer
Louis Wolheim
El Brendel

FUGITIVES
Dir. William Beaudine
Cast Madge Bellamy
Don Terry
Arthur Stone
Earle Foxe

GHOST TALKS, THE
Dir. Lewis Seiler
Cast Helen Twelvetrees
Charles Eaton
Carmel Myers
Stepin Fetchit

GIRL FROM HAVANA, THE
Dir. Benjamin Stoloff
Cast Lola Lane
Paul Page
Kenneth Thompson
Natalie Moorehead

GIRLS GONE WILD
Dir. Lewis Seiler
Cast Sue Carol
Nick Stuart
Roy D'arcy
Leslie Fenton

HEARTS IN DIXIE
Dir. Paul Sloane
Cast Stepin Fetchit
Clarence Muse
Eugene Jackson
Dorothy Morrison

HOT FOR PARIS
Dir. Raoul Walsh
Cast Victor McLaglen
Fifi Dorsay
El Brendel
Polly Moran

IN OLD ARIZONA
Dir. Raoul Walsh
Irving Cummings
Cast Warner Baxter
Edmund Lowe
Dorothy Burgess
J. Farrell MacDonald

JOY STREET
Dir. Raymond Cannon
Cast Lois Moran

Nick Stuart
Rex Bell
Sally Phipps

LOVE, LIVE AND LAUGH
Dir. William K. Howard
Cast George Jessel
Lila Lee
David Rollins
Henry Kolker

LUCKY STAR
Dir. Frank Borzage
Cast Janet Gaynor
Charles Farrell
Guinn Williams
Gloria Grey

MAKING THE GRADE
Dir. Alfred E. Green
Cast Lois Moran
Edmund Lowe
Albert Hart
Lucien Littlefield

MARRIED IN HOLLYWOOD
Dir. Marcel Silver
Cast J. Harold Murray
Norma Terris
Walter Catlett
Irene Palasty

MASKED EMOTIONS
Dir. David Butler
Howard Hawks
Cast George O'Brien
Nora Lane
James Gordon
J. Farrell MacDonald

MASQUERADE
Dir. Lumsden Hare
Russell Birdwell
Cast Leila Hyams
Alan Birmingham
J. Farrell MacDonald
Lumsden Hare

NEW YEAR'S EVE
Dir. Henry Lehrman
Cast Mary Astor
Charles Morton
Arthur Stone
Helen Ware

NIX ON DAMES
Dir. Donald Gallagher
Cast Mae Clarke
Robert Ames
Maude Fulton
William Harrigan

NOT QUITE DECENT
Dir. Irving Cummings
Cast June Collyer
Louise Dresser
Allan Lane
Marjorie Beebe

ONE WOMAN IDEA
Dir. Berthold Viertel
Cast Rod La Rocque
Marceline Day
Ivan Lebedeff
Sharon Lynn

PLEASURE CRAZED
Dir. Charles Klein
Cast Marguerite Churchill
Kenneth MacKenna
Rex Bell
Dorothy Burgess

PROTECTION
Dir. Benjamin Stoloff
Cast Dorothy Burgess
Robert Elliott
Paul Page
Ben Hewlitt

RED WINE
Dir. Raymond Cannon
Cast Conrad Nagel
June Collyer
Sharon Lynn

RIVER, THE
Dir. Frank Borzage
Cast Charles Farrell
Mary Duncan
Ivan Linow
Margaret Mann

ROMANCE OF THE RIO
GRANDE
Dir. Alfred Santell
Cast Warner Baxter
Mary Duncan
Antonio Moreno
Mona Maris

SALUTE
Dir. John Ford
David Butler
Cast George O'Brien
Helen Chandler
Stepin Fetchit
Joyce Compton

SEVEN FACES
Dir. Berthold Viertel
Cast Marguerite Churchill
Lester Lonergon
Paul Muni
Russell Gleason

SIN SISTER
Dir. Charles Klein
Cast Nancy Carroll
Lawrence Gray
Josephine Dunn
Myrtle Stedman

SONG OF KENTUCKY
Dir. Lewis Seiler
Cast Lois Moran
Joseph Wagstaff
Dorothy Burgess
Hedda Hopper

SOUTH SEA ROSE
Dir. Allan Dwan
Cast Lenore Ulric
Charles Bickford
Kenneth MacKenna
J. Farrell MacDonald

SPEAKEASY
Dir. Benjamin Stoloff
Cast Stuart Erwin
Sharon Lynn
Lola Lane
Paul Page

STRONG BOY
Dir. John Ford
Cast Victor McLaglen
Leatrice Joy
Clyde Cook
Slim Summerville

SUNNYSIDE UP
Dir. David Butler
Cast Janet Gaynor
Charles Farrell

Majorie White
El Brendel

TAKING A CHANCE
Dir. Norman Z. McLeod
Cast Rex Bell
Lola Todd
Richard Carlyle
Billy Watson

THEY HAD TO SEE PARIS
Dir. Frank Borzage
Cast Will Rogers
Irene Rich
Owen Davis, Jr.
Marguerite Churchill

THRU DIFFERENT EYES
Dir. John Blystone
Cast Mary Duncan
Warner Baxter
Edmund Lowe
Sylvia Sydney

TRENT'S LAST CASE
Dir. Howard Hawks
Cast Raymond Griffith
Marceline Day
Raymond Hatton
Donald Crisp

TRUE HEAVEN
Dir. James Tinling
Cast George O'Brien
Lois Moran
Oscar Apfel
Phillips Smalley

VALIANT, THE
Dir. William K. Howard
Cast Paul Muni
Marguerite Churchill
Johnny Mack Brown
Dewitt Jennings

VEILED WOMAN, THE
Dir. Emmett Flynn
Cast Lia Tora
Paul Vincenti
Walter McGrail
Ivan Lebedeff

WHY LEAVE HOME
Dir. Raymond Cannon
Cast Sue Carol
Nick Stuart
Dixie Lee
Ilka Chase

WOMAN FROM HELL, THE
Dir. A. F. Erickson
Cast Mary Astor
Robert Armstrong
Roy D'arcy
Dean Jagger

WORDS AND MUSIC
Dir. James Tinling
Cast Lois Moran
Tom Patricola
David Percy
Frank Albertson
Helen Twelvetrees

1930

ARE YOU THERE?
Dir. Hamilton MacFadden
Cast Beatrice Lillie
John Garrick

Olga Baclanova
Jillian Sand

ARIZONA KID, THE
Dir. Alfred Santell
Cast Warner Baxter
Mona Maris
Carole Lombard

BIG PARTY
Dir. John Blystone
Cast Sue Carol
Dixie Lee
Walter Catlett
Frank Albertson

BIG TRAIL, THE
Dir. Raoul Walsh
Cast John Wayne
Marguerite Churchill
El Brendel
Tully Marshall

BORN RECKLESS
Dir. John Ford
Andrew Bennison
Cast Edmund Lowe
Catherine Dale Owen
Lee Tracy
Marguerite Churchill

CAMEO KIRBY
Dir. Irving Cummings
Cast J. Harold Murray
Norma Terris
Douglas Gilmore
Myrna Loy

CHEER UP AND SMILE
Dir. Sidney Lanfield
Cast Arthur Lake
Dixie Lee
Olga Baclanova
Whispering Jack Smith

CITY GIRL
Dir. F. W. Murnau
Cast Charles Farrell
Mary Duncan
David Torrence

COMMON CLAY
Dir. Victor Fleming
Cast Constance Bennett
Lew Ayres
Tully Marshall

CRAZY THAT WAY
Dir. Hamilton MacFadden
Cast Joan Bennett
Kenneth MacKenna
Regis Toomey

DANCERS, THE
Dir. Chandler Sprague
Cast Phillips Holmes
Lois Moran
Mae Clarke

DEVIL WITH WOMEN, A
Dir. Irving Cummings
Cast Victor McLaglen
Mona Maris
Humphrey Bogart

DOUBLE CROSS ROADS
Dir. Alfred Werker
George Middleton
Cast Lila Lee
Montague Love
Robert Ames
Ned Sparks

FAIR WARNING
Dir. Alfred Werker
Cast George O'Brien
Louise Huntington
Mitchell Harris
George Brent

GOLDEN CALF, THE
Dir. Millard Webb
Cast Sue Carol
Jack Mulhall
El Brendel
Majorie White

GOOD INTENTIONS
Dir. William K. Howard
Cast Edmund Lowe
Marguerite Churchill
Regis Toomey

HAPPY DAYS
Dir. Benjamin Stoloff
Cast Warner Baxter
Frank Albertson
El Brendel
Walter Catlett
Charles Farrell
Janet Gaynor
George Jessel
Dixie Lee
Edmund Lowe
Victor McLaglen
Will Rogers

HARMONY AT HOME
Dir. Hamilton MacFadden
Cast William Collier, Sr.
Marguerite Churchill
Rex Bell
Dixie Lee

HIGH SOCIETY BLUES
Dir. David Butler
Cast Janet Gaynor
Charles Farrell
William Collier, Sr.
Hedda Hopper
Joyce Compton

JUST IMAGINE
Dir. David Butler
Cast El Brendel
Maureen O'Sullivan
John Garrick
Marjorie White
Frank Albertson

LAST OF THE DUANES
Dir. Alfred Werker
Cast George O'Brien
Myrna Loy
Lucille Brown
Walter McGrail

LET'S GO PLACES
Dir. Frank Strayer
Cast Joseph Wagstaff
Lola Lane
Sharon Lynn
Dixie Lee
Ilka Chase

LIGHTNIN'
Dir. Henry King
Cast Will Rogers
Louise Dresser
Joel McCrea
Helen Cohan

LILIOM
Dir. Frank Borzage
Cast Charles Farrell

Rose Hobart
Estelle Taylor
Lee Tracy

LONE STAR RANGER
Dir. A. F. Erickson
Cast George O'Brien
Sue Carol
Walter McGrail
Warren Hymer

MAN TROUBLE
Dir. Berthold Viertel
Cast Dorothy Mackaill
Milton Sills
Kenneth McKenna
Sharon Lynn
Roscoe Karns

MEN ON CALL
Dir. John Blystone
Cast Edmund Lowe
Mae Clarke
William Harrigan
Warren Hymer
Sharon Lynn

MEN WITHOUT WOMEN
Dir. John Ford
Cast Kenneth McKenna
Frank Albertson
Warren Hymer
Stuart Erwin

NEW MOVIETONE FOLLIES OF 1930
Dir. Benjamin Stoloff
Cast El Brendel
Marjorie White
Frank Richardson
William Collier, Jr.

NOT DAMAGED
Dir. Chandler Sprague
Cast Lois Moran
Walter Byron
Robert Ames
Inez Courtney

OH FOR A MAN
Dir. Hamilton MacFadden
Cast Jeanette MacDonald
Reginald Denny
Marjorie White
Warren Hymer
Bela Lugosi

ON THE LEVEL
Dir. Irving Cummings
Cast Victor McLaglen
Fifi Dorsay
Lilyan Tashman

ON YOUR BACK
Dir. Guthrie McClintic
Cast Irene Rich
Raymond Hackett
H. B. Warner
Ilka Chase

ONE MAD KISS
Dir. Marcel Silver
Cast Jose Mojica
Mona Maris
Antonio Moreno

PART TIME WIFE
Dir. Leo McCarey
Cast Edmund Lowe
Leila Hyams
Tommy Clifford
Walter McGrail

PRINCESS AND THE PLUMBER, THE
Dir. Alexander Korda
Cast Charles Farrell
Maureen O'Sullivan
H. B. Warner

RENEGADES
Dir. Victor Fleming
Cast Warner Baxter
Myrna Loy
Noah Beery

ROUGH ROMANCE
Dir. A. F. Erickson
Cast George O'Brien
Helen Chandler
Antonio Moreno

SCOTLAND YARD
Dir. William K. Howard
Cast Edmund Lowe
Joan Bennett
Donald Crisp

SEA WOLF, THE
Dir. Alfred Santell
Cast Milton Sills
Raymond Hackett
Jane Keith
Nat Pendleton

SKY HAWK, THE
Dir. John Blystone
Cast Helen Chandler
John Garrick
Gilbert Emery

SO THIS IS LONDON
Dir. John Blystone
Cast Will Rogers
Irene Rich
Frank Albertson
Maureen O'Sullivan

SONG O' MY HEART
Dir. Frank Borzage
Cast John McCormack
Alice Joyce
Maureen O'Sullivan

SOUP TO NUTS
Dir. Benjamin Stoloff
Cast Ted Healy
Frances McCoy
Stanley Smith

SUCH MEN ARE DANGEROUS
Dir. Kenneth Hawks
Cast Warner Baxter
Catherine Dale Owen
Hedda Hopper
Bela Lugosi

TEMPLE TOWER
Dir. Donald Gallagher
Cast Kenneth MacKenna
Marceline Day
Henry B. Walthall

THREE SISTERS
Dir. Paul Sloane
Cast Louise Dresser
Tom Patricola
Kenneth MacKenna
Joyce Compton
June Collyer

UNDER SUSPICION
Dir. A. F. Erickson
Cast J. Harold Murray
Lois Moran

478

On location for a Buck Jones western in Lone Pine Canyon, California, near Bishop, with Mt. Whitney in the background. Jones is in the center in the Stetson.

Marian Nixon and Buck Jones.

John Gilbert in *The Madness of Youth*. (1923)

Edmund Lowe and Warner Baxter in *In Old Arizona*. (1929)

George O'Brien and Janet Gaynor in *Sunrise*. (1927)

Tom Mix in *Catch My Smoke*. (1923)

Buck Jones in *Gold and the Girl*. (1925)

John Wayne and Marguerite Churchill in *The Big Trail*. (1930)

Victor McLaglen, Dolores Del Rio, and Edmund Lowe in *What Price Glory?* (1926)

George O'Brien and Mitchell Harris in *Fair Warning*. (1930)

Charles Farrell and Janet Gaynor in *Sunny Side Up*. (1929)

Warner Oland as Charlie Chan.

Charles Farrell and Janet Gaynor in *Seventh Heaven*. (1927)

J. M. Kerrigan
George Brent

UP THE RIVER
Dir. John Ford
Cast Spencer Tracy
Claire Luce
Warren Hymer
Humphrey Bogart

WILD COMPANY
Dir. Leo McCarey
Cast Frank Albertson
H. B. Warner
Sharon Lynn
Joyce Compton

WOMEN EVERYWHERE
Dir. Alexander Korda
Cast J. Harold Murray
Fifi Dorsay
George Grossmith

1931

ALWAYS GOODBYE
Dir. Kenneth MacKenna
William C. Menzies
Cast Elissa Landi
Lewis Stone
Paul Cavanaugh
John Garrick

AMBASSADOR BILL
Dir. Sam Taylor
Cast Will Rogers
Greta Nissen
Marguerite Churchill
Ted Alexander

ANNABELLE'S AFFAIRS
Dir. Alfred Werker
Cast Victor McLaglen
Jeanette MacDonald
Roland Young

BAD GIRL
Dir. Frank Borzage
Cast Sally Eilers
James Dunn
Minna Gombell

BLACK CAMEL, THE
Dir. Hamilton MacFadden
Cast Warner Oland
Sally Eilers
Bela Lugosi
Dorothy Revier

BODY AND SOUL
Dir. Alfred Santell
Cast Charles Farrell
Elissa Landi
Humphrey Bogart
Myrna Loy

BRAT, THE
Dir. John Ford
Cast Sally O'Neil
Alan Dinehart
Frank Albertson
Virginia Cherrill

CHARLIE CHAN CARRIES ON
Dir. Hamilton MacFadden
Cast Warner Oland
John Garrick
Marguerite Churchill
Warren Hymer

CISCO KID, THE
Dir. Irving Cummings

Cast Warner Baxter
Edmund Lowe
Conchita Montenegro
Nora Lane

CONNECTICUT YANKEE, A
Dir. David Butler
Cast Will Rogers
Maureen O'Sullivan
Myrna Loy
Frank Albertson

DADDY LONG LEGS
Dir. Alfred Santell
Cast Janet Gaynor
Warner Baxter
Una Merkel
John Arledge

DELICIOUS
Dir. David Butler
Cast Janet Gaynor
Charles Farrell
El Brendel
Lawrence O'Sullivan

DOCTOR'S WIVES
Dir. Frank Borzage
Cast Warner Baxter
Joan Bennett
Cecilia Loftus
Ruth Warren

DON'T BET ON WOMEN
Dir. William K. Howard
Cast Edmund Lowe
Jeanette MacDonald
Roland Young
Una Merkel

EAST LYNNE
Dir. Frank Lloyd
Cast Ann Harding
Clive Brook
Conrad Nagel
Cecilia Loftus

GIRLS DEMAND EXCITEMENT
Dir. Seymour Felix
Cast Virginia Cherrill
John Wayne
Marguerite Churchill

GOLDIE
Dir. Benjamin Stoloff
Cast Spencer Tracy
Jean Harlow
Warren Hymer
Lina Basquette

GOOD SPORT
Dir. Kenneth MacKenna
Cast Linda Watkins
John Boles
Greta Nissen
Hedda Hopper
Alan Dinehart

HEARTBREAK
Dir. Alfred Werker
Cast Charles Farrell
Madge Evans
Paul Cavanaugh
Hardie Albright

HOLY TERROR, THE
Dir. Irving Cummings
Cast George O'Brien
Sally Eilers
Rita LaRoy
Humphrey Bogart

HUSH MONEY
Dir. Sidney Lanfield

Cast Joan Bennett
Myrna Loy
Hardie Albright
Owen Moore

MAN WHO CAME BACK, THE
Dir. Raoul Walsh
Cast Janet Gaynor
Charles Farrell
Kenneth MacKenna
William Holden

MERELY MARY ANN
Dir. Henry King
Cast Janet Gaynor
Charles Farrell
Beryl Mercer

MR. LEMON OF ORANGE
Dir. John Blystone
Cast El Brendel
Fifi Dorsay
William Collier, Jr.
Ruth Warren

NOT EXACTLY GENTLEMEN
Dir. Benjamin Stoloff
Cast Victor McLaglen
Fay Wray
Lew Cody
Robert Warwick

ONCE A SINNER
Dir. Guthrie McClintic
Cast Dorothy Mackaill
Joel McCrea
John Halliday
Ilka Chase
George Brent

OVER THE HILL
Dir. Henry King
Cast Mae Marsh
James Kirkwood
James Dunn
Sally Eilers

QUICK MILLIONS
Dir. Rowland Brown
Cast Spencer Tracy
Marguerite Churchill
Sally Eilers
John Wray
George Raft

RIDERS OF THE PURPLE SAGE
Dir. Hamilton MacFadden
Cast George O'Brien
Marguerite Churchill
Noah Beery

SEAS BENEATH, THE
Dir. John Ford
Cast George O'Brien
Marion Lessing
Warren Hymer
John Loder

SIX CYLINDER LOVE
Dir. Thornton Freeland
Cast Spencer Tracy
Edward Everett Horton
Sidney Fox
William Collier, Sr.

SKYLINE
Dir. Sam Taylor
Cast Thomas Meighan
Hardie Albright
Maureen O'Sullivan
Myrna Loy

SOB SISTERS
Dir. Alfred Santell

Cast James Dunn
Linda Watkins
Molly O'Day

SPIDER, THE
Dir. William C. Menzies
Kenneth MacKenna
Cast Edmund Lowe
Lois Moran
Howard Phillips
Earle Foxe
El Brendel

SPY, THE
Dir. Berthold Viertel
Cast Kay Johnson
Neil Hamilton
John Halliday

SURRENDER
Dir. William K. Howard
Cast Warner Baxter
Leila Hyams
Ralph Bellamy
C. Aubrey Smith

THEIR MAD MOMENT
Dir. Hamilton MacFadden
Chandler Sprague
Cast Warner Baxter
Dorothy Mackaill
Zasu Pitts

THREE GIRLS LOST
Dir. Sidney Lanfield
Cast Loretta Young
John Wayne
Lew Cody
Joyce Compton
Joan Marsh

TRANSATLANTIC
Dir. William K. Howard
Cast Edmund Lowe
Lois Moran
John Halliday
Greta Nissen
Myrna Loy

UNDER SUSPICION
Dir. A. F. Erickson
Cast J. Harold Murray
Lois Moran
J. M. Kerrigan
George Brent

WICKED
Dir. Allan Dwan
Cast Elissa Landi
Victor McLaglen
Una Merkel

WOMEN OF ALL NATIONS
Dir. Raoul Walsh
Cast Victor McLaglen
Edmund Lowe
Greta Nissen
Humphrey Bogart
Fifi Dorsay

YELLOW TICKET, THE
Dir. Raoul Walsh
Cast Elissa Landi
Lionel Barrymore
Laurence Olivier
Mischa Auer

YOUNG AS YOU FEEL
Dir. Frank Borzage
Cast Will Rogers
Fifi Dorsay
Lucien Littlefield

YOUNG SINNERS
Dir. John Blystone
Cast Thomas Meighan
Hardie Albright
Dorothy Jordan
Cecilia Loftus

1932

AFTER TOMORROW
Dir. Frank Borzage
Cast Charles Farrell
Marian Nixon
Minna Gombell
William Collier, Sr.

ALMOST MARRIED
Dir. William C. Menzies
Cast Violet Heming
Ralph Bellamy
Alexander Kirkland
Alan Dinehart

AMATEUR DADDY
Dir. John Blystone
Cast Warner Baxter
Marian Nixon
Rita LaRoy
Lucille Powers

BACHELOR'S AFFAIRS
Dir. Alfred Werker
Cast Adolphe Menjou
Minna Gombell
Rita LaRoy
Joan Marsh
Alan Dinehart

BUSINESS AND PLEASURE
Dir. David Butler
Cast Will Rogers
Jetta Goudal
Joel McCrea
Dorothy Peterson

CALL HER SAVAGE
Dir. John Francis Dillon
Cast Clara Bow
Monroe Owsley
Gilbert Roland
Thelma Todd
Estelle Taylor

CARELESS LADY
Dir. Kenneth MacKenna
Cast Joan Bennett
John Boles
Minna Gombell

CHANDU THE MAGICIAN
Dir. Marcel Varnel
William C. Menzies
Cast Edmund Lowe
Irene Ware
Bela Lugosi

CHARLIE CHAN'S CHANCE
Dir. John Blystone
Cast Warner Oland
Alexander Kirkland
H. B. Warner
Marian Nixon

CHEATERS AT PLAY
Dir. Hamilton MacFadden
Cast Thomas Meighan
Charlotte Greenwood
Ralph Morgan

CONGORILLA
(*Documentary*)
Prod. Mr. and Mrs. Martin Johnson

CRY OF THE WORLD
(*Documentary*)
Editor Louis de Rochemont

DANCE TEAM
Dir. Sidney Lanfield
Cast James Dunn
Sally Eilers
Ralph Morgan
Minna Gombell

DEVIL'S LOTTERY
Dir. Sam Taylor
Cast Elissa Landi
Victor McLaglen
Alexander Kirkland
Ralph Morgan

DISORDERLY CONDUCT
Dir. John W. Considine, Jr.
Cast Sally Eilers
Spencer Tracy
El Brendel
Ralph Bellamy
Ralph Morgan

DOWN TO EARTH
Dir. David Butler
Cast Will Rogers
Dorothy Jordan
Irene Rich
Mary Carlisle

FIRST YEAR
Dir. William K. Howard
Cast Janet Gaynor
Charles Farrell
Minna Gombell
Leila Bennett

GAY CABALLERO, THE
Dir. Alfred Werker
Cast George O'Brien
Victor McLaglen
Conchita Montenegro
Linda Watkins

GOLDEN WEST, THE
Dir. David Howard
Cast George O'Brien
Janet Chandler
Marion Burns

HANDLE WITH CARE
Dir. David Butler
Cast James Dunn
Boots Mallory
El Brendel

HAT CHECK GIRL
Dir. Sidney Lanfield
Cast Sally Eilers
Ben Lyon
Ginger Rogers
Monroe Owsley

ME AND MY GAL
Dir. Raoul Walsh
Cast Spencer Tracy
Joan Bennett
Marion Burns
George Walsh

MYSTERY RANCH
Dir. David Howard
Cast George O'Brien
Cecilia Parker
Charles Middleton

PAINTED WOMAN
Dir. John Blystone
Cast Spencer Tracy
Peggy Shannon
William Boyd
Irving Pichel

PASSPORT TO HELL, A
Dir. Frank Lloyd
Cast Elissa Landi
Paul Lukas
Warner Oland
Alexander Kirkland
Donald Crisp

RACKETY RAX
Dir. Alfred Werker
Cast Victor McLaglen
Greta Nissen
Nell O'Day
Alan Dinehart

RAINBOW TRAIL
Dir. David Howard
Cast George O'Brien
Cecilia Parker
Minna Gombell

REBECCA OF SUNNYBROOK FARM
Dir. Alfred Santell
Cast Marian Nixon
Ralph Bellamy
Mae Marsh
Alan Hale

SHE WANTED A MILLIONAIRE
Dir. John Blystone
Cast Joan Bennett
Spencer Tracy
Una Merkel
James Kirkwood

SHERLOCK HOLMES
Dir. William K. Howard
Cast Clive Brook
Miriam Jordan
Ernest Torrence
Reginald Owen
Alan Mowbray

SILENT WITNESS
Dir. Marcel Varnel
R. L. Hough
Cast Lionel Atwill
Greta Nissen
Helen Mack
Alan Mowbray

SIX HOURS TO LIVE
Dir. William Dieterle
Cast Warner Baxter
Miriam Jordan
John Boles
George Marion

SOCIETY GIRL
Dir. Sidney Lanfield
Cast James Dunn
Peggy Shannon
Spencer Tracy
Walter Byron

STEPPING SISTERS
Dir. Seymour Felix
Cast Louise Dresser
Minna Gombell
William Collier, Sr.

TESS OF THE STORM COUNTRY
Dir. Alfred Santell

PAINTED WOMAN *(column)*

Cast Janet Gaynor
Charles Farrell
Dudley Digges
June Clyde

TOO BUSY TO WORK
Dir. John Blystone
Cast Will Rogers
Marian Nixon
Dick Powell

TRIAL OF VIVIENNE WARE, THE
Dir. William K. Howard
Cast Joan Bennett
Donald Cook
Skeets Gallagher
Zasu Pitts

WEEK ENDS ONLY
Dir. Alan Crosland
Cast Joan Bennett
Ben Lyon
John Halliday

WHILE PARIS SLEEPS
Dir. Allan Dwan
Cast Victor McLaglen
Helen Mack
Jack LaRue
Rita LaRoy

WILD GIRL
Dir. Raoul Walsh
Cast Charles Farrell
Joan Bennett
Ralph Bellamy
Irving Pichel

WOMAN IN ROOM 13, THE
Dir. Henry King
Cast Elissa Landi
Ralph Bellamy
Neil Hamilton
Myrna Loy

YOUNG AMERICA
Dir. Frank Borzage
Cast Spencer Tracy
Doris Kenyon
Tommy Conlon
Ralph Bellamy

1933

ADORABLE
Dir. William Dieterle
Cast Janet Gaynor
Henry Garat
C. Aubrey Smith
Herbert Mundin

AFTER THE BALL
(*Gaumont-British*)
Dir. Milton Rosmer
Cast Esther Ralston
Basil Rathbone
Marie Burke
Jean Adrienne

ARIZONA TO BROADWAY
Dir. James Tinling
Cast James Dunn
Joan Bennett
Herbert Mundin
Sammy Cohen

BERKELEY SQUARE
Dir. Frank Lloyd
Cast Leslie Howard

Heather Angel
Valerie Taylor

BEST OF ENEMIES
Dir. Rian James
Cast Buddy Rogers
Marian Nixon
Frank Morgan
Greta Nissen

BONDAGE
Dir. Alfred Santell
Cast Dorothy Jordan
Alexander Kirkland
Isobel Jewell
Jane Darwell

BROADWAY BAD
Dir. Sidney Lanfield
Cast Joan Blondell
Ricardo Cortez
Ginger Rogers
Adrienne Ames

CAVALCADE
Dir. Frank Lloyd
Cast Margaret Lindsay
Clive Brook
Bonita Granville
John Warburton

CHARLIE CHAN'S GREATEST
CASE
Dir. Hamilton MacFadden
Cast Warner Oland
Heather Angel
John Warburton
Virginia Cherrill

CUANDO EL AMOR RIE
(WHEN LOVE LAUGHS)
Dir. David Howard
Cast Jose Mojica
Mona Maris
Carlos Villarias
Carmen Rodriquez

DANGEROUSLY YOURS
Dir. Frank Tuttle
Cast Warner Baxter
Miriam Jordan
Herbert Mundin
Florence Eldridge

DEVIL'S IN LOVE, THE
Dir. William Dieterle
Cast Loretta Young
Victor Jory
David Manners
Vivienne Osborne

DOCTOR BULL
Dir. John Ford
Cast Will Rogers
Vera Allen
Marian Nixon
Rochelle Hudson

EL PRECIO DE UN BESO
(PRICE OF A KISS)
Dir. Marcel Silver
Cast Jose Mojica
Mona Maris
Antonio Moreno

EL REY DE LOS GITANOS
(KING OF THE GYPSIES)
Dir. Frank Strayer
Cast Jose Mojica
Rosita Moreno
Julio Villarreal

F. P. 1
(*Gaumont-British*)
Dir. Karl Hartl
Cast Leslie Fenton
Conrad Veidt
Jill Esmond
George Merritt

FACE IN THE SKY
Dir. Harry Lachman
Cast Spencer Tracy
Marian Nixon
Stuart Erwin
Sam Hardy

GOOD COMPANIONS, THE
(*Gaumont-British*)
Dir. Victor Saville
Cast Jessie Matthews
Edmund Gwenn
John Gielgud

HELLO SISTER
Dir. Alan Crosland
Cast James Dunn
Boots Mallory
Zasu Pitts
Minna Gombell

HOLD ME TIGHT
Dir. David Butler
Cast James Dunn
Sally Eilers
Frank McHugh
June Clyde

HOOPLA
Dir. Frank Lloyd
Cast Clara Bow
Preston Foster
Richard Cromwell
James Gleason
Minna Gombell

HOT PEPPER
Dir. John Blystone
Cast Edmund Lowe
Victor McLaglen
Lupe Velez
El Brendel

HUMANITY
Dir. John Francis Dillon
Cast Ralph Morgan
Boots Mallory
Alexander Kirkland

I LOVED YOU WEDNESDAY
Dir. Henry King
William C. Menzies
Cast Warner Baxter
Elissa Landi
Victor Jory
Miriam Jordan

INFERNAL MACHINE
Dir. Marcel Varnel
Cast Genevieve Tobin
James Bell
Chester Morris

MY LIPS BETRAY
Dir. John Blystone
Cast Lilian Harvey
John Boles
El Brendel
Irene Browne

MY WEAKNESS
Dir. David Butler
Cast Lilian Harvey
Lew Ayres

Charles Butterworth
Harry Langdon

NO DEJES LA PUERTA ABIERTA
(DON'T LEAVE THE DOOR OPEN)
Dir. Frank Strayer
Cast Raul Roulien
Mona Maris
Tom Patricola

OLSEN'S BIG MOMENT
Dir. Mal St. Clair
Cast El Brendel
Walter Catlett
Susan Fleming
Barbara Weeks

PADDY THE NEXT BEST THING
Dir. Harry Lachman
Cast Janet Gaynor
Warner Baxter
Margaret Lindsay
Walter Connolly

PILGRIMAGE
Dir. John Ford
Cast Henrietta Crosman
Heather Angel
Norman Foster
Marian Nixon
Maurice Murphy

PLEASURE CRUISE
Dir. Frank Tuttle
Cast Genevieve Tobin
Roland Young
Ralph Forbes
Una O'Connor

POWER AND THE GLORY, THE
Dir. William K. Howard
Cast Spencer Tracy
Colleen Moore
Ralph Morgan
Helen Vinson

ROBBERS ROOST
Dir. Louis King
Cast George O'Brien
Maureen O'Sullivan
Walter McGrail
Reginald Owen

SAILOR'S LUCK
Dir. Raoul Walsh
Cast James Dunn
Sally Eilers
Frank Morgan

SECOND HAND WIFE
Dir. Hamilton MacFadden
Cast Sally Eilers
Helen Vinson
Ralph Bellamy
Victor Jory

SHANGHAI MADNESS
Dir. John Blystone
Cast Spencer Tracy
Fay Wray
Ralph Morgan
Eugene Pallette

SMOKE LIGHTNING
Dir. David Howard
Cast George O'Brien
Nell O'Day
Frank Atkinson
Clarence Wilson

SMOKY
Dir. Eugene Forde

Cast Victor Jory
Irene Bentley
Frank Campeau
Hank Mann

STATE FAIR
Dir. Henry King
Cast Will Rogers
Janet Gaynor
Sally Eilers
Lew Ayres
Norman Foster

TRICK FOR TRICK
Dir. Hamilton MacFadden
Cast Ralph Morgan
Victor Jory
Sally Blane

WALLS OF GOLD
Dir. Kenneth MacKenna
Cast Sally Eilers
Norman Foster
Ralph Morgan
Rochelle Hudson

WARRIOR'S HUSBAND, THE
Dir. Walter Lang
Cast Elissa Landi
David Manners
Ernest Truex

WORST WOMAN IN PARIS, THE
Dir. Monta Bell
Cast Benita Hume
Adolphe Menjou
Helen Chandler

ZOO IN BUDAPEST
Dir. Rowland V. Lee
Cast Loretta Young
Gene Raymond
Wally Albright

1934

ALL MEN ARE ENEMIES
Prod. Al Rockett
Dir. George Fitzmaurice
Cast Helen Twelvetrees
Mona Barrie
Hugh Williams

AS HUSBANDS GO
Prod. Jesse L. Lasky
Dir. Hamilton MacFadden
Cast Warner Baxter
Helen Vinson

BABY TAKE A BOW
Prod. John Stone
Dir. Harry Lachman
Cast Shirley Temple
James Dunn
Claire Trevor

BACHELOR OF ARTS
Prod. John Stone
Dir. Louis King
Cast Tom Brown
Anita Louise
Arline Judge

BOTTOMS UP
Prod. B. G. DeSylva
Dir. David Butler
Cast Spencer Tracy
John Boles
Pat Patterson
Thelma Todd

BRIGHT EYES
Prod. Sol M. Wurtzel
Dir. David Butler
Cast Shirley Temple
Jane Withers
James Dunn
Judith Allen

CALL IT LUCK
Prod. John Stone
Dir. James Tinling
Cast Pat Patterson
Charles Starrett

CARAVAN
Prod. Robert T. Kane
Dir. Erik Charrell
Cast Charles Boyer
Loretta Young
Jean Parker

CAROLINA
Prod. Winfield Sheehan
Dir. Henry King
Cast Janet Gaynor
Robert Young
Lionel Barrymore

CAT'S PAW, THE
(*Harold Lloyd Production*)
Prod. Harold Lloyd
Dir. Sam Taylor
Cast Harold Lloyd
Una Merkel

CHANGE OF HEART
Prod. Winfield Sheehan
Dir. John Blystone
Cast Janet Gaynor
Charles Farrell

CHARLIE CHAN IN LONDON
Prod. John Stone
Dir. Eugene Forde
Cast Warner Oland
Ray Milland
Mona Barrie

CHARLIE CHAN'S COURAGE
Prod. John Stone
Dir. George Hadden
Cast Warner Oland
Drue Leyton
Donald Woods

COMING OUT PARTY
Prod. Jesse L. Lasky
Dir. John Blystone
Cast Frances Dee
Gene Raymond

CONSTANT NYMPH, THE
(*Gaumont-British*)
Dir. Basil Dean
Cast Brian Aherne
Victoria Hopper
Peggy Blythe

DAVID HARUM
Prod. Winfield Sheehan
Dir. James Cruze
Cast Will Rogers
Evelyn Venable
Kent Taylor

DEVIL TIGER, THE
Prod. Clyde E. Elliott
Dir. Clyde E. Elliott
Cast Marion Burns
Kane Richmond
Harry Woods

DOS MAS UNO DOS
(Two and One Two)
Prod. John Stone
Dir. John Reinhardt
Cast Rosita Moreno
Valentine Parera

DUDE, RANGER THE
(*Principal Production*)
Prod. Sol Lesser
Dir. Edward Cline
Cast George O'Brien
Irene Hervey

ELINOR NORTON
Prod. Sol M. Wurtzel
Dir. Hamilton MacFadden
Cast Claire Trevor
Gilbert Roland
Hugh Williams

EVER SINCE EVE
Prod. Sol M. Wurtzel
Dir. George Marshall
Cast George O'Brien
Mary Brian
Peggy Blythe

FIRST WORLD WAR, THE
(*Documentary*)
Prod. Truman Talley
Narrator Pedro de Cordoba

FRONTIER MARSHAL
Prod. Sol M. Wurtzel
Dir. Lewis Seiler
Cast George O'Brien
Irene Bentley
George E. Stone

GAMBLING
(*Harold B. Franklin Production*)
Prod. Harold B. Franklin
Dir. Rowland V. Lee
Cast George M. Cohan
Dorothy Burgess
Wynne Gibson

GEORGE WHITE'S SCANDALS OF 1934
Prod. Robert T. Kane
Dir. George White
Harry Lachman
Thornton Freeland
Cast Rudy Vallee
Jimmy Durante
Alice Faye
Gregory Ratoff
Adrienne Ames

GRAND CANARY
Prod. Jesse L. Lasky
Dir. Irving Cummings
Cast Warner Baxter
Madge Evans
Marjorie Rambeau
H. B. Warner

GRANADEROS DEL AMOR
(GRENADIERS OF LOVE)
Prod. John Stone
Dir. John Reinhardt
Cast Raul Roulien
Conchita Montenegro

HANDY ANDY
Prod. Sol M. Wurtzel
Dir. David Butler
Cast Will Rogers
Peggy Wood
Mary Carlisle

HEART SONG
(*Gaumont-British*)
Prod. Erich Pommer
Dir. Friedrich Hollander
Cast Charles Boyer
Lillian Harvey
Maurice Evans

HELL IN THE HEAVENS
Prod. Al Rockett
Dir. John Blystone
Cast Warner Baxter
Conchita Montenegro
Russell Hardie

HOLD THAT GIRL
Prod. Sol M. Wurtzel
Dir. Hamilton MacFadden
Cast James Dunn
Claire Trevor
Gertrude Michael

I AM SUZANNE
Prod. Jesse L. Lasky
Dir. Rowland V. Lee
Cast Lillian Harvey
Gene Raymond
Leslie Banks

I BELIEVED IN YOU
Prod. Sol M. Wurtzel
Dir. Irving Cummings
Cast Rosemary Ames
John Boles
Gertrude Michael

I WAS A SPY
(*Made in England*)
Dir. Victor Saville
Cast Madeleine Carroll
Herbert Marshall
Conrad Veidt

JUDGE PRIEST
Prod. Sol M. Wurtzel
Dir. John Ford
Cast Will Rogers
Tom Brown
Anita Louise
Rochelle Hudson

LA CIUDAD DE CARTON
(CARDBOARD CITY)
Prod. John Stone
Dir. Louis King
Cast Antonio Moreno
Catalina Barcena

LA CRUZ Y LA ESPADA
(CROSS AND THE SWORD, THE)
Prod. John Stone
Dir. Frank Strayer
Cast Jose Mojica
Anita Campillo

LAS FRONTERAS DEL AMOR
(LOVE'S FRONTIERS)
Prod. John Stone
Dir. Frank Strayer
Cast Jose Mojica
Rosita Moreno

LOVE TIME
Prod. Sol M. Wurtzel
Dir. James Tinling
Cast Pat Patterson
Nils Asther
Herbert Mundin

MARIE GALANTE
Prod. Winfield Sheehan

Dir. Henry King
Cast Spencer Tracy
Ketti Gallian
Helen Morgan

MELODIA PROHIBIDA
(FORBIDDEN MELODY)
Prod. John Stone
Dir. Frank Strayer
Cast Jose Mojica
Conchita Montenegro

MURDER IN TRINADAD
Prod. Sol M. Wurtzel
Dir. Louis King
Cast Nigel Bruce
Heather Angel
Victor Jory

MUSIC IN THE AIR
Prod. Erich Pommer
Dir. Joe May
Cast Gloria Swanson
John Boles
Douglas Montgomery
June Lang

NADA MAS QUE UNA MUJER
(ONLY A WOMAN)
Prod. John Stone
Dir. Harry Lachman
Cast Berta Singerman
Alfredo del Diestro

NOW I'LL TELL
Prod. Winfield Sheehan
Dir. Edwin Burke
Cast Spencer Tracy
Helen Twelvetrees
Alice Faye
Shirley Temple

ORIENT EXPRESS
Prod. Sol M. Wurtzel
Dir. Paul Martin
Cast Norman Foster
Heather Angel

PECK'S BAD BOY
(*Principal Production*)
Prod. Sol Lesser
Dir. Edward Cline
Cast Jackie Cooper
Jackie Searle
Thomas Meighan

PURSUED
Prod. Sol M. Wurtzel
Dir. Louis King
Cast Rosemary Ames
Victor Jory
Russell Hardie

SERVANTS' ENTRANCE
Prod. Winfield Sheehan
Dir. Frank Lloyd
Cast Janet Gaynor
Lew Ayres
Walter Connelly

SHE LEARNED ABOUT SAILORS
Prod. John Stone
Dir. George Marshall
Cast Alice Faye
Lew Ayres
Harry Green

SHE WAS A LADY
Prod. Al Rockett
Dir. Hamilton MacFadden
Cast Helen Twelvetrees
Donald Woods
Ralph Morgan

SLEEPERS EAST
Prod. Sol. M. Wurtzel
Dir. Kenneth MacKenna
Cast Wynne Gibson
　　　Preston Foster
　　　Mona Barrie

SPRINGTIME FOR HENRY
Prod. Jesse L. Lasky
Dir. Frank Tuttle
Cast Otto Kruger
　　　Nancy Carroll
　　　Heather Angel

STAND UP AND CHEER
Prod. Winfield Sheehan
Dir. Hamilton MacFadden
Cast Warner Baxter
　　　Madge Evans
　　　James Dunn
　　　Shirley Temple

SUCH WOMEN ARE DANGEROUS
Prod. Al Rockett
Dir. James Flood
Cast Warner Baxter
　　　Rosemary Ames
　　　Rochelle Hudson

365 NIGHTS IN HOLLYWOOD
Prod. Sol M. Wurtzel
Dir. George Marshall
Cast James Dunn
　　　Alice Faye

THREE ON A HONEYMOON
Prod. John Stone
Dir. James Tinling
Cast Sally Eilers
　　　Johnny Mack Brown
　　　Charles Starrett
　　　Zasu Pitts

WHITE PARADE, THE
Prod. Jesse L. Lasky
Dir. Irving Cummings
Cast John Boles
　　　Loretta Young
　　　Jane Darwell
　　　Joyce Compton

WILD GOLD
Prod. Sol M. Wurtzel
Dir. George Marshall
Cast John Boles
　　　Claire Trevor
　　　Harry Green
　　　Monroe Owsley

WORLD MOVES ON, THE
Prod. Winfield Sheehan
Dir. John Ford
Cast Madeleine Carroll
　　　Franchot Tone
　　　Reginald Denny
　　　Raul Roulien

1935

BABOONA
(Documentary)
Prod. Mr. and Mrs. Martin Johnson

CHARLIE CHAN IN EGYPT
Prod. Edward T. Lowe
Dir. Louis King
Cast Warner Oland
　　　Pat Patterson

CHARLIE CHAN IN PARIS
Prod. Sol M. Wurtzel
Dir. Lewis Seiler
Cast Warner Oland
　　　Mary Brian

THE COUNTY CHAIRMAN
Prod. Edward Butcher
Dir. John Blystone
Cast Will Rogers
　　　Evelyn Venable
　　　Mickey Rooney

CURLY TOP
Prod. Winfield Sheehan
Dir. Irving Cummings
Cast Shirley Temple
　　　John Boles
　　　Rochelle Hudson

DANTE'S INFERNO
Prod. Sol M. Wurtzel
Dir. Harry Lachman
Cast Spencer Tracy
　　　Claire Trevor

THE DARING YOUNG MAN
Prod. Robert T. Kane
Dir. William Seiter
Cast James Dunn
　　　Mae Clarke
　　　Neil Hamilton

DOUBTING THOMAS
Prod. B. G. DeSylva
Dir. David Butler
Cast Will Rogers
　　　Billie Burke
　　　Allison Skipworth

DRESSED TO THRILL
Prod. Robert T. Kane
Dir. Harry Lachman
Cast Tutta Rolf
　　　Clive Brook
　　　Nydia Westman

THE FARMER TAKES A WIFE
Prod. Winfield Sheehan
Dir. Victor Fleming
Cast Janet Gaynor
　　　Henry Fonda
　　　Charles Bickford
　　　Jane Withers

THE GAY DECEPTION
Prod. Jesse L. Lasky
Dir. William Wyler
Cast Francis Lederer
　　　Frances Dee
　　　Benita Hume

GINGER
Prod. Sol M. Wurtzel
Dir. Lewis Seiler
Cast Jane Withers
　　　Jackie Searle

THE GREAT HOTEL MYSTERY
Prod. John Stone
Dir. Eugene Forde
Cast Edmund Lowe
　　　Victor McLaglen
　　　Rosemary Ames

HARD ROCK HARRIGAN
Prod. Sol Lesser
Dir. David Howard
Cast George O'Brien
　　　Irene Hervey

HELLDORADO
Prod. Jesse L. Lasky
Dir. James Cruze
Cast Richard Arlen
　　　Madge Evans
　　　Ralph Bellamy

HERE'S TO ROMANCE
Prod. Jesse L. Lasky
Dir. Alfred E. Green
Cast Nino Martini
　　　Genevieve Tobin
　　　Anita Louise

IN OLD KENTUCKY
Prod. Edward Butcher
Dir. George Marshall
Cast Will Rogers
　　　Dorothy Wilson
　　　Russell Hardie

IT'S A SMALL WORLD
Prod. Edward Butcher
Dir. Irving Cummings
Cast Spencer Tracy
　　　Wendy Barrie

LADIES LOVE DANGER
Prod. Edward T. Lowe
Dir. Bruce Humberstone
Cast Mona Barrie
　　　Gilbert Roland
　　　Adrienne Ames

LIFE BEGINS AT FORTY
Prod. Sol M. Wurtzel
Dir. George Marshall
Cast Will Rogers
　　　Richard Cromwell
　　　Rochelle Hudson

LILIOM
Prod. Erich Pommer
Dir. Fritz Lang
Cast Charles Boyer
　　　Madeleine Ozeray
　　　Viviane Romance

THE LITTLE COLONEL
Prod. B. G. DeSylva
Dir. David Butler
Cast Shirley Temple
　　　Lionel Barrymore

THE LOTTERY LOVER
Prod. Al Rockett
Dir. William Thiele
Cast Lew Ayres
　　　Pat Patterson

MYSTERY WOMAN
Prod. Sol M. Wurtzel
Dir. Eugene Forde
Cast Mona Barrie
　　　Gilbert Roland

ONE MORE SPRING
Prod. Winfield Sheehan
Dir. Henry King
Cast Janet Gaynor
　　　Warner Baxter

ORCHIDS TO YOU
Prod. Robert T. Kane
Dir. William A. Seiter
Cast John Boles
　　　Jean Muir

OUR LITTLE GIRL
Prod. Edward Butcher
Dir. John Robertson
Cast Shirley Temple
　　　Rosemary Ames
　　　Joel McCrea

REDHEADS ON PARADE
Prod. Jesse L. Lasky
Dir. Norman Z. McLeod
Cast John Boles
　　　Dixie Lee
　　　Jack Haley

SILK HAT KID
Prod. Joseph Engel
Dir. Bruce Humberstone
Cast Lew Ayres
　　　Mae Clarke

SPRING TONIC
Prod. Robert T. Kane
Dir. Clyde Bruckman
Cast Lew Ayres
　　　Claire Trevor
　　　Jack Haley

STEAMBOAT 'ROUND THE BEND
Prod. Sol M. Wurtzel
Dir. John Ford
Cast Will Rogers
　　　Ann Shirley
　　　Irvin S. Cobb

TEN DOLLAR RAISE
Prod. Sol M. Wurtzel
Dir. George Marshall
Cast Edward Everett Horton
　　　Karen Morley

THUNDER IN THE NIGHT
Prod. John Stone
Dir. George Archainbaud
Cast Edmund Lowe
　　　Karen Morley

UNDER THE PAMPAS MOON
Prod. B. G. DeSylva
Dir. James Tinling
Cast Warner Baxter
　　　Ketti Gallian

UNDER PRESSURE
Prod. Robert T. Kane
Dir. Raoul Walsh
Cast Edmund Lowe
　　　Victor McLaglen
　　　Florence Rice

WAY DOWN EAST
Prod. Winfield Sheehan
Dir. Henry King
Cast Rochelle Hudson
　　　Henry Fonda

WELCOME HOME
Prod. B. G. DeSylva
Dir. James Tinling
Cast James Dunn
　　　Arline Judge

WHEN A MAN'S A MAN
Prod. Sol Lesser
Dir. Edward Cline
Cast George O'Brien
　　　Dorothy Wilson
　　　Paul Kelly

Heather Angel and Leslie Howard in *Berkeley Square*. (1933)

Shirley Temple and Bill Robinson in *The Little Colonel*. (1935)

Will Rogers and Dorothy Wilson in *In Old Kentucky*. (1935)

Diana Wynyard and Clive Brook in *Cavalcade*. (1933)

Will Rogers and Janet Gaynor in *State Fair*. (1933)

John Boles, Rochelle Hudson, and Shirley Temple in *Curly Top*. (1935)

Alice Faye in *The George White Scandals of 1934*.

James Dunn and Shirley Temple in *Stand Up and Cheer*. (1934)

FOX FILM CORPORATION ACADEMY AWARDS FOR 1927–1928

JANET GAYNOR: Best actress in *Seventh Heaven, Street Angel,* and *Sunrise.*

FRANK BORZAGE: Best direction for *Seventh Heaven.*

BENJAMIN GLAZER: Best adaptation for *Seventh Heaven.*

CHARLES ROSHER, KARL STRUSS: Best cinematography for *Sunrise.*

SUNRISE: Special award for artistic quality of production.

ROCHUS GLIESE: Honorable mention for art direction of *Sunrise.*

HARRY OLIVER: Honorable mention for art direction of *Seventh Heaven.*

FOX FILM CORPORATION ACADEMY AWARDS FOR 1929

WARNER BAXTER: Best actor for *In Old Arizona.*

FOX FILM CORPORATION ACADEMY AWARDS FOR 1931

FRANK BORZAGE: Best direction for *Bad Girl.*

EDWIN BURKE: Best adaptation for *Bad Girl.*

GORDON WILES: Art direction for *Transatlantic.*

FOX FILM CORPORATION ACADEMY AWARDS FOR 1933

CAVALCADE: Best picture.

FRANK LLOYD: Best direction for *Cavalcade.*

WILLIAM S. DARLING: Art direction for *Cavalcade.*

FOX FILM CORPORATION: Honorable mention for technical developments.

THE TWENTIETH CENTURY PICTURES

When Darryl F. Zanuck founded 20th Century Pictures in 1933, the motion picture industry was almost totally controlled by the major companies—MGM, Paramount, Warner Brothers, RKO-Radio, Fox and, to a lesser extent because they did not own any theaters, Columbia, Universal, and United Artists. Zanuck had enormous confidence in his venture and in his abilities to create popular movies. Generally, independent producers were no match for the majors, largely because the majors had huge amounts of talent under long-term contract and the big-name performers and directors were never loaned out unless another studio could offer an equal talent in return. 20th Century Pictures had no immediate contracts with talent and the company would have had a tough time had it not been for a political arrangement made by Zanuck with Louis B. Mayer. By taking on William Goetz, Mayer's son-in-law, Zanuck was able to secure not only some financing but a tacit guarantee of cooperation in the matter of loan-outs. This was to be one of the most important factors in the success of 20th Century Pictures.

However, there was no doubt in anyone's mind that the future of the company lay in the abilities of its thirty-one-year-old production head, who was to be paid $250,000 annually for his services and who would prove himself well worth it.

The elements which Zanuck had cultivated in his own stories for Warners and in the stories he put into production were to reappear over and over. Action was a prerequisite—there was always something going on in a Zanuck picture—but there was often a curious abandon of logic. The public didn't seem to mind. With a goodly amount of humor and romantic interest, the films provided sufficient, and sometimes extraordinary, entertainment.

Zanuck was fortunate in having all the story elements blend well in his first release, *The Bowery,* a rousing and robust yarn directed by Raoul Walsh. Drawing upon fact, but well laced with fiction, the film recounted the endless rivalry between the characters played by Wallace Beery and George Raft.

The plot has Beery as a tough, good-hearted saloon owner, who watches over a mischievous orphan (Jackie Cooper). When Beery takes in a pretty Fay Wray, the orphan runs off to join his friend's arch-rival (Raft). On a bet, Raft stages a jump from the Brooklyn Bridge and Beery loses everything. However, Beery suspects that Raft faked the jump, challenges him to a fistfight, emerges the winner and regains his saloon and prestige. In the end, Beery and Raft make up long enough to enlist in the army but still argue over who really won the fight.

Because of its elaborate sets, period flavor, and fine cast, *The Bowery* proved a winner. But would Zanuck be as lucky with his next pictures? Creatively, no. In November of 1933, a little over a month after the release of *The Bowery* 20th Century brought out *Broadway Through a Keyhole.* The story made use of the public's fascination with gangsters and involved an innocent girl (Constance Cummings) who wants nothing more than to be a successful singer. She looks up an old friend (Paul Kelly), unaware that he has become a racketeer, and he gets her a job in a night club. When he falls in love with her, he does his best to make her a star, and when a rival gangster starts gunning for him, he ships her off to Miami for safekeeping. There she meets a band leader (Russ Colombo) and falls in love with him. Her racketeer benefactor at first objects, but comes to realize he has to let her go. Other than Walter Winchell's debut on screen, *Broadway Through a Keyhole* had nothing to distinguish it from a flock of other programmers of the time.

Blood Money did little to right the wrongs of the previous release. Running a meager sixty-five minutes, it was Zanuck's most bizarre venture of the 20th Century period. Again set in the underworld, the film featured Judith Anderson as a tough, fast-talking gang leader with ice in her veins, and the beautiful Frances Dee as a spoiled kleptomaniac socialite with a pronounced masochistic streak. The ludicrous plot climaxed with Anderson saving her boyfriend from a death plot in which the murder weapon was an exploding eight ball on a pool table. Not a milestone in moviemaking.

Advice to the Lovelorn, released in December, 1933, was a change of pace for Zanuck, but not much more successful. Lee Tracy played a fast-talking, wisecracking reporter who is so unreliable that his boss assigns him the "Lonely Hearts" column as a punishment. Instead of answering letters with typical replies, he makes outrageous and unorthodox suggestions, thinking this will get him released from the assignment. He is chagrined to find that the column becomes a success and results in bigger sales for the paper. The film is amusing when sticking to this light line but goes off the track with later melodramatics.

Making a transition from the light to the dramatic, Zanuck followed with the heaviest of his stories, *Gallant Lady,* with Ann Harding expressing perpetual suffering in endless close-ups. The lady is left pregnant and alone when her husband-to-be is killed in a plane crash. She has her child secretly and puts him up for adoption. Six years later on an ocean cruise, she just happens to meet her son, who is on his way to his father. Conveniently, the father is about to remarry and Harding does her best to work her way into his life. An obligatory happy ending brings relief to her sufferings.

Although *Moulin Rouge* was not the best of Zanuck's features, it was a definite step forward from the previous three pictures. It featured Constance Bennett in a dual role as twin sisters, both entertainers. One is married to a songwriter who doesn't want to see her return to the stage and the other takes her place when she is hired to star in a musical. The plot lines become increasingly complex when the first girl's husband falls in love with the woman he thinks is the sister. The plot was recycled only a year later in *Folies Bergere,* where it was used with much more effect. *Moulin Rouge* would have probably been better had Constance Bennett been more believable as the tremendously talented singer-dancer she was portraying, a casting problem arising from the dearth of talent Zanuck had available to him.

Fortunately, 20th Century Pictures came up with a film which proved to be both entertaining and financially successful. It was the kind of film which Zanuck would eventually realize he could do best—the his-

488

Jackie Cooper and Wallace Beery in *The Bowery.*

Constance Cummings and Paul Kelly in *Broadway Through a Keyhole.*

Judith Anderson and George Bancroft in *Blood Money.*

Lee Tracy and Sally Blane in *Advice to the Lovelorn.*

Constance Bennett and Russ Columbo in *Moulin Rouge*.

Ann Harding and Clive Brook in *Gallant Lady*.

Jack Oakie and Spencer Tracy in *Looking for Trouble*.

George Arliss and Boris Karloff in *House of Rothschild*.

Loretta Young and Cary Grant in *Born to Be Bad*.

Ronald Colman in *Bulldog Drummond Strikes Back*.

torical biography. After four mediocre releases, *The House of Rothschild* put the company back on the right track. Not since the *Bowery* had Zanuck mounted such a lavish, expensive production, and there was no doubt that Nunnally Johnson's literate screenplay contributed to its excellence. But it was probably George Arliss' riveting portrayal of Nathan Rothschild that sealed the film's success.

Broad in scope, the film spanned an entire generation in the history of the renowned family. Beginning with a lengthy prologue, a device Zanuck often used, the film presented Mayer Rothschild, a moneychanger in the Frankfurt ghetto in 1770, instructing his sons to establish banking institutions in each of the major European countries. The story follows the ascendancy of the banking family in European society and ends with the knighting of Nathan Rothschild. The excellent cast included Boris Karloff as a sinister Prussian minister and C. Aubrey Smith as the stately Duke of Wellington. The final four-minute sequence was photographed in the new three-strip Technicolor process, which added regal glamor to Nathan Rothschild's audience with Queen Victoria. It was the finishing touch to a tasteful and, for its time, daring film.

It was business as usual though with *Looking For Trouble*, another comedy-drama involving two troubleshooters for the telephone company who wiretap their way into an attempted robbery. Naturally, there's a young lady who's unwittingly tied in with the thugs but proves to be true to the hero, Spencer Tracy. Aside from Tracy, the film had only two other assets—Jack Oakie, as his wisecracking partner and a spectacular re-creation of the Long Beach earthquake as the climax of the film, which skillfully blended newsreel footage to advantage. Directed by William Wellman, it had enough elements to be accepted as standard movie entertainment.

Almost rivaling *Blood Money* in its bizarre attitude, *Born to Be Bad* starred Loretta Young and Cary Grant. The film ran into censorship problems in telling the story of a woman who is emotionally scarred by past experiences and determined to survive on any terms. The script called for Young to be a model who does not wear underclothes when trying to get buyers interested in product. With the Hays Office in full power in 1934, Zanuck was forced to drop this element, which resulted in the scenes not making much sense. Another problem was the girl's constant snubbing of Grant, with him always coming back for more. It was hard to accept Grant in the role of a sap and equally had to present the innately wholesome Young in a nasty guise. *Born to Be Bad* was born to be 20th Century's only financial failure.

With the exception of *The House of Rothschild*, which was based on a play, all of Zanuck's features were filmed from original material. This made sense on two counts. Zanuck had been a writer and felt comfortable with his grasp of story construction. After all,

Fredric March and Constance Bennett in *The Affairs of Cellini*.

it had been his strength as production head at Warners. Secondly, it was cheaper to develop properties than pay for authors' rights.

When Zanuck bought the rights to one of the Bulldog Drummond series, the results were wildly successful. The tongue-in-cheek detective mystery proved to be a real audience pleaser. As the Hollywood Reporter described *Bulldog Drummond Strikes Back:* "It's Ronald Colman at his debonair best. It's Nunnally Johnson having a swell time writing a lot of things he always wanted to see in a murder mystery. It's Roy del Ruth directing at a pace and with a sly sense of humor that mystery stories have been crying out aloud forever since the first Bulldog Drummond story hit the screen." In short, a box-office hit.

The formula for adapting popular entertainment from another medium was repeated when Zanuck bought the rights to Edwin Justus Mayer's play *The Firebrand,* later titled *The Affairs of Cellini.* Although the results were more like a filmed play, the lavish sets and costumes more than made up for the lack of exterior locations. There were also energetic performances by Fredric March as Benvenuto Cellini, the Florentine artist and bon vivant, and Frank Morgan, delightfully re-creating his stage role as the bumbling Duke Alessandro. The plot centers on Cellini's involvement in court intrigue when the Duchess (Constance Bennett) picks him to be her lover and his foiling of an attempt to take over the throne. Directed with a fine comedic flair by Gregory LaCava, *The Affairs of Cellini* is a spoof on swashbuckling romances and except for a few dull stretches it was a successful undertaking for 20th Century Pictures.

George Arliss as *Cardinal Richelieu.*

Fredric March and Charles Laughton in *Les Miserables.*

The Last Gentleman, released in October of 1934, was the last "small" picture to be produced by Zanuck. It was clearly designed as a star vehicle for George Arliss and it was one of his few nonhistorical portrayals. Again, very stagey in concept, the film was buoyed by the sardonic style of Arliss and his skillful delivery of lines. An elderly, wealthy misanthrope nearing the end of his life, Arliss despises his relatives, whom he believes hover around him solely to gain his money. With the aid of a film taken before his death, he tells each of his relatives what he thinks of them as he reads his final wishes. Basically a series of sketches, the film contains a number of amusing passages, but the key factor is the talent of Arliss.

With *The Mighty Barnum,* released for Christmas, 1934, Zanuck once again revived the spirit of rowdy adventure which had set off 20th Century in the first place. Wallace Beery played an oafish, crass, and crude Phineas T. Barnum, but somehow made him a sympathetic character. The star of the film, though, was the spectacular fire which temporarily ended Barnum's career. Utilizing fine special effects, Zanuck climaxed his film with an unforgettable inferno. According to this account Barnum was an unsuccessful merchant who always yearned for a museum in which to display his collection of oddities. Once successful, he then turned to creating a freak show, but also flirted with one of his stars, the beautiful Jenny Lind (Virginia Bruce) and moved toward bankrupcy. His literate partner,

Frank Albertson, George Arliss, Charlotte Henry, Rafaela Ottiano, Donald Meek, Janet Beecher, Edna May Oliver, and Ralph Morgan in *The Last Gentleman.*

Virginia Bruce and Wallace Beery in *The Mighty Barnum.*

Maurice Chevalier and Merle Oberon in *Folies Bergere.*

Ronald Colman, Loretta Young, and C. Aubrey Smith in *Clive of India.*

Bailey Walsh (Adolphe Menjou), saves the day by bringing in Jumbo, the world's largest elephant. Later they added other exotic animals and toured the country with them. Thus was born the Barnum and Bailey Circus—at least according to Zanuck. As with later films, this was his retelling of history, always with strong, colorful central characters and with historical facts condensed and changed for dramatic effect.

The most spectacular of his productions, *Clive of India,* also became his most expensive. Incredible battle scenes were filmed on sound stages, using elephants as well as hordes of soldiers. But to keep the film from losing its personal appeal, the story was built around Clive's inner conflict between glory and domesticity. With Ronald Colman in the leading role, the film highlighted the famous Englishman's career from a clerk to the leader of Britain's forces in India. Naturally, it was Clive's campaigns in India which supplied the main interest, but Clive's unhappy wife (Loretta Young) provided the personal drama. With a strong cast and fine production values, including the photography of Peverell Marley, who would be a Zanuck man for years to come, *Clive of India* advanced the stature of 20th Century Pictures.

To continue the streak, the next release was *Folies Bergere,* a delightful, rollicking musical comedy of mistaken identity starring the greatly popular Maurice Chevalier as a roguish entertainer and Merle Oberon in her first American film. The film was enhanced by lavish dances, almost equaling the best of Busby Berkeley and squads of pretty chorus girls. The plot concerned Chevalier's dual appearance as an impressionist and a wealthy French industrialist. For business reasons the impressionist appears in public as the industrialist, but things become complicated when he falls in love with the wife (Oberon) of the industrialist. Comedic confusion follows in the wake, with the husband realizing he had better be more loving

Loretta Young, Jack Oakie, and Clark Gable in *Call of the Wild.*

and caring on the home front. Unlike the episodic films released by 20th Century to date, *Folies Bergere* was the company's most tightly constructed feature. The plot was so much to Zanuck's liking that he used it twice thereafter—in 1941 as *That Night in Rio,* with Don Ameche in the dual role, and ten years later as a Danny Kaye vehicle, *On the Riviera.*

Another big-budget feature, *Cardinal Richelieu,* followed, this being George Arliss' third and final film for Zanuck. Again success was guaranteed, for it combined all the elements which Zanuck and his staff at 20th Century had learned so well. There was spectacle, a star-studded cast, a good script, and an appealing condensation of history. It was a perfect vehicle for Arliss, an expert in conveying the cool slyness and brilliant scheming of palace intrigue.

Les Miserables was destined to become one of 20th Century's most popular and best remembered pictures, largely because of the inspired casting of Fredric March as Victor Hugo's persecuted hero, Jean Valjean, and Charles Laughton as the relentless police pursuer, Inspector Javert. Under Richard Boleslavsky's fine direction, both actors added to their prestige. Running 108 minutes, it was the longest Zanuck film to date, with enough plot twists for two films. The acting and the production values gave the film a quality that endures. It can rightly be considered a Hollywood classic.

The last of the 20th Century pictures was released in August, 1935, and again Zanuck called on his director friend William Wellman. *The Call of the Wild* had less to do with the Jack London novel than it did with Clark Gable and Loretta Young falling in love, but audiences didn't mind. It was basically a Western set in Alaska dealing with gold prospectors fighting off greedy villains. It was a lusty, brawling outdoors movie with plenty of romance and adventure—and irresistible, mammoth St. Bernard dog named Buck. The film originally ended with Gable left alone when his friend, played by Jack Oakie, is murdered by the villains, but audiences reacted so negatively at the previews that Zanuck removed the death sequence and shot a new ending with Gable and Oakie being reunited. With this upbeat touch, *The Call of the Wild* proved a bonanza for 20th Century.

By this time Zanuck had learned enough about movie audiences and enough about production techniques and methods to want something more than merely running a film company. His experiences with the two years of guiding 20th Century Pictures and making eighteen movies had given him—and the industry—every reason to believe that his period as an apprentice tycoon was over. His formative years as a filmmaker had come to an end. His era as a producer extraordinaire was about to begin. And the elements, the ideas, the concepts of these eighteen movies would surface over and over again in his next twenty years as production head for 20th Century-Fox.

491

TO THE FILMS OF 20th CENTURY-FOX

Page numbers in *italics* denote illustrations.

SUPPLEMENTAL INDEX TO THE FILMS OF 20TH CENTURY-FOX, 1979-1984 ▬▬▬▬▬